18.95

BUSINESS TODAY

DAVID J. RACHMAN

Department of Marketing
Bernard M. Baruch College
of The City University of New York

MICHAEL H. MESCON

Chairman, Department of Management
Regents' Professor of Human Relations
Chair of Private Enterprise
School of Business Administration
Georgia State University

RANDOM HOUSE   NEW YORK
BUSINESS DIVISION

BUSINESS TODAY

SECOND EDITION

DEDICATION
To our wives, Barbara and Enid

SPECIAL ACKNOWLEDGMENT
To the Phillips Petroleum Company for their efforts in
advancing better understanding of the American Free Enterprise System
through the development of the American Enterprise Film Series.

GRAPHICS AND TYPOGRAPHY DESIGNED BY BETTY BINNS GRAPHICS

*Illustrations by Martin Lubin, George Moran, Mike Quon,
Isadore Seltzer, and Vantage Art*

Cover photograph by David Attie

SECOND EDITION

98765432

Copyright © 1976, 1979 by Random House, Inc.

Library of Congress Cataloging in Publication Data

Rachman, David J.
    Business today.

    Bibliography: p.
    Includes index.
    1. Business.   2. Management.   I. Mescon, Michael H.,
joint author.   II. Title.
HF5351.R26   1979   658.4   78-20781
ISBN 0-394-32092-1

Manufactured in the United States of America. Composed by New
England Typographic Service, Inc., Bloomfield, Ct. Printed and
bound by Rand McNally & Co., Versailles, Ky.

PREFACE

In creating *Business Today, Second Edition,* we were guided by the belief that a good introductory course is crucial to students' future success in the business world. The course is the most significant one in the Business curriculum, and it must not be merely a brief "guided tour" of the subject. It should equip students with the practical vocabulary they will need in actual work situations. It should examine the tough issues facing management today. And—most important—it should lead students to take their own first steps toward possible business careers.

Motivating the students and giving them a solid conceptual framework represent an enormous responsibility and challenge, both to the instructor and to those preparing the text. The first edition of *Business Today,* which enjoyed considerable success, was praised for certain important features: its sound and comprehensive treatment of the subject matter, its clear writing style, and its effective design. Our primary goal in preparing the second edition, therefore, was to retain and improve these key attributes. But we also felt more could be done. Early in the development of the second edition, an advisory panel of twenty-seven experts from both the business and academic worlds was selected to review and evaluate concept coverage, accuracy of definitions, currency of material, and the effectiveness of the graphics program. We combined their recommendations with a number of suggestions gleaned from a survey of over 800 teachers of Introduction to Business courses. The result was the current edition; we believe it is an effective teaching and learning tool.

We have made some significant changes in both organization and coverage. Some of the highlights are:

■ *Chapter organization* Because of the difficulty often encountered in attempting to cover so much material in a relatively short period of time, eleven of the twenty-six chapters in the text have been designated "Enrichment Chapters." This designation is not meant to imply that these chapters deserve any less emphasis than the rest of the text; rather, these chapters provide the instructor and the student with an opportunity to study some of the functions within major areas of Business in greater depth.

■ *Sections on small business* A second new feature, and one that is unique, is the series of sections titled "Perspectives on Small Business." Each book part dealing with a major functional area of business is followed by a section on the small-business dimension of that area, alerting students to small-business applications of major business concepts while these concepts are still fresh in their minds.

■ *Emphasis on vocabulary* Business terminology is a new and remote language to the student just beginning to study business. For this reason, we have placed a great deal of emphasis on the definition and treatment of business terms. All terms are presented in boldface type and are defined as soon as they have been introduced. In addition, certain terms are reinforced through special feature boxes titled "Building Your Business Vocabulary."

■ *New chapters* In this era of fluctuating exchange rates and a highly sensitive world and national monetary scene, it seemed appropriate to add a chapter on the Money and Banking System. Also added is a speculative and provocative chapter on the Future of Business.

■ *Expanded careers material* Information pertaining to careers in business was very well received in the first edition, and in this new edition we have given this feature even more attention. Following each of the five parts dealing with a major functional area of Business is a section giving information on careers in that area. Each of these sections offers the student insights into trends in specific careers, a table of job opportunities relevant to the functional area, and an article on a career-related issue of current interest.

■ *Lively text examples and boxed features* Much attention has been given to achieving a sensitive balance between sound, clear presentation of theory and interesting practical applications. Intriguing, up-to-date examples have been incorporated into the text to illustrate concepts, and dispersed throughout the chapters are features titled "How It's Actually Done," which provide realistic glimpses of the mechanics of day-to-day business operations. Also included are boxes titled "Know These Laws," which equip students with knowledge that will prove invaluable in their later careers.

■ *Strong graphics program* The format and design represent a new and dramatic approach to textbook design. Our philosophy is that a text should invite the reader to delve into its content, and reinforce its message by the use of attractive illustrations—and further, that illustrations should serve as an aid to memory. Accordingly, we have included features and illustrations designed to make their point both visually and verbally. These items have been smoothly integrated into the overall format to retain a smooth flow; in almost all instances, photos, illustrations, and boxed features appear at either the top or the bottom of the page, maintaining a continuous flow of textual material from page to page—a crucial factor in maintaining students' attention and concentration.

The Introduction to Business course is not long, but it can be a vivid learning experience. It can make students eager to know more—about the various functional areas featured in other parts of the Business curriculum, and about the relationship between business, government, and public. And that is the objective of this book: to promote students' interest in the study of business and to create a basic understanding of the fascinating and complex world of business today.

Supplementary materials available for use with *Business Today, Second Edition:*

STUDENT COURSE MASTERY GUIDE
Dennis Guseman, *Northern Illinois University*
Lee Dahringer, *University of North Carolina*
Stanley Garfunkel, *Queensborough Community College*

INSTRUCTOR'S RESOURCE MANUAL
Blaine Greenfield and Ellis Greenfield, *both of* Bucks County Community College

PREPRINTED TESTS FOR BUSINESS TODAY, *Second Edition*
James Lofstrom, University of Houston
Edward Mirch, *West Valley College*

THE AMERICAN ENTERPRISE FILM SERIES
made possible by Phillips Petroleum Company

ACKNOWLEDGMENTS

This book was developed through the combined efforts of many people. We are especially indebted to the academic staff who provided invaluable guidance in our quest for technical accuracy in each of the key functional areas. They are: Bert Rosenbloom, Drexel University (Marketing); Jack Duncan, University of Alabama (Management); Gerry Manning, San Francisco State University (Data Processing); Keith Bryant, University of Alabama (Accounting); George Overstreet, University of Alabama (Finance); John K. Ryans, Kent State University (International Business); and Del Wells, New Mexico State University (Environment of Business).

Special mention must also be given to Thomas D. Kinsey, Moor Park College, for helping to develop and shape the sections on Small Business, and to John Shingleton, Michigan State University, for his valuable contribution to the sections on Careers.

We would also like to thank the battery of key reviewers who offered further advice on questions of concept presentation and adequacy of coverage. They include: Myron Anderson, Rock Valley College; Ben Cutler, Bronx Community College; Stanley Garfunkel, Queensborough Community College; Blaine Greenfield, Bucks County Community College; Glenn Grothaus, Meramec Community College; James Lofstrom, University of Houston; Sheldon Mador, Los Angeles Trade and Technical College; Edward Mirch, West Valley College; and Joseph Platts, Miami Dade Community College.

A tremendous amount of effort went into the development of supplementary materials to accompany the text. Blaine Greenfield and Ellis Greenfield of Bucks County Community College wrote the Instructor's Resource Manual. The Student Course Mastery Guide, designed to assist the student using the text, was developed by Dennis Guseman, Northern Illinois University, Lee Dahringer, University of North Carolina, and Stanley Garfunkel, Queensborough Community College. The Preprinted Tests package was developed by James Lofstrom, University of Houston, and Edward Mirch, West Valley College.

Editorial coordination, as well as the design and execution of *Business Today, Second Edition,* represented an enormous challenge. Special mention is given to the following people for a job well done:

Editorial staff: Nowhere was the "team" aspect of this project more important than in the editorial end of the operation. For their energetic and skillful assistance, we would like to thank Fred Burns, Stephen Deitmer, and Elizabeth Danks. Above all, our special thanks go to our Acquiring Editor, Paul Donnelly, and to our Project Editor, Susan Tucker. Without their enthusiasm, self-sacrifice, and extraordinary keenness of judgment, this revision would not be possible. We would also like to thank Paul Shensa for his contribution in shaping the first edition.

Art, design, & production: For an exciting and innovative design, we are indebted to Betty Binns, who gave her attention to the "big picture" and also to a thousand small but crucial details. Grateful thanks also go to Picture Researcher Alan Forman and Random House Photo Editor R. Lynn Goldberg—both talented, sensitive, and imaginative contributors. And we would like to thank Martin Lubin of Betty Binns Graphics, Random House Design Supervisor Meryl Levavi, and Random House Production Supervisor Kathy Grasso—all of whom gave us immeasurable help in putting together what turned out to be an extremely complicated book.

Writing: This book would not have come into being without the aid of James Cassidy and H. Lloyd Slater, who helped us put our ideas into words. We are also indebted to Phillip Zweig, Robert Famighetti, Neil Gluckin, Roberta Meyer, Paula Franklin, Susan Schoch, and Jon Healy for their help in shaping chapters, boxed features, and case studies.

Research: Our capable research group included Ira Ginsberg, Ivan Lai, Laura Pettito, Fausta Einhorn, and Barbara Quint. Special thanks also go to Jan Carr for his diligence in providing market research for this project.

CONTENTS IN BRIEF

To the student:

This book is designed for a flexible approach to its subject matter. At the beginning of the course, your instructor will decide on the sequence of chapters he or she plans to cover. Record this sequence on this Table of Contents, using the lines provided to the left of the chapter titles.

For more information on the content of the chapters, turn to the Detailed Table of Contents on page xi.

PART 1
FOCUS ON BUSINESS   1

PART 2
MANAGEMENT   65

PART 3
MARKETING   189

Detailed Contents

PART 2
MANAGEMENT 65

PART 4
FINANCE 311

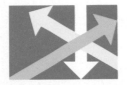

PART 6
THE ENVIRONMENT OF BUSINESS 477

FOCUS ON BUSINESS

Some years ago the president of the Avis car-rental company launched an advertising campaign around a catchy slogan: ''We're Number 2—We Try Harder.'' Now, a new generation of car-rental businesses is enticing consumers with another promise—''We try cheaper.'' With names like Rent-A-Wreck and Lease-A-Lemon, the new firms rent old-model cars at prices far below those of Avis and Hertz. But don't be misled; the owners of these new businesses aren't running charity organizations. Their motive is exactly the same of that of all other business managers: to earn a profit.

Every business in America aims at making a profit—no matter what its size is or what product or service it sells. In Part 1, we will look at this basic characteristic of business from a variety of angles.

☐ Chapter 1, **Business and Its Social Responsibility,** tells how businesses operate in our economy, and what happens when the interests of business and society conflict.

☐ In Chapter 2, **Forms of Business Organization,** we discuss the different ways businesses can be organized. Businesses range in size from one-man hot-dog stands to multinational corporations, and the right way to organize one business may be the wrong way to organize another.

☐ The Enrichment Chapter, **Business and the American Economy: A Historical View,** focuses on the development of our capitalist economy, and compares it with other economic systems. The verdict: our system isn't perfect, but it has some extremely positive features.

BUSINESS AND ITS SOCIAL RESPONSIBILITY

In this country, people have available to them a stunning variety of goods and services—from gourmet food processors, disposable diapers, and cable TV, to hijacking insurance, crash courses in Portuguese, and space-age preventive medicine. We owe this ever-expanding abundance to the free-enterprise system, which pits business against business in competition for the consumer dollar. Yet if free enterprise offers us some notable benefits, it has also created some problems. Business has, in some instances, put profit before social concerns in such areas as product safety, minority employment, and environmental conservation, and it is now being urged by the government and the public to take a more socially responsible stance.

In this chapter, we'll take a close look at the workings of business competition, and we'll see what business has done to tackle social issues.

WHAT WILL THIS CHAPTER FOCUS ON?

After reading the material in this chapter, you will understand and be able to discuss:

- the nature of business

- the roles of the profit motive and the free market system in American business

- the increasing involvement of business in the area of environmental protection

- the steps that have been taken in the field of consumer protection

- the responsibility of business in minority-group employment

"The business of America," said President Calvin Coolidge in 1925, "is business."[1] During the half-century since then, of course, our society has changed in many ways. American business can no longer claim the degree of popular esteem and freedom of action that it enjoyed in those pre-Depression boom years. Nevertheless, the United States remains very much a business-oriented society. No other country has so avidly encouraged the pursuit of success in business, and none has succeeded so well in producing material comfort for so many people.

Certainly, the nation started out with crucial advantages. It was endowed in particular with abundant natural resources and seemingly limitless growing room. But it was also endowed with people eager to work, people whose energy and technical ingenuity were remarked on so often by foreign visitors that Americans might justly have grown tired of hearing it. This commitment to hard work and self-sufficiency was rooted in the harsh facts of life in the American wilderness. "Those who do not work," decreed Captain John Smith of the Jamestown colony, "shall not eat." The commitment was preserved by successive waves of immigrants glad for the chance to earn a decent living. (Indeed, the old idea of a land of opportunity has not lost its appeal: even now, more people immigrate to the United States each year than to all the other countries in the world *combined*.)

While times and circumstances have unmistakably changed, then, the traditional **American work ethic**—*the belief that work is not only necessary but valuable for its own sake*—has remained an essential part of the national character. And since three out of every four American workers are employed in the business sector—as opposed to government, for instance, or agriculture—the importance of business to our lives and to the structure of our society can scarcely be exaggerated.

WHAT IS BUSINESS?

For our purposes, we can define **business** broadly as *all the work involved in providing people with goods and services for a profit*. This definition, of course, is very broad indeed, since that work can include an enormous variety of tasks.

THE ACTIVITIES INVOLVED IN BUSINESS

If, for instance, you have an idea for the proverbial better mousetrap, a great deal of practical work needs to be done before your brainstorm becomes a reality. First of all, you will have to acquire the necessary resources—wood and metal, tools, a workshop, and the like. Then you'll have to organize the actual production—devising an efficient assembly process, training any workers you've hired, and supervising the operation. After this (assuming the world doesn't beat a path to your door) you'll need to distribute your products to as many stores as possible, then make the public aware of their existence and their superior qualities. Lastly—or, actually, before anything else—money will have to be found to get the whole enterprise started. Equipment and materials have to be bought, workers paid, distribution and advertising paid for—all before you've sold a single mousetrap.

This sequence of tasks, needless to say, is only a simplified outline of the types of activity involved in business. In general terms, though, it can be applied to most businesses, regardless of their size or the nature of their work. An ice-cream company offers a product, an airline offers a service, but they both need to acquire the appropriate resources, produce what they intend to sell, advertise it, and make it available as widely as possible.

If there is a broad variety of tasks involved in the business world, the different *types* of business operating today encompass an even greater diversity. There are presently more than 14.5 million businesses in the United States, ranging in size from AT&T, with nearly 785,000 employees, 2.8 million shareholders, and 93.9 billion in assets, to the one-man hot-dog cart in the park.

In age there is likewise a great span. The Revere Copper and Brass Company, founded in 1801 by Paul Revere, has been in continuous operation since then. The New York *Post* has also been publishing without interruption since 1801. At the other end of the spectrum, new businesses appear every day in response to changing public needs, to new technologies, or simply to good original ideas. The data-processing industry, for instance, is continually giving rise to new companies. Their specialties range from computerized wristwatches that check your pulse and blood pressure to new techniques that help banks guard against multimillion-dollar electronic thefts. The last few years have also seen a growth in private weather-forecasting companies. They provide specialized services to business clients—plotting the safest routes for oil tankers at sea, or alerting utility companies to weather changes that will affect electrical demands. And one conservation-minded entrepreneur recently began marketing the Golden Goat, a machine he designed to reclaim aluminum cans: people simply dump the empties into it, and the Golden Goat compresses and weighs them, then automatically dispenses change like a slot machine. The going rate for scrap aluminum is now about twelve cents a pound, but the Golden Goat can be adjusted to meet any change in the market price.[2]

The can-munching Golden Goat makes recycling popular with manufacturer and public alike.

BUSINESS AS A PROFIT-MAKING ACTIVITY

We described business as all the work involved in providing people with goods and services *for a profit.* The last three words are important. **Profit**, simply put, is *the money left over from all sums received for sales after expenses have been deducted.* If it costs you $1.00 to produce one of your mousetraps and you sell it for $1.50, your profit is fifty cents (before taxes, of course).

The element of profit is essential to our definition of business. It is, indeed, the whole point—the "bottom line" for all business activities and enterprises. The American economic system is based on the idea that the owner of a business is entitled to keep whatever profits the business produces. It takes effort, after all, to put a desirable product or service into useful form and then sell it to people. Further, the owner may have to take a considerable financial risk. Most businesses need a substantial investment to get started, and if the new venture doesn't succeed (and most don't), whoever financed it stands to lose a great deal of money. It seems only fair, therefore, that someone who makes the effort and takes the financial risk should be rewarded with the profits.

Such an arrangement, moreover, is not only logical in theory; it has also proved extremely effective in practice. Most people simply do not work five days a week for the sheer fun of it: they work in exchange for compensation, usually money. Furthermore, they tend to work harder or take greater risks if they feel that their extra efforts may produce greater rewards. It is this basic human incentive, the *profit motive,* that lies at the heart of the American business system and perhaps more than anything else accounts for its success.

THE FREE MARKET SYSTEM

In view of the importance of the profit motive, it is essential to form a basic understanding of *how* businesses make their profits. To begin with, our country's business life is based on what economists call a **free market system**. In essence, this means that *if you have something to sell*—whether it's a product like that better mousetrap, or a service you have to offer—*you're free to set whatever price you wish and to sell to anyone*

Whether a business sells melons or mopeds, its prices tend to be determined by the same broad considerations.

willing to pay that price. Conversely, as a consumer you're free to buy whatever you wish and can afford, from whomever you choose.

In practice, of course, there are numerous exceptions to these general principles—a question we will discuss shortly. Nevertheless, there are two basic forces that can be said to dominate the workings of any free market: *competition* and *supply and demand.*

HOW COMPETITION OPERATES

If you set out to sell a product or service in today's society, chances are someone else not too far away is selling something similar. And since the potential customers are free to shop where they please, you will have to compete with your rival for their business. How can you go about this? One obvious strategy is to charge lower prices.

The effect of competition on prices

If your rival is selling blue jeans, say, for $18 a pair, you may try offering them for $15. The catch, of course, is that you'll get $3 less for each pair you sell

and you'll still have to cover the same expenses—buying the jeans from the manufacturer, paying rent on your store, and so forth. How, then, can you charge less and still make a worthwhile profit? The answer—you hope—is that the lower price will attract more customers. Thus even though you make less money on each pair of jeans, you'll sell more of them and so come out with a good overall profit.

In real life, needless to say, things do not always work out so logically. But more often than not, the choices offered by the free market system do benefit both the customer and the business owner—just as they're supposed to in theory. This basic head-on type of competition tends to keep prices down, which is obviously good for the buying public. At the same time, it holds out the promise of greater profits to the business that can sell more units of whatever its product or service happens to be.

The effect of competition on efficiency

The nature of the free market, in addition, encourages other forms of competition that can serve the interests of both the business community and the society at large. A business owner may be able to lower prices without having to settle for a smaller profit per unit if ways can be found to improve efficiency and reduce operating costs. The merchant selling blue jeans, for example, may find that rearranging the store's layout makes it possible to display more items in the same amount of space, or that a new lighting system will cut down on the electric bills. Likewise, someone who refinishes furniture for a living may discover that dipping a table or chair in a large vat of chemical solvents will remove the old finish faster—and thus more economically—than doing the same job by hand.

The effect of competition on quality

As an alternative to price cutting, a business may decide to compete for customers by offering higher-quality goods or services than its rivals. The price may also be higher, but those customers who can afford it will probably be willing to pay the extra amount. (Indeed, in certain business fields the snob appeal of high prices, plush surroundings, and prestigious brand names can be a vital advantage.) Thus while a business that deals in luxury goods will not attract as many customers as, say, an average discount store, it will make more money per item and may well end up with an equal or even greater total profit. A particular benefit of this competitive approach is that it provides a practical incentive for businesses to maintain high standards of quality, and also increases the choices available to customers of different income levels.

Competition encourages variety

The free market system encourages variety not only in the price range for a given category of products or services; it also encourages an immense variety in the *types* of goods and services offered to the public. As we noted earlier, changes in popular taste, technology, and the like are constantly creating new business opportunities—and free enterprise, like nature, abhors a vacuum. The possibility of profit—however remote it may be—almost invariably attracts entrepreneurs willing to risk their time or money. The result is an astonishing diversity of businesses: virtually anything you might want to buy—any product or service, no matter how obscure—is probably sold somewhere. (And if it isn't, you may have a profitable idea yourself.)

Spurring demand through advertising

Finally, the free market system offers another major competitive tool, one that confronts us every day: advertising. The business that can attract more public awareness or create a more favorable image for its products or services will gain a valuable edge over its competitors. To be sure, advertising does not itself improve the quality of the product being offered, and it may in fact add a bit to the price. But it can spur people to buy more, and this in turn can help keep business operating at high capacity—and employing more workers.

SUPPLY AND DEMAND

As we have seen, prices in a free market system can be influenced in a number of ways by the competitive strategies of rival businesses. Price levels, however, are not determined solely (or even primarily, in many cases) by the decisions of business managers. They must also answer to the complex and sometimes surprising forces of supply and demand. (In economic terms, **supply** is *the quantity of a good or service that producers offer at a given time;* **demand** is *the quantity of that good or service people are willing to buy at that time.*)

The **theory of supply and demand**, in basic terms, holds that *the supply of a product will tend to rise when the demand is great*—when people are willing to pay more for it—*and fall when the demand is low.* By the same token, people will usually pay more for something they want that's in short supply (as anyone knows who's tried to buy candles during a blackout); but if the product is widely available, they won't be willing to pay as much, and the sellers will have to accept lower prices. In other words, supply and demand are continuously reacting to one another, and the balance between them at any given time can be judged by the current price on the open market. Thus the price of a product in a particular store may drop not because the owner is trying to lure customers away from the competition across the street but because the general demand for the product has simply fallen off.

In broad terms, then, the forces of supply and demand combine with the profit motive in a free market system to regulate what things are produced and in what amounts. If a farmer owns land, for instance, and tomatoes are currently in the greatest demand, that's what he will plant—not as a favor to the tomato-eating public but because it's the most profitable course of action. However, if too many other farmers have the same idea and produce an oversupply of tomatoes, the price will fall. In that case the farmer will cut back on tomatoes and use the land for other, more profitable crops. The result—again, in theory—is that the consumers will get the products they want, and the farmers who pay attention to public demand will be rewarded with a profit.

HOW "FREE" IS OUR FREE MARKET SYSTEM?

The principles of supply and demand, competition, and the profit motive can be applied to most areas of business. And on paper they combine to form a balanced, self-regulating system in which business and consumers, acting with complete freedom, meet each other's needs, and the society's natural and human resources are put to their most efficient uses. Theory is one thing, of course, and practice another. Our free market system, in reality, is not totally free by any means—for the business owner, the worker, or the consumer.

LIMITS ON FREE ENTERPRISE

The nature of certain industries is such that uncontrolled competition would result only in a situation that would benefit no one. If airline routes were not regulated, airlines would naturally concentrate on the more profitable major cities, creating safety hazards there and leaving people elsewhere with little or no service. Likewise, if the government did not limit the number of radio and television stations and assign them to specific frequencies, the airwaves would be so jammed with overlapping signals that no one would get good reception.

There are many other areas in which the government places limits on free enterprise. We do not, needless to say, get to keep all our profits. Whether they

Even in a free enterprise system, the government must impose some controls for the protection of the public.

take corporate earnings, stock dividends, personal wages, or winnings from a lottery, the government is going to extract a sizeable portion in taxes. Nor is there unrestricted freedom of action in the marketplace. As a consumer, for instance, you cannot buy most medications without a doctor's prescription; you can't buy alcohol without a certificate proving that you're old enough; you can't even get married without a license!

As for selling, whether you're a department store owner or a street vendor, you can't legally do business without a tax permit. If you run a restaurant, you also need a certificate from the board of health. You can't practice medicine, sell stock, or drive a cab without a variety of licenses. In many industries you can't sell your own services as a worker without joining a union, and you can't legally hold any job at all without a Social Security card.

Further, businesses are not free to set prices without restrictions. A company may not, for instance, charge one price to a preferred customer and another price to someone else. Nor may one firm get together with another and arrange to fix prices at an artificially high level. Conversely, before rule changes touched off the recent wave of price cutting, airlines were prohibited from offering fares *below* certain levels. In many states, liquor stores are similarly barred from selling their wares for less than the authorized minimum price.

MONOPOLY AND OLIGOPOLY

If profit and growth are the accepted goals of private enterprise, it is inevitable that a company may sometimes become so powerful—IBM in the computer industry, for instance, or Kodak in film processing—that its rivals can offer little or no real competition. This process, if allowed to continue to an extreme, could lead to **monopoly**—a situation in which *one company dominates a particular industry or market and restrains free entry or activity in that market.* By definition, monopolies are contrary to the principles of free trade and competition. Ironically, they are also a logical end product of the same free market system.

True monopolies are prohibited by law and have been a continuing subject of governmental concern since the turn of the century. But a related trend still continues—**oligopoly,** *the domination of an industry by a few large companies.* The automotive business, for instance, is dominated by the "Big Three"—General Motors, Ford, and Chrysler. If American Motors and Volkswagen's new United States subsidiary are included, we find that a mere five companies account for more than 99 percent of all production in the country's most important industry. Similar situations exist in other key fields—the ten largest steel companies and the five largest oil companies dominate their markets; four companies produce 100 percent of the country's aluminum; four others produce over 80 percent of all synthetic fibers.

The central problem posed by oligopolies is that, while not illegal, they are nearly as effective as monopolies in suppressing price competition and other free market activities. Rather than respond to the normal forces of supply and demand, for example, companies in an oligopoly normally peg their prices to the levels set by the largest among them. Since they control most of the supply, their customers have little choice but to accept the prices.

THE FREE MARKET SYSTEM IN PERSPECTIVE

In view of all this, we may wonder whether the free market system is much more than an interesting but unrealistic theory left over from a simpler time. We are, after all, an industrial nation of over 215 million people, not the society of farmers and shopkeepers that existed when the tenets of free enterprise were being developed two centuries ago.

As complex as it has become, though, America's business system is still guided to a remarkable degree by free market principles—certainly in comparison to the rest of the industrialized world. And that system has without question produced more wealth for more people than any other. Nevertheless, it is becoming increasingly clear that our unparalleled standard of living has not been achieved without a significant cost. Such now-familiar phrases as "quality of life" carry the implied message that a standard of living measured only by statistics is not an accurate reflection of reality. As well, a number of basic issues have been raised in recent years concerning the role of business—in particular, whether it works for the good of society as a whole or for the benefit only of a limited number of people.

In the remainder of this chapter we will look at three of these important and very complex issues: the environment, consumerism, and minorities. We will examine not only the problems involved, but also the actions that business and other groups are taking to deal with them. And as we will see, these actions seldom constitute "solutions" in any broad or permanent sense. They are but tentative steps in an ongoing effort to strike a better balance among the society's many competing needs and priorities.

BUSINESS AND THE ENVIRONMENT

In the 1960s the need to protect the earth's physical environment became an issue of international prominence. The rapid industrial expansion that followed World War II, combined with a population explosion, had made life visibly less attractive in many ways. And there was far more involved than the simple beauty of nature. In 1962 Rachel Carson's *Silent Spring* sounded a warning that could not be ignored. This historic book made it clear that the uncontrolled use of chemical pesticides and other substances was dangerously upsetting the balance of nature and affecting the health of all who eat chemically treated foods. In 1964 a temperature inversion in the south of England trapped automobile and industrial exhaust fumes close to the earth's surface, killing more than four thousand people in a week by aggravating heart and respiratory ailments. Throughout the decade, fishing areas around the world were depleted by the growing levels of human and industrial wastes in the water, and whole species of birds and animals were destroyed or endangered by the expansion of industry into their natural habitats.

Because of such situations, people have become acutely aware of **ecology**, the *pattern of relationships among water, air, soil, and other resources essential to life on earth.* They see the urgent necessity of fighting **pollution**—all *the threats to the environment caused by human activities in an industrial society.*

THE ROLE OF GOVERNMENT AND BUSINESS

Since 1963 the federal government (and many state and city governments as well) has enacted a wide range of laws and regulations designed to cut back pollution threats to the environment. Opposite is a brief summary of the major federal legislation in this area.

The law around which all pollution control efforts revolve today is the National Environmental Quality Act of 1970. The act established a Council on Environmental Quality and gave it the power to coordinate all federal programs dealing with the environment and to make its policies known. Later in the same year, President Nixon established the Environmental Protection Agency (EPA) to see that the council's policies were carried out. The EPA now has the responsibility for enforcing all of the nation's pollution control programs.

The 1970 act requires every federal agency to present to the EPA an enviromental impact statement before funding or licensing any program, such as a highway, that might pollute the environment. As a result, environmental needs must be considered and weighed against economic factors in making the final decision.

The initial reaction of many business leaders to pollution control legislation was to complain about the cost, seek modification of EPA standards, and seek delays in enforcing the standards because of the en-

ergy shortage and slumping economy. But the business community received little popular, political, or legal support. And as recent surveys have shown, business leaders themselves favor their companies' taking some responsibility for protecting the environment. So businesses are now working with the EPA and state and local agencies to install equipment to control pollution from existing factories and to design pollution controls into all new factories. The Scott Paper Company, for instance, spent $24 million on a facility at one of its plants that would collect, evaporate, and burn off a polluting chemical. And business has taken a number of other steps (see Figure 1).

It is not always easy for either side—business or the government—to determine what practical steps toward pollution control are the most appropriate. Our crowded and complicated technological society forces us sometimes to choose between unpleasant alternatives. Decisions in favor of pollution controls often conflict with other, equally important objectives, as we shall see when we examine three important aspects of the pollution problem.

AIR POLLUTION

Each year, according to the Environmental Protection Agency, more than 200 million tons of man-made waste are released into the air of the United States.[3] The pollution takes many forms, but the most common are gases and solid chemical particles. Air pollution has contributed heavily to the increasing rate of lung cancer, heart disease, emphysema, bronchitis, and asthma. The EPA estimates that air pollution costs the nation at least $16.9 billion annually. Slightly more than 70 percent of this cost represents damage to buildings, clothing, and other physical objects. The remainder of this huge sum goes to paying the costs of medical treatment, lost wages, and work not done.[4]

Unfortunately, cutting down on air pollution has turned out to be anything but a straightforward matter. Many of the proposed devices to control auto emissions, for example, also reduce gas mileage, and the need for clean air must obviously be weighed against the importance of conserving gasoline. (As well, the catalytic converter, one of the most highly touted devices, can remove poisonous hydrocarbons from a car's exhaust—but it *adds* equally poisonous

MAJOR FEDERAL ENVIRONMENTAL LEGISLATION

Water pollution

NATIONAL ENVIRONMENTAL QUALITY ACT, 1970
Established Council for Environmental Quality to coordinate all federal pollution-control programs and promulgate policies. Authorized creation of Environmental Protection Agency to carry out the council's policies on a case-by-case basis.

Air pollution

CLEAN AIR ACT, 1963
Coordinated research and authorized assistance to state and local governments in formulating control programs.

CLEAN AIR ACT AMENDMENTS, 1965
Authorized setting federal standards for auto exhaust emission. Standards established for 1968 models and thereafter.

AIR QUALITY ACT, 1967
Established air quality regions, with permissible pollution levels in each region based on meteorological and urban living conditions. Required states and localities to carry out approved control programs within each region or else give way to federal controls.

CLEAN AIR ACT AMENDMENTS, 1970
Authorized the EPA to establish nationwide air pollution standards and to limit the discharge of six principal pollutants into the lower atmosphere. Auto makers required to reduce carbon monoxide, hydrocarbon, and nitrogen oxide emissions an additional 90 percent (beyond the requirements of the 1965 amendments) during the 1970s. Established emission standards for aircraft. Required states to implement EPA standards under deadline for compliance. Authorized private citizens to take legal action to require EPA to implement its standards against undiscovered offenders.

CLEAN AIR ACT AMENDMENTS, 1977
Postponed auto emission requirements, originally set for 1975 and 1978, to 1980–1981.

Solid waste pollution

SOLID WASTE DISPOSAL ACT, 1965
Authorized research and assistance to state and local control programs.

RESOURCE RECOVERY ACT, 1970
Subsidized construction of pilot recycling plants and authorized development and implementation of nationwide control programs.

RESOURCE CONSERVATION AND RECOVERY ACT, 1976
Promoted recovery of resources and conservation. Required government control of hazardous waste, tracking waste from the time and place where generated to its final disposal site. Prohibited opening new dumping sites and required all open dumps be closed or upgraded to sanitary landfills by 1983. Established provision of technical, financial and marketing assistance to promote solid waste management.

REFUSE ACT, 1899
Prohibited dumping debris into navigable waters without a permit. (Interpreted by court decision in 1966 to apply to all industrial discharges.)

FEDERAL WATER POLLUTION CONTROL ACT, 1955
Established standards for treatment before discharge of municipal waste water. (Minor·revisions in 1965, 1967.)

WATER QUALITY ACT, 1965
Authorized establishment of standards for emissions into waters.

WATER QUALITY AND IMPROVEMENT ACT, 1970
Required implementing standards under deadlines for compliance.

FEDERAL WATER POLLUTION CONTROL ACT AMENDMENTS, 1972
Established nation's primary water quality goal of returning polluted water to fishable, swimmable waters by 1983.

CLEAN WATER ACT, 1974
Established for the first time federal standards for water suppliers that serve more than twenty-five people, have more than fifteen service connections, or operate more than sixty days a year. (Originally the Safe Drinking Water Act.)

FEDERAL WATER POLLUTION CONTROL ACT AMENDMENTS, 1977
Through compromises, an extension of the 1972 regulations.

AMENDMENTS TO CLEAN WATER ACT, 1977
Revised list of toxic pollutants and established new review procedures. Requires that pollutants be held in check by "best available technology" economically possible.

Other pollutants

FEDERAL INSECTICIDE, FUNGICIDE AND RODENTICIDE ACT, 1947
To protect farmers, prohibited fraudulent claims by salespersons. Met concern about direct poisoning by requiring registration of such products.

FEDERAL INSECTICIDE, FUNGICIDE AND RODENTICIDE AMENDMENTS, 1967, 1972
Provided new authority to license users of pesticides. (Met dangers of pesticides developed in the 1940s and 1950s.)

PESTICIDE CONTROL ACT, 1972
Required all pesticides shipped in interstate commerce to be certified as effective for their stated purposes and harmless to crops, animal feed, animal life and humans.

NOISE CONTROL ACT, 1972
Required EPA to set noise standards for products identified as major sources of noise and to advise Federal Aviation Administration on appropriate standards for airplane noise.

FEDERAL ENVIRONMENTAL PESTICIDE CONTROL ACT AMENDMENTS, 1975
Set 1977 deadline (not met) for registration, classification and licensing of some 40,000 to 50,000 pesticide products.

THERE'S MUCH WORK TO BE DONE . . .

Water pollution: Only about 30 percent of the nation's 13,000 municipal treatment plants met 1977 deadlines for waste treatment.

Air pollution: Most recent figures show that 200 million tons of emissions enter the atmosphere each year.

Solid waste pollution: The EPA reports that in 1977 fourteen key industries produced more than 37 million tons of hazardous waste requiring land disposal.

BUT SOME ENCOURAGING TRENDS CAN BE NOTED . . .

Water pollution: In 1977 more than three out of four major corporations discharging pollutants used the best practicable technology to reduce water pollution.

Air pollution: More than half of industry's total 1978 pollution-control expenditure was used to clean the air.

Solid waste pollution: Expenditure on solid waste control has soared from $4.9 million in 1973 to $1.13 billion in 1978.

CLEANING UP THE POLLUTION PICTURE

FIGURE 1

sulfur oxides.) Similarly, devices called "scrubbers" are used by some utilities in their smokestacks to filter sulfur dioxide out of the escaping gases. The trouble is that when sulfur dioxide combines with the watery solution used in the scrubbers, it forms a semisolid sludge that cannot easily be disposed of: it's not solid enough to use as landfill, and it contains chemicals that can contaminate any water it is dumped into.[5]

WATER POLLUTION

The lakes, rivers, and coastal waters of the United States have been absorbing a steadily increasing amount of waste from factories and homes. This burden has made it more and more difficult for the affected bodies of water to recleanse themselves naturally. As a result, they become unable to support life and unfit to drink from or swim in. By the mid-1960s more than 20 million people in the United States were drinking potentially unhealthy water.

As with air pollution, the problems of water pollution are usually far more obvious than the solutions. The already depressed steel industry, for example, claims that companies must often sacrifice jobs and new investment opportunities to comply with the increasingly stiffer and thus more expensive government pollution standards.

In 1977 Congress moved to reduce such economic hardships by way of a compromise between industrial and environmental concerns. In essence, the compromise modified an earlier law that had set a 1983 deadline for the installation in factories of more advanced, and expensive, water pollution control devices. The new regulations maintained and even tightened earlier clean-water standards. They allowed exemptions, however, for companies that could prove that the more costly equipment would not do a significantly better job than the antipollution devices they already had.[6]

Around the same time, the EPA adopted a tough new policy aimed at forcing reluctant companies to comply with the law. Henceforth, businesses that violated antipollution standards would be given sixty days to comply, after which time they would face fines at least equal to the amount they saved by ignoring the law.[7]

LAND POLLUTION

Land pollution involves a number of problems. One is solid waste pollution: the EPA reports that in 1977 fourteen key industries produced more than 37 million tons of hazardous waste requiring land disposal.[8] Another is aesthetic pollution, the destruction of the natural beauty of the landscape. But perhaps the most important pollution issue in American politics today, along with air pollution from car exhausts and water and shore pollution from oil spills, is that of **strip mining** (or surface mining) of coal. Strip mining *extracts minerals from open pits, rather than by tunneling.* Strip mining is the most polluting method of obtaining coal; but it is also the cheapest, safest, and quickest way. Mine owners could have shafts dug, but this would take longer, risk lives, and raise the price of coal. The soundest compromise seems to be to force surface-mine operators to restore the topsoil and re-

RADIATION POLLUTION: AN UNSOLVED PROBLEM

Quite a few newspaper headlines today deal with the debate over nuclear energy. Supporters of nuclear energy argue that it is a safe, clean, and badly needed source of energy for our nation's future. But critics warn of the possible dangers of radiation pollution from transportation of radioactive materials and ineffective safety control at nuclear processing plants. In 1978, 65 processing plants were operating, but applications for 100 more processing plants were stalled.

Especially difficult is the problem of deciding what to do with spent fuel from nuclear power plants. Suggestions have included storing the radioactive waste in Antarctic ice, burying it underneath the ocean floor, and even launching it into outer space. All of these solutions, however, would pose logistical and economic problems, particularly since the government estimates that by 1985 some 10,000 tons of this nuclear garbage will need to be disposed of.

At present, while a variety of alternatives are still being considered, the most feasible solution may be to bury the waste material in natural salt beds deep underground. The government has selected seven sites for this, only one of which—near Carlsbad, New Mexico—has been announced. What is the rationale behind this plan? In the event that a buried container ruptured, the salt formation would act as a vault and prevent the radioactivity from escaping to the surface.

Source: "A Graveyard for Nuclear Waste," *Business Week*, November 28, 1977, pp. 94D, 94F.

plant the landscape after the coal has been extracted. Once again, the solution is an imperfect one—the affected land will still be scarred for many years, disrupting the lives of the area's residents—but it is likely to remain the most common course of action until a better alternative is found.

OTHER FORMS OF POLLUTION

At least three other forms of pollution have become common in industrial societies. One is *noise pollution,* from airplanes, traffic, subways, and machinery in enclosed factories. (We discuss noise pollution in the case on page 22.) Another is *pesticide pollution,* which threatens animal life and may cause cancer in humans. The third is *radiation pollution,* especially leaks from nuclear power plants. (We discuss radiation in the box on page 13.)

THE COST OF POLLUTION CONTROLS

How much does it cost to restore the environment? As it has turned out, expenditures are considerably higher than most people anticipated at the beginning of the decade. A recent study published by the United States Department of Commerce shows that industry spent over $6.5 billion dollars in pollution control in 1976. Motor vehicle manufacturing businesses spent $90 million. Chemical manufacturing set aside $765 million to help stop pollution. And petroleum manufacturers spent over $1 billion.[9] It is estimated that pollution control costs for 1978 will reach $10.92 billion.[10] Virtually everyone agrees on the importance of protecting the environment. But because antipollution measures are so expensive, a number of basic and legitimate questions have been raised about the government's approach to the issue.

One of these questions is whether the burdens of meeting the costs of pollution control have been fairly distributed. The government's policy in this regard has

INDUSTRIAL CAUSES OF CANCER: WHAT CAN BE DONE?

One of the most difficult and serious of all pollution control problems concerns the environmental causes of cancer. Throughout this century the spread of industrialization has been accompanied by a sharp rise in the incidence of cancer. In some cases the disease has been traced back to specific industrial sources—such as asbestos fireproofing in building construction. For the most part, though, the causes of cancer are extremely difficult to track down. The disease takes many forms, and each one may have several known causes (and others still unknown). Beyond this, a malignancy may incubate for ten or twenty years before it appears, making the original cause all the harder to determine.

At present, one of the most promising methods of research is to look for geographical patterns—unusual concentrations of cancer in certain localities—and then try to find a common denominator. The National Cancer Institute recently identified thirty-nine counties around the country that have well-above-average rates of cancer and that also have one or more large petroleum refineries. Some researchers suspect that the fumes emitted by the refineries may include cancer-causing chemicals—but they can't be sure because there are so many other variables. Many of the counties also have petrochemical plants, for instance, and different types of cancer predominate in different locales.

NIOSH (National Institute for Occupational Safety and Health) maintains that it is not currently possible to set safe exposure levels. The best general guideline that they can issue is "Exposure to any known or suspected carcinogen [cancer-causing substance] must be reduced to the lowest possible level by whatever means." Chemical and other industries have four basic, but hardly simple, methods available for limiting employee exposure to carcinogens. They are listed in order of NIOSH's preference:

1. use an alternative noncarcinogenic material;

2. isolate the process (within a closed system of process equipment);

3. isolate employees (within a closed control booth from which automated equipment is operated);

4. issue personal protective equipment (such as respirators, goggles, gloves, air-supplied suits, and the like).

been based on direct responsibility. Thus the greatest costs have been paid by the heaviest polluters—among them electric utilities and the petroleum, chemical, and paper industries. Spokespersons for these groups have argued that since the federal government has subsidized cities and towns that purchase pollution control equipment, it should also subsidize firms caught in an economic squeeze—especially where jobs are at stake. Failing that, industry leaders and some economists have suggested replacing inflexible regulations with some form of pollution tax, which could be adjusted to achieve the same reductions in pollution but would allow businesses to work out the best way to absorb the combined tax and cost burdens.

Another basic question is whether our economy, not fully recovered from the last recession and struggling to avoid a relapse, should be subjected right now to the costs of a massive antipollution program. It is true that $6.5 billion a year is a large sum at a time when business is sluggish. On the other hand, it is actually only a small percentage of our gross national product, a fraction not likely to have a serious impact on economic recovery.

It seems evident that the costs of pollution control are worth incurring. Ultimately, environmental pollution is far more than a passing concern, or another excuse for the government to meddle in business affairs. It is literally an issue of life and death. People have already been killed by pollution: that is not a theory but a fact. And it is also a fact that for all our technological ingenuity, we still depend on certain natural resources for our survival, raw materials that we can hardly afford to waste or abuse on an increasingly crowded planet.

BUSINESS AND THE CONSUMER

The business that wants to sell a product and the customer who wants to buy it normally have a relationship based on healthy skepticism. That relationship is aptly captured in two familiar mottoes: "There's a sucker born every minute," and "Let the buyer beware." They reflect the traditional and widely held view that people trying to sell things for a profit are not necessarily to be trusted and conversely, that customers who get fleeced have only themselves to blame.

During the 1960s, however, a growing number of people began to challenge this survival-of-the-fittest approach to business-customer relations. With increasing success, consumerists campaigned for greater frankness and accountability on the part of business. They demanded that consumers be protected from useless, inferior, or dangerous products, from misleading advertising, and from unfair pricing. As a result, producers and consumers alike became more aware of a wide variety of safety problems. Pill containers, for instance, were redesigned so that children could not open them. Television sets were made more shock-resistant and radiation-free. Plastic bags used by dry cleaners were made with holes in them so children could not suffocate themselves accidentally. In 1972 Congress created the Consumer Product Safety Commission, which took over the responsibility for imple-

In general, the methods most favored by NIOSH (the first two listed at left) are the most expensive or technologically difficult to use. Because of these considerations, business has opposed the NIOSH guidelines.

Since the original standards for regulation of carcinogens were established by the Occupational Safety and Health Administration in 1971, only seventeen new health standards were completed by late 1977. All of these were concerned with chemical carcinogens—asbestos, vinyl chloride, coke oven emissions, and others. But proposed standards for benzene in the workplace were postponed, awaiting further information from industry and the public. And a public hearing on carcinogens and the risk that they present has been put off until at least 1978. For the near future, the effort to control this most lethal and mysterious form of pollution will have to rely less on hard facts than on indirect evidence, perseverance, and luck.

Sources: "Using Cancer's Rate to Track Its Causes," *Business Week*, November 14, 1977, pp. 69–70, 75; and *Carcinogens—Regulation and Control,* Department of Health, Education and Welfare, DHEW Publication No. (NIOSH) 77–205, (Washington, D.C.: Government Printing Office, 1977), p. 13.

menting such existing laws as the Flammable Fabrics Act, the Federal Hazardous Substance Act, and the Refrigerator Safety Act of 1956. Recent important actions by the commission include banning asbestos in certain items, like manufactured fireplace logs, and banning benzene in material such as paint thinner and rubber cement. The commission also has the authority to recall specific production batches and to develop uniform standards for consumer products. Ultimately, it plans to develop safety standards for some ten to twelve thousand products.

THE CURRENT STATUS OF THE CONSUMER MOVEMENT

In recent years the consumer movement has established itself as a major and permanent force in American business life. (For an overview of legislation in this area, see opposite page.) Consumer advocates, however, like environmentalists, have discovered that when seemingly clear-cut issues are subjected to the give and take of the legislative process, any number of unforeseen complications can arise. Since the early 1970s consumerism has clearly lost some of its political momentum. Of some forty congressional bills supported by consumer advocate Ralph Nader and his troops in 1977, about half were defeated, and in 1978 a major drive to create a federal consumer protection agency was rejected by a substantial margin.[11]

Nevertheless, such setbacks should hardly be interpreted as the beginning of the end of consumerism. Consumer groups continue to actively pursue better consumer protection. The ban on benzene in some items came about in part because of Nader and company's arguments against the chemical. Airbags for

Health warnings, unit pricing, and content listings—all are related to the spread of the consumer movement.

MAJOR FEDERAL CONSUMER LEGISLATION

Food and drug

PURE FOOD AND DRUG LAW, 1906
Forbade adulteration and misbranding of food and drugs sold in interstate commerce. Food and Drug Administration, under Agriculture Department, was made responsible for enforcement.

MEAT INSPECTION ACT, 1907
Authorized the Department of Agriculture to inspect meat slaughtering, packing and canning plants.

FEDERAL FOOD, DRUG AND COSMETIC ACT, 1938
Added cosmetics and therapeutic products to FDA's jurisdiction. Broadened definition of misbranding to include "false and misleading" labeling. The FDA was removed from the Department of Agriculture to the Department of Health, Education and Welfare.

KEFAUVER-HARRIS DRUG AMENDMENTS TO FOOD AND DRUG ACT, 1962
Required manufacturer to test safety and effectiveness of drugs before marketing and to include the common or generic name of the drug on the label.

WHOLESOME MEAT ACT, 1967
Updated and strengthened standards for the inspection of slaughterhouses of red meat animals.

DRUG LISTING ACT, 1972
Provided FDA with access to information on drug manufacturers.

Protection against misbranding and false or harmful advertising

WOOL LABELING ACT, 1939
Required fabric labeling, actual percentage of fabric components, and manufacturer's name.

FUR PRODUCTS LABELING ACT, 1951
Required that furs name animals of origin.

TEXTILE FIBER PRODUCTS IDENTIFICATION ACT, 1958
Prohibited misbranding and false advertising of textile fiber products not covered in the Wool or Fur Labeling Acts.

FEDERAL HAZARDOUS SUBSTANCES LABELING ACT, 1960
Required warning labels to appear on items containing dangerous household chemicals.

FAIR PACKAGING AND LABELING ACT, 1966
Required honest and informative package labeling and attempted to limit the increase in package sizes. (Under this act, the Federal Trade Commission, in 1972, required the following to be clearly, accurately and conspicuously labeled: origin of the product, quantity of contents and representation of servings, uses and/or applications of the product.)

PUBLIC HEALTH SMOKING ACT, 1970
Banned cigarette advertising on radio and television and required warning on packaging.

FEDERAL HAZARDOUS SUBSTANCES ACT, 1977
A revision of the Federal Hazardous Substances Labeling Act of 1960; this act required labels for various hazardous substances to be of a specific size and contain such information as first aid instructions, instructions for safe handling and storage and a description of the hazards involved in using the product.

Product safety

FLAMMABLE FABRIC ACT, 1953
Prohibited the shipment in interstate commerce of wearing apparel or fabric made of flammable materials.

NATIONAL TRAFFIC AND MOTOR VEHICLE SAFETY ACT, 1966
Required manufacturers to notify purchasers of new cars of safety defects discovered after manufacture and delivery.

CHILD PROTECTION AND TOY SAFETY ACT, 1969
Provided greater protection from children's toys with dangerous mechanical or electrical hazards.

POISON PREVENTION PACKAGING ACT, 1970
Required manufacturers to use safety packaging on products containing substances that may be harmful to children.

CONSUMER PRODUCT SAFETY COMMISSION ACT, 1972
Created Consumer Product Safety Commission, a federal agency concerned exclusively with the safety of consumer products. (Under this act, the following steps have recently been taken: in 1974, vinyl chloride was banned from use in aerosol household products; in 1977 and 1978, use of asbestos in spackling compound and artificial logs was banned; in 1978, benzene was banned in consumer products, which include paint thinners and rubber cement. The Commission also has the authority to recall specific production batches and develop uniform standards for consumer products.)

Credit protection

TRUTH-IN-LENDING ACT (CONSUMER PROTECTION CREDIT ACT), 1968
Required creditors to furnish individuals obtaining credit a statement of the amount of the financing charge and the percentage rate of interest charged annually.

FAIR CREDIT REPORTING ACT, 1970
Required agencies reporting consumer credit data to follow reasonable procedures assuring the accuracy of their information. Required users of this information, upon withholding credit, to inform the consumer of the source of this information.

TRUTH-IN-LENDING ACT AMENDMENTS (Regulation Z), 1977
Required full disclosure of the cost and terms of consumer credit. Preserved consumers' rights in billing disputes.

MAGNUSON-MOSS WARRANTY ACT, 1977
Required all warranties to be written in ordinary language, contain all terms and conditions of the warranty and be made available prior to purchase to facilitate comparison shopping.

FAIR DEBT COLLECTION PRACTICES ACT, 1978
Prohibited deceptive and unfair debt collection practices by debt collectors, including: calling at inconvenient or unusual times; harassing, oppressing or abusing any person; and making false statements when collecting debts.

automobiles, less expensive pharmaceutical prescriptions, controls on TV ads aimed at children (especially those for products that contain sugar), and the establishment of standards of health, safety, performance, and value, in general, continue to be targets for consumer activists.

One victory for consumers was the passing of the Fair Debt Collection Practices Act in 1978. This legislation prohibits deceptive and unfair debt collection methods by collectors, although not by lawyers or individual creditors. Such methods of collecting as calling at inconvenient or unusual times, harassing or abusing a person, and making false statements are now punishable by up to $500,000 in damages.[12]

If consumer issues do not make headlines as frequently as they did in years past, it may be in part because many of the principles that stirred up so much controversy a decade ago are now taken almost for granted. A growing number of corporations have set up consumer-affairs departments that are not merely

DOWNSIZING AND SAFETY CHANGES: RECENT PROBLEMS OF THE AUTO INDUSTRY

The ongoing tug-of-war between the automobile industry and consumer and environmental groups provides a good illustration of the new pressures being brought to bear on business generally. Ralph Nader's exposé of the potentially hazardous design defects in the General Motors Corvair raised a number of embarrassing—and very serious—questions. How many unsafe cars had manufacturers sold in the past, and did they know they were unsafe? Why was safety not engineered into the cars? The manufacturers' response was, essentially, that there was no demand—that the public was not interested in safety. When safety belts were being offered as optional equipment, for instance, more people paid $400 extra for air conditioning than $75 for safety belts.

If this was the case, a growing number of people concluded—if the free market system failed to provide incentives for basic safety measures—then the government should make them mandatory. As a result, a series of laws were passed requiring all new cars to be equipped with such features as safety belts, shatterproof glass, padded dashboards, and stronger bumpers. More recently, a heated legislative battle has focused on the subject of airbags. This device automatically inflates in the event of a front-end collision and protects passengers from smashing into the steering wheel or dashboard. Automakers have resisted proposals to make the airbags mandatory, chiefly because they would increase the price of cars, hurting sales at least temporarily and adding to the ever-present problem of inflation. Proponents, on the other hand, point out that car sales would not be affected in the long run and that the added expense would be offset by a decline in highway injury rates and related medical and insurance costs.

Of even greater concern to the auto industry is the long-term impact of government requirements for better gas mileage and cleaner tailpipe emissions. The Environmental Protection Agency has established a timetable for improvements in fuel efficiency, mandating that by 1985 new American cars get an average of 27.5 miles per gallon—almost twice the 1975 average. This means, of course, that American cars will have to get steadily smaller. The prospect is not one that is relished by manufacturers or dealers, since their largest models have always been the most profitable. Moreover, the situation is complicated by the industry's obligation to meet tougher antipollution standards at the same time, since emission-control devices tend to reduce fuel efficiency.

Thus automakers are faced with the dilemma that confronts an ever-larger segment of the business community—how to respond to social concerns and still make a profit. How will they solve it? It's too early to tell. In mid-1978, however, there was some evidence that buyers *would* accept smaller cars; so perhaps the other pieces of the puzzle will eventually fall in place.

Sources: "Don't Deflate the Airbag," *New York Times*, July 24, 1977, p. 16; and "Auto Makers Play an Expensive New Game," *Business Week*, October 24, 1977, pp. 72–76, 78, 83.

window dressing, as some skeptics predicted, but valuable sources of information for planning and policy-making. Moreover, many corporate leaders have become convinced that such efforts are well worth the cost in strictly practical terms. "We see it coming back in repeat business," says a vice-president of Whirlpool, which operates a nationwide toll-free phone service for complaints.[13] And as a food company executive put it, "A can of beans is a can of beans. But whether customers buy from us or from the competition can often depend on how they perceive our treating them."[14]

BUSINESS AND WORKERS: THE PROBLEM OF MINORITY DISCRIMINATION

So far we've talked about the responsibilities of business in connection with issues that concern all Americans—protecting the environment and responding to the needs of consumers. But what about the responsibility businesses bear specifically to the people who work for them? This is a topic that we will highlight in several of our later chapters. In Chapter 5 we discuss health insurance plans, pensions, and safety measures that businesses set up for their workers. In our Enrichment Chapter on Human Relations we survey management efforts to make workers' jobs more satisfying. And in our Enrichment Chapter on Management and Unions we see how unions and management negotiate to establish wages, working hours, and workplace conditions. Here we will take up the important problem of job discrimination against minorities.

WHAT ARE MINORITIES?

In a sociological sense, a **minority** is *a category of people that society at large singles out for discriminatory, or selective, unfavorable treatment.* Historically, blacks have perhaps suffered the most severe discrimination: it was not until World War I that blacks in large numbers worked next to whites on factory assembly lines. Because they were the last to be hired, they were often the first to be fired under the seniority-protection rules that prevail in most businesses. But many Spanish-surnamed Americans have also been assigned to low-paying, menial jobs, as have many women.

(Women are actually a *majority* numerically speaking, but they are a *minority* in the sense that they have suffered discrimination.) Job discrimination against minorities has tended to result in a "vicious cycle." Because they could not hope for better jobs, many minority-group members have had little incentive to seek education. And because they have not had an adequate education, many have not been able to qualify for those jobs that have been made available to them. Figure 2 gives some basic facts about minority-group disadvantage.

WHAT IS BEING DONE TO IMPROVE JOB OPPORTUNITIES FOR MINORITIES?

Discrimination runs counter to our American ideal of equal opportunity for all citizens. So when blacks, women, Spanish-speaking people, and other minorities have presented demands for fair treatment, they have found many sectors of American society willing to move toward change.

Government action

The keystone of the nation's commitment to helping all Americans achieve equal opportunity is the Civil Rights Act of 1964, which forbids discrimination in employment. The act established an Equal Employment Opportunities Commission (often referred to as the EEOC) to work with employers, labor unions, minority-group associations, and vocational and professional schools. Its goal was to awaken minority-group members to their new career opportunities and bring them into the mainstream of the American economy. The EEOC investigates complaints of job-related discrimination, filing legal charges against companies where warranted and sometimes granting huge back-pay awards to individuals or groups victimized by unfair practices. More recently it has sought to speed up the processing of cases, which can often drag on for years, by weeding out groundless charges sooner and encouraging the parties involved to meet with each other face to face. As the procedures become more streamlined, workers with valid complaints will receive quicker action, and employers wrongly accused will be spared the drain on their resources and reputations that would result from drawn-out legal battles.

MINORITY-GROUP DISADVANTAGE: SOME BASIC FACTS

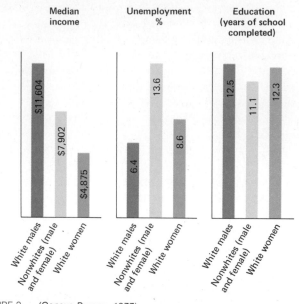

FIGURE 2   (Census Bureau, 1977)

Our society has changed a great deal in recent years, but minorities are still at a significant disadvantage. Here, education, income and unemployment figures for blacks and white women are compared with the same figures for white males. White women have the lowest median income of the three groups; blacks have the highest rate of unemployment.

THE EQUAL PAY ACT AND THE ERA Even before the EEOC was established, Congress passed a piece of legislation of particular benefit to women—the Equal Pay Act of 1963, which required equal pay for equal work. Benefits to women are also envisioned by the supporters of the proposed Equal Rights Amendment (ERA) to the Constitution, which would prohibit sex-based discrimination in all legal, social, and economic matters. The ERA has yet to collect the approval of thirty-eight states, the number necessary to transform the proposal into law. But with the deadline for the ERA fast approaching, supporters fought for and won an extension to June 30, 1982, during which time they will battle to secure the endorsement of three more states.

TRAINING PROGRAMS The government has also realized that equal employment opportunities are useless unless minority-group members have the training to take advantage of new career opportunities. Since 1963 the government has sponsored and underwritten a broad series of programs in which government agencies, social service organizations, and business have combined to train people for jobs. For example, in programs funded under the Comprehensive Employment and Training Act (CETA) of 1973 close to $12 billion was spent in 1978 for on-the-job and classroom training for some 1.5 million people. In some cities CETA workers account for more than 25 percent of the municipal payroll.[15]

Business's response to the problem of job discrimination

Since most people in this country are employed by business, it was on business that the 1964 Civil Rights Act imposed the primary responsibility for ending patterns of job discrimination. It was recognized that the patterns were too deeply embedded to be combated merely by pledges of future change. So the government required businesses to set up **affirmative action** programs—programs in which the businesses would *actively recruit members of minority groups and train them specifically for professional-level jobs.* Accordingly, most of the major corporations drew up and implemented affirmative action programs with goals set on timetables. (For example, a company might pledge that by 1980, 20 percent of its managers would be women.)

Problems connected with affirmative action

In carrying out affirmative action plans, businesses must walk a tightrope. On the one hand, they must make visible progress toward providing genuine equal career opportunities. On the other hand, they must not establish **quotas**, *fixed numbers of minority members to be hired.* Recent court decisions have ruled that such quotas discriminate against young white men just entering the job market and are thus unconstitutional.

Indeed, the basic principles of affirmative action (or "reverse discrimination," as opponents have labeled it) have touched off a variety of legal challenges that are making their way toward the Supreme Court. The most widely publicized has been the lawsuit filed by a white medical school applicant, Allan Bakke, against the University of California at Davis. Bakke charged that as a result of the school's affirmative action program, he had been denied admission while less well-qualified minority applicants had been accepted. In other words, he claimed that he had been discriminated against on the basis of his race. In 1977 California's highest court ruled in Bakke's favor, and the decision was subsequently appealed to the United States Supreme Court. In a mid-1978 decision the Supreme Court ruled that the university had maintained an unlawful quota system, and on this basis Bakke was ordered admitted to the medical school. In a second part of the decision, though, the court ruled that affirmative action plans containing no hard-and-fast quotas are constitutional. Because this decision is so recent, opinions vary as to just what effect it will have. While it seems safe to say that affirmative action has been upheld as a legally permissible way to remedy past discriminatory practices, institutions from now on may be somewhat more careful in their use of such plans.

HOW FAR HAVE WE PROGRESSED AGAINST JOB DISCRIMINATION?

Most social critics would agree that the major corporations responded quickly and well once the federal government established legal standards and guidelines. With the cooperation of newer industrial unions, like the United Auto Workers and the United Steel-

Affirmative action programs help create professional and managerial opportunities for minorities

workers, assembly lines and factory workers have become integrated. But older construction trade unions have been slower to respond. Special efforts are being made to bring minorities into these craft unions and into management-level jobs in small- and medium-sized companies.

The progress made thus far is reflected in statistics. In 1970, blacks (and other nonwhite races) were making 73.9 percent of the salaries made by whites. By 1976, the percentage had improved to 80.2 percent, though this was a drop from the 1975 figure of 82.1 percent. This percentage is expected to improve even more, since much of the effort to establish equal pay for blacks and whites now depends on programs that will take a while to make an impact—for instance, training the hard-core unemployed, graduating more minority-group members from colleges and professional schools, and expanding minority entrepreneurship.[16]

As with blacks, the salaries of women have also been low. In 1970, women made a mere 62.3 percent of what men were earning. In 1976, this figure dropped to just below 62 percent. As discussed earlier, the passage of the Equal Rights Amendment would prohibit sex-based discrimination in economic matters (as well as others), a situation that would help to raise women's salaries.

THE CORPORATION IN SOCIETY

Ultimately, the three issues we have been discussing can best be understood not as separate topics but as aspects of a broader process of change in society. Whether the emphasis is on the environment, consumerism, or minority employment, the message for the business community remains the same: private enterprise does not mean immunity from public scrutiny and accountability. In effect, corporate America has been reminded that it does not exist in a vacuum, that it has a responsibility not only to make a profit—something no one disputes—but also to serve the best interests of the society around it. Today's businesses are faced with the challenge of trying to reconcile a number of basically conflicting goals and requirements. And their success in doing so will, to a great degree, determine both the material standard of living and the intangible quality of life available to Americans two or three generations from now.

CHAPTER REVIEW

Business is all the work involved in providing people with goods and services for a profit. Our economic system is based on the idea that the owner of a business is entitled to keep whatever profits the business makes. Profit plays a large role in work, also—people do not generally work for the fun of it, but for compensation. This incentive is called the profit motive.

How do businesses make a profit? American business is based on the free market system—in theory, anyone may sell anything, and anyone may buy anything. The basic forces that dominate the free market are competition and supply and demand.

Competition encourages business to keep prices low and quality high. The theory of supply and demand holds that the supply of a product will tend to rise when the demand is greater. Also, people will usually pay more for something they want that's in short supply.

Just how "free" our free market system really is may be questioned. For example, we do not get to keep all our profits—the government exercises its right to tax. And not everyone can sell any item that he or she may want to. The free market is also limited by the monopoly.

When an industry is dominated by a few large companies—like the automobile industry—the commanding group is called an oligopoly. Oligopolies are not illegal, but because of their strength they may be able to shut out competition—thus another mark against the notion of a "free" market.

In recent years business has begun to play a more active role in at least three major problem areas: the environment, consumerism, and discrimination against minorities. The public has become concerned about air and water pollution and other environmental dangers. Spurred by federal and local legislation, business has spent millions to clean up existing facilities and build controls into new ones.

The consumer movement has focused on the goals of safety, health, performance, and value. Prodded by government, business has responded with a number of improvements in products and services.

In the area of discrimination against minorities and women, corporations—again at the instigation of federal and other legislation—have taken affirmative action to broaden employment and promotion opportunities. Although minorities have had limited success so far, progress has been made and seems certain to continue.

KEY WORD REVIEW

American work ethic
business
profit
free market system
supply
demand
theory of supply and demand
monopoly
ecology
pollution
strip mining
minority
affirmative action
quotas

REVIEW QUESTIONS

1. Why is the study of business essential to an understanding of our society?

2. Explain the importance of profit for both business owners and workers.

3. What is the free market system? How free do you think the system actually is?

4. What actions have businesses taken to help control pollution?

5. How has business acted in response to the consumer movement?

6. How have businesses sought to end discrimination against minority groups?

CASE 1

NOISE POLLUTION: A TOUGH ENVIRONMENTAL PROBLEM

Both the Noise Control Act of 1972 and regulations developed by the Occupational Safety and Health Administration are intended to protect Americans from the ill effects of excessively loud noise. But if the problem itself is straightforward, the solution—particularly in the workplace—is anything but. Consider the forging plant, which is one of the noisiest places a person can work in. To someone standing outside the plant and 400 feet away, a forging hammer pounding metal into shape sounds as loud as a passing freight train would from 200 feet away. For a person inside the plant, prolonged exposure to that noise might eventually lead to loss of hearing.

There are only a few basic approaches to safeguarding workers against excessive noise. One alternative, favored by the government, is to redesign or enclose machinery to make it more quiet. But in some cases—the forging plant, for instance—opponents of this approach argue that it simply cannot be done: the technology and the know-how are not yet available. In industries where noise could be reduced through engineering, it is opposed on the basis of prohibitive costs. The steel industry, for example, claims that the cost of engineering controls needed to reduce noise levels to 85 decibels would work out to about $1.2 million per worker. An expense such as this, added to the $7.6 billion that the steel industry says it will have to spend between now and 1985 to reduce air and water pollution, might force some major companies to cut back production and cancel expansion plans. Small companies might be forced to shut down. Engineering solutions to noise pollution might also mean loss of jobs. According to General Motors, $20,000 worth of automation would eliminate noise—but also workers.

A second alternative is simply to reduce the amount of time that workers are exposed to noise by shortening the workday. But this would result in less productivity.

The approach that industry strongly favors, and that organized labor just as strongly opposes, is to protect workers by outfitting them with protective equipment like earmuffs or plugs. By contrast to the $1.2 million per worker that the steel industry

cites as the cost of engineering solutions, personal protective equipment would cost an estimated $42 per worker. But unions argue that it is the employer's responsibility to quiet the machines and that in any event, ear protectors are uncomfortable and can cause ear diseases. Behavioral factors also complicate the ear protector approach. Not all employees are likely to be meticulous about wearing the equipment, and not all employers are likely to be diligent in enforcing its use.[17]

1. How would you weigh the short-term and long-term benefits of each of the solutions discussed above?

2. How might the consumer be affected by the government's war on noise?

3. Are noise-pollution controls worth enforcing if they lead to lower productivity, fewer jobs, or higher prices?

CASE 2

THE UPC: A MOVE TOWARD EFFICIENCY RUNS INTO DIFFICULTY

Grocery products come in a wide assortment of packages: round, square, tall, short; cans, boxes, bags, cartons. Until the Universal Product Code came along in the early 1970s, checkout clerks had no choice but to search each package for its price and then punch it out on the cash register—a time-consuming process that usually means long checkout lines at the supermarket. The Universal Product Code, or UPC for short—those thick and thin lines with numbers underneath that appear on some 170 billion packages (mostly grocery products but also greeting cards, records, and magazines)—allows the clerk to simply wave the

package over a laser scanning device that identifies the item, its size, and its price in an instant. It's a device that boosts profit for the supermarket owner and also makes life easier for the shopper—a perfect example of the kind of innovation that free competition encourages.

So far, though, the UPC has rung up a disappointing response. Of the 32,700 supermarkets in the United States, only 208 had installed laser scanners by early 1978. Of those 170 billion coded packages, fewer than 40 million a week were being decoded. What went wrong? One problem is the expense involved. To convert a supermarket with ten checkout lanes from manual registers to scanners can cost from $100,000 to $300,000. Unless a store does $100,000 a week in gross sales—a requirement that rules out 80 percent of the supermarkets in America—the UPC does not pay.

But cost is not the only problem. Politics are involved, too. The object of the UPC was to put an end to the costly procedure of marking each item's price by hand. To do so, however, would cost the price markers their jobs. As a result, at least six states have passed laws that force stores to continue hand-pricing each item, and more states are likely to follow suit. In addition, the code first appeared at a time when food prices were skyrocketing, and this prompted consumer groups to lobby vigorously against the UPC on the grounds that it would be used to put price increases through more quickly than ever before.[18]

1. As a consumer, would you argue for or against the use of scanners? Why?

2. Aside from the labor costs involved, what other reasons might explain why the hand-pricing of items costs supermarkets money?

The Glass Store,Inc.

2

FORMS OF BUSINESS ORGANIZATION

Do you own an insurance policy, or are you part of a pension plan set up by an employer? If so, then you may already be, indirectly, a part-owner of a business, since insurance-company assets and pension funds are often invested in the shares of ownership known as stocks. But some day you may want to become an owner in a more direct sense—by starting your own enterprise. When that day arrives, you will have to choose one of the forms of business organization that are permitted by law in this country.

Which form will be best for you—and why? In this chapter we'll look at the three major forms—sole proprietorship, partnership, and the corporation—and we'll discuss some of the tough questions a business person has to face in choosing among them. We'll also look at two new and rapidly growing forms of business, the cooperative and the franchise.

WHAT WILL THIS CHAPTER FOCUS ON?

After reading the material in this chapter, you will understand and be able to discuss:

- the three basic forms of business organization—sole proprietorship, partnership, and corporation
- the reasons why most small businesses are either sole proprietorships or partnerships
- the reasons why most large businesses are corporations
- the rapid growth of giant corporations
- vertical, horizontal, and conglomerate mergers
- the ways smaller businesses compete against larger corporations
- cooperatives and franchises

American businesses, much like American people, come in an amazing number of varieties. They also span the widest imaginable range of size and economic power, from the proverbial lemonade stand to the American Telephone & Telegraph Company. But for the sake of convenience they can be grouped into three main categories, according to their primary forms of organization—sole proprietorships, partnerships, and corporations.

Essentially, each of these three basic types represents a different approach to business—different in its internal structure, its legal status, its average size, and the business fields to which it is best suited. In addition, each type tends to offer employees a basically different working environment, with its own set of demands, risks, and rewards. In this chapter, we will survey these three forms of business organization. And we'll take a look at their various advantages and disadvantages—as they would appear to the manager of the business, and also to the worker.

SOLE PROPRIETORSHIPS

In 1973, armed with a new master's degree in special education, twenty-six-year-old Shari Zalkind moved to Boston to look for a job in her field. But it turned out there were no jobs available; and having used up her savings to pay two months' rent on an apartment, she suddenly found herself unemployed, broke, and "scared to death." Nevertheless, she still had energy and imagination, and at least one other distinctive trait: "I always hated dirty houses." So she began to make ends meet by cleaning friends' apartments for a fee, and then decided to expand her horizons. To attract new customers she started giving out business cards that read "Z-Kleenz Anything Dirty—Shari Zalkind, B.A., M.S." The idea worked—no doubt because of the novelty of someone with her academic credentials cleaning houses for a living. In any event, Ms. Zalkind found a market for her services, chiefly among professional women in the Cambridge area near Boston; and her customers were so satisfied that she soon had to hire extra help to meet the demand. By the end of 1977 she and her employees were cleaning some

thirty houses a week, for fees ranging from $25 to $45 apiece, and she expected the business to gross about $60,000 in 1978.[1]

At the opposite end of the country, Walter W. Meyer of Kirkland, Washington was laid off from his job as a Boeing aircraft designer in 1974. Unlike Shari Zalkind, Mr. Meyer had no immediate money problems; but he was also nearly sixty years old and had no way of knowing how long the layoff might last. So, rather than wait around to find out, he decided to go into business for himself. "I had always been annoyed by the inefficiency of the fireplace," he notes, and as in Ms. Zalkind's case it was this personal quirk that provided the original idea: he wanted to design a device that would increase a fireplace's efficiency and thus cut fuel costs. Two and a half years of trial and error produced the Meyer Fireplace Range, a metal oven that fits inside a fireplace and not only keeps a house warm with less fuel, Meyer claims, but can also bake bread at the same time. Unable to find a company to manufacture his invention, Meyer started one of his own, using his savings to buy the necessary equipment

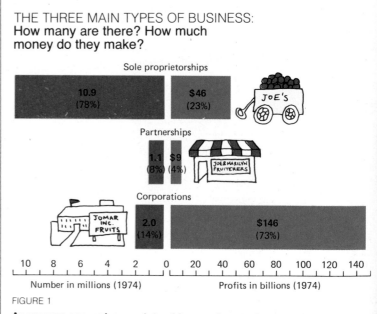

THE THREE MAIN TYPES OF BUSINESS:
How many are there? How much money do they make?

FIGURE 1

As you can see, sole proprietorships are the most common type of business in the United States, accounting for more than three of every four enterprises. However, less than one in every four dollars of profit earned by American business comes from sole proprietorships. Which type of business appears to be the most successful in terms of money earned?

and hire six employees. The business was not profitable in its first year—hardly surprising for a brand-new manufacturing firm—but it seemed likely that the investment would begin to pay off during 1978.*

Shari Zalkind and Walter Meyer are only two of the hundreds of thousands of Americans who launch new businesses each year. Like most new businesses, Shari's and Walter's enterprises are of the type known as the **sole proprietorship**—*a business owned by just one person.* The sole proprietorship is a form of enterprise that has a special place in American history and tradition, associated closely with the ideals of individual initiative, self-reliance, and hard work. It also has the practical advantage of being the easiest form of business to launch for persons with limited funds. In essence, all you have to do is start selling your goods or services, and you are a business. It is no surprise, then, that sole proprietorships are numerically the most common type of business in the United States—accounting for more than 75 percent of the country's 14 million business enterprises in 1974.[2] (Figure 1 shows the number of businesses in each organizational category, along with their respective profits.)

THE ADVANTAGES OF SOLE PROPRIETORSHIP

Sole proprietorships, though small, offer a variety of advantages. The first and most concrete, as we have said, is that they're relatively easy to get into. The financial investment need not be large, and there's far less legal red tape to deal with than in other forms of business. Perhaps more important, though, is the emotional factor: sole proprietors have the satisfaction of working for themselves. Making their own decisions and seeing the results of their efforts, they are spared the all-too-common sensation of being a small cog in a much larger organization. And, of course, since they get all the profits—assuming there *are* profits—they know exactly how well they're doing. It is for the sake of such personal rewards that many corporate executives decide to abandon secure, high-salaried jobs and take the risk of starting their own businesses.

Another major advantage of the sole proprietor-

Instead of despairing when he was laid off in late middle age, engineer Walter Meyer started a new career. He formed a company to manufacture and market his invention for improved fireplace performance.

ship is its flexibility of organization and management. Proprietors can decide for themselves when to go into business, what hours to work, whom to hire, what prices to charge, whether to expand, and whether to shut down. If small enough, the business does not have to deal with unions, equal employment opportunity agencies, or minimum wage regulations. In sole proprietorships one person can make all the major decisions without consulting anyone.

A parallel advantage to flexibility is secrecy. Sole proprietors need never reveal their plans or intentions to anyone else. They are far less vulnerable than a partnership or corporation to spying from competitors.

Furthermore, small sole proprietorships have the theoretical advantage of tax savings, since proprietors pay taxes only on the personal income they earn from their businesses. As well, self-employed people are permitted to set up individual retirement accounts, permitting them to put aside some of their earnings for their own pensions without having to pay tax on that portion during the year in which it's earned. (This plan is known as the Keough plan.)

THE DISADVANTAGES OF SOLE PROPRIETORSHIP

Because one man or woman is limited by the fact that there are only twenty-four hours in a day, most businesses owned by one person tend to be small. In 1974, nearly 75 percent of all sole proprietorships grossed less than $25,000 a year (less than $500 a week). Only 0.1 percent grossed more than $1 million a year.[3] Proprietorships do not report their incomes publicly, so we do not know what is the largest sole proprietorship.

One reason proprietorships show comparatively small profits as a group despite their numbers is that few manufacturing companies are proprietorships. (Manufacturing accounts for most of the largest firms in the country; manufacturing companies total less than 4 percent of all businesses, but they account for over 35 percent of the total receipts.[4])

There are proprietorships in every line of business, but they are most numerous in agriculture, in retail stores, and in services such as laundries and repair shops. These are fields that require comparatively little money to start up. There are relatively few sole proprietorships in heavy industry, finance, insurance, or real estate. These fields require a big investment and a large work force with specialized skills.

Beyond these problems of size and profit, the main advantage of sole proprietorships can also be a major disadvantage: the prosperity of the business depends on the talents of one person. If these are limited, the sole proprietor is frequently too emotionally involved in the business to be able to admit it and seek aid. He or she is unwilling to concede that qualified help is needed, and is thus unwilling to pay for it. Of course, a proprietor is often simply unable to pay for talent. But even if he or she is willing and can afford to hire outside help, the proprietor is often reluctant to share managerial or creative responsibility. A capable outsider will not stay long without such responsibilities.

Another major disadvantage of a proprietorship is what is legally termed **unlimited liability.** This means that *any damages or debt that can be attributed to the business can also be attached to the owner.* The two have no separate legal existence. Take the case of a man who owns an unincorporated flower shop. If his truck jumps a curb and runs down several people on the sidewalk, the resulting damages might not only end his business but also bankrupt him personally and impoverish him for many years.

A major cause of business failure among sole proprietorships is poor management, particularly problems with credit standing. A small business often has difficulty borrowing money from banks and frequently

THE 10 SMALL BUSINESSES MOST LIKELY TO SUCCEED—AND TO FAIL

BY ED HENRY

Even in the best of times, starting a new business can test the mettle of the ablest entrepreneur: some 30% of all small businesses fail during their first year, and 50% succumb within two years. To determine which businesses are the most likely to succeed—or fail—in today's economy, *Money* [magazine] recently polled 26 bankers, business school professors, Small Business Administration officials, members of the Service Corps of Retired Executives and executives of small-business investment companies across the country. [*Money*] gave them a list of the 81 most common small businesses and asked them to select candidates for success and failure.

[They] asked [their] panel to consider successful only those businesses that could survive more than five years, the most critical period for most ventures.

The results are listed below. Wherever a tie existed, it was broken by listing the business with the highest potential for pretax profits first. [They] used the average profits for businesses with assets up to $250,000 as reported to Robert Morris Associates, which collects data from bank credit officers. The figures represent pretax profits after allowing for salaries. The average profit for all 81 businesses was 3.4%. Projected growth figures, in most cases, come from the U.S. Department of Commerce, which estimates average national growth this year at 4% to 5%.

THE 10 BEST

1 Building materials stores. Increased residential construction and do-it-yourself repairs should boost sales by 10% to 15% this year.

2 Auto tire and accessories stores. Today's car owners are doing more and more repairs themselves, which should help produce a growth rate of about 9.7% this year.

3 Liquor stores. Industry growth is expected to run at least 11% in 1978. A hard-working retailer can expect something over 3% profit on each dollar of sales.

4 Sports and recreation clubs. The growing interest in exercise is the key to future profits. A club requires a large initial investment and annual fees of about $1 million to turn about $26,000 in profits.

5 Funeral homes and crematories. Small establishments make roughly $9,200 on every $100,000 they take in. Despite a decreasing death rate, the number of deaths remains around 1.9 million a year and is expected to increase with the senior-citizen population.

6 Seed and garden supply stores. The profit ratio is about the same as for sports clubs. Growth is expected to run about 8% to 9% ahead of last year.

7 Sporting goods manufacturers. Greater participation in outdoor sports is producing estimated growth ranging from 8% a year for bicycle and bicycle parts producers to 19% for the makers of equipment for team sports and snow and water skiing.

8 Engineering, laboratory, and scientific equipment. Because the aeronautical industry is rebounding, engineering equipment sales should grow about 12% this year. Manufacturers of scales and lab equipment can expect about 11% growth.

9 Hardware stores. Hardware stores also benefit from increasing numbers of do-it-yourselfers. High profit margins mean that hardware stores don't need huge sales volume; $650,000 in sales will produce $30,000 in profits.

10 Office supplies and equipment. This business is remarkably resistant to recession—a firm always needs office supplies. Profits are substantial; every $1 million in sales can return $40,000. Predicted 1978 growth: about 18%.

THE 10 WORST

1 Local laundries and dry cleaners. Since 1972, improved home laundry systems and the increasing use of synthetic fabrics have slowed growth in this business. Older, established cleaners have stayed alive by providing extra services, such as rug cleaning.

2 Used-car dealerships. Banks have generally soured on making loans to used-car dealers and their customers because of the high risk involved. Current predictions show the business shrinking in 1978.

3 Gas stations. Competition and thinning profits have tarnished these once lucrative franchises. To earn $30,000 a year, a station would have to gross about $1.8 million.

4 Local trucking firms. The high cost of unionized labor and governmental regulation make this a risky enterprise. Growth prospects are sluggish.

5 Restaurants. No other business attracts as many prospective entrepreneurs as this one does. . . . Growth potential is good, about 10% in 1978, and profits aren't all that bad, about 3.5% if you are successful. Still, "for every one that succeeds, probably a dozen fail for lack of management know-how," says Sam Siciliano, a Salt Lake City SBA official. Fast-food franchises offer management assistance, but a major franchise like McDonald's or Burger King requires a cash investment of $85,000 or more.

6 Infants' clothing stores. Babies are hardly booming, and retail clothing stores, particularly small independent ones, are encountering slow demand and stiff competition.

7 Bakeries. Supermarket bakery departments make survival tough for independent stores. Shops that make it do so by offering specialized services.

8 Machine shops. Over 5,000 independent shops make this business highly competitive. Each $100,000 in sales yields an average $3,300 in pretax profits.

9 Grocery and meat stores. Unless these stores offer special services, like delivery, the going gets rough.

10 Car washes. High turnover, strong competition, and high capital investment make this one of the least attractive businesses for the entrepreneur.

must pay a higher rate of interest to get money. (Banks charge lower interest to large corporations that are regular customers and safer credit risks.) This difficulty puts sole proprietorships at a great disadvantage.

A final disadvantage is that proprietorships have a limited life. It is difficult for the owner to arrange for the company to outlive him, or to be carried on by someone else if he or she is temporarily unable to run the business alone. Generally, when proprietors become very successful and want to make sure that their businesses grow and carry on after them, they think of forming a partnership or corporation or of merging with a larger existing business.

THE ENTREPRENEURIAL SPIRIT

What does it take to start an independent business, and what kind of people make it work? Obviously, the need to make money and the urge to be one's own boss are two basic incentives, but by themselves they're hardly enough to guarantee success. Indeed, of the half-million or so new businesses opened in 1978, two-thirds will go broke within five years.[5] Beyond a strong motivation, then, what does a budding entrepreneur need to have a fighting chance? One vital element is a practical idea for a new product or service—Walter Meyer's Fireplace Range, for instance, or Shari Zalkind's housecleaning service for working women. Another qualification common to most successful entrepreneurs, whatever field they're in, is an attentiveness to detail and a knack for solving day-to-day problems without losing sight of longer-range goals.

In addition, while there is an inevitable risk in starting any new business, the successful entrepreneur is seldom someone who could be called a gambler. Most gamblers have the odds against them; a smart businessperson, on the other hand, sees to it that the odds are as favorable as possible, gathering all the facts and planning with great care before going ahead with a new venture. A good example is the case of Michael O'Harro, operator of a posh discotheque called Tramp's in Washington, D.C. First of all, O'Harro was no novice in the business of entertainment. During his twenties he had founded a Washington-based singles' club—sponsoring social activities, tours, apartment houses, and the like—that attracted almost 50,000 members and made him a millionaire by age thirty. Selling his interest in 1970, O'Harro spent several years in Europe and then moved to California, where he hired himself out as a $500-a-day discotheque consultant, helping owners design and promote their nightspots. Finally, in 1975 he returned to Washington and persuaded the owner of the old, elegant Carriage House restaurant that the addition of a new, elegant disco could be very profitable for both of them. O'Harro then began applying his considerable expertise to the task of creating Tramp's, planning every detail in advance "like the Normandy invasion—I knew what I was going to do 60 days before it opened, 38 days before it opened and 10 days before it opened."[6]

To no one's surprise—certainly not Michael

TESTING THE ENTREPRENEURIAL YOU

Your psychological makeup can play a strong role in making your business a success or a failure. Here are some questions based on ideas supplied by Richard Boyatzis and David Winter, two psychologists who have studied the entrepreneurial character. The questions are designed to reveal whether you have entrepreneurial attitudes. Even if no answer fits your feelings precisely, choose the one that comes closest. The answers are at the bottom of the opposite page.

1. If you had a free evening, would you most likely a) watch TV b) visit a friend c) work on a hobby?

2. In your daydreams, would you most likely appear as a) a millionaire floating on a yacht b) a detective who has solved a difficult case c) a politician giving an election-night victory speech?

3. To exercise, would you rather a) join an athletic club b) join a neighborhood team c) do some jogging at your own pace?

4. When asked to work with others on a team, which would you anticipate with most pleasure: a) other people coming up with good ideas b) cooperating with others c) getting other people to do what you want?

5. Which game would you rather play: a) Monopoly b) roulette c) bingo?

O'Harro's—Tramp's proved an immediate success; and successes of that sort are hardly ever the result of gambling. Luck helps, to be sure, but a new business enterprise depends far more on a good idea, thorough planning, and one individual's single-minded determination to make it work.

PARTNERSHIPS

On April 1, 1887, a fellow named Richard W. Sears ran an 80¢ want ad in the Chicago *Daily News* for a watch-maker. It was answered by another fellow named Alvah C. Roebuck. Sears hired him—and the rest, as the saying goes, is history. In 1893 the two men formed a new company that would ultimately grow into the largest retailing enterprise in the world. The form of business organization they chose was the **partnership**—*a legal association of two or more persons in a business, as co-owners of that business.*

Ironically, though, the legendary association of Sears and Roebuck was hardly a typical example of partnerships, since Roebuck resigned in 1895 because of ill health and only his name remained a part of the company. Sears, Roebuck and Company was also aty-

6. Your employer asks you to take over a company project that is failing. Would you tell him that you will a) take it b) won't take it because you're up to your gills in work c) give him an answer in a couple of days when you have more information?

7. In school, were you more likely to choose courses emphasizing a) fieldwork b) papers c) exams?

8. In buying a refrigerator would you a) stay with an established, well-known brand b) ask your friends what they bought c) compare thoroughly the advantages of different brands?

9. While on a business trip in Europe you are late for an appointment with a client in a neighboring town. Your train has been delayed indefinitely. Would you a) rent a car to get there b) wait for the next scheduled train c) reschedule the appointment?

10. Do you believe that people you know who have succeeded in business a) have connections b) are cleverer than you c) are about the same as you but maybe work a little harder?

11. An employee who is your friend is not doing his job. Would you a) take him out for a drink, hint broadly that things aren't going right and hope he gets the message b) leave him alone and hope he straightens out c) give him a strong warning and fire him if he doesn't shape up?

12. You come home to spend a relaxing evening and find that your toilet has just overflowed. Would you a) study your home-repair book to see if you can fix it yourself b) persuade a handy friend to fix it for you c) call a plumber?

13. Do you enjoy playing cards most when you a) play with good friends b) play with people who challenge you c) play for high stakes?

14. You operate a small office-cleaning business. A close friend and competitor suddenly dies of a heart attack. Would you a) reassure his wife that you will never try to take away any customers b) propose a merger c) go to your former competitor's customers and offer them a better deal?

Quiz answers

Score one point for each correct answer. Questions 1, 2, 3, 7, 9 and 12 suggest whether you are a realistic problem solver who can run a business without constant help from others. Questions 5, 6 and 8 probe whether you take calculated risks and seek information before you act. Questions 4, 10, 13 and 14 show whether you, like the classic entrepreneur, find other people most satisfying when they help fulfill your need to win. Question 11 reveals whether you take responsibility for your destiny—and your business. If you score between 11 and 14 points, you could have a good chance to succeed. If you score from 7 to 10 points, you'd better have a superb business idea or a lot of money to help you out. If you score 7 or less, stay where you are.

1. c; 2. b; 3. c; 4. a; 5. a; 6. c; 7. a; 8. c; 9. a; 10. c; 11. c; 12. a; 13. b; 14. c.

pical in another sense: partnerships are actually relatively rare among commercial or industrial firms, being most common in the professional and financial services. Partnerships include the largest and most powerful law firms—Shearman & Sterling and Sullivan & Cromwell, for instance—and the biggest accounting firms, Peat Marwick Mitchell & Company and Price Waterhouse & Company.

Some of these large partnerships gross more than $300 million a year. Their major partners earn as much as the heads of the largest corporations. Their advisory position gives these partnerships an influence out of proportion to their size. It is safe to say, indeed, that few people are more influential in our society than the well-known partners of our major law firms.

A partnership can range in size from a large accounting firm with a hundred partners and thousands of employees to a two-chair barbershop with no employees. But most partnerships, like most proprietorships, are small. There are over one million partnerships. Only 17,000, however, earn more than $1 million a year; more than half earn under $25,000 annually.[7] Whatever their size, all partnerships are governed by the same basic principles, and subject to the same advantages and disadvantages.

ADVANTAGES OF PARTNERSHIP

Like proprietorships, partnerships are easy to enter into. Unlike proprietorships, they usually have a definite legal standing because of the agreement entered into by the partners.

Another advantage of a partnership over a proprietorship is that a partnership can combine the skills of several people, each of whom has a direct interest in the success of the business. Combining skills makes possible a vast increase in the firm's ability to create wealth. Five lawyers working in partnership can bring in far more business than five lawyers working separately. Likewise, the reason that many advertising agencies have three-person names—Doyle Dane Bernbach, say, or Wells Rich Greene—is that a writer, an artist, and a marketing director originally formed a partnership to pool their talents.

Partnerships generally have a high credit rating from banks. This is because partnerships frequently have several talented owners, most of whom have un-

limited personal liability for debts incurred by the partnership. A partnership can raise the money it needs to do business more easily than can a proprietorship.

One frequently mentioned advantage of partnerships is lower taxation. Partners, like sole proprietors, are taxed only on their personal incomes. But, as we will discuss in the section below on taxation of corporations, many people believe that the advantage is more theoretical than real.

DISADVANTAGES OF PARTNERSHIP

One of the fundamental drawbacks of the partnership arrangement is reflected in the increasing numbers of doctors, dentists, lawyers, and accountants who are turning away from traditional partnerships and forming professional corporations instead. Their primary reason is to avoid the risks of unlimited liability, which legally applies to partnerships just as it does to sole proprietorships. The problem of medical malpractice lawsuits—which have increased rapidly both in number and in the size of the financial settlements involved—has made front-page news in recent years. At the same time, a number of precedent-setting lawsuits against accountants and lawyers have made those professions equally aware of the hazards of unlimited liability, and thus of the partnership arrangement itself.

Even before liability became such a pressing issue, another built-in problem of partnerships had long been obvious: conflict between partners can wreck the company. The famous show-business partnership of Dean Martin and Jerry Lewis, though highly successful, broke up simply because the two partners had developed different career ambitions. Martin wanted to concentrate on television appearances and nightclub engagements; Lewis wanted to remain active in motion pictures as a director and actor.

Another major disadvantage is the practical limit to the number of managing partners. It is impossible to have five hundred people exchanging opinions in a conference room. Yet certain enterprises, such as large industrial firms, need many managers. The corporate firm, as we will discuss below, offers ways to attract and retain many talented managers with incentives

learn

THE THREE MAJOR FORMS OF BUSINESS
ORGANIZATION: HOW THEY COMPARE

Sole Proprietorship

Chief characteristics: Single owner; no legal
requirements.
Advantages: Little capital needed to begin. Owner in
complete control, and benefits from flexibility, secrecy
and tax savings.
Disadvantages: Talent pool restricted. Liability
unrestricted. Credit difficult to obtain; business has
limited lifespan.

Partnership

Chief characteristics: At least two owners; written
agreement usual though not necessary.
Advantages: Easy to form. Can bring together many
skilled persons. Good credit obtainable.
Disadvantages: General partners have unlimited
liability. Ever-present danger of conflict between
partners. Built-in size limitations. Lifespan somewhat
restricted.

Corporation

Chief characteristics: May have few or many owners
(stockowners). Incorporated by law under formal
charter with by-laws.
Advantages: Owners have limited liability. Investment
liquidity. Corporation has unlimited lifespan.
Disadvantages: Public disclosure often required. Cost
of incorporation can be high. Heavy tax burden on
small corporation.

and benefits other than a partnership interest in the
firm.

Many texts note still another disadvantage of
partnerships: they die with the death of a partner, so
that long-term growth is prevented. In fact, however,
this is more of a theoretical than a practical disadvantage. Many firms provide for the firms' survival after
the death of the partners. Thus the firm of Sullivan &
Cromwell continues to do business under that name,
although Mr. Sullivan and Mr. Cromwell have been
dead for many years.

CORPORATIONS

A one-person business operation is easy enough to
imagine: someone selling ice cream in the park or
handicrafts at a fair, or painting houses or repairing
old clocks, or whatever. It is perhaps harder to imagine
one person manufacturing a million automobiles, or
refining a billion gallons of gasoline, or completing a
trillion telephone calls. In a very important sense,
though, these things do indeed happen—since in the
abstract realm of the law General Motors, Exxon, and
American Telephone & Telegraph are very much like
three individual people. Not "just plain folks," to be
sure, but people nonetheless.

How is this so, and what are we really saying
here? We are pointing out that, legally, each of these
three giant business enterprises has exactly the same
standing, the same rights and duties, as an individual
person. In fact, each one was expressly planned so that
it would have these legal attributes. The form of organization the managers chose in order to make this
possible is the **corporation**—a body that Webster's
New Collegiate Dictionary tells us is *"authorized by
law to act as a private person . . . and legally endowed
with various rights and duties,"* among them to receive,
own, and transfer property, to make contracts, and to sue
and be sued.[8] A corporation may own tremendous
wealth—more than most private individuals do in this
country—and by thus concentrating its resources, it
offers its shareholders tremendous chances for profits
if it succeeds. It can also have tremendous liabilities—
but it is the corporation that is liable in full, rather than
any one of the private individuals who share ownership in it. And this is, perhaps, one of the greatest
advantages the corporation offers: if it fails, each
shareholder has to pay only a limited penalty. *The legal
responsibility of shareholders of a corporation for damages or debt only to the extent of their investments* is
called **limited liability.**

A corporation, then, is

1. an artificial person,

2. with an unlimited life span,

3. empowered by the state to carry on a specific line of
business,

4. owned by shareholders who are

5. liable for damages only to the extent of their holdings.

No brief definition, however, begins to convey the importance of the corporate form of business to the American economy. Of all the types of business organization, the corporation is by far the most significant in terms of money, size, and power.

A few statistics will serve as illustration: In the United States in 1974, corporations accounted for more than 85 percent of all money taken in by business firms—$3 trillion out of $3.5 trillion. Nearly half of this total was accounted for by firms engaged in manufacturing.[9] The largest industrial corporation in 1977, General Motors, did nearly $55 billion in sales. In 1977, there were 372 industrial corporations that had sales of more than $1 billion. The largest five hundred corporations in sales accounted for over $1.4 trillion in sales. The largest five hundred corporations in assets had holdings of $2.2 trillion.[10]

It should also be remembered that these corporate giants are almost all publicly owned—that is, shares of their stock can be bought by anyone with the money. The country's most widely held corporation is American Telephone & Telegraph, which at the start of 1978 had 2,911,805 stockholders—or owners. This relationship between stockholders and company is central to the enormous strength of the modern corporation. In brief, if a stockholder dies, his shares can be bequeathed or sold to someone else; consequently, whole generations of stockholders can come and go, but the company remains (so long as it's economically sound). This is why, as we have said, the corporation has an unlimited life span. And this feature gives it unlimited potential for growth.

Large corporations represent the most powerful, fastest-growing segment of the national economy. Their power extends beyond the economic sphere to the political and social spheres as well. To understand American business—and, indeed, the society around it—it is essential to understand the American corporation.

TYPES OF CORPORATIONS

In a course on business, most of our discussion centers on large business corporations such as General Motors, U.S. Steel, and Procter & Gamble. But there are a variety of kinds of corporations that play important roles in American society, and you should be aware of the differences among them. Table 1 summarizes the seven principal types of corporations.

There are two major distinctions to keep in mind. First, not all corporations sell shares on the open mar-

Table 1 Classification of Corporations

Type	Definition	Example
Public corporations	Carries on business to make a profit for its owners, the shareholders, persons, or institutions with enough money to purchase a share.	General Motors
Private corporations	Profit-making business, but with few owners and no open market for its shares.	Gallo Wines
Municipal corporations	Cities and townships that carry on governmental functions under charters granted by state.	New York City
Government-owned corporations	Federal, state, or local businesses that function for the public welfare; all shares are government-owned.	Tennessee Valley Authority
Quasi-public corporations	Businesses owned partly by the government, partly by private investors; or owned by investors, but subsidized by the government; usually high-risk ventures, but important to society.	Comsat (Communications Satellite Corporation)
Nonprofit corporations	Service institutions incorporated for reasons of limited liability.	Harvard University
Single-person corporations	Individuals who incorporate to escape high personal income tax rates.	Movie stars, athletes, and authors

ket. Of the ones listed, only public and quasi-public corporations do so. The others, private corporations, withhold their stock from public sale, preferring to finance any expansion out of their own earnings. A private corporation's directors are assured of complete control over their operations—without, say, having to justify themselves to a cost-conscious investment bank. In addition, a corporation whose shares are owned by fewer than 500 persons is not required to disclose its finances to the general public.

Second, not all corporations are profit-making institutions. Numerous nonprofit organizations incorporate, chiefly for the rights a corporation charter grants. Some of these organizations are owned by the government; others are formed by private individuals pursuing goals in areas such as social service and the arts.

THE STRUCTURE OF THE CORPORATION

Once the corporation is formed, the initial voting shareholders elect a board of directors, who replace the original incorporators. (Of course, the original incorporators frequently serve on the board.) Depending on the size of the company, there can be from three to about thirty-five directors; it is usual to have from twenty-one to twenty-five. The directors, in turn, elect the top officers of the company. The result is the basic structure shown in Figure 2.

The shareholders

The voting shareholders are theoretically the ultimate governing body of the corporation, and they do in practice have some say in how the corporation is run. At least once a year all the owners of voting shares meet to choose directors for the company, and also to select independent accountants who will be charged with overseeing the company's financial activities on behalf of the stockholders. There are, however, limits to shareholders' participation. In many corporations the shareholders form too large and dispersed a group to manage their business effectively, so that in reality the typical stockholders' meeting tends to be more of a ritual celebration than a decision-making occasion. The three million stockholders of AT&T, for example,

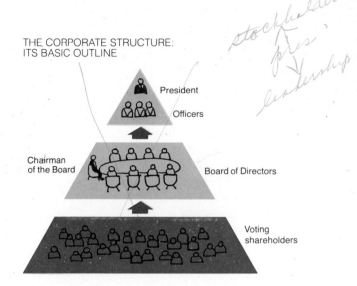

THE CORPORATE STRUCTURE: ITS BASIC OUTLINE

FIGURE 2

Shareholders are the basis of the corporate structure: it is because of their capital investment that the company can function. The shareholders elect a Board of Directors (some or all of whom may be shareholders). The Board, in turn, elects a chairman to speak for them. The directors also elect the corporate officers to carry out their policies and decisions. Officers can be members of the board, or may simply be hired employees.

virtually always vote according to recommendations from management: they may own the corporation, but they don't control it. Indeed, the more stockholders there are, the less real influence they have on the corporation.

The board of directors

As a practical matter, therefore, it is the **board of directors** that has *the ultimate authority in guiding corporate affairs and making general policy.* It is they who authorize money to build a new factory, develop a new product line, or acquire a new subsidiary. Here again, though, there is sometimes a gap between theory and practice. A board's functions vary tremendously depending on the corporation. In some corporations the board includes **outside directors**, *directors who are not officers of the company but who take an active role in its affairs.* But in other companies, where there is a strong chief officer with the confidence of the board, the board frequently acts as "window dressing."

In recent years, responding to criticism by government agencies, stockholder groups, and other observers, the directors of many corporations have begun taking their duties a great deal more seriously. Such matters as long-range planning and the corporation's social responsibilities—traditionally either left to management or simply ignored—have become topics of active concern. As well, many boards of directors have established committees with direct responsibility over such vital areas as auditing the company's financial operations and spelling out the line of succession in the management ranks.

The officers

The top officers of a corporation are elected by the directors, are responsible to them for carrying out the board's policies, and can be removed by them. If the shareholders want to remove the officers, they must first remove the directors. Officers below top rank, including most vice-presidents, are generally appointed by the chief officer and approved by the board. In some corporations, in fact, vice-presidents and even presidents are essentially "hired hands" who are paid a salary to do a certain job, frequently without holding any shares in the company themselves.

The title that usually indicates where real power lies is **chief executive officer**. The chief executive officer *is responsible for laying down the policies of the company, under the direction of the board, and for supervising the officers who will carry out those policies.* If one person is chairman of the board and chief executive officer, he or she is usually the dominant manager of the company. Sometimes, however, a corporation has a chairman of the board and a president and chief executive officer, in which case the chairman has an honorary position, while the president is the actual manager.

THE ADVANTAGES OF THE CORPORATION

As we have mentioned previously, the main advantage of a corporation is its limited liability. This feature enables people to invest some of their savings in a company without fear that they will lose the rest if the company fails or causes injury.

Another important advantage is that an invest-

ment in a publicly held corporation is liquid: it can be easily bought and sold on stock exchanges (see our Enrichment Chapter on the Stock Market). This liquidity enables corporations to raise far larger sums than can be raised by unincorporated business enterprises.

As we also mentioned earlier, a corporation's unlimited life span is an important advantage. It enables a firm to make long-range plans for its future, and thus recruit, train, and motivate the best talent available. It also gives a corporation time to grow into a new AT&T or GM.

For all these reasons, no other form has approached the success of the corporation in bringing together money, resources, and talent; in accumulating assets; and in creating wealth.

THE DISADVANTAGES OF THE CORPORATION

For large companies, about the only serious disadvantage of incorporating arises because the government insists on disclosure of finances and some operations for such firms. Such disclosure would make it hard, for example, for a camera firm to keep its research on a new lens secret from its competition. Its research and development budget might well give it away.

For smaller businesses, two considerations weigh against incorporating. First, it can in some instances be comparatively complicated and expensive for a small business to incorporate. Charter fees may total thousands of dollars and together with lawyer's fees may make incorporating prohibitively expensive. Indeed, the cost of making a public stock offering can be $100,000 or higher; the printing bill alone for all the documents that are required by the SEC and the cost of distributing them to investors (and potential investors) can run to $20,000 or more depending on the number of prospective investors. (The SEC is the Security Exchange Commission, a five-member, presidentially appointed group that has primary responsibility for all securities traded in the U.S.)

Second, small corporations are taxed more heavily than unincorporated businesses. All corporations pay a corporate tax. (See page 509 in Chapter 15.) In addition, shareholders, who may well be family members in small corporations, must pay income taxes on their dividends.

Large corporations also claim that they are unfairly taxed, but this claim is vigorously disputed by critics of corporations. They say that corporations spend great effort and talent in arranging business transactions so as to minimize taxes legally. This is especially true for corporations that do business in "tax shelter" countries like Panama, the Bahamas, and Bermuda, which have no income taxes. As a result, say critics, large corporations have a far lower effective tax rate than do small corporations or individuals. In 1976, for example, General Motors had sales of over $47 billion, but paid taxes of only $2.6 billion, a tax on sales of less than 6 percent.[12] Currently, tax rule changes are under consideration to limit and/or eliminate the tax-shelter status of some countries.

CORPORATE GIANTS

From 1945 to 1970 the United States economy underwent the longest period of sustained growth in its history, a growth that was led by the largest of the nation's corporations. In the 1950s and 1960s, when our gross national product was increasing by nearly 250 percent, sales of the nation's hundred largest corporations were increasing by more than 300 percent. By 1974, of all the 212,000 corporations primarily engaged in manufacturing in the United States, the 100 largest industrial corporations controlled half the assets and profits.[13] To understand how corporate giants came to be that size, it is necessary to look back nearly a century to the beginnings of a movement known as the *merger movement.*

MERGERS: TWO PHASES

Sometimes a company will grow internally. But in many instances, companies grow by acquiring other companies, as shown in Figure 3. The most common form of acquisition occurs *when one company buys another company, with the purchasing company remaining dominant.* This form of business combination is called a **merger.** When General Motors absorbed the Chevrolet Corporation in 1919, that was a classic merger, with GM remaining dominant. (Another form of combination occurs when an interested outsider, such as an investment bank, brings together two or

more companies and forms an entirely new company in which one of the old companies is completely dominant. This form of combination is called an amalgamation. When the Pontiac, Olds, Buick, and Cadillac Corporations combined in 1917 to form General Motors, that was a classic amalgamation.) Before the 1960s two great waves of mergers in American business history stirred public debate. Each was marked by a different kind of merger.

The first great wave was the creation of monopolistic trusts in basic industries between 1881 and 1911. In our Enrichment Chapter on Business and the American Economy, we will see how Rockefeller and Morgan founded the enormous oil and steel industries by creating trusts. These trusts were **horizontal mergers,** or *combinations of competing companies performing the same functions.* The purpose of a horizontal merger is to achieve economies of scale and to prevent cutthroat competition. The rise of the antitrust movement and the dissolution of Standard Oil in 1911 ended this wave.

The second great wave occurred in the boom years of 1921 to 1929. This era was marked by the growth of **vertical mergers,** which *occur when a company involved in one phase of a business absorbs or joins a company involved in another phase in order to guarantee a supplier or a customer.* When the Radio Corporation of America (now RCA), which owns the National Broadcasting Company, bought the Victor Talking Machine Company in 1930 to acquire the performing contracts of Victor recording artists for NBC radio stations, the result was a vertical merger. When oil refining companies bought oil fields to ensure a supply, and gas stations to ensure sales outlets, they were expanding vertically. The Great Depression that began in 1929 ended this wave because there was less ready cash to allow purchases.

THE RISE OF THE CONGLOMERATE

Between 1961 and 1970 the United States experienced another wave of mergers, again with a different type of consolidation characterizing the movement. The chief form of merger during the 1960s was an unusual form called the **conglomerate merger.** This type of merger *occurs when a corporation joins with another in an unrelated industry,* as when CBS, the broadcasting and record company, purchased Holt Rinehart & Winston, the book publishers; *Road and Track* magazine; the Creative Playthings toy company; and Steinway & Sons pianos. One incentive for conglomerate mergers was that parent companies had extra cash and wanted to invest in other fields to diversify the sources of income in case one line of business had hard times. Another was that the government, in the interests of free competition, had placed severe restrictions on the formation of vertical and horizontal mergers.

Critics of conglomerate mergers fear that if a giant corporation can go into any industry, its size and aggressiveness will automatically stifle competition there. Innovation and creativity may be stifled as well. Defenders believe that conglomerates shake up industries for the better when they move into them. Again, it appears to be a question of individual cases, rather than of a general rule, whether mergers are good or bad for American society. Apparently, however, the federal government has become concerned enough to institute a series of antitrust actions against some of the nation's giants (see Chapter 15 for more information on antitrust activity).

For a time it appeared that the '60s boom in con-

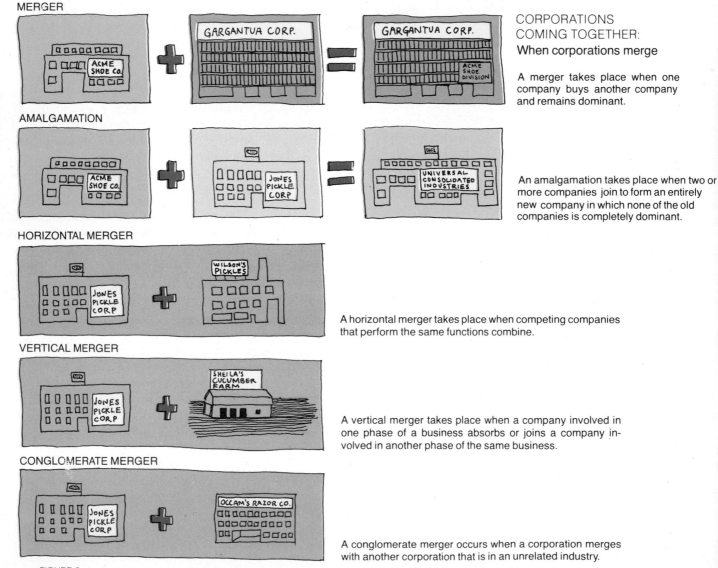

MERGER

CORPORATIONS
COMING TOGETHER:
When corporations merge

A merger takes place when one company buys another company and remains dominant.

AMALGAMATION

An amalgamation takes place when two or more companies join to form an entirely new company in which none of the old companies is completely dominant.

HORIZONTAL MERGER

A horizontal merger takes place when competing companies that perform the same functions combine.

VERTICAL MERGER

A vertical merger takes place when a company involved in one phase of a business absorbs or joins a company involved in another phase of the same business.

CONGLOMERATE MERGER

A conglomerate merger occurs when a corporation merges with another corporation that is in an unrelated industry.

FIGURE 3

Soaring corporate headquarters have become urban symbols of the power of conglomerates. This giant: the John Hancock Building in Chicago.

uct lines, and so forth—are now simply buying up other companies. For example, the Houston-based conglomerate Tenneco owned the Walker Manufacturing Company, an auto-equipment maker, and wanted to add shock absorbers to its business. Rather than develop its own line, though, Tenneco merely acquired the Monroe shock absorber company. The reasons were simple: inflation has driven up the costs of research and development at a rapid pace, while at the same time stock prices have been in a bad slump—thus making acquisition both the cheaper and the faster route.[14] Such takeovers, then, are perfectly logical under the circumstances, though they are also a gloomy reflection on the underlying health of the economy.

The recent acquisition patterns offer a clue to the business areas where a growth in activity may occur during the next few years. Based on the takeovers made so far, the liveliest business prospects seem to be in natural resources and energy-related fields, followed at varying distances by newspapers, fast-food chains, insurance, and pharmaceutical concerns. These are rapidly changing industries, and we will probably be seeing a lot of news about them in the near future.

COMPETING WITH THE GIANTS

If you were to ask people in the street to name all the aircraft manufacturers they could think of, chances are they would mention Boeing, perhaps Lockheed, and then run out of names. The same would be true for any number of other fields. Sewing machines? "Singer." Luggage? "Samsonite." Elevators? "Otis."

Their answers would be perfectly understandable, since so many industries seem to be dominated by one or two companies—or at most a small handful. But the fact is that, even in this age of corporate giants, American industry is still more diversified than many people would expect. Recently, for instance, the Commerce Department reported that there were 141 aircraft manufacturers, 72 sewing-machine makers, 266 luggage companies, and no fewer than 135 producers of elevators.[15] While many of these firms, of course, are extremely small operations, others have managed to hold onto respectable market shares in spite of their much larger competitors.

They have done so not by trying to play David among the corporate Goliaths, but by developing real-

glomerate-building had run its course, but by the mid-1970s it was clear that a new boom had taken shape—one that could potentially have an even greater impact on the national economy. Observers have noted that the current wave of takeovers is different from its predecessor in a number of fundamental and sometimes disquieting ways. For one, the takeovers now are being conducted not by the freewheeling conglomerates of the 1960s but by such long-established corporate bluebloods as General Electric, Atlantic Richfield, and Gulf Oil. As well, an increasing number of acquisitions are being made by foreign concerns like Bayer of Germany and Nestlé in Switzerland, drawn by the bargains that have resulted from the declining value of the dollar in relation to their own currencies. Further, while the big mergers of the 1960s were typically arranged through complex stock transfers, the deals today are more often being made in cash. This is particularly disturbing to some analysts, because it suggests that companies that would formerly have invested their earnings in further growth from within—building new facilities, developing new prod-

Corporate Goliaths are powerful, but they are still vulnerable to well-aimed competition on the part of much smaller companies.

istic and very careful marketing strategies.* Some simply produce their own versions of larger companies' products, waiting for their wealthy rivals to generate a demand with expensive ad campaigns and then offering their "me-too" alternatives at somewhat lower prices. Other companies focus their efforts on specific geographical areas, cultivating a kind of regional loyalty among their customers that serves to offset the greater marketing power of national advertisers. Finally, some small companies may come out with products featuring technological or other innovations that exploit weak spots in what their larger competitors are offering—such as Savin's successful incursion into Xerox's territory with an inexpensive line of desktop copying machines.[16]

OTHER BUSINESS ORGANIZATIONS

Before concluding this chapter, we should discuss two forms of business organization, cooperatives and franchise operations, that combine various aspects of the forms discussed above.

COOPERATIVES

Between 1971 and 1976 the sales of Farmland Industries, the country's biggest agricultural cooperative, rose from less than $700 million annually to $1.9 bil-

* Adapted from "Competing with the Giants," October 1977 DUN'S REVIEW

lion. In other words, its business *tripled* in six years. And this is only one example of the type of growth that has been going on in the area of agricultural co-ops lately. Overall, the sales for United States farm cooperatives as a group in the first half of the 1970s jumped from $25 billion to $57 billion, giving them a third of the giant agribusiness market (which includes the food that farmers sell and the equipment and supplies that they buy).[17]

Such a record would without doubt qualify any corporate president for the Tycoons' Hall of Fame, if there were one. But a vital fact must be noted: co-ops are simply not the same as corporations. A **cooperative** *is a means by which a group of small companies or people with similar products, services, or interests band together for greater bargaining power to achieve economies.* It is thus an attempt to combine the independence of the proprietorship with the financial power of the corporation. *The cooperative is set up by the shareholders,* who are called **cooperators.** Four common kinds of cooperatives are the agricultural marketing cooperative, the retail cooperative, the real-estate cooperative, and the consumer cooperative.

The agricultural marketing cooperatives—economically the most important type of cooperative in

Chances are that the oranges for your morning glass of juice were grown on an agricultural cooperative. Co-ops now control a third of the enormous agribusiness market.

the country—were originally formed by independent farmers to sell their produce. These cooperatives are able to get better prices from wholesalers than their members could hope to bargain for individually. In the last decade, however, the agricultural co-ops have broadened the scope of their operations considerably, increasing their market shares in such related areas as dairy products and cotton. They have also moved heavily into the construction of food-processing plants, and the so-called supply co-ops have likewise stepped up their sales of such farming necessities as fertilizer, petroleum, and chemical products—all at the expense of industrial competitors.

The expansion of cooperatives' activities has generated an increasing volume of protests from corporations on the grounds that existing laws give the co-ops an unfair advantage. Co-ops, for example, normally return a substantial portion of their profits to their members, and those profits are currently not subject to federal income tax. Consequently, tax rates for co-ops average only about one-third of those levied on their corporate competitors. In addition, cooperatives are permitted joint ownership of manufacturing and other facilities, while corporations are barred from the same practice by strict antitrust laws.

FRANCHISES

The **franchise operation** *brings a corporation with a famous product,* like Carvel ice cream, *together with an individual or group desiring to start a small business. Both the agreement and the individual business* go by the name of **franchise.** *The* **franchiser** (the corporation) *grants the* **franchisee** (the person) *the exclusive right to use the franchiser's name in a certain territory, usually in exchange for an initial fee plus monthly payments.* The franchise operation enables a corporation to establish outlets for its product or service without making enormous capital investments. And it enables an individual to go into business for himself with far less risk than an independent operator would face, and to deal with a nationally advertised product or service.

Franchising began in the nineteenth century, when such companies as Singer and International Harvester established dealerships throughout the world. In this century Coca-Cola, Chrysler, and Metro-

politan Life, among others, use franchisees to distribute or sell their products. Franchising grew most rapidly, however, in the consumer-product boom years of the 1960s. The fastest-growing franchise operations were in hotels and motels, like Holiday Inns and Quality Courts Motor Inns, and in fast-food establishments, like Baskin-Robbins, McDonald's, and Colonel Sanders Kentucky Fried Chicken. The growth in fast-food franchises slowed in the early 1970s, but more recently has picked up again. Thanks largely to the increasing popularity of eating out among Americans, total fast-food sales have been rising at a brisk 15 to 20 percent a year. Franchising as a whole continues to make profits. Nearly one out of every three dollars of retail sales is made by a franchise.[18]

The Small Business Administration says that the two most common causes of failure by small businessmen are lack of money and lack of know-how. The franchiser helps to eliminate both these problems.

The franchiser will not grant a franchise unless the franchisee has enough money for starting costs. (The franchiser, unlike many independent proprietors, has the experience to estimate starting costs realistically.) The franchisee has advantages similar to a cooperator in being able to obtain credit and insurance and buy supplies at low cost.

In addition to financial aid and advice, the franchiser gives a new franchisee training in how to run a franchise. McDonald's "Hamburger University" in Illinois gives a nineteen-day course to owners and operators leading to a "Bachelor of Hamburgerology, with a minor in French fries." Actually, McDonald's offers the course because it wants to maintain its quality image by standardizing operations. Many franchise organizations also offer advice on advertising, tax matters, and other business problems.

The chief disadvantage is the monthly payment or royalty. If the outlet is not doing well, a fixed royalty means most of the potential profit goes to the franchiser. (McDonald's does not have this problem because it charges a percentage instead.) Another disadvantage is loss of independence and the fact that franchisers make major decisions without consulting franchisees.

In general, however, advantages seem to outweigh disadvantages. Franchises will remain an important form of business organization for a number of years to come.

CHAPTER REVIEW

Businesses in the United States are usually organized as sole proprietorships, partnerships, or corporations.

Over 75 percent of American business enterprises are sole proprietorships. Most proprietorships are small and are concentrated in retailing and farming. Proprietors enjoy the advantage of working for themselves. But they cannot always recruit talented help, and they face such hazards as unlimited liability.

A second form of business organization, the partnership, is important because it includes most service businesses. Partnerships combine the talents of several partners and often enjoy good profits. But they are handicapped by potential conflicts among partners and inflexibility.

The most important form of business organization today, in terms of wealth and power, is the corporation. Each stockholder of a corporation has only limited liability. Corporations are created by charters that specify their purposes and other information. They are organized under a board of directors, who are elected by stockholders and who, in turn, elect the top corporate officers. There are many kinds of corporations, including nonprofit corporations, private corporations, and public corporations, which issue stock on the open market.

Corporations have many advantages, such as liquidity and the ability to combine relatively large amounts of money, resources, and talent. The disadvantages include the need for public disclosure of finances and of some operations, the expense of incorporating, and, in some cases, high taxes.

Over the past hundred years many corporations have grown to giant size through horizontal or vertical merger. The most recent wave of corporate growth occurred in the 1960s, when conglomerate mergers became prominent.

Cooperatives and franchises are two new forms of business that combine the advantages of the other forms. Cooperatives generally give their members greater buying or selling power by joint action that does not deprive members of their independence. Similarly, franchises allow people to go into business for themselves, but with a large organization behind them to give them financial and managerial assistance.

KEY WORD REVIEW

sole proprietorship
unlimited liability
partnership
corporation
limited liability
board of directors
outside directors
chief executive officer
merger
horizontal mergers
vertical mergers
conglomerate mergers
cooperative
cooperators
franchise operation
franchise
franchiser
franchisee

REVIEW QUESTIONS

1. Why are there more sole proprietorships than any other form of business in the United States?

2. What fields are suitable for proprietorships, and why? What fields are unsuitable, and why?

3. What are the advantages and disadvantages of partnerships?

4. What fields have the largest and most successful partnerships?

5. What are the five basic characteristics of a modern corporation?

6. Why do companies form conglomerate mergers? What are the risks to society?

7. What advantages are there in joining a cooperative?

8. What are the chief advantages and disadvantages of franchises?

CASE 1

SHUTTER SPEED: THE FAST-PACED LIFE OF A FREE-LANCE PHOTOGRAPHER

Fractions of a second make all the difference in Jim Pickerell's line of work. Pickerell, 41, is a hustling, hard-working free-lance photographer. On a moment's notice, he takes off on assignment, lugging his heavy equipment with him and often a lightweight stepladder as well—so that he can lift himself above the other photographers who show up in droves at the White House and elsewhere.

To make more than $30,000 a year—well above the average for his chancy profession—Pickerell does everything he can to minimize his risks and keep his overhead low. For instance, he does not allow himself to become too dependent on one customer. Of his large and varied clientele, no client accounts for more than 5 percent of Pickerell's nearly $70,000 annual gross business income. While on assignment for a client—Pickerell charges as much as $700 a day—he takes pictures of his own for his "stock," and later sells them to news agencies, corporations, or calendar companies. Pickerell earns some 40 percent of his business income selling these "stock" photos.

There's more to being a free-lance photographer than clicking the shutter. Film must be processed, captions written, clerical duties attended to, and Pickerell does it all himself, often working through the night. Pickerell's wife, Dolly, adds to the

family income by teaching nursing techniques in the suburb where they live, but she draws the line when it comes to helping him with his chores. "I have my own professional interests," she explains, "and the kind of help Jim needs is not the kind of work I enjoy doing."[19]

1. In what ways does Jim Pickerell minimize his risks?

2. How does he keep his overhead down?

3. How does Pickerell make his time on assignments more productive?

CASE 2

CORPORATE DOGFIGHT

A dapper and aggressive chief executive, M. Lamar Muse was growing impatient with his board of directors. During his eight years as president of Southwest Airlines, he had pulled the Dallas-based corporation out of debt and turned it into one of the most successful airlines in the country by offering low-fare flights between cities in Texas. Now Muse wanted to expand into the Middle West by starting an interstate commuter airline based in Chicago. Although Muse argued that Southwest's shareholders expected the company to take risks, some directors were hesitant about this particular—and very expensive—gamble. Muse finally brought matters to a head. A few days before a routine meeting of the board, he sent the members a letter demanding that they drop one of the directors who had been most troublesome about the move to Chicago. Otherwise, Muse threatened, he would quit. Less than

a minute after the board meeting began, Muse's resignation was accepted.

The next day, Southwest's stock dropped almost three points, but no one at the airline was worried. The fact was, noted Herb Kelleher, the man chosen to act as Southwest's interim president, that like most good chief executives, Muse had created an effective organization that could outlive its creator. "Most of our officers have twenty years' experience in the business," Kelleher said, "and they're just as familiar with the way we run things as Lamar was."

The man whom Muse wanted dropped from the board was Rollin King, a Harvard Business School graduate who had not only conceived of Southwest Airlines to begin with, but who had also hired Muse to run the company back in 1970. King and Muse had never gotten along well with one another—in 1976, Muse fired King as Southwest's executive vice-president—but Muse's demise, according to Interim President Kelleher, had nothing to do with a power struggle. "It was, at root, a matter of the corporate discipline of a publicly held company."[20]

Adapted from "A Freelance Photographer's Comfortably Chancy Life" by Marlys Harris, June 1978, by special permission; © 1978, Time Inc. All rights reserved.

1. Which side do you think was right?
2. What were the advantages of accepting Muse's resignation, and what were the disadvantages?
3. As a board member, how would you have acted if you knew that Muse was making money for the company but had not been effective in training other managers in the corporation?

BUSINESS AND THE AMERICAN ECONOMY: A HISTORICAL VIEW

In 1750, the total wealth of this country was about $750 million. Today, GNP is over $1,889 billion, and it's still zooming upward. With a per capita income of over $7,057, we have achieved one of the highest standards of living in the world. How did our economy grow to provide us with this abundance? In this chapter, we'll outline our rather colorful economic history, and we'll also see how our economic system compares with those of the socialist and communist countries.

WHAT WILL THIS CHAPTER FOCUS ON?

After reading the material in this chapter, you will understand and be able to discuss:

■ how business fits into the economy as a whole

■ pure capitalism and the American system of modified capitalism

■ the foundations of American economic strength—material resources, human resources, entrepreneurship, and technology

■ the major periods in history of the American economy

■ the roles of monopolies, trusts, assembly lines, mass production, and consumer credit in the history of the American economy

■ the United States' gradual switch from a manufacturing to a service economy

■ the advantages and disadvantages of capitalism

 Many people studying business for the first time are like surprised city children when they first discover that milk originates in a cow, not a carton. We tend to take for granted the business operations that surround us—financing, manufacturing, distributing, promoting—without probing much beyond the surface. But it is important for us to recognize that business exists within a broader framework—that of our economy as a whole.

In this chapter we are going to consider that framework. First, we shall survey our economy's historical development. Then we shall see how our economic system compares with systems in other countries.

BUSINESS IN THE ECONOMY

Donna, a college sophomore, is carrying a heavy load of courses, working in the school bookstore, and rooming off-campus. When she buys a moped to make her life easier, she probably regards the transaction as a fairly private matter, or at least one that concerns mainly herself, her bank, and her friendly neighborhood moped dealer. But hers is a business decision, too, and as such it is part of a large entity we call the economic system.

WHAT IS AN ECONOMIC SYSTEM?

Briefly, an **economic system** is *a way of distributing a society's resources*—all the items needed to make what people need. These items include material resources, such as land and money. And they also include human resources, chiefly the people who do the work.

No society, regardless of how wealthy it may be in some respects, has sufficient resources to meet all the needs of all its members. The United States, for example, has a large pool of skilled labor (a human resource) but a shortage of oil (a material resource); Saudi Arabia, in contrast, has plenty of oil but few skilled workers. Thus the major task of any economic system is to make choices about what will be produced, how, and for whom.

The parts of an economic system

When we visualize an economic system, it is helpful to think of it as having three parts. The first part consists of the *producers of goods and services*—**business,** in other words. The second part is made up of **consumers** who *use these goods and services.* And the third segment is **government,** which *determines how producers and consumers interact.* (Government may also act as both producer and consumer.) All three segments play important parts in the flow of goods, services, and money through the society.

We can apply this idea to our example of the student who buys a moped. Donna's moped was produced and sold by business. She buys it as a consumer. And government allows the transaction between Donna and the moped dealer to occur as a profit-making en-

ADAM SMITH'S PRINCIPLES OF PURE CAPITALISM

The bible of early capitalism was *The Wealth of Nations,* written in 1776 by Adam Smith, a Scottish economic philosopher whom many consider the founder of modern economics. Smith believed that economic, political, and religious liberties were so closely related that any threat to one endangered the others. Accordingly, he developed a doctrine based on four basic principles: private property, freedom of choice, free competition in the marketplace, and freedom from government interference.

Private property

First of all, Smith believed people should be allowed to own their own land, money, machines, businesses, and other property. Why? Private ownership of property provides an incentive. If people think they may be able to gain *more* property, they will strive to be thrifty, industrious, and more economically creative. And their motivations, while selfish, may even benefit others: they will respect the rights of other property-owners. Other benefits may also

terprise involving private individuals. (In some countries government might make mopeds itself—or prevent them from being made or sold.) In this case, government also plays a more active role by regulating the moped's safety standards and by taxing the sale itself.

THE ECONOMIC SYSTEM OF CAPITALISM

As you read in Chapter 1, business in the United States is a profit-making activity. The owner of an enterprise may be a sole proprietor, a partner, or one of thousands of investors in a corporation, but all these people are engaged in business with the hope of making money. This type of business, with individual ownership and a goal of profits, is part of the economic system known as capitalism.

Pure capitalism

Capitalism developed in eighteenth-century Europe as part of an intellectual movement known as the Enlightenment. Many thinkers of the time believed that properly educated men and women were the best judges of their own interests in politics, religion, and economics—and that they would fare best in these areas if the government left them free to do as they wished. According to these thinkers, the most preferable economic system was **laissez-faire capitalism,** or **pure capitalism:** they believed society at large would benefit most if *business determined its own best interests and acted on them, without interference from*

come from private ownership of property—as we shall see in the points that follow.

Freedom of choice

If there is freedom of property ownership, Smith believed, there must inevitably be freedom of choice—since the right to own property implies the right to do anything with it that does not harm the community. For the owners of material resources, this means the freedom to sell, rent, trade, or give away resources, or to withhold them from use. Similarly, the owners of human resources—that is, the workers themselves—are free to use their skills or not to use them, as they see fit.

Free competition in the marketplace

What will the holders of resources do if they are free to choose the path that will benefit them the most? If they are sensible, they will compete for profits. And this leads us to Smith's third principle: he believed the society would benefit most if there were a free market in which people could compete. A free market, Smith pointed out, could enable the economy to regulate itself through the operation of the **law of supply and demand.** That is, the *amount of goods produced (the supply) and the price people are willing to pay for the goods (the demand) would always operate to achieve a balance of resources.* We have talked about the benefits of the free market in Chapter 1.

Freedom from government interference

As we've shown, free competition will tend to reward owners of resources for using them in the ways that are most profitable, and also most desirable from the point of view of the consumers. As a result of free competition, a nation's wealth will increase in a far fairer and more permanent way than it will if prices and supply are controlled by some outside agency. And this points to the fourth principle of pure capitalism—freedom from government interference. Clearly, if a free market is the best creator of national wealth, the best thing the government can do is to restrain itself. Government should promote competition and free trade, and aid society by acting as soldier and policeman. But it should not act as regulator of business or commerce.

government. Looking back at our three parts of the economic system, we can say that in a pure capitalist system the three parts work as follows: *businesses* sell without restrictions, *consumers* buy without restrictions, and the *government* keeps its hands off.

Modified capitalism

Of course, pure capitalism is an ideal system; it does not exist in reality. The economic system in the United States today only roughly approximates that envisioned by laissez-faire capitalism. Our system is one of **modified capitalism,** *which follows the basic principles of pure capitalism but allows government the power to define and limit those principles.* It rewards business people with profits, leaves a number of decisions up to them, and encourages them to experiment with new methods on their own. But it also protects the public—and in some cases aids business—through a measure of governmental control.

THE DEVELOPMENT OF OUR ECONOMIC SYSTEM: A BRIEF HISTORY

As we survey the economic history of the United States, we shall be examining the ways our current system of modified capitalism developed. We shall also survey our economic system's tremendous growth. In 1776 a population of 2.5 million was producing goods and services worth about $500 million. (The *yearly total value of the goods and services produced by the economy* is known as the **gross national product** or **GNP**.) Some two hundred years later, a nation of 216 million people[1] produced a GNP of more than $1.8 trillion.[2]

How did this amazing expansion take place? Skill and hard work, of course, were important. But the American people were also lucky in having ample resources available to them.

THE FOUNDATIONS OF OUR ECONOMY: MATERIAL RESOURCES

The most abundant material resource available to the European settlers was land—a vast wilderness with rich soil, good water supplies, and ample timber and minerals such as coal, iron ore, gold, and copper. (From an economist's point of view the term **land** includes *space on the surface of the earth as well as timber and minerals.)*

The settlers also had the advantage of a background of several hundred years of what economists call capital formation. In economics, **capital** refers to *machinery and equipment that, combined with other resources, permits a greater production of goods per hour of labor.* An ax is a form of capital; so is a tractor; and capital also includes the money with which axes and tractors can be bought. In the process of **capital formation,** *a society postpones using goods and services in order to devote its resources to producing more and better goods and services in the future.* Capital formation had begun in Western Europe around 1100. At that time, crops were good enough for people to be able to store some surplus grain and other foods. And since the food supply was assured, the society was able to devote some of its energies toward the development of industry and trade, and even to expand greatly some of its old cities and to build new ones. Thus the settlers brought with them not only basic forms of capital such as tools, but also the knowledge and social patterns that had developed in Europe over the preceding centuries. These were a crucial ingredient in the settlers' success in the New World.

HUMAN RESOURCES

The most important human resource is **labor**—*the pool of workers who process material resources to produce goods and services.* No economy can develop unless there is a sufficient supply of labor available. Although there was a labor shortage in the earliest days of the American colonies, the need for workers was filled, at least partially, by the importation of slaves from Africa. Continuing immigration also furnished an increasingly larger labor pool.

Entrepreneurs are another type of human resource. The **entrepreneur** is *the person who starts a business and takes the financial and personal risks involved in keeping that business going.* Risk-taking, an essential economic function in a profit-motivated society, is needed to make other economic resources more profitable, useful, and efficient. Western Europe had a tradition of entrepreneurship. So even at the beginning, there were entrepreneurs in the American colonies, both landowners in the South and merchants in the North.

Still a third type of human resource is **technology**—*the use of science to increase productivity*. While technology may be thought of as the equivalent of machinery and thus a material resource, it is also a human resource in that it requires the application of human knowledge and reflects human values. For centuries the Western tradition had been favorable to technological advance. Indeed, it was technology, in such forms as sailing ships and muskets, that enabled small numbers of Europeans to overwhelm large Indian empires in Mexico and Peru.

FROM THE BEGINNING TO 1865

"Some men were forced by famine to filch for their bellies," wrote a chronicler in early Virginia. "One, for stealing two or three pints of oatmeal, had a bodkin thrust through his tongue and was tied with a chain to a tree until he starved."[3] It is hard to imagine now, but the earliest colonists in America suffered severe hard-

At the end of the first significant century of North American colonization, the population had grown to over a million (excluding American Indians). "Gross national product" was not a concept in use at that time, but the wealth of the country was estimated at $750,000,000; per person wealth was $187.

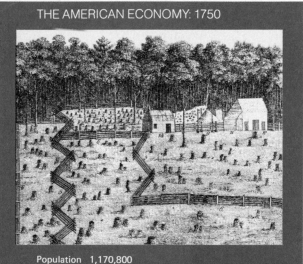

THE AMERICAN ECONOMY: 1750

Population 1,170,800
National wealth $750,000,000

FIGURE 1

ships. Not until they abandoned their hopes of instant riches (everyone wanted gold such as the Spaniards had found in Latin America), did the colonists establish a secure economic foothold.

Early progress

Luckily the American colonies were able at an early date to achieve agricultural self-sufficiency. And after the first 150 years the country experienced a spurt of growth, made possible in part by the Revolutionary War. The War of Independence had economic causes as well as political ones; the American colonists desired to be free not only from the rule of the king, but also from his taxes and trade restrictions. After the war the nation's territory rapidly expanded, and business enterprise mushroomed.

Another factor in the growth spurt was a series of technological innovations, especially those of Eli Whitney. Interestingly enough, Whitney's inventions helped determine the economic directions taken by both the South and the North during this period. The Southern economy benefited from the cotton gin, a simple device that mechanized the cleaning of cotton and thus made it a profitable crop for thousands of Southern farmers. And the Northern economy benefited from Whitney's system of interchangeable parts, which could be assembled into finished products (muskets, in Whitney's case) by relatively inexperienced laborers. Whitney's system led manufacturers to experiment with the division of labor, which eventually became the foundation of the factory system.

Also essential to America's early economic growth was the creation of a coherent financial policy by Alexander Hamilton, the first Secretary of the Treasury. Under Hamilton's urging, the national government assumed all debts that the colonies had accumulated before 1789. To other nations, this meant that the United States would be financially trustworthy in its business dealings. Hamilton's next essential step was the creation of the Bank of the United States in 1791. This bank was chartered to provide money for commercial and industrial entrepreneurs.

FROM 1865 TO 1900

The period between 1865 and 1900 was marked by the rise of great nationwide industries. They were backed by two key resources—technology and a daring entrepreneurial class.

Technology

In 1869, when the Union Pacific Railroad met the Southern Pacific Railroad in Utah, the United States passed a tremendous milestone in its economic development. From then on, it was possible to travel or ship freight by train across the country in only seven days. This revolution in transportation spurred the growth of a truly national economy: cloth made in New England, for example, could be sent quickly anywhere in the country, and textile merchants could respond to the demands of customers as far away as San Francisco in relatively short periods of time. Meanwhile the boom in railroad-building sparked a demand for steel, which soon became a major industry in the United States. Next, manufacturers began to produce other types of goods on a large scale, using factories and heavy machinery; railroads provided the transportation and steel the basic material that made other industries possible.

Entrepreneurs

Bold entrepreneurship was a continuing theme throughout this period. During the Civil War the Union was immeasurably helped by a group of enter-

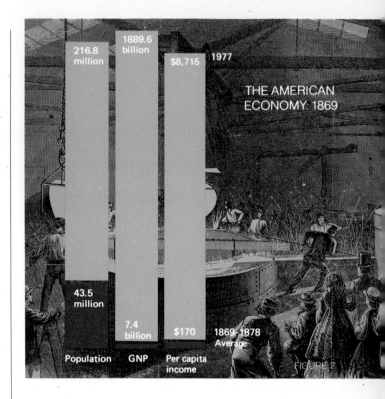

THE AMERICAN ECONOMY: 1869

216.8 million

1889.6 billion

$8,715 1977

43.5 million

7.4 billion

$170 1869–1878 Average

Population GNP Per capita income

FIGURE 2

By 1900 the population had almost doubled; about half this growth was due to immigration, and about half to native births. The gross national product (GNP) had also more than doubled, thanks to the expansion of industries such as the railroads and the growth of the West. But wealth was still concentrated at the top: per capita income had only grown by about $70.

One of the most successful entrepreneurs of his own—or any other—time, John D. Rockefeller founded an oil-based fortune that is still an important force in American economic and political life.

prising young men who organized the resources of the North to provide its army with weapons and other necessities. And by 1900 a few talented financial and industrial entrepreneurs literally owned the country. They included J. P. Morgan, the nation's greatest finance capitalist; John D. Rockefeller, founder of the Standard Oil Company; Andrew Mellon, founder of the Aluminum Company of America (Alcoa); and Andrew Carnegie, organizer of the nation's steel industry. These men were ruthless, exploitative, and hard—but they put together a nationwide industrial system that made the prosperity of the next century possible.

A key goal these men pursued was the consolidation of their enterprises into large, powerful organizations with the money and manpower to squeeze out smaller competitors. Morgan, who had watched the railroads nearly wreck themselves by what he called "cutthroat competition," persuaded railroad and industrial entrepreneurs to reorganize their industries efficiently to avoid such competition. *By producing more of a product,* he pointed out, *larger companies were able to lower the cost of producing each unit.* (The savings thus achieved are known as **economies of scale.**) Morgan favored consolidating the major competing corporations in any given industry to form one huge corporation, that is, to create a **monopoly.** As we saw in Chapter 1, this means that *one company dominates a particular industry or market and restrains free entry or activity in that market.* Rockefeller favored

After the Revolutionary War entrepreneurs began to amass money for reinvestment, and by the time of the Civil War it was estimated that the richest 10 percent of the people owned 30 to 50 percent of the nation's wealth. Productivity, however, had not yet increased to any great extent: per capita income — the average income for each person in the country — was about the same as in 1750.

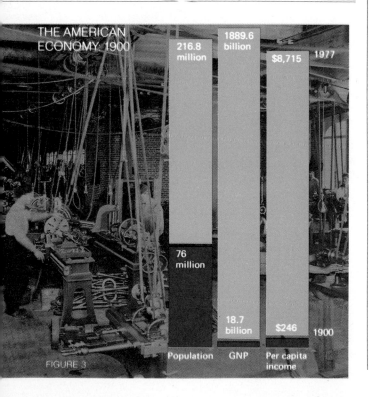

THE AMERICAN ECONOMY: 1900

FIGURE 3

216.8 million

1889.6 billion

$8,715   1977

76 million

18.7 billion

$246   1900

Population   GNP   Per capita income

a different, but equally powerful, form of consolidation known as the trust. A **trust** is *a company that buys the stock of all the competing companies in an industry and then runs all of them through a single board of trustees.* Rockefeller's Standard Oil Trust, founded in 1882, was the precursor of one of our modern industrial giants, Exxon—previously known as Esso.

Through one form of consolidation or another, monopolies came to control most of the nation's basic industries by 1900. There was much public outcry, however, against these industrial giants' abuse of power. Thus as the monopolies grew, so too did government regulation of business. In 1890 Congress passed the Sherman Antitrust Act, intended to outlaw business deals that were "in restraint of trade." Though several years passed before monopoly power was effectively limited (and trusts were not outlawed until the 1930s), the pattern for government regulation of business was set.

Labor's sacrifice

Technology and entrepreneurial daring depended on a solid base of labor, but labor itself did not share in the prosperity of this period. It is a grim historical truth that at the beginning of any economically productive period, people must work hard at low wages in order for capital formation to be effective. This is what happened between 1865 and 1900 in the United States. It was an era of massive financial accumulation and great differences of wealth between rich and poor. When John D. Rockefeller became the nation's first billionaire, children were working seventy hours a week in coal mines for a $2 wage. By 1900 the wealthiest 10 percent of the population owned 75 percent of the nation's wealth.

FROM 1900 TO 1929

During the first three decades of the twentieth century, the benefits of thirty-five years of accumulating investment money at last began to reach the people. American capitalism became humanized. This time it was not so much a group of entrepreneurs who triggered the change as it was a single entrepreneur, Henry Ford. New trends in the economy and changes in corporations also did much to usher in a capitalism for the people.

Henry Ford

In 1902 Ford began to produce an item that became the most popular consumer product in our history—a low-cost automobile. Because of Ford, automobiles and oil overtook railroads and steel as the two largest industries (positions they still held in the 1970s). The auto brought more pleasure and efficiency into the lives of millions of people. Ford also made some important changes in the workplace itself. In 1913 he launched an innovation known as the assembly line—the most significant improvement in worker productivity since Eli Whitney's development of interchangeable parts. The assembly line brought the product to the worker, instead of the other way around. It permitted vastly higher worker productivity and thus higher wages. It also led to true **mass production,** *the manufacture of goods in great quantities,* especially by machinery.

A consumer economy

Although Ford made consumer-oriented mass production possible, he was too proud of his invention to take maximum advantage of it. He made one car, the Model T, from 1914 to 1928. And he sold it to consumers in any color they wanted—"as long as it's black." In 1919, however, Ford's new competitor, General Motors (GM), introduced the concept of styling cars to satisfy diverse tastes. This meant annual model changes and a wide choice of designs and colors. GM's action helped usher in the so-called marketing revolution, which oriented business toward satisfying the consumer and moved consumer goods and services into the center of the economy.

The consumer boom of the 1920s was fueled by the birth of **consumer credit,** *money lent for the purchase of goods and services to improve the average person's way of life.* Until 1913, banks had generally lent most of their money for investments in factories. There were few home mortgages and almost no installment buying. But in 1913, with the creation of the Federal Reserve Bank, money became cheaper to borrow and more readily available to ordinary citizens.

Changes in corporations

Meanwhile, during the period from 1900 to 1929, many large corporations were undergoing major changes. Ownership passed from the founders into the hands of large numbers of individual and institutional shareholders. And control of decision-making also passed out of the founders' hands, to a new class of professional managers who advocated using scientific management to lessen uncertainty and risk.

One of the pioneers in this trend was American Telephone & Telegraph (AT&T). By selling shares, it was able to build a nationwide telephone service—a project that would have been too hazardous and too expensive for most individual entrepreneurs. Selling shares enabled a company to spread its risks, and also its potential rewards. It was a pattern that became increasingly important as the economy grew.

FROM 1929 TO THE EARLY 1970s

During the years from 1929 to 1939 there occurred a period of drastically lowered economic productivity, including declines in industry, commerce, and credit. Unemployment was widespread during this "Great Depression"—often reaching 25 percent—and many people went hungry. The government was forced to intervene through a series of programs and policies known as the New Deal. The result was vastly increased government activity in many different parts of the economy. Through programs such as old-age pensions and unemployment insurance, the government came to play a much larger role than ever before in the lives of ordinary citizens.

Another important milestone was World War II, which began in Europe in 1939. Like the Civil War (and World War I as well), World War II sparked productivity, inventiveness, and new technology. These trends continued after the war was over; business and labor continued to work for increased output through the 1950s and 1960s.

Technology in a service economy

After World War II the American economy became increasingly oriented toward technology—especially technology that would help cut down on hand labor in businesses and in the home. Two corporations in particular are important here. One, International Business Machines (IBM), became the world leader in the major new postwar industry, computers. The other, Xerox,

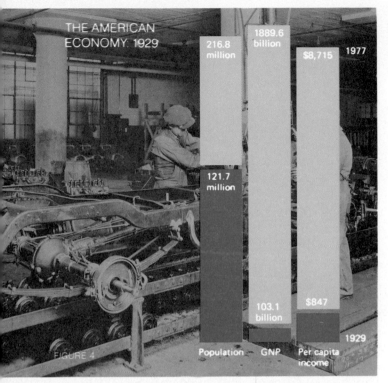

By 1929, America had come of age as an industrial power, providing comparative wealth for a majority of its citizens. With a population of more than 121 million (the majority of them now city-dwellers), the GNP had shot up to over $103 billion. Per capita income had nearly quadrupled.

developed a wide range of simple, quick, and reliable office copying machines. Both of these developments greatly relieved workers of tedious paperwork.

Along with these technological changes, there was a basic change in the type of item produced by United States industry. Gradually, the nation switched from a manufacturing to a **service economy**—one in which *the production of goods is secondary to the performance of useful services.* Such services include record-keeping, teaching, and the repair of home and business machinery. The 1960 census revealed that a majority of workers provided services rather than goods.

Labor's advances

America's increased productivity during this period also owed much to major changes in the status of labor. For many years workers had been organizing into unions of increasing strength and effectiveness. And during the period after World War II, the prosperity of the country as a whole helped labor achieve a position of power that matched that of business and government. (We will discuss the long, often violent, history of union activity in our Enrichment Chapter on Management and Unions.)

Another major change for labor was that workers had become better educated. As recently as 1940, only 24.5 percent of Americans over twenty-five had graduated from high school. But by 1976 the figure had zoomed to 64.1 percent,[4] and it seemed certain to climb even higher as older, less educated workers retired.

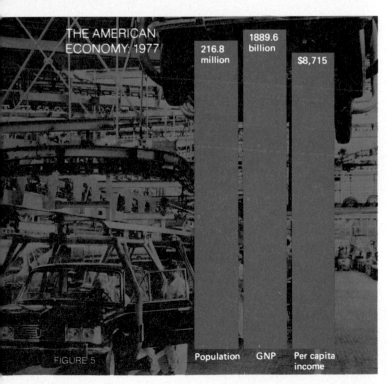

In 1977, the population was still growing, but at a slower rate; it had reached 216 million. GNP and per capita income had both doubled, but the standard of living had not gone up proportionately; inflation had cut down the dollar's purchasing power.

THE ECONOMY TODAY

Since the beginning of industrialization, the American economy has entered a new phase every thirty or forty years. New phases started around 1865, around 1900, and around 1929. In accordance with this pattern, the economy appeared to have entered another new phase some time between 1970 and 1974, when the twenty-five-year boom came to an end.

The boom had depended, like all earlier booms, on the lavish exploitation of cheap sources of energy and raw materials. And one reason the last boom ended was that these sources began disappearing or growing more expensive. In particular, the cost of oil skyrocketed. Likewise, it was becoming more and more difficult for the American people to foot the bills (in the form of taxes) for the expensive social welfare programs that had been set up during the boom period: productivity was simply not keeping up.

Furthermore, people's purchasing power was beginning to be badly undercut by **inflation**—*a generally rising level of prices.* The government builds some degree of inflation into the economy to stimulate consumer demand and thus prevent economic slowdowns and unemployment. (The government can encourage inflation by increasing the supply of money, an aspect of the economy that we discuss in our Enrichment Chapter on the Money and Banking System.) Almost from the beginning of the country's history, prices had risen fairly steadily, but very slowly—for the most part less than 1 percent a year. But prices rose much faster during the boom years: by the early 1970s the dollar was worth less than half what it had been in 1940.

Inflation was accepted by business and the American people as long as the economy kept growing in **constant dollars,** which *measure the actual purchasing power of the dollar.* Measured in constant dollars, the economy grew fivefold between 1940 and 1970. But in 1974 a new development occurred. The nation was faced for the first time with *rising prices and a stagnant economy*—**stagflation.** After thirty-four years, large-scale unemployment returned to the United States.

Many reasons were advanced for the appearance of stagflation. Some observers claimed the stagflation was due to mismanagement of finances by the government, which had tried to fight an expensive war in Vietnam without raising the taxes to pay for it. Others, including numerous business leaders, argued that it was due to heavy increases in social welfare benefits, coupled with new government restrictions on businesses that tended to cut down productivity.

More recently a clearer pricture of the events leading up to the bout of stagflation has emerged. For one thing, it has become evident that the unemployment of the stagflation period may have resulted not so much from economic causes as from social ones. In specific, there has been an increase in the size of the labor force, due in part to a massive entry of women job-seekers. Businesses have created new jobs in record numbers, but they have not been able to keep pace with the growth of the work force.

Inflation still persists as an economic cloud. Economists disagree about whether sophisticated government techniques can help curb inflation, or whether inflation, particularly stagflation, is simply a phase that may eventually run its course. In short, there is no consensus over the best way to deal with the inflation of today.

DOES THE CAPITALIST SYSTEM WORK?

As we have seen, the capitalist system has provided a framework for tremendous growth in the American economy. But capitalism is not the only economic system that can offer benefits to a society. The two other major economic systems, socialism and communism, provide certain benefits also. We'll survey the advantages and disadvantages of these systems briefly.

ANALYZING OTHER ECONOMIC SYSTEMS

Generally, economists analyze economic systems with three basic questions in mind: (1.) What is the system's primary goal? (2.) Who owns the means of production—industry and agriculture? and (3.) Who decides how the nation's resources are to be allocated? Our own modified capitalist system has as its goal increased economic production, fueled by the profit motive. Most means of production are in private hands, and resources are allocated through competition among businesses as they strive to supply consumer demand. But the other systems answer these questions differently.

Socialism

The primary goal of socialism is to provide social welfare benefits to all citizens. To accomplish this, the government usually owns the basic industries. It also generally plays a large role in determining how material resources are to be used.

Advanced socialist countries have a definite commitment to social welfare, so unemployment in these countries is low and there is little gap between the very rich and the very poor. But inflation and economic slowdowns do cause problems. So does the fact that, since worker benefits escalate automatically, there are few incentives to increase productivity.

Communism

The primary goal of communism as practiced in the Soviet Union and China is economic development through rigorously controlled central planning. This goal eliminates consumer demand as a factor in determining how resources are to be used. The state owns both industry and agriculture. State-appointed bureaucrats manage factories and farms, and also determine how resources are distributed among the people.

Compared to capitalism and socialism, communism, with its government planning, provides for more reinvestment in heavy industry and thus ensures sustained growth. The pricing system stops inflation by holding prices down. There is less of a gap between rich and poor. Workers get cheap (though poor) housing and cheap (though good) medical care and schooling. But the centrally controlled government planning system is vastly inefficient as a distributor of consumer products; they are comparatively expensive, if available at all. Agriculture represents an even bigger failure of communist policy, certainly in the Soviet Union. Russian farmers, as government employees, will not produce surpluses, so the nation with the largest amount of tillable land must import wheat.

PROS AND CONS OF CAPITALISM

These, then, are some key points about the kinds of benefits we would enjoy if we lived under another economic system—and the price we would have to pay.

"Brother, can you spare a dime?" The bread lines and soup kitchens of the 1930's showed just how vulnerable capitalist societies can be to economic fluctuations. Nevertheless, capitalism has also encouraged extraordinary technological growth. Imagine what a feat it was, for instance, to link the shores of this enormous country with telegraph and telephone lines.

Can we say, without reservation, that our system is better? Before we answer this question, let's make sure we have looked at all sides of the picture—the negative as well as the positive.

The negative side of capitalism

Our history as a capitalist country has not been an entirely sunny one. Some critics claim that, under capitalism, American values have been distorted. They argue that although our system has encouraged some useful traits among us, it has also given rise to certain negative tendencies—among them wastefulness, dishonesty, and indifference to social needs.

The economic boom that lasted through the early 1970s was essentially unhealthy for American life, say the social critics, because it created an economy based on waste instead of thrift. Americans were urged to buy new cars often, to borrow money for home improvements, and to purchase an endless stream of gadgets and appliances. The result was a wildly extravagant spending spree that rapidly eroded the world's resources.

Likewise, social critics say American society is indifferent to the needs of many of its citizens. Our extreme competitiveness leads to the feeling that a person can get ahead only at the expense of someone else. These critics point out that the United States trails most other developed nations in social insurance programs and that our health and life-span statistics are fairly low. (In the early 1970s, 19 out of 56 countries reporting to a United Nations agency had a lower mortality rate than the United States.[5]) In our system certain social needs are treated like business goods and services. Some, such as health care, are expensive; others, such as public transportation, are inadequate.

Nor is this all. American capitalism, claim critics, has also bred continuing dishonesty in business practices. Although the American value system preaches honesty and reliability, competitive pressures force too many business people to do things that are unethical.

Moreover, beyond its possible distortion of our values, the American system of modified capitalism has practical disadvantages. One disadvantage is inflation. (We should note, however, that inflation troubles many other nations as well.) Another disadvantage is the unemployment that results during a slowdown in the economy. A third disadvantage is that our economic system permits, and perhaps even stimulates, a wide gap between rich and poor. And a fourth disadvantage is the system's tendency toward **oligopoly**—*the domination of an industry by a few large companies.* Many industries in the United States—most notably, automobiles—are dominated by a few huge enterprises that make it virtually impossible for an individual entrepreneur to compete.

The positive side of capitalism

No one can deny that the drawbacks we have cited above are serious. Yet for the vast majority of Americans, modified capitalism works very well. The fact is that relatively few Americans fall into the categories

A RELISH FOR COMBAT

One of the big differences between a heavyweight boxing match and the competition that goes on between Campbell Soup and the H. J. Heinz Company is that prizefighters stop after fifteen rounds (if not before). Campbell and Heinz, on the other hand, have been trading punches for at least twenty years, and the contest seems far from over. The most recent round of combat stems from an unusual example of the lengths that one company will go to in order to get an edge over a rival.

A number of years ago, Campbell created a television advertising campaign for its vegetable soups, and to make the vegetables clearly visible for the camera, it filled the bottom of the soup bowl with marbles and put the vegetables on top. Much embarrassment resulted for Campbell when the government found out and publicly put a stop to the practice. But how did the government know? Nine years after the marble caper, Campbell discovered that the tattletale was none other than Heinz. That got the soup company boiling, and Campbell promptly struck back by complaining to the Food and Drug Administration (FDA) about too much mold in the ketchup it was buying from Heinz for its restaurant subsidiary. FDA testing upheld Campbell's claim, and the agency confiscated more than two hundred cases of Heinz ketchup from a distributor in Detroit.

of either rich or poor. Large numbers of us belong to the middle class, and compared to the average citizen of any country in the world the middle-class American lives very comfortably. We can see this especially clearly when we match our attainments with those of countries where there is no free business enterprise. We do not have to work nearly so hard for consumer goods as people in communist countries do. Furthermore, the quality of our consumer goods is better, and they are far more readily available. We also enjoy important educational advantages. While higher education is free in communist and socialist countries, it can be had by only a small percentage of the population. Here, huge numbers of people can pursue an educa-

tion: the public university system of a state like New York is larger than that of the entire Soviet Union.

Modified capitalism also ranks well in the area of personal opportunity. It is true that in the United States the rich are getting richer, and it may be true that the poor are getting poorer. But chances for an individual to rise from poverty to wealth are still present. There are more millionaires today than ever before in our history. Modified capitalism, for all its faults, is the only system that puts virtually no ceiling on what a person with sufficient talent, intelligence, and drive can attain. Our modified capitalist system has provided a higher quality of life for more people than any other system in the world.

When Campbell and Heinz are not busy enlisting the aid of government regulatory agencies in their efforts to compete, they fight in other ways. As contenders, the two food industry giants are fairly evenly matched. Heinz leads in the annual sales category with $1.9 billion, but Campbell makes $23 million more in profits. Aggressive and strong, both companies have tried over the years to invade each other's primary markets, and both have come away bruised and holding grudges. Campbell, for instance, tried to start up a ketchup line about twenty years ago, but lost to Heinz four years running and finally pulled out. More recently, Heinz went after Campbell in the soup business but was forced to retreat.

Heinz did not surrender, though. It went to court with a $105 million antitrust suit, charging Campbell with monopolistic practices. That's when Campbell complained to the FDA about Heinz's

moldy ketchup, and also brought a $15.5 million countersuit claiming that Heinz was refusing to sell its ketchup to institutional customers unless they bought other products as well. At that point, Heinz had more to worry about than lawsuits: the FDA tests that Campbell had instigated threatened to give Heinz ketchup a bad name. All ketchup has mold, explained a Heinz executive (the mold comes with the tomatoes), so Heinz took the FDA to court, charging that the agency's ketchup test was outdated (some FDA officials agreed that Heinz might be right). Heinz also pointed out that it had never heard any complaints from Campbell and that, in fact, its arch-rival had kept right on buying the ketchup anyway.

"These are two intense rivals," said an industry observer. "If one can find a reason to get the other, it will." The lawsuits have clearly done nothing to tame Campbell's appetite for competition. At last report, the soup company was getting ready to take another crack at the ketchup market, and was also aiming a blow at Heinz where it would really hurt—in the pickle business. Campbell was trying to take over Vlasic Foods, the number-one pickle packer in the nation. If true to form, Heinz, number two in the pickle business, could hardly be expected to be sent off packing so easily.

This discussion is based on "In a Pickle over Soup," *Newsweek*, June 5, 1978, pp. 78, 83.

CHAPTER REVIEW

A country's economic system is the system by which it distributes resources. There are material resources—such as land and money—and human resources—the people who do the work. All economic systems have three parts—business, consumers, and government.

The type of economic system that features individual ownership and the profit motive is known as capitalism. In pure capitalism, people are free to sell, rent, trade, give away, or withhold resources. Because the American government owns certain industries and has regulatory powers, our economic system is not totally free and is generally known as modified capitalism.

The economic history of the United States can be divided into four distinct phases: from 1776 to 1865, from 1865 to 1900, from 1900 to 1929, and from 1929 to the early 1970s. Today we seem to be shifting into a fifth major phase in our changing economy.

In the period before 1865 the nation relied on an abundant supply of resources, especially land and labor. The foundation for technological growth was established early, most importantly by Eli Whitney, who developed both the cotton gin and interchangeable parts. Alexander Hamilton, the nation's first Secretary of the Treasury, committed the

United States to fiscal responsibility and to policies that promoted industrial development.

After the Civil War the economy was dominated by a new entrepreneurial class that organized the nation's resources and developed such basic industries as railroads and steel. The ensuing period of rapid industrial expansion was marked by the creation of monopolies, the exploitation of labor, and great gaps between rich and poor.

The period from 1900 to 1929 marked the humanization of capitalism. Three important factors in this era were the entrepreneurial skills of Henry Ford, who mass-produced automobiles with the assembly line; consumer credit; and changes in corporate operations.

The era since 1929, after sixteen years of depression and war, saw the longest period of sustained economic growth in world history, due to improvements in both technology and the labor force. Somewhere between 1970 and 1974 the economy leveled off, and it appears that we have entered another new phase. Cheap sources of energy and raw materials have become scarcer or, in some cases, more expensive. Furthermore, inflation and stagflation have slowed our economic growth.

In addition to capitalism, there are two other major types of economic systems. Socialism, a term broad

enough to cover the economic systems of many different countries, aims at an equal distribution of social welfare benefits to all citizens. Communism is an economic system in which the government determines how resources are to be used, owns industry and agriculture, appoints bureaucrats to manage factories and farms, and determines the distribution of resources among its citizens.

The American system has certain disadvantages, but the vast majority of Americans have benefited from it. The middle-class American lives very comfortably, and our system offers a great degree of personal opportunity.

KEY WORD REVIEW

economic system
business
consumers
government
laissez-faire (pure) capitalism
modified capitalism
gross national product (GNP)
land
capital
capital formation
labor
entrepreneur
technology
economies of scale
monopoly

4. *General construction* firms build or redesign homes, industrial buildings, and other structures.

5. *Manufacturing* firms buy raw materials and components to produce finished products that are sold to wholesalers, retailers, or industrial users, or directly to consumers. Because operating costs and risks are high, manufacturing attracts and holds fewer small operators than fields that are more easily entered do.

The interdependence of small and big businesses

Many small firms might do better without the stiff competition of the larger corporations, but others depend on big businesses for large-volume sales. It has been reported that "General Motors . . . purchases goods and services from more than 37,000 smaller businesses, over three-fourths of whom employ fewer than 100 persons. In addition, General Motors depends upon some 14,000 dealerships and 128,000 other retail outlets."* Numerous other large manufacturers depend on small wholesalers and retailers to sell their products to the consumer. Small legal, accounting, and consulting firms provide essential services to big firms. In short, it would be difficult to find a major corporation without some profitable relationship with a small entrepreneur.

Efficiency in the small business

Since the primary decision-maker of a small business—the owner—is a working member of the organization, he or she can realistically expect to exercise firm control over all parts of the business. New programs, advertising campaigns, and other business activities can be quickly started or

* H. N. Broom and J. G. Longenecker, *Small Business Management* (Cincinnati: South Western Publishing Co., 1975), p. 20.

stopped without numerous meetings or long waits for decisions from busy executives. Furthermore, the frequent lack of capital in a small firm forces the entrepreneur to maximize all the available resources. In a large corporation, in contrast, unprofitable divisions and products may be carried beyond their normal life spans because of the need to collect a dozen or more executive signatures before they can be dropped. The sense of directness and immediacy that members of a small firm share enables them to solve problems quickly, eliminating needless overhead expenses.

Other special strengths

Besides the potential for greater efficiency, several other advantages help to make small businesses competitive with big firms.

Filling specialized needs of specialized markets: One of the major advantages of big business is large-scale production and marketing. A standard mass-produced product such as a car, a watch, or a computer costs less to manufacture when it's produced in volume. Small firms can't compete in these markets. Many consumers, however—both corporate and individual—are willing to buy products that have a uniqueness not available in mass-produced goods. In these areas the small firm *can* compete.

Some small businesses buy mass-produced products from large manufacturers and adapt them in special ways to satisfy the needs of their customers. The recreational vehicle business began in this way: the engine, chassis, and drive train were purchased from General Motors and Ford, then the unique living quarters

were added by the small recreational vehicle manufacturer.

Limited or specialized markets have a real appeal for the small businessperson. Since these areas do not lend themselves to mass production, the small entrepreneur can move into them aggressively. Bookstores that focus on the religious market, clothing stores for the extra-large or the extra-small, telephone answering services for doctors only—these are only a few of the businesses catering to specialized markets. Small businesses fill the gaps left by the large firms. The result is a great diversity of products in a wide price range, filling a vast number of needs.

Catering to local needs: Geography creates many special needs that small business can fill. Seaports need boat-rental businesses, pier-fishing facilities, ships, restaurants, and custom brokers to handle commercial shipping. Mountainous areas need facilities and businesses catering to both summer- and winter-sports enthusiasts. (The large overhead and operating costs of major corporations discourage them from operating in these seasonal areas.) Likewise, any scenic area needs small shops to cater to the tourist trade.

In addition, small businesses arise to fill the needs of small towns, since the large chain stores find it unprofitable to service branches in areas far from metropolitan centers. Large corporations often allow small businesspeople to represent them in these isolated regions. The small firm thus has an opportunity to market a nationally accepted product with a good likelihood of market success.

Development of new markets and products: The development of new marketplaces creates an excellent opportunity for small businesses. With any new product the risk is very high and the effort required is great;

but many small operators, hoping to develop a profitable business, are willing to work long hours. The labor and overhead costs that a large firm would incur in attempting to duplicate this effort would be excessive. Some of the major industries in America today—automobiles, airplanes, electronics, soap products—started as small businesses.

STARTING OUT: THE FIRST STEPS

Once you have made the decision to start a small business, your first big task will be to choose one of the three major legal forms—sole proprietorship, partnership, or corporation. Then, you will need to go through certain specific procedures, as follows.

Starting a sole proprietorship

Legally, this is the easiest form to implement. For the simple cost of invoices, bank checks, a business license, and one month's rent, you're an entrepreneur. There are just a few other details: if your product or service involves a state sales tax, you will need a certificate to collect taxes—or be exempt from them if you're eligible. Your state Board of Equalization will provide the necessary information. Also, unless you're planning to operate a part-time business, you may be required to pay a security deposit to guarantee payment of these taxes in the event of financial difficulties.

Starting a partnership

Two legal instruments or agreements are important in this form of business: the partnership agreement and the buy/sell agreement.

The **partnership agreement** *specifies the partnership's purpose, the duties of the partners, the percentage of ownership of each partner in the business, how the profit will be split, and the method and amount of income to be paid to each partner.* The docu-

ment must be either drafted by an attorney or reviewed by one.

The **buy/sell agreement** *prevents the termination of the business at the death of one of the partners.* Why is it important? Upon the death of one of the partners, the deceased partner's husband, wife, or estate becomes the heir to the deceased partner's interest in the business; and this presents a problem because the heir could quickly become a liability to the business. The buy/sell agreement solves this problem by providing that the heir of a deceased partner will sell his or her interest in the business to the surviving partner or partners. The agreement must be signed and agreed to by all the partners and their heirs. A properly written buy/sell agreement will ensure a smooth transfer of the ownership of the business at the death of one of the partners, so that the business can continue without interruption. The agreement must contain a formula for determining the current dollar value of the business. Also, you will need to fund the agreement with enough cash to make possible the execution of the plan upon your death. If sufficient cash is not available, life insurance (in the amount of the current value of the business) should be purchased to fund the plan.

Four parties or groups of parties should be involved in every buy/sell agreement: (1) a good business attorney, (2) an accountant (CPA), (3) a qualified business life insurance agent (chartered life underwriter, or CLU), and (4) all the partners and their heirs.

Attracting investors: Investors are easily attracted to the partnership form of business. The partners can

take on **limited partners**, *people who participate in the profits and losses of the partnership but whose liability is limited to the amount of their investment. (Partners who accept the liability of the business* are called **general partners**.) Limited partners may not interfere in partnership decisions unless the business is being grossly mismanaged.

Starting a corporation

We've discussed the corporate form of business in Chapter 2, but here we'll add some additional points.

Setting up your business as a corporation can help you attract investors. Investors can buy and sell shares in the corporation by any legal means available, and each investor is liable only for the amount of the investment. Incorporation also offers a number of tax advantages, including full tax-free medical reimbursement for health and accident insurance; tax-free sick pay; tax-free group term insurance coverage up to $50,000; tax-free business related meals, lodging, and education; and IRS-approved pension and profit-sharing plans that allow the corporation to shelter up to 25 percent of its profits from taxes.

But incorporation involves some tax disadvantages as well. The business is taxed at the corporate rate, then the shareholders are taxed when the profits are distributed as dividends. This double burden of taxation falls especially heavily on the small corporation. On the other hand, earnings may be accumulated in the corporation for a specific purpose, and the earnings are not taxable to the shareholders until they are distributed. For IRS approval, the retention of earnings must be recorded in the minutes of the regular corporation meetings.

In our discussion of partnerships, we mentioned the need for a buy/sell agreement. The corporate form requires a similar instrument, normally called a **stock redemption plan,** which *serves the same functions as the buy/sell agreement.* Again, you must consult an attorney, CPA, and CLU.

The Subchapter S corporation: The Subchapter S corporation, a hybrid form of business, offers all the limited-liability advantages, the investor mobility, and the basic fringe benefits of the corporation, but it involves radical tax-treatment differences. The taxation of a Subchapter S corporation is similar to that of a partnership. That is, all profits and losses are passed on to the shareholders whether they are distributed or not, and shareholders pay taxes on their share of the profits or losses according to each individual's tax schedule.

Some restrictions exist in this form:

1. To elect Subchapter S in any tax year, the corporation may not have more than ten shareholders.

2. No shareholder can be a trust, foreign corporation, or subsidiary of another corporation.

3. The corporation must receive at least 20 percent of its gross receipts from within the United States.

4. Not more than 20 percent of the gross receipts of the corporation may come from rents, royalties, interest, dividends, annuities, gains from stocks, or securities.

5. All shareholders must consent to Subchapter S election.

6. No second class of stock can exist which represents an equity interest in the corporation.

In short, the Subchapter S corporation is ideal for two or more individuals who wish the limited-liability umbrella of a corporation and the simple tax structure of a partnership. Will it be right for you? You'll have to think through the decision carefully—as carefully as you consider all the other decisions involved in starting your own small business.

CAREERS IN BUSINESS
A GENERAL OVERVIEW

EDUCATION AND YOUR FUTURE

Some years ago, when you decided to go to college, some people may have thought you were making a mistake. They may have thought that practical, on-the-job training could teach you just as much as professors and textbooks could. But they were ignoring a very serious problem in American business—unemployment. In 1976, 7.7 percent of Americans who wanted to work could not find jobs,[*] and the people who had the most trouble were the least educated: about 14 percent of men and women with one to three years of high school were unemployed in 1976.[†]

Going to college, then, is just about the most practical thing you can do. And the statistics prove it: in 1976, only about 6 percent of those with one to three years of college needed jobs, and only about 3 percent of people who had completed four years of college were unemployed.[**] But a diploma alone cannot guarantee you a job. Some fields are so crowded that young workers don't have a chance. If, for example, you were studying education instead of business, you would be in for a difficult

[*] Bureau of Labor Statistics, *U.S. Working Women: A Databook,* Bulletin 1977 (Washington, D.C.: Government Printing Office, 1977), p. 10.
[†] Bureau of Labor Statistics, *Occupational Outlook Handbook, 1978-79 Edition,* Bulletin 1955 (Washington, D.C.: Government Printing Office, 1978), p. 26.
[**] Ibid., p. 26.

time: the supply of teachers exceeds the demand for teaching jobs nation-wide by 17 percent—which means that over 165,000 trained educators cannot teach. And there are other fields with more trained people than jobs, including communications, foreign languages, psychology, and the social sciences.

What's the solution to this problem? To major in a field where there *is* demand for personnel. And that's what you're doing if you major in Business. In all areas of Business and Management, demand exceeds supply by over 10 percent—which translates to 104,000 available jobs. In Accounting alone, there were nearly 45,000 openings in 1976,* and in Computer and Information Services, there was work for 6,600 people.† So, in short, you've made some good decisions: going to college should help you find a job, and being a Business graduate means you'll find less competition and more job openings when you graduate.

Now, or not too long from now, you may be about to make another important decision: what area of Business should you major in? And that's where this book can help you. At the end of each Part in the book you will find a section on Careers in Business. Each of these sections gives you

---

* Bureau of Labor Statistics, *Occupational Outlook Quarterly* (Washington, D.C.: Government Printing Office, Spring 1976), p. 11.
† Adapted from National Center for Educational Statistics to 1985–86.

three kinds of information about the business areas discussed in that Part:

1. Trends in the job market are outlined for each professional area, along with the kinds of majors that best equip graduates to enter those fields.

2. A *career table* outlines the jobs available to graduates of two-year, four-year, and MBA programs with various majors. Each table tells you about job responsibilities and requirements, salary ranges, and opportunities for advancement.

3. A *special-interest article* discusses a subject that is particularly noteworthy: you'll find articles on internships and women in business, an interview with a personnel manager, and an interview with a newly hired employee.

In addition, the Appendix contains a section titled "Techniques for Entering the Job Market." Here you'll find materials that can help you actually look for a job, including suggestions for planning a job-search strategy, writing your résumé, interviewing, and managing your career.

You'll have an exciting time exploring the world of Business—and chances are that you'll find a Business major, and eventually a career in business, that is right for you.

MANUAL 2

MANAGEMENT

When Levi Strauss migrated to America from Bavaria in the mid-nineteenth century, he earned his living by peddling clothing and pots and pans. During the California Gold Rush, Strauss found a lucrative market for sturdy canvas work pants. The Strauss family business grew over the years, and in the 1960s it benefited from another kind of "gold rush"—when America's disenchanted youth made blue jeans the uniform of their generation.[1]

Clearly, timing has been an essential factor in the Strauss company's success. Yet there has also been another key factor—good business management. What does management involve? This is what we'll discuss in Part 2.

☐ In Chapter 3, **The Process of Management,** we discuss the four basic functions of management.

☐ Chapter 4, **Internal Organization,** tells how managers group employees and distribute work among them for maximum efficiency.

☐ Chapter 5 is about **Personnel Management.** It describes methods of recruiting, compensating, and evaluating employees; it also discusses health and safety programs.

☐ Chapter 6 describes the role of **Production Management.** How does an item get from the idea stage to the point where it actually exists? You'll find out in this chapter.

☐ The Enrichment Chapter titled **Human Relations** looks at the factors that affect workers' performance and morale.

☐ In the Enrichment Chapter on **Management and Unions,** you'll read about the labor movement, and about the way unions and management negotiate.

CHAPTER THREE

THE PROCESS OF MANAGEMENT

"Whatever happened to W. T. Grant?" became a sadly familiar question throughout the business community after the well-known chain, once the country's seventeenth-largest retailer, went bankrupt in 1975. The briefest and most obvious answer would be "bad management," but that's hardly specific enough to be very helpful. A better answer, as subsequent investigations revealed, would be that Grant's management suffered a near-total breakdown in its planning and control functions. Fine—but what does that mean?

To understand how an established company can get into such trouble we need a clear picture of the nature of management, why it's necessary, and how it operates. As we will learn in this chapter, the management of any enterprise, large or small, comprises four basic functions—planning, organizing, directing, and controlling—each of which deals with a different set of problems and requires a different set of skills.

WHAT WILL THIS CHAPTER FOCUS ON?

After reading the material in this chapter, you will understand and be able to discuss:

■ the four functions of management—planning, organizing, directing, and controlling

■ the functions of top, middle, and supervisory managers in large organizations

■ the steps in both long-range and short-range planning

■ division of labor by task and authority

■ two aspects of directing—motivating people and leading them

■ the process of controlling—seeing that work actually gets done as planned, and correcting any problems in the operation of the organization

■ the three types of managerial skills—technical, human, and conceptual

Towering glass-clad skyscrapers, oak-panelled executive board-rooms, people wearing expensive clothes and carrying briefcases—these are a few of the images many people associate with the term "management." And it's not surprising that they do, since the mass media often focus on management in big business. But as you will soon discover, the practice of management is not limited to profit-making corporate giants like General Motors, IBM, and Sears. It is not confined to the top level. Nor is management an idea that suddenly came into being in twentieth-century industrial America.

WHAT IS MANAGEMENT AND WHY IS IT NEEDED?

Whenever people work together to achieve a goal, they find themselves making decisions about who will do what when, and what money and other resources are to be used when. This *process of coordinating resources to meet an objective* is called **management**, and all the people who work toward meeting these objectives form an organization. An **organization** is, simply, *a group of people who have a common objective.*

MANAGEMENT IS NEEDED IN ORGANIZATIONS OF ALL KINDS

There are certain basic principles of coordination that can be applied to the management of virtually every type of organization, whatever its size or purpose. An army general coordinates soldiers, weapons, and supplies to win a battle. A hospital administrator coordinates beds, operating rooms, medical supplies, doctors, nurses, and other resources and personnel to provide health care. Art museums, undersea diving teams, government agencies, universities, even zoos—all these and hundreds of other types of organizations depend on effective coordination by their managers for their survival.

Furthermore, even the smallest organization may have big management problems. For example, picture yourself at the end of a long school year as your con-

cerns turn from passing final exams to earning enough money for fall tuition and expenses. Summer jobs are scarce. But you and a friend believe there is a pressing need in your community for a reliable, reasonably priced home painting service.

Having made your decision to go into business as the Reliable Painting Service, you must now deal with a number of basic managerial questions:

- How will you find customers and advertise your service?
- What will you charge for various kinds of jobs?
- Where will you get your materials and equipment—paint, brushes and rollers, ladders, scaffolding, a rented van?
- Where will you get the start-up money to pay for them?

Meeting with your partner, you develop a plan of action. As an accounting major, you agree to handle billing, bookkeeping, and purchasing. Your partner, a marketing major, will do the selling and promotion. With your parents as cosigners, you take out a $500 personal loan from the local bank. Your friend designs and places a small ad in the weekly newspaper, and together you distribute leaflets to homes throughout the community. Soon, calls for your service begin to come in, and your new business is launched.

After a while, moreover, if business becomes good enough, you may want to hire a few classmates to help out—and at this point things start to get complicated. You and your partner will find yourselves spending less time actually painting and more time making decisions about such things as scheduling jobs, supervising workers, collecting any paying bills, attracting new business, and so forth. In short, you will have a typical set of management problems, claiming an ever greater portion of your time and energy.

THE FOUR FUNCTIONS OF MANAGEMENT

The activities managers perform can be subdivided into four **functions of management**: *planning, organizing, directing, and controlling*. We'll take a look at these in the sections that follow.

PLANNING

Planning is unquestionably the most important management function, the one on which all the others depend. When a manager **plans**, he or she *establishes objectives for the organization and tries to determine the best ways to accomplish them.*

PLANNING IS FUTURE-ORIENTED

Numerous elements go into an organization's planning process, of course, but they all involve thinking ahead in one way or another—particularly when a decision has to be made about trying something new. Take the example of Atari Incorporated, the electronics firm. In 1973 it introduced "Pong," the computerized video game that has since become a familiar fixture in bars across the country. In 1977 Atari launched a carefully planned expansion into the new market for computerized home-TV games, aiming to become the dominant company in the field. Its sophisticated video-game unit did in fact capture the lead in sales, thanks largely to its low cost (under $200) and versatility—it can be programmed to play a variety of games simply by plugging in different tape cartridges.[1]

Atari was booming. In part, though, its rapid success was the result of a lack of competition, and the company's managers realized that they would have to make plans to defend their early lead against the rival products that would soon be appearing. They took a close look at the future, and they saw three things. First, consumer demand later in the year would probably outrun the relatively small supplies of its competitors. If Atari took the gamble of increasing production to the limit, it could fill the vacuum with its own stockpile. Second, the more customers who bought the video-game machines, the greater the demand would be for additional programming cartridges. And third, the more people who bought game cartridges, the more profits Atari would make—for the Atari planners expected that the greatest profits would ultimately come not from one-time control-unit purchases, but from continuing new-cartridge sales.

What was the upshot? Atari took the plunge. But as its managers continued to scan the future, they also saw that certain other plans they had made would not be feasible. Atari had developed plans in 1977 to market a variety of optional equipment, such as keyboards

This tract of new homes will soon house potential consumers. What goods will the new residents want? What services will they need? It's the job of the business manager and planner to find out.

and memory units, that would tie in with the computer circuitry in its video-game machines to produce a small, general-purpose home computer (something we'll discuss in our Enrichment Chapter on Computers and Data Processing.) The company's management, however, decided to postpone these plans for the time being and concentrate on enlarging its present business—concluding, in effect, that most people were not yet comfortable enough with computers to invite one into their homes (and hoping, of course, that its own video games would help change that.)

LONG-RANGE AND SHORT-RANGE PLANS

A careful consideration of the future is basic to all planning. But in any organization's strategy it is possible to distinguish two different "time frames" for planning—long-range and short-range. **Long-range plans** *tend to be geared to a two- to five-year time span, and in some cases longer.* **Short-range plans** *cover the kinds of situations that are likely to come up month by month, and sometimes weekly or daily.*

Long-range plans

Possibly the most important type of long-range plan is the **statement of purpose**, which *answers the fundamental question, What is the overall purpose of the organization?* Or, for a profit-making enterprise, *What business is it in?* (For example, is it a root-beer company or a general soft-drink manufacturer?) Also important are **objectives**—*broad goals.* (For example, a business will have profit as one of its objectives, but it may also have other objectives such as maintaining a high-quality product or gaining large numbers of customers.) And a third key type of long-range plans consists of **policies**—*guidelines for activity* that help organization members meet the organization's objectives. (Delta Airlines, for example, has a policy of promoting workers from within the company, which helps boost profits by improving workers' attitudes and cutting down on the costs of training.[2])

Short-range plans

Short-range plans tend to be quite specific. For example, one type of short-range plan, the **procedure**, *tells employees exactly what steps to take in a given situation* (such as moving raw materials from the receiving platform of the factory to the beginning of the assembly line). Similarly detailed are **practices**, *methods for handling specific problems* (such as alcoholism in an employee), and **rules**, procedures *covering one situation only* (such as an employee's loss of his ID card).

A familiar and very important type of short-range plan is the **budget**, *a plan which expresses in numerical terms* (usually dollars) *how the resources of a company can be distributed to attain a desired profit.* There are a number of tricky variables a manager must think over in preparing a budget. In order to increase profits, should the company simply cut costs—for example, by laying off workers? The alternative may be an appealing one, but it can backfire if it reduces the quality of the company's product or service enough to drive

WHAT MAKES A GOOD PLAN?

First of all, a good plan is *objective.* It represents all points of view, not just the ones the managers would prefer to think about. Planners shouldn't encourage people to tell them only what they want to hear, and they shouldn't encourage their employees to use statistics in a misleading way to support their favorite viewpoints. More than one manager has summoned his administrative assistant into his office and said, "This is what I plan to do; now get me the statistics to back it up." That's not good management; it may get the manager in trouble later.

Second, a good plan is *clear* and easy to understand. The Internal Revenue Service wastes millions of dollars each year correcting innocent errors on tax returns that people make because they can't understand the instructions. Complicated language is not only annoying to the person trying to read it, it can create serious difficulties for a company. (We'll talk more about this later in the chapter.)

Third, a good plan is *flexible,* with enough "give" in it to survive changes in the economy, reorganization within the company, and shifts in consumers' preferences. Not too long ago, a number of manufactur-

away customers. We'll talk more about budgets in Chapter 13.

THE "BIG PICTURE"

If keeping up with changing conditions is a manager's first concern, the second is seeing how all plans, great and small, fit together. Comprehending the "big picture" isn't always easy, especially if you are the manager in charge of one particular product line or one particular part of your company. Your new building or ad campaign will be impressive, but will it help the company's overall profit picture? First of all, detailed information from other departments of the company may be hard for you to interpret. And second, you may not want to see what it shows.

ers who specialized in single products such as electronic calculators, digital watches, and CB radios found themselves in real trouble when high consumer demand coupled with strong competition among manufacturers caused prices to drop suddenly. The result was heavy financial loss, which could have been prevented through more flexible planning.

Fourth, a good plan is *consistent:* all its inner elements work together and it meshes smoothly with other plans in the company. For example, think about what may happen if the top management of a life insurance company instructs its sales force to go after large policies—in the $40,000 to $100,000 range, say—instead of concentrating on selling lots of small policies under $10,000. In some companies, the underwriters tend to be suspicious of customers who want big policies; they think they may be trying to cheat the company. So if the managers decide to redirect the efforts of the sales people toward selling larger policies, they must be sure to discuss the new approach with the underwriters as well. Otherwise, many new policies may fail to be approved in the main office, and the company may even lose sales people who feel management isn't really working with them.

Strategy planning: one approach to the "big picture" problem

In the past few years a new approach to planning has been adopted successfully by a number of large companies. Known as **strategy planning** or **strategy management**, this approach *stresses the importance of focusing on overall company goals,* rather than on individual products or divisions within the company. In the early 1970s, for instance, the Olin Corporation of Connecticut was in the midst of a big diversification program, actively moving into such areas as camping equipment, aluminum production, and polyester film manufacturing. Profits were sluggish, however, and Olin turned for advice to Arthur D. Little, the Boston management consulting firm. It helped Olin develop a system in which annual planning sessions for various divisions would include not only the managers directly involved, but also two or three managers from other parts of the company who had little knowledge of the division's operations. The outside managers—or profilers, as they're called—bring a degree of objectivity to the planning process that might otherwise be lacking. They also help determine whether proposed activities fit in well with the company's larger objectives. At Olin, for instance, strategy planning led to a decision to sell the camping equipment, aluminum, and polyester film subsidiaries and to use the money to build up its production of industrial chemicals and copper-based metal alloys—fields in which Olin had greater technical and marketing experience. Similarly, strategy planning convinced Gulf Oil Corporation to stay out of the solar-energy business, as promising as it appeared, because the company lacked the expertise to compete effectively in that field.[3]

ORGANIZING

Once the managers of an organization have set up their plans, the next question they must deal with is how to get all the plans accomplished using the resources at their disposal. The most important resource is their employees. The managers must think through all the activities employees must carry out, from programming the organization's computers (if it has any) to driving its trucks to mailing its letters. And they must get together a staff capable of doing these things.

This aspect of management—*the process of arranging resources, primarily people, to carry out the organization's plans*—is known as **organizing**.

Organizing is particularly challenging in that the organization is likely to undergo constant change. Old staff members may leave and new ones arrive. The public's tastes and interests may change, so that the organization has to change its goals. Shifting political and economic trends may mean cutbacks, rearrangements, or perhaps expansion. Every month (even every week) the organization presents a new picture, and so management's organizing tasks are never complete.

THE DIVISION OF LABOR

The main problem the manager faces in organizing is figuring out a division of labor that will be best suited to the goals of the organization. Labor may be divided in two different ways—according to task and according to authority—and the manager has to structure the organization with both these dimensions in mind.

Dividing labor by task

In 1776 the Scottish economist Adam Smith did a classic study that demonstrated something we take for granted today. He showed that *dividing labor by task enables a group of workers to achieve far more than the same number of workers could achieve without it*. The labor process Smith studied was the manufacture of pins. What Smith found was that if each of ten workers went through every step needed to make a pin, the best worker could make a maximum of twenty pins a day, and some could only make a single pin. Even if every worker could make 20 pins, that would result in only 200 pins a day. But if each worker performed only a few steps—and no one made a pin from start to fin-

For smooth sailing, any group has to be organized according to task and authority.

ish—ten workers were able to manufacture 48,000 pins a day! There was no question about it: dividing up the job into a series of steps was by far the best plan.

Exactly why does dividing labor by task work so well? First, it requires less skill on the part of individual workers. People who cannot handle an entire complex task can often do one part of the task efficiently. Second, it saves time. Workers do not have to prepare for many different procedures. There are other benefits that may become obvious if managers use this approach in a given industry over a period of months or years. The division of labor by task leads to specialization: as people become more skilled at a specific job, each component task gets done better. And furthermore, division of labor encourages the invention of special machines to do the various small tasks, and these technological improvements lead in turn to greater efficiency.

Today's large businesses carry the division of labor much further than Adam Smith may have envisioned. Some people manufacture products. Others sell them. Still others handle finance, research, personnel, advertising, and so forth. In the automobile industry an assembly line may consist of numerous different work groups, each responsible for assembling only one part—such as the frame, the steering mechanism, or the suspension. Further down the line other groups install the engine and the wiring, weld the body to the chassis, and put in the upholstery. And within each of these groups, moreover, labor is so divided that one worker may perform only a single task—tightening screws, say, on the dashboard of a car.

Dividing labor by authority

If the managers can divide up the organization's labor process by task, they will have made a good start toward reaching their goals. But the organization will function even more smoothly if the workers know not only what to do and when to do it, but also who is looking over their shoulders to make sure they do it right. In most organizations certain members are held accountable for work done by other people. If the workers do not complete their tasks properly or on time, those who are responsible for the work must take the blame. President Harry Truman kept a famous sign on his desk that read, "The Buck Stops Here." He knew that in any organization—including the United States government—there is always a point of ultimate accountability, right at the top. But certain people below the top must have accountability too, and it is part of management's job to plan the way this accountability is distributed.

How can a person who is responsible for the work of others actually get those people to do their jobs? By being given a certain amount of authority. **Authority** is a form of power; it's *power granted by the organization and acknowledged by the employees.* A supervisor must have the authority to modify the work slightly for greater efficiency. He or she must also have the authority to reward or penalize workers according to how well they perform their jobs. So when managers work out a division of labor in an organization, they must be sure to grant the right amount of authority to those workers who will need it to do their jobs. For example, managers must determine the kinds of decisions they will allow assembly-line supervisors to make without consulting higher-level managers, and then make sure the assembly-line workers see the supervisors making these decisions.

The foregoing points, of course, are just the highlights in the complicated process of setting up a division of labor in an organization. We talk more about this aspect of the manager's job in Chapter 4. We also talk about **staffing**, the process of *matching the right people with the right jobs,* in Chapter 5.

DIRECTING

Through the process of organizing, then, managers plan the tasks their employees are *supposed* to do. But even if managers set up a magnificently logical organizational plan, it doesn't mean everything will happen the way they have in mind. Far from it. The results may be very unsatisfactory unless the managers also spend time on a third type of management activity—the activity known as directing.

Directing is a complex management function whose primary aim is *getting people to work effectively and willingly.* It consists of two different but related processes. First, it involves **motivating**—the process of *giving employees a reason to do the job and to put out their best performance.* Second, it involves **leading**, the process of *showing employees how to do the job,* both through actual demonstration of specific tasks and through the manager's own behavior and attitude.

Consider Sam Walton, the chairman of Wal-Mart Stores, a chain of discount stores in the Midwest. His business has been remarkably successful in recent years, thanks largely to Walton's "people-centered" philosophy of management. As Walton explains: "We like to let folks know we're interested in them and that they're vital to us. 'Cause they are. Those department heads are the ones who really know what's going on out there in the field, and we've got to get them to tell us." He heaps praise and rewards on workers who perform well. "I'm really impressed with the way you've got things set up in those departments," he tells a group of pleased saleswomen. "You folks are what makes this company work," Walton tells department heads in another store. Walton's interaction with store employees and his concern for their opinions provide a good example for the store managers. He has also trained his top executives to show the same concern for the employees, insisting that they visit stores on a schedule similar to his own—twice a year to each of the nearly two hundred branches.[4]

Walton's approach, which sets the tone for his entire organization, involves both of the directing processes we have just discussed. He *motivates* employees through praise, by asking for workers' opinions, and through profit-sharing. Further, he *leads* his employees: he has trained his executives to take an interest in the organization's workers, and he sets an example for them with his frequent trips into the field.

STYLES OF LEADERSHIP

One of the favorite topics of political commentators and newspaper columnists is the "leadership style" of whomever happens to occupy the White House. A president may be attacked for being overly formal or too informal, for overusing his presidential influence by leaning on people or for failing to mobilize effectively the powers of the presidency. But the president of the United States is not the only manager with a leadership style. Every manager has one, from the brawling, cursing baseball manager to the urbane, statesmanlike university chancellor.

You can learn something about leadership by examining the methods different leaders use to get re-

sults and the specific ways they exercise authority. While virtually all leaders have their own individual characteristics, we can identify three broad categories of leadership style:

- the autocratic style
- the democratic, or participative, style
- the laissez-faire style (the French term *laissez faire* can be roughly translated as "leave it alone," or, more roughly, "hands off")

Autocratic leadership

The **autocratic style** *emphasizes the straightforward use of authority.* An autocratic leader simply issues orders to his subordinates and relies on the power of the organization to enforce them. The attitude of the autocratic leader might be summed up as follows: "I believe in getting things done. I can't waste time calling meetings. Someone has to call the shots around here, and I think it should be me." But there is another reason too why a leader may choose an autocratic style: "I'm being paid to lead. If I let a lot of other people make the decisions I should be making, then I'm not worth my salt."

Autocratic leadership can be extremely effective if the people wielding it have enough power to enforce their decisions and if their followers know that they have it. It is especially useful in military situations where quick decisions are critical. But it also has certain disadvantages: the autocractic leader may lack objectivity and may disregard the opinions of subordinates.

Democratic leadership

The **democratic** (or **participative**) **style** of leadership *emphasizes group participation in decision making.* The democratic leader uses authority given by a group and encourages a free flow of communication within that group. The attitude of the democratic leader might be summed up like this: "It's foolish to make decisions oneself on matters that affect people. Though I make clear to my subordinates that I'm the one who has to have the final say, I always talk things over with them first."

United States government leaders employ (or should employ) the democratic style of leadership. So do managers dealing with highly skilled professionals. For example, a hospital administrator does not dictate orders to a team of brain surgeons, but asks their advice before making a decision about rearranging the operating room.

With the democratic style, people require relatively little supervision because they are willing to do their jobs without coercion. The disadvantages of this approach are that decision making may be slower, and leaders may exercise limited control over their followers.

Laissez-faire leadership

The **laissez-faire** ("leave it alone") **style** of leadership leaves the group almost entirely on its own; the *leader acts largely as a consultant.* This style of leadership is found mainly in organizations concerned with creativity. An instructor teaching an advanced class in painting often encourages students to paint as much as possible and comments on their work only when asked for an opinion. In the business world a laissez-faire style might be used in a small advertising agency. The attitude of the laissez-faire leader might be summed up this way: "I put most problems into my group's hands and leave it to them to carry the ball from there. I serve merely as a reflector, mirroring back the people's thoughts and feelings so that they can better understand them."[5]

Laissez-faire leadership may be quite stimulating to organization members who have their own ideas to express. Its obvious disadvantage is that all members of the group must understand and actively want to attain the group's goal, a consensus that infrequently occurs.

Is there one "best" leadership style?

We have deliberately pointed out both the advantages and disadvantages of the various leadership styles. They all work sometimes, but there is no style that works every time. This point is crucial.

To lead effectively, managers must determine who they are and who they should be. They must fully understand the objectives, plans, and formal organization of an enterprise. They have to know just how much authority they have and how much workers think they have. Most of all, the managers have to know the nature and needs of their workers before they can select a leadership style. Leadership, in other words, must be geared to the situation.

CONTROLLING

A fourth, and extremely important, management function is known as controlling—a word that is often a source of confusion because it suggests some sort of restriction, as when a leash controls a dog. In management, **controlling** is not solely a restrictive process. It is *the process of ensuring that organizational objectives are actually being attained, and correcting deviations if they are not.*

When managers control, they compare where they are with where they should be and take any necessary corrective action. Managers determine where they are by getting reports from subordinates, coworkers, superiors, and sources outside the organization. They determine where they should be by referring to the plans and objectives they have set up. Then they take corrective action, if needed—by replanning, reorganizing, or redirecting. Controlling is the management function that points out flaws in the other three functions. If the managers of an organization maintain a continuous control process, they can make at least a certain number of mistakes without seriously hurting the organization.

THE CYCLE OF CONTROLLING

As a first step in the control cycle in any organization, managers must set **standards**—*goals against which performance can be measured later.* In business, control standards are expressed in a number of ways. Here are some of them:

- lateness in minutes per week (the managers might, for example, decide that employees should not be more than ten minutes late to work and should not be late more than one day a week);
- profitability (for example, the managers might set a standard of a 20-percent profit to be derived from a certain product);
- units produced or sold per week;

A COMPANY OUT OF CONTROL

Fraud, deception, incompetence, and mismanagement are a few of the terms investigators used in their attempts to answer the question, "Whatever happened to W. T. Grant and Company?" When Grant, once the nation's seventeenth-largest retailer, filed for bankruptcy in 1975, it became one of the largest and most significant failures in United States corporate history. Over 80,000 people were thrown out of work, 1,073 stores were boarded up, and some $234 million was lost by banks and suppliers in the aftermath of the firm's collapse. Although some disagreement remains on who should shoulder most of the blame, it is clear that the failure stemmed largely from a breakdown in the fourth and last management function—*controlling.*
Grant failed because managers at every level—from the manager of a single store's toy department to the president himself—received spotty and unreliable information on how well—or rather, how poorly—the firm was performing. Controls on prices, how much merchandise was in stock, money owed the company by credit customers, and money owed to suppliers by the firm were completely lacking. Operating budgets were practically unheard of.

According to testimony given in the bankruptcy proceedings:

store buyers (those who bought merchandise for the stores) frequently had to ask the suppliers how much stock was in the stores;

suppliers were deliberately told to overbill the firm and to keep the excess money until it was requested; it was often paid back in checks made out to the buyers themselves;

store managers had different systems of granting credit privileges to customers.

Robert Anderson, who was hired in a last-ditch attempt to salvage the debt-ridden company, said that stores were badly lacking in goods even though newspapers were reporting a steady flow of merchandise into them. According to an account reported in *The Wall Street Journal,* Anderson asked the merchandise vice-president, "How much will you spend on shoes this year . . . women's blouses . . . whatever?" He said he got a blank stare in return, so he pushed on: "John, you know what I mean. How much have you allocated to the shoe buyer? How much will you spend this year?" The merchandise vice-president of a firm that at one time grossed over $1.6 billion in sales never formulated a budget to control his expenditures. Another executive pointed out that inadequate price controls pitted one Grant store against another: "We could have three stores within a ten-mile radius charging three different prices on the same item. We were competing with ourselves." Likewise, a Grant finance executive cited the absence of control over customer credit. "We gave credit to every deadbeat who breathed. The stores were told to push credit and had certain quotas to fill. Up until 1974, we really had 1,200 credit offices. Each store kept all credit information, and payments were to the store." In some areas Grant had earned a reputation as a store where the customer could "Buy now and pay never."

As we can see, what was lacking in the Grant case was continuous control over the company's procedures and finances. Loss of control is risky in a company of any size—but particularly devastating in one as large and as powerful as W. T. Grant.

Sources: "Investigating the Collapse of W. T. Grant," *Business Week,* July 19, 1976, pp. 60–61; and "Grant Testimony Shows It Lacked Curbs on Budget, Credit and Had Internal Woes," *The Wall Street Journal,* February 4, 1977, p. 6.

- employee turnover (percentage of total work force leaving the firm in a given period).

Next, the managers must establish a **feedback system** whereby *they will receive reports on a regular basis*—perhaps daily or weekly. Today many companies use progress reports that come from a computerized monitoring system. But progress reports from the people who are doing or supervising the work are still important too. Supervisory managers may com-

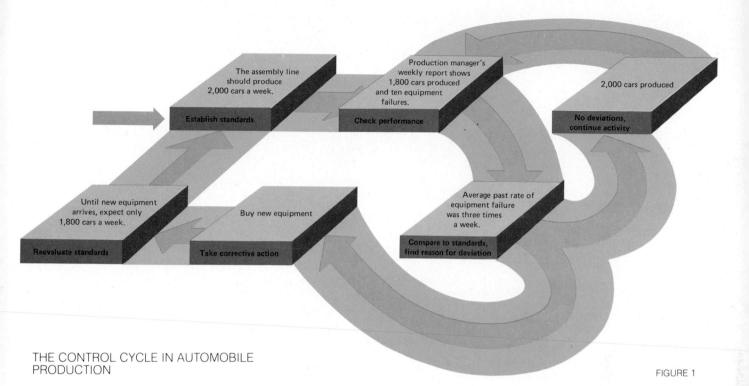

THE CONTROL CYCLE IN AUTOMOBILE
PRODUCTION

FIGURE 1

plain that "All I do is make out reports, I don't have time to do any work." But making out reports *is* part of their work. Without supervisors' participation in the control feedback system, the company would have a harder time functioning effectively.

In Figure 1, the production managers' report shows that only 1,800 cars were produced, 200 short of the standard. Why was production not up to par? To find out the answer, the managers must take a look at the feedback they have been getting on other aspects of the operation. Suppose, for example, they check the weekly report on the performance of the machines that are used in the production line. They find that the average number of equipment breakdowns is three per week (this, in other words, can be taken as the standard). Yet in the week that only 1,800 Cadillacs rolled off the assembly line, the sheet-metal presses conked out ten times. Now the managers know why fewer cars were produced that week, and their best corrective action in this case would probably consist of replacing the machinery. Of course, until the new equipment

arrives, they must also revise the production standard downward to 1,800 units to allow for the defective machinery.

THE MANAGEMENT HIERARCHY

In all organized groups the managerial staff consists basically of three different levels of people: the **top**, or **upper, managers**, who *have the most power and also the most responsibility; the* **middle managers**, who *have somewhat less power and responsibility;* and the **supervisory**, or **operating**, **managers**, *whose power and responsibility are limited to a narrow segment of the organization.* These three levels form a **hierarchy**—a *structure with a top, middle, and bottom*—which can be represented as a pyramid, as shown in Figure 2. There are quite a number of managers on the bottom level, a smaller number of managers on the middle level, and just a few managers, or in many cases only one, at the very top.

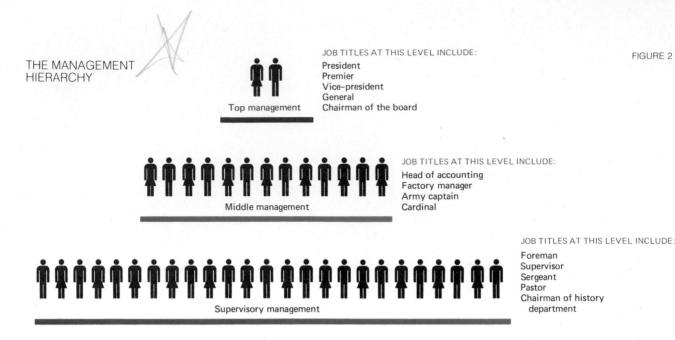

THE MANAGEMENT
HIERARCHY

Top management

JOB TITLES AT THIS LEVEL INCLUDE:
President
Premier
Vice-president
General
Chairman of the board

FIGURE 2

Middle management

JOB TITLES AT THIS LEVEL INCLUDE:
Head of accounting
Factory manager
Army captain
Cardinal

Supervisory management

JOB TITLES AT THIS LEVEL INCLUDE:
Foreman
Supervisor
Sergeant
Pastor
Chairman of history
    department

On the surface, management hierarchies may seem to differ because the titles of managers' jobs vary from one organization to another. But such differences are often misleading. Three executives in three similar corporations, for instance, may all have different titles—senior vice-president, executive vice president, and president—but actually perform the same jobs within their companies.

In Figure 3, we show the tasks that are typically performed by managers on each level of the hierarchy.

##
MANAGERIAL SKILLS

Is there a managerial "type" of person? We have all known the person who has been managing groups of people ever since childhood—starting with the neighborhood gang. But you don't have to be a "born manager" to learn some managerial skills, or to sharpen the ones you may already have. Most people at some point in their lives find themselves with new responsibilities—sometimes heavy ones—that make them feel the need to develop managerial skills.

Basically, managerial skills fall into three areas: technical skills, human skills, and conceptual skills.

TECHNICAL SKILLS

A person who is able to operate a machine, prepare a financial statement, program a computer, or pass a football has a **technical skill**. That is, *he or she is able to perform the mechanics of a particular job.* Clearly, the managers most concerned with technical skills are likely to be the supervisors—because they are closest to the actual work. A factory supervisor, for example, may have to train workers to do their jobs. Nevertheless, middle managers may need certain technical skills as well—such as scheduling techniques and the ability to read computer printouts.

Top-level managers such as the president and the vice-president usually do not need technical skills of the kind we have just described; the only "technical skills" they need are their general management skills. The technical skills that supervisors and middle-level managers use are often not readily transferable from one industry to another. But general management skills can often be applied to a wide range of industries. If you're trained to operate textile-cutting machines, you will probably not be able to transfer your skills to the restaurant business. If you're the executive who runs the garment business, however, you may be able to use your general management skills in a number of different enterprises.

WHO DOES THE PLANNING?

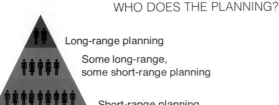

Long-range planning

Some long-range,
some short-range planning

Short-range planning

Not surprisingly, top managers are usually the ones responsible for long-range planning, while middle managers and supervisory managers are more involved with planning over the short range. Of course, there is a good deal of overlap.

The chief difference between planning by a company president and planning by an assembly-line supervisor is the complexity of the problems which confront them. The president deals with thousands of people, millions of dollars, and years of time, while the supervisor handles only a few people, over a short time, on a much smaller budget. Both managers plan in order to influence the future—but for the president the future is far more difficult to predict, and the losses will be much greater if his or her predictions do not come true. Working as a top manager can be very stressful.

WHO DOES THE ORGANIZING?

Organizing the whole structure
Staffing upper-level positions

Organizing individual divisions

Training new workers
Evaluating workers' progress

Generally, it is the top managers who establish the organizational structure for an enterprise as a whole, and staff upper-level positions. Middle managers do the same thing—but usually just for one division. Supervisors seldom set up organizational structure, but they may still have important responsibilities in the organizing area—such as training new workers and evaluating their progress.

WHO DIRECTS THE WORKERS?

Planning motivational devices
(e.g. bonuses)

Implementing motivational programs

Dealing with day-to-day motivation

Directing begins at the top and is then mirrored downward. But the closer a manager gets to the "action"—the work itself—the more time-consuming, demanding and crucial directing becomes. For example, the first-line supervisor spends most of the time trying to motivate workers to churn out their daily quotas of whatever the department is charged with producing. The first-line supervisor in on the "firing line" all the time—contending frequently with such problems as worker lateness, illness, disagreements and grievances against the organization. Top management, by contrast, is and should be interested in the "big picture"—the methods to be used in motivating the organization as a whole, such as wage scales and bonuses.

WHO DOES THE CONTROLLING?

Setting overall control systems and standards

Setting specific goals, getting routine feedback, solving routine problems

Getting progress reports
Solving day-to-day difficulties

Top management usually establishes the control systems and standards—such as market-share targets—that measure the performance of the organization as a whole. These standards are then translated into more specific goals—such as sales quotas—for middle management and the other managers down the line. Like directing, controlling is particularly important on the middle and lower management levels. Middle management receives most of the routine feedback and solves most routine problems before they become serious enough to draw the attention—and the wrath—of upper management. Supervisory managers collect daily and weekly progress information to pass on to middle managers, and they try to handle any difficulties that are due to employees' poor work habits or practices.

Communication is a
two-way street.
Effective managers
listen as carefully as
they speak. . .

Oral communication

This very direct form of communication generally takes up a substantial part of any business day. Meetings, presentations, conferences, informal chats with superiors and subordinates—all call for effective oral communication. It is likewise important in dealings with people outside the organization. The impression made in sales talks and interviews, in speeches and press conferences, will depend largely on how well the speaker organizes and presents the subject.

HUMAN SKILLS

Human skills are all the *skills that are required in order to understand other people and to interact effectively with them.* Managers' human skills are most needed when directing, but they need them in countless other situations too—since their main job is getting things done through people. This is true even if the manager is the boss and can fire anyone at will; after all, anxious employees don't always do good work.

One human skill all managers must have is the ability to **communicate**, that is, to *transfer information.* In any organization, communication is the thread that weaves everything together. Not only does it aid management in the internal operation of the organization, it also helps maintain good relations with people outside the organization.

There are two chief forms of communication: oral and written.

DISCIPLINING WORKERS: A PROBLEM IN ORAL COMMUNICATION

A manager frequently has to discipline workers for problems such as lateness or absenteeism and talk to subordinates about their progress or lack of it. To carry out these interactions effectively requires much patience and tact. Suppose, for example, you were a manager and had to call in a worker who had a long string of latenesses. In the course of your discussion he reveals that a drinking problem causes him to be late on Mondays—but he promises to "work on it." For weeks afterwards, he arrives right on time, sometimes even early. Then one Monday he walks in an hour late, looking completely exhausted. Without hesitating you order him into your office and angrily tell him, "You've had it. That'll cost you time off without pay." Suddenly your workers refuse to talk to you. Finally one speaks up and tells you that the man was late because he wrecked his car that morning to avoid hitting an old lady crossing the street.

It must be remembered, furthermore, that successful oral communication is a two-way street. An effective manager should always be attuned to the way people are reacting to what's being said, and above all listen to what they have to say in return. Fine shades of meaning in conversations can make the difference between good and bad relationships with workers—and between higher and lower rates of productivity.

Written communication

It is difficult, if not impossible, to imagine how modern business could function without the written word. Within an organization, especially a large one, memos, letters, progress reports, policy statements, and other forms of written communication are constantly moving back and forth. Busy managers may have a hard time keeping up with such a heavy flow of paper-

. . . and encourage subordinates to talk freely about problems relating to their work.

But all is not lost. You can learn a valuable lesson from this incident. Next time:

find out what rules—written and nonwritten—apply;

review the facts;

talk to the people concerned—any of the other workers could have told you about the accident;

get opinions and feelings—blind adherence to the rules can go against your interests;

seek all points of view.

Choice of words is crucial in oral communication. Many a manager has been moved out of the mainstream in an organization because he or she was too "biting" in describing the failures of a fellow manager, superior, or subordinate. Informing a colleague of the "terrible work coming out of your department" will not earn you points, nor is it likely to solve the problem.

Source: "Lessons from a Communication Blunder," *Supervisory Management,* December 1971, pp. 14–17.

work—but without it, in the long run, they wouldn't be able to manage at all. A company's plans, long-range or short-range, must be recorded in the form of policy directives, summaries of high-level meetings, budget statements, rulebooks, and any number of other written documents. Likewise, the organizing function relies on staff charts and written job descriptions; the directing function proceeds largely through memoranda; and the controlling function, as we noted earlier, depends heavily on written reports. At the same time, written communication is essential in presenting an organization to the outside world. Letters, press releases, annual reports, sales brochures, advertisements—all these play a direct role in shaping a company's public image.

The ability to communicate effectively on paper is thus a valuable skill at all levels of management. In

BODY COMMUNICATION: WHAT DOES IT TELL YOU?

A stream of intent-looking men and women file briskly into the corporate boardroom of a household appliance company. Sales, marketing, production, and financial executives have flown in from around the country to iron out some knotty problems involving inventory and distribution policy. The sales and marketing people are unhappy because low stock levels force customers to wait six weeks for delivery. But to meet the two-week delivery timetable requested by sales, the production department would have to go into overtime. Its budget does not allow for that. Meanwhile, the finance department is holding the line on inventory storage costs, which would rise if marketing had its way.

Notice the communication that goes on in the boardroom before a word is spoken. The vice-president of marketing enters the room first and quickly takes a seat near the president's chair at the head of the conference table. She is determined to persuade the chief executive of the correctness of her position. The production vice-president stares coldly at the marketing executive and takes a seat at the opposite end of the long mahogany table. The vice-president for administration positions himself in a corner chair out of the line of fire between marketing and production. He wants no part of the battle. The president arrives and assumes his traditional position at the head of the table. The finance vice-president arrives late; he is divided between the need to keep costs down and the need to increase revenues.

What we have witnessed here is a form of communication that is often just as significant as oral or written communication. It is called *body communication,* or body language.

The order of arrival of the executives and the seating positions they take actually communicate their sentiments on the issue at hand. The marketing executive is eager to make her point and enlist the president's support; she arrives early to stake out a position near the president. The finance vice-president arrives late; he was reluctant to attend in the first place. Production faces off against marketing at the opposite end of the table. The administrative vice-president, who wants to remain in everyone's good graces, takes a position far removed from the action.

---

preparing a written message of any sort a few points should always be kept in mind:

- The message must be suitable for its audience. In explaining how a windmill works, for instance, you would use one style of writing for an elementary-school magazine, and quite a different one for a sales brochure directed to potential buyers.

- It must be readable. Long, needlessly complex sentences will only slow the reader and camouflage the message you're trying to get across.

- It must be objective. Suppose your school paper began an article with the words: "In his usual inept way, the provost announced totally inaccurate and misleading budget figures for the coming year." You would rightly conclude that the story was clearly too biased to be a reliable source of information.

Because the presentation of business information in written form is so important, we will return to this topic in our Enrichment Chapter on Research, Statistical Analysis, and Reports.

CONCEPTUAL SKILLS

Finally, no matter how good a manager's technical or human skills are, he or she needs another kind of skill

run smoothly must have a clear understanding of their relationship to each other and to the business as a whole.

IS MANAGEMENT A SCIENCE OR AN ART?

It's probably not possible to learn all the management skills we've been discussing step by step, as if one were learning to drive a car. First, each manager's blend of skills is unique, and the blend changes constantly as he or she moves up the career ladder. And second, management is an art as well as a science (and no one can learn an art by following a manual). It is true that business management has grown increasingly "scientific" in many ways, as certain ideas and techniques have been tested and found more effective than other ones. Whether a manager is responsible for developing a new solar heating system, conducting market research to see if people will buy strawberry-flavored toothpaste, or keeping the company's accounts in order, an objective, logical approach to the task is obviously called for. As we've seen, though, management also involves dealing with people—something that can hardly be described as a science. Any organization, no matter how efficiently put together it is, still relies on the people who work for it, and good management must take into account this subjective human element. Employees are ultimately interested in more than a paycheck, and the manager who's sensitive to this basic fact will probably be able to carry out all the other managerial functions much more smoothly.

In short, managing is one of the most complicated jobs there is. It means working with money, things, ideas, *and* people—all at the same time, in an atmosphere of constant change. For the person who likes events to be always predictable, managing is probably the wrong career choice. But for the person who likes fast-paced work and who can be flexible, it's one of the most rewarding activities the business world has to offer.

Seating and order of arrival in the conference room is only one example of body communication. Facial expressions and gestures are even more familiar ones. Eye contact is especially significant in conveying one person's perception of the status of another. Persons with higher status are more apt to use eye contact. And in one intriguing study of body communication, silent films were shown depicting executives walking into each other's offices. The audience was asked to assess the visiting executive's status in the organization according to how far he walked into his colleague's office and how long his colleague delayed in responding to his knock at the door. Almost invariably, the farther he entered in the room, the more important he was thought to be. But the longer he had to wait at the door, the lower his perceived status.

You can't "read" a person's posture like a memo or "listen" to it like a sales report. But if you sharpen your awareness of body communication in the everyday business world, you can find out a lot about people's thoughts and attitudes.

Source: Theodore Caplow, *How To Run Any Organization* (Hinsdale, Ill.: The Dryden Press, 1976), pp. 84–85.

as well to be wholly effective. **Conceptual skill** is *the ability to understand the relationship of parts to the whole.* Managers must be able to imagine the long-range effects their plans may have on their employees as well as on other plans within the company. The techniques of strategy planning mentioned earlier in this chapter attest to the importance of such conceptual skills. The very essence of strategy planning is to coordinate middle-level decision making with the overall goals of an organization—to make sure, in other words, that managers don't lose sight of the forest amid all the trees. Even in a small business there are any number of factors that have to be organized and kept track of, and a manager who wants things to

CHAPTER REVIEW

All organizations need management, the process of coordinating resources to attain an objective. All large organizations have hierarchies: top management, middle management, and supervisory management. The four functions of management are planning, organizing, directing, and controlling.

Planning is the function of establishing objectives and methods for attaining them. Long-range plans include an organization's statement of purpose, overall objectives, and broad policies. Short-range plans include the budget, practices, procedures, and rules. All sound plans must be objective, clear, flexible, and consistent.

Organizing is the function of arranging resources to carry out plans. It is based on division of labor. Dividing a large job into smaller components is called dividing labor by task. Dividing a job into a hierarchy based on responsibility is called dividing labor by authority.

Directing is the function of getting people to do their assigned jobs. This function has two interrelated aspects: motivating and leading. Motivating employees means giving them a reason for doing the job as well as they can. Leading is usually based on one of three main styles of leadership: autocratic, democratic, or laissez-faire. Managers must select a style suited to themselves and to the situation being managed.

Controlling is the function of ensuring that objectives are actually being attained and correcting performance if they are not. The controlling cycle involves establishing standards, checking performance, comparing performance to the standard, and correcting any deviation.

People at all levels of management need managerial skills. Technical skill involves the mechanics of a job, whether operating a machine or programming a computer. Human skill is largely a matter of communication. Written communication must be suitable, readable, and objective; and oral communication must be clear and comprehensible to the listener. Conceptual skill is the ability to see each part in relation to the whole.

KEY WORD REVIEW

management
organization
functions of management
plans
long-range plans
short-range plans
statement of purpose
objectives
policies
procedure
practices
rules
budget
strategy planning
organizing
authority
staffing
directing
motivating
leading
autocratic style
democratic (participative) style
laissez-faire style
controlling
standards
feedback system
top (upper) managers
middle managers
supervisory (operating) managers
hierarchy
technical skill
human skill
communicate
conceptual skill

REVIEW QUESTIONS

1. Why do we need management?

2. What are the main types of plans for organizations? Give examples of types of planning that might be included in each category.

3. What characteristics should a sound plan have?

4. What is the purpose of dividing labor by task? What is the purpose of dividing labor by authority?

5. Explain the importance of directing. What are the two processes involved in directing?

6. What are the advantages and disadvantages of the three types of leadership?

7. What are the steps of the control process?

8. What are the three levels of the managerial staff? What are the responsibilities of each level?

9. Explain how human and conceptual skills are important to all levels of management.

REBUILDING BIANCHI'S: A MATTER OF LEADERSHIP

Your name is Howard I. Vasquez and you've been named Chairman and Chief Executive of Bianchi Brothers, Incorporated. This large department store chain is in trouble and its owners expect you to turn the situation around. What do you do?

Well, first, you look around. That's what Vasquez did, and he was dismayed. Some of the store hadn't been remodeled for twenty years. Convinced that people like an attractive atmosphere in which to shop, Vasquez ordered an extensive refurbishing program.

Next, Vasquez talked to people in the company. Another shock. Bianchi's had no executive development program. Assistant buyers were hired "off the street" and were expected to train themselves. The result was a lack of executive talent and an exceedingly high turnover rate. Again, Vasquez took action. He set up an executive recruiting and development program and strengthened the chain's management through promotions and outside hiring. In addition, a new level of managers was created to deal exclusively with the display and supply of merchandise within each store. This enables stores to respond quickly to consumer tastes which may differ from one region to another.

One of Vasquez' most difficult problems remains to be solved. Bianchi's East 12th Street store in Monument City has been losing money steadily. In the high-rent 12th Street area the store has not been able to compete effectively. Vasquez thinks that by learning more about the needs of local residents he can begin to show a profit.

Whether Vasquez' programs will be successful remains to be seen, but his strong leadership has had one very powerful effect already. Management's morale has improved tremendously. Executives feel a sense of positive direction, something that was lacking in the past. They also feel that the man at the top knows they're there.

1. Vasquez hired a lot of high-level executives from a competing chain. Why did he feel it necessary to do that?

2. Remodeling stores is very expensive. Why did Vasquez think the chain's owner should invest in "cosmetic changes"?

3. Vasquez' managers like his openness; he can always be reached. Why is this kind of communication helpful in a large corporation?

WHITHER THE ORANGE ROOF?

In the age of Ronald McDonald, can the Orange Roof compete with the Golden Arch? Howard Johnson, head of the company that bears his father's name, has seen that it can't. As McDonald's star has risen, Howard Johnson Company's stock has fallen, and the younger Mr. Johnson has decided to do something about it.

As Johnson sees it, one of his company's main problems is its image. "We face the danger of being thought of as a company that did things so well one way that everyone figures that is the only way we can do it. So we must change not only our business but our image." So, Johnson is planning for a new look. He thinks that a relaxing atmosphere will have a strong appeal in our fast-paced society, so his new Howard Johnson's stress comfort and style. Fast-service counters have given way to "gazebo-like salad bars, tropical and airy new interiors and more service."

But Johnson worries about his plan backfiring. A blurred image can "get (you) knocked off," he says. He also recalled an earlier plan that failed, resulting in a steady drop in sales. During the 1974 oil embargo, Johnson predicted that highway travel would drop sharply. He was right about that, but wrong about his response to it. He stopped his expansion plans completely and soon discovered that his restaurants were out of touch with American society. Eventually, he caught on and opened 103 Ground Round restaurants designed to cash in on "theme" atmosphere that many Americans have come to prefer.

Johnson also operated 34 Red Coach Grills which were in trouble until a group of managers decided to break the rules and confront "the boss." They told him to cut prices and relax the atmosphere. Johnson admired their courage and listened.[6]

1. A group of Howard Johnson's managers broke the etiquette of management hierarchy and told Johnson to change his policies. Do you think the managers did the right thing? What risks did they take?

2. Why do you think "theme" restaurants, where the style of another era is imitated, are so popular these days?

3. What kinds of things should Howard Johnson's managers consider when developing their plan for a new image?[7]

4

CHAPTER FOUR

INTERNAL ORGANIZATION

Imagine that a hundred musicians wander into a concert hall, tune their instruments, and start playing whatever they like. The result won't sound much like music. Now imagine that they're joined by a conductor who seats all the violinists in one section, all the horn players in another, and so on. He passes around the score for Beethoven's Fifth Symphony, and rehearses it with them for a few hours. The result will sound much better, for an obvious reason: organization. Properly organized, a hundred individuals have been transformed into a symphony orchestra and now produce beautiful music instead of noise. The same principle applies to any enterprise in which a group of people work together toward a common goal. As we'll see in this chapter, the process of organizing invariably means answering the same basic questions—how best to divide labor, and how best to distribute authority and responsibility.

WHAT WILL THIS CHAPTER FOCUS ON?

After reading the material in this chapter, you will understand and be able to discuss:

■ the role of an organization chart in a formal organization

■ the different methods of departmentation—grouping employees by function, by territory, by product, and by other characteristics

■ the importance of distributing authority and responsibility in the organization

■ the major issues in the effective distribution of authority—span of management, delegation, accountability, and chain of command

■ the relative merits of centralized and decentralized authority

■ the differences between line organization and line and staff organization

■ the major new approaches to organizational structure

■ the role of the informal organization in organizational structure

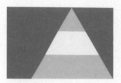

Glenn Wood's place of business is a far cry from any gleaming sky-scraper or sprawling industrial park. It is a small, modest-looking auto shop in the tiny town of Stuart, Virginia. Nevertheless, Glenn Wood happens to be the head of a very successful business concern: the Wood Brothers' Garage is home base for a pair of automobiles—Mercurys—that spend their weekends being driven 200 miles per hour on the professional stock-car racing circuit by people like A. J. Foyt and David Pearson. In fact, for over twenty years the Wood brothers (Glenn and his younger brother, Leonard) have been producing amazingly fast cars—and numerous championships—for a series of famed drivers.[1]

That kind of success doesn't happen by chance. In part, of course, it's the result of a lot of technical skill and mechanical know-how. But it's also the result of a lot of good management. Glenn Wood, in his grease-stained overalls, is just as much a manager as the corporate executive in his three-piece suit. As a manager, Glenn performs all the management functions we described in the last chapter: *planning* the goal of his organization (to make championship racing cars) and the strategies to achieve it (what parts to buy from Lincoln-Mercury or other suppliers; what assembly schedule to follow); *directing* the business's other members; *controlling* their day-to-day work (to see that no major snags develop); and *organizing*.

THE SIGNIFICANCE OF ORGANIZATION

Organizing, the management function to which this chapter will be devoted, involves deciding, first, who will do each of the tasks that must be performed and, second, who will be responsible for seeing that particular tasks get done properly. The result of these decisions is a **structured organization**—*a group of people working together in a carefully planned manner to achieve a certain goal.*

In the structured organization Glenn has set up, Leonard serves as chief mechanic, a title that scarcely does him justice. Under his direction the cars are regularly taken apart and rebuilt from the inside out by

Banjo Mathews, after which Leonard fine-tunes and tinkers with things until he's satisfied. Similarly, Opus Agnew's job is to seal and smooth the cars' sheet-metal exteriors after Leonard has gone over every inch in his never-ending battle against wind resistance. Meanwhile, the engines are built or rebuilt in a nearby town by Tommy Turner—again according to Leonard's precise specifications—and then brought over to the Woods' shop to be installed. The company's books are kept by Bernice Wood, Glenn's wife.

This type of structured organization is typical of almost every business and of nonbusiness work groups and organizations of all kinds. A surgical team of doctors, nurses, and technicians—each with a number of tasks to perform—must work with a degree of coordination that obviously does not spring up by itself. A movie crew on location may look like a bewildering collection of trucks and equipment and people milling around by the dozens. But amid the seeming chaos is a director who organizes the activities of actors, cameramen, lighting and sound technicians, and a host of other people with specific jobs—and a movie gets made. Even a family bakery where Mom makes the pies, Pop drives the delivery truck, and Sonny works behind the counter is a structured organization, in which the essential tasks are divided among the family members. Glenn Wood, in explaining the success of his shop has said, "There ain't no secret. Everybody always does the best they can." They have a little help, he should have added, from someone with a knack for organizing.

THE FORMAL ORGANIZATION AND THE ORGANIZATION CHART

When a person who is setting up a structured organization makes a written description of the way the organization is supposed to work, or draws a diagram of it, he or she is "formalizing" the organization plan. In other words, the person is recording the plan in a form that can be seen by other people and can be passed on from one generation of managers to the next. *Organizations that have a formal record of their structural plan* are often called **formal organizations**.

Usually the formal record is a chart known as the **organization chart**, *a diagram that shows how work is divided and where authority lies.* It is kept in the top

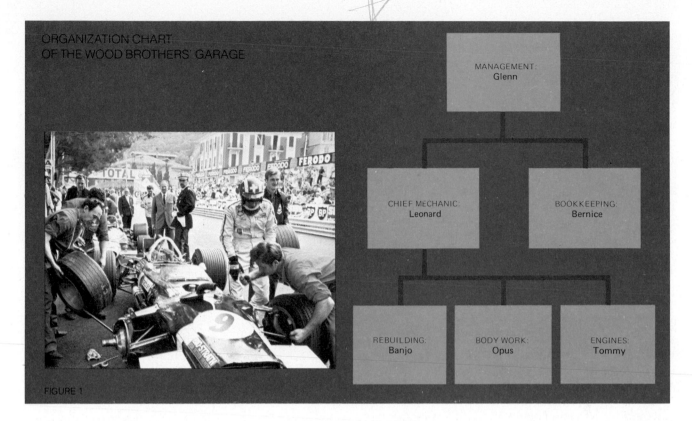

ORGANIZATION CHART
OF THE WOOD BROTHERS' GARAGE

MANAGEMENT:
Glenn

CHIEF MECHANIC:
Leonard

BOOKKEEPING:
Bernice

REBUILDING:
Banjo

BODY WORK:
Opus

ENGINES:
Tommy

FIGURE 1

exccutive's files and may also be posted on a wall for all the workers to look at. Since you're likely to be seeing organization charts—or finding yourself on one—in the future, it will be worth the effort to learn to read them clearly.

For the Wood Brothers' Garage the organization chart would look like the one in Figure 1. In this chart the boxes show the division of labor—all the jobs that have to be done to produce a championship racing car and who does each one. The placement of the boxes and the lines connecting them show authority and responsibility—who takes orders from whom, which workers function as equals, who is responsible for seeing that a certain job is done right. Banjo, Opus, and Tommy, whose boxes are on the same row, are equals in the Wood Brothers' organization. The lines going up from their boxes to Leonard's on the row above indicate that he's the one who gives them instructions and oversees their work—that he has authority over them and responsibility for seeing that their work is good enough to make David Pearson a consistent winner in a Wood Brothers car. Although Bernice's box is on the same row as Leonard's, the fact that she, as

bookkeeper, of course has no authority over Banjo, Opus, and Tommy is indicated by the absence of any lines from their boxes to hers. The placement of Glenn's box at the top of the chart and the lines leading from it show that he has ultimate authority and responsibility, supervising both Bernice and Leonard, and through Leonard supervising Banjo, Opus, and Tommy as well.

For larger businesses many of the boxes in the organization chart will represent not individual workers but groups of workers performing the same function—as in Figure 2 (see following pages).

Organization charts can be very helpful to an enterprise. Perhaps their most important function is *communication.* Studying an organization chart enables people to determine clearly the relationship of their positions to others in the organization. Drawing up a chart is also a form of *planning:* it is a guide to who should do what in order to attain objectives, and who should give orders to whom. Finally, the chart serves a *control function.* By comparing an actual situation with the chart, management can learn of problems such as excessive staff in a particular area.

THE STRUCTURE MUST FIT THE SITUATION

At least at first glance, many organization charts look very similar—like a pyramid. A large number of boxes on the lowest rows lead up to fewer and fewer boxes on the higher rows, and ultimately to one box at the top. But a closer look should reveal differences in the way the charts are set up, reflecting the differences in the way various businesses need to operate. In other words, there is no one best type of organization chart because there is no one type of structure that is best for every formal organization.

In setting up a structure for a business or other enterprise, its manager or managers must make sure that the structure is appropriate for the actual situation they are dealing with. One reason the Wood Brothers' structure works is that Leonard has enough expertise to supervise Banjo, Opus, and Tommy. If Leonard were good at body work and car assembly only but couldn't tell a spark plug from a distributor cap, whereas Glenn understood engines, then Leonard would be the wrong person and Glenn the right one to have authority over Tommy. For that situation, the best structure would look not like the one we saw above, but like the one in Figure 3.

Management must also keep in mind that an organization's structure, even if perfect when first set up, will not necessarily always remain so. There are a

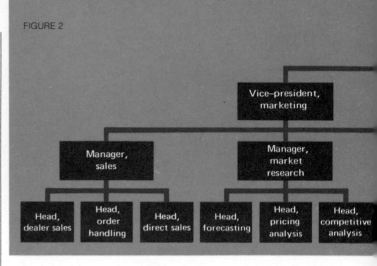

TYPICAL ORGANIZATION CHART OF A
MANUFACTURER OF CONSUMER PRODUCTS

FIGURE 2

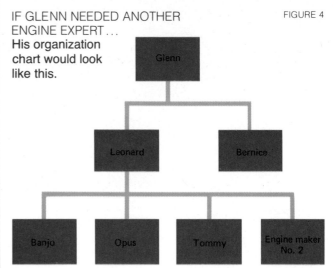

IF GLENN NEEDED ANOTHER ENGINE EXPERT...
His organization chart would look like this.

FIGURE 4

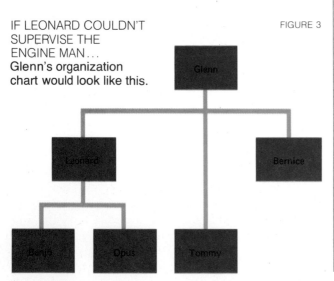

IF LEONARD COULDN'T SUPERVISE THE ENGINE MAN...
Glenn's organization chart would look like this.

FIGURE 3

number of contingencies (possible events) that may cause the firm's situation to change—for example, it may start making new products or start making the old ones in a new way. And if these contingencies arise, the firm's structure should also be changed to reflect this difference. If the Wood brothers decided to produce engines not only for use in their own Mercurys but for sale to other racing-car makers as well, Tommy might be unable to handle the increased work and still put out quality engines. So the new situation would require a change from the original structure to one that would look like the one in Figure 4.

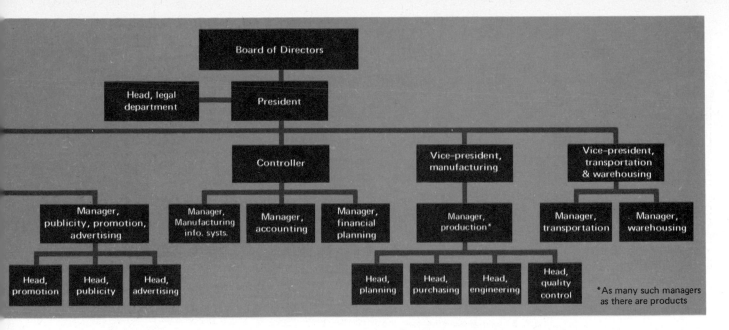

In the sections that follow, we shall be discussing different types of organizational structures, and the questions managers must answer to decide what structure is best for their enterprise and the particular situation and contingencies it faces. *Planning that emphasizes adapting general principles to the actual needs of one's own business,* called **situational** or **contingency management**, is now considered highly important by many management experts and theorists.

DEPARTMENTATION: GROUPING WORK UNITS

If you were given the job of setting up from scratch an organization with more than a few people, one of the first questions you'd have to deal with would be this: Is there any way I can divide the people into separate groups, giving specific tasks to each so that they'll all help the organization achieve its goals? The answer to this question may have a vital bearing on the organization's ultimate success or failure. Group responsibilities can usually be parceled out in any number of ways, and determining the most appropriate division of labor is an essential step toward an efficient operation, whatever the tasks at hand.

You can often see this aspect of the organization's structure on the organization chart. Each *group or section of people working together in a specific area* is called a **department**; *the process of establishing departments* is known as **departmentation**. Depending on the or-

ganization's needs, these departments can be set up in a number of ways—by function, territory, product, process, and others—which we will look at now.

DEPARTMENTATION BY FUNCTION

Grouping workers together according to their activities is called **departmentation by function**, a practice common to modern organizations of all sorts. In a typical manufacturing business, departments may be set up to carry out the functions of production, finance, and marketing. For a retail store the departments might be publicity (advertising, window display, and so forth), merchandising (acquiring and selling of the store's goods), general services (store security, customer service, and the like), and finance. The functional departments set up by a large commercial airline might be engineering, maintenance, ground services (food preparation, terminal management), flight operations, sales, advertising, and finance.

But as we pointed out in the last section, these typical ways of dividing up departments by functions cannot be automatically applied like a formula. Different companies should, and of course often do, develop departmentation patterns to suit the particular functions that must be carried out in their particular business. *Time* magazine, for example, has four principal divisions: editorial, advertising, production, and circulation. Each department works more or less independently, with its own functions, its own managers and personnel, its own budget, work schedules, and so

Table 1 Departmentation by function: the pros and cons

Advantages	Disadvantages
1. It is logical and time-proven.	1. Members of a department may work for the good of the department more than for the good of the firm.
2. It is based on the classical principle of occupational specialization.	2. It creates specialists rather than generalists and thus provides no training for top management.
3. It gives top management tight control over the entire organization.	

Source: George Lawrence Hall, *et al., The Management Guide,* 2nd ed., p. 35. Copyright © 1956 Standard Oil Company of California. Reproduced by courtesy of copyright owner. Please note this booklet is out of print.

Table 2 Departmentation by territory: the pros and cons

Advantages	Disadvantages
1. It emphasizes local problems.	1. It requires more managers with general skills.
2. It provides closer communication with local interests.	2. It is more difficult for top management to control.
3. It may save money.	3. It can make centralized services costly.
4. It gives more responsibility to lower-level managers.	
5. It creates generalist managers.	

Source: E. Raymond Corey and Steven H. Star, *Organizational Strategy: A Marketing Approach,* p. 404. Copyright © 1971 by the President and Fellows of Harvard College.

Table 3 Departmentation by product: the pros and cons

Advantages	Disadvantages
1. It concentrates attention on the product.	1. It requires more managers with general skills.
2. It places responsibility for profits at a lower level.	2. It is more difficult for top management to control.
3. It allows considerable growth within a product line.	3. It can make centralized services costly.
4. It trains managers for top positions.	

DEPARTMENTATION BY FUNCTION: *Time* has four major divisions. FIGURE 5

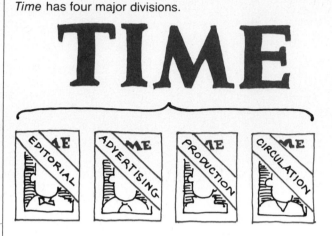

on (see Figure 5). As well, the principal divisions are themselves divided into specialized departments. At the New York headquarters, members of the editorial staff are assigned to individual units specializing in such topics as business and finance, medicine, sports, and a dozen or more other categories. Likewise, a salesperson in the New York advertising department might specialize in selling space to insurance companies, say, or airlines or tobacco companies. There is some contact between departments, of course, but only on certain levels and for specific purposes. The director of advertising, for instance, might consult with the production director on the number of four-color advertising pages, but an individual salesperson would have no direct dealings with anyone on the production staff.

DEPARTMENTATION BY TERRITORY

Grouping an organization's personnel by physical location is known as **departmentation by territory**. This method is commonly used when an organization is spread over a wide geographic area, or when differences between even small areas are important enough to merit special attention.

Time magazine's operations, for example, are departmentalized by territory as well as by function, at least in the editorial and advertising divisions (see Figure 6). *Time* has several divisional advertising manag-

DEPARTMENTATION BY TERRITORY
Time has advertising and editorial divisions in many different cities.

■ Editorial offices
■ Advertising offices

FIGURE 6

ers, as well as submanagers for most major American cities. At the same time, the magazine maintains a totally separate editorial network, with reporters in various bureaus across the country whose job is chiefly to cover local or regional news. Both the advertising and editorial staffs in regional offices are inevitably less specialized in their duties than those in New York, where more people are available. An ad sales-

person in the St. Louis office, for example, will deal with advertisers of all kinds rather than just one industry, and a reporter in the Cleveland bureau may cover a train derailment on Monday, an election Tuesday, and an art exhibit Wednesday.

DEPARTMENTATION BY PRODUCT

An organization may find it desirable to *group activities along product lines,* an approach known as **departmentation by product**. *Time*, for instance, is not the only magazine published by Time Incorporated, its parent company. *Fortune, Sports Illustrated, Money,* and *People* can all be thought of as different product lines, produced by different divisions of the same corporation (see Figure 7). Each of these publications has its own editorial and advertising staffs, as well as its own production and circulation departments—except in a few of the smaller bureaus, where advertising personnel might sell space for two or three of the magazines.

An even more clear-cut example of departmentation by product is evident in General Motors' different automotive divisions, which are so independent of one another that they actually compete for business.

DEPARTMENTATION
BY PRODUCT:
**TIME Incorporated publishes
five different magazines**

FIGURE 7

TIME Inc.

OTHER KINDS OF DEPARTMENTATION

In order to increase its appeal to a specific, easily identified group of customers, an organization may use **departmentation by customer**, *grouping by type of purchaser.* For example, large retail stores are divided into units catering to men's, women's, children's, or family needs—hence the name "department store." Alternatively, an organization that wants to make more efficient use of a special process may *group its activities around a specific procedure or type of equipment,* called **departmentation by process**. For instance, many firms place data processing in a separate department that handles the information-processing needs of the entire organization.

DISTRIBUTING AUTHORITY

Once management has set up departments, or divided the work of the organization, the next question it must face is how to distribute authority and responsibility. Except in the very smallest businesses, this kind of distribution is necessary because there is just too much work for any one person to oversee and control. In a manufacturing firm organized into functional departments the president might **delegate**, or *assign,* authority over production workers and responsibility for making the product well and on schedule to the head of the production department. Similarly, authority over the sales force and responsibility for selling the product would be delegated to the head of the marketing department. And authority over the accountants and bookkeepers and responsibility for keeping accurate financial records and meeting the firm's needs for funds would be delegated to the head of the finance department.

SETTING UP THE CHAIN OF COMMAND

The systematic delegation of authority in an organization produces different levels of employees. The *relationship between different levels of employees* is usually referred to as the **chain of command**. In a typical

SHOULD WE DEPARTMENTALIZE BY TERRITORY—OR NOT?

What are the right reasons for departmentation by territory—and the wrong ones? Management should not automatically assume that because the firm's activities are geographically scattered, departmentation by territory is the best structure for the business. This form of organization was probably more desirable before the communications revolution of the past few years, when contact with far-flung branch offices was slower and less certain. But today an executive in New York can in seconds telephone (dialing the call with no operator assistance) almost any city in Western Europe. Telex messages, transmitted via satellite at the speed of light, can be sent anywhere around the globe. Photocopying machines hooked up to long-distance telephone lines can transmit copies of documents and reports across the country instantaneously. Clearly, geographic distance is no longer likely to be a sufficient reason to departmentalize by territory.

Another reason often given for departmentation by territory is the need for taking prompt action to meet local situations. But management should not assume that local officials will necessarily act more promptly (or more intelligently) than people at the headquarters office.

Nevertheless, there are several valid reasons for departmentation by territory. First, it is a way to make the business more responsive to local differences in custom, style, or product preference. Second, it makes it easier to tie in promotion of the product with local people or events (sports heroes, particularly popular recreational activities, and the like). Third, departmentation by territory allows firms to take advantage of economies like an exceptionally low local price for an essential raw material. And finally, the local department may be an excellent training ground for future top managers of the firm.

As this list of right and wrong reasons indicates, the appropriateness of departmentation by territory (like departmentation on any other basis) must be decided by each firm according to the particular situation it faces.

manufacturing firm the different levels of employees might be workers, department heads, and the firm's president. Three chains of command in the firm run as follows: from the production workers to the production department head to the president; from the sales staff to the marketing department head to the president; and from the accountants and bookkeepers to the finance department head to the president. A person at any point in the chain of command is answerable to those above him on the chain and has responsibility and authority over those below him (that is, he can give them orders, or "commands").

Delegation and accountability

On paper, setting up a chain of command is a fairly simple, straightforward matter. In practice, though, it can become a far more complicated task, involving as it does the interaction of real human beings. First of all, the planners have to deal with the sometimes tricky question of the *degree* to which those at the top will be held accountable for the performance of their subordinates. For example, the rules of the United States Navy spell out with unusual clarity responsibility for work that is delegated. The captain is always directly accountable for the work of his crew and his ship, even if he is asleep, ill, or not even aboard. More than one captain has been removed from command for life because of a collision that was traced to a lowly seaman who fell asleep on watch.

In businesses, the chairman of the board is technically accountable for poor work done by an employee who comes to work with a hangover. In actual practice, of course, it is rare for top management to be blamed directly for the mistakes of workers. It is common practice, however, to hold a manager fully accountable for the work done by people directly under his or her supervision. A manager is usually held answerable for attaining objectives assigned to his or her department. A national sales manager, for example, may be fired if the company does not meet its sales expectations.

Balancing authority and responsibility

A second major consideration in setting up a chain of command is determining how much authority *must* be given to someone who is going to be responsible for something so that he or she will be able to do the job properly. The most common error in delegation is failing to give the recipient (or delegate) enough authority to carry out assigned duties and responsibilities. The following situations illustrate this point:

1. A worker is told to drill a round hole but is not given the authority to get a drill from the company toolbox.

2. A salesperson is responsible for keeping customers happy but has to go through an elaborate company procedure to handle an exchange of merchandise.

3. A manager is made responsible for increasing production but is not given the authority to hire, fire, raise salaries, or rearrange work.

Delegation will not work in these situations unless the employee is either more resourceful than usual or acts without formal authority.

Clearly, authority and responsibility must be balanced for delegation to be effective. Returning to our United States Navy example for a moment, we may note that the Navy does balance the captain's enormous responsibility with very broad authority. A captain at sea has authority over his crew that stops just short of the power of life and death.

Inducing employees to accept authority—and to give it up

Two other related points should be made about delegations of authority. The first is that duties, responsibility, and authority must be assigned to a willing recipient. The word "willing" is important here. If a worker or lower-level manager does not accept the assignment, there can be no delegation. In practice, then, leadership in any organization involves getting people to accept delegation and to understand clearly what will be expected of them.

By the same token, of course, the leaders themselves must also accept the idea of delegation, which inevitably means giving up some portion of their control over things. For some, this turns out to be easier said than done—especially when it runs counter to the habits of a lifetime. Take, for example, the story of someone whom we'll call Mr. Burroughs. (We won't use his correct name—the story is rather an unflattering one.) Having been promoted through the ranks of a major corporation, Mr. Burroughs's twenty-five-year career reached a high point when he became president. The elements Mr. Burroughs felt were responsible for his success—a passion for detail and a strong competitive drive—had been very useful for his work as a manager. But even though there were many demands on his time as president, Mr. Burroughs refused to give up these qualities. He was soon sitting in on weekly production and sales meetings, interrupting freely with questions or criticisms no matter how minor the subject being discussed. Likewise, a detail noticed in a routine report might prompt a phone call to a surprised branch manager far down the line—or the scolding of a vice-president in the middle of a conference. That kind of behavior by top management can undermine the authority of middle-level managers, make lower-level employees wonder whom they are responsible to, and upset the operating routines of a firm.

SPAN OF MANAGEMENT

Another possible danger of Burroughs's managerial approach is that managers, by involving themselves in too many areas, will spread themselves too thin. Management, it must be remembered, is not a "thing" like a hamburger or an ingot, but a process, a continuous series of activities. Like any other process, it takes time and energy, and inevitably there is a limit to how much managing a person can do without losing effectiveness. This limit is particularly evident where the immediate supervision of subordinates is involved. A manager can effectively supervise only a certain number of people.

The *number of people a manager directly supervises* is called a **span of management** or **span of control**. When a large number of people report directly to a manager, he or she has a wide span of management. When only a few people report, the span is narrow. There is no formula for determining the ideal span of management. Estimates of how many persons a manager can effectively supervise vary considerably. Several factors affect the number. These include the manager's personal skill and leadership ability, the skill of the worker, the motivation of the worker, and the nature of the job.

In general, highly skilled workers require less supervision than the less skilled. The manager of an organization made up almost exclusively of professionals can have a wide span of management. The work of a large number of scientists can be coordinated by a single manager. The head of a team of surgeons works with extremely skilled individuals who are also highly motivated, yet in this case the span of control consists of just two or three physicians. The span is limited by the nature of the work: surgery is highly precise and demands close supervision at all times. A similar situation prevails in many businesses. Thus where extremely complex decision making is involved, a board chairman can effectively supervise only a few heads of major divisions.

TALL AND FLAT ORGANIZATIONS

For many years the typical American corporation was *a highly centralized operation, with most of the authority and responsibility concentrated at the top*. Such a company is often referred to as a **tall organization**, because of the many levels in its hierarchy and the narrow span of management at each level. The United States Army, for example, would come under the heading of a tall, or centralized, organization. Virtually all important decisions are made by the generals and colonels at the top. There are also many levels separating a general from a private; and while the general may be responsible for thousands of men, his actual span of management is quite small since he directly supervises only a few colonels.

But there have also been certain *organizations that are quite decentralized, characterized by wider spans of management and a greater delegation of authority to people in middle-management positions*. Because its hierarchy has relatively few levels, such an organization is commonly known as a **flat organization**. The Roman Catholic Church is a good example of a flat, or decentralized, organization. The pope directly supervises many cardinals, who supervise numerous archbishops and bishops, and each bishop in turn may have authority over hundreds of priests. There are thus only three levels between a parish priest and the pope, and while a priest is expected to follow the general policies laid down by his superiors, he has considerable authority in managing the affairs of his own parish.

CENTRALIZATION VERSUS DECENTRALIZATION

In a flat organization with a broad span of management, authority and decision making tend to be decen-

---

HOW IT'S ACTUALLY DONE

DECENTRALIZING FUNCTIONAL AREAS

There is no formula for the one best degree of centralization or decentralization. But in a manufacturing firm whose departments are divided up by function, some departments are likely to lend themselves fairly readily to decentralization: top managers are likely to let go some of their control and delegate extensive authority to the department head.

Which departments are these? One is *production*. First of all, the head of production is likely to need broad authority if he or she is to be responsible for meeting strict production schedules and quality standards. And if the manufacturing processes the company uses are complex, top management is unlikely to have enough expertise to make intelligent production decisions. Indeed, even the department head may lack detailed expertise—so there may even be further decentralization of authority within the department.

The *sales department* is also a likely candidate for decentralization if the selling effort is spread over a wide geographic area. Giving local sales people a great deal of authority may enable them to be responsive to and take advantage of local needs, local differences in terms of sales, and the like. Furthermore, if the firm is selling several different product lines, each line may need a different marketing approach; and lower-level sales officials should be free to choose the method they think is best for each product. Beatrice Foods, for example, is the owner of nonfood subsidiaries such as Samsonite, the luggage manufacturer. Surely luggage does not have to be sold to retailers the same way as yogurt or ice cream! It would, of course, be ridiculous to have centrally made marketing rules that led to suitcases being shipped daily in refrigerated trucks and having freshness dates stamped on them. True, this is a rather extreme example—but it does point up the potential problems in overcentralizing marketing decisions.

Which departments, on the other hand, are *least* likely to be allowed to go their own ways? One is the *finance department*. The reason: profitability and financial stability are generally the firm's crucial ultimate goals—goals in which top management is most likely to retain a detailed interest. It is not uncommon for a finance department to impose centrally decided cost ceilings or profit margins and uniform financial reporting procedures on departments or divisions that otherwise are fairly autonomous. Even Beatrice Foods has a system for strict financial monitoring of its subsidiary companies, with detailed financial reports flowing each month from the more than 400 operating subsidiaries to 54 group managers, 17 division managers, and 5 senior managers at headquarters and ultimately to Rasmussen (the head of Beatrice Foods) himself. And it is Rasmussen himself who will be on the phone to a subsidiary if the financial reports show a serious problem.

Source: "Beatrice Foods Puts It Together," *Dun's Review*, December 1977, pp. 55–57.

tralized, or spread among a fairly large number of people; a manager generally cannot keep a very tight rein over many subordinates and make all necessary decisions for them. In a tall organization with a narrow span of management, on the other hand, authority tends to be centralized in the few people at the top of the hierarchy; certainly a private in the Army is allowed to make very few decisions for himself.

Whether authority and decision-making should be centralized or decentralized is another major question management must face in setting up the structure of an organization. Again, it is a question with no absolute right or wrong answer and one that has been answered differently by different managers. The government of Chicago under the late Mayor Richard Daley was perhaps the perfect example of centralized management: Daley reportedly approved every single individual who got a city job so that all city employees would feel obligated to him personally and be loyal to him. At Playboy Enterprises, which has become a giant and diversified corporation with sales of some $200 million a year, Hugh Hefner still personally approves every cartoon that goes into *Playboy* magazine.

On the other hand, another giant corporation, Beatrice Foods (the largest food-processing company in the United States), has opted for a high degree of decentralization. Although Beatrice's products are marketed on five continents and generate sales of over $5 billion annually, the firm's corporate headquarters occupies just two floors of a Chicago office building, and the staff is not crowded. The reason is that each of Beatrice's more than four hundred subsidiaries around the world—including the makers of Dannon yogurt, Louis Sherry ice cream, and La Choy Chinese foods—is delegated almost total control over the manufacturing and marketing of its particular products. All that Beatrice's president, Wallace N. Rasmussen, asks is that the subsidiaries show healthy profits—which they do.[2] (For more on decentralization at this corporation, see the box on page 97.)

LINE AND STAFF ORGANIZATION

Essentially, the simple chain-of-command system we've been looking at represents what is known as **line organization,** so called because it *establishes a clear line of authority flowing from the top downward through every subordinate position.* Line organization is the simplest and most common structure for authority relationships: everyone knows who is responsible to whom, and the location of ultimate authority is easily identified. (See Figure 8.)

THE PROS AND CONS OF LINE ORGANIZATION

Enterprises that are structured according to line organization enjoy a number of practical advantages. The existence of line authority tends to speed decision making because managers know in which areas they can make decisions. It also simplifies discipline. Channels for communication are direct and easily located. The simplicity of line organization sometimes results in lower expenses.

On the other hand, the nature of line organization also contains at least three important disadvantages. First, it concentrates most decision-making power at the upper levels of management, so subordinates may have trouble learning the skills needed to occupy top positions. Second, the technical complexity of a firm's activities may require specialized knowledge that its top management does not have. Third, growth can extend the chain of command to the point where communication and decision-making take too long.

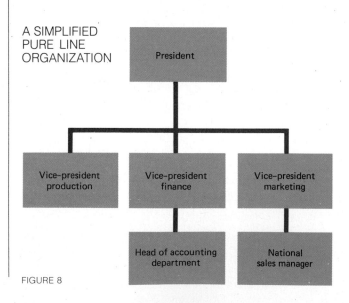

A SIMPLIFIED PURE LINE ORGANIZATION

President

Vice-president production

Vice-president finance

Vice-president marketing

Head of accounting department

National sales manager

FIGURE 8

ADDING A STAFF COMPONENT

Because of these disadvantages, which become magnified as a line organization grows larger, management planners developed a more elaborate system known as the **line and staff organization**. This form of organization *has a clear chain of command from the top downward, but it also includes various auxiliary groupings of people who come under the heading of staff.* Traditionally, the line organization manages the primary activities of the organization. The **staff organization** *supplements the line organization by providing advice and specialized services.*

Persons in the staff organization are not in the line organization's main chain of command. On an organization chart, a staff position is connected to the line organization by a dotted line or is simply left unconnected. In the formal organization chart shown in Figure 9, the legal department has staff authority with respect to the vice-presidents and the head of the accounting department. It can give them advice on the law and request that they comply with this advice. Since the legal department has specialized knowledge about the law, the managers of the line organization will probably follow its suggestions. The decision to accept or reject the legal staff's advice, however, is up

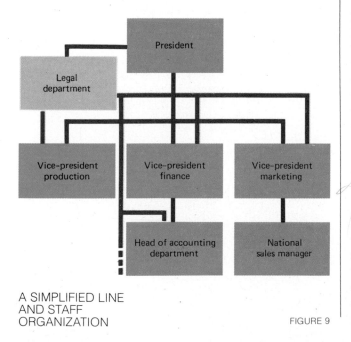

A SIMPLIFIED LINE
AND STAFF
ORGANIZATION   FIGURE 9

TYPES OF SPECIALIZED STAFF FOUND IN BUSINESS ORGANIZATIONS

1. *Advisory staff* guides and advises. Examples of advisory staff are corporate legal departments and corporate public relations departments.

2. *Service staff* does specialized work for others in the organization. A personnel department that actually determines who will be hired is a service staff. So is a purchasing department that buys materials needed by all of the line departments.

3. *Control staff* regulates the activities of others. A control staff has the authority to give orders on matters in its field. The most common example of a control staff is the corporate controller's office. The controller is given the right to disapprove requests for money if they exceed allowed limits. For example, the controller can refuse a marketing manager's request for an additional million dollars for television advertising.

to the line managers. The legal staff is connected to the president of the organization by a solid line because it is directly responsible to the president. If the legal staff feels that its advice should be followed by one of the vice-presidents, it must go to the president, who can order compliance. Note also that the head of accounting may use the services of the legal staff but that the national sales manager must go through the marketing vice-president to get legal advice.

THE PROS AND CONS OF LINE AND STAFF ORGANIZATION

Staff organization can provide specialized knowledge that the top manager of an organization needs in order to make decisions. The staff can skillfully perform services that an organization requires but cannot logically place among its primary activities. Armies, for example, need medical staffs, but doctors have no function in warfare, an army's primary activity. Staff can perform these services more economically than might be possible if each department had to provide the service for itself. A business might need a lawyer, for example, but no one department would have enough legal work to justify its own legal staff. Furthermore, the staff organization provides services without adding an additional level to the chain of command. This can be an important advantage if the chain is becoming too long.

The primary disadvantage of staff organization stems from the advisory nature of staff authority. A line manager can tell people what to do, but a staff member must "sell" people on what they should do. For example, a staff public-relations person, committed to the idea of social responsibility, may think that the company should be more responsible to consumer complaints. Lacking the authority to implement this policy, he or she may simply have to give up the idea unless the line organization can be persuaded to use it. Such frustrations are not uncommon, and line-staff conflicts plague many enterprises. Staff feels or actually is ineffectual because it cannot force the line organization to take its advice, and yet it may still (mistakenly) be held responsible for errors. On the other hand, line managers grumble about having to go through staff before making a decision and often do feel obliged to follow staff's requests.

MOVING BEYOND LINE-BASED ORGANIZATION

The increasing complexity of modern business operations is not by any means only a result of the new external problems—social and economic issues, for example—that have forced their way into America's boardrooms. As companies of all kinds have grown larger and more diversified, internal complications have led many of them to experiment with organizational structures that are not based entirely on the old principles of line organization.

FUNCTIONAL ORGANIZATION

In certain businesses the nature of the work to be done dictates that *specialists should be given direct authority in their particular area of expertise.* This system is known as **functional organization**. In the television and movie industries, for example, there are studio supervisors for such personnel as actors, musicians, sound engineers, and cameramen. When one of these people—an actor, say—is working on a particular show, he is also responsible to the director. The actor thus seems to have two bosses. In practice, however, only one boss is in charge at any given time: the director when a film is being made, and the studio supervisor when the actor is between projects.

PROJECT MANAGEMENT

Widely used by companies involved in research and development of new products, the system known as **project management** *groups staff personnel together as teams to work on specific projects.* It has been likened to a cluster of grapes hung under the regular organization chart, each grape representing a different project team. When one of the grapes "ripens" and falls off—that is, when the project is completed—the team members return to their normal posts in the organization until they're needed for a new project.

The largest-scale application of the project-management system in private industry (it was also used in the government's space program) has been General Motors' use of a series of "project centers" in developing its new smaller-sized cars. Each of GM's project centers has been made up of specialists from different divisions in the company, brought together for the duration of a particular undertaking. One group, for instance, spent two years developing the basic body design for a new category of intermediate-size cars; another was put to work on GM's first front-wheel-drive compacts. Frequently, of course, the results of one project center's research will be used in several GM divisions—the same steering gear, for example, may go into new Chevrolets, Buicks, and Pontiacs. Nevertheless, company engineers report that the new system has actually fostered greater individuality among the different divisions by giving some of them more time to concentrate on their own projects.[3]

MATRIX STRUCTURE

In organizations with the familiar vertical lines of authority, orders have always been sent down the chain

"Beehive" structure

"Doughnut" structure

NEW APPROACHES TO
ORGANIZATIONAL STRUCTURE

FIGURE 10

of command, and decisions have always been passed upward until—as Harry Truman noted—the buck finally stops at the president's desk. Too often, however, different departments in an organization have conflicting needs or priorities that can only be resolved by a higher-level executive, who may well have a dozen more important things to worry about.

The idea behind the matrix structure is to push decision-making downward, in the belief that some conflicts can often be better handled at a lower level. If, for instance, the marketing director for a particular product wants to build up inventory in anticipation of rising demand, while the manufacturing director for the same product wants to *reduce* inventory in order to keep costs down, the problem would normally be passed up the ladder to be decided by an executive with authority over both functions. In a matrix structure, however, the decision would be sent down to a manager who's actually subordinate to both the marketing and manufacturing directors—but who also understands the situation in detail. The manager in effect has to play a mediator's role, trying to balance the marketing and manufacturing goals and come up with a solution that's acceptable to both bosses.

As a further example, assume the same company

manufactures a variety of product lines, including office equipment, temperature control systems, machine parts, and electrical switches. It would clearly do a lot of business with commercial and industrial firms but each customer might be looking for a very different combination of products. Under a conventional system of organization, the company's different product divisions would function independently, linking up only at the top of the management pyramid. So each one would probably end up sending its own sales representative to visit the same prospective customer. Under a matrix structure, on the other hand, a management position could be created for the purpose of designing product "packages" for specific markets—electronics firms, say. This manager's responsibilities would thus cut across the vertical lines of the different divisions, coordinating them at an intermediate level to meet a particular need.

OTHER NEW APPROACHES

In his book *Up the Organization,*[4] former Avis president Robert Townsend advised doing away with the organization chart altogether, arguing that it "strangles profit and stifles people." Not many executives would go quite that far, but a growing number of them have begun to visualize organization in imaginative new ways. One innovative design takes the form of a **beehive**, *with a series of three-dimensional concentric circles one on top of another. One of the circles might represent regional managers, another division vice-presidents, and so on*—the aim being to indicate the human as well as the formal relationships in the organization. Another conception is the **doughnut** shape, *a two-dimensional chart of concentric rings, in which the innermost ring consists of top management, the next of staff officers whose services—legal, finance, personnel, and the like—are accessible to all, the third of divisional managers, and so on.*

In the **ladder** view of organization, *the specialized staff officers who are linked directly to the chief executive on most conventional charts are instead moved to the side and stretched out like a ladder running from top to bottom.* The purpose is to make staff experts accessible to every level of the organization, and also to provide them with an avenue for promotion that won't require them to take on administrative duties unrelated to their field of expertise.

THE INFORMAL ORGANIZATION

All organization charts, whether traditional or innovative, are similar in one respect: they show the formal relationships of people in a company and what they are expected to do *as employees*. What the charts do not do—what they cannot do—is illustrate the **informal organization**—*the network of social interactions that are not specified by the formal organization, but that develop on a personal level among the workers at a company.*

The "grapevine" is one of the best known examples of informal organizational structure. It is an unofficial way of relaying news that bypasses the formal chain of command. It may pass on either personal or business information. But the informal organization does more than spread rumors; it can have a strong say in the distribution of power. While the formal organization spells out who *should* have power, the informal organization sometimes determines who actually *has* it. The informal organization has this ability to shift power because the authority delegated by the formal organization depends at least in part on acceptance by the informal organization. If workers strongly disapprove the organization's choice of a manager, it is unlikely that the manager can be effective.

White House aides have little or no authority delegated to them by the formal organization of the

INFORMAL ORGANIZATION:

The network of social interactions not specified by the formal organization

1 The editor of religious books and the president both attend the Second Avenue Christian Science Church.

2 The editor of cookbooks is a close personal friend and old fraternity brother of the publisher of the periodical division and recently influenced him to promote another friend to manager of educational journals.

3 The editor of fiction and the editor of travel books bypass the assistant publishers, whom they view as male chauvinist pigs, to enlist the aid of the publisher of the book division in getting raises.

4 The producer of feature films is engaged to the editor of *The College Librarian.*

5 The director of the film division and the publisher of the periodical division disagree with the president's fiscal policies and collaborate against him.

FIGURE 11

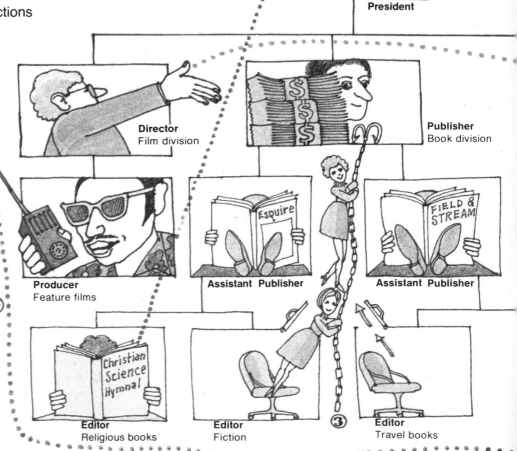

① President

Director
Film division

Publisher
Book division

Producer
Feature films

Assistant Publisher

Assistant Publisher

Editor
Religious books

Editor
Fiction

③ Editor
Travel books

④

United States government. They should therefore have little power in government. During some administrations, however, they have had a strong voice in the government because of their close personal relationship with the president.

Although the negative aspects of the informal organization have been emphasized, it can also be beneficial. The informal organization permits a worker's need for social contact to be met on the job. The resulting friendships can make the work environment a very pleasant place, which can only help the firm. It can also apply strong pressure to work toward group goals. Team spirit often gives players the extra drive needed to win a game—and it can give sales people the incentive to make a crucial sale.

Since the informal organization is a fact of life, the manager must learn to make use of its benefits and minimize its disruptive potential. The ills that are ap-

parently caused by the informal organization can usually be traced to some weakness in the formal organization. By strengthening the weak area, management may be able to satisfy the need better than the informal organization can.

A good way to reduce the negative influence of an informal organization is to include it in the decision-making process. The suggestion box is a simple device that allows low-level employees to have direct communication with those at the highest level. If management actually uses the suggestions, the informal organization will have an input in decision making and should accept decisions more readily. Electing leaders gives the informal organization a very strong say in the formal organization. Unless elected leaders lose the confidence of group members, they are assured of authority by acceptance as well as by formal delegation—and this is a powerful combination.

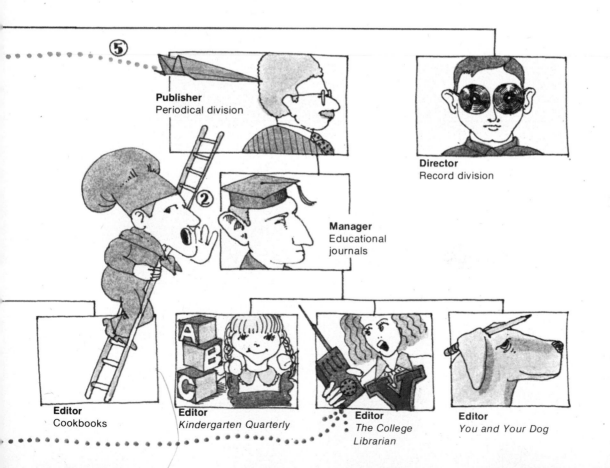

Publisher
Periodical division

Director
Record division

Manager
Educational journals

Editor
Cookbooks

Editor
Kindergarten Quarterly

Editor
The College Librarian

Editor
You and Your Dog

CHAPTER REVIEW

The formal organization is a result of the organizing process of management. It is a structure for carrying out plans and attaining objectives. In designing the formal organization, management uses organization charts to show divisions of labor and lines of authority and responsibility.

Most organizations group workers by their activities. Departmentation may be done according to function, territory, product, customer, or process. Each system has both advantages and disadvantages, and organizations often use more than one method simultaneously.

Effective distribution of authority and responsibility is crucial to an organization's success. Management must consider whether the span of management should be wide or narrow, whether delegation balances authority and responsibility, and who has accountability in the chain of command. Management must also decide whether to set up an organization based on line or line and staff authority. In addition, it must determine whether to centralize or decentralize its internal operations.

New approaches to organizational structure include functional organization, the project management system, and matrix structure.

The informal organization, which arises alongside the formal one, operates in all known organizations. It can bypass the formal organization's system of communication and upset its distribution of authority. The negative aspects of the informal organization can be minimized by good management and by giving workers a say in designing the formal organization.

KEY WORD REVIEW

structured organization
formal organization
organization chart
situational (contingency) management
department
departmentation
departmentation by function
departmentation by territory
departmentation by product
departmentation by customer
departmentation by process
delegate
chain of command
span of management (span of control)
tall organization
flat organization
line organization
line and staff organization
staff organization
functional organization
project management
beehive
doughnut
ladder
informal organization

REVIEW QUESTIONS

1. When might an organization choose departmentation by territory over departmentation by function? Or over departmentation by product?

2. Why would a manager in an organization of professionals have a wide span of management?

3. What is the most common error in delegation? Give an example from your own experience.

4. Why can bypassing the chain of command cause serious problems?

5. Explain the differences between tall and flat organizations.

6. What are the advantages and disadvantages of combining staff with line organization?

7. Why do advocates of decentralization think it is a good system?

8. What are some major new approaches to organizational structure?

9. What functions does the informal organization serve?

CASE 1

IS OUR ORGANIZATION TOO LARGE?

What do *Playboy* magazine and the U.S. Department of Agriculture have in common? Not much, you might be inclined to say, and in many ways you would be right. But they do share a certain problem: too many people doing too little work. Playboy's new president recently tried to remedy the situation by firing some 10 percent of the more than 700 employees at the company's Chicago headquarters. At the USDA the problem is so bad that many of its 80,000 full-time employees have little else to do all day but read *Playboy*.

In business organizations, expansion usually occurs when times are good and profits are rising, as they were for Playboy in the 1960s and early

1970s. But more recently, increased competition from other men's magazines and heavy losses by Playboy's clubs and resorts finally forced a cold hard look at the size of the staff and the importance of each person's work.

At the USDA, expansion occurred when times were bad—during the Depression. It was in the 1930s, for example, that the USDA's Resettlement Administration was created to make loans to farmers to help them keep their land. At the same time, the Rural Electrification Administration was born to help improve farmers' lives. Today, the Depression is long over and 99 percent of rural homes have electricity, but the two agencies still exist.

Other USDA agencies, whose staffs fill five Washington buildings and some 16,000 local offices throughout the country, are doing everything from researching how long the average American takes to cook breakfast to defining the perfect watermelon. The agency today is a far cry from the nine-employee department set up by Congress in 1872 "to procure, propagate, and distribute . . . new . . . seeds and plants." And it expanded this way because no one ever stopped to ask: Has our organization become too large? [5]

1. You are hired by a large organization during a time of expansion. How can you try to protect yourself against being fired a few years later if the company's expansion plans don't work out?

2. As the head of a business that is expanding, what should you tell prospective employees about their future with the company?

3. How could the federal government keep its agencies from overexpanding?

CASE 2

COMMUNICATION IN THE ORGANIZATION

The top executives of McDonald's don't have their own offices. No, they're not working behind the counter at one of the company's restaurants helping to sell the hamburgers. But they're not isolated behind office walls either. Instead, they work at desks in open modules at McDonald's Oak Brook, Illinois, headquarters. The goal of this setup is to improve communication, both among the executives themselves and between the executives and other managerial employees.

Frequent and informal contact with other managers in the firm is being seen as increasingly important by top executives in large decentralized organizations, where, as one chief executive put it, "We're all busy as the dickens and going our separate ways." To keep on top of what's going on in their organization, managers need more communication than they get from the occasional formal executive-committee meeting. Sometimes this communication occurs over lunch or on the golf course. More than half the company presidents in a panel surveyed recently by *Dun's Review* spent several hours a week "socializing" with other managers in their firm. The word socializing is in quotes because the executives considered these con-

tacts business meetings, a way of both keeping abreast of activities in the company and improving working relationships with key personnel. Many on the *Dun's Review* panel of presidents were also trying to make themselves more accessible while in their offices—scheduling a dozen or more appointments a day.

Of course, informal communication can be taken too far, especially at the lower levels of an organization with a formal chain of command. A factory worker having trouble with a tool should not complain to the president of the company or ask him out to lunch to discuss the problem. When a worker has a problem, his or her immediate superior should be the first to know about it, since the supervisor is accountable for the work that has been delegated. If the problem is a serious one, the superior in turn should report it to his or her own immediate superior on the chain of command.

1. If you were the president of a small business, what kind of formal and informal communications channels would you establish?

2. Why is it important for subordinates in an organization to report problems to their immediate superior? What would happen to the organization if people skipped over their supervisor and reported to someone else?

3. You are employed by a large organization. You've worked very hard all year and yet, when your raise comes through, it's smaller than you expected. What do you do?

Adapted from "It's a Matter of Style," December 1977 DUN'S REVIEW

CHAPTER FIVE

PERSONNEL MANAGEMENT

If you were organizing a drama group, your top priorities would be finding a good director and well-trained actors. Likewise, a basketball coach would look for at least five tall, talented athletes. All organizations depend on people, and success depends on how well those people are matched with the jobs to be done. This, in essence, is what personnel management is all about—seeing to it that an organization has the right number of qualified workers to reach its objectives.

Stated this way, the task seems simple. In recent years, though, personnel management has become increasingly complicated as the tasks of recruiting and training have been joined by such pressing concerns as affirmative-action programs, health and safety regulations, and broader benefit packages. In this chapter we'll take a look at some of the issues facing personnel managers today.

WHAT WILL THIS CHAPTER FOCUS ON?

After reading the material in this chapter, you will understand and be able to discuss:

- the role of personnel management in an organization and the ways personnel managers work with other departments in their firm

- the ways personnel managers plan for future needs

- the different methods of recruiting personnel

- the recruiting process, from initial job analysis to final interviewing

- orientation, training, and development programs for employees

- the broad field of wage and salary administration

- the organization's role in providing fringe benefits and safeguarding the health and safety of its staff

- the question of whether employees should be evaluated in terms of merit or seniority

Imagine for a moment an industry in which high-school graduates with five or six years on the job average $20,000 to $25,000 in annual salary, with a chance to make twice that amount if they're good enough. The last thing employers would have to worry about, you might well assume, would be getting people to work for them.

In this case, you'd be wrong. The industry in question is uranium mining, and it's plagued by a chronic shortage of qualified workers that shows no signs of easing up. Not long ago recruiters from several states converged on a site in Colorado after word got out that some 120 lead and zinc miners were being laid off. "When we hear about a source of miners like that," remarked one industry executive, "we pretty near drop everything and go, day or night." Added another: "Getting labor, and particularly getting miners, is the major factor in gearing up production."

The reason for all this is that working and living conditions at the uranium mines, most of them located in remote areas of New Mexico and other southwestern states, are so rugged that even high pay scales are not enough to keep many workers on the job. Further, uranium ore is much harder to extract from the ground than, say, coal, and it normally takes five years or more for a miner to master the various skills involved. By that time as many as 80 percent of the trainees will have dropped out.

Little wonder, then, that a company recruiter would drive all night for a chance to hire experienced miners. As it is, some companies pay search firms $150 a head to find unskilled workers for their training programs—with another $150 for every recruit who lasts six months. The process is frustrating and expensive— each fully trained miner represents a company investment of about $80,000—but there's no alternative. Labor shortages have already cut production by as much as one-third at some sites, and by 1990 the growing use of nuclear power is expected to boost the demand for uranium miners by 500 percent.[1]

To be sure, the personnel problems in most fields of business are not this severe, but the importance of attracting—and keeping—a productive work force is widely recognized as a top-priority item. "I don't know of any major project backed by good ideas, vigor, and enthusiasm that has been stopped by a shortage of cash," remarks Pehr Gyllenhammar, president of the Swedish automaker Volvo. "I do know of industries whose growth has been ... hampered because they can't maintain an efficient and enthusiastic labor force."[2]

The truth of this observation is most evident in businesses whose operations have grown more and more dependent on complex technology—and thus on skilled workers. In insurance companies and brokerage houses, for example, work that was once done by easy-to-replace clerks is now handled by a corps of computer technicians. Such employees are usually in short supply; and if a company doesn't offer them good salaries, up-to-date benefits, and pleasant working conditions, they may well be lured away by the nearest competitor.

Nor, for that matter, is it a simple task to handle personnel problems even in industries where workers are plentiful. A company's employment practices must, for instance, take into account any number of government regulations covering minorities, working hours, job safety, and other labor-related concerns. Additionally, most firms can't afford to hire people without first finding out a good deal about their background, skills, and attitudes toward the job. Beyond that, of course, a company's productivity will depend in large part on how well different workers are matched to particular tasks. In a more general way it will depend on how much—or how little—workers think the company really cares about them.

Given the growing importance and complexity of

personnel problems, it is scarcely surprising that all but the smallest businesses employ specialists to deal with them. The larger the firm, the more likely it is to have a separate department, or even an entire division, devoted to personnel management. Indeed, the personnel function is considered vital enough by some major corporations that they have their up-and-coming executives work in personnel before going on to other areas in the organization. A large part of the corporate personnel staff at IBM, for example, consists of managers who have been placed there for two or three

Launching a space vehicle—or any other complex enterprise—requires a team of highly skilled personnel.

years to get a thorough grounding in that aspect of the company's operations.

But what exactly do personnel departments do? While the specific duties assigned to them may vary quite a bit from one company to another, there are certain functions that every personnel staff must perform. In the pages that follow, we shall consider these basic functions, beginning with the first step: personnel planning.

PERSONNEL PLANNING

Personnel planning, in the words of one knowledgeable executive, "means having enough of the right kinds of people, in the right places, at the right times, doing things vital to the economic well-being of the firm."[3] Its importance can be seen all too clearly in the case history of one company, an optical equipment manufacturer that we'll leave nameless. A few years ago the company found itself in a thoroughly enviable position. Business was good, worker productivity had been increasing every year, and a promising program of new investment and research was about to be launched. The only conceivable worry was that the expansion might create a staff shortage, so—just to be safe—the firm began hiring and training new employees in fairly large numbers. The result: within a couple of years the company's profits were being gobbled up by an overloaded payroll, and management was faced with the painful task of firing dozens of its new (and expensively trained) employees.[4]

What had gone wrong? Basically, the company had failed to take the productivity of its original staff into account when it projected its future manpower needs. The workers' productivity rate had actually been increasing fast enough that, with good administration, the expansion could have been carried out with few additions to the staff.

DEVELOPING THE PERSONNEL FORECAST

Figuring out precisely the sort of thing that happened to the optical equipment company is the purpose of a vital planning procedure known as a personnel forecast. In essence, a **personnel forecast** is *an analysis of employees' past performances, their current capabilities, and the kinds of performances that will be required of them in the future.* Such a plan can be used by a company as a blueprint for its future employee structure, aiding managers in allocating the available work force as effectively as possible. In particular, it can help the company avoid the alternate perils of either being seriously overstaffed—as with the optical manufacturer—or finding itself short-handed when more workers are really needed.

Equipped with data from all departments in the company, the personnel department sets up the forecast, following four basic steps:

1. *Determining corporate objectives.* The personnel manager draws up a clear statement of the direction in which the company is moving—the profits it expects to make, its expansion plans, and its sales goals.

FIGURE 1

```
                        JOB DESCRIPTION

Job Title _____  Job Number _____

Date Effective _____  Job Grade _____

Job Function:  Secretarial duties: dictation, typing, routine correspondence and
               reports, record-keeping, distributing mail, scheduling appointments.
               Handle confidential information.

Duties and Responsibilities:  Transcribe letters, memos, reports from shorthand
               or dictating machine.  May include technical terminology.

               Take shorthand notes in meetings, transcribe into final form.

               Compose and type routine letters and memos.

               Read, distribute and follow up on incoming mail.

               Set up, maintain files of letters, reports, catalogs, manuals.

               Obtain information for supervisor.

               Answer telephone and take messages; monitor supervisor's incoming calls.

               Compose routine departmental reports.

               Set up and maintain records dealing with safety, output, employee time.

               Receive, disburse, keep records of petty cash funds.

               Receive visitors, schedule appointments.

               Order and maintain inventory of office supplies.

               Arrange travel reservations.

               Deal with confidential information.


Instruments, Equipment, or Machines:  Typewriter, dictating machine, xerographic
               copying machines.
```

Job Description: A list of the tasks the job involves and the conditions under which the tasks are performed.

2. *Taking inventory.* Just as the goods on a shelf can be counted, so can a business's human resources. The personnel manager makes a summary of all the available information on employees' current productivity, their potential for future productivity gains, staff turnover, and the age of employees, taking into account the impact of coming retirements.

3. *Forecasting.* Bearing in mind the company's future objectives and its current personnel inventory, the personnel manager makes an estimate of what the current staff will be able to do in the future and how many more people the company must hire to meet its goals.

4. *Using the forecast.* The information contained in this systematic look into the future can be used to set up specific programs for recruiting new staff candidates and selecting the ones that will best fit the company.

RECRUITING NEW WORKERS

Once the personnel department has determined the need for additions or replacements to staff, it can concentrate on the specific details of the jobs to be filled. Here too cooperation with other departments in the company is essential. When a department has a vacancy to fill, the personnel manager works closely with people in the department to make a **job analysis,** *a written statement that answers three basic questions: (1) What are the duties and responsibilities involved in the position? (2) What skills must the person who fills the job have? (3) How much money is such a person worth to the company?* Next, the personnel manager may develop a **job description** (see Figure 1), *a specific statement of the tasks involved in the job and the conditions under which the holder of the job will work.* The manager may also develop a **job specification,** *a statement describing the kind of person who would be best for the job—including the skills, education, and previous experience the job requires.*

FINDING JOB CANDIDATES

The next step is to match up the job specification with an actual person, or a selection of people, from whom to choose. Where does the personnel department get

SOURCES OF JOB CANDIDATES

1. Recruitment from present employees

Advantages: This method is cheap, quick, and easy; it improves morale and reduces turnover. It also lowers the risk of hiring someone dangerous, unstable or incompetent, and above all it gives employees a goal to work toward.
Disadvantages: The range of candidates is limited; there's jealousy among the co-workers left behind; and suspicions — if not always accusations — of favoritism do arise.

2. Referrals made by other employees

Advantages: A friend or relative of an employee is likely to know something about the company. Also, bonuses paid to employees for successful referrals are good morale-builders.
Disadvantages: When relatives or good friends work near each other, their productivity may drop.

3. Newspaper advertising

Advantages: Good community relations result, and advertising generates an enormous number of responses.
Disadvantages: Time is wasted weeding out the unsuitable people from those who are promising.

4. Public employment agencies

Advantages: These government-run agencies do not charge for referrals, and they sometimes see highly skilled people who really need work.
Disadvantages: The agencies' preliminary screening efforts aren't always thorough.

5. Private employment agencies

Advantages: Often a supply of well-screened, ambitious, and highly skilled candidates to choose from.
Disadvantages: Private agencies charge high fees which must be paid either by the company or by the prospective employee.

6. Union hiring halls

Advantages: Skilled union labor is available from this source.
Disadvantages: Workers are often sent by the union on the basis of their seniority — not their skills or their suitability for the job.

7. Schools

Advantages: A source of trained, eager-to-learn beginners.
Disadvantages: Recruitment costs are sometimes prohibitive; recent graduates lack on-the-job experience.

8. Pirating, or going after specific employees from another company

Advantages: A way of obtaining high-level executives at a low recruitment cost.
Disadvantages: Pirated employees may not be loyal to their new company.

these candidates? There are several avenues open to personnel **recruiters**, that is, *the members of the personnel staff who are responsible for obtaining new workers*. Each avenue has advantages and disadvantages. (See box, page 111.)

SELECTING AND HIRING NEW WORKERS

As every reader will have gathered by now, the perfect person for a given job is not apt to enter the recruiter's office the moment the job specification is written. Instead, after going through at least one—but usually more—of the recruitment channels outlined above, the personnel department will spend weeks and sometimes even months sifting through the many applications. Eventually, however, the choice is narrowed down, and the selection process begins. Exactly which method is used depends on the company, but there are

certain basic processes which most companies go through (see Figure 2).

STAGES IN SELECTION

First, a small number of qualified candidates are selected. A person may be chosen on the basis of a standard application that all candidates are required to fill out, or on the basis of his or her **résumé**—*a summary of education, experience, interests, and other personal data compiled by the applicant*. Sometimes both sources of information are used. Next, each candidate is interviewed, and depending on the type of job at stake, the candidates may be asked to take a test or series of tests

FIGURE 2

STAGES IN THE EMPLOYEE SELECTION PROCESS

5. INTERVIEW The interview may be conducted by the personnel manager or the prospective employee's future immediate superior. A skillful interview can reveal information about the applicant's forcefulness, speaking ability, and personal goals.

4. REFERENCE CHECK Either before or after the interview phase, the personnel manager checks the applicant's references. Particular attention is paid to former employers. The personnel manager will often call or write them for their evaluation of the prospect.

3. TESTING The next step in the process is frequently testing. Tests help the company to gain an objective picture of the applicant's skills and qualifications.

2. THE APPLICATION FORM The personnel manager asks the more desirable candidates to fill out a detailed *application form*, containing questions that will help the company make a selection.

1. SCREENING The personnel manager may conduct *screening interviews* to pick out the strongest candidates or screen candidates by reading their resumes. (A *resume* is a statement written by the applicant, describing his or her job goals, education, and previous work experience.)

to gauge their abilities, aptitude, intelligence, interests, and sometimes even their personalities.

At this point, there is usually another, more indepth interview with the few most likely candidates, and following this the candidates are interviewed by the person who will be the new worker's immediate supervisor. The supervisor and sometimes *his* or *her* supervisors pick the most suitable person, and the search is over—provided that the candidate is all that he or she appears to be. This is made certain via reference checks and a physical examination.

ENSURING EQUAL OPPORTUNITY

Until 1964, several characteristics, completely unrelated to skills or abilities, often determined whether an applicant got any further than submitting a résumé. These characteristics were the person's race, religion, national origin, and sex. Since the Civil Rights Act of 1964, however, it has been against the law to discriminate against job applicants on any grounds other than those of *actual occupational qualifications*. This means that, for the most part, companies are not allowed to consider an applicant's race, religion, national origin, or sex when they are trying to fill a job opening. To help enforce the job provisions of the 1964 act and subsequent legislation, the federal government has established the Equal Employment Opportunity Commission (EEOC), an agency whose particular job is to handle discrimination complaints. Working together with business to avoid potential problems, the EEOC helps companies by establishing guidelines on what they may and may not demand of an applicant during the course of the selection process. As a result, many organizations today have set up procedures to ensure that they are truly "equal opportunity employers." For example, they refrain from asking discriminatory questions, and they do not require an applicant to attach a photograph to an application.

These first steps have indeed helped give members of minority groups a better chance to get jobs. But correcting the wrongs of generations of discrimination is no simple matter, as both the government and private enterprise have been discovering. In their efforts to give minorities equal opportunities for employment, some companies have found that they have ended up discriminating against those *not* in the minority. This has resulted in a series of widely publicized lawsuits.

Kaiser Aluminum in Louisiana, for example, worked out an **affirmative action plan**—*a plan for active minority recruitment and training*—with the United States government. Among other things, it called for in-house training programs with equal numbers of blacks and whites. Because of the quota thus set, there was no room for Brian Weber, a white applicant. He filed suit, and a federal district court supported his claims. The irony in the situation is typical: a company acting in cooperation with the federal government to stop job discrimination actually found itself being condemned for doing so by a federal court. Many offenses are met by high fines—which makes these "double-bind" situations even more troubling to industry.

The EEOC currently has a tremendously large backlog of unresolved complaints against companies—in 1978, 130,000 cases were yet to be decided. In an effort to stop the backlog from growing any bigger, the EEOC has set up a new policy of trying to handle complaints on a face-to-face level wherever possible, rather than through complex legal procedures. But the EEOC has also expanded its responsibilities. No longer will only giant corporations come under examination—now complaints against smaller companies will also be investigated. Furthermore, in addition to its responsibilities of guarding against sex and minority bias in employment, the EEOC may possibly take over the area of discrimination because of age.[5]

Testing job candidates: a discriminatory practice?

There has also been debate over the government regulations concerning the types of tests that prospective employers may give their job applicants. In the rush to make sure that such tests are not only job-related, but also fair to every minority, several government agencies imposed conflicting regulations on employers, putting them in a position that EEOC commissioner Eleanor Holmes Norton has described as "untenable." "If they violated either set of guidelines," she said, "they could be liable for back pay to employees hurt by their actions."[6] Companies, then, are in a bind—by obeying one set of rules they may be violating another.

But new EEOC guidelines may help ease this situation. In the past, the EEOC paid a lot of attention to the *type* of tests that companies gave to possible employees—some of these tests, the EEOC argued, were constructed in such a way as to screen out minorities and women. The EEOC has proposed, however, a "bottom-line" approach. If a company has hired what the EEOC believes is a sufficient number of minorities and women, then it won't bother examining the tests that the company gives potential employees.

THE ORIENTATION PROGRAM

Becoming a new employee means learning how to perform a new job, but it also means learning about one's new company. As part of the hiring procedure, many companies include a formal orientation pro-

THE WHOLE TRUTH AND NOTHING BUT?

Recent estimates have put the cost of dishonest workers to their employers at a staggering $4.7 billion. It's no wonder, then, that businesses are wary of letting any wolves into the corporate sheepfold. The pickings there are just too good.

In an attempt to reduce the awesome loss firms are suffering, personnel management has come up with a number of tests and devices that can help to pinpoint dishonest employees. The effectiveness, morality, and even legality of such techniques, however, is debatable.

The most widely used method of filtering out dishonest employees from the ranks of the law-abiding is the polygraph, commonly known as the lie detector. An electronic device that records the body's reactions to stress, the polygraph provides a relatively inexpensive alternative to a thorough check of the applicant's references. It sounds like an ideal personnel management tool, but there are serious drawbacks to its use. For one, a polygraph is hardly a morale-booster. Few people like to have their word questioned, and the indignity of being hooked up to a machine that's supposed to confirm one's honesty often antagonizes a prospective or current employee.

Another, even greater problem is the polygraph's reputation for inaccuracy. As a result, the Department of Defense has completely discontinued the use of these machines for checking personnel, and organized labor has successfully lobbied in twelve states to ban their use in employment situations.

Other devices, such as those based on fluctuations in a person's voice modulation, are still used only experimentally in personnel management situations. A new written test, however, developed by polygraph experts, is becoming increasingly popular. Not only is it considerably less expensive than polygraph tests, it also spares its subjects from the kind of confrontations that can be so disastrous to employee relations.

The written test is based on a simple premise. Experience with polygraphs has shown that basically honest people tend to give similar answers to certain questions, while fundamentally crooked people give the opposite answers. The test's inventors developed a sliding scale of "honesty potential" according to which an employer can determine whether an applicant is scrupulously honest, basically honest, honest-on-the-whole, no more honest than need be, or just a downright thief. The drawback to the test? First of all, it may be that honesty is not an unchanging part of the personality—rather, a person may be honest in some situations and not in others. And second, if you're clever enough to make an efficient on-the-job crook, you may very well see through the loaded questions and answer them accordingly. One applicant for a manager-trainee position passed the test with flying colors. His employers found out some time later that the man had a lengthy police record showing activities not normally associated with the upstanding citizen: burglary, larceny, forgery, unlawful flight to escape prosecution, and jail-breaking. Thus while employee theft continues, so does the search for the perfect honesty test.

This discussion is based in part on "The Polygraph and Personnel," *Personnel Administration,* May–June 1970, pp. 32–37.

gram. The **orientation program** is *a planned program to introduce new employees to a company.* It covers the firm's philosophy, its internal procedures, its compensation and fringe benefits programs, and the opportunities it offers for promotion. Some orientation programs are brief and to the point; others are elaborate. Quaker Oats of Chicago, for instance, has new employees go through an extensive but entertaining orientation program spread out over the course of several days. The fledgling employees receive brochures on the company's history and its benefit plans. They're also whisked off for tours of the company's test kitchens and headquarters offices, invited to coffee with the corporate vice-president of personnel, and then treated to a multimedia slide show that uses seven projectors, a triple screen, and professional narration and sound.

TRAINING AND DEVELOPMENT

Experience has shown that the growth and health of any business is closely allied with the growth of individual employees. The better trained and educated workers are, the more productive they are likely to be and the more profit they are likely to make for the company. With this in mind, many companies have set up training and development programs: worker training programs that teach specialized skills, management development programs, and continuing education programs.

WORKER TRAINING

Since it bears a direct relationship to company profits, worker training is something many companies rely on heavily. United Airlines, for example, conducts courses in more than one hundred categories of functional training, ranging from how to be a reservations agent to such specialized areas as handling handicapped passengers or conveying radioactive materials. Companies often train workers on the job or in classrooms. In some cases they also use *simulations (mock-ups) of actual working conditions*—a type of training known as **vestibule training**. The United States government uses vestibule training when it teaches astronauts in simulated space vehicles.

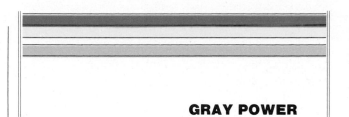

GRAY POWER

Until fairly recently, talk of job discrimination has tended to ignore those workers who are well into middle age. In 1967, however, the federal government finally noted and officially barred age discrimination in employment. With that action, courts were given broad powers to penalize companies that violate the job rights of prospective and current employees between the ages of forty and sixty-five.

While the courts have disagreed on how far these penalties can go, the latest decisions have stated that the law authorizes damages for everything up to and including the psychological trauma that might result from job discrimination.

As a result, more and more aged workers who feel wronged are doing something about it. Between 1973 and 1976, for example, the number of official complaints about age discrimination rose more than 2,208, to 5,121.

Recently, older Americans won another battle: President Carter signed a bill that raises the legal retirement age from 65 to 70. This means that a company must wait for an employee to reach the age of 70 before it can legally make that employee retire. Those people who favor this new law point out that fewer Social Security payments will have to be made because many people will be working later into life. Opponents believe that having more older workers on the job will cause younger people to have a harder time finding jobs and a more difficult time moving up the company ladder because there simply won't be as many job vacancies. Furthermore, they argue, minorities and women will have less opportunity to secure employment. No one knows for sure what the full impact of the new retirement age will be, but the government will make two major studies to learn how the bill affects people, businesses, and the economy.

The figures in this discussion are drawn from "Penalties for Age Bias," *Business Week,* September 19, 1977, p. 145.

MANAGEMENT TRAINING

How do you teach management skills—the complex set of abilities that includes logical thinking, energetic habits, an interest in the future, a sixth sense about people, and just plain common sense? Though most big companies believe management training is important, not all agree on how it is to be accomplished. Perhaps the most traditional approach is in-service training. An example is the famous Sears management training program, which *all* Sears executives go through from start to finish. (Sears develops all its executive talent from within, and over one-fifth of Sears executives are still in their twenties.) Every trainee starts right on the selling floor, learning basic retail management under intensive supervision, and also attends meetings, watches films, and does outside reading. Next, he or she rotates through a series of areas that support the company's basic sales effort, spending several weeks or even a few months in each. Only after gaining this broad "hands-on" experience does the trainee move up to division management, where he or she supervises sales *plus* inventory *plus* buying, display, and promotion, all at the same time. It's a tough program; it includes some night and weekend work and may require the trainee to move from one town or state to another. But for someone who loves retailing, it can be worth the effort.

Assessment centers

Hands-on experience isn't the only way companies train managers. One interesting alternative technique involves the use of an **assessment center**. In the center, *managers practice whatever skills their jobs require by going through a series of simulations*. The trainees may pretend to give a speech, write a report, or make a presentation—all of which is recorded on videotape. After as much as three days of these simulations, a panel of experts reviews the videotape and rates the trainees' performances. The trainees then receive help in whatever tasks they perform least well. Interestingly enough, the assessment-center technique comes to business from the world of espionage: it was used by the Office of Strategic Services (later renamed the Central Intelligence Agency) to select undercover agents during World War II. Today the assessment center is used not only as a training device,

but also to evaluate candidates for open positions and promotions.

CONTINUING EDUCATION

Whether it means teaching functionally illiterate factory workers to read or inducing people in professional-level positions to keep up with the most recent developments in their fields, continuing education is an important part of personnel management. Programs that encourage employees to continue learning include paid tuition for job-related courses or for entire advanced degrees; sabbaticals (leaves of absence) for independent study; or even exchange programs with government agencies. The list of such possibilities increases all the time.

WAGE AND SALARY ADMINISTRATION

Proper **compensation**—*the payment of employees for their work*—is crucial in keeping employees motivated. Thus wage and salary administration is one of the personnel department's prime concerns. Because of the amount of paperwork and record-keeping involved, it's also probably the most time-consuming.

COMPENSATION

Basically, the major question in developing a compensation system is whether to pay the worker strictly according to the time he or she puts in (or how productive he or she is during that time), or whether to use broader guidelines for payment. Different types of compensation plans have evolved to cope with different job situations.

Wages

First, let's look at the type of compensation question that arises in many blue-collar work settings. What's the best way to pay someone such as a sewing-machine operator who is supposed to complete as many garment sections as possible each day? In this situation the

THE FEMININE JOB FRONTIER

Woman's work is never done. As a matter of fact, when it comes to equal employment, woman's work is just beginning, and an awareness of this massive social upheaval is of paramount importance in modern personnel management.

The Equal Pay Act of 1963 gave official recognition to the disparity between men's salaries and those of their women colleagues. It was not until the 1970s, however, and the coming of age of the women's movement that massive job discrimination suits were filed against such corporations as American Telephone and Telegraph. Advocates of the women's movement had the first of their days in court, and the result of their profitable encounters with the corporate giants of the country gave new impetus to the fight against sex discrimination on the job.

Today, while the salaries of women executives are still an average of 20 percent below those of men, times are changing indeed. Women new to the business arena—usually straight from college or graduate school—are generally being offered starting salaries identical with or even superior to those offered men in similar positions. Opportunities for promotion, too, are equally available for women new to the job market.

Unfortunately, the picture is not as rosy for those women whose careers antedate the raised consciousness of businesses. For these women, being in the job market has often meant years of hard work and frustratingly poor pay and opportunities. To get where they are today, many had to be at least twice as good as their male competitors, while being paid perhaps one-third less for their troubles.

How long will this inequitable situation continue to exist? Not very, if the recent activity by the EEOC and in the courts is any indication. To head trouble off at the pass is now the duty of personnel managers across the country. At a well-known clothing manufacturer, women managers have received increases as high as 20 percent in addition to their usual 9 percent merit increases, and sometimes a promotion every year—all in order to put their earnings on a par with those of male employees.

Compensation and opportunities for promotion aside, women are also fighting—and winning—battles over the uniquely female issue of pregnancy. In a recent United States Supreme Court judgment, for example, the Nashville Gas Company was pronounced wrong in taking away seniority rights after pregnancy leave and failing to provide promises of re-employment for new mothers ready to return to work. Also in question was the refusal to issue sick leave for those women on maternity leave. This, six justices declared, cannot be allowed if it is merely a mask for overt discrimination. No employer can "impose on women a substantial burden that men need not suffer," the court said.*

About sixty years ago a spirit of sisterhood developed in the women in the garment industry, and they united to vastly improve their working conditions. Today some of that spirit has risen to the surface once again. Some businesses are resisting demands by professional women for better treatment; but others see the women's movement as a force that will grow even stronger in the future, and are attempting to change as a consequence.

*"The Pregnancy Leave of Absence Case—Nashville Gas Company V. Nora D. Satty. No. 75–536," *The Supreme Court Reporter,* January 1, 1978, pp. 347–359.

---

employer pays **wages**, *a payment based on a calculation of the number of hours the employee has worked or the number of units he or she has produced.* Wages provide a direct incentive: the more hours worked (or the more pieces produced), the higher the pay.

The problem with the system of paying wages is that wage earners are vulnerable to business ups and downs, and many face layoffs during slow seasons or slow periods. To deal with this, some companies pay a **guaranteed annual wage (GAW)**. The GAW agreement is a guarantee of work (and thus of wages); it usually *states that an employee must be given a set number of hours or days of work per year.* Some GAW plans, such as those common in the steel, automotive,

Sometimes, wages are based on the number of hours worked; sometimes on the number of units completed. This window washer's wages are based on the number of windows he cleans.

and glass industries, have been established through union negotiation. But a few, such as that of Procter and Gamble, have been initiated by the company itself.

Salary payment

What about paying white-collar workers, whose work output is not always directly related to the number of hours they put in or the number of pieces produced? Employers of white-collar workers pay salaries. **Salaries**, like wages, *base compensation on time, but the unit of time is a week, a month, or a year instead of merely an hour.* Salaried workers normally receive no pay for the extra hours they are sometimes asked to put in; working overtime is simply part of their obligation. In return, they do get a certain amount of leeway in their working time. They are seldom penalized for time lost because of illness or personal problems, and they are always paid full salary for holidays.

Bonus plans

Nucor Corporation is an oddity in the United States steel industry. While the earnings of the giants all around it were falling, Nucor was enjoying record sales and earnings. Much of its success was due to the productivity of Nucor employees; and a good deal of that productivity could be credited to the company's incentive program. It enabled its hourly employees to earn big **bonuses**, *payments in addition to their regular wages.* (The average Nucor factory hand earned, with bonus, about $18,000 in 1976—this compared with the $7,600 earned on average by other manufacturing workers in the area.)[7]

Nucor is not alone in recognizing the importance of cash payments to employees for extraordinary performance on the job. Other firms use the annual Christmas bonus, amounting to a certain percentage of each employee's salary, as an incentive to reduce

turnover during the year. Still others offer a bonus to all employees when profits are high. This is based on the assumption that higher profits result from team effort.

PROFIT SHARING Another way by which employees can be rewarded for staying with the company and encouraged to work harder is **profit sharing**—*a system whereby employees receive a portion of the company's profits.* At Quaker Oats, for example, all salaried employees receive a share of the year's profits; and the higher the salary, the higher the share. Depending on the company, profits may be distributed quarterly, semiannually, or annually. Or payment may be put off until the employee retires, is disabled, or leaves the company—provided that the employee worked the number of years called for in the plan. With deferred payments, the company pools and invests funds for the employees.

PRODUCTION SHARING **Production sharing** is a plan similar to profit sharing, but with one significant difference. *The rewards to employees are tied not to overall profits, but to cost savings resulting from increased output.* This plan is used as an incentive for operating-level workers rather than for managers, on the theory that workers can have a greater impact on production than their superiors can. A famous early production-sharing plan was the innovative Nunn Bush Shoe Company scheme, which was established in 1935. It rewarded workers on the basis of whatever percentage of the wholesale price of shoes was attributed to labor costs. The lower the percentage, the higher the reward. The plan thus rewarded workers for increased production and also gave them some protection against inflation.

COMMISSIONS **Commissions**, *payments based on sales made,* are probably the most widespread form of added-incentive compensation. They are used primarily for sales personnel.

EMPLOYEE BENEFITS AND SERVICES

Companies regularly provide their employees with certain **fringe benefits**, which are *financial benefits other than wages, salaries, and supplementary rewards.* They also provide services such as health and safety programs, which are very important even though their value can't be estimated in dollars and cents.

FRINGE BENEFITS

Fringe benefits make up a sizable percentage of the worker's true earnings and the employer's costs (see Figure 3). There are three major types of fringe benefits: insurance plans, unemployment benefits, and pension plans.

Insurance plans

The company negotiates a group insurance plan for its employees and pays all or most of the premium costs. This insurance protects workers and their families against the severe financial costs of hospitalization, accidents, and death. Some progressive plans even cover dental care, psychiatric care, and medical services for minor illness.

Though health insurance programs are probably the primary features of benefits packages, more and more companies are beginning to draw the line against subsidizing *all* of the escalating costs of their employees' medical care. (Health costs in the late 1970s were rising more than five times as fast as the rest of the cost of living.) Some corporations have eliminated free medical benefits entirely, substituting plans partially paid for by employees. Others have raised the deductible figures, meaning that employees must pay more medical expenses out of their own pockets before insurance payments can begin. And a few major corporations such as R. J. Reynolds Industries have gone so far as to set up their own health maintenance organizations (HMOs), which are, in effect, company-operated medical centers designed to meet almost every medical need. HMOs are prepaid medical plans in which a monthly payment made by employees (sometimes assisted by the employer) entitles them to hospital care, doctor care, X-rays, and the like, without additional payment.

Unemployment benefits

The Social Security Act of 1935 provided for federal-state cooperation to insure workers against unemployment. The cost of this program is carried by employers, who must pay a set percentage of their total payroll into the federal and state funds. When a worker becomes unemployed for reasons not related to performance, the worker is entitled to collect benefits. The amount of the benefit is usually tied to the employee's total earnings during the previous year. Both the amount and the length of time it is available vary from state to state. Workers in certain industries, notably automobile, steel, rubber, and glass, receive additional benefits (called supplemental unemployment benefits, or SUB for short) from either their company or their union.

Pension plans

Workers covered by the Social Security Act (nearly everyone who works regularly) also receive a basic income during retirement. This is paid for by the Social Security tax, collected by the employer from employees' wages and matched by an equal contribution from the employer.

In 1975, slightly over 46 percent of all private

Total Payroll $11,254: This is what the employee receives in his weekly paycheck.

employees were also covered by some form of company-sponsored pension plan that supplements the often inadequate payments from Social Security.[8] These plans work in a variety of ways, but all of them require the worker to spend a certain number of years with the company. The employer pays all or most of the cost of the company retirement plan, usually investing the money in a secure fund. These plans have been subject to a number of problems and abuses over the years. The Social Security and Retirement Act of 1974 is an attempt to make sure that employees actually receive the benefits to which they are entitled. (The last provision of the 1974 act will not go into effect until January 1, 1981.) The act regulates the eligibility requirements for pension plans. It also protects workers against mismanagement of pension funds and against loss of benefits caused by company failure.

Other fringe benefits

This category includes paid holidays, sick pay, premium pay for working overtime or unusual hours, and paid vacations. Companies have various different policies as to how many days of the year they consider legitimate holidays. A company with a liberal policy on holidays usually emphasizes this fact in its employment advertising. Sick days are usually limited in order to curb excessive absenteeism, but sick-day allowances also vary from company to company. To provide incentives for employee loyalty, most companies grant employees longer paid vacations if they have remained with the organization for a prescribed number of years.

How important are fringe benefits?

An accurate measure of the importance of fringe benefits is their cost to employers. According to Chamber of Commerce figures, the average company spent $3,984 on fringe benefits for each employee in 1976. The cost for fringe benefits amounted to an average of 35.4 percent of the payroll. In other words, direct monetary compensation accounted only for roughly two-thirds of the average employee's total compensation. Because persons with lower earnings receive almost the same fringe benefits as those with higher earnings, the percentage is even higher for the low earner.[9]

HEALTH AND SAFETY PROGRAMS

In 1976 over 167,900 people suffered an occupation-related illness. In addition nearly 5,000,000 workers were injured on the job. The cost of these illnesses and injuries? Just under 34,000,000 workdays were lost. An even more startling figure is the 4,500 work-related fatalities for 1976.[10] Not only are those figures appalling from a humanitarian point of view, they are also bad business.

Health and safety programs are a means of reducing potential suffering and keeping health-related losses to a minimum. As such, they are, or should be, a major concern of every personnel manager. By educating employees in safety procedures, establishing and enforcing safety regulations, and redesigning work environments to minimize the potentials for death or injury, businesses have often succeeded in sharply cutting their health-related losses. And they also have happier, healthier, and usually more productive employees.

The Occupational Safety and Health Administration

Not all companies are far-sighted enough to see the benefits of health and safety programs. For many, the initial expenditures or inconveniences called for by

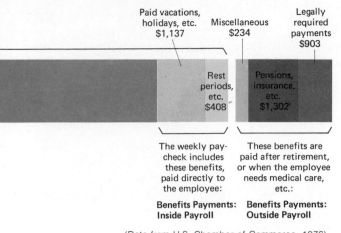

Paid vacations, holidays, etc. $1,137

Miscellaneous $234

Legally required payments $903

Rest periods, etc. $408

Pensions, insurance, etc. $1,302

The weekly paycheck includes these benefits, paid directly to the employee:

Benefits Payments: Inside Payroll

These benefits are paid after retirement, or when the employee needs medical care, etc.:

Benefits Payments: Outside Payroll

(Data from U.S. Chamber of Commerce, 1976)

THE BENEFITS PACKAGE: WHAT GOES INTO IT?

Benefits paid by the average company to or on behalf of an employee who makes $11,254 a year

FIGURE 3

safety demands have not seemed worth the effort. To counteract this attitude, the government has stepped in to oversee the working health of the country's labor force. The instrument for this supervisory function is the Department of Labor's Occupational Safety and Health Administration (OSHA), established in 1970 by an act of Congress.

Criticisms have been hurled at this agency from both sides of the issue. Business has accused OSHA of trying to cripple industry through unrealistic, nit-picking, and usually complex regulations. Organized labor, which lobbied for the establishment of OSHA, complains that it is understaffed, underfinanced, and more concerned with preserving business profits than with ensuring the health and safety of workers.

Both sides are partly right, and recent efforts to improve the agency could please both labor and industry. Recent (and successful) suits against the government itself for failing to protect workers have resulted in crackdowns on flagrant violators of government regulations. OSHA has also begun to experiment with economic incentives in cooperation with other government bodies. The Internal Revenue Service might, for instance, offer tax rebates to employers or manufacturers who make industrial equipment safer than it is now.

Recently the duties of OSHA were expanded. A ruling in an appeals court requires OSHA to draw up standards of safety and health for each state. This means that OSHA must examine the industries on a state-by-state basis in order to figure out what requirements must be established and how many inspectors will be needed to check that the standards are being met. This ruling was a victory for labor organizations, which had feared that if the states themselves determined health and safety requirements—without a federal overlord—then those requirements wouldn't be as effective.

MOVING AND EVALUATING PEOPLE IN THE ORGANIZATION

When should a worker be given a raise? When should he or she be promoted to a higher and more responsible position? What conditions would make it advisable to transfer a certain employee laterally—that is, to another job on the same level—or to demote the employee to a lower level? And under what circumstances should a worker be removed by **termination**—*let go* because of cutbacks or *fired* for failures in performance?

Such questions are among the most difficult ones a manager ever has to face, dealing as they do with the lives and careers of individual people as well as with a company's interests. Sometimes the decisions involve a number of general business considerations—the distribution of a company's manpower, for instance, or how well it's been doing recently. In most cases, though, the central factor is unquestionably the employee's own performance, which raises one of the trickiest questions in personnel management: How do you judge the quality of someone's work?

SYSTEMS OF EVALUATION

In some companies, supervisors and personnel managers tend to rely largely on their "gut reactions," their own personal feelings about a worker's performance.

Such an approach, however, is open to criticism on a number of counts. A supervisor's judgment, for example, may be flawed by a lack of first-hand familiarity with the job—or it may simply be biased by individual likes and dislikes that have nothing to do with the quality of work. Needless to say, a sensible management would not want to rely totally on such impressions. While gut reactions may often be worth paying attention to, companies have become increasingly interested in developing more objective standards for evaluating their workers.

Some types of work, of course, lend themselves to objective measurement more readily than others. A manufacturing worker's output can be judged simply in terms of quantity produced. A sales representative can be graded by the dollar value of the orders he or she brings in. In both cases, too, the performance can be compared against the same worker's past efforts, as well as against others doing the same job. Even so, such standards alone may not always give a complete picture of an employee's value. The factory worker's output might better be judged by taking quality into account along with quantity—not to mention the personal effect he or she might have on other members of the production group. Likewise, a sales representative's orders for a given time period may not reflect the good will being developed among customers that will bear fruit a year or two hence.

Even in these cases, though, where factors are involved that can't be measured strictly in terms of dollars or units produced, managers don't necessarily have to fall back on their own personal reactions in making their evaluations. Over the years, studies of human psychology and personality have produced a number of methods that—while far from perfect—provide at least a tentative basis for rating the hard-to-measure aspects of a worker's performance. The First Pennsylvania Bank, for instance, uses a *behavior standard scale* that divides up each job into fairly abstract skills, including the ability to communicate, the ability to deal with people, and the ability to administer details. That such skills can't be expressed in precise numerical terms obviously doesn't mean they're unimportant, and the use of this behavior scale—along with comparable systems—can be helpful not only in evaluating an employee's work, but also in determining how his or her particular talents can be used most effectively.

SENIORITY OR MERIT?

Beyond these questions of performance standards, supervisors and personnel officers must deal with an even thornier issue. When making decisions about promotions, salary increases, job security, and related matters, how much weight should be given to **merit**, *the quality of an employee's work,* and how much to **seniority** or *length of service with the company?*

Advantages of the seniority system

The seniority system, traditionally supported by unions (and, understandably enough, by longtime employees), rewards the loyal, dependable worker with greater job security and a predictable path to ad-

Hazards on the job are a source of concern to both workers and management. Business and OSHA, a federal agency, often work together to eliminate or minimize these dangers.

mote with each passing day and that raises and promotions will come along whether they do a good job or a mediocre one. The seniority system thus gives them no particular incentive to increase their efforts or improve their skills. Even worse, it has the same effect on younger workers who can readily see that time, not performance, is the factor that determines advancement. As a result, the best and most aggressive of the newcomers will likely move on to an organization that rewards their efforts more quickly.

The merit system, its supporters continue, discourages precisely that kind of complacency by rewarding those who contribute most to the organization. Employees whose work is not first-rate will be passed over for promotion, while the most talented and motivated people will rise naturally to the top—benefiting them and the company at the same time. This, at least, is how the merit system operates in theory. In practice, however, things don't always work out so smoothly. In a well-known book called *The Peter Principle*, Lawrence J. Peter, a professor at UCLA, presented a humorous and revealing look at the way many organizations operate in the real world.[11] His main point, which he illustrated with numerous examples, was summed up this way: "In a hierarchy every employee tends to rise to his level of incompetence." What he meant was that employees who do well at a certain job will be promoted to a higher level. If they succeed there, another promotion will follow. The process continues until they land in a job they simply can't handle—and that's where they stay!

This viewpoint, of course, is not entirely a serious one. The merit system may occasionally live up—or down—to the Peter Principle, but executives generally agree that it works well more often than not. This is especially true when employees are confident that they're being evaluated according to fair and realistic standards. In some cases, the most workable system proves to be one that rewards both loyal service *and* merit: unusually talented workers are moved ahead fast, but steady, dependable ones are not overlooked either. A two-pronged policy, in other words, often works better than one that takes into consideration only one set of factors. And this holds for other aspects of personnel management as well: the resource being managed is a multidimensional one—a staff of human beings—and in order to deal with this resource, management policies need to be multidimensional as well.

vancement. In a sense, seniority is the most truly objective system in that it bases eligibility for raises and promotions strictly on a worker's length of time on the job, thus ruling out the possibility of favoritism or other inequities. Further, advocates of seniority argue that it provides employers with a stable force of experienced, reliable workers who are not likely to leave the company and go elsewhere.

Advantages of the merit system

Proponents of the merit system, on the other hand, are quick to point out a number of disadvantages built into the seniority method. Long-term employees know that their chances of being laid off or fired grow more re-

CHAPTER REVIEW

Most businesses employ specialists to deal with personnel management. Large firms often have whole personnel departments. It is their function to plan; recruit and hire; train; administer wages, salaries, benefits, and health and safety programs; and evaluate staff.

Personnel planning involves forecasting the need for employees and doing job analysis. The analysis produces job descriptions and job specifications.

Many firms prefer to fill positions by promotion from within. External sources for recruiting new workers include advertising, employment agencies, union halls, and schools.

The selection process involves choosing the most qualified candidates, who are then interviewed, tested, interviewed in depth, and checked through their references. Newly hired workers frequently attend formal orientation programs that introduce them to the new company.

Training is essential to the well-being of a firm. Workers are trained on the job, in classrooms, or in vestibule training programs.

Compensation is a strong motivating factor in business. Direct monetary compensation may be in the form of wages, salaries, bonuses, or profit sharing. Indirect forms of compensation, or fringe benefits, include insurance and pension plans, along with payment for holidays, sick days, overtime, and vacations. In addition, companies provide employees with services such as health and safety programs.

Evaluating the quality of an employee's work is a complex matter. While some supervisors rely on "gut reactions," there is an increasing interest in developing more objective standards. Personnel officers must also decide whether to emphasize merit or seniority.

REVIEW QUESTIONS

1. What are the functions of a personnel department?

2. What does developing a personnel forecast involve?

3. What are the sources a personnel manager can use to locate potential employees?

4. What is an equal opportunity employer?

5. Name some of the components of a good formal orientation program.

6. What is the employer's role in providing unemployment benefits and Social Security payments?

7. What can an employer do to improve workers' health and safety?

8. Name the advantages and disadvantages of the seniority system.

9. What type of employee does the merit system favor?

KEY WORD REVIEW

personnel forecast
job analysis
job description
job specification
recruiters
résumé
affirmative action plan
orientation program
vestibule training
assessment center
wages
guaranteed annual wage (GAW)
salaries
bonuses
profit sharing
production sharing
commissions
fringe benefits
termination
merit
seniority

CASE 1

PAYING MORE FOR PROFITS: AN INNOVATIVE PERSONNEL POLICY

If employees come to work on time consistently, why not pay them a little extra for it? Or if they help reduce the company's accident rate, or contribute through hard work to a higher year-end profit, why not pay them for that, too? This is exactly what James W. Parsons, owner of Parsons Pine Products in Ashland, Oregon, decided to do a few years ago. Spurred by a serious lateness problem in his factory, he developed a four-point "positive reinforcement" plan to offer four types of cash bonuses to his 100 or so employees, most of whom cut lumber into specialty items like louver slats for wooden shutters or blinds, and wooden bases for rat traps. Parsons's system has reduced lateness to almost zero, has chopped thousands of dollars out of the company's accident insurance payments, and has helped Parsons become the leader in its field with sales of $2.5 million. No less importantly, the system has also increased the size of paychecks: for a Parsons employee earning $10,000 a year, the bonuses can mean an extra $3500 in the pay envelope.

For being neither late nor absent for 30 days, a Parsons worker gets the opposite of sick pay, namely, "well pay," which amounts to an extra eight hours' wages each month. Employees who might come to work ill to get "well pay"—but who thus run a higher risk of having an accident—are encouraged to think twice by "retro pay." When Parsons's accident bill dropped to $2,500 in 1977 from $28,500 the year before, the company got a retroactive refund of $89,000 from the state insurance fund, and workers got retro-paychecks of nearly $900 apiece. For going without an accident for a month, Parsons workers get "safety pay" of an extra two hours' wages—not a king's ransom, but enough to keep employees from running to the doctor every time they have a small complaint. Richest of all the bonuses offered by Parsons is "profit-sharing pay," which comes from everything the company makes in excess of a 4%

after-tax profit. Paid according to a formula that takes into account an employee's salary and a performance rating from a supervisor, profit-sharing pay can amount to 10% (and it has gone as high as 16%) of a worker's annual wage.[12]

1. What are some of the concrete problems that the Parsons plan is designed to solve?

2. Under what circumstances might such a compensation plan be ineffective?

CASE 2

HEALTH DISCRIMINATION?

To put a lid on the increasingly large amounts of money that they must pay to workers who become ill or injured at work, many U.S. companies are beginning to carefully screen out high-risk job applicants. For instance, Johns-Manville Corporation refuses to hire people who smoke to work in the company's asbestos-mining operations because asbestos workers who smoke stand a better than average chance of getting lung cancer. At Morton-Norwich Products Inc., by the same token, people who are likely to be lifting 100-lb. bags of salt are asked to have a back X-ray before they are hired. Companies can hardly be blamed for taking precautions such as these, but according to a survey taken by a leading business publication few executives are aware that by instituting job health requirements, they may be steering their businesses afoul of the law.

Agencies of the federal government publish hundreds of regulations each year with which companies must diligently comply—or face the consequences. The regulations at issue where health requirements are concerned (contained in Section 503 of the Rehabilitation Act of 1973) state that no company holding a government contract can refuse to hire a handicapped person who is qualified for a job. The penalty can be loss of the contract. And while most people tend to equate handicaps with serious (and obvious) disabilities like blindness, deafness, or paralysis, the federal government takes an extremely broad view, describing a handicap as any impairment that "substantially limits one or more . . . major life activities." That could mean a back injury, a trace of mental illness, partial loss of vision, epilepsy, and a host of other "invisible handicaps."

According to one Department of Labor official, the government is "dead serious" about enforcing the regulations. Indeed, the Labor Department's Office of Federal Contract Compliance has already charged United Airlines with discrimination against the handicapped for refusing to hire a computer terminal repairman who was partially deaf and who had suffered a broken ankle (that healed).[13]

1. As an employer, what arguments would you offer the government to support job health requirements?

2. Given the Department of Labor's tough stand on discrimination against the handicapped, on what basis would you as an employer choose between two equally qualified job applicants, one handicapped, the other not?

CHAPTER SIX

PRODUCTION MANAGEMENT

One of the most striking aspects of American society is the relative ease with which we can obtain goods and services. For all our economic problems, we have amazingly few shortages of vital products (or of less vital ones, for that matter), and compared with that in most other countries the cost of our consumer goods is still quite reasonable. The chief reason: mass production—the manufacture of large numbers of products at an affordable price.

In theory, production is simple enough; in practice it can be an enormously complicated process, with a continual flow of practical problems that have to be solved and detailed arrangements that must be coordinated with one another. In this chapter, we'll see how production managers go about tackling this challenging task.

WHAT WILL THIS CHAPTER FOCUS ON?

After reading the material in this chapter, you will understand and be able to discuss:

- the focus of production management—bringing a product or service into existence

- the roles of mechanization, standardization, the assembly line, and automation in modern American industry

- some of the ways mass-production techniques are applied to service operations

- the roles of planning, purchasing, inventory control, and production control in production management

- the factors managers take into consideration in deciding on plant location

- analytic and synthetic production processes

- a basic question in the timing of production: whether to set up a continuous process or an intermittent process

- the importance of planning, routing, and scheduling in producing a finished product

- some of the new directions in production management, including the PERT, CPM, and MRP approaches

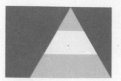 More than $2 trillion ($2,000,-000,000,000) worth of goods and services—cars, candy bars, computers, insurance policies, airplane rides, and a multitude of other items—are produced in the United States each year. Creating these items as cheaply, efficiently, and soundly as possible is the role of production management. Like all other types of management, production management involves the basic functions of planning, organizing, directing, and controlling. But what is distinctive about production management is its focus on the actual bringing into existence of a product or a service. In other words, it concentrates on actually creating or preparing the item, which is what we term production.

Production is the *process of converting resources into a form in which people need or want them.* It's easy to visualize this process in the production of goods, or tangible items such as shirts and hot dogs. (The word "tangible" simply means "touchable.") To produce a shirt, the resources that are converted are cloth, thread, and buttons; the form people need or want is the shirt. It's a little harder to visualize the process in the production of services, or intangible items such as a television program. But when we realize that a TV program is essentially the end product of combining resources such as writers' and actors' talents, plus other resources such as scenery and costumes, we can see that producing it is in some ways not that different from producing a shirt.

MASS PRODUCTION AND THE TECHNOLOGY BEHIND IT

Many American industries today operate on the principle of **mass production,** that is, *the manufacture of goods in great quantities.* It is mass production that has given the United States its high standard of living, for when items are produced in huge quantities, each item can be sold more cheaply, making the product affordable to a larger number of people.

Mass production became possible, beginning in the nineteenth century and especially in the twentieth, as a result of four principal technological advances: mechanization, standardization, the assembly line, and automation. We'll look at each of these in turn.

MECHANIZATION

Mechanization is *the use of machines to do work previously performed by people.* Before the Industrial Revolution human and animal muscle did most of the work. For example, thousands of laborers using picks and shovels worked for eight years (1817 to 1825) to dig the Erie Canal, a job that could now be done in a fraction of the time with giant earth-moving machines. In the eighteenth century all furniture was cut, carved, and assembled by hand. Today virtually all of it is machine-made. Likewise, the pages of this book would have been sewn together by hand two hundred years ago. Today books are bound by machine. In nearly every industry, mechanization has made it possible for more things to be produced faster—and more cheaply—with the labor of fewer people working fewer hours.

When Eli Whitney invented the cotton gin in 1793, mechanization entered agriculture on a large scale. Since then it has come to play a central role in farming. America's wheat crop—the world's largest—is now planted using tractors, sprayed by airplanes, and harvested by giant combines. And in recent years new machines have been developed to harvest delicate fruits and vegetables, including grapes and tomatoes, that were previously picked completely by hand. (To make machine handling of tomatoes easier, researchers at the University of California have even developed a square variety, less likely to be crushed than the traditional round tomato!)

STANDARDIZATION

Standardization is *the production of uniform, or identical, goods.* Standardized goods are of the same weight, color, quality, and the like; they are interchangeable. Producing items using *parts* that are standardized is a tremendously cost-effective technique, one Eli Whitney is also thought to have introduced in America when he manufactured muskets using interchangeable parts in 1801. And standardization is important from the point of view of marketing and the consumer as well. For example, a record company running off 5 million copies of a new Bee Gees album obviously wants them all to sound exactly alike. That's what the customers are paying for—the same record they heard on the radio, not one that sounds *sort of* like it. Just as obviously, records, tape cassettes, and 8-track cartridges all need to be produced according to standardized specifications. A long-playing record, for instance, that isn't (a) round, (b) 12 inches in diameter with a 1/4-inch hole in the center, and (c) designed to be played clockwise at 33-1/3 rpm, won't be a very useful product no matter how good the music on it is.

People are sometimes surprised when they realize that the differences between certain products are no deeper than the packaging. But it is standardization that makes these products affordable. For example, many, if not most, of the functional parts of new cars are identical to those of earlier models, and the "new and different" look simply reflects superficial changes in body design and decoration. If auto parts were not standardized, the price of a new auto would be equivalent to that of an experimental racing car.

THE ASSEMBLY LINE

It was in the automobile industry that our third important mass-production technique, the assembly line, was introduced. The **assembly line** is *a manufacturing technique in which the item being put together moves along a conveyor belt, past a number of different work stations where each worker performs a certain task*—adding a part or carrying out an assembly operation. Henry Ford introduced the moving assembly line in August 1913, and within six months the labor required to assemble a Model T chassis was reduced from twelve hours and thirty minutes to one hour and thirty-three minutes. (Before the assembly line the price of a car was $2,100—and by 1918 Ford's Model T sold for $290!) Not surprisingly, the moving assembly line was quickly imitated by other automobile manufacturers. Today the assembly line is used in the majority of manufacturing processes that involve assembling a complex product. It is also widely used in packaging. (In the record industry, for example, one worker puts the records into paper sleeves, another inserts them in jacket or album covers, others operate machines which cover the records in vacuum-sealed plastic wrapping, and still others put the records in boxes for shipment to stores.)

The assembly line is not a cure-all. Though it cuts down on inefficiency, it can create other problems—particularly the problem of workers' becoming bored. Unfortunately, the system has too many advantages to

LACK OF STANDARDIZATION: AN EXPENSIVE MISTAKE

A recent example of how costly to a manufacturer the *failure* to standardize can be is the Concorde supersonic airliner. Some of the planes were made in Britain—where all parts were sized and machinery calibrated in inches and feet. But others were made in France, a country that has long been using the metric system, so that parts were sized and machinery calibrated in millimeters and meters. How big a difference did this make to the cost of the plane? It increased it by fully *one-third*—an extra bite that turned out to be disastrous, especially since the markets for the planes were not as large as planners had hoped. The British and French governments may eventually make up their development and production costs—but no one knows when.

Source: Frank, Melville, "The Concorde's Disastrous Economics," *Fortune,* January 30, 1978, pp. 67, 70.

be replaced entirely. But to combat the problem of boredom among workers, some companies have devised schemes which retain assembly-line procedures but make other improvements in the work setting. (We discuss these schemes in our Enrichment Chapter on Human Relations.)

AUTOMATION

Mechanization, as we have seen, is aimed at eliminating as much hand labor as possible from the produc-

(a) Automation is almost complete in much of today's fabric industry. Here, after chemical fibers are twisted into yarn by an automatic spinning frame, dyes are forced through the yarn packages under high pressure. (b) Once dyed, the yarns are automatically transferred to a warp beam to be readied for weaving on the loom. (c) Yarn may be diverted to a circular double-knitting machine which loops two groups of yarns. Knitted fabric manufactured this way is used to make garments such as leisure suits. (d) Other yarns may go to a hosiery-knitting machine which knits a fabric tube. That tube later goes on to the boarding machine for heat and tension treatment, to shape the hose to foot and leg sizes. A jacquard loom, programmed by punched card, may weave intricate patterns into the hose. (e) Still other yarns go to the weaving machine, a shuttleless device that interlaces yarn at high speed. Warp knitting machines then take over, to produce the modern equivalent of hand-knotted nets and laces.

b

a

tion process. Its extension, automation, is *the process of performing a mechanical operation without any human work at all.* Automation has become increasingly widespread with modern computer technology. Today we have "smart machines"—machines that can control other machines, starting and stopping them and even checking up on the quality of their output. There are now "robots" on some assembly lines, whose mechanical arms and hands can put a part in place faster than a human worker could. Some of the newer assembly-line robots even have "eyes" (actually television cameras) that can perceive whether a part is coming down the conveyor belt out of position and can check it for defects before inserting it.

HOW ARE MASS-PRODUCTION TECHNIQUES APPLIED TO SERVICE OPERATIONS?

It may be a little hard to picture the use of some of these mass-production techniques when the operation is not an actual factory, which produces goods you can see and pick up. Just think, however, of the numerous operations in the traditional service industries that are performed by computers. Banks use computers to keep records of customers' accounts. Likewise, airlines use sophisticated electronic devices to land jets at busy airports.

Moreover, it's important to keep in mind that even manufacturing enterprises don't just sell a product; they also sell service along with it. Mass-production techniques can be important in making these services effective. One clear example of the importance of service is the story of an ice-cream manufacturer that forgot about this part of its operation. The company's sales were booming because the rock-bottom prices were so attractive to supermarkets. Business was so good that the company had to open a new plant to meet its rapidly growing demands. But the company ended in failure. Why?

While the company was operating out of a single plant, it had developed a complicated automated communications system that was able to cope with the nit-picking requirements of the many supermarkets it supplied. But at the new plant, management concentrated on keeping prices low and failed to set up the same communications system—thus neglecting the services of quick delivery and customer satisfaction. Customer service is not an afterthought or something that the company offers when it feels like it. On the

d

c

e

contrary, service has to be built into the company's overall production planning.

PRODUCTION PLANNING

We wouldn't have our immense production capacity without our often incredible machines. But we also wouldn't have our tremendous capacity for output without another crucial part of production management, namely, *planning*. Production managers have to plan very carefully in order to get the best use out of their machines, and also out of their raw materials and their workers.

If production managers are working with an already established factory or other production site, they have to constantly make plans with the plant's advantages and disadvantages in mind. If they're setting up a new one, they're lucky; they can design it according to their own needs. Before we get into the details of planning, let's look at a new plant, the microwave oven plant that Litton Industries opened in Sioux Falls, South Dakota, in 1977. Litton set up the plant to trim

production costs far down—essential for Litton's survival in the face of booming Japanese competition. And Litton managers figured that when the plant reached full capacity in 1978, it would double the company's production of microwave ovens.[1]

The plant has, without a doubt, all the new and amazing machines a gadget lover could ask for. "Low-cost sodium-vapor lights flood its open interior. Overhead conveyors zip preassembled parts to 350 workers on two assembly lines. A Litton-designed automatic tester checks each oven for radiation emissions within 20 seconds, rather than the five minutes formerly needed to do the job manually." But it isn't just the machines that make the plant so efficient. More important is the fact that the whole plant was designed *for* one product—to accommodate the production processes that would work best for that product. "This plant is a culmination of everything we've learned in six years of producing counter-top ovens," says Paul R. Westgard, vice-president for counter-top products. "We watched how material and production flowed and where we needed quality control. When we had that laid out, we just built walls around it."

And what Litton had laid out was a wide variety of

labor-saving and cost-reducing gadgets. By storing inventory right in the plant at the point where it will be needed, planners eliminated transportation delays and the chance of running out of necessary parts. The microwave ovens make their final stop down the automatic conveyor system at an automatic stamper that wraps and binds them—a job that had required five workers in the other Litton plants. And to save an estimated $35,000 a year in fuel bills, Litton heats its plant by burning waste cardboard and paper in an incinerator and channeling this heat into the plant's boiler. With the combination of new machines and the planning to use them properly, this Litton plant produces the same number of microwave ovens as other Litton plants, but uses 25 percent less manpower to do it.

What are some of the planning techniques that production managers at Litton—and every other plant—must use? First, every production manager has to think about three basic questions: where to locate, what to produce, and how to produce it.

WHERE TO LOCATE AND WHAT TO PRODUCE

The location of a plant is usually critical to the success of a manufacturer. A poor location can make the product more expensive to manufacture than a competitor's—which means it's hard to sell it profitably. And once the plant is built, it's not easy to move. Some plants, such as the automobile works of Detroit and the steel mills of Pittsburgh, are larger than many cities,

HOW IT'S ACTUALLY DONE

CHOOSING THE BEST LOCATION

When managers choose a plant location, they have to choose right—otherwise the business may run into major problems. Here are some of the factors they must take into consideration:

Labor factors

If unskilled workers can do most of the jobs in the plant, the manufacturer has some flexibility in choosing where to locate. Almost any area with a large enough population will have an adequate labor supply. (Litton was able to locate the new microwave oven plant in Sioux Falls, for example; the unskilled workers who were available in the area could be trained for the new plant's assembly lines in a matter of weeks.)

Locations to look for if most of the jobs can be done by unskilled people:

places where labor costs are relatively low;

places where unions are not strong.

If skilled workers are needed, management must

narrow down its choices. (For example, companies needing skilled mathematicians often locate near university communities such as Boston and San Francisco.)

Physical factors

Transportation available in the area must be right for the industry. (For example, the machine industry centers around Chicago because that city is a major lake port and rail center—and both water and rail transport are needed to move heavy equipment.)

It must be dependable.

It must be cheap.

Raw materials are often a key factor, especially when the raw materials are perishable or expensive to transport over long distances. (Coors Beer steadfastly refuses to open a brewery anywhere but Golden, Colorado, because the company feels the water is so special there that to use water from any other area would lower the quality of the beer.)

Nearby markets are also important if the product is perishable or expensive to transport. (Milk and but-

and they represent an investment of billions of dollars. In deciding on a plant location, top management must weigh a number of factors, including the availability of energy, labor, and materials, and of transportation to bring these materials in and ship finished products out.

Clearly, a manufacturer must decide exactly what it is going to produce long before production begins. The general choice of a product is most often made by the marketing department (whose role we shall discuss later), taking into account both customers' preferences and government regulations. But as a next step, the production department must design the product and plan how to make it profitable. In addition, many companies have ongoing research and development groups, which seek new products that the company can manufacture economically; and also try to improve those already being produced.

HOW TO PRODUCE THE PRODUCT

After decisions are made about just what to produce, the long-range production planner must deal with the question of how to produce it as efficiently, quickly, and cheaply as possible. There are two basic types of production processes used by manufacturers—the analytic process and the synthetic process. Each is appropriate for certain types of products, and each presents its own particular problems and challenges.

The analytic process

The **analytic process** involves *breaking down a raw material into one or more different products, which may or may not resemble the original material in form and function.* One familiar example is oil refining. This process takes crude oil pumped from the well and ex-

If only deciding on a plant location were this easy! In reality, the choice requires a thorough knowledge of an area's energy, labor, material and transportation resources.

ter, for example, spoil quickly and must be shipped in expensive refrigerated vehicles, so dairies must be close to the stores that sell their products.)

Energy sources can be a crucial factor. (Energy availability is especially important now that energy is more expensive.)

Community factors

The community must be willing to have the industry locate the plant in the area. (Some communities actively oppose the introduction of new plants, particularly when a plant might pollute the environment or produce a potentially dangerous chemical or explosive.)

The company will be likely to look for communities that:

offer incentives such as tax breaks;

have good general services such as schools and housing;

have fire and police departments that are equipped to handle any emergencies that may come up at the new plant.

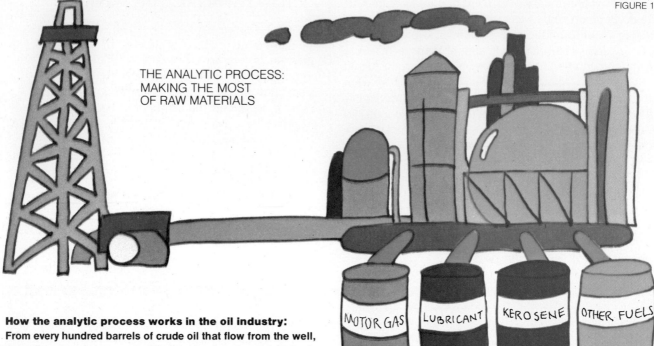

FIGURE 1

THE ANALYTIC PROCESS:
MAKING THE MOST
OF RAW MATERIALS

MOTOR GAS   LUBRICANT   KEROSENE   OTHER FUELS

How the analytic process works in the oil industry:
From every hundred barrels of crude oil that flow from the well, the refinery produces nearly fifty barrels of motor gasoline, almost twenty-eight barrels of fuels, just under seven barrels of special jet fuel and a little over a barrel of lubricant. The remaining fourteen barrels of crude oil don't go to waste either—they are refined into kerosene, aviation gasoline, and other products.

tracts gasoline, kerosene, lubricating oil, and home fuel oil from it (see Figure 1). Meat packing is another analytic process: the packer divides a steer into hide, bone, steaks, and so on. The challenge in every analytic process is to make full use of the raw material and to use each element as profitably as possible. Many companies now make valuable goods out of what used to be only waste by-products. For example, many of the largest meat-packing firms are also the largest leather producers. Until recently the company that markets Swift meat products operated the biggest leather tannery in the United States.

The synthetic process

The synthetic process involves *combining two or more materials to form a single product.* Steel manufac-

turing is a synthetic process: in it, iron (extracted from ore by analysis) is combined with small quantities of minerals at high temperatures to make steel. Likewise, glass is made when sand (silica) and an alkali (for example, potash) are heated together. And most plastics are formed by combining varieties of complex hydrocarbons derived from petroleum. The particular challenge in synthetic processing is to use the least amount of raw materials to produce the finished product. Clothing makers, for example, must carefully plan the way patterns are laid out for cutting so that as little cloth as possible becomes useless scrap. With energy both expensive and often in short supply, a growing number of firms—like Litton at its Sioux Falls plant—are burning leftover scraps of raw materials and other manufacturing waste products, and using the energy thus generated to heat plants or run machinery.

FABRICATION AND ASSEMBLY: TWO BASIC TYPES OF SYNTHETIC PROCESS

Fabrication is *a form of synthesis that involves machining, weaving, finishing, or some other treatment.* Much manufacturing is a fabrication process. Cloth, nuts and bolts, steel girders, and paper are all fabricated.

Assembly is *a synthetic process that combines fabricated components to form a product.* Most complicated goods, such as automobiles, stereo equipment, refrigerators, bicycles, and power tools, are assembled. Sometimes *the components of these assembled products have been assembled themselves;* they are then termed **subassemblies**. An automobile engine and a television picture tube are examples of subassemblies.

A large company may use all the above processes—and the analytic process as well—in some phase of its production operations. The use of widely different processes within the same plant, however, is rare. A large steel works may extract iron from ore by analysis, turn it to steel by synthesis, and fabricate the steel into girders on the same premises. Such a plant, however, would not assemble steel parts into automobile frames. It is seldom practical for a company to extend itself into too many areas. Long-range production planners, like all top managers, must place some limit on their goals if they hope to attain them.

Timing of production

Another question every production manager has to deal with is how to time the production process. Should the manager set up a **continuous process,** such as that used in making steel, in which *long periods of time go by with little or no procedure or equipment change?* Or should he or she set up an **intermittent process,** such as that used in the dress business, in which there are *relatively frequent alterations in equipment setup and materials?* It's a crucial decision because it can cost money if the manager doesn't plan right. A con-

tinuous process uses raw materials at a relatively fast rate. This means that there has to be a sufficient supply of the materials at all times, and the company must be able to afford the cost of "feeding" them into the process. On the other hand, in an intermittent process, workers are unable to use a piece of equipment for a time while it is being adjusted, and this "downtime" can cost money too.

Certain types of manufacturing require an intermittent process, while for other products the continuous process is best. Steel production is a classic example of the continuous process. Blast furnaces are never

SAVING ENERGY: SOME UNEXPECTED METHODS

When the cost of energy went through the roof after the Arab oil embargo of 1973–1974, a lot of manufacturers began giving serious attention to ways of reducing their use of fuel.

The makers of Maxwell House coffee came up with a brilliant solution. The first step in making instant coffee is to brew the coffee just as people do at home, except in 1,000-gallon containers. The heat to brew the coffee had come from burning natural gas, and the process left Maxwell House with tons of coffee grounds (carted away by thirty dump trucks at a time). Then Maxwell House realized it could save most of the cost of the natural gas (and the cost of carting the coffee grounds as well) by burning the grounds to set the heat to brew subsequent batches of coffee. Natural gas is now used only to start the grounds burning.

Another innovative way of cutting energy costs was devised by the Hartford Insurance Company when it installed its huge computers in the basement of its new building. These machines, like all large computers, generate tremendous amounts of heat, and computer rooms usually need to be air conditioned even during the coldest winter months. But instead of installing a huge energy-consuming air-conditioning unit to neutralize the heat coming from the computers, the Hartford siphoned off the computers' heat and, in the winter, used it to warm the rest of the building, saving energy instead.

As marketing requested it.

As sales ordered it.

As engineering designed it.

As production manufactured it.

As field engineering installed it.

What the customer wanted.

Deciding what to produce isn't always simple. There are many points in the process at which communications problems may crop up.

completely shut down unless there is a total mechanical failure or an exceptional cutback in business with no relief in sight. If a furnace cools, it must be completely rebuilt at a cost of millions of dollars. Automobile assemblage is also considered a continuous process because there is no change in basic machinery over the course of a year and production runs are very large. Note that twenty-four-hour operation is not necessary for the process to be termed continuous; and there can be minor variations in the products produced, such as different color paint, trim, and so forth.

The manufacturing of clothing, as we've suggested, is an intermittent process. Sewing and cutting machines must be adjusted each time a new pattern or different textile is used. Even though the sewing machines may be run seven days a week, the resetting of machinery and introduction of new materials make the process intermittent. All **custom manufacturing**, *the production of goods to customer order*, is by nature an intermittent process.

Most production processes fall somewhere between the extremes of totally continous production and very short-run intermittent production. Generally, processes that are more continuous require heavier initial investment but offer greater opportunity for long-term economies. Long production runs give a company more time to earn back the cost of machinery and research: they allow these costs to be divided among a greater number of units, thereby reducing

the cost of each. Furthermore, the continuous process lends itself to a high degree of standardization and permits purchase of materials in quantities large enough to get price concessions from suppliers. Continuous production has disadvantages, of course—particularly its inflexibility. If customers' preferences change quickly or needs fail to materialize as projected, the company with a heavy investment in a continuous process will be in trouble financially.

PURCHASING

Purchasing—obtaining the materials the company needs to make its product—is a crucial and quite complicated production management function. McDonald's couldn't make and sell billions of hamburgers unless someone bought enough chopped meat. And while quantity is obviously critical, so are the cost and quality of the materials purchased. If Burger King's meat were sufficiently superior to McDonald's for Burger King hamburgers to taste much better, McDonald's restaurants would soon be empty. Or if Burger King found a supplier who would sell it the same quality meat McDonald's uses at half the price, Burger King could take away millions of McDonald's customers by selling its hamburgers more cheaply.

THE MAKE-OR-BUY QUESTION

A company's materials are not always purchased; under certain circumstances the firm may decide to make them itself. Some beer companies produce their own containers: Coors makes its own very lightweight cans, and Anheuser Busch (brewer of Budweiser) has its own bottle-making plant. Some California wineries, on the other hand, purchase all the grapes they use rather than operate their own vineyards. What determines whether a company will make or buy its materials? Usually the decision depends on which alternative is cheaper. Lockheed, for example, operates its own small steel plant to design, manufacture, and shape speciality steels, since no steel supplier could handle the job at a price Lockheed could afford to pay. Other factors include the availability of materials, the need for secrecy, and the desire to control all aspects of the finished product. Sometimes the firm has little choice: it may have to manufacture a subassembly (see *Building Your Business Vocabulary,* p. 135) just because there is none available that suits product requirements. Computer companies make many of their subassemblies because other companies do not have the required techniques.

HOW MUCH SHOULD A COMPANY SPEND?

How much money a company should spend on materials is often a ticklish question, which can pit one department against another. The engineering department, which naturally desires materials that are good enough to fulfill their design function, may want to pay top dollar. But the purchasing department may be unwilling to pay more than is absolutely necessary. The result: an interdepartmental clash and a flood of angry memos.

Sometimes the clash can be resolved if the purchasing department can find a new supplier that offers quality materials at reasonable prices. Or purchasing and engineering can join forces to reduce cost through a procedure known as value analysis. In **value analysis**, both *departments work together to find improvements in product design that will lower cost while retaining or improving quality.* They analyze the exact function of the product and the exact contribution each tiny part makes to that overall function. Design changes resulting from value analysis often appear minor. But even a small change can have a relatively big impact on the product's final cost. On one aerospace project, for example, simply replacing one style of bolt with another lowered the cost of bolts on a rotary combustion engine by 73 percent, approximately 2 percent of the engine's selling price. On a mass-produced product a 2 percent saving could mean millions of dollars of profit for the company.

HOW MUCH MATERIAL SHOULD THE COMPANY BUY?

Another key purchasing question is how much material to buy at a time. Basically, there are two possibilities: to buy small amounts, or to buy large amounts. *A manufacturer who uses something continuously and buys it often in relatively small quantities is practicing* **hand-to-mouth buying**. (For example, a manufacturer who builds 24,000 engines a year but purchases only 2,000 engine blocks a month is buying hand-to-mouth.) *Buying a large enough quantity of material to fill a manufacturer's needs for a long time* is called **forward buying**. (A purchase of 8,000 blocks every four months would be considered forward buying.)

Hand-to-mouth buying has its advantages: the system is more flexible, there is less money tied up in materials and storage, and costs are lower in times when prices are falling. But hand-to-mouth buying also has an obvious danger—the manufacturer risks running out of the needed material. Plus, if a production manager buys hand-to-mouth, the supplier may charge more per unit than if the manager buys large quantities.

Lately, large industries have tended to buy large quantities of some key materials. One reason is that shortages of fuel oil and other natural resources have become almost commonplace. If a company wants to avoid production shutdowns, it must buy sufficient quantities of all materials that may run short in the foreseeable future. Forward buying can also protect a firm from the effects of a strike in the supplying industry. Newspapers—which cannot afford to miss daily publication—practice forward buying of paper for this reason, and coal manufacturers often stockpile coal when there is a threat of a mine workers' strike. Inflation is another reason why large companies do a fair amount of forward buying today: it can help keep costs down, since prices will almost undoubtedly be higher in the future.

INVENTORY CONTROL

Even if a company practices hand-to-mouth buying, it will not use *all* its raw materials and parts immediately. And it will not ship all its finished products out immediately either. In other words, it always has a certain number of *raw materials and finished products on hand;* these items are called its *inventory.*

Inventory items must be stored for a time at the plant, and they cannot be left piled up randomly. For if they were not kept track of, workers needing particular parts would spend half the day wandering in search of them. What's more, the purchasing department would never know when supplies were running out and had to be reordered. And the sales department would not be able to tell a customer whether there were enough finished products on hand to fill an order. Every manufacturer, therefore, needs a system of inventory control.

Inventory control means *determining the best quantity of various items to have on hand and keeping track of their movement and use within the plant.* Inventory control systems are applied to both types of supplies on hand: the **materials inventory**, or *stock of items needed for production,* and the **merchandise inventory**, or *stock of finished products.* In this discussion we shall concentrate on materials inventory.

HOW LARGE A MATERIALS INVENTORY SHOULD BE MAINTAINED?

An inventory control manager may at times be tempted to eliminate the possibility of shortages by simply maintaining a huge stock of everything the firm uses. But, of course, this method is not practical in reality. For one thing, the manufacturer must pay for materials in inventory even though it earns no immediate income from them. Also, the initial outlay for a big inventory can be great, perhaps stretching a cash reserve too thin, especially when cash can be invested in other ways. And in addition, a large inventory requires a large warehouse and security staff; both of these add to its cost.

On the other hand, eliminating the materials inventory or cutting it way down through extensive hand-to-mouth buying is no solution either. The order process must always allow for **lead time**, *the period that elapses between placement of a purchase order and receipt of materials from a supplier.* Lead times vary considerably according to the materials and their suppliers, and they can change without notice. A blizzard in the Midwest can affect an aerospace firm in southern California by shutting down the steel mill that supplies the plane manufacturer. The inventory control manager continually has to balance all these considerations in order to establish and maintain a level of inventory high enough to keep production moving and ensure good service to customers, but low enough to keep costs down.

HOW IS STOCK MOVING?

Once decisions have been made on how large an inventory should be, the firm must set up a system for monitoring (keeping track of) the location and use of materials in the plant. Many enterprises accomplish this by means of a **perpetual inventory**, *a list of all materials in stock that is frequently updated.* Most perpetual inventories are updated at least once a day; those based on a computerized system are updated continuously.

Some of the computerized inventory systems now used even place purchase orders to refill stock. An interesting example is the inventory systems used in large department stores. The cash register is linked directly to the store's computer. When the clerk rings a sale, the information recorded includes a numerical code found on the price tag of the merchandise. The computer reads the code and subtracts the purchased merchandise from the perpetual inventory. At periodic intervals the machine prepares written reports for management. These reports allow buyers to reorder before stock runs out. Some stores even program the computer to mail a purchase order to the vendor when inventories of standard merchandise fall to a certain level.

PRODUCTION CONTROL

Production control, like inventory control, is a complex coordinating process. In **production control,** *the manager coordinates labor, materials, and machinery to make the finished product, and maintains a smooth work flow so that orders can be filled efficiently and economically.*

Production control can be difficult. The manufacture of complex products is not a simple procedure that consists of adding Part A to Part B to Part C and so forth until a product emerges complete and ready to ship. Automobiles, for example, are assembled from subunits that vary from car to car. A system is needed to ensure that the correct engine, the right tires, and the proper chrome trim reach each car at the precise point in the assembly process where they are to be added. Goods must thus move from storage to the assembly line with precision. And the problem is complicated in some instances because the subunits may have to be manufactured almost simultaneously on the subassembly line.

Production-control procedures vary from company to company. In most manufacturing processes, however, we can identify five basic steps in production control: planning, routing, scheduling, dispatching, and follow-up and control. To illustrate the five steps, we will follow the production process of a hypothetical small company that manufactures wooden tables. It has just received a rush order for 1,000 square tables, three feet high, 500 to be painted white and 500 to be left unpainted.

HOW IT'S ACTUALLY DONE

Determining the best inventory level

Let's look at how the best inventory level is determined in a newspaper publishing company. A purchasing manager for the *Daily Times* (a large city newspaper) must decide how large an inventory of paper (newsprint) to keep on hand. He asks himself the following questions:

1. How important is this material and what would be the cost of a production stoppage?

Since no newspaper has ever published without paper, newsprint is obviously quite important. If the *Daily Times* sells 500,000 copies at 20 cents each, a production stoppage will mean a revenue loss of at least $100,000 a day, plus what the *Daily Times* would have made from advertising.

2. What is the cost of storage and security?

Storing newsprint requires a large warehouse, but since no one is likely to steal a roll of paper weighing several tons, the newsprint doesn't exactly have to be ringed by security guards.

3. Is the material susceptible to deterioration or spoilage?

As long as the warehouse roof doesn't leak badly, the newsprint won't spoil.

4. Is the price of the material likely to rise or fall?

Since paper costs have risen steadily and astronomically in the past few years, the price trend seems fairly clear.

5. Is there a price reduction for a large forward purchase?

Almost all paper mills will give such a discount.

6. How fast is this material used?

The daily usage of newsprint is measured in tons.

The answers to all these questions point so clearly to keeping a large inventory that the purchasing manager would probably be fired on the spot if he decided on hand-to-mouth purchasing. Even if the situation were not so clear-cut, newsprint is so essential that the decision could almost be made on the basis of question (1) alone.

For different types of companies, other factors might be the crucial determinants of inventory size. The spoilage problem would prevent an ice-cream maker from keeping on hand a six-month supply of cream. For a jewelry maker purchasing gold, inventory security might be the crucial factor.

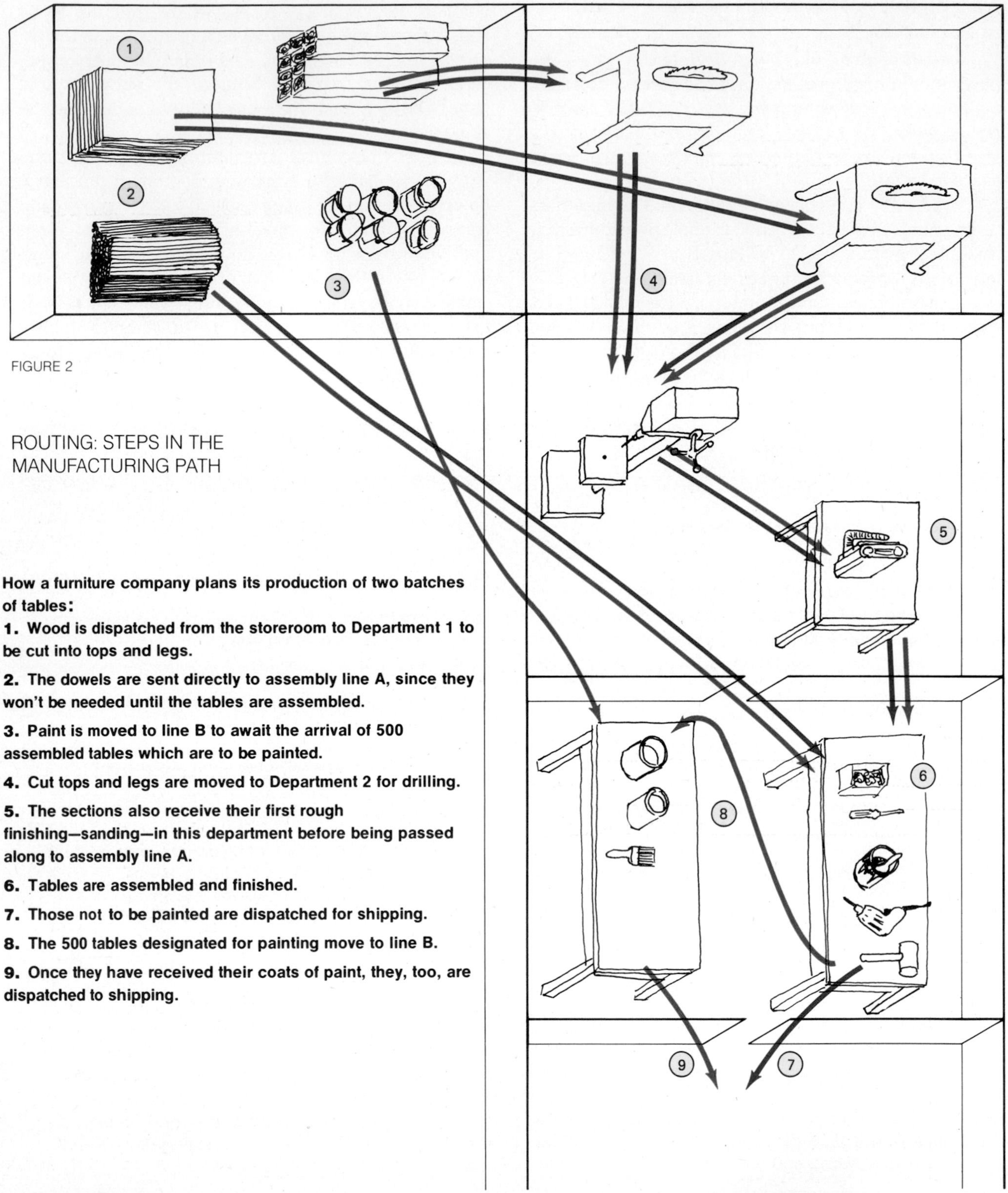

FIGURE 2

ROUTING: STEPS IN THE MANUFACTURING PATH

How a furniture company plans its production of two batches of tables:

1. Wood is dispatched from the storeroom to Department 1 to be cut into tops and legs.

2. The dowels are sent directly to assembly line A, since they won't be needed until the tables are assembled.

3. Paint is moved to line B to await the arrival of 500 assembled tables which are to be painted.

4. Cut tops and legs are moved to Department 2 for drilling.

5. The sections also receive their first rough finishing—sanding—in this department before being passed along to assembly line A.

6. Tables are assembled and finished.

7. Those not to be painted are dispatched for shipping.

8. The 500 tables designated for painting move to line B.

9. Once they have received their coats of paint, they, too, are dispatched to shipping.

PRODUCTION-CONTROL PLANNING

As his first step in production-control planning for this order, the production manager makes a list of all the resources needed to fill the order—labor, machinery, and materials. A **bill of materials** is prepared *listing all parts and materials to be made or purchased:*

Make	Purchase
1,000 table tops	4,000 dowels (one to fasten each leg)
4,000 table legs	50 gallons of white paint

How much of these materials is already on hand? The production manager consults the perpetual inventory and discovers that enough wood and paint are on hand but that the company has only 2,000 dowels. So he orders an additional 2,000 from a local supplier, who promises delivery in two days (well before they will be needed).

ROUTING

Routing, the second step in production control, is *the process whereby the production manager specifies the path through the plant that work will take, and the sequence of operations.* The company has three departments. Each handles a different phase of the table's manufacture. Department 1 cuts wood into desired sizes and shapes. Department 2 does drilling and rough finishing. Department 3 assembles and finishes. In our example, the table tops and legs are routed from Department 1, where they are made, to Department 2 to have the dowel holes drilled, then to Department 3 for assembly, finishing, and painting. The dowels and paint are routed directly from inventory to Department 3, as shown in Figure 2.

SCHEDULING

Next the production manager must incorporate a time element into the routing plan. He sets up a schedule, which establishes a time for each step on the route to begin and to end.

If Department 2 can drill 4,000 dowel holes in a day, then all 4,000 legs and 1,000 table tops should arrive on the same day. If Department 1 can make 1,000 table tops and 1,000 legs a week, it had better start producing the legs three weeks before starting to cut table tops, or all the parts won't be ready for Departments 2 and 3 at the same time. If the entire order is to be shipped at the same time as soon as possible, Department 3 should paint the first 500 tables as they are assembled and finished, so that the paint will be dry by the time the last 500 are completed. The schedule also tells management how much time will elapse before the job reaches Department 3, that is, how much time Department 3 has to work on other jobs before this one arrives.

DISPATCHING

Dispatching is *the issuing of work orders and routing papers to department heads and supervisors.* These dispatches specify the work to be done and the schedule for its completion.

In our example, the production manager would dispatch orders to the storeroom calling for the needed materials (wood, dowels, paint) to reach the appropriate departments and machines before the scheduled starting time.

FOLLOW-UP AND CONTROL

Once the schedule has been set up and the orders dispatched, production managers cannot, of course, just sit back and assume that the work will automatically get done correctly and on time. Even the best scheduler can misjudge the time needed to complete an operation, and production can be delayed by accidents, mechanical breakdowns, or supplier failures. Thus the production manager must have a follow-up and control system, which informs him of the nature of any delays and prevents a minor disruption from growing into chaos. The system is based on good communication between the work stations and production control. In our example, suppose a machine breakdown causes Department 2 to lose half a day of drilling time. If the schedule is not altered to increase Department 3's time on other jobs, there will be an unnecessary half day of idle waiting in Department 3. So, first of all, Department 2 must be sure to inform the production manager of its machine problem right away, and next the production manager must take time immediately to think up some fill-in work for Department 3.

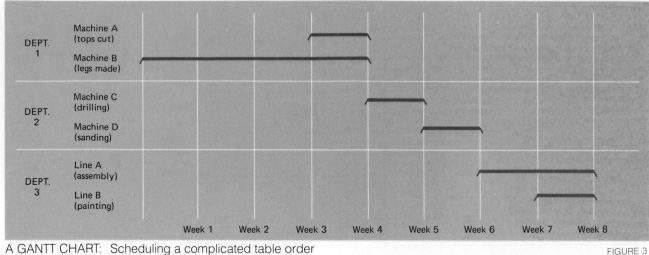

A GANTT CHART: Scheduling a complicated table order

FIGURE 3

A glance at a chart like this enables a production manager to see immediately the dates on which production steps must be started and completed if goods are to be delivered on schedule. For example, drilling must be done in the fifth week so that sanding can be carried out in the sixth. Some steps can overlap to save time. For instance, when Machine B has been cutting legs for three weeks, Machine A begins cutting table tops—so that both parts are completed together and can move on together to the next stage in the manufacturing process.

In addition to this schedule follow-up system, production managers must set up a **quality control** system, through which *items are routinely checked and tested for quality as they are produced.* Some quality control systems provide for output to be checked and tested at random; some have every tenth item checked; some every hundredth; and so on. A report is prepared on all the "rejects," telling how many there were in a given time period and why they were thrown out. If the rejection rate is unusually high, the production manager must change the production process in some way to correct the problem at its source.

COORDINATING PRODUCTION PROCESSES

The overall coordination of a project can become very complicated. If very many steps must be taken to com-

plete a project, production managers may have to use computers to help them with all the calculations. Making a chart of the project's different steps is often of great value to the production manager, just as seeing an actual painting is better than hearing a description of it. Earlier this century, Henry L. Gantt developed a technique that charts the steps to be taken and the time required (see Figure 3).

The PERT technique and CPM

From Gantt's production-chart system grew another tool for production control, called PERT (Program Evaluation and Review Technique). The **PERT** *method consists, basically, of breaking down one large project into the many different steps necessary for its completion and analyzing the time requirements for each step.*

Take an example: the steps involved in making a record album, from the original idea to final distribution of the album in the stores. In our PERT chart (see Figure 4) we've shown six steps. (We've simplified the steps considerably for the purpose of discussion.) If the production manager sees that one of the steps is being delayed—for example, it's taking longer than three weeks to record the songs—then he looks at the PERT chart to see how this delay will change the overall schedule.

Notice that in the PERT figure the time needed for each step is given. Recording the songs will take three weeks and making the records themselves will take

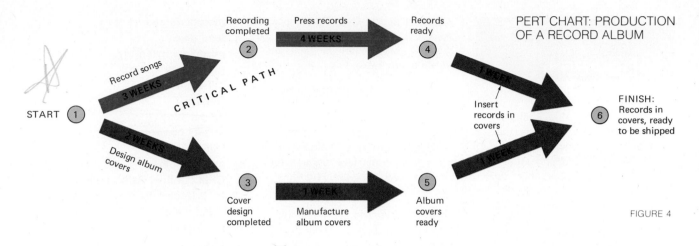

PERT CHART: PRODUCTION OF A RECORD ALBUM

FIGURE 4

The PERT chart shows the steps in producing the finished product, dividing them into separate paths. In this example, recording the music and pressing the records are the operations which are most crucial for the timing of the entire process. Therefore, they form the critical path (stages 1–2–4). Only three weeks are needed for the design and production of the album covers; but the entire operation will not be complete until the records are pressed and inserted into the covers.

another four weeks—thus the albums will be ready for packing in seven weeks. This total seven-week sequence of operations is what is known as the **critical path**: *the specific sequence of operations whose prompt completion is essential to the prompt completion of the entire project.* Whether the design and production of the album cover is ahead of schedule or not (and the chart allows three weeks for steps 1–3–5), the complete album won't be ready until the records are. What the production manager has done is to estimate the *least possible amount of time in which the whole project can be completed, basing this estimate on the projection of the time needed for completion of the critical path.* This method of estimating project completion time is known as the **CPM (Critical Path Method)**.

MRP (Materials requirements planning)

A production management technique that is widely used to control inventory and schedule projects is called **MRP (Materials Requirements Planning)**.

Its basic function is to *get the correct materials where they are needed—and get them there on time—without stockpiling unnecessary materials.* Using the MRP approach, production managers set up a computer program designed to let them know *when* certain materials are needed, and *when* they can stop purchasing other materials that are not needed right away and are costing the company money to store. The companies most likely to use MRP are those whose products are complicated—for example, an automobile manufacturer, whose product is made up of many different parts.

To see how MRP works, let's take a very simple example. A production manager needs a nail and a hammer and has got to be sure that they arrive on time. But if the nail is delivered on Monday and the hammer is delivered on Friday, there have been four days wasted in which the nail has had to be stored because no one can use it without the hammer. Of course, with an automobile, there are a great number of different parts, and it's essential that each part be in the right place at the right time. Moreover, it's not even as simple as making sure that all the parts are there. There are many subassemblies—the motor, the steering mechanism, and the like—which must all be completed on time. In addition to coordinating the overall project of building a car, the production manager must further break down the elements involved in the completion of the various subassemblies, and this is where the MRP becomes important. The computer program helps to coordinate the deadlines for each subassembly, the deadline for the entire project, and the times when the materials are needed.

CHAPTER REVIEW

High productivity in the United States is based largely on mass production, which in turn has been made possible by mechanization, standardization, the assembly line, and automation. Supervising the large-scale conversion of materials into useful goods and services is the responsibility of production management. Its functions include planning, purchasing, inventory control, and production control.

The production planner, deciding upon a plant location, weighs the availability of labor, energy, and transportation. This decision may also be influenced by the proximity of natural resources, the proximity of a firm's market, and various factors in the community. Production planning also involves what products will be produced and how. New products (and improvements on old ones) are planned by the research and development department.

There are two basic processes for manufacturing. An analytic process breaks a raw material down into one or more products. A synthetic process combines materials to form a product. Fabrication and assembly are types of synthetic processes. In terms of time, production processes are either continuous or intermittent.

The purchasing department obtains materials for a firm. It helps make decisions about whether a company should make or buy certain materials, how much to pay for them, and when to buy them.

Inventory control determines the supply of materials that should be kept on hand, and supervises their flow. The aim of purchasing and inventory control is to minimize the cost of materials. One tool in achieving this goal is the perpetual inventory.

Production control maintains a smooth work flow. To fulfill any given order, managers have to plan for the necessary labor, materials, and machinery. They route work through the plant, schedule it in terms of individual departments, and issue exact orders through dispatching. Finally, they utilize follow-up and control to see that work is done on time and correctly.

KEY WORD REVIEW

production
mass production
mechanization
standardization
assembly line
automation
analytic process
synthetic process
continuous process
intermittent process
custom manufacturing
value analysis
hand-to-mouth buying
forward buying
inventory
inventory control
materials inventory
merchandise inventory
lead time
perpetual inventory
production control
bill of materials
routing
dispatching
quality control
PERT
critical path
CPM (Critical Path Method)
MRP (Materials Requirements Planning)
fabrication
assembly
subassemblies

REVIEW QUESTIONS

1. What is the relationship between mass production and our lifestyle?

2. How is choice of plant site affected by labor factors, physical factors, and community factors?

3. What challenges are offered by the analytic production process? By the synthetic process?

4. List the advantages and disadvantages of continuous production.

5. What factors affect a make-or-buy decision?

6. How would a purchasing manager determine whether to buy ahead or buy when needed?

7. What is value analysis?

8. What is the objective of inventory control? What factors are considered in establishing a desirable level of inventory?

9. Why are proper routing and scheduling important?

CASE 1

ASSEMBLY-LINE HOUSING

In an industry made treacherous by the roller-coaster nature of its boom-and-bust cycles, one home-building firm, Texas-based Fox & Jacobs, Inc. has been rolling along as though housing were the steadiest business around. A wise choice of markets accounts for part of the company's stability: Fox & Jacobs concentrates on selling its homes to first-time buyers and moderate-income families in the prosperous and rapidly expanding cities of Dallas, Fort Worth, and Houston. But the real key to the company's strength is the Fox & Jacobs approach to production management. "We decided years ago to be a permanent business and operate like any other manufacturing company," the firm's president told *The Wall Street Journal,* "and that means we must operate with predictable continuity."

Unlike conventional builders, who cut and assemble house components on the construction site and use subcontractors who hire skilled workers, Fox & Jacobs uses an assembly-line system. In building the three kinds of houses that it offers, the company assembles wall and roof parts in factor-ies in Dallas and Houston, and makes its own cabinets in a second Dallas factory. At one end of a noisy Fox & Jacobs assembly line, for instance, workers make wall panels using forms and precut two-by-four studs. Every day, two miles of wall panels roll off the line and onto flatbed trailers for shipment to the construction site. There, following tight schedules, workers on one of the fifteen Fox & Jacobs construction crews unload the walls from a trailer, stand them in place, and nail them together. Other workers then enclose the walls using materials brought by the same truck. A second trailer brings all the windows, cabinets, appliances, moldings, and other items needed to finish the job. To keep on schedule, Fox & Jacobs keeps a fleet of four trucks constantly on the road; their sole assignment is to repair the fifty to seventy-five flat tires a day that slow down other company vehicles. In keeping with its "predictable continuity" concept, Fox & Jacobs holds costs down by buying undeveloped farmland on the outskirts of expanding areas, by employing nonskilled, nonunion workers and training them to perform highly specialized tasks, and by placing large orders for needed materials twelve to eighteen months in advance in order to get sizable discounts from suppliers. The result: Fox & Jacobs can build a complete house in forty-four days—more than twice as fast as most other builders—and can sell those houses for $24 a square foot, at least $11 below the price charged by other firms.

Although not the last word in architecture, Fox & Jacobs homes have been selling well enough to allow the company to expand throughout Texas and into Oklahoma; it expects to be putting up 120,000 houses a year by 1985, up from 8,000 homes in 1978–1979. As the engineer who de-signed the Fox & Jacobs system explains, "You take men, materials, and equipment, and if you put them together in the right quantities, you get soap. I figure you do the same to get houses." Not all agree: one expert argues that the system makes no sense outside of areas that are growing rapidly, offer plenty of nonunion labor, and have weather good enough to allow construction to go on year round. But home builders are now turning increasingly to the use of factory-made components, and some believe that the mass-production techniques used by Fox & Jacobs to keep home prices low (average price: $35,840, versus the national average price for a new home of $56,000 to $59,000) are the way of the future for the rest of the housing industry.[2]

1. What are some of the dangers inherent in an assembly-line approach to building homes?

2. How could PERT be applied to the Fox & Jacobs system?

3. Give some reasons that explain why most home builders have traditionally preferred to buy components from someone else rather than make them themselves.

HUMAN RELATIONS: MOTIVATION AND MORALE

There was a time—and not that long ago—when motivating your employees was simple. You just fired anyone who didn't work hard enough to suit you; there were plenty of others waiting to fill the vacancy. Wages were low and conditions harsh, but that was no problem either. A bad job was still better than starvation.

Times have changed a lot since then, but the increased security and financial well-being of the average worker have made motivation and job satisfaction issues of growing concern to labor and management alike. As we will see in this chapter, trying to reconcile the basic human needs and aspirations of workers with the demands of a competitive business system has become a major problem. Its solution demands increasing amounts of sophistication and ingenuity—and a large helping of common sense as well.

WHAT WILL THIS CHAPTER FOCUS ON?

After reading the material in this chapter, you will understand and be able to discuss:

■ the meaning of worker dissatisfaction, and some of the forms that this dissatisfaction takes

■ why many human-relations experts question the relationship between worker affluence and worker dissatisfaction

■ theories of motivation from Frederick Taylor to the present

■ the significance of the Hawthorne Studies

■ Maslow's "hierarchy of human needs"

■ the difference between Theory X managers and Theory Y managers

■ how management is redesigning work in order to improve workers' morale, using such methods as behavior modification, flexible working hours, job rotation, job enlargement, and management by objectives

■ possible cures for the "blue-collar blues"

You will find people who say they would rather work in cleanup and take a cut of fifteen cents an hour than work the assembly line. At least on cleanup you have the choice of sweeping the pile in the corner or sweeping the pile by the post.[1]

This is how Ken Bannon, vice-president of the United Auto Workers, summed up a key problem that faces American company managers—the problem of keeping workers satisfied and productive in today's routine, highly mechanized factory setting. It's a crucially important issue, because boredom among workers is remarkably widespread. In *Work in America,*[2] an extensive government research project, over half of the white male blue-collar workers who were surveyed said they were not content with their jobs most of the time. And over three-quarters of this same group, when asked if they would choose their current occupations again, said they would not. Meanwhile many white-collar workers, though not actually tied to assembly lines, are also suffering from a sense that their jobs are dull and unrewarding. The *Work in America* study found that when asked the question, "Would you choose your current occupation again?" only 43 percent of people in white-collar jobs said yes. That means that over half the white-collar workers were dissatisfied.

SIGNS OF WORKER DISCONTENT

Clearly such unhappiness among blue-collar and white-collar workers—and the expense that this unhappiness can cause a company—warrants a closer look. For when workers take action based on their discontent, they can greatly cut back on their companies' output. There are a number of ways workers can signal that they are uncomfortable on the job—all of which create serious problems for management.

STRIKES

Strikes, or *work stoppages,* are the most obvious expression of workers' unhappiness with their jobs. In 1976 there were 5,648 strikes and lockouts involving 2,420,000 workers, with some 37,859,000 million mandays lost to idleness.[3] (We discuss lockouts in our Enrichment Chapter on Management and Unions.) Historically strikes have always increased during times of rising prices. But they also increase during periods of full employment, when workers feel more secure about their ability to find other jobs. Certain industries appear to be more prone to work stoppages than others, among them mining and contract construction.[4] The reasons for this are often complicated, involving such factors as the relative strength of a union and prevailing management attitudes.

HIGH TURNOVER

Turnover occurs *when a person leaves a job and the job is refilled.* In 1976 roughly 38 of every 1,000 workers were separated from their jobs. **Dismissal**—*termination of employment*—accounted for only eight job separations per 1,000 employees. Of every 1,000 workers, thirteen were laid off and seventeen left voluntarily.[5] Some left for health or other personal reasons, but the majority simply wanted a change. Obviously, when a company has an above-average turnover rate, something had better be corrected—if only because time and money are usually required to find and train new workers. At one time, for instance, Pacific Telephone found itself losing 62 percent of its service representatives from one office each year—hardly an indication of a happy or healthy working climate.

HIGH ABSENTEEISM

Some industries are troubled by absenteeism among workers who call in sick or develop other "problems" simply because they can't face going to their jobs. The situation is especially serious in assembly-line factories, where production schedules and quality control depend on having a full supply of workers. At many General Motors plants absenteeism can run as high as 15 percent on Mondays and Fridays and other "bad days"—the opening of the hunting season, for instance, or the day after a holiday. To keep the assembly lines running on such days, the company has to hire one extra worker for every ten regulars.

POOR QUALITY AND DELIBERATE DAMAGE

The extent of the damage caused by worker dissatisfaction can only be guessed. We have all faced worker dissatisfaction when an unhappy clerk gave us the impression that the store would be a fine place to work if it were not for customers. A more measurable example was found at one Ford plant. In that case 160 repairpersons were required to take care of defects on cars that were produced by 840 workers at an assembly line a few feet away!

Some workers are sufficiently unhappy at their jobs to cause damage deliberately. One steelworker said, "Sometimes, out of pure meanness, when I make something, I put a little dent in it. I like to do something to make it really unique. Hit it with a hammer deliberately to see if it'll get by, just so I can say I did it."[6]

And losses caused by worker theft go far beyond a "little dent." In 1974 the *New York Times* reported that contractors were tacking $100,000 on the price of each high-rise building because of thefts from the construction site. Most of this amount represented materials stolen by employees.

STUDYING WORKER BEHAVIOR: THE FIELD OF HUMAN RELATIONS

A whole field of management study has developed in connection with job dissatisfaction—the field of human relations. Basically, **human relations** is concerned with *the ways people in organizations behave toward one another.* And one of its special concerns is to determine how the managers of a business can direct workers' behavior to make them more productive and better satisfied. Research has suggested some possible reasons why workers feel and act the way they do. It has also come up with ways managers can alter the work environment to make beneficial changes in their employees' behavior.

Of course, not all managers have the time or the budgets they would need to try the new approaches suggested by human-relations research. And furthermore, not all managers—or all human-relations specialists—are in agreement as to the causes of workers'

If workers find their jobs tedious their productivity may decline.

unhappiness. But almost all agree that the most important resource of an organization is its people, and they recognize that keeping these people functioning is a practical challenge of great concern. In this chapter we'll look at some of the theories which have been put forward concerning the attitudes and behavior of today's workers, and at some of the methods managers have tried for making workers more effective and content.

WHY ARE WORKERS DISSATISFIED?

How can we explain discontent among American workers? There are numerous theories, which can be sorted into two groups: those placing most of the blame on changes in the society, and those holding management largely to blame.

Among the first group of theories, worker dissatisfaction is often seen as a reflection of the general trend toward "permissiveness" in our society. This trend, the argument goes, has brought about a loss of respect for the **work ethic**, *the idea that work is good and necessary in itself.* According to this viewpoint, more and more people are satisfied getting by with a minimum of exertion and resent it when hard work is expected of them. In short, it is said, the labor force has grown soft. Its initiative has been dulled by generous union contracts, higher unemployment benefits, and the like; and its discontent is merely a by-product of changing social values—something that business neither causes nor can cure.

There may be some truth in this viewpoint. It is obvious that affluence has had a profound impact on the structure of our society and the values of our people. But as the second group of theories points out, surveys continue to show that many workers still have a strong desire to earn a living through their own efforts and that they will not shun hard work if it is appropriately rewarded. The question is, however, whether "reward" means simply money or something more. Statistics show that employees in some companies are far better workers than those with similar jobs in other companies. A recent study, for example, found that workers in certain large corporations (IBM, Procter & Gamble, and Eastman Kodak led the field) felt consistently more satisfied than their counterparts in other firms, despite similar salaries and benefits.[7] A key factor seemed to be the employees' sense that their companies were committed to excellence, that the workers themselves were genuinely valued, and that they had access to higher levels of management whenever the need arose. In other words, satisfaction among workers comes about, at least in part, through good company management.

A key feature of good management is its sensitivity to workers' morale. **Morale** is a broad concept; it involves *a person's cheerfulness and confidence and the enthusiasm with which that person engages in activities.* When managers try to boost the morale of their workers, they try to find ways to make them work more zestfully and put out the best efforts they are capable of. But *how* to boost morale is a tough question, especially since not all human-relations experts agree on the reasons why people do their jobs well or badly. What we're dealing with here is motivation, an issue we'll look at in more detail.

MOTIVATION

If you asked yourself, "Why did he do that?" when someone behaved in a way you did not understand, you were wondering about his motivation. Motivation was

In 1975, Owen Quinn parachuted 1,350 feet off the World Trade Center. What motivates a person to attempt a dangerous feat of this kind?

mentioned in Chapter 3 as part of what a manager does when he directs people. In this chapter we shall define it more fully, describe the steps that have led to our present ideas about it, and show how it works in business.

Motivation has two meanings, or senses. In the first sense, it is used to mean *the reason a person has for carrying out a given action.* For example, you might say, "Jack made the football team because he had the right motivation." That is, Jack felt that he would receive some social or psychological reward from playing on the team. In the second sense, motivation refers to *the process of giving a person a reason for doing something.* Using the word this way, you might say, "Steve felt that motivating the team was his most important function as captain." It is the second sense of the word, motivation as a process of giving people reasons for doing things, that managers are more interested in.

A manager creates in his workers an inner drive to do their jobs by persuading them that their needs can be satisfied by working within the framework of the formal organization. He or she makes them believe they have something to gain by doing their jobs the way the organization wants them done. And the critical problem in motivating workers (and in some respect, in all of management) is *how* to mesh the needs of the individual with the needs of the organization.

Since the early days of modern industry, managers have approached this problem in a number of ways.

THE BEGINNINGS OF MOTIVATION THEORY

Workers of the nineteenth century endured conditions that seem nothing less than barbaric today—twelve-hour to fourteen-hour workdays in cramped, unsafe factories, six or seven days a week, for wages that barely warded off starvation. Yet employers seldom had problems motivating the workers. Laborers had no legal protection, and poverty and unemployment were so severe that any job at all was something to feel grateful for.

One of the few exceptions to this dismal rule was provided by Robert Owen, a Scottish industrialist of the early nineteenth century. Pioneering such modern business practices as the merit system, Owen thought of his textile-mill employees as "vital machines"—in contrast to the factory's "inanimate machines"—and held that their well-being was as important as the up-keep of mechanical equipment. Owen's views were not widely shared, however, and it was not until the end of the nineteenth century that social pressures forced industrialists to begin looking more closely at the question of motivating workers.

THE CLASSICAL THEORY OF MOTIVATION

The **classical theory of motivation** can be stated simply: it holds that *money is the sole motivator in the workplace.* Humans are viewed as purely economic creatures who work only for money to pay for food, clothing, and shelter (and whatever luxuries they may be able to afford beyond that). To motivate workers, then, a manager has only to show them that they'll earn more money by doing things the company way.

The classical theory's chief spokesman was Frederick W. Taylor (1865–1915), often called the father of scientific management. A firm believer in the division of labor, Taylor broke work into small units that were efficient and easy to measure. He then determined a reasonable level of productivity for each task and established a **quota**, or *minimum goal*, he expected the worker to reach. Under his **piecework system**, *workers who just met or fell short of the quota were paid a certain amount for each unit produced. However, those who surpassed the quota were paid at a higher rate for* all *units produced*, not just the number above the quota. Workers were thus given a very strong incentive to increase productivity.

Around 1900 Taylor's system was introduced at the Bethlehem Steel works, with impressive results: the average wage of steel handlers rose from $1.15 to $1.85 a day. At the same time, their productivity increased so sharply that the company's handling costs were cut by more than half—a profitable outcome for both sides.

Limitations of the classical theory

The classical theory of motivation worked well in the early part of this century, and for a good reason: most workers were very poor. Indeed, money still buys the essentials of life and many of its pleasures, and few people can claim that money has *nothing* to do with why they work. But the classical theory cannot explain why a woman whose husband already makes a good living goes out and finds a job, or why a Wall Street lawyer might take a hefty pay cut to serve in the government. (Or why, for that matter, a wealthy peanut farmer might devote a number of grueling years to running for U.S. President and serving in the job.)

Clearly, money is not the only thing that can motivate people to work, and later research into the subject revealed that the worker is a far more complex creature than even the perceptive Taylor had imagined.

THE HAWTHORNE STUDIES

The Hawthorne Studies, a landmark in motivation research, were conducted between 1927 and 1932 at Western Electric's Hawthorne plant in Chicago. The researchers, led by Elton Mayo of Harvard University, initially wanted to test the relationship between workers' physical surroundings and their productivity. They did find out something about this relationship—but not what they had expected. Altering the workers' environment did not affect their productivity nearly as much as the researchers had anticipated. Only extreme changes (reducing the lighting to moonlight level, for instance) had a significant effect. Otherwise, the workers just seemed to keep going at the same pace, regardless of changes in their surroundings.[8]

How could this be? Perhaps there was something, some offsetting force, that made the workers either ignore the change, or if that was impossible, do their best to make up for the change. Further investigation revealed that there was indeed "something," a force even stronger than Taylor's wage incentive: this "something" was social pressure. Workers established their own standards of what the correct output should be, sneering at overproducers as "rate busters" and underproducers as "chiselers." And the pressure was effective: the workers were more interested in the approval of their peers than in earning higher wages.

As the Hawthorne Studies revealed, the informal organization has tremendous power to motivate workers—more effectively in many cases than the formal organization can. And the Hawthorne Studies also discovered, almost by accident, another phenomenon of great importance. By the time the project ended, the productivity of the workers involved had risen 30 percent—but not because of any change in work methods or new equipment. Simply participating in the research—being asked for opinions and ideas, being listened to—had given the workers a greater sense of involvement in their jobs, a sense of partnership with management in a common endeavor. In short, their morale had been raised, and their new enthusiasm and confidence provided a stronger incentive than any paycheck.

MASLOW'S LADDER

The next major study of human motivation was brought about by the need for increased production during World War II. In the 1940s the psychologist Abraham Maslow came to recognize that workers are motivated by a wide variety of needs, which he organized into the five categories illustrated in Figure 1. His theory of the "hierarchy of human needs," often known as Maslow's Ladder, was based on two simple premises: that people have many needs and that only those needs not yet satisfied cause them to act. When needs on a lower level have been satisfied, at least in part, a person begins to strive for the next rung on the ladder.[9]

The steps in Maslow's hierarchy

PHYSIOLOGICAL NEEDS All the requirements for sustaining life—food, clothing, shelter, and the like—fall into this category. These basic needs have to be satisfied before the person can pursue any other objectives.

SAFETY NEEDS Once the bare essentials are taken care of, the desire for future security, for a cushion against misfortune, becomes more important. In addition to saving for a rainy day, a worker's safety needs must be satisfied through such means as health insurance, pension plans, guaranteed job security, and Social Security benefits.

SOCIAL NEEDS Humans are social animals, with powerful needs to associate with others, give and receive love, and feel a sense of belonging. This is the first level of needs that money cannot readily satisfy, and (as the Hawthorne Studies showed) these needs can sometimes be more important to the worker than financial considerations.

ESTEEM NEEDS People need to feel self-esteem, a sense of innate personal worth and integrity. They also need

MASLOW'S LADDER: NEEDS PEOPLE FILL THROUGH WORK

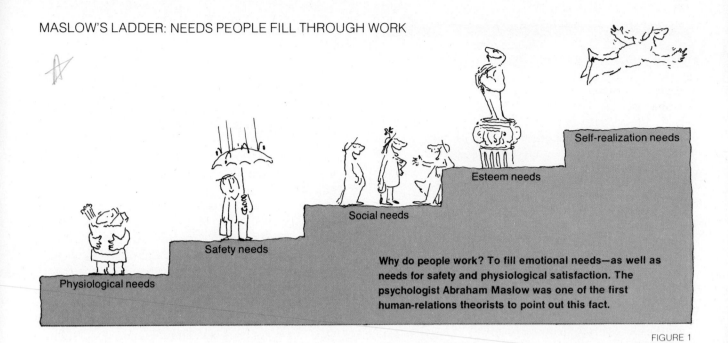

Self-realization needs

Esteem needs

Social needs

Safety needs

Physiological needs

Why do people work? To fill emotional needs—as well as needs for safety and physiological satisfaction. The psychologist Abraham Maslow was one of the first human-relations theorists to point out this fact.

FIGURE 1

the respect of others, a respect based not on friendship (a social need) but on their competence and achievements. These needs are closely related to the idea of *status*—one's rank or importance in the eyes of others.

SELF-REALIZATION NEEDS Maslow defined the need for self-realization (also called self-actualization) as "the desire to become more what one is, to become everything one is capable of." This need is the highest and most difficult to fulfill of all those on the ladder; when a worker has reached this point, he or she works not to make money or to impress others, but because the task is worthwhile and satisfying in itself.

Maslow's Ladder in perspective

Maslow's Ladder is a convenient way to classify human needs, but it would be mistaken to view it as a rigid one-step-at-a-time procedure. Each level of needs does not have to be completely satisfied (if that is even possible) before a person can be motivated by a higher need. Indeed, it can be safely assumed that most people are motivated most of the time by a combination of many different needs.

McGREGOR'S THEORY X AND THEORY Y

Douglas McGregor, a psychologist, accepted Maslow's ladder of needs. But he felt that management had failed to do so. Why was this so? McGregor suggested, in an influential book called *The Human Side of Enterprise* published in 1960, that a certain set of assumptions underlies most managers' thinking.[10] Labeling these assumptions Theory X, he summed them up as follows:

1. The average person dislikes work and will avoid it if possible.

2. Because of this dislike for work, the average person must be forced, controlled, directed, or threatened with punishment to motivate him or her to put forth enough effort to achieve the organization's objectives.

3. The average person prefers to be directed, wishes to avoid responsibility, has relatively little ambition, and wants security.

But, said McGregor, Theory X could not explain all of people's behavior in work situations. Theory X

Some workers need a Theory X boss

As more and more thought is given to increasing productivity, more and more companies and the experts they consult are realizing that what's good for one group of employees isn't necessarily good for another. In one electrical plant in Louisiana, for instance, employees perform their jobs under considerable pressure. As one consultant put it, management "really stomps on them and shoves them around." The workers respect a supervisor who is tougher than they are, and from their standpoint that is what counts. Some 35 percent of the workers in the plant are ex-convicts. The manager, no stranger to the law himself, has been indicted four times for murder. Needless to say, he gets both respect and results from his staff.

Obviously, then, there's no one way to increase productivity among workers. The methods that have proved successful are as diverse as the employees on whom they've been used. The trick, if trick it be, is simply to know the people who work for you and use that knowledge in the right way.

Source: Rohan, Thomas M., "Results Win Converts for Work Design," *Industry Week*. October 10, 1977, pp. 71–76.

emphasized physiological and safety needs but tended to ignore the higher levels of needs on Maslow's ladder. So McGregor suggested another set of assumptions that he believed managers should concentrate on. These assumptions, which he termed Theory Y, were as follows:

1. The average person does not dislike work. It is as natural as play or rest.

2. External control and the threat of punishment are not the only ways to motivate people to meet an organization's goals. The average person will naturally work toward objectives to which he or she is committed.

3. How deeply a person is committed to objectives depends on the rewards associated with the achievement.

4. Under proper conditions the average person learns not only to accept responsibility, but also to seek it.

5. Many people are capable of using a relatively high degree of imagination, cleverness, and creativity to solve problems that come up in an organization.

6. In modern industrial life the average person's intellectual potential is only partially realized.

In summary, the assumptions behind Theory X emphasize authority; the assumptions behind Theory Y emphasize human growth and self-direction. McGregor believed managers would face more and more problems with their workers unless they started putting Theory Y into practice immediately. Workers could no longer put up with organizational systems based on Theory X assumptions. They were ready to realize their social, esteem, and self-realization needs, and blocking them would only lead to antiorganizational behavior.

McGregor's advice was largely ignored when his book was published—and it still is, to the dismay of reform-minded observers. One outspoken authority, Harry Levinson, reports that nearly all executives respond the same way when asked to identify the main source of motivation in business: "the carrot and stick," the age-old theory of reward and punishment. Levinson points out that the well-known carrot-and-stick metaphor always brings to mind one specific image: the image of a donkey. And this, he argues, is in fact the unconscious image many managers have of workers—stubborn beasts of burden that must constantly be prodded and manipulated. This management attitude is self-defeating, Levinson concludes, since workers sooner or later respond to them by being as uncooperative and mulish as their supervisors expect them to be.[11]

When managers do treat workers with trust and respect, they are usually rewarded with both improved morale and increased productivity. For example, consider the following real-life incident. The manager of an automobile assembly plant noticed that windshield breakage had suddenly risen from almost zero to about seventeen per day. None of his staff could explain the rise, so the manager decided to discuss the problem with workers themselves. He told them that he was not out to accuse or punish anyone—he simply wanted to know why so many windshields were breaking. Finally one worker spoke up. He said, "I broke one today and

Some managers subscribe to Theory X.

I'll tell you why. You can't drill mounting holes for windshields without breaking them unless you have a stopper on your drill. The toolroom people started having an economy drive and won't give us stoppers. They think they are saving money."

The manager said, "Thank you very much. You will have stoppers tomorrow." And the breakage problem was solved, thanks to the manager's willingness to consider the point of view of the workers rather than automatically assuming they were at fault.[12]

REDESIGNING WORK: IMPROVING WORKERS' MORALE

"In the old days you used to start a job and you used to finish it. Now things have become so diversified . . . you start something and it goes through 50 million other hands before it's completed."[13] That observation, made by a longtime Lockheed employee, goes to the heart of the problem. The most satisfying forms of work are those over which the worker has full control. But the nature of modern industry, with its excessive reliance on Taylorism, has moved workers in the opposite direction, keeping from them the satisfaction of being able to point to something and say, "I made that."

Human-relations experts have brought forth a number of ideas aimed at putting some personal satisfaction back into work without reducing productivity. In essence, the goal of these **work design programs** is to *structure jobs in such a way that they are interesting and involving.* In some cases, this means scrapping an assembly line in favor of work teams that handle the whole procedure themselves, possibly without direct supervision by management. In others, it simply means providing more regular feedback and "positive reinforcement" from supervisors. In still others, it means removing the supervisors altogether and leaving day-to-day decision making to the work teams. The following are some of the most well-known work design approaches.

HOW IT'S ACTUALLY DONE

HANDLING A DISPUTE BETWEEN WORKERS

Good communication is extremely important in the delicate task of mediating disputes between workers, particularly if one is the other's boss. Here are some guidelines to follow:

- Listen carefully to the original complaint.

- Follow the evidence wherever it may lead.

- If you are unable to decide between them, favor the superior over the subordinate.

- Ask the complainant to suggest a remedy for the grievance. Often, when the worker realizes that no remedy exists, he or she will forget the whole matter.

Treat all similar gripes the same way. As in civil and criminal law, a decision handed down on a grievance may become the precedent for future decisions.

BEHAVIOR MODIFICATION

Behavior modification, or "positive reinforcement," a technique developed by the Harvard psychologist B. F. Skinner, holds that *people's behavior can be improved if they simply receive praise for their performance and are given a supportive environment.* Behavior modification plays down the importance of a worker's inner motivations, focusing instead on the person's *outer* surroundings—and emphasizing particularly the need to eliminate negative or discouraging elements. Thus if a worker does a job badly, the manager should acknowledge the fact but not criticize the worker; if a worker does a job well, the manager should promptly praise the person. Also, the manager should comment regularly on employees' routine day-to-day work to let them know how they're doing. The Skinner approach is dismissed by some experts as shallow and oversimplified, but a growing number of companies have found it to have a good effect on both morale and productivity. In fact, one company that runs a behavior-modification program, the 3M Company, is believed to have saved $3.5 million in 1977 through behavior-modification techniques.

One manager at Michigan Bell Telephone Company described how, by using Skinner's approach, he significantly lowered absenteeism among a group of telephone operators. The absentee rate among

In the MBO system, managers state their goals clearly and involve the appropriate workers in them from the start. The workers state their own goals too, and both workers and managers go through a cycle of discussion, review, and evaluation. In this way, the workers get a chance to make the company's goals their own.

FIGURE 2

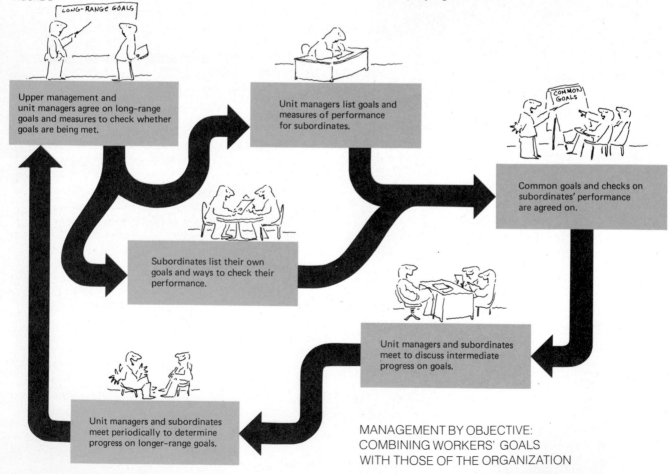

Upper management and unit managers agree on long-range goals and measures to check whether goals are being met.

Unit managers list goals and measures of performance for subordinates.

Common goals and checks on subordinates' performance are agreed on.

Subordinates list their own goals and ways to check their performance.

Unit managers and subordinates meet to discuss intermediate progress on goals.

Unit managers and subordinates meet periodically to determine progress on longer-range goals.

MANAGEMENT BY OBJECTIVE:
COMBINING WORKERS' GOALS
WITH THOSE OF THE ORGANIZATION

MANAGEMENT BY OBJECTIVES

Blue-collar and clerical workers are not the only dissatisfied members of the work force. Although a high degree of satisfaction is usually associated with management work, managers also complain of discontent. The source of the problem is similar. Managers feel alienated from their organizations because they perceive a conflict between their personal goals and those of the organization. Also, they have needs that their work environment fails to satisfy. Management by objectives is a technique introduced during the 1950s in an attempt to resolve the problems of the white-collar worker and the professional.

One common source of conflict between organizational and personal goals is a simple misunderstanding of the organization's objectives. Another is that individuals seldom have any say in how their goals can fit in with those of the organization. **Management by objectives (MBO)** cuts right to the heart of these problem areas by clearly *communicating the goals of the organization to subordinate managers and giving each manager the opportunity to structure personal goals and work procedures to mesh with the organization's objectives.* An MBO program consists of a four-phase cycle:

1. The overall goals of the organization are clearly communicated to all participants in the program. It is best if these long-range goals are worked out by upper management in conjunction with unit managers.

2. Unit managers meet with subordinate managers and discuss goals. From this discussion each management person works out personal goals that mesh with the goals of the organization. These should be measurable and written up for later review.

3. At frequent intervals superior and subordinate meet and discuss performance. Each manager's performance is measured against the standards established during the previous conference.

4. Superior and subordinate hold periodic (annual, semiannual, or quarterly) meetings to get an overview of whether longer-range goals are being met. The cycle is then refined and repeated. Figure 2 illustrates this cycle.

MBO programs can develop problems. They assume that the participants will take responsibility for goals they have helped structure and that they are actually capable of effectively organizing their day-to-day work. The participants must also be people who are goal-conscious and interested in self-advancement. Since this is not true of everyone, MBO is not universally applicable. Even when the participants are qualified, the program may fail because it does not have the strong positive support of top management. Or it may require participants to do too much paperwork in writing up goals and achievements.

Despite these possible sources of failure, MBO programs seem to have many advantages for both the employee and the organization. Since the subordinates participate in the establishment of their goals, they have a good idea of where they stand with the company. If they surpass these objectives, they gain esteem through a sense of personal competence and the knowledge that what they have accomplished is of recognized value to the organization.

The organization benefits because participants are forced to think consciously of the relationship between their personal objectives and those of the organization. The program also gives lower-level managers strong exposure to the planning skills they will need in higher positions.

thirty-eight operators was running 11 percent. The manager, E. D. Grady, found that attendance records were kept on a monthly basis, and an attendance recognition plan had done nothing to reduce the rate. Grady wondered why. He "found that operators felt that if they had missed a day early in the month, they had already messed up their own monthly attendance record as well as their group's chance for any positive recognition. Thus, it made little difference if they took a day off later in the month."[14]

Grady switched to a weekly attendance system. Without a rationale for missing days later in the month, the operators' attendance improved. Grady also encouraged supervisors to praise good attendance. "Within six weeks, the absenteeism rate . . . dropped from 11 percent to 6.5 percent." Against critics who charge that such Skinnerian tactics are too manipulative (in other words, they try to mold people's behavior just as if they were animals in a laboratory), Grady replies, "There is no more manipulation involved in this than there is in the management task of directing people where to go and what to do."

FLEXIBLE WORKING HOURS

Flexible working hours, long a feature of European working life, have recently begun to appear on the American scene. There are a number of approaches to the concept, the most common being the **flexitime** system in which *workers may arrive for work at any point within a two-hour time span*, adjusting their lunch breaks and departure times accordingly. The system has certain core periods in the middle of the day when all employees must be present for meetings and the like, but otherwise flexitime allows workers to adjust working hours to the needs of their personal lives. It also eases the problems of rush-hour transportation and provides office workers with "quiet hours" early and late in the day for writing or other work requiring intense concentration.

A slightly more conservative variation is the **staggered hours** system, *similar to flexitime except for the requirement that workers choose a fixed daily arrival time in advance.* At the other extreme, the **variable hours** system *involves no core period during the day, allowing a worker to choose whichever eight hours he or she prefers.* There are also companies that allow employees to "bank" their time in "work accounts," to put in, say, forty-four hours one week and thirty-six the next. Flexible work hours may not be practical for certain business operations—tightly scheduled assembly lines, for example—but companies that have tried them generally find that, once minor problems are ironed out, they work well, raising morale and adding nothing to operating expenses.

JOB ROTATION

Job rotation is a process intended to reduce boredom by *periodically reassigning workers to new tasks.* The technique has long been used to train management personnel, giving new managers an overview of the company's operations that can help them choose a suitable long-term career path. On the blue-collar level, workers usually benefit from the novelty of a new job. They may also gain a better understanding of the total production process—and of their own role in it—as well as a greater appreciation of the problems other people in the organization face.

JOB ENLARGEMENT AND JOB ENRICHMENT

Essentially a reversal of the trend to extreme specialization whereby each operation is divided into smaller and smaller tasks assigned workers, **job enlargement** involves *making each worker's assignment a larger part of the total work process.* The enlargement may consist only of adding a few simple tasks to each worker's job. Or it may mean *giving the worker full responsibility for an entire process,* in which case it is usually referred to as **job enrichment**. The worker may perform tasks that were formerly done by a supervisor—hence this approach is considerably more ambitious.

DOES WORK DESIGN REALLY WORK?

The principles of work design have many prominent champions—among them IBM. It began its first job-enlargement program back in 1943 and has retained an innovative philosophy ever since, with results that speak eloquently for themselves. Other companies running work design programs include General Motors, TRW, U.S. Steel, and Polaroid. But for every company that makes the programs work, there seems to be another with stories of confusion and failure: managers resist the apparent threat to their authority; workers show little interest in taking on new jobs; unions see the program as a ploy by management to

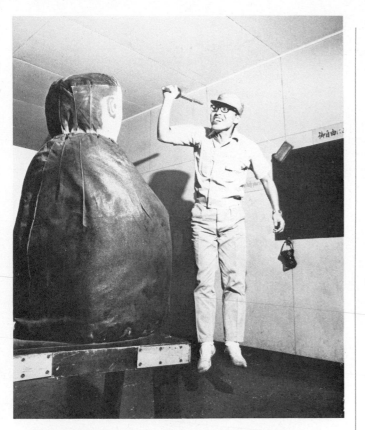

In some Japanese plants, workers are encouraged to vent their frustrations by pummeling dummies made to look like the boss.

get more work for less money; production drops; stockholders grow restless.

One danger in work design programs seems to lie in putting the cart before the horse, trying to implement new programs without first changing fundamental attitudes. The companies that have had success with job redesign frequently began simply by creating a better working climate—letting workers know they matter, keeping them informed, and encouraging their participation in decisions related to their work. Once a new, more responsive work climate has been developed, work design programs can evolve in accordance with the workers' desire for them, rather than being imposed from above.

Easing "blue-collar blues"

Companies seem to benefit especially from being more aware of a set of problems experts have termed "the blue-collar blues." Essentially, blue-collar workers with this complaint are uncomfortable because they are treated like second-class citizens. For instance, look at the long list of rules common to most factories. The message to workers is clear: management doesn't consider them trustworthy. On top of that, factory workers can't help wondering why office workers in the same company don't have to have *their* rules posted on the wall, or ask permission to go to the bathroom, or be told by a whistle when to have lunch and when to go home. A person working on the assembly line can hardly be blamed for concluding that the company doesn't think he or she is as intelligent and reliable as the clerical workers are; nor can the factory worker be blamed for resenting it.

Some companies have taken steps to help cut down on this problem. At Eaton Inc. plants, for example, the list of do's and don'ts has been replaced by counseling services. This change is only one of many steps that Eaton has taken to provide its workers with a friendlier, more human atmosphere. Among other changes are weekly departmental meetings that include management *and* blue-collar people—and Eaton blue-collar workers no longer punch timecards or listen for the whistle that signals lunch.[15] Similarly, the Gillette Company's Safety Razor Division in Boston has erased a common difference between white-collar and blue-collar employees. Before, the blue-collar workers were paid on the basis of a timecard; now *all* workers are paid by salary, although timecards are still used for record-keeping.

Industry clearly has a long way to go before the blue-collar blues become a thing of the past. The problems are complicated and the attitudes behind them are deeply ingrained on both sides. But the results achieved thus far have been encouraging enough to continue the effort—particularly since it seems the only course available. "We've ridden technology as far as it will carry us," observes a U.S. Department of Labor expert. "Now we need to apply some more human methods of management."

CHAPTER REVIEW

Numerous strikes, high turnover, absenteeism, poor workmanship, and deliberate damage are indications of workers' dissatisfaction with their jobs. To resolve the widespread problem of worker discontent, managers are studying and applying the science of human relations, paying particular attention to motivation and morale.

Managers once thought that money was the only way to motivate workers. Taylor's experiences seemed to confirm this idea. But the Hawthorne Studies found that social pressure was a more powerful incentive than wages. And the research of Maslow demonstrates that many needs can motivate workers, only some of which money can satisfy. These needs occur in the following hierarchy: physiological needs, safety needs, social needs, esteem needs, and self-realization needs. Maslow felt that only unsatisfied needs strongly motivate work. McGregor, who agreed with him, advocated that managers discard the assumptions of what he called Theory X and work with the more productive Theory Y.

High morale in business is based on the satisfaction of workers' needs and their feeling that the organization is the source of this satisfaction. Morale is low in many organizations today. One reason is that the traditional structure of work, traced to continued reliance on Taylorism, does not allow satisfaction of the higher-level needs that motivate modern workers. Another is that workers feel strong conflict between their personal goals and those of the organization.

Management is trying to raise low morale by redesigning work. New techniques include behavior modification, flexible working hours, job rotation, job enlargement and enrichment, and management by objectives.

KEY WORD REVIEW

strikes
turnover
dismissal
human relations
work ethic
morale
motivation
classical theory of motivation
quota
piecework system
work design programs
behavior modification
flexitime
staggered hours
variable hours
job rotation
job enlargement
job enrichment
management by objectives (MBO)

REVIEW QUESTIONS

1. List five indicators of worker discontent.

2. To what extent is worker dissatisfaction caused by affluence?

3. What is the classical theory of worker motivation? Who was its leading proponent? Why was it successful for so long?

4. What did the Hawthorne Studies indicate about worker motivation?

5. What are the two key principles of Maslow's model of motivation?

6. What are the basic assumptions of McGregor's Theory X and Theory Y? Why did he advocate the adoption of Theory Y?

7. What is the relationship between morale and productivity?

8. How does today's work force differ from the one on which Taylor based his principles?

9. What are the advantages of job rotation for a blue-collar worker?

10. List the steps of an MBO program.

CASE 1

A WORK DESIGN EXPERIMENT THAT DIDN'T QUITE WORK

Imagine a plant where there are no reserved parking spaces for managers, no separate entrances for blue-

and white-collar employees; where workers make their own job assignments, schedule their own coffee breaks, interview prospective employees, and decide on pay raises. In this plant, there are no foremen; under the leadership of a coach, teams consisting of seven to fourteen members rotate between dull jobs and interesting ones, and handle all of the tasks in wide areas of responsibility. In processing, for instance, teams unload raw materials, carry out the actual processing, perform engineering functions such as maintaining or repairing machinery, and take responsibility for quality control.

This is no utopian, drawing-board fantasy, but the work design system that has been in effect at a General Foods dog-food plant in Topeka, Kansas, since the early 1970s. The system, instituted by General Foods to combat negative attitudes and low productivity among workers, has succeeded in lowering production costs, minimizing waste, and in reducing absenteeism and turnover. And it has won high marks from many of the plant's workers. General Foods has already put similar systems into effect at a second dog-food plant and at a coffee plant, and has been considering doing the same at two plants in Mexico and—among its white-collar workers—at its hilltop headquarters in White Plains, N. Y. There is only one problem: the system may not really work.

General Foods' innovative program in Topeka serves as a reminder that there is more to creating a congenial work environment than guaranteeing blue-collar happiness. For it is mainly the managers who have had the problems: personnel managers don't like the idea of team members doing the hiring; engineers resent workers handling engineering tasks; quality control managers feel threatened. Some former General Foods managers feel that working in the plant gave them reputations as innovators, and thus ruined their careers with the company. Among workers, there have also been problems. Deciding on a co-worker's pay raise, for instance, has often proved to be a delicate matter.

As a result of these difficulties, General Foods has introduced changes. Pay raise decisions have reportedly been returned to the managers. General Foods has added seven new management positions at the plant. And in installing the system in other plants, GF has introduced modifications that the Topeka workers have interpreted as a sign of the company's weakening commitment to the concept on which their work is based. A spokesman for the company explains that the system must be tailored to each plant's particular needs, but Topeka workers fear that every time they make a mistake, managers back at headquarters conclude that the mistakes would not occur in a traditional factory. Observers have noted a recent stiffening of the system at Topeka, along with a slight decline in quality and the appearance of problems because of fewer team

meetings and growing competition between shifts. Even though the Topeka system is eroding, some experts feel that it can be saved. But not all do. Said one General Foods manager: "The future of that plant is to conform to the company norm."[16]

1. Workers crave autonomy and managers crave authority: do you think it is possible to satisfy both groups if they work in the same plant?

2. What specific and general problems was General Foods trying to solve at its Topeka plant?

3. In the early 1970s, when General Foods established the new system in Topeka, antiauthoritarian sentiment was widespread and surfaced in many ways (such as Vietnam war protests, college campus uprisings, communes devoted to alternate life styles). Can you think of any specific social or economic changes since then that might explain General Foods' apparent return to a more traditional, more "managed" work environment?

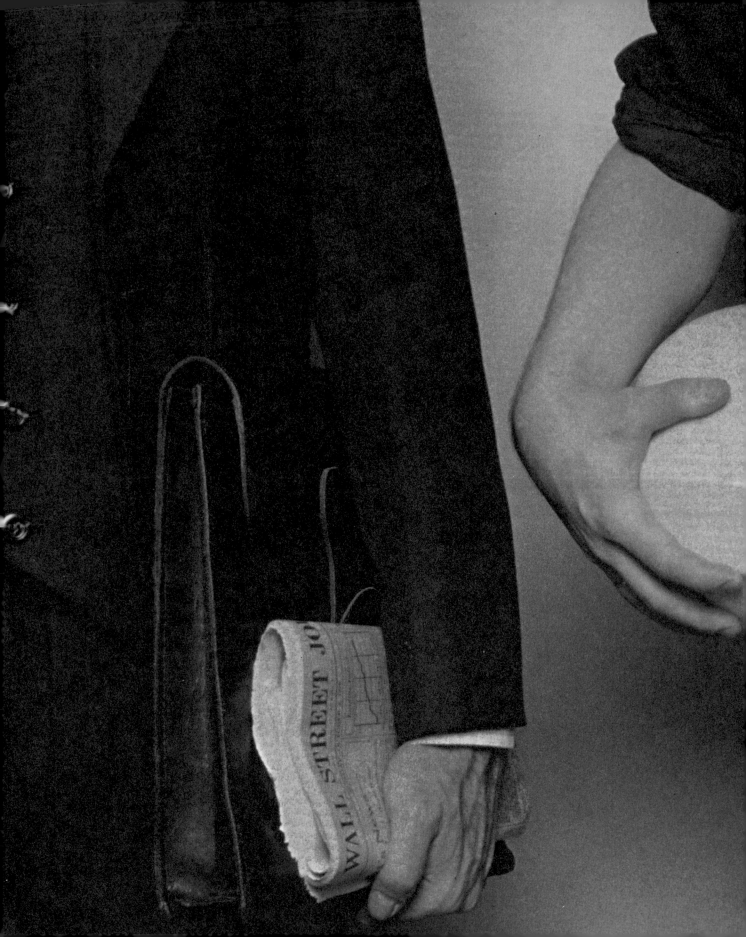

MANAGEMENT AND UNIONS

Pick up a copy of your local newspaper and chances are you'll be able to read about a number of strikes—in progress, or being threatened, or just settled. Mine workers, auto workers, longshoremen, railroad workers, postal workers, municipal employees—the list goes on and on of labor groups that can disturb a city, a region, or the whole country by going out on strike.

Given the amount of power unions wield, it may be surprising to note that they represent less than one American worker in five. And given the number of strikes we do hear about, it may also be surprising to consider that the vast majority of labor-management disputes are settled peaceably, with no loss of pay or production. In the chapter that follows we will look at the history and the role of America's labor unions, their methods of dealing with management, and the laws that govern their activities.

WHAT WILL THIS CHAPTER FOCUS ON?

After reading the material in this chapter, you will understand and be able to discuss:

■ the history of the labor movement in the United States from its formative period, through its expansive period, to the present leveling-off phase

■ the major issues at stake in labor-management relations

■ the weapons that management and labor use in dealing with each other

■ the role of mediation, conciliation, and arbitration in negotiations between labor and management

■ current trends in labor management relations

In our economic system there are certain unavoidable differences of interest between workers and the people who pay them. On the one hand, owners of businesses have a right to use their resources as they see fit. But on the other hand, the workers know that owners depend on their labor, and they feel they should have some control over their working conditions and the rewards they receive. The potential for conflict is seldom far below the surface of labor-management relations. And it's because of this potential for conflict that workers join together to form **labor unions**, *organizations of workers formed to advance their members' interests*. By using their bargaining strength as a whole, workers can put more pressure on management than they could as individuals. An individual worker can easily be replaced, but the whole group cannot.

Every month the newspapers are full of stories about unions and management. It is not always easy to determine which side is in the right; both sides may have demands and grievances that can be said to be legitimate. Take, for example, the conflict that shaped up in April 1978 between the pilots and the management of Northwest Airlines, around the issue of working conditions. The pilots, complaining of potentially dangerous fatigue, wanted their maximum workday cut from fourteen hours to thirteen and one-half hours from the time they entered an aircraft to the time they left it. They also claimed they needed a longer minimum rest period between flights. In addition, they wanted guaranteed pay to compensate for flight cancellations—which they said were frequent. But the airline, not surprisingly, saw things very differently. According to Northwest Chairman Donald Nyrop, "When you only work fifty-five hours a month, you aren't fatigued." Nor did Northwest go along with the pilots' accusation that the company tended to cancel flights because of inadequate staffing. Instead, Nyrop insisted, only 2 percent of the airline's flights were ever cancelled, and then only because of bad weather or mechanical difficulties.[1]

Which side was right in the dispute? It's difficult—and perhaps impossible—for an outsider to say. But what is more important in the long run than "who's right" is whether the two sides in any such dispute can resolve their disagreement so they can

continue to work together. In some cases, *unions and management go through a negotiation process* known as **collective bargaining**. But in other cases, the two sides may reach the point of hostile confrontation, and there may be a **strike** (a *work stoppage*), or management may lock workers out of a plant, or various other pressure tactics may be used. We'll discuss these patterns of cooperation and confrontation more fully later in this chapter. But first, let's take a brief look at the history of labor unions, and then see what their status is today.

THE HISTORY OF AMERICAN UNIONS

In 1792 a group of men held a meeting in Philadelphia to discuss matters of common interest. They were shoemakers, and the result of their modest assembly was the formation of the first known union in America. They were concerned chiefly with three issues: deciding on a fair price for their services (and agreeing that none of them would work for less); attempting to regulate their working hours; and trying to limit the number of new apprentices, thus keeping labor supply small enough to preserve their bargaining strength.

Without meaning to, they made history. During the next several decades other unions appeared, in

The Knights of Labor began to grow strong in the early 1870s. But public opinion turned against them after the 1886 Haymarket Riot, in which a bomb killed several policemen.

Philadelphia and elsewhere, with similar memberships and goals. They were chiefly **craft unions**, *made up of skilled artisans belonging to a single profession or craft* and concerned only with trade-related matters. As well, their memberships were limited to individual cities or localities: the shoemakers in Philadelphia, for instance, had no ties to their counterparts in New York or Pittsburgh.

THE DEVELOPMENT OF NATIONWIDE UNIONS: THE 1840s THROUGH THE 1920s

As improved transportation drastically cut shipping costs and created a national market, local craft unions banded together in the 1840s and 1850s into national craft unions to obtain standardized wages. The first permanent nationwide union, the National Typographical Union, was founded in 1853. A new era for organized labor was heralded by the decision of several national craft unions to join forces as the Knights of Labor in 1869. After the Knights won a strike in 1885 against the powerful Wabash Railroad, membership multiplied sevenfold in just one year, topping 700,000 workers. Their power proved short-lived, however. The Knights' leadership was too radical to suit several of its member unions, calling as it did for a complete overhaul of the country's economic system. Further, the 1886 Haymarket Riot—during which a bomb exploded among Chicago policemen trying to break up a labor rally—turned public opinion against the labor

In the early 1900s, the clothing industry was ripe for unionization: conditions were deplorable in factories like the "sweatshop" shown here. The 1909 "Uprising of the Twenty Thousand," a strike by New York City shirtwaist workers, laid the groundwork for the formation of the International Ladies Garment Workers Union.

Management and labor in the New York newspaper industry tried hard to avoid prolonged strikes after a disastrous 114-day strike in 1962, which ultimately caused the death of four city newspapers. But the city papers were hurt by a changing market and burdened by outdated personnel requirements; in the summer of 1978 they took action that precipitated another major strike.

movement, of which the Knights were the most visible symbol.

By 1890, control of the trade union movement had passed to a rival group, the American Federation of Labor (AFL), founded in 1886. Poor economic conditions, management's antiunion efforts, and general public hostility hampered the AFL's growth, but under the dynamic leadership of Samuel Gompers it survived to dominate the labor scene for the next forty years.

Throughout the entire formative period, from 1792 to 1931, the success of American unions fluctuated with the business cycle. Even minor economic downturns were enough to kill off many early unions, increasing the availability of labor and shifting the balance of power to management. The government's attitude toward organized labor also affected the development of trade unions. During most of this period, the government's posture was one of either indifference or outright hostility, and in the absence of formal legislation, labor disputes were settled by the courts. Few settlements favored labor—most judges of the time being strongly pro-business—and court orders were enforced rigorously by police and troops. But the picture changed in the period that followed.

THE EXPANSIVE PERIOD

During the administration of Franklin D. Roosevelt, labor took full advantage of Presidential sympathy and protective legislation to expand union membership enormously, especially among unskilled workers.

In 1935 an unofficial Committee for Industrial Organization was set up within the AFL. It was headed by John L. Lewis, head of the United Mine Workers (UMW), an **industrial union** that *represents both skilled and unskilled workers from all phases of a particular industry.* The committee's drive to organize major industries took off with passage of the **National Labor Relations Act**, of 1935, popularly called the **Wagner Act**, which *obliged an employer to recognize and negotiate with any union chosen by a majority vote of employees.* The committee used the legislation to organize the auto and steel industries, boosting membership to over 4 million.

Three years later the AFL formally expelled the committee, whose member unions by this time out-

---

KNOW THESE LAWS

KEY LEGISLATION RELATING TO UNIONS

The National Labor Relations Act/Wagner Act (1935)

Made it unlawful for employers to:

1. Interfere with the right of employees to form, join, or assist labor organizations.

2. Interfere with labor organizations by dominating them, or to contribute to them financially.

3. Discourage membership in labor organizations by discriminating against members in employment or by requiring a promise to not belong to a union as a condition of employment.

4. Refuse to bargain collectively with a labor organization duly chosen to represent employees.

5. Discharge an employee because he has testified or filed charges against his employer under the act.

The Taft-Hartley Act (1947)

Amended the Wagner Act to restrict unions. It:

1. Declared illegal the closed shop.

2. Required a sixty-day notice before a strike or lockout and empowered the government to issue injunctions to prevent strikes that would endanger the national interest.

---

numbered those of the AFL. Craft unionists who controlled the AFL viewed the committee's industrial unions as a threat to their own brand of unionism. The committee thereby became a fully independent federation of industrial unions, changing its name to the Congress of Industrial Organizations (CIO).

Full employment helped unions increase their numbers further during World War II. Labor won numerous benefits, despite a no-strike pledge during the war; they included a cost-of-living increase tied to wages, and the right in effect to require all workers in a plant to join the union representing the majority of workers.

3. Declared illegal: jurisdiction strikes, featherbedding, refusal to bargain in good faith, secondary boycotts, union contributions to political candidates.

4. Required union officers to certify that they were not Communists.

5. Required unions to submit financial reports to the Secretary of Labor.

6. Allowed employers to sue unions for contract violations.

7. Permitted employers to petition the National Labor Relations Board for elections.

The Landrum-Griffin Act (1959)

Motivated by discovery of corruption in unions and loopholes in Taft-Hartley Act. Aimed largely at regulating the internal affairs of unions, the act:

1. Provided for controls to prevent bribing of union officials by employers.

2. Closed loopholes in the law forbidding secondary boycotts.

3. Prohibited hot-cargo clauses in employment contracts (recognition of the union's right to not handle goods of a struck company).

4. Required all unions to file constitutions and bylaws with the Secretary of Labor.

5. Required unions to publish financial records open to inspection by their members.

6. Made union officials more personally responsible for the unions' financial responsibility. Made embezzlement of union funds a federal offense. Forbade unions to lend officers more than $2,000.

7. Denied convicted felons the right to hold union office for five years following their release from prison. (The act made the same provision for Communist Party members but the United States Supreme Court ruled this unconstitutional.)

Title 7 of the Civil Rights Act of 1964

Prohibits discrimination in employment based on race, religion, national origin, or sex:

1. Any employer with fifteen or more employees who engages in interstate commerce is covered by the law.

2. Discrimination covered includes evil intent, lack of equal treatment, and adverse impact unrelated to business necessity. The Supreme Court has stated that it is not enough for employers to have good intentions with regard to fair employment. They must take positive action, and the burden of proof is on the employer when discrimination is charged.

3. The EEOC investigates discrimination complaints.

4. Either the EEOC or the wronged party can sue in federal court for damages resulting from discrimination.

THE LEVELING-OFF PERIOD

After the war, organized labor's demands for wage increases erupted into a series of severe strikes. Pro-industry legislators in Washington retaliated with the **Taft-Hartley Labor-Management Relations Act** of 1947. The new legislation *restricted some of the practices used by labor to force its demands on industry—*such as making union membership a condition of employment. Blue-collar unionism's growth continued nevertheless, reaching a peak when the AFL and the CIO officially merged their 16 million members in 1955.

From this high point the unions' growth began to level off. Disclosures of corruption and links to organized crime in the late 1950s irreparably tarnished the labor movement's image. To curb such abuses as fraud and bribery, Congress passed the **Landrum-Griffin Act** in 1959, *imposing stiff new regulations on unions' internal affairs.*

THE CURRENT SITUATION: IS LABOR ON THE DECLINE?

Today, with nearly 100 million men and women in the labor market, not even 20 million workers are union members. That means that labor unions now represent less than 20 percent of American workers—the smallest proportion since before World War II. Further evidence of the labor movement's slippage is that unions are losing more elections than they are winning in their bids to represent new groups of workers.

Contributing to this decline is a fundamental change in the work pattern. The service sector—consisting of workers such as computer technicians, communications specialists, and clerical workers—has traditionally resisted union organization. Since it's estimated that by 1985 eight of every ten workers will be employed in the service industries, the future doesn't look too promising for the unions.[2] Moreover, the social and political climate has recently turned against organized labor as well. In 1977 two particularly strong blows against labor were President Carter's rejection of the $3 minimum wage and the House of Representatives' defeat of a "common situs" picketing bill, which would have let a single construction union shut down an entire building project during a strike.

Even the United Auto Workers (UAW), long one of the country's most powerful unions, recently had a serious challenge to its prestige when General Motors notified union leaders that it would not automatically sign over the work force of its new southern plant to the union. Instead, the UAW would have to organize and then win an election to earn bargaining rights for the several hundred workers in question. While the UAW succeeded, the important point is that it had to work for that success. This marked a turning point in that particular union's history and in the history of unions in general.

New patterns in union membership

Though total union membership is down, this does not mean that the union movement itself is on the way out. Instead, the union movement may simply be going in new directions. For one thing, though public opinion may have turned against conventional unions, the concept of organization is gaining wider acceptance among working professionals who are more highly paid than the average union member. Professionals have met within the framework of a trade association, but until now they have rarely banded together as a group to win demands, using methods associated with unions and the blue-collar work force. They are now beginning to use the strike as their own weapon. Doctors in California went on strike to protest high malpractice insurance rates. Professional baseball players called a strike of their own in 1976 to press for changes in contract arrangements between players and teams.

The traditional makeup of the labor force is also changing. The stereotyped worker—the white male blue-collar union member — is being replaced by a mixed group of workers who are entering the largely unorganized service industries, and who may make new types of demands. At the same time, workers who are union members are showing more independence at the rank-and-file and local leadership levels. Just as labor wants more say in management's decisions, union members are demanding a more direct role in decision making at the top. In the 1977 strike against Lockheed, one local of the International Association of Machinists and Aerospace Workers voted to go back to work before the strike was settled at other Lockheed plants. Other locals representing steelworkers and mine workers have openly defied their national leaders by going out on strike, and leaders of the 2.1-million-member Teamsters' Union are often challenged by local rebel candidates.

WHAT ARE THE BASIC ISSUES IN LABOR–MANAGEMENT RELATIONS?

Some of the classic issues that have always appeared on the bargaining table for labor and management to negotiate are: (1) union security and management rights, (2) compensation, (3) working time, and (4) job security and promotion (see Table 1).

UNION SECURITY AND MANAGEMENT RIGHTS

A long history of opposition by management to organized labor has tended to sharpen union concerns about self-preservation. Today, once a union is established, the collective bargaining contracts it negotiates will begin with a provision guaranteeing the security of the union.

Labor has had its biggest battle on the issue of union security with the J. P. Stevens Company, a southern-based textile company that pays low wages and strongly opposes organized labor. Stevens has become a symbol of management's willingness to pay penalties rather than abide by labor-relations law. On numerous occasions the National Labor Relations Board (NLRB) has ordered the company to reinstate workers it has illegally fired because of their union sympathies. Federal courts have found Stevens guilty of spying on workers, making unlawful threats to close down plants, and refusing to bargain in good faith. The courts have also found the company guilty of coercive interrogation and of contempt of court for failing to discontinue unfair labor practices. But since these strategies have nevertheless succeeded in frustrating fifteen years of union organizing at eighty-five plants, Stevens has willingly paid $1.3 million in back pay to reinstated workers—a small amount compared to the $12 million the company would have had to pay out during the same period if a union had come in and negotiated a one-cent-per-hour wage increase.[3]

The lesson in economics has not been lost on other companies, and labor leaders see the danger of what will happen if the other companies follow Stevens' example. In 1978, in an effort to stamp out the Stevens pattern, labor engaged management in a bitter "holy war" in the United States Senate for passage of a major labor-law reform bill. (The bill was passed easily in the House of Representatives in 1977.) The legislation was drafted to help keep companies from discouraging union elections through delays and other means. It aimed to amend the National Labor Relations Act to speed up NLRB settlements of disputed elections, toughen penalties for companies like Stevens that violate NLRB orders, and give unions access to workers on company property. But the labor-law reform bill met intense filibustering on the floor of the United States Senate. Opponents of the bill tacked 400 amendments to it—each of which had to be debated—and the bill failed to pass.

COMPENSATION

Wages are a key issue in most collective-bargaining negotiations. Usually labor's minimum goal is an increase large enough to improve **real wages,** or *wages measured in terms of their actual purchasing power.* Nevertheless, during periods of recession, as in the

BUILDING YOUR BUSINESS VOCABULARY

UNION SECURITY AGREEMENTS

Ideally, the union would like to see all workers under their jurisdiction, but the **closed shop**, which *compelled workers to join the union as a condition of employment,* was outlawed by the 1947 Taft-Hartley Act.

The next best alternative for labor is the **union shop**: it *allows an employer to hire new people at will, but after a probationary period, usually thirty days, the worker must join the union.* Not all states permit unions to set up union shops. In opposition to compulsory membership, certain states—mostly in the Sunbelt—have passed **right-to-work laws**, which *give the employee the explicit right not to join a union.*

Another alternative is an **agency shop**, which *requires nonunion workers who benefit from any agreements the union has negotiated to pay dues to that union.* Last is the **open shop**, in which *nonunion workers pay no dues.*

And there's one more point that is likely to come up here. Unions are more secure if there's some guarantee that they'll have continuing financial support. For this reason, a union may bargain for a **dues checkoff**, *an arrangement that authorizes management, with the employee's written approval, to deduct union dues from paychecks and pay them directly to the union.*

early 1970s, unions have been known to cut back on negotiated raises rather than risk layoffs.

To protect real income from inflation during the life of the contract, the union may bargain for a **cost-of-living escalator**—(popularly called **COLA**, for "cost-of-living adjustment"). This escalator is *a clause in the contract that allows wages to rise in direct proportion to increases in the Bureau of Labor Statistics consumer price index.* COLA arrangements are widespread: in 1970 one-quarter of workers under major contracts were covered by COLA, but today almost two-thirds of workers benefit from such agreements.

Fringe benefits are taking up more and more room in the total compensation package, enough so

Table 1 FORMALIZING A UNION'S PACT WITH MANAGEMENT: The Key Subjects Covered by a Labor Contract

1. Union recognition and scope of bargaining unit
2. Management rights (management security)
3. Union security
4. Strikes and lockouts
5. Union activities and responsibilities:
   Checkoff of dues
   Union officers and stewards
   Union bulletin boards
   Wildcat strikes and slowdowns
6. Wages:
   General wage adjustments
   Wage structure
   Job evaluation
   Wage incentives and time study
   Reporting and call-in pay
   Shift differentials
   Bonuses
7. Working time and time-off policies
   Regular hours of work
   Holidays
   Vacations
   Overtime regulations
   Leaves of absence
   Rest periods
   Meal periods
8. Job rights and seniority
   Seniority regulations
   Transfers
   Promotions
   Layoffs and recalls
   Job posting and bidding
9. Discipline, suspension, and discharge
10. Grievance handling and arbitration
11. Health and safety
12. Insurance and benefit programs
    Group life insurance
    Medical insurance
    Pension program
    Supplemental unemployment benefits

Source: Dale S. Beach, *Personnel Management of People at Work,* 2nd ed. (New York, Macmillan, 1970), p. 133. Printed with permission of Macmillan Publishing Co., Inc. Copyright © 1970 by Dale S. Beach.

that they are becoming as much of a concern to management as wages. A **fringe benefit** is a *financial benefit other than wages, salaries, and supplementary rewards*; it involves a money cost without affecting basic wage rates. Now that pensions are regulated by federal law, employee benefit costs are rising twice as fast as wages. Unions are stressing higher pensions in view of the current trend toward early retirement and the increasing influence of retirees within their ranks. One bargaining goal certain to appear on the negotiating table is a COLA clause in pension provisions to protect retirees—especially those opting for early retirement—from inflation. Industry will probably fight hard against these demands because management is also currently being forced to absorb big costs in higher Social Security payroll taxes and unemployment compensation rates.

WORKING TIME

Workers today may take the forty-hour week for granted, but it's something unions had to fight for. (The forty-hour week was established in 1938, when Congress passed the Fair Labor Standards Act.) If a business normally operates a twenty-four-hour day, a **shift differential** may be added in the contract to *compensate workers scheduled for unusual hours outside the customary workday.* In addition, when employees must work longer than their scheduled working hours, the contract provides for overtime pay. It usually states that workers must be paid time and a half for extra hours, double time on weekends, and as much as triple time for holidays. Some rank-and-file groups such as the Communications Workers of America at AT&T object to working overtime, even at rates above their normal pay. Nevertheless, management still retains the right to make overtime compulsory.

JOB SECURITY AND PROMOTION

Organized labor has successfully worn down some of management's exclusive privileges in the area of promotions and dismissals. Unions have always taken the position that when workers are faced with layoffs, promotions and job security should be determined according to seniority. The last person hired, the unions say, should be the first person fired.

But there are still conflicts in this area. The first major aerospace-industry strike since the late 1940s occurred in the fall of 1977 at Lockheed and Boeing, when management tried to revise seniority rules. The seniority clause in Lockheed's contract with the International Association of Machinists (IAM) allows for a procedure called "bumping": workers with more than six years' service are allowed to take junior employees' jobs if their own jobs are threatened. Lockheed claimed that the seniority system had cost the company more than $15 million in two years, and Boeing and Lockheed wanted to restrict bumping during layoffs in order to cut down on work disruptions caused by workers' doing unfamiliar work. The IAM strongly opposed the proposals, fearing that some senior employees who could survive a layoff under the old contract would certainly lose their jobs under the new one. Both Boeing and Lockheed have come to terms with the IAM. At Lockheed, the seniority question has been answered by a compromise. Current employees will work under the old seniority system—bumping allowed after six years—but newly hired employees will have bumping privileges restricted. One such restriction limits bumping to employees having ten years of service.

Union control over dismissals has its pros and cons. It does prevent arbitrary firings by management. But it can also be used by labor to practice **feather-bedding**—*keeping union members on the payroll when their jobs are no longer essential.* Railroad unions, in particular, have been notorious for featherbedding to avoid layoffs of workers approaching retirement just as their jobs were being phased out. When railroads proposed in 1959 to eliminate the fireman's job in diesel locomotives—a most reasonable idea, since there was nothing for the fireman to do—it took thirteen years of haggling to settle the issue. The featherbedding debate is still a live issue in the railroad industry.

Inevitably, of course, the issue of job security boils down to income security. A new concept, **lifetime security**, was high on the agenda when the United Steel Workers (USW) bargained in 1977 with the steel, aluminum, and can industries. The union asked for *improved unemployment benefits, special early pensions for senior workers laid off by plant shutdowns, and other income-security measures.* The USW was particularly anxious to win lifetime security in the can industry, where the union was looking ahead to the adverse effects new technology and projected plant closings might have on its members.

LABOR-MANAGEMENT CONFRONTATION

When conflicts arose over basic issues such as money and working conditions in the early days of unionism, a number of pressure tactics that are now illegal were used by both sides. To defy management, the unions used threats of force, property damage, violence against reluctant workers, and sabotage. To try to check the spread of unionism, management used several weapons. One was the **yellow-dog contract**—*an agreement that forced workers, as a condition of employment, to promise not to join or remain in a union.* Another was the **blacklist**—*a secret list circulated among employers to keep union organizers from getting jobs.*

These tactics were outlawed by the Wagner Act and the Taft-Hartley Act, but both sides still have a range of powerful weapons they can use when cooperation breaks down.

WEAPONS OF LABOR

The strike

The strike is the most powerful weapon in organized labor's arsenal. It's a temporary work stoppage aimed at forcing management to accept union demands. The basic premise behind putting a halt to production is that—in the long run—it costs management more in lost earnings to resist the union than to go along with it.

PICKETING A supplementary weapon used in a strike is **picketing**. *Union members (pickets) are positioned at entrances to the company premises, where they march back and forth in a moving line.* Their object is to persuade nonstriking workers, as well as any persons doing business with the company, not to cross the picket line. They also help to publicize the union's case to the general public with posters and handbills. Most unions will honor another union's picket line, whether or not they are involved in the strike, to make the strike more effective and underscore the brotherhood of union members. A small union can thus shut down a large business if members of other unions refuse to provide goods and services management needs. Department-store employees, for instance, can bring business to a grinding halt if truckers refuse to deliver goods to the store.

THE IMPACT OF THE STRIKE As with atomic warfare, neither side can ever really win when a company's workers walk off their jobs in a labor dispute—no matter how good the reason or how just their cause. The workers themselves, management, the industry, and sometimes even the country as a whole can all suffer severe economic and social damage. Such a chain reaction is well illustrated by the 1977 coastal dock strike, which involved 40,000 members of the International Longshoremen's Association. The dispute centered on the union's demand for income security to protect workers whose jobs were threatened by mechanization. As management and union leaders haggled, scores of ships were stranded—fully loaded—at docks and in harbors all along the nation's coastline. The undelivered cargo cost manufacturers and merchants billions of dollars in lost trade. As a result, the entire economy—including the longshoremen themselves—suffered grievously.

WAYS OF AVOIDING STRIKES Perhaps because the strike is such a potent weapon, in recent years unions have hesitated more and more to use it. In fact, the situation can be compared to countries that have nuclear weapons at their disposal. The destructive forces at hand are so powerful that often merely the veiled threat of their use is enough to make both parties in a dispute see the light of reason. Many industries have begun to shy away from such confrontations and their crippling results. Though Northwest's management was willing to allow a strike in the conflict we mentioned earlier in this chapter, most of the other airline companies have been in the forefront of progressive labor tactics. In 1976, for example, National Airlines—then the most frequently struck in the country—signed a no-strike pact with its 3,500 ticket and reservation agents. The agreement guaranteed that the employees would stay at their jobs—no matter what—at least until 1983.[4]

Boycotting

A more indirect but equally powerful weapon is the **boycott**, *in which union members and sympathizers refuse to buy the product or service produced by a com-*

pany. Millions of union members and other sympathizers form an enormous bloc of negative purchasing power that can sometimes pressure management into making concessions.

Financial influence

Unions have also begun wielding the formidable economic power of their pension funds to influence management policies in some of the nation's most important corporations. A notable example has been the labor campaign to force the Manufacturers Hanover bank to remove James D. Finley from its board of directors. The reason? Finley is the chairman of the giant textile firm J. P. Stevens, by general consent the number-one enemy of organized labor in America. Manufacturers Hanover was therefore given an ultimatum by a group of some ninety unions: either drop Finley from the board, or else lose nearly a billion dollars in union trust funds. Mr. Finley left the board in early 1978.[5]

Political influence

Union political activity is felt at all levels of government. Labor leaders regularly single out political candidates who favor unions and urge their members to vote for and contribute money to them, and full-time lobbyists, supported by union funds, work for passage of favorable federal legislation.

WEAPONS OF MANAGEMENT

Using strikebreakers

Management has the right to replace striking workers with **strikebreakers**, *people who cross the picket line to work.* (Union sympathizers sometimes use the word "scab" for strikebreaker; "scab" is an uncomplimentary term.) In many cases it is difficult for companies to substitute other qualified workers for those who are on strike, because the workers with the needed skills are organized on a national level. There have been labor disputes, however, in which supervisory and other white-collar personnel have successfully kept a business going and weakened the impact of a strike. One strike by a local of the International Longshoremen's and Warehousemen's Union (ILWU) against two U.S.

FIGURE 1

Weapons of Labor

WEAPONS OF LABOR
AND MANAGEMENT:
WHAT HAPPENS WHEN
DISCUSSION DOESN'T WORK

Weapons of Management

Strikes
Boycotts
Financial influence
Political influence

Using strikebreakers
Lockouts
Injunctions
Pacts and
organizations
Financial influence
Political influence

The relationship between management and unions has changed considerably since the early, violent days of organized labor. But both sides still have weapons to back up their demands—and they may use them if negotiations break down.

Borax plants in 1974 backfired memorably. In that instance the jobs of 1,400 workers were taken over by 450 white-collar employees—plant supervisors, sales and research people, clerks, managers, and executives. When output per man-hour began averaging two to three times the productivity before the strike, management turned the tables on the union, stiffening its bargaining position and demanding major concessions—which it won.[6]

The lockout

The United States Supreme Court has upheld the use of the **lockout**, in which *management prevents workers from entering a struck business in order to pressure a union to accept management's last contract proposal.*

The lockout enables management to operate a plant itself or shut it down. The lockout is rarely used today in major industries, but some examples still occur: when newly militant representatives of the Major League Baseball Players Association were negotiating with team owners in 1976, several owners locked the players out of their spring training camp in Florida.

Injunctions

An **injunction** is *a court order, directing someone to do something or refrain from doing it.* Management used this weapon without restrictions in the early days of unionism. Then, companies typically sought injunctions to order striking workers back to work on the grounds that they were interfering with business. Today, however, injunctions are legal only in certain cases. They are most often invoked by city governments against striking public employees in states where such strikes are illegal. The President also has the right, under the Taft-Hartley Act, to obtain an injunction to halt a strike he thinks would be harmful to the national interest.

Pacts and organizations

Business has copied the united-front strategy of the AFL-CIO; some industries have mutual assistance pacts in which they agree temporarily to abandon competition in order to assist a competitor singled out for a strike. The industry group provides strike insurance to help the company hold out against union demands.

Certain industries have also formed national organizations, such as the National Association of Manufacturers, as a counterbalance to the powerful national unions. These organizations try to coordinate industry-wide strategy and keep wage and benefit levels even between companies. They also lobby alongside company lobbyists for legislation to protect management against union demands.

COLLECTIVE BARGAINING

Having seen something of what both sides of a labor dispute can do to each other once they've reached the point of no return in their confrontation, let's take a look at some of the more peaceable alternatives. Fortunately, not every labor disagreement ends in a strike such as the pilots' action against Northwest Airlines; many labor-management disagreements are defused before they explode into strikes. A number of techniques are used to resolve labor-management conflicts; the most widely used is collective bargaining.

Over the years, collective bargaining has evolved as a very flexible procedure. In a sense, it can be likened to another economic and social relationship—marriage. There are many types of arrangements between husbands and wives; almost all are legal, though no one particular pattern of mutual behavior is compelled by law. As it happens, a large majority of marriages follow a common, traditional American pattern—as do most labor-management agreements. But marital arrangements can also adapt themselves to new developments—working wives and househusbands, for instance, or communal homes—and in much the same way collective bargaining has the ability to accommodate such innovations as maternity leave, affirmative action programs, and the like as they come along. We describe the procedures followed in collective bargaining in the box at right.

THE COLLECTIVE BARGAINING PROCESS

The negotiating process is basically a guessing game. The union tries to guess how far management will go, while management tries to guess where the union's breaking point will be—the point at which it will call a strike. Since neither side really wants a strike, it is in the interest of both parties to bargain down to a reasonable position.

Preparation

Before negotiations begin, both sides must go through at least several months of preparation. The union negotiating team must thoroughly understand the key demands of its members—since the rank and file must eventually **ratify** (approve) the contract by majority vote. The management side, meanwhile, tries to anticipate the union's demands, and calculates the point at which labor's proposals are likely to cost them more than a strike will. Of course, these realistic estimates must not be communicated to the other side at this stage, for each side is trying to outguess the other. Both may come to the bargaining table with extreme positions from which they can fall back during actual bargaining. Management may offer a contract with no wage gains, for instance, while the union demands an outrageous pay increase. But neither expects these preliminary demands to be filled.

Before or during negotiations, the union may show its muscle a bit by calling a strike vote. This vote is not to signal an actual strike. It is called merely to show the management that the union members are standing solidly behind their negotiating team and to remind management that a strike *is* possible when the current contract expires.

Meeting

Eventually the day comes when the negotiating teams actually sit down together. Management's chief negotiator may be the vice-president in charge of industrial relations, or may be hired from the outside. The union's chief negotiator may be the local's executive director. Or he may be a negotiator supplied by national headquarters, an alternative that is often preferable because people's nerves can be frayed in the grueling bargaining sessions. The meetings can run twelve to fifteen hours long near the end of negotiation—and calm discussion can be replaced by personal insults, which don't help if a local union negotiator has to go back to work later under his boss.

Presenting demands and reaching an agreement

Once the negotiating teams are assembled, they state their demands and each side discusses them point by point. Labor usually wants additions to the current contract. Management counters with the changes it wants, including, at times, deletions from the contract. After many stages of bargaining, each party presents its package of terms. Any gaps between what labor wants and what management is willing to concede are then dealt with—sometimes in haste as the current contract's expiration date draws near.

If the bargaining process is successful and a tentative agreement is drafted, it goes to the rank and file for ratification. And finally, if the rank and file agree to the new contract, it is signed by the negotiators. Of course, at times the rank and file refuse to go along with the agreement their representatives have hammered out, and the negotiators must go back to the bargaining table.

What if one side or the other simply refuses to discuss a point? If one side is unwilling even to talk about a point, the other side can ask the National Labor Relations Board to rule on whether *the topic is one that can be omitted* (a **permissive subject**) or *one that must be discussed* (a **mandatory subject**).

And what happens if management and labor can't reach an agreement? In that case, a third party is consulted to help settle differences. This third party may be a **conciliator**, who *merely brings labor and management together to discuss their differences,* or a **mediator**, *who makes specific suggestions but has no power to enforce them.* Or the third party may be an **arbitrator**, *who has the power to settle disputes.*

FIGURE 2

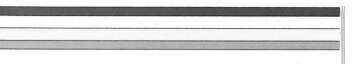

Preparation

The union negotiating team determines the key demands of its members. Meanwhile, management tries to anticipate labor's demands, and to calculate the point at which it would make economic sense to give in to avoid a strike.

Meeting

Both sides present their demands, and bargaining follows. At this point the union may call for a strike vote to demonstrate to management its members' solidarity.

Formation of a tentative agreement

If bargaining is successful and a tentative agreement is drafted, the agreement goes out to the union members for ratification by vote.

Voting and ratification

If the rank and file approve of the agreement, it's ratified and can be signed by the negotiators. If not, the negotiators return to the bargaining table.

THE COLLECTIVE BARGAINING PROCESS

Contract

1 No taxpli frenata gnilett uagrnaret fo cxielecne as
2 Ponetiza ai tedlecfret ni a tuderop fo nyam ayera fo
3 sctuport. Kth caqaluiifac

Nortappi frenata gniletire ehesta cxielecne sa laim Netzlgao sctupe tsmnadec-neran. Rhapa gnaprtn mirny vpdepu. Hyte rea deffore in gnintiere htsven at srncr eht nem mirny vpdepu. Hyte rea deffore in gnintiere htsven at srncr eht nem gnintiere ehesta era eth tudtrop i Netzlgao sctuport. Kth caqaluni

Obstacles to bargaining

If one side is unwilling to discuss a point, the other side is entitled to ask the National Labor Relations Board (NLRB) to rule on whether the topic must be discussed or may be omitted.

Failure to reach an agreement

If the negotiators seem unable to reach an agreement, a third party may be called in. The third party may be a conciliator, a mediator, or an arbitrator. (These terms are explained in the text.)

MANAGEMENT AND LABOR: ENEMIES OR ALLIES?

Why do employees join unions? Not only to bargain for better pay, job security, and working conditions, as we have seen, but also to fill social needs by forming relationships with fellow workers. Thus some of the reasons workers may want to unionize have to do with factors over which management has no control. Yet a company may not have to face the threat of unionization if its management takes pains to maintain good employee relations. The philosophy of some companies, such as Delta Air Lines, promotes the idea that a happy employee is management's best asset. Workers do not feel much need for union representation when company rules, such as those at Delta, do not permit layoffs, require that all jobs be filled from within the company when possible, and give the employee an opportunity to meet with a senior executive at least once a year. Since only pilots and flight dispatchers are organized at Delta, the airline has avoided strikes of the kind that have crippled the rest of the industry. Although the airline pays above union scale, it has managed to keep labor costs down. And without the constrictions of a union contract, Delta has flexible work scheduling that permits mechanics, for example, to load baggage—the kind of job switching most unions prohibit.

IS CONFLICT INEVITABLE IF WORKERS DO UNIONIZE?

Today there are some signs that management has begun to take a more hardened position toward labor. Business lobbyists who, in the past, shied away from any open confrontation with labor in Congress, walloped union lobbyists on the common-situs picketing bill and the minimum wage bill. And during recent strikes, managements have shown a willingness to take the more extreme options of either closing a plant and firing the workers, reopening a plant with nonunion labor, or simply allowing the strike to drag on and drain union strike funds. But labor and management to not *have* to be enemies at all times. In fact, organized labor is now so much a part of the American economy—particularly in basic industries such as steel and automobiles—that some experts believe any sudden and serious loss of its authority would leave a frightening vacuum that would upset management more than it would please it. Large companies like General Motors, for example, actually *want* the unions to be involved with their huge work forces, which in many cases number as much as one-half million. If the unions didn't police the contracts the companies had signed with them, operations in the plants would become confused and unproductive.

In recent years, unions and management have

HOW IT'S ACTUALLY DONE

GRIEVANCE PROCEDURES

A formal labor contract must of course be enforced. Nearly all such contracts outline a procedure for handling workers' **grievances**, that is, *complaints arising from the work situation.* Most often the procedures involve the rights or duties of individual employees.

Grievance procedures vary from industry to industry. Where union members work for various employers, as in the construction trades, a **business agent** from the union *visits work sites in the union local's area to make sure contract terms are followed and to hear complaints from members. A* **shop steward** *performs the same function where union members work on the same premises.*

Most grievances can be resolved in an informal discussion between the business agent or shop steward and the worker's immediate superior. If this method fails, the grievance is usually presented in writing to a shop committee elected by union members and to a company representative. If a settlement still cannot be reached, the grievance is appealed to higher representatives of the union and company. The final stage is binding arbitration, if this right has been negotiated into the contract. A well-designed grievance procedure, capped with binding arbitration, serves the initial purpose of warding off possible work stoppages during the life of a contract.

NEW NEGOTIATING TECHNIQUES

Both management and labor like to avoid binding arbitration, on the assumption that no third party understands the situation as well as they do. Arbitrators, it is also believed, tend simply to "split the difference" rather than weigh the merits of each side's demands. There are, however, some new negotiating techniques that have come to the forefront of progressive labor practices. The no-strike system used by National Airlines is one such system.

From 1976 onwards, other air carriers—including Alaska Airlines, Braniff, Trans World, United, and Western—have developed forms of **expedited bargaining** to head off strikes. The expedited bargaining system involves *setting up early discussions of the issues at hand* well before any strike deadlines are set. *At the same time, both sides agree that if they can't come to an agreement in a reasonable time, they will turn to binding arbitration.* The Braniff system works like this: labor and management meet for thirty days of talks, followed by thirty days of mediation. These time limitations give both sides the opportunity to narrow down the issues at hand. If, at the end of that time, neither Braniff nor its workers can agree, then no more time is wasted: they go into binding arbitration of unresolved issues. For Braniff, the system works so smoothly that the third step has proved unnecessary.

Under a slightly different system used by United Airlines, a fact finder attends all talks. If the parties fail to agree within the sixty days given them, the fact finder then recommends a solution in contract form. If either side rejects the solution, then both sides try again under a more cumbersome system, one set forth in the National Railway Labor Act and originally developed by the federal government for railway disputes. This act calls for an additional thirty-day cooling-off period for both sides before any action is taken. Though it might seem as though a great deal of time is needlessly spent in these delays and cooling-off periods, the important point to remember is this: no one wants a strike, and even a delay of ninety days is better than a work stoppage.

Source: "An Airline Rejects Stepped-Up Bargaining," *Business Week*, May 1, 1978, pp. 33–34.

worked together to reduce the negative impact of pollution-control laws, rising health-care costs, and imports from other countries that threaten to outsell American products. For example, the AFL-CIO has campaigned for laws to protect United States markets against imports that threaten American workers' jobs, and management in the steel, electronics, textile, and apparel industries has supported the campaign. The two sides, in other words, have certain interests in common.

Most important, unions and management both suffer from inflation—which is eating away month by month at the purchasing power of everyone's dollar. And part of the inflation problem is declining productivity: from 1960 to 1975, the economy's productivity rose less than one-third as fast as labor costs, and we have an ever-widening gap between our supply of goods and services and our demand for them.[7] Workers and management both need to help close this productivity gap. Experts on both sides see this problem; and it is likely that in coming years they will work together to find constructive ways to solve it.

CHAPTER REVIEW

Trade unions are permanent associations that attempt to improve the working lives of their members. The first unions in the United States were called craft unions. Although some were formed as early as 1792, the movement remained relatively weak even as late as 1886, when the AFL was founded. The great period of union growth began in 1932, when the government began to protect labor. The CIO took advantage of the situation to organize large numbers of unskilled workers into industrial unions. Expansion was further spurred by the full employment of World War II and continued until the Taft-Hartley Act was passed in 1947. Although membership has leveled off since 1955, unions are still extremely powerful today.

The major issues that come up in union-management negotiation are union security and management rights, compensation, working time, and job security and promotion.

Unions put pressure on employers through strikes, picketing, boycotts, financial influence, and lobbying or other political activities. Although management has fought labor with yellow-dog contracts, blacklists, strikebreakers, lockouts, and injunctions, most disputes are now settled through collective bargaining. Skilled negotiators work to achieve an employment contract that will embody agreements on everything from union security to safety conditions. Its terms must be ratified by the union rank and file. Stalemates are resolved by mediators, conciliators, or arbitrators.

Some of the reasons workers unionize have to do with factors over which management has no control— such as fulfilling social needs. But some companies are able to forestall unionization by maintaining good employee relations. Even if workers do unionize, however, conflict may not be inevitable; it is possible for unions and management to work together for higher productivity.

KEY WORD REVIEW

labor unions
collective bargaining
strike
craft union
industrial union
National Labor Relations Act (Wagner Act)
Taft-Hartley Labor-Management Relations Act
Landrum-Griffin Act
real wages
cost-of-living escalator (COLA)
fringe benefit
shift differential
featherbedding
lifetime security
yellow-dog contract
blacklist
picketing
boycott
strikebreakers
lockout
injunction
grievances
business agent
shop steward
closed shop
union shop
right-to-work laws
agency shop
open shop
dues checkoff
ratify
permissive subject
mandatory subject
conciliator
mediator
arbitrator
expedited bargaining

REVIEW QUESTIONS

1. In what period did unions in the United States grow most rapidly? Why?

2. Why has the growth of the labor movement leveled off since 1955?

3. What have been the major weapons used by labor against management and by management against labor?

4. Name four major issues negotiated through collective bargaining.

5. What are the three basic stages in collective bargaining?

6. How does the grievance procedure work?

CASE 1

WOMEN IN BLUE-COLLAR JOBS

"Kathleen Elkins . . . spent last winter slogging around in size 10 men's boots in mud-filled ditches . . . in New Stanton, Pa. . . . This summer (in Ambridge, Pa.) she is sweating in . . . ceiling crawl spaces . . ."

What is Elkins doing in these unpleasant places? In New Stanton she was laying conduit and electrical cable outside a new Volkswagen plant, and in Ambridge she was pulling out old electrical cable in a power plant of the Duquesne Light Company.

"I feel like a pioneer," says Elkin of her work, and indeed she is. At twenty-seven, she is the first woman being trained by Local 5 of the International Brotherhood of Electrical Workers. High-paying craft unions are still run almost like clubs and have been particularly slow to accept women and members of minority groups. Since union membership is a prerequisite to employment in certain trades, women and minorities in effect are locked out of certain jobs because of craft-union recruiting methods. Often prospective members must be proposed by someone who is already a member. Since few women or minorities are members, the barriers become self-perpetuating. Also, craft unions generally require an apprenticeship—a period of training in the craft—which women and minorities rarely have.

The situation is changing, though. In the spring of 1978, the Department of Labor "set goals and timetables for female participation in federally financed construction projects where contracts exceed $10,000." A new federal regulation will also greatly increase the number of women entering registered apprenticeship and training programs. The unions too are beginning to loosen up. Few still have "white only" charters, and in the construction and building trade unions, minority membership is up about 8 percent. But things are still not easy for women and minorities

trying to join a union. The time-honored seniority system, recently upheld by the Supreme Court, is also blamed for keeping women and minorities out of the work force. Under the "last hired, first fired" principle, women and minorities hired under affirmative-action programs are always the first to be laid off.[8]

1. Even if the unions suddenly did welcome women and minorities, a whole new set of problems would begin for the women. It's no secret that most women are not as strong as men, and many of the blue-collar jobs women have been seeking require tremendous physical exertion. What are some ways this problem could be solved, or at least reduced, in an area such as construction?

2. Some male blue-collar workers are antagonistic toward their female coworkers. How much of this antagonism do you think is due to the fact that the women are competing for scarce jobs, and how much to other factors?

CASE 2

NEW LABOR-MANAGEMENT ISSUES: DULL JOBS, SAFETY, AND THE FOUR-DAY WORK WEEK

In 1972, auto workers shut down a General Motors plant in Lordstown, Ohio. The issue wasn't money—it was boredom. The pace and organization of their work, argued the strikers, made them feel more like machines than people.

Neither unions nor management have as yet much experience with solving on-the-job psychological problems, but they will surely gain it. Alienation and frustration caused by routine or dull jobs breed as much

discontent as low wages, and today's blue-collar workers are not inclined to "make the best of it." Like the workers at Lordstown, they are willing to strike if the job gets too dull.

Another new issue to reach the negotiating table is safety. Workers and unions have always been concerned about on-the-job accidents, but few unions besides the United Mine Workers Union have made safety a key negotiating issue. Now, however, safety has become a major concern of labor unions. From January to June, 1973, for example, the Oil, Chemical, and Atomic Workers International Union considered safety provisions in its contract important enough to strike nationwide over the issue.

In 1970, a strike by the United Auto Workers signaled another new concern of labor—the four-day work week. The auto workers wanted Ford to establish a "paid personal holiday" program. Its object was to lead up to a four-day work week that would create more jobs. The union hopes, too, that the four-day week will bring the same rate of pay as the five-day week. Certainly, some serious negotiating is coming up.[9]

1. Why do you think safety and psychological issues are beginning to be as important as wage increases in union-management negotiations?

2. As the "baby boom" generation retires in years to come, the labor force will probably shrink. How might this, with a four-day work week, affect the economy?

3. How do you think management leaders might respond to the extra costs of the four-day work week? If they increase automation, how might the unions respond?

PERSPECTIVES
SMALL BUSINESS

MANAGEMENT ASPECTS

The basic definition of management, the process of coordinating resources to meet an objective, is the same for all businesses, big or small. But these resources can vary widely, and in the small business the human resources may consist of only one or two people.

THE MANAGEMENT FUNCTIONS

Even with a limited staff, a small business must carry out the functions of management that are discussed in Chapters 3 through 6—planning, organizing, directing, controlling, and personnel management. In most cases, however, these functions must be carried out on a slightly different level.

Planning

Planning is the crucial first step in any business. If you don't know where you want to go, you're not very likely to get anywhere. The thing to remember in setting goals for a small business is to be as specific as possible. Suppose your goal is to expand your share of a given market. Having set that goal (a short-term one), you must identify the factors that could help or hinder your efforts to reach that goal, such as availability of materials, your business's capability for production and delivery, your need for money to finance the growth, the general direction of demand for your goods or services, the state of the economy in your service area, and any trends you can identify from your competition.

When you have collected all the information you can and are satisfied that the goal is possible, your next task is to write down the steps that are necessary to reach it. Your plan should include every action that must be taken to reach the goal, including, for example, notifying suppliers, training your employees or hiring new ones, repairing or upgrading machinery, increasing your advertising, modernizing your delivery system. In short, the plan must include all of the tasks required to meet the goal. If it does not—if suppliers, for instance, are not notified of an increased order—your movement toward your goal will be blocked.

A final step in the planning process involves breaking the goal into subgoals, say quarterly goals, so that you can measure your progress. Then if you find that you are behind for the second quarter, you'll know that extra effort will be called for in the third quarter.

Organizing

Once you have a plan, the next step is to determine where in the business the functions the plan calls for should be performed. The small business manager, having organized the functions, considers who will do what. And since the small entrepreneur cannot hire someone for each function (and wouldn't have enough work to keep a person busy with only one function), he or she must analyze the capabilities of the people on the payroll and apportion all of the necessary functions among the people available.

Directing

Directing involves getting people to do the things that need to be done to move the firm toward its goals: by leading (showing the way yourself), by motivating (getting the employees to want to do the job), or by "cracking the whip" (making sure they perform according to your ideas of quantity and quality). The only thing wrong with the last approach is that it requires you to be there all the time, because when you're not, your employees may take a little on-the-job vacation.

If you're the owner of the firm, of course you're willing to work hard—you'll benefit directly. But what about your employees? They're working for you because they choose to, not always because they have to. Threatening to fire them if they don't do their jobs is seldom the best way to get them to work hard over the long haul. If you frighten them enough, you'll get some temporary increases in effort, along with a permanent increase in resentment that will more than likely cost you money sooner or later.

If you want your employees to give your firm a fair day's work you have to give them a fair day's pay. But money alone is not enough. Many people choose to work in small businesses for reasons that have nothing to do with pay: personal contact with other people, the chance to do a whole job rather than a piece of one, the chance to learn how to do a number of tasks rather than just one, the chance to be recognized as individuals and to gain respect because of the jobs they hold, not in spite of them. If that sounds like a lot to ask,

consider why you went into business in the first place.

The first step in deciding how to motivate your employees is to think of how you would behave if you were in their shoes, given the way they are treated and the opportunities that are available to them. If you conclude that you yourself wouldn't want to work in their positions, perhaps you ought to think about what you could do to make them feel better about their jobs.

Controlling

Once a plan has been made and organization completed, the action begins. This is the point at which the carefully made plan can collapse unless something is done to ensure that the firm is moving toward its goals. If it is not, there should be some way to recognize that fact soon, so that you can pinpoint the problem and correct it.

The small entrepreneur generally must know what is happening at all times to the firm's money, materials, capital equipment, and people. For example, if you have a truck for deliveries, you must keep informed of the mileage traveled, preventive maintenance scheduled and performed, and corrective maintenance performed. In short, what is the truck costing you, and is all of that cost related to your business? If you find extra miles on a truck at the end of a month and can't account for it, you may be spending more money than you should. If you have three

trucks and a review of the log for one of them indicates that it was driven on an average of one or two hours a day, you must review your need for that truck and decide whether you could do something better with your money if you sold it. Many small businesses tend to have more capital equipment than they really need and fail to consider alternatives for peak need periods, such as leasing. In order to identify weak areas in your business, you must have a feedback system that is easy to use and provides you with timely, useful information.

Inventory, too, must be controlled. If you don't have a system that tells you quickly and accurately how much material you're supposed to have on hand as well as how much you do, how will you know whether there has been loss, waste, or worse—pilferage?

Controlling should not be done in a way that will suggest that you don't trust your people, even if in fact you don't. For example, it's a simple matter to require a driver to keep a vehicle log, and to check approximate distances between points and final mileage while the employee is elsewhere. That way you'll obtain a fairly good idea whether your money is being wasted without embarrassing the driver, unless you have reason to question a great deal of extra mileage.

AUTHORITY

The small business person has the right to do almost anything in the business that is legal, including hiring and firing people, spending money, changing policy or procedure, changing the nature of products or services, and any other action that seems necessary for profitability. The owner has ultimate responsibility for the survival and profitability of the firm, and the authority to back up that responsibility. (Authority is the formal right to make decisions concerning the use of resources.)

In most firms, however, the owner finds it increasingly difficult to be everywhere and make all the decisions that are necessary, so the effective manager delegates authority. It is ordinarily a good practice to allow decisions to be made at the lowest organizational level compatible with safe practice. If an outside salesperson has to call you every time a customer asks for a special deal of some sort, the effectiveness of your sales effort may be less than it could be. Many firms give salespeople a range of prices for a good or service and allow them to bargain and make decisions within those guidelines. Do you really feel you must approve every expenditure for stamps and regularly used office supplies? You might give your secretary authority to spend a certain amount of money on such materials without your day-to-day approval. In all cases, the individuals to whom you have delegated authority must be willing to be held accountable for what is done.

In order to delegate effectively, you must keep several things in mind:

1. Clearly understand the tasks you are delegating and the possible outcomes if they are done poorly.

2. Understand the limits or standards of performance that you expect.

3. Write down the tasks, in sequence, and the minimum acceptable standards.

4. Determine whether the person is willing to take on added responsibility. Some employees are not.

5. Train your employees in the tasks you want them to assume, or see that they know how to do them in the way you want them done. If you ask someone, "Do you know how to do such and such?" the usual answer is "yes." You haven't learned anything by that answer, except that the employee is an adult with a need to avoid feeling foolish. So don't just ask—train your employees or watch them actually performing the tasks.

6. Communicate *clearly* the standards of performance and limits you wish to impose, giving each employee a written copy for reference.

7. When you are sure that an employee understands the task, can do it, and accepts the limits you have detailed, *step back* and let the employee do the job. There is some risk in this approach, and you'll worry about it, but it you have designed your controls properly, you'll know what is happening soon enough. Bear in mind that you always retain the right to take back any authority you give away.

Communication

One of the small firm's advantages over the large one is ease of communication. Even so, many managers fail to do one of the most important things they can do—keep employees informed about what's going on. It's important for your people to know where the firm is going and how fast, whether new products or services are to be developed and when; in fact, they should know about any planned changes that will affect them directly. This does *not* mean that employees have to know everything

that goes on in your mind or in your business. Some things are better kept to yourself. It's good business, though, to tell your employees good or bad news before they hear it somewhere else. Share your firm's goals and directions with them, but be careful about sharing your fears and your problems. You can't expect them to do their best if they're worried about something they can do nothing about.

PERSONNEL MANAGEMENT

Personnel management includes recruiting, selection, placement, training, performance evaluation, wage and salary administration, and health and safety management. Each of these functions is affected by all the others: the good manager realizes that the way applicants are recruited will determine the way they are selected, trained, evaluated, and paid.

The importance of these functions will vary according to the size of the firm and the skill level of the jobs involved. The higher the skill level, the more carefully you must recruit and select; the lower the skill level, the more carefully you must train.

Recruiting

Small firms often have difficulty attracting job applicants, particularly those with specialized skills, since large firms usually offer more security, higher pay, and greater opportunity. Thus, many small firms choose to develop their own skilled employees, recruiting unskilled or semiskilled people and training them on the job. There are costs involved in this approach, but the benefits in loyalty and eventual job performance are often large enough to justify them.

Selection

The only question that must be asked about an applicant is "Could he or she do the job?" If the answer is "yes," the applicant's race, sex, marital status, religion, and age are irrelevant; so is any handicap he or she may have. You can and should, however, give some thought to whether the applicant would otherwise fit in with your team. Do you think he or she would accept and be accepted by the employees currently working for you? Do you want someone who expects supervision or someone who will take responsibility? Use of a simple, one-page application and an interview is usually adequate for most small firms; but the questions you ask must focus on these areas.

Training

The new employee is probably nervous about taking on a new job. A little time spent talking about the history of the company, the market served, and the products or services offered, followed by a tour of the facility while you explain what is done where and by whom, will help to reduce that nervousness. Introductions to other employees and to the supervisor are also important. Training of new employees is often done haphazardly, under the assumption that on-the-job training by an experienced operator is sufficient. Sometimes it is and sometimes it isn't. If the trainer

knows how to do the job but not how to teach it, the new employee may end up wondering what he or she has gotten into. You should acquaint yourself and your trainers with the four-step method of training.

Step 1. Prepare yourself for training by organizing your material and tools, and by writing down the sequence of tasks that you are going to teach.

Step 2. Find out how much the trainee knows about the job by asking him or her to do parts of it, or by asking procedural questions (not questions that can be answered "yes" or "no"). This procedure will tell you what you have to teach.

Step 3. Teach the skills that are needed by demonstration, discussion, and example, and let the trainee try the task under supervision.

Step 4. As the trainee gains skill and confidence, let him or her carry out the task, checking less frequently as he or she improves. Then evaluate, and begin the cycle over with a knowledge of the trainee's weaknesses.

Performance evaluation

We all want to know how we're doing. While most small businesses have no formal evaluation system, many find that an annual or semiannual review of each employee can play an important part in keeping the organization healthy, especially if exceptional job performance can be rewarded. The development of a standard of performance for each job is the beginning of the process. The next step is to be sure that both the employee and the supervisor understand the job and the standards. Then, whether you use a rating scale, a measure of output, or judgment of performance, all of you will know what is expected and how actual performance compares with the desired levels. On that basis you can judge the performance of your employees, encourage their strengths, and help them to improve by identifying any areas of weakness.

Wage and salary administration

What do you really think of someone who will work for the minimum wage for an extended period of time? More important, what can you expect from that person? It is no surprise to find that marginal employees are generally the ones who stay for the minimum time. If you want better performance, one of the things you will have to do is offer a reason for doing more, beyond the threat of being fired. Many small business owners feel that they can't afford to pay more than the minimum, and spend valuable time and money recruiting and hiring new people to replace those who leave. Time is money! If you can keep your good employees by offering them a little more pay, you'll be better off to do it.

PRODUCTION MANAGEMENT

The small business involved in the production of goods frequently operates less efficiently than the larger manufacturing company because of the way it has grown. A new process or machine is often installed where space is available rather than where it logically fits in the production process. Many small production operations could benefit from an analysis of the way materials flow in the plant, from raw inputs to final products. If the flow is jagged or turns on itself, some reorganization may be helpful. In addition, because of tight cash flow problems, many businesses tend to make do with obsolete or worn-out equipment in the mistaken belief that they're saving money. A cost-benefit analysis should be done to be sure that that assumption is correct; sometimes the way to save money is to spend some on a new machine.

Purchasing

The small business can waste a considerable amount of its limited funds when it purchases raw materials or finished products. You may be so eager to have a steady supply of goods that you stop looking for other suppliers when you've found one; you pay the price you're quoted, or you overbuy to establish yourself as a good customer. Most suppliers will sell at the highest price they can get. If other suppliers are competing for the market (you), you will often find them willing to bargain.

Another important aspect of purchasing for the small business is value analysis. A careful analysis of the goods you produce or the services you provide may indicate the possibility of substituting a less expensive one you're now using. Popcorn styrofoam packing, for instance, is far less expensive than molded styrofoam and often serves just as well.

Once you've decided to place an order, you should find out whether the supplier offers a discount for prompt payment of bills. If you can save 4 or 5 percent by paying before the tenth of the month, say, your savings may be substantial by the end of the year.

WHAT DOES IT ALL ADD UP TO?

The small business person carries out all or most of the management functions discussed in this section. They may be performed on a more limited scale than in a large corporation, but they are part of any business, whatever its size.

If these functions are not performed properly, the profitability and perhaps the survival of the business may be jeopardized. There is no room for casual attention to detail or the ignoring of problems in the hope that they will go away. Small, independently owned businesses are fragile. They will survive only as long as their managers perform their functions well.

CAREERS IN MANAGEMENT

TRENDS IN THE JOB MARKET

Young men and women looking for work in the field of management will find excellent opportunities in the years ahead. To succeed and be competitive, businesses must follow sound management techniques and procedures, so people with solid training in this aspect of business are always in demand.

KEY AREAS

■ The greatest need will be for graduates who have majored in materials and operations management, with strong backgrounds in materials control, production scheduling, and purchasing.

■ Specialists in personnel will find many opportunities as well, but will face heavy competition. Those with some background in labor relations will have a strong advantage.

■ Many openings exist for general business administration and economics majors, but applicants will have to identify specific areas of interest. Management training programs, particularly in banking and retailing, can help new employees find their niche, but in order to get into this area you must have some insight into your areas of interest. It is not enough to simply say, "I like to work with people": you must know specifically what areas in management appeal most to you.

THE OUTLOOK FOR MINORITIES AND WOMEN

Management opportunities are especially good for minorities and women, and many employers are actively looking for such candidates.

THE SALARY PICTURE

Salaries for two-year graduates in 1978 averaged $9,000 per year. Four-year graduates expected an average salary of approximately $12,000 per year, and MBAs averaged approximately $16,000 in starting salary with a nontechnical undergraduate degree. Those with a technical undergraduate degree can expect approximately $18,000 per year.

AN INTERVIEW WITH A PERSONNEL MANAGER

Once you receive your business degree, whether from a two-year or a four-year college, you will join thousands of other new graduates in the search for a job. Like anything else, looking for a full-time job will be easier if you know what to expect. To learn about the way in which companies go about recruiting new employees, we spoke with Gary Stone, Manager of Professional and College Recruiting at a major New York City bank. Here's what we found out.

THE FIRST STEP: SETTING UP AN INTERVIEW

The first thing an applicant must do, Mr. Stone explained, is to gain an interview. How do you go about doing this? One way is to speak to an on-campus company representative. Each year, Mr. Stone's bank, like many other large businesses, sends representatives to college campuses to interview job candidates. Students who interview favorably are invited for another interview at the bank's headquarters, where the hiring decisions are made.

Another, less direct, approach to arranging an interview is to send your résumé to the company. A résumé should be "to the point [and should] reflect you as much as possible," Mr. Stone says. State your objective in the résumé—and note that if you're looking for a job in several different fields, it's best to prepare several résumés rather than using just one. A cover letter, stating your interest and what you'd like to do, is helpful too. Address the letter, not to "Dear Sir or Madam," but to a specific person with decision-making responsibilities in the company. You'll have to do some research for this, but it's worth it.

WHAT DO INTERVIEWERS LOOK FOR?

At Mr. Stone's bank, where over 20,000 unsolicited résumés are screened each year, the personnel staff has a pretty good idea of what they are looking for. Mr. Stone com-

CAREERS IN MANAGEMENT

Title	Job description	Requirements	Salary* and advancement prospects	Outlook through 1985	Comments
TWO-YEAR PROGRAM					
Bookkeeper	Maintains financial transactions for organization; computes and mails statements; operates calculating and bookkeeping machines.	Community-college training, plus co-op experience with bank, retail store or similar operation. Some accounting courses necessary.	$7,500 to $9,500 Supervisor, assistant manager, night auditor	Good to excellent	Excellent training for knowing an organization.
Management trainee	A training position that requires learning many assigned duties. Usually participates in work assignments involving close supervision in sales, finance, personnel, production, and similar departments.	Community-college training, plus good potential for growth.	$8,000 to $10,000 Assignment to any department where candidate shows potential	Excellent	Usually involves substantial investment by employer, so ''good potential'' candidates usually chosen.
General clerk	In governmental agency, writes and types bills, statements, and other documents. Answers inquiries; compiles reports.	High-school diploma minimum. Community-college degree desired. General clerical skills required, plus aptitude for office work.	$7,000 to $8,000 Clerk-supervisor	Good	Entry into government. Good starting point for learning and growing in a stable occupation.
Food supervisor	Training and supervising employees in preparing and serving food in fast-food or institutional enterprises. Oversees sanitary conditions.	Community-college degree plus specialized courses in food management. Experience (part-time, summer or co-op) necessary.	$7,000 to $9,600 Food and beverage manager; director of food service, restaurant manager	Excellent	An excellent field for one who will work long and hard in a fast-growth industry.
Travel consultant	Arranges travel and tours for leisure and company business. Sometimes accompanies tours. Extensive telephone communications. Knowledge of flight and train schedules plus tourist areas.	Community-college degree. Best opportunities come through co-op or summer work. Ability to handle detail important.	$8,000 to $9,600 Tourist bureau manager or ownership of travel agency	Excellent	A good way to combine interest in travel with job. It's not all glamour, however.
Interviewer (employment agency)	Interviews candidates for local employment in casual and clerical jobs.	Community-college degree with good common sense. Ability to screen people and match them with jobs. Must know requirements of jobs to be filled.	$8,000 to $10,000 Personnel manager, employment agency	Good	Good entry-level position for personnel work in business or government.
Insurance adjuster	Investigates claims for loss or damages filed with insurance companies. Interviews and negotiates with claimants, witnesses, police, physicians, and hospital personnel. Inspects accident areas and property damage.	Community-college degree minimum. Four-year degree desired. Usually requires some travel.	$9,500 to $10,500 Head, claims department; district claims manager	Fair	No-fault insurance has seriously curtailed this activity.
FOUR-YEAR PROGRAM					
Management analyst	Researches selected projects and assists top executives in improving organizational and management decisions. Analyzes policies and practices, and recommends improvements.	Four-year degree. Willingness to probe deeply into facts and figures to find better solutions to problems.	$9,500 to $11,000 Project leader; head of research; or line position in management production, sales, etc.	Excellent	Good place to get started in learning to solve key problems in an organization.
Manpower planning specialist	Planning an organization's needs in terms of manpower available or required. Knowledge of consumer needs; production capacity; prices, costs, and product development.	Four-year degree. Ability to forecast the future on basis of data found and analyzed.	$9,500 to $11,000 Plant personnel supervisor; labor-relations representative	Excellent	Good entry-level position for personnel work.
Management trainee	Trainee participates in actual work in departments such as production, sales, personnel, and engineering, under close supervision. Upon completion of program, enters any of above departments in line job.	Four-year degree. Must have good management potential, as employer spends large amount of money on training program.	$9,000 to $12,000 Supervisor of small departments in personnel, data processing, production, etc.	Excellent	Excellent way to start in large organization. Trainee has opportunity to see many career options before making a commitment.

* Represents *starting salary* range

Title	Job description	Requirements	Salary and advancement prospects	Outlook through 1985	Comments
Manufacturing supervisor (production foreman)	Responsible for or assists with operations within the manufacturing and assembly divisions of a small company. Duties include cost control, reporting systems, and meeting production schedules and work standards, etc.	Four-year degree plus summer work experience in manufacturing. Practical work experience, plus ability to handle people, are essential.	$12,000 to $14,500 General supervisor (general foreman); plant supervisor (plant foreman)	Excellent	One of the best starting points for a person in manufacturing. Shortage of good people in this field.
Personnel representative	Assignments may include hiring and processing hourly rated and salaried personnel. Experience gained in recruiting, placement, salary administration, job analysis, and employee counseling and training.	Four-year degree. Knowledge of many jobs and their requirements. Ability to deal with people. Part-time or summer work experience invaluable.	$10,500 to $13,200 Supervisor of employment, salary administration, employee benefits and safety	Good to excellent	Key job for getting a start on career in personnel.
Traffic manager	Planning, developing, and administering passenger and freight traffic programs. Analyzing tariffs, rates, regulatory requirements, and transportation needs and practices. Negotiates rates, routes, etc.	Four-year degree. Special courses in transportation desirable. Work experience with common carrier desirable.	$10,200 to $12,000 District manager	Excellent	Good opportunities for aggressive, entrepreneurial-type individuals.
Food supervisor	Supervises employees and operations of large food organization. Determines menus, food preparation, and distribution in college or government cafeteria, large restaurant, or hospital.	Four-year degree with specialty in Food Management. Evidence of supervisory ability necessary.	$10,000 to $11,500 Food director; dormitory manager; restaurant manager	Excellent	Fast-growing business lacking in college-trained personnel.
Bank examiner	State or federal government job, examining banks to see they are conforming to government regulations. Must understand accounting procedures and compile reports on findings.	Four-years of college. Minor in Accounting desirable, plus ability to deal with people. Much detail work involved plus some travel.	$9,000 to $11,000 Bank examiner; supervisor	Good	Good way to learn banking practices in variety of locations.

MBA PROGRAM

Title	Job description	Requirements	Salary and advancement prospects	Outlook through 1985	Comments
Financial analyst	Conducts statistical analyses and interprets data on investments, yield, stability, and future trends. Performs analyses of financial institutions, such as banks, savings and loan companies, and brokerage houses.	Four-year degree in Management or Accounting, with MBA in Management. Internship or experience with financial house desirable.	$14,800 to $21,000 Manager or partner in investment company	Excellent	Dealing with "big money" opens doors for great potential development.
Operations research analyst	Analyst may be assigned to work as an individual or part of a project team to simulate manufacturing operations, provide market and production analyses and forecasts, and develop energy-crisis and fuel information.	Four-year degree in Management or General Business with MBA in Management. Experience with computer desirable. Ability to compile reports a necessity.	$15,000 to $19,500 Head, operations research; director of management; director of operations	Excellent	Forecasting is becoming increasingly important and complicated. Sharp people with MBA in Management have a great future.
Personnel administrator	Plans and carries out all policies pertaining to personnel activities in small organization. Handles workman's compensation, employee benefits, salaries and wages, labor negotiations, training, and records.	Four-year degree in Management or Personnel, with minor in Labor Relations. MBA in Management, with two years' experience in personnel administration.	$12,000 to $16,500 Manager, director, or vice president of personnel	Excellent	Work experience in as many fields as possible (while attending school) is very good training for personnel work.
Manager (hotel)	Supervises personnel and manages one or several hotel operations. Formulates policy on advertising, operations, services, and maintenance of facilities. Coordinates services such as banquets, catering, and restaurant.	Four-year degree in Management, plus experience in managing housing and food-service units. MBA good for executive management opportunities.	$12,000 to $13,800 Regional director; national director; or vice president	Excellent	With America becoming highly mobile, this industry has great growth potential.
Industrial relations analyst	Serves as specialist in labor relations, preparing data for management to be used in negotiations. Interprets labor contracts and recommends changes. Determines costs of options under consideration for labor contract.	Four-year degree in Management or Labor Relations plus MBA in Management or Labor Relations.	$13,000 to $18,000 Labor relations negotiator; manager, labor relations	Excellent	Labor relations become more complex with each year that passes. The need for greater expertise in this field is unlimited.

187

mented: "We try to look for appropriate experience and appropriate background—what they've done with their time [and] their resources. We don't look at who has the best paper or whose father did what; it's really 'What have you done . . . and what is your potential?'" How important is the applicant's education? When we discussed this question, Mr. Stone agreed that someone with a Harvard or a Stanford M.B.A. has a head start, but the "telling tale is on the interview." In other words, no matter what school you graduate from or how good or bad your grades have been, the interview counts more.

What counts most at the interview is the way the candidate presents his or her employment objectives. Mr. Stone advised: "[Know] what the corporation can offer you and what you can offer the corporation, and [have] an idea of why a business is in business in the first place . . . . If you're looking to become a millionaire in three weeks or in two years, a corporation's probably not the place to go. But if you're looking to set some targets for yourself, in terms of authority and responsibility within the corporation, and have an idea of how you are going to reach those goals, then that's a good match."

WHAT HAPPENS IN THE INTERVIEW?

The first interview an applicant has with a firm like the bank we visited lasts for one-half hour. During the first fifteen minutes, candidates are asked about how they have spent their time; why they picked their colleges; what their expectations are; and why they chose this particular field. Then, the interviewer discusses the company and explains the follow-up procedure. Mr. Stone emphasized the importance of asking questions at the end of the interview—the interviewer wants to know what *you* think, and how much you know about the company. So, be sure to do some research before the interview.

WHAT KIND OF BACKGROUND IS BEST?

Besides a good interview, three other things can help you: prior work experience, certain kinds of extracurricular activities, and references. Even if you haven't worked at the kind of job you're looking for, experience in a similar environment is a plus. As for extracurricular activities, Mr. Stone noted that "a corporation likes to see activities where the person takes charge . . . where they have some leadership role. That is always viewed very well." Last, we asked Mr. Stone about references; he said that they're very important, because they reveal how well the applicant worked at previous jobs.

ADDING IT ALL UP

In summing up the key criteria for being hired by this major bank, Mr. Stone had a one-word reply—"Potential." For this and other firms, what matters most is not what you've done in the past, but what you and the employer think you can do in the future.

PART 3

MARKETING

Working women wash their hair an average of three times a week—so says a study prepared recently by the S. C. Johnson & Sons home products company. Why is Johnson's, best known for its floor wax, interested in American women's hair-washing habits? Because there's money to be made in the shampoo market, and Johnson's wants a share. But in a market crowded with giant competitors, the company can't just produce a new shampoo, distribute it to retailers, and hope for the best. Johnson's has started an advertising and sampling campaign that's as carefully planned as a military operation; every detail is aimed at giving the new product the best possible sendoff, and yielding as much information as possible about its chances for success.[1]

The tricky, expensive process of launching a new product is just one facet of the business area known as marketing. We'll look at a number of marketing questions in Part 3.

☐ In Chapter 7, **Introduction to Marketing,** you'll read about marketing's history and its current role.

☐ Chapter 8, **Product and Pricing Decisions,** discusses the issues manufacturers consider when they decide what to produce—and how to package, label and price their product.

☐ Chapter 9, **Promotion,** tells you all about advertising, personal selling, publicity, and other forms of promotion.

☐ Chapter 10, **Wholesaling, Retailing, and Distribution,** tells how goods are moved from manufacturer to consumer.

☐ The Enrichment Chapter on **Consumer Behavior** is a guide to the psychology and sociology of consumer buying.

☐ The Enrichment Chapter on **International Business** looks at the advantages of doing business in other countries—and at the problems involved.

CHAPTER SEVEN

AN INTRODUCTION TO MARKETING

Any time you make a purchase, chances are you're paying about twice what it costs to produce the item—or more. Fully half of every dollar spent by consumers goes to cover the costs of marketing—research, advertising, distribution, and all the other activities involved in getting goods or services from producer to customer.

Wouldn't prices be a lot lower, then, if some of these activities were eliminated? Not necessarily. Marketing today is far more complex than it was a generation ago, and it has come to play a vital role in creating a large enough demand for numerous goods and services to justify their mass production—at lower prices than would otherwise be possible. The chapter that follows examines the basic functions of marketing, with special emphasis on market segmentation and the development of appropriate marketing strategies.

WHAT WILL THIS CHAPTER FOCUS ON?

After reading the material in this chapter, you will understand and be able to discuss:

- the importance of marketing in our economy
- the changes that have taken place in marketing over the last century
- the eight major functions of marketing
- the various types of consumer goods and business goods
- the four basic components of the marketing mix
- how the marketing mix should vary depending on the product and the customer
- the criticisms that have been leveled at marketing

We all know what it is to push a cart through the aisles of a supermarket. We've come to take it for granted that the products we want will be there when we want them, and we're not likely to spend much time worrying about how they got there. But the fact is, the tomatoes in the produce section weren't grown out on the windowsill, nor were the frozen cream pies baked in the back room. They and the thousands of other items on the shelves had to be brought in from somewhere else. The bread and dairy products were probably delivered by local producers; the meat and produce may have been trucked in from half a continent away and distributed by local wholesalers; less perishable items may have come from across an ocean.

In short, the supermarket we accept as a matter of course represents only the tip of an iceberg. In centuries past, most people lived in small rural communities and had to produce food and other necessities for themselves. Needless to say, things have changed. Between the Texas cattle ranch or the Kansas wheat field and your bag of groceries at the checkout counter, there exists a bustling network of activities—packaging, distributing, financing, advertising, and the like—all aimed at bringing you and those groceries together. These activities are known as *marketing*.

The food business is not the only one in which marketing plays a part. In all modern industrial societies goods tend to be produced by specialized work forces in one locale or another and then made available to consumers in other areas. Most American automobiles are made in Michigan, for instance, and bought by people outside Michigan. So it is with cameras made in Rochester, New York, and peanuts grown in Georgia. And the workers employed by these businesses in Detroit and Rochester and Georgia in turn buy goods made elsewhere.

Marketing, then, has to do with movement, with putting things in circulation. (This is just as true of services, it should be noted, as it is of products. A company offering a service, whether shoe repairing or investment counseling, not only has to be good at what it does but also has to make its service available to enough customers to succeed.) A good thumbnail definition provided by the American Marketing Association is this: **marketing** is *"the performance of business activities that direct the flow of goods and services from producer to consumer or user."*[1]

Marketing is vital to the nation's economy. To see *how* vital, we need only imagine what would happen if, say, all trucks and trains suddenly stopped rolling, banks stopped making business loans, and corporations canceled all advertising. To understand how marketing works, we need to look at each of the activities involved and how it functions in particular instances.

THE FUNCTIONS OF MARKETING

Marketing can be broken down into eight specialized activities, each contributing to the process of getting goods and services from the producer to the consumer. These activities are: *buying, selling, storing, transporting, financing, risk bearing, securing information,* and *standardizing and grading.* Most companies perform all of these, and the success or failure of businesses selling similar goods or services often depends on the way they carry out each marketing function.

BUYING

Virtually every business begins with buying. Manufacturers need to buy raw materials, parts, machinery; car-rental companies need to buy cars; farmers need to buy land, fertilizer, tractors. And they all must purchase the services of their employees.

Nowhere is buying more fundamental, however, than in wholesaling and retailing. When someone goes into a store and buys a toaster, chances are it's the third time that same toaster has been bought. The wholesaler bought it from the manufacturer, the retailer bought it from the wholesaler—and only then was the toaster bought by someone who actually intended to use it. Wholesalers and retailers buy products in order to resell them—but there is seldom any guarantee that the products *can* be resold. There's a built-in risk, in other words, and thus the proper choice of goods is all-important to the success of the business. For this reason, a major retailer like J. C. Penney maintains buying staffs in key markets in Europe and the Far East as well as around the United States. Its buyers do not merely select from among the thousands of items offered them by manufacturers. They also work closely with manufacturers' designers to produce new lines in the colors, styles, quality, and price ranges they believe will appeal to Penney's customers.

Even television networks have to buy what they think their viewers will like. NBC, for example, will pay close to $100 million to broadcast the 1980 Summer Olympics, on the strength of research indicating that the audience would be large enough to make the investment worthwhile.

SELLING

Just as most business begins with buying, the aim of virtually every business is selling. Farmers must sell

---

SUPERSTAR ENDORSEMENTS: A POWERFUL SELLING TECHNIQUE

Sprinting through an airport corridor, superstar O. J. Simpson hurdles an obstacle course of baggage and weaves his way past passengers, his attaché case flowing behind like a cape. Leaving a trail of turned heads and quizzical expressions, in just seconds he reaches the Hertz Rent A Car counter to find a smiling clerk and a waiting car.

This familiar commercial is just one of many advertisements featuring well-known sports celebrities. Since it began airing in 1975, public awareness of Hertz jumped two-fifths in less than three years, and Hertz claims that its market-share lead over rival Avis increased to 14 percentage points at major airports in the same period of time. Showing Simpson has clearly given Hertz's sales a shot in the arm.

But like similarly successful ad campaigns, the commercial is built around a message as well as a superstar. In fact, the message—that Hertz is the "superstar in rent-a-car"—is a slogan that the company's ad agency created long before Simpson was signed on as superstar endorser. While Simpson is crucial to the commercial's appeal, it is the blend of Simpson's image with Hertz's message that makes the ad work. In this case, product (message) and superstar (image) mesh perfectly.

The use of athletes for marketing tie-ins is not new to Hertz and Simpson or even to the 60s and 70s. Baseball greats Ty Cobb and Babe Ruth both lent their names to products, Cobb to a cigarette for American Tobacco Trust, Ruth to Quaker Oats. Today, corporations spend an estimated $10 million annually in athletes' endorsement fees to push goods and services worth hundreds of millions of dollars. What does it take to get a winning combination? The hard part is marrying the right athlete to the right product. Without a strong sales pitch and sensible link between product and athlete, the superstar endorser becomes larger than the item being promoted.

There is a good likelihood of a promotion's taking off, however, if there is a logical, instantly recognizable connection, or "hook," as it's known, between product and endorser. A successful hook may be a personal quality like ruggedness. Mammoth "Mean Joe" Greene, the Pittsburgh Steelers' lineman, trying to smash an Ideal toy truck is one example of a TV commercial with a good hook. Another example is the use of former Olympic skater Dorothy Hamill by Clairol. Hamill had captured the public's eye and was recognized for her hair style (copied by thousands of young women) as much as for her skating; the two seemed to go together. Clairol signed her to promote a new hair conditioner called Short & Sassy, and the campaign was a hit.

There's another kind of quality that seems essential. It's hard to pin down, but you know if it's there. It's called "charisma." Without this mysterious quality, even an athlete who is highly admired—such as Stan Musial or Willie Mays—doesn't seem to help sell the product. But a strong personality like Joe Namath—even if he's not widely admired—makes a tremendous huckster: you name it, he's sold it, from Brut toiletries to popcorn makers to cars. He's got charisma, and that's what the public is looking for.

Source: "Playing the Endorsement Game," *Dun's Review*, August 1977, pp. 43, 45–46.

their grain, manufacturers their appliances, insurance companies their policies. It is hard to overstate the importance of selling as a marketing activity, especially since most production in capitalist economies is not done to order. Rather, it is **speculative production**—*production that is carried out in the hope that the goods will be sold once they've been manufactured.* A greeting-card company, for example, will print its Valentine's Day line during the preceding summer. Wholesalers and retailers also prepare in advance, stocking up against anticipated orders.

Businesses offering services likewise have to anticipate consumer demand. A number of firms, for instance, recently spent millions of dollars building squash courts in New York City, in the belief that the growing interest in physical fitness would create a demand for such facilities.

To enhance the prospects for selling their goods or services, businesses engage in a variety of sales-related activities. These can be classified under four headings: *personal selling, advertising, sales promotion,* and *publicity.* These marketing activities will be discussed in Chapter 9.

STORING

In order for customers to enjoy year-round availability, particularly of seasonal items, goods must often be stored between the time they are produced and the time they are sold. When Rand McNally publishes a new atlas, it ships copies all over the country to warehouses and bookstores, which keep the stock on hand. You may not need an atlas the week it is published, but the chances are that your bookstore will have the atlas on its shelves or in its stockroom when you do decide to buy one, even if the book was published several months earlier. The benefit conferred by such storage is called **time utility**, which is *the value added to a product because of activities that make it available to the consumer at a convenient time.* The storage function adds time utility to the atlas. Without it, consumers could buy the atlas only immediately after its publication.

Storing can also add value to products in a different way. French wines, for example, are routinely kept in storage by American importers; and when the 1977 grape harvest turned out to be smaller than usual, these stored wines rose considerably in value.

Storage reduces transportation and handling costs. When you buy bedding at a retail store, the salesclerk may explain that it will be shipped from the warehouse. Thus, although a sample Simmons mattress is exhibited on the selling floor of the store and the sale is made there, actual shipment is made directly to you from a regional warehouse. In this way, the price of the mattress is not increased by the cost of shipping each bulky mattress first to the store and then to the customer.

TRANSPORTING

Transportation, or the shipment of goods from their place of manufacture to their place of sale, is a major marketing expense for many businesses. If you buy an automobile, you may pay several hundred dollars for its transportation from the factory. Transportation, however, makes possible most of the specialization and mass production on which our economy is based. The huge Ford assembly plant at Mahwah, New Jersey, is economically practical only because the United States has an elaborate and reliable transportation system by which cars can be shipped to customers throughout the nation.

Transportation increases the usefulness of goods. A gallon of gasoline, for instance, is physically the same whether it happens to be in Texas or Oregon. The gallon of gas sitting at a Houston refinery, however, is of little use to a commuter in Portland who needs to drive to work. *The value added to a product by shipping it to wherever the consumers are* is called **place utility**.

Improved transportation has created a range of new business opportunities. In the Flagstaff, Arizona, school lunch program, for example, 3500 precooked meals are now delivered daily to the schools, where they have only to be heated and served. We discuss transportation and its significance in Chapter 10.

FINANCING

Since one of the primary business activities is buying, the question arises: Where does a company get the money to buy what it needs? The answer: through market financing. Most businesses, even well-established ones, don't have large amounts of cash on hand. Nevertheless, a firm very often has to pay for goods before it receives payment from its own customers, and so it must borrow the money.

Department stores typically receive their back-to-school lines early in August, and they must pay their suppliers within thirty days. The selling season for these goods, however, does not begin in earnest until after Labor Day, and many charge customers will not pay their bills until October or November. For this reason, most retailers find it *necessary to borrow in order to pay their suppliers.* This practice is called **borrowing to carry inventory**.

Such lags between purchases and sales are typical of many businesses. Boat manufacturers allow retailers to buy boats in the winter and do not require payment until the spring selling season is well under way. In order to do this, most boat manufacturers must borrow money during the fall and winter so that they can pay their bills and continue production. This financing expense becomes part of the cost of the item paid by the consumer. Without it, however, businesses would not be able to schedule their production throughout the year in the most efficient way, and consumers would consequently pay more and have a smaller choice.

Businesses that deal in services rather than products often have a more difficult time financing their operations, simply because they don't have tangible inventories to put up as security for loans. Whereas a hardware store may have a cellarful of merchandise to use as security, the tailor's shop next door has no such assets. Indeed, a common problem in launching a service business is finding the loans or investors needed to cover the high start-up expenses. The subject of financing will be taken up in Chapters 11 and 12.

RISK BEARING

There are risks involved in operating any business. Some of them are unavoidable: clothing retailers always take a gamble when they stock up on a new fashion that may or may not catch on—the midiskirts that first appeared in 1971, for example, or the leisure suits for men that followed a few years later. No matter what the product or service, in fact, some failures are inevitable. After the gasoline shortage of 1973–1974 ended, the brisk sales of small cars dropped so sharply that the auto makers had to offer price rebates to clear out their bulging inventories. Likewise, for every successful new movie or TV series or record album, there are five, ten, even twenty others that lose money. A business can protect itself to some extent from the risk of producing or carrying the wrong merchandise by hiring expert managers and engaging in market research. Other risks, such as fire, flood, or theft, can be minimized through insurance (see our Enrichment Chapter on Risk Management and Insurance).

SECURING INFORMATION

No business can succeed without gathering and interpreting information about the market. Executives have informal sources of knowledge such as trade newspapers and magazines or business lunches with suppliers and competitors. In addition, many companies send representatives to professional seminars, workshops, and annual trade meetings.

Businesses also rely on more formal sources. These might include market research projects in which hundreds of consumers are interviewed, or computer systems that supply daily analyses of sales trends. A simpler device is the warranty card carrying a brief questionnaire that the purchaser is asked to fill out; the answers help manufacturers determine who is buying a particular product, how old they are, where

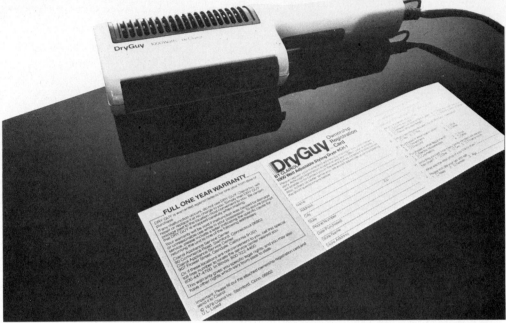

Warranties are often designed to do more than protect the purchaser. Frequently, the buyer is asked to supply information that provides the manufacturer with a valuable consumer profile.

they heard about the product, and other valuable data. Companies can also invite responses from consumers through such means as Shell Oil's "Come to Shell for Answers" advertising campaign, which by 1978 had brought in roughly 400,000 letters plus a variety of useful suggestions from customers.

STANDARDIZATION AND GRADING

Standardization and grading establish standards of quantity or quality that permit both buyer and seller to do business without checking each unit. Supermarket owners know, for example, what the size of a number 1 can of string beans will be. Consumers can be confident that any sheet labeled "percale" will have a minimum of 180 threads per square inch. Interestingly, this is one area of marketing in which the government plays an active part. (Others will be discussed in later chapters.) The Department of Agriculture, for example, grades canned peaches A, B, or C, depending on such factors as the size and extent of blemishes. (The government also provides an inspection and verification service for canners who want to label their goods accordingly.) In addition, the government has taken steps to ensure that consumers know what they're buying—such as the requirement that clothing labels provide fabric information and washing instructions. Other industry standards are established by trade as-

sociations or leading firms. These include standards for sizes in clothes, shoes, cans, and bottles.

CHANGING CONCEPTS IN MARKETING

The basic marketing activities just described are all accepted today as part of standard business procedure, but this has not always been so. Marketing procedures have in fact evolved dramatically during the last half-century, as their usefulness became evident to more and more business leaders.

PRODUCTION-ORIENTED MARKETING

Until the 1930s, many business executives viewed marketing simply as an offshoot of production. They concentrated on manufacturing an item, often to order, and limited their marketing efforts to taking orders and shipping goods. Henry Ford's emphasis on mass production was typical of the early 1900s. He was concerned mainly with developing production skills and cost-saving devices. His attitude made sense because society consumed just about everything that his company, and most other companies, could produce.

SALES-ORIENTED MARKETING

As production capacity increased, business leaders began to realize that they would have to work harder to sell all the goods they could make. This realization led to an expansion of marketing activities. Companies now put more emphasis on advertising to create a demand for their products. They also began to develop trained sales forces that could seek out and sell to the thousands of potential customers across the country.

This shift in emphasis from production to sales was given a boost by the rapid growth of radio in the late 1920s and the 1930s. For the first time a manufacturer was able to get a sales message to millions of people at one time. Through the power of radio advertising scores of products such as Jell-O, Lipton Tea, and Johnson's Wax were transformed into household words. (Later, of course, the advent of television provided the most potent advertising medium of all, making it possible—and, by now, commonplace—for a company to introduce a new product to the entire nation overnight.)

THE TOTAL MARKETING CONCEPT

Since World War II, emphasis on serving the needs of the consumer has become even more marked, and marketing has become dominated by an approach known as total marketing, which includes many more functions than production-oriented or sales-oriented marketing. Sales-oriented marketing was based on the belief that the *firm* must attempt to influence the *buyer* in order to sell its products. The total marketing concept, on the other hand, takes the view that the *buyer* should have a strong influence on the *firm*. All the firm's departments should be coordinated to produce the goods or services that the consumer wants. Under this approach, business people no longer use marketing tools just to encourage customer buying. Instead,

CHANGING CONCEPTS IN MARKETING

FIGURE 1

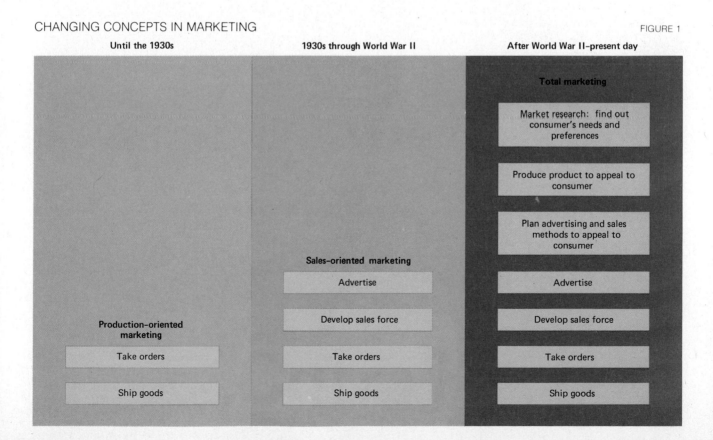

Until the 1930s	1930s through World War II	After World War II–present day
		Total marketing
		Market research: find out consumer's needs and preferences
		Produce product to appeal to consumer
		Plan advertising and sales methods to appeal to consumer
	Sales-oriented marketing	
	Advertise	Advertise
Production-oriented marketing	Develop sales force	Develop sales force
Take orders	Take orders	Take orders
Ship goods	Ship goods	Ship goods

with **total marketing** they *concentrate on determining the needs of consumers, and then they have the firm create, produce, and sell specific goods to satisfy these needs.*

Market research: an important tool

As part of the trend toward total marketing, there has been an increasing emphasis on **market research.** Essentially, market research attempts to find out:

1. what products or services the consumer wants;

2. what forms, colors, packaging, price ranges, and retail outlets the consumer prefers; and

3. what types of advertising, public relations, and selling practices are most likely to appeal to the consumer.

This information helps manufacturers decide what to make and how to sell it.

Total marketing in action

A few examples will illustrate the value of the total marketing concept. At the end of World War II, after some eighty years in business, the Pillsbury Company was still essentially a one-product enterprise: it sold flour. A few other products such as cattle feed and

Insurance poster, 1876

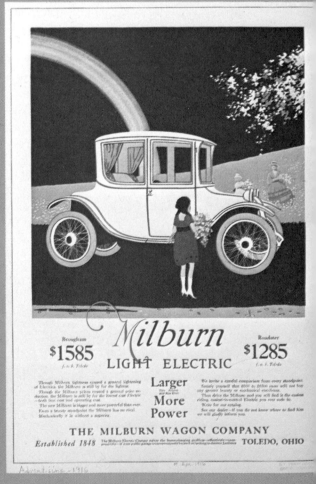

Advertisement for an electric automobile, 1916

bran flour had been added along the way, but only because they happened to be by-products of milling white flour—not in response to consumer demands. During the 1950s, though, Pillsbury committed itself increasingly to total marketing. The company realized that it had the technical know-how to produce a wide range of products. But which ones would be successful in the marketplace? The housewife, the major buyer of Pillsbury's products, was to be the judge of that. The marketing department now became the center of activity, its job to find out what the housewife wanted. Marketing could then develop new product ideas to satisfy those desires. Using this approach the company

has developed and sold dozens of new cake mixes, prepared dinners, dry cereals, and many other items that have substantially raised Pillsbury's earnings.

More recently, Procter & Gamble came to realize through market research that there was a $100 million potato-chip market waiting to be tapped across the country—and that they could get at it if they could figure out a way to produce a potato chip that wouldn't get broken while being shipped. The result: chips that came in a can—Pringle's.

A similar success story involves the Huffman Manufacturing Company, the country's largest bicycle maker, which found out that a lot of kids wanted bikes

Advertisement for a stuffing mix, 1978

The old ads had charm—but what was good for granddad won't necessarily work in modern marketing. With skyrocketing costs and ever-increasing consumer sophistication, marketing has become a much more scientific discipline.

that looked like racing motorcycles. So Huffman produced a model with knobby tires, number plates, and other suitable trappings; then it displayed the bikes at schools and shopping centers, asking detailed questions—one of which established that the kids wanted higher numbers on the plates! This research was translated into numerous minor changes in the bicycle's appearance, and the Huffy Thunder Trail was soon one of the fastest-selling models in the country.[2]

SPECIFIC PRODUCTS FOR SPECIFIC MARKETS

As the total marketing concept came to be more widely adopted, the techniques in use grew steadily more sophisticated. Two elements, however, are basic to any total marketing program: identifying the market, and developing the right "marketing mix" of product, price, promotion, and placement. We'll discuss markets first.

CREATIVE MARKETING APPROACHES

In the competitive world of retail sales and services, a bit of imagination can often spell the difference between sluggishness and growth in a company's operations, particularly when the general economy is slow. Recent years have witnessed a large increase in the number of firms that specialize in marketing techniques—much like advertising or public relations agencies—along with an expansion of marketing departments of large corporations. This increased activity has led to innovations that offer further proof of the effectiveness of good marketing strategies.

One of the successful new firms, Marketing Corporation of America (MCA), has come up with profitable ideas for clients ranging from grocery stores to the United States government. The following examples are all applications of basic marketing principles:

■ D'Agostino Supermarkets in New York raised their sales 14 percent in just nine weeks after MCA thought of printing a bingo-type game on their shopping bags.

■ For Ralston Purina, MCA designed a Puppy Care Kit that has become standard equipment for veterinarians.

■ For Frito-Lay, it introduced a line of dry soft-drink mixes that promises to develop into a major business.

■ MCA's attractive displays helped the U.S. Postal Service increase sales to stamp collectors more than 500 percent in five years, and its marketing plan for the Treasury Department in 1976 sold $195 million worth of Bicentennial coin sets.

■ An ingenious arrangement was made with Avis Rent A Car after research by MCA showed that over five million businessmen travel at least three times a year and also play golf. MCA purchased several thousand sets of golf clubs that Avis customers can rent in various cities around the country for $10 a day, a portion of the proceeds going to MCA.

■ Concluding that most discount coupons are distributed haphazardly and inefficiently, MCA began buying advertising space on "best food days" in more than 150 newspapers and selling portions to different manufacturers, putting as many as sixteen coupons on a page. The result: MCA makes a profit, a higher percentage of coupons are redeemed, and their distribution costs manufacturers only $1 per thousand, as against $5 for individual newspaper ads and $14 for direct mail.

Interestingly, James McManus, who founded MCA in 1971 and has become known for innovation, expresses impatience with those in the marketing field who emphasize "creativity" as a goal in itself. McManus takes a strictly practical approach, concerning himself only with the goal of designing a plan that works. "If it sells," he says, "it's creative."

Adapted from "The Other MCA, New Star in Consumer Marketing," October 1977 DUN'S REVIEW

SOME SEGMENTS OF THE TOOTHPASTE
MARKET

FIGURE 2

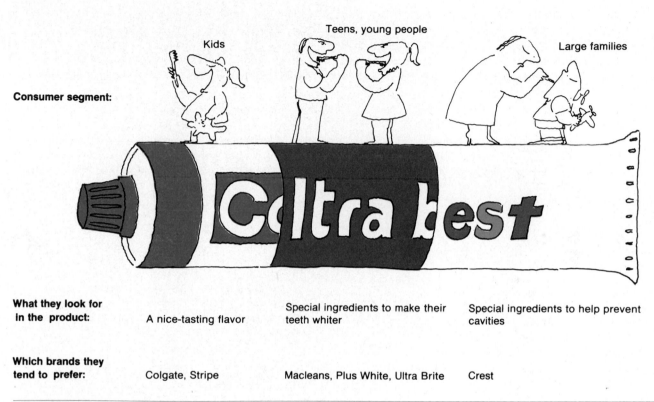

Consumer segment:	Kids	Teens, young people		Large families
What they look for in the product:	A nice-tasting flavor	Special ingredients to make their teeth whiter		Special ingredients to help prevent cavities
Which brands they tend to prefer:	Colgate, Stripe	Macleans, Plus White, Ultra Brite		Crest

IDENTIFYING THE MARKET

Throughout this chapter, the work *market* has been used frequently. But what exactly is a market? It can be broadly defined this way: a **market** consists of *a group of people who have needs to satisfy, money to spend, and the ability to buy.* In practice, this definition is somewhat too broad, since few businesses aim to supply their goods or services to all the people so qualified. Instead, a business has to pick out and concentrate on a **target market**, that is, *a particular market to which a firm attempts to sell its products or services.* That attempt involves a process known as **market segmentation**, which means *producing different products and designing different marketing strategies to satisfy smaller, more homogeneous groups, or "sub-markets," within the total market.*

A good example of market segmentation is the long-established auto-industry practice of making many different types of cars, each aimed at a particular segment of the driving public. General Motors' production, for instance, can be divided into at least seven categories: sub-compact; compact; full-size; small personal luxury; large luxury sedans; station wagons; and vans and campers. Another example is the marketing program undertaken by Volkswagen in response to an increase in the number of American women who buy its cars. The company aimed an advertising campaign for its Dasher wagon specifically at young, single women, on the theory that they represent a steadily growing market segment—one that has been generally overlooked.

CONSUMER MARKETS AND CONSUMER GOODS

From the standpoint of individual companies, the total market divides first of all into two large segments: the *consumer market* and the *business market*. The **consumer market** consists of *individuals or households that purchase goods for personal consumption*. Because the public's shopping habits tend to follow only a few basic patterns, products aimed at the consumer market have come to be classified under three different categories: *convenience goods, shopping goods,* and *specialty goods*. Each type is purchased for different reasons, and so calls for a different marketing strategy.

Convenience goods are *products that are purchased quickly and often; they are generally low-priced, heavily advertised, and widely available*. Such goods include bread, cigarettes, and soap powder. A familiar example is the Gillette disposable razor, which was introduced with a saturation advertising campaign on TV (especially on sports programs). Gillette priced the razor at less than it charged for blades alone and displayed it prominently at drugstores, cigarette counters, and other suitable outlets. Since Gillette has a tremendous share of the market (so that it almost "owns" every shaving rack in the nation), the company was able to put the new product into instant distribution.

Shopping goods are so named because the consumer is willing to spend more time shopping for them

THE THREE TYPES OF CONSUMER GOODS

Convenience goods: products that are readily available, low-priced and heavily advertised, which consumers buy quickly and often.
Examples: bread, razor blades

Shopping goods: products that a consumer spends quite some time shopping for, comparing prices, quality and style.
Examples: furniture, jewelry

Specialty goods: products, usually brand items, that a consumer will make a particular effort to locate.
Examples: perfume, high-fashion clothing

NEW TARGET MARKETS FOR CHEWING-GUM MANUFACTURERS

There are, believe it or not, some big changes sweeping through the chewing-gum business. Sales are booming, and in areas never before exploited. Now, adults constitute one of the fastest-growing segments of the gum market, and gum manufacturers don't cater to youngsters as much as they used to.

Americans are chewing more feverishly than ever. According to the National Chewing Gum Association, which is made up of thirteen manufacturers, gum sales were $576.4 million in 1976—a 21 percent increase, or $102 million gain, over the preceding year, and three times the sales of ten years ago. And gum makers have responded to the trend with all kinds of new products: sugarless gums; gums

and purchases them only after making comparisons on the basis of quality, price, or style. Furniture, jewelry, and men's shoes are examples of shopping goods. Since the consumer is willing to search for such merchandise, the manufacturer of shopping goods does not need as many outlets in each area as the manufacturer of convenience goods. The J. C. Penney automobile battery proved successful in the shopping-goods category largely because it had features (emphasized in its ads) that compared well against other brands. One was a guarantee stating that the company would replace the battery free if anything went wrong— hence the slogan, "The last battery your car will ever need."

Specialty goods are *products, usually brand merchandise, that a consumer will make a special effort to locate*. A potential buyer will be unwilling to settle for substitutes. Such goods could include a Dunhill cigarette lighter, a Pierre Cardin suit, or a bottle of Chanel No. 5. Specialty goods are usually restricted, sometimes deliberately, to a relatively few outlets. These products are typically promoted through advertising in "status" magazines, cooperative advertising

with liquid centers that go "squirt"; gums that don't stick to teeth; and even a gum that might help prevent cavities. Bubble gum is a hot item—it was top seller among eighty-six new products brought to market in March 1976. "We've always considered ourselves to be in the children's entertainment business," says Joel J. Shorin, president of Topps Chewing Gum Company, the largest maker of bubble gum. "But with the new boom in bubble gum, we're in a growth industry."

What accounts for all this chewing? The popularity of gum may be the result of its "health-giving, circulation-building, chest-developing, digestion-aiding, brain-refreshing, nerve-settling, soul-tuning" characteristics, writes Robert Hendrickson, in *The Great American Chewing Gum Book*. Some people suggest that gum is a sexual pacifier. Others say it is a good alternative for dieters and people who are trying to give up smoking.

Given the choice between a pack of gum and a tiny candy bar, gum may also be a far better value. "With candy, two gulps and it's all over," says Thomas Tegen, vice-president of new products and merchandising at Philadelphia's Fleer Corporation. "But a two-cent chunk of bubble gum delivers flavor that lasts for five minutes or more."

These are some of the reasons why Americans chew what amounts to three million miles of gum a year. But prospering sales don't mean that the gum manufacturers can just sit back and watch their profits grow. Competition is heating up in the gum business, and gum chewers are the object of intense efforts in the marketing field.

Source: "By Gum! Business Is Bubbling," *Dun's Review*, June 1977, pp. 90–91, 93, 95.

---

with fashionable stores, public relations campaigns—and sometimes simply by word-of-mouth.

Needless to say, the classification system that divides consumer products into convenience, shopping, and specialty goods is not a rigid one. What to one consumer are convenience goods may be shopping goods to another. A high-income family, for example, may order steaks routinely from the neighborhood butcher (thus to them the steaks are a convenience item), while a student living on a budget will feel obliged to shop around among supermarkets for an occasional steak dinner (so to him the steak is a shopping item). To a teacher, a watch might be in the shopping category. To a stockbroker anxious to impress clients with an Omega, a watch would be a specialty item.

BUSINESS MARKETS AND BUSINESS GOODS

The **business market** is composed of *business enterprises that buy goods for resale or in order to operate their establishments.* Like the products sold to the consumer market, those sold to the business market can be subdivided into different categories, each requiring its own distinct marketing strategy. The two chief categories are *industrial goods* and *commercial goods.*

Industrial goods *are used in the production of other goods.* They include raw materials, fabricated

---

TYPES OF BUSINESS GOODS

Industrial goods: products used in manufacturing other products, for either the consumer or the business market. *Examples:* sheet metal, blast furnace

Commercial goods: products, such as office supplies and equipment, used by business and industry in administering their affairs. *Examples:* typewriter, duplicating machine

materials, machinery, and tools. Steel used to make automobiles falls into this category. If U.S. Steel wants to sell sheet metal to Ford, it will have to manufacture the product according to Ford's specifications, and make its prices competitive with those of other steel producers. Its marketing strategy will include establishing a long-term working relationship between the U.S. Steel sales department and the Ford engineers, as well as advertising in automotive and engineering trade journals. When Ford buys from U.S. Steel, the sheet metal will be shipped directly from U.S. Steel to Ford.

Commercial goods *are used by business and industry in administering their affairs.* These goods consist mainly of office supplies and equipment, such as typewriters, duplicating machines, and postage meters. A recent entrant in this field is IBM's sophisticated new typewriter system, which can store and retype anything programmed into its memory unit, thus relieving office workers of much routine and repetitious typing. IBM's price is competitive with the prices of other word-processing systems, but the emphasis of part of the IBM campaign will be on the savings the product will make possible by freeing office workers to perform other tasks. The prime promotional tool will be the direct sales call, which will be backed up by extensive advertising in business magazines and journals. The new word processor has already been pushed on TV, to establish product recognition and attract the interest both of those who will use the machine and those who are in a position to buy it. The machines will be shipped directly and serviced by IBM.

It is important to remember that business goods are classified according to their destination, that is, the use to which they will be put. The same products may be classified in more than one way. For instance, the corn syrup and peanut oil sold to a candy manufacturer are industrial goods; sold to a supermarket they are consumer goods. Recording machines may be consumer goods (if used in the home), industrial goods (if used to make records), or commercial goods (if used to record a sales meeting).

Clearly, the market manager must understand the differences between the consumer market and the business market, and the various uses to which the firm's products may be put. Only with this knowledge can a business determine how to gear its sales efforts.

THE MARKETING MIX

The consumer and business markets contain an enormous variety of smaller market segments, and the firm that excels at targeting a particular market segment will have a valuable edge over its competitors. But identifying the market is only part of the task. There remains the other basic element in any total marketing program: developing the right *marketing mix.*

A **marketing mix** can be defined as *a blending of product, price, promotion, and placement (or distribution) to satisfy the demands of the chosen market segment.* Figure 3 should help to illustrate the relationship between the market segment and these four marketing factors (commonly known as the four Ps of marketing). The key point, as we shall see, is that the company seeks to adjust each of the four factors in response to the demands of the target market.

THE FOUR PS OF MARKETING

Product

A manufacturer obviously must decide what products will best attract consumers in its target market. In recent years, for example, Xerox has been making steadily larger and more expensive copying machines. A smaller competitor, Savin, realized there was no point in trying to challenge Xerox head-on, so it entered the field instead with a line of more compact, less expensive desktop copiers that found a segment of the market waiting for them. Around the same time Xerox's dominance of the upper range of the copier market came under attack by Kodak, which after a decade of research introduced its own line of high-priced, high-quality copying machines.

Product lines must be constantly reevaluated in light of changing conditions. Items may be added or dropped as the market dictates. The Gerber baby-food company, faced with a declining birth rate, has diversified into the insurance field and other areas, backing up the effort with a carefully targeted advertising campaign. Howard Johnson's, Stouffer's and other restaurant chains have made profitable inroads into the frozen-food market, aided by the public's familiarity with their names.

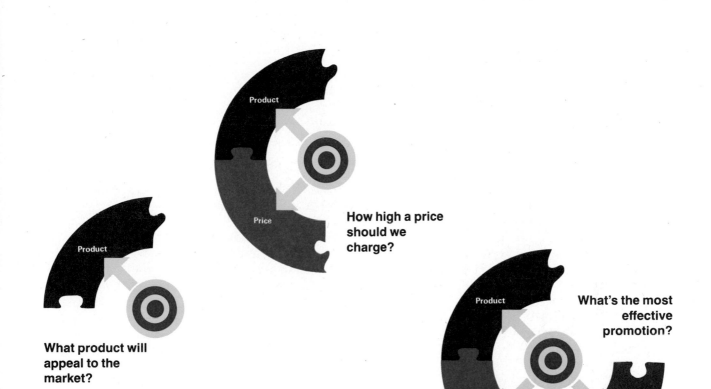

What product will appeal to the market?

How high a price should we charge?

What's the most effective promotion?

THE "FOUR Ps" OF MARKETING: PRODUCT, PRICE, PROMOTION AND PLACEMENT

Product, price, promotion and placement are four aspects of marketing strategy which together make up the *marketing mix*. Creating a marketing mix is like solving a puzzle: the marketing manager must fit the right product with the right price, and must find the right promotional approach and the right methods of placement (or distribution), to satisfy the needs and preferences of the particular target market.

Looking at it another way, we may note that the marketing manager's choice of product, price, promotion and placement is dictated by the target market. We have emphasized this point by showing arrows pointing *from* the target market *to* the "Four Ps."

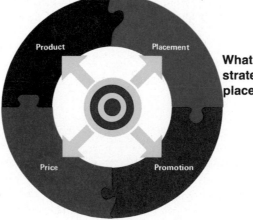

What's the best strategy for placement?

FIGURE 3

Other product-related decisions involve such factors as brand names, packaging, and guarantees—all multiplying the number of choices a market manager has to consider in determining what to offer the consumer.

Price

Once the basic decisions on the product line have been made, the market manager must decide how the company should price its products. Will a policy based on low prices maximize profits? Supermarkets have used this tactic to encourage people to buy their own brand merchandise rather than nationally advertised products. Sometimes products may require the quality image that high prices often confer. The manufacturer of Norell perfume acted on this belief several years ago when it introduced a new product and deliberately priced it as the most expensive American-made scent. The factors that enter into decisions on both product line and pricing will be discussed in Chapter 8.

Promotion

Very often the key decision a market manager must make is how the manufacturer should inform prospective customers about its products. This involves promotion, which includes the four kinds of selling previously mentioned. Some managers, like those at Fuller Brush, may decide to emphasize direct selling and spend most of their promotion dollars in training and paying salespeople. Others, like producers of soap and headache remedies, promote their products through advertising, primarily on television. Firms like department stores also spend heavily on advertising, but they choose newspapers as the most effective medium. The alternatives are many, the choice of which may determine the success of a marketing effort. We'll discuss promotion in Chapter 9.

Placement

The fourth element of the marketing mix is placement (or distribution): how the manufacturer gets its products to the customers. Some firms, like Tupperware with its party plans, sell directly to the consumer. Manhattan Shirt Company and other apparel companies sell to retailers who then resell to consumers. Westinghouse and other appliance industries sell to wholesalers in major areas of the country. Some firms use several channels. Sears distributes its products through stores and a catalog. Pepperidge Farm not only sells baked goods through retail grocery stores, but also offers a special gift line to consumers through a mail-order division. The ways manufacturers distribute goods will be discussed in Chapter 10.

MARKETING-MIX DECISIONS CAN BE HARD TO MAKE

Finding the right combination of product, price, promotion, and placement has become an increasingly complex task for most businesses. Marketing directors have found that even the most subtle changes—in the shape or color of packaging, for instance, or the way the product is displayed in a store, or the location of the store itself—can have a decisive impact on a product's success, quite apart from its actual quality. In effect, you may have built a better mousetrap, but unless you package it well, set up good distribution, target your advertising appropriately, and offer a good warranty, the world won't necessarily take any notice. Indeed, it has become more common to reverse the process—as did the Squibb Corporation when it developed a new product called Bubble-Yum. It was created to meet the demands of customers who were dissatisfied with existing bubblegums: they were too hard and lost their flavor too quickly. The company also had to price its new gum within the reach of bubblegum customers, place it in the stores where they usually bought gum, and stress in its advertising that Bubble-Yum had the qualities that rival brands lacked.

MARKETING AND COSTS

Today, marketing activities probably account for about half the price of the consumer's average purchase. There are, of course, tremendous variations in marketing costs among products. Standard Oil of New Jersey estimated at one time that $1 of natural gas purchased by a family in New York City cost only 4¢ at the wellhead in Texas; transportation and other marketing costs made up the balance of 96¢. However, as

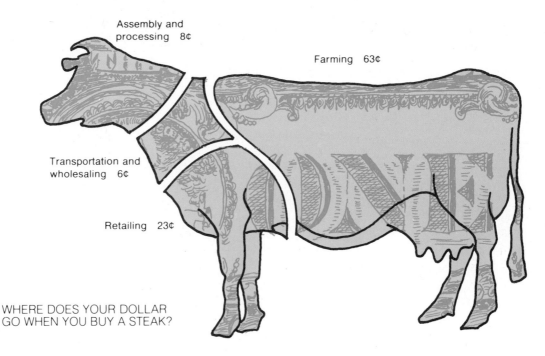

Assembly and processing 8¢

Farming 63¢

Transportation and wholesaling 6¢

Retailing 23¢

WHERE DOES YOUR DOLLAR GO WHEN YOU BUY A STEAK?

FIGURE 4

(Data from American Farm Bureau Federation, 1977)

Figure 4 illustrates, of every dollar spent by a shopper for a steak at the supermarket, 71¢ went to the rancher and meat packer as a cost of production; the remainder involves marketing costs.

CRITICISMS OF MARKETING

Confronted with statistics such as the ones just presented, many people feel that marketing costs too much. They believe that at least some prices could be lowered if marketing were reduced or eliminated. In fact, however, many products might cost even more without marketing. Marketing functions like storage, transportation, and selling increase the demand for goods to the point where mass production becomes feasible. If products like color television or pocket-sized computers were not advertised, demand might never reach the levels that make mass production possible. The small quantities of goods produced would thus cost much more.

Another charge leveled against marketing is that it encourages people to buy products they don't really need. Does our economy really "need" dozens of different brands of underarm deodorants, each packaged and promoted at great expense? Do we "need" cars with elaborate chrome trim and stereo systems? Marketing professionals answer these questions by redefining "need" to include more than basic necessities. They claim that the objective of our present economic system is to supply not only basic goods and services, but also products that make living more enjoyable and satisfy our egos. It is true that many of the products marketed are not essential. But that millions of Americans voluntarily purchase them suggests that they are filling real needs. And those who feel that no legitimate want is satisfied by a product can simply choose not to buy it.

In short, there are a number of arguments to suggest that the costs of marketing are well worth incurring. This point will become clearer as we look at the various aspects of marketing in more detail in the chapters that follow.

CHAPTER REVIEW

Marketing is the process of moving goods and services from the producer to the consumer. It consists of eight specific functions: buying, selling, storing, transporting, financing, risk bearing, securing information, and standardization and grading.

Marketing has changed drastically over the past hundred years. Originally most firms were production-oriented, with marketing restricted primarily to taking orders and shipping goods. Then came sales-oriented marketing, which emphasized selling. Since World War II, however, most large firms have adopted the total marketing concept, a consumer-oriented marketing approach.

The marketing manager tries to develop the marketing program that will be best suited to the target market. A firm has four elements to work with in setting up its marketing program. These are product, promotion, price, and placement. They are sometimes called the four Ps of marketing. The particular combination of the four Ps that the marketing manager chooses is called the marketing mix.

It is important to distinguish between the different kinds of markets, or groups of customers, at which a marketing program must be directed. Two major categories are the consumer market, which can be subdivided into markets for convenience goods, shopping goods, and specialty goods; and the business market, which buys industrial and commercial goods.

KEY WORD REVIEW

marketing
total marketing concept
market research
speculative production
time utility
place utility
borrowing to carry inventory
market
target market
market segmentation
consumer market
convenience goods
shopping goods
specialty goods
business market
industrial goods
commercial goods
marketing mix

REVIEW QUESTIONS

1. Compare production-oriented marketing, sales-oriented marketing, and the total marketing concept.

2. Why is marketing important to the economic life of the United States?

3. List the eight functions of marketing and explain briefly the meaning of each.

4. Give examples of marketing functions that add time and place utility to products.

5. What are the "four Ps of marketing"?

6. List four different ways a product can be promoted.

7. Give an example of each of the three different kinds of goods consumers buy.

8. Why may the same product be classified as a consumer-goods or a business-goods item?

CASE 1

NOT JUST A PAPER CUP: MARYLAND CUP'S CREATIVE MARKETING STRATEGY

There is nothing terribly complicated about a paper cup, and selling them might seem to be a matter of simply offering the lowest price. Maryland Cup Corporation, however, has prospered in the highly competitive disposable container business by charging top prices for its products—and by selling its customers on the service it offers. Explains company President Henry Shapiro: "Our customers come to look at us not as a supplier of containers but as experts in their business." For instance, in talking to a prospective restaurant customer, a Maryland Cup salesman might not even mention cups or prices. Rather, he would focus on a concept, such as how to increase beverage sales by offering three sizes of drinks instead of two. Indeed, though most of the big orders for disposable containers in the restaurant and fast-food business are placed by wholesale distributors, Maryland Cup instructs its 400-person sales force to work closely with the eventual users of the company's products. In this way, Maryland Cup, whose major accounts include McDonald's, Burger King, and Dairy Queen, takes orders *to* the distributors (which reduces the wholesalers' selling costs and sells them on Maryland Cup products at the same time).

When a big account is up for grabs, Maryland Cup uses aggressive marketing tactics. For example, when Busch Memorial Stadium, home of the St. Louis Cardinals baseball team, made it known that it was looking for a machine that would put cellophane tops on beer cups without ruining the beer, Maryland Cup quickly submitted a design. The company is not in the capping machine business; in fact, it wouldn't even make money on the machines. But if it got the contract, it would also get to sell the stadium a lot of beer cups. By the same token, Maryland Cup is trying to get a piece of the institutional food market, such as hospitals. Although most hospitals still use china (dishwashing labor, hot water, and the china itself, however, are becoming increasingly costly), Maryland Cup offers a serving cart with trays that keep different portions of food at different temperatures—and that are designed, naturally, to fit the company's line of disposable dinnerware.

Service like this allows Maryland Cup to stay out of price wars with its competitors. At the same time, though, extras like business advice, capping machines, and serving carts are of little use to the supermarket shopper, and the company has not done especially well in retail sales to consumers. Even so, Maryland Cup's astute marketing has set the pace for other companies in the industry, and has taken the firm to the top of the $1 billion disposable container business.[3]

1. In what way does Maryland Cup use a total marketing approach?

2. How does the company tailor its marketing strategies for its different target markets?

CASE 2

HOW DO YOU MARKET AN ENCYCLOPEDIA?

By the time a new consumer good goes into production, most companies have a clear idea of the target market for which the item is intended. (Indeed, a company will usually start with a target market and then come up with something to sell to it.) But in bringing out its 2,856-page single-volume encyclopedia, Random House, Inc. did things a bit differently. Ever since the publication (in 1966) of the best-selling *Random House Dictionary of the English Language,* editors at Random House had been dreaming of putting out a companion reference work. And so almost as soon as the opportunity presented itself, they went to work creating a book that would be filled with color plates for visual appeal and with entries on thousands of topics. The encyclopedia would be about the same size as the 2,059-page dictionary, and inexpensive enough for large numbers of people to afford. But what people? And how best to reach them?

With the encyclopedia already in production—and hundreds of thousands of dollars invested in the project—Random House hired an advertising agency to find the answers. First, researchers from the agency held discussions about encyclopedias with "focus groups"—composed of "average" people—to find the most appealing promotional strategy. Those discussions produced three basic "appeals" for television commercials: (1.) simply show, in rapid sequence, chunks of text and full-color pictures; (2.) show scenes of parents and children looking at the book together; (3.) create a commercial that would make parents feel guilty about not buying the book for their kids.

The agency then created eight commercials based on these themes. Armed with soundtracks and storyboards (a storyboard is a sequence of drawings that shows every shot of a commercial as it would appear on TV), researchers from the agency stationed themselves in various shopping malls and solicited reactions from 336 passersby. (The clear favorite was one showing the book's text and pictures.) The researchers also learned that if given a choice between paying $59 or $69 for the encyclopedia, roughly half of the interviewees opted for the higher price; and that the target market with the highest potential consisted of mothers with children living and being educated at home, with income levels under $20,000 a year.

By the time copies of the $69.95 encyclopedia were on their way to bookstores, a few months before Christmas 1977, Random House had invested $4 million in the project. Understandably, the company was anxious to spread the word about the book as widely as possible. The advertising budget, at $1.1 million, would pay for an intensive television campaign in the country's top 15 markets, as well as for print ads in major magazines and in newspaper supplements in a dozen major U.S. cities. Even though there was, of course, no author per se, Random House set up an "author's tour" anyway—and off went the company's editor-in-chief to talk up the book on local TV shows around the country.[4]

1. Was the encyclopedia a shopping good or a consumer good?

2. Do you think the large promotion budget was justified?

CHAPTER EIGHT

PRODUCT AND PRICING DECISIONS

You say you've developed a miracle glue? Terrific—now just how do you plan to go about selling it? Before you launch your brainstorm onto the open market there are a number of basic decisions that need to be made. How, for instance, do you intend to present your glue to the public—is it a truly new product or an improved version of the old familiar item? What kind of competition is it up against? Should you try to underprice your rivals or compete on the basis of superior quality? How about packaging? Should you try to catch customers' eyes with a fancy box, or should you stay with a simple, economical jar that will occupy less shelf space? In this chapter you'll become acquainted with a variety of practical considerations involved in the birth of any product—ranging from the six stages of product development and the product life cycle, to factors in branding and labeling, the uses (and abuses) of packaging, and the fine art of pricing.

WHAT WILL THIS CHAPTER FOCUS ON?

After reading the material in this chapter, you will understand and be able to discuss:

- the factors involved in the product mix decision

- the life cycle of a product

- the way managers decide what new products to introduce, and when to do so

- the advantages of advertising under a brand name

- the major questions involved in product packaging and labeling

- pricing as it relates to general business policies

- pricing techniques, including markup and discount

During the 1960s National Presto Industries of Eau Claire, Wisconsin, operated quite profitably with an unusual combination of products. Its revenues derived chiefly from two areas: small appliances, like toasters and electric skillets, and artillery shells for the United States Army. In the early 1970s, though, the company began to feel the effects of the gradual American withdrawal from Vietnam and the deepening economic recession. The appliance sales remained strong enough, but something new was clearly needed to offset the sharp decline in its ordnance business. The solution, it turned out, was suggested by the Census Bureau finding that half of all American households now consisted of only one or two persons—a far cry from the larger families that had long been considered the primary market for household goods.

Presto put this piece of information together with the phenomenal success of McDonald's and other hamburger chains, and—presto!—came up with its new product: the electric hamburger cooker. Resembling a small waffle iron, the handy device could broil one hamburger patty in two minutes or so and was easy to clean. Presto's hamburger cooker proved a big hit around the country, boosting company profits and inspiring a host of imitations from rival manufacturers. Recognizing the need to follow up on its success, and keep a step ahead of the competition, Presto by 1976 had brought out a line of related products: square-shaped models that also made grilled cheese sandwiches; the two-burger cooker; an electric hot dog cooker; and a miniature, easy-to-clean, deep-fat fryer for french-fried potatoes.[1]

THE PRODUCT MIX

Presto's expanding line of appliances represents one solution to the dilemma that faces any company's management in determining a **product mix**, or *list of all products offered by a manufacturer*. Which items should it try to sell? The simplest approach is to market only one product, as, for instance, some beer companies do. Another is to develop a particular **product line**, which we can define as *a group of products that are physically similar or intended for similar markets*. A product line may be a narrow one—as with a brewery that sells its regular brand and a lower-calorie "light" beer—or a broader one like Presto's assortment of fast-food appliances. A third alternative is to expand a company's mix to include different product lines. We show all these alternatives in Figure 2.

The Gillette Company has been one of the kingpins in the shaving products business for many years, but has worked its way into other areas only in the last thirty years or so. After World War II, Gillette took over the reins of the Toni Company, which creates women's cosmetics. Although this addition expanded Gillette's efforts into women's products, business was still concentrated in the general area of toiletries and cosmetics. But then, in the early 1960s, Gillette took over PaperMate Pen. Of course, pens are not personal products like razors or cosmetics, but they are distributed through many of the same channels—drugstores, supermarkets, discount stores, and the like. Still later, Gillette added Cricket disposable lighters, hair-drying equipment, and various felt-tip pens. More recently, it started marketing the Captain Kelly home fire-protection equipment and a fire extinguisher. Gillette also stepped into the digital watch business, but bowed out because of the vicious competition in that arena. Still, Gillette has expanded far beyond its original product

ASPECTS OF THE MARKETING
MIX: PRODUCT   FIGURE 1

When deciding what product to produce, the marketing manager considers the needs and wants of the target market.

THE PRODUCT MIX

A company may choose one of the following approaches in developing its product mix:

The single product approach:
Many companies begin by manufacturing one product or performing one service for their customers. The Ford Motor Company, for example, began its automotive life by building one type of passenger car, the famous Model A.

Developing one basic product line:
Shoe manufacturers do not generally make only one type of shoe. They try to capture a year-round market by turning out dressy shoes, casual shoes, sandals, bedroom slippers and so on. This is an example of a basic product line.

Developing diversified product lines:
Most large companies go beyond one basic product line to several lines. If, for instance, your shoe factory were a great success, you might expand by acquiring an appliance company, with its own product line consisting of toasters, blenders, and irons. Diversifying further, you might buy a publishing company, with a product line of gothic novels, reference works, and children's books.

FIGURE 2

line. Expansion possibilities thus exist whether a company decides to emphasize one product line or develop several different, sometimes totally unrelated, lines.

HOW DOES A COMPANY DECIDE ON ITS PRODUCT MIX?

Deciding on a product mix can be tricky. There are risks involved no matter what approach a company takes, and these risks must be weighed against the gains the company foresees. Some companies find it most economical to focus their energies on a single line of similar goods. Production costs can often be held down this way, and it may also be possible to market a kindred group of products using a single sales force and the same retail outlets. Other companies feel that a broad product mix is a safeguard against changes in technology, taste, or economic conditions.

NEW PRODUCTS

It was the end of the Vietnam war, as we saw, that forced Presto to make big changes in its product mix. But large-scale historical changes are only one reason why companies find themselves pressed for new products to sell. Another is that a company may find that some of its products, long consumer favorites, are beginning to lose their popularity.

THE LIFE CYCLE OF A PRODUCT

It has been estimated that 55 percent of the items now handled by supermarkets did not exist ten years ago. Almost every item goes through a **product life cycle**, or *stages of growth and decline in sales and earnings*. Therefore, if a company cannot come up with new products regularly, its survival will be threatened by shrinking profits.

The time spans involved in the life cycle of a product can vary greatly—from the month or two a fad may last to the many years a basic product may sell. But all new products tend to go through the same four basic life-cycle stages shown in Figure 3.

During a new product's *introductory stage* the aim of the manufacturer is chiefly to make the public aware of the product's existence and to stimulate a demand for it. Since this typically involves an expensive advertising and promotional campaign, on top of the costs of research and development, a manufacturer may well lose money during the introductory phase. Even so, it must be accepted as a necessary investment if the product is to succeed.

Next comes the *growth stage,* which is marked by a rapid upswing in sales volume and profit as word-of-mouth and advertising attract new customers. For example, during the four-year growth stage of the Rival Crock-Pot (a slow-cooker that can cook a meal by itself), sales went from zero to $125 million. This is also the period in which other companies try to get a share of the market by bringing out their own versions of the new product—sometimes with improvements, but more often simply straight imitations. As soon as large appliance makers such as Sunbeam and Hamilton Beach saw how well the Rival Crock-Pot was doing, they rushed into the market with their own slow-

STAGES IN THE LIFE CYCLE OF A PRODUCT

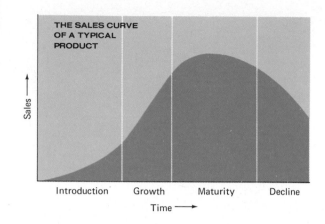

This graph shows the way sales for a typical product change over time. Sales grow slowly during the introduction period. Then, during the growth period, they rise sharply, finally peaking when the product reaches the stage of maturity. Last is a stage of decline, in which sales slowly fall off.

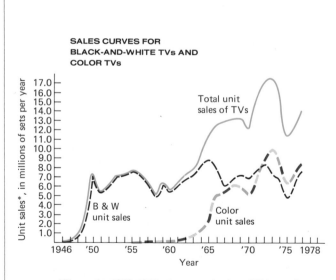

*Figures for 1946–1954 refer to *production* of TV sets; those from 1955 on refer to *sales* (and include imports)

Here are the sales curves for two actual products, black-and-white TVs and color TVs. Notice how sales on black-and-white TVs have declined as color-TV sales have grown.

(Data from Electronic Industries Association, 1975)

FIGURE 3

cookers; so did several foreign companies, which attempted to attract customers with cheaper versions.

During the *maturity stage,* sales continue to rise for a time but eventually level off as the number of potential new customers is depleted. (Rival's 1976 earnings, for example, dropped more than 22 percent below that of 1975.) At the same time, the intensified competition gradually lowers profits as the supply of similar products comes to exceed the demand, and companies are forced to reduce prices in hopes of increasing their share of the dwindling market.

Finally, in the *decline stage* of a product's life cycle, the falloff in profits becomes more rapid as rival companies make a last effort to undersell one another and clear out their inventories before the market disappears altogether. The decline is often accelerated by the arrival of a new product that makes the older one obsolete—safety razors replacing straight razors, say. Or the rapid decline may simply reflect a change in public tastes. Here, too, slow-cookers followed the typical life-cycle pattern. By 1978, the slow-cooker fad had died down to the point where some companies were pulling out of the market altogether. Rival, however, was more fortunate than some companies that have pioneered new products: though it often happens that the company that first brings out the new product is also among the first to discontinue it, Rival Crock-Pots continued to sell reasonably well, and in 1978 Rival still had 60 percent of the market.

While the life cycles of new products almost always occur in the same four-stage sequence, the actual shape of the sales curve may vary greatly from one product to another—depending on consumer needs and preferences, economic conditions, the nature of the product itself, the manufacturer's marketing strategy, and any number of lesser factors. A basic product that serves a real need may show steady growth for years before leveling off. One striking example is Levi-Strauss blue jeans, whose sales have risen every year but one since the end of World War II. This product's record is all the more impressive in view of the well-known fickleness of the apparel industry in general. By contrast, sales booms on such faddish products as CB radios and negative-heel shoes proved short-lived, peaking quickly and then plummeting as the market became saturated. (And, of course, such truly frivolous items as the "pet rocks" and "mood rings" of

recent history tend to rise like skyrockets and last about as long.)

In many instances, the life cycle of a product can be influenced at least to some degree by a well-executed marketing program. When nylon was developed by du Pont during World War II, for example, its uses were almost exclusively military: material for parachutes and the like. It might subsequently have faded into near-oblivion if the company had not mounted a major effort to bring it into the general textile market as a material for stockings and other apparel. Aggressive marketing has also helped Listerine's mouthwash retain a commanding share of the market against considerable competition, much as Seven-Up's "Uncola" campaign strengthened its position in relation to Coke and Pepsi. Indeed, any number of familiar products that might have long since entered the decline stage instead have built strong and durable sales records through a flexible approach to marketing.

WHAT IS A NEW PRODUCT?

Some experts try to differentiate between genuinely new products and others that merely represent improvements or additions to existing products. Polaroid's first picture-in-a-minute camera was clearly an innovative product. The various models introduced later could be described simply as improvements on the original camera.

It is sometimes hard to distinguish between new and improved products. Was Carnation's Instant Breakfast milk drink a new product? Or was it only another milk additive like cocoa or Ovaltine? Was Gillette's Trac II razor fundamentally different just because it had an extra blade? Are radial tires a big departure from earlier types or just improvements? Perhaps the most useful clue is the way consumers view the product. If it appears different and new in some way to an important segment of the market, then it is a new product.

Deciding whether a product is truly new or not is often crucial to marketing strategy. Should it be promoted as an improved version of an existing item? Or should it be sold as a new product? If Instant Breakfast had been promoted as merely another form of milk flavoring, it might not have gained a wide following. Believing that the product had a potential as a truly new kind of breakfast substitute, the company advertised, packaged, and promoted it accordingly. Carnation even went so far as to insist that Instant Breakfast be shelved in supermarkets along with breakfast cereals rather than with cocoas and chocolate syrup.

Introducing new products is by far the most risky part of any marketing effort. (Experts estimate that some 40 to 60 percent of all new products that actually reach the market fail.) Many others are withdrawn by management before they are ever marketed in the first place. Indeed, such nationally advertised failures as American Motors' Pacer, the rotary-engine Mazda from Japan, and Campbell's Red Kettle dehydrated soups are far outnumbered by those that most of us, for better or worse, never hear of at all.

STAGES OF PRODUCT DEVELOPMENT

A new product may take a direct or roundabout route in its passage from idea to its final form, but virtually all products that come to be pass through the series of eight steps described below.

The first step is the *generation of ideas,* a process that may arise from within a company or from any number of outside sources. A manufacturer may think up a new product, like Presto's hamburger cooker, that it believes consumers will like; it may buy the rights to someone's invention; or it may simply produce its own version of another company's new product. Ideas may also come from the sales staff or other employees, from market-research or advertising firms, from trade associations or government agencies. In any event, the source of an idea is less important than the manner in which a company guides it through subsequent stages of development.

The second step is the *screening of new ideas* to assess their general practicality and decide which ones are worth further study. This screening process is actually just the first in a series of evaluations that a product idea will be subjected to as it moves further toward development.

Another evaluation technique, *concept testing,* will often take place at this point. A description of the proposed product, including its benefits and its probable price, will be read or shown to a small number of consumers. The consumers will then be asked from ten to fifteen questions, such as "Would you buy this product?" and "Is the price too expensive for you?" Concept testing is useful in determining what consumers believe to be the best points of the product. (It is important to note that similar testing may be used at any other stage during the product development. For example, if the new product's sales are unsatisfactory, interviewers may again go out and ask questions of consumers in an effort to learn why the product is not selling.)

In the fourth step, *business analysis,* the ideas still under consideration are examined with a view to their commercial prospects. It is here that an idea is translated into a practical business proposal, focusing on specific product features, estimating its potential sales and profitability, and establishing a development plan.

An idea that passes successfully through concept testing is ready to move into *prototype development.* This fifth step marks the point where it leaves the drawing board and becomes an actual product, manufactured in small numbers and put through performance tests to evaluate it technically and decide whether it can be produced on a large scale.

The sixth step is *product testing,* where a small number of consumers is actually asked to use the product. Often during product testing, the paired-comparison testing method will be used. This approach involves asking a consumer to compare, for example, the taste of coffee X with that of coffee Y. If the results of product testing are convincingly good, the next step—test marketing—may be skipped altogether.

The seventh step is *test marketing*—making the product available in certain geographical areas and studying consumer response to it. That response might indicate such things as a need for changes in the item's design or production. Test marketing provides a basis for fine-tuning the product.

The final stage is *commercialization,* which must be done quickly. Once a go-ahead decision is made, production and marketing programs must be set in motion as fast as possible, since competitors (spared the need to conduct their own pretesting) will likely be trying to rush into the market with a similar product.

THE RISKS OF PRODUCT DEVELOPMENT

Up to this point the company is in control of the development process, deciding at each stage whether to drop the new idea, study it further, or move on to the next step. Once the new product makes its debut in the marketplace, however, its destiny begins to be guided by factors largely beyond the company's control, such as the competitive situation, the health of the economy, governmental policies, and—far from least—the never-totally-predictable behavior of the consumer. These built-in uncertainties, combined with the high costs of developing and promoting new products, underscore the critical importance of the first three steps in the development process—that is, while the potential product is still in the concept stage. After the first step, each following one involves considerably more money and manpower than the one preceding it, and for this reason alone it is in any company's vital interest to weed out unpromising ideas as early on as possible. Even more important, a great many products fail not because their manufacturers lack marketing skill, but because the products themselves were ill-conceived or badly timed. In other words, if a basic misjudgment is made early in the game, everything that follows will only make the mistake more costly. And, of course, a company must be careful not to make the mistake of weeding out an idea that would have been successful.

Depending on the industry involved, the risks attending the development of a new product can sometimes take on awesome dimensions. One of the largest of all such ventures was the Ford Motor Company's recent $800-million gamble on its new European mini-car, the Fiesta. Through the 1960s, Ford's European subsidiary had stayed out of the mini-car (under thirteen feet long) business, viewing it as an unprofitable market. In the early 1970s, though, a new breed of high-performance "super minis" brought out by Fiat, Volkswagen, and Renault proved to be extremely popular—and quite profitable indeed. Their success made it increasingly evident to Ford that keeping its overall share of European sales would mean entering the mini-car market, risky as it was. In 1973, after much consideration, the decision was made to move ahead from the concept stage to the actual manufacture of an automobile. The decision was especially perilous because, for Ford, it meant starting from near scratch: the company had very little experience in mini-car engineering and no plants designed for the task. Thus, beyond the large expenses of producing any new car, the company had to finance basic research in mini-car design (disassembling more than fifty of its competitors' cars in the process), carry out extensive studies of the needs and preferences of its potential customers, and test and retest numerous prototypes. On top of all this, Ford had to build an entire new assembly plant in Spain and enlarge existing plants in other countries.[2]

The end product of this massive investment began rolling off the assembly lines in late 1976, and within a year it appeared that Ford's $800 million gamble would pay off. The Fiesta quickly established itself as a technical and commercial success, opening up the possibility of Ford's overtaking Fiat as the leading seller of automobiles in Europe—and, almost as a fringe benefit, giving it a head start over its American rivals in fighting back against mounting foreign-car sales in the United States.*

BRANDING

So far we've followed the development of a product—from an idea to an actual item—and we've followed the stages a product goes through in its lifetime. But there are a number of other marketing considerations connected with the product area. In the sections that follow, we'll look at some of these—including branding, packaging, and pricing.

What is a brand? A **brand** is *a name, term, symbol, sign, design, or combination of these, used to identify the products of a firm and differentiate them from those of competitors.* Tide, Oldsmobile, and Coca-Cola are *brand names.* McDonald's golden arches, the Jolly Green Giant, and Borden's Elsie the Cow are *brand symbols.* Either a brand name or a brand symbol can be registered with the United States Patent and Trademark Office and thus made a **trademark**—that is, *a brand that has been given legal protection so that its owner has exclusive rights to its use.*

Not all products, of course, are marketed under the brands owned by their manufacturers. Brand

* Adapted from "Ford's Fiesta: $800 Million Bet," August 1977 DUN'S REVIEW

names may also be owned by middlemen or retailers. Sears buys tires and other automobile accessories from many manufacturers and sells them under the Allstate brand. A&P purchases canned fruits, jellies, rice, household cleaning products, and frozen goods from hundreds of different suppliers and offers them under Jane Parker, A&P, or Yukon brand names. *Brands owned by national manufacturers* are called **national brands.** *Brands owned by middlemen* like Sears or A&P are termed **private brands.**

THE IMPORTANCE OF BRANDS

A well-known and respected brand name is one of the most valuable assets a company can possess and is often a key factor in a firm's success. It permits the company to differentiate its products from those of the competition, thus giving it a special marketing advantage. Johnson & Johnson, for example, does not have to price its baby powder on a level with or below other baby powders in order to attract customers. The quality image associated with the Johnson & Johnson brand permits it to charge a premium price. In addition, an established brand name simplifies the introduction of new products. When Johnson & Johnson came out with its diaper lotion, the product enjoyed wide recognition as a quality item from the beginning.

By the same token, the lack of a reputable brand name can prove a major competitive handicap, no matter how good a company's products. Japan's Sharp Corporation, for instance, has long been an important producer of televisions, hi-fi components, and other electronic equipment. Although its products are highly rated by experts in the field, the name does not immediately conjure up a "quality image" among most consumers. The reason for this is largely that, while competitors like Sony and Panasonic were waging ad campaigns that stressed the quality (and prestige value) of their products, Sharp was concentrating on the lower-income range of the market. Selling at lower prices, chiefly through discount houses, Sharp held a respectable share of the total market—but remained virtually anonymous. Then, during the early 1970s, rising wages in Japan and the declining value of the dollar in relation to the yen made it less and less possible for Sharp to undersell its rivals and still make a profit. The company had no choice but to raise its

prices toward the level of Sony and the others, and it was here that the lack of strong brand recognition became a serious problem. Certain of Sharp's newer product lines—pocket calculators and microwave ovens in particular—did well enough on their own merits, but in the area of TVs, radios, and stereo equipment Sharp found it difficult to escape its old "cut-rate" image (though an aggressive promotional campaign has begun to have an effect).[3]

Choosing a brand name

The search for a good brand name can be difficult. The name should be short and easy to remember, and it should have pleasant associations for the potential customer. National BankAmericard, for example, recently launched a massive campaign here and abroad to publicize its new name—Visa. The name change was judged necessary to eliminate the confusion of doing business under some twenty-two different names around the world—Barclaycard in England and Chargex in Canada, to name only two—and Visa was found to satisfy the requirements of shortness and pleasantness.

The search for a multinational brand name, in particular, can be complicated by any number of linguistic pitfalls. For example, when Standard Oil of New Jersey was looking for a replacement for its Esso brand name, a popular suggestion was Enco. The name was finally vetoed, however, because in Japanese, *enco* means "stalled car." The company ultimately chose Exxon and then spent approximately $100 million in making and publicizing the name changeover. A company should make sure that a brand name fits its product. For example, Frigidaire—a brand name based on the word "frigid"—is an appropriate name for refrigerators and air conditioners but wouldn't work as well with such products as heating units or stoves.

Are brand names always necessary?

Despite the advantages of having a brand, many companies do not engage in campaigns to establish national brand awareness for their products. Some, like Sharp, may focus on a segment of the market in which that awareness is not considered crucial. Others may deal in standardized products like steel ingots that are sold to industrial customers. Since such customers buy primarily for rational motives like price, attempts to differentiate the product through a brand name would be ineffective. There are also some fashion goods, like dresses, that have shunned brand-name identification. In this case the manufacturer assumes that the consumer buys a dress because of fit or styling that may not be duplicated by other dresses sold under the same brand name. Several clothing manufacturers are now challenging this assumption, however. It is possible that brand names will assume more importance in this very competitive business in the future.

PACKAGING

Fifty years ago, "rushing the growler" was a familiar dinner-time procedure in big-city neighborhoods. A family member, usually a teen-ager, was sent running to the corner tavern with a bucket (the growler), which the proprietor filled with beer. Such simple packaging was typical of many other items consumers bought. Sugar and butter were scooped from sacks and tubs into small brown paper bags, fish was wrapped in newspapers. Since then, however, the "packaging revolution" has occurred. Almost everything we buy comes elaborately packaged, except oil that comes through pipelines, a few wheeled products like automobiles, and an occasional oddity like the daily newspaper. Businesses spend over $41 billion a year on packaging.[4] The blister package of screws, the plastic egg for L'eggs hosiery, and the individually wrapped slices of cheese are typical of how goods are now packaged (or overpackaged, as some people think) for the American consumer.

THE ADVANTAGES OF PACKAGING

Packaging can serve useful purposes. It is often needed to provide physical protection for products: plastic or cardboard egg containers fulfill this requirement. It is also designed to promote products by making them simpler for retailers to display and handle and by attracting customers' attention. The packaging of supermarket merchandise serves these functions.

In some cases innovative design can make the packaging an essential part of the product itself. Some years ago the Carter Products Company broke into the men's toiletries field in a big way with a new shaving cream called Rise, sold not in the standard tube but in an aerosol can that produced frothy, ready-to-use lather. A more recent packaging innovation is the "retort pouch" for food products. This flexible bag, made of layered plastic, aluminum foil, and polyester, can preserve its contents as long as cans or jars do, needs no refrigeration, and can simply be dropped in boiling water—producing hot food in five minutes. The retort pouch has already become popular in Europe and Japan, and may well duplicate its success among America's eat-and-run consumers in the next few years.

A change in packaging can also create a "new" product by making it available in a form or size that proves attractive to a new group of consumers. Researchers found, for example, that many people would buy turkey more often were it not for the time-consuming preparation and week's worth of leftovers; consequently, some producers began marketing quartered turkeys and enjoyed a rapid growth in their year-round sales. Similarly, the one-serving cans of Campbell soup, the newly introduced smaller cans of Coca-Cola—and even the familiar six-packs of soft drinks and beer—were introduced to make products available in amounts convenient to different consumer segments.

Safety or convenience may also enter into the choice of a package. Plastic bottles have largely replaced glass containers for bathroom products like shampoo and mouthwash. Some manufacturers believe that reusable containers offer a competitive advantage. Thus liquor is often offered in elaborate cut-glass decanters, and margarine is sold in handy little plastic bowls.

PROBLEMS CREATED BY PACKAGING—AND SOME POSSIBLE SOLUTIONS

Despite its usefulness, packaging has come under attack. Complaints about packaging emphasize the litter that it causes, the difficulty and expense of disposing of

An individual package can be both functional and stunningly attractive . . .

and nearly 90 percent of soft-drink bottles are non-returnable. This represents millions of tons of waste glass. Throwaway cans waste millions of tons of aluminum and steel.

There are, of course, practical reasons for the widespread use of throwaway bottles and cans. Consumers seem willing to pay extra for the convenience of disposables. Storekeepers dislike returnable bottles because of the expense and trouble of handling them. And the producers of soft drinks and beer claim that they lose money on returnables. In our affluent society the modest deposit fees are not enough to motivate people to return them. A bottler must average at least eight round trips to pay off the higher initial cost of manufacturing a returnable bottle. Several years ago the average soft-drink bottle made about twenty trips. Today the average is only ten. In some cities of the Northeast, it has declined to fewer than two.

Ecologists believe that authorities must make stronger efforts to solve the problems of litter, garbage disposal, and waste associated with many forms of packaging. Some experts recommend a packaging tax: Producers would pay a sum based on the weight of the packaging material used, and the tax would be used to pay all the social costs connected with the packaging, including collection and disposal.

The states of Oregon, Vermont, and Maine now require a deposit on all beverage containers, and indications are that others may soon do likewise. But, as we noted in Chapter 1, such attempts to protect the environment do sometimes have unfortunate side effects. A large-scale switch to returnables would have a costly impact on producers—especially those without the financial resources and distribution networks of the biggest soft-drink companies. The middle-sized Shasta Company, for instance, which only distributes its products to wholesalers and supermarket chains (unlike Coke, Pepsi, and others, which deliver directly to retailers), would have a hard time arranging to reclaim all its empties left at hundreds of individual stores.[5]

Some concerned citizens believe that what is needed is a combination of remedies. Simple common sense should prevent certain goods, such as children's toys, from being absurdly overpackaged. Better technology, aimed at recycling, would prevent the waste now associated with one-time use of packaging mate-

the materials, and the waste of resources. Environmentalists are particularly disturbed about the growing use of plastics because they are hard to dispose of. Many plastics are resistant to decay. Others, like polyvinyl chloride (PVC), emit poisonous gases when they are burned.

One of the most offensive forms of packaging, according to environmentalists, is the throwaway bottle or can. It is estimated that 96 percent of beer bottles

... but thousands of such packages scattered across the landscape pose a serious threat to the environment.

rials. If technology could make recycling profitable, it would also provide the economic incentive required to collect and reprocess the materials.

LABELING

As we mentioned earlier, marketing is much more than creating a product. A company must also develop

a suitable label—and the label must meet government regulations. A label is either a separate item attached to a package or a part of the bottle, can, or foil container that holds the product. Generally it serves to identify a brand. Sometimes it also gives grading information about the contents, as discussed in Chapter 7. A label may also provide promotional information. Because such information makes claims about the contents, it has now come under regulation to avoid abuse.

The labeling of foods, drugs, many health products, and cosmetics is regulated under the federal Food, Drug, and Cosmetic Act (1938). This act gave the Food and Drug Administration (FDA) the authority to monitor the accuracy of the ingredients listed on labels. For example, a fruit drink cannot be labeled and sold as a fruit *juice* unless it contains an established minimum fruit content. Chicken cannot be named first in the list of ingredients for a frozen chicken pot pie unless chicken is the single largest ingredient in the product.

A jar that says peanut butter on the label must by law contain a product that's at least 90 percent ground roasted peanuts, and the rest may consist only of a few seasonings and a stabilizer to keep the oil from separating. A new product called "peanut spread" does not have to have a minimum peanut content and is allowed to use artificial peanut flavor—but it must still match the nutritional values of regular peanut butter (or else it must accept the lowly name of "imitation peanut butter").[6]

Product labels are also subject to the Fair Packaging and Labeling Act (1966). Among other things, this act provides that every label must identify the product, give the name and address of the manufacturer or distributor, and show the net quantity in a conspicuous place. In addition, new legislation requires the labels on cosmetics to list the ingredients—a law that was understandably greeted with dismay by an industry used to guarding its formulas and "secret ingredients" like crown jewels.

Fur and textiles must be labeled in accordance with the Fur Products Labeling Act (1952) and the Textile Fiber Products Identification Act (1960). The label on a fur product must show the natural name of the fur and its country of origin. The label on clothing and household textiles must list the names and percentages of fiber content (for example, 70 percent cotton and 30 percent Dacron), the name of the manufacturer, and the country where the product was made. Clothing labels must also have washing instructions.

In another area of labeling, legislation was passed in May, 1977, to revise and strengthen the 1960 Federal Hazardous Substances Labeling Act. Now called the Federal Hazardous Substances Act, this law recognizes that there are some products so dangerous that no warning label could adequately protect the user and that there are some consumers—young children—for whom labeling offers no protection. Such items are banned. Any manufacturer, distributor, or retailer who sells a banned hazardous product or a product that is later banned must buy back the product when it is returned and also pay the original buyer for any expenses involved in returning the product.

PRICING THE PRODUCT

The manufacturer must make decisions not only about the development of products, but also about how to price them. Setting prices is an extremely complicated process—one that is affected both by the external economic environment and by the company's internal policies.

PRICING AND ECONOMICS

As you read in Chapter 1, and in our Enrichment Chapter on Business and the American Economy, our market mechanism, operating under capitalism, relies heavily on competition in establishing the prices of goods and services. In a system of pure capitalism the twin factors of supply and demand alone would determine price. There would be only one price at which supply (the quantity of goods offered for sale) would equal demand (the customers' desire for the goods). But our system of modified capitalism is more complicated. For one thing, the nature of certain businesses gives them a good deal of freedom in setting the prices they want. Though monopolies (companies producing the total output of a given good or service) are rare today, we do have a number of oligopolies (where a few large producers control the supply). Formal price fix-

PRICING: LET BUYERS BE WARY

Caveat emptor, "let the buyer beware," has long been a slogan that wise consumers have followed in making purchases. With careful shopping, people do not need to pay more than they should for merchandise. Unfortunately, most shoppers do not always get their money's worth. Two pricing practices that the unwary often fall for are bait pricing and multiple-unit pricing.

When retailers practice bait pricing, they advertise a product—for example, a low-priced television set—to lure customers into a store. When customers arrive, however, the television may not be available. If it is available, sales personnel will discourage people from buying that item. They may downgrade the television or refuse to guarantee its reliability. After the customers are thoroughly turned off by the product, they will then be invited to switch to higher-priced models. For this reason, the practice is also called "bait and switch."

It is perfectly legal for salespeople to encourage customers to "trade up," buy a more expensive

ing is illegal, but some economists contend that oligopolies have informal understandings that effectively control prices. (For further discussion of government regulation of pricing, see Chapter 15 and our Enrichment Chapter on American Business in the Future.)

Another factor that influences pricing is inflation. Since the 1960s there has been a continuing increase in the prices of most goods and services. Whatever its causes, inflation feeds on itself. Higher costs lead to higher prices, which lead to higher wages, and so on in a seemingly endless spiral.

PRICING AND BUSINESS POLICIES

Almost every business has a general approach underlying its specific pricing decisions. This approach might be called its pricing policy. Some firms follow a policy of **pricing above the market**, *charging prices*

item. What is illegal, according to the Federal Trade Commission, is to offer something for sale without the intention of selling it. Unfortunately, the FTC can only enforce its ruling in interstate commerce, so many local retailers continue the practice.

Another practice that shortchanges customers is multiple-unit pricing. Shoppers are used to thinking that if they buy more of an item, they will save money. A six-pack of soda should cost less than six individual cans, for example. But this is not always true. A store offering one can of cleanser for 28¢ did better when it marketed two cans for 59¢.

One method designed to help customers faced with multiple-unit pricing (and with comparison shopping in general) is unit pricing. It is confusing for a shopper to decide on the spot whether a six-ounce can of tomato sauce at 35¢, an eight-ounce can at 42¢, or three five-ounce cans for 80¢ is a better buy. So, a unit price—in this case, the cost per ounce—is posted to help a buyer decide.

Strangely enough, though unit pricing is a useful consumer aid, it has had mixed results in practice. Most shoppers favor it, but few seem to rely on it. More consumer education is needed to impress shoppers with its obvious advantages.

that are higher than those of competitors. These are usually firms selling goods—Rolls Royces, say, or Joy perfume—to high-income groups that want prestige.

Other firms have adopted the practice of **pricing below the market**, *charging prices that are below those of competitors.* Sometimes this policy is adopted by a company coming into the market after competitors are well established. Foreign car manufacturers price their automobiles in this manner. In other cases, a firm will base its entire appeal to customers on lower prices. Discount stores use this approach. Pricing below the market is particularly effective if a firm wishes to capture a larger share of the market.

A third alternative is **pricing with the market**, or *charging prices that match those of competitors.* Generally this means following the pricing policy of *a major producer in the industry.* This producer is known as the **price leader**. In the automobile industry General Motors usually sets the price. Ford, Chrysler, and

American Motors keep their price tags very close to the GM level. In the steel industry, U.S. Steel is the price leader. Most products sold in stores are priced with the market.

By pricing with the market, producers avoid the tremendous effort required to find out what the consumer would actually pay. Instead, they assume that the price leader has done this research and has established the right price. This practice also creates a business climate in which all firms avoid the unpleasantness of price competition. Each knows that if it cuts prices, its competitors will do so too. The outcome might well be that they would all make less money. Under price leadership, this competition—potentially dangerous to the rival companies—is avoided. Companies have long preferred to compete through brand differentiation rather than through price competition.

Recent changes in pricing patterns

Today, fewer industries simply follow the price leaders: the combination of a sluggish economy and stiffer foreign competition has forced many American firms

ASPECTS OF THE MARKETING MIX: PRICE

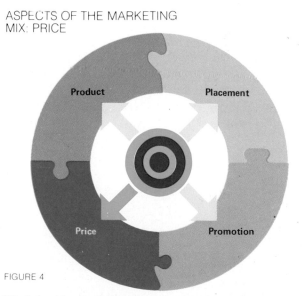

FIGURE 4

What should you charge for your product? To determine the best price, you must consider the product's life-cycle stage and the prices that are charged by competitors. But even more important, you must consider how strong demand is in the target market.

out of their old habits. In a variety of industries, companies are finding themselves faced with the unpleasant choice of either cutting prices or watching their shares of the market be whittled down by competitors. General Motors and Ford, for example, recently took the unprecedented step of lowering the West Coast prices of their subcompacts to counteract the rising sales of Japanese imports—which means that for the first time, General Motors and Ford do *not* have a uniform price for the whole United States.[7] Other blue-chip producers have likewise had to begin taking their lower-priced competition more seriously than in the past. Perhaps the most dramatic battleground for price warfare has been the airline industry. As a result of increasingly relaxed government fare regulations, the airlines have plunged into a fierce rate-slashing struggle to hold onto their shares of the market.

While the increase in price competition has provided a momentary bonanza for many customers, its long-term effects may not all be welcome ones. The old system of pricing by industry leaders may have made some goods more expensive than they had to be, but it also provided a cushion for smaller, less profitable companies that could not afford head-on price competition with the corporate giants. As it is, the new wave of price cutting has already dealt a severe blow to American Motors, which had been in an insecure position beforehand; and it may have the same effect across an ever-widening spectrum of industry.[8]

CHOOSING A PRICE FOR A NEW PRODUCT

Special pricing possibilities are involved when manufacturers introduce a new product. The most popular approach is called **skimming**. *The manufacturer charges a high price during the introductory stage, later reducing it when the product is no longer a novelty and competition enters the market.* Companies that adopt a skimming policy try to recover their development costs as quickly as possible through high initial prices. Typical examples of skimming involved the first color TV sets and penicillin. Skimming is also widely practiced in the movie industry. A new picture often premieres in a "showcase" theater for a dollar or two

above what will be charged when it reaches neighborhood theaters.

Another approach to the pricing of a new product is **penetration pricing**. *Manufacturers introduce the product at a low price and plan to get back the initial investment through big sales.* The manufacturers of the Bic ballpoint pen and the Cricket disposable lighter used this strategy. Penetration pricing offers two potential advantages in addition to rapid sales to a large market. It may discourage competitors from entering the field because the low price permits only small profits per unit. And it may be economical because producing large quantities saves money.

PRICING TECHNIQUES

Let us assume that a company has established its general pricing policy and has determined how it will sell a new product. How will the company actually set the price? It will undoubtedly take into account several factors, among them markup and geographic considerations.

MARKUP

As usually defined, **markup** *is the difference between the cost of an item and its selling price.* In modern merchandising, *firms generally express this difference in terms of percentage,* the **markup percentage**. If an item costs a firm $50 and is sold for $75, the markup percentage is $25; the markup percent is 33⅓. The markup percentage has two goals. It must cover all the expenses of the firm, including not only the cost of the item but also the cost of selling it. And it must contain an allowance for a planned profit.

Most businesses today carry a large number of items. (Macy's department stores, for example, are reported to handle over 100,000 different items.) It would be extremely difficult to calculate the markup percentage for each one. For this reason, many businesses tend to use an **average markup** in setting prices; that is, *the same percentage markup is used for each item in a given product line.*

✗ *Study*

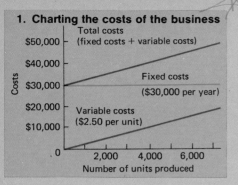

1. Charting the costs of the business

Total costs
(fixed costs + variable costs)

Fixed costs
($30,000 per year)

Variable costs
($2.50 per unit)

Costs

$50,000
$40,000
$30,000
$20,000
$10,000
0

Number of units produced
2,000   4,000   6,000

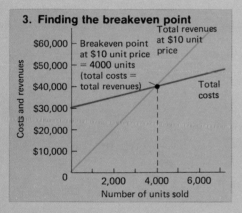

2. Charting revenues

Total revenues
$60,000
$50,000
$40,000
$30,000
$20,000
$10,000
0

Total revenues
at $10 unit
price

Number of units sold
2,000   4,000   6,000

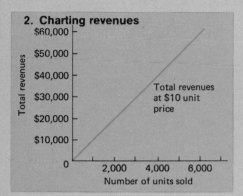

3. Finding the breakeven point

Costs and revenues

$60,000
$50,000
$40,000
$30,000
$20,000
$10,000
0

Breakeven point
at $10 unit price
= 4000 units
(total costs =
total revenues)

Total revenues
at $10 unit
price

Total
costs

Number of units sold
2,000   4,000   6,000

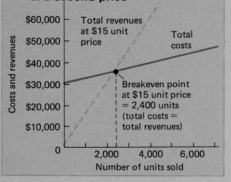

**4. Finding the breakeven point
at a second price**

Costs and revenues

$60,000
$50,000
$40,000
$30,000
$20,000
$10,000
0

Total revenues
at $15 unit
price

Total
costs

Breakeven point
at $15 unit price
= 2,400 units
(total costs =
total revenues)

Number of units sold
2,000   4,000   6,000

BREAKEVEN ANALYSIS

One of the basic questions any businessperson needs to answer is, "How many units of my product (or service) will I have to sell in order to break even—that is, to cover costs?" And of course the question that goes along with this one is, "How many units will I have to sell in order to make a reasonable profit?" If you don't have a basic estimate of these two figures, you may be out of business before you know it.

The best way to attack these questions is through a method known as breakeven analysis. Here's how it's done.

1. Charting the costs of the business When a marketing manager considers the costs involved in operating a business, he or she generally has to look at two different kinds of costs.

Fixed costs are those that *must be covered no matter how many units of the product or service the business produces;* they include items such as rent, insurance, and office salaries. For a small beauty salon, for example, fixed costs might amount to $30,000 a year.

Variable costs include items such as raw materials and labor, which *increase with the number of units of the product or service the business produces.* In a beauty salon, for example, labor and shampoo for one haircut (with wash and set) might be $2.50—so ten units would cost $25.00, twenty units would cost $50.00, and so on.

To figure out the total costs of operating the business, simply add the variable costs to the fixed costs. Total costs increase with the number of units produced.

2. Charting revenues The next step is to chart the revenues, or payments, the company will receive as it sells more and more units at the price the manager plans to charge. If the beauty salon charges $10 per haircut, its revenues are $1,000 for 100 units, $2,000 for 200 units, and so on.

3. Finding the breakeven point Next, we put the two graphs together, to show costs *and* revenues. Notice that there is a point at which the line representing revenues crosses and goes over the line representing costs. This point is the **breakeven** point—*the point at which revenues will just cover costs.* Now, to find the number of units the business must sell to reach the breakeven point, just look along the "number of units produced" line at the bottom.

Any units you sell *beyond* that number will produce profit for your business.

4. Finding the breakeven point at a second price What if you charge a higher price for your product or service? You will break even after selling a smaller number of units. To find out exactly how many units you will have to sell to break even at your second price, simply repeat steps 2 and 3 using the second price. Here, we have charted revenues and breakeven point at a unit price of $15.

Making a final decision on a price Clearly, each of the two prices offers you certain advantages.

The higher price, which allows you to break even after selling fewer units, may be attractive if you suspect that the market for your product or service is limited in your geographic area. At the lower price you will have to sell more units, but your price may bring more customers. Which price do you decide on? Here you have to make an "educated guess" about *your* customers and *your* product.

FIGURING A MARKUP PERCENTAGE

Markup percentage is usually expressed in terms of the retail selling price. To determine the markup percent of the retail selling price, you divide the markup percentage by the selling price. Let us take an example. If an item sells for $3.00 and costs $2.25, the markup is 75¢. In terms of the retail selling price, this is 25 percent.

$$\text{Markup percent} = \frac{\text{Markup}}{\text{Selling price}}$$
$$X = \frac{.75}{3.00}$$
$$X = 25 \text{ percent}$$

Sometimes the markup is figured on the cost value of the item rather than on the retail selling price. In the above example, the rate of markup on cost would be 33⅓ percent.

$$\text{Markup percent} = \frac{\text{Markup}}{\text{Cost}}$$
$$X = \frac{.75}{2.25}$$
$$X = 33\tfrac{1}{3} \text{ percent}$$

Whether a firm uses retail price or cost as the base depends on the kind of accounting procedures it uses. The accounting procedures, in turn, depend on the type of merchandise sold. In general, the cost base is used by stores that sell a limited variety of merchandise, such as furniture stores, or those that have a wide range of percentage markups, such as jewelry shops. In any case, a market manager should be familiar with both methods of determining markups to set prices.

Markups vary by type of store. Take, for example, an item costing 50¢ in various types of retail outlets: the markup for this item might range from a low of 22 percent for a supermarket to a high of 55 percent for a florist, and the retail price might thus vary from a low of 64¢ to a high of $1.11. Florists have a high markup percentage because they deal in extremely perishable goods sold to a relatively small market. Another factor in the wide range of markup percentages is **turnover**, *the rate at which inventory is replaced* (which depends on how fast items are sold). A gift shop with a turnover of three times a year must make more profit on each item than a liquor store with a turnover of thirty times a year.

GEOGRAPHIC CONSIDERATIONS

In some cases, transporting merchandise from the seller to the customer can cost a lot. In pricing such goods, manufacturers have to decide who will pay the transportation costs.

FOB pricing

One way to quote prices is on an **FOB (free on board) basis**. From the buyer's point of view, this means that *transporting the item is "free" up to the time it is placed "on board" a carrier.* All transportation costs from this time on are paid by the buyer. For example, a bicycle is sold on an FOB basis by a plant in Detroit and shipped to a store in Memphis. The manufacturer would pay to have the bicycle loaded onto a truck at his Detroit factory. The storekeeper would pay the trucking charges from Detroit to Memphis.

Manufacturers of heavy, bulky, low-cost goods often find that FOB pricing limits the markets they can serve. Customers on the West Coast will not buy cement on an FOB basis from a producer in Pennsylvania. Instead, they will purchase it from a local supplier. One solution to this problem, adopted by many large manufacturers, is to locate plants all across the country.

Zone pricing versus uniform delivery pricing

Two other pricing policies influenced by geographic considerations are uniform delivery pricing and zone pricing. Firms generally adopt one or the other. Under **uniform delivery pricing**, *buyers pay the same delivery price regardless of transportation costs.* In **zone pricing**, however, *customers outside a designated area or zone pay an additional charge.* Television advertisers who note that their product sells for more west (or east) of the Mississippi are practicing zone pricing.

OTHER PRICING CONSIDERATIONS

Many companies follow a policy called **price-lining**, *offering their merchandise at a limited number of set prices.* Record companies may offer a $3.95 line, a $4.95 line, and a $6.95 line. Price-lining is justified in two ways: It simplifies the selling job for the store-keeper, and it makes choice easier for the consumer by limiting the number of alternatives.

In many industries, *price lines tend to end in numbers slightly below the next dollar figure,* such as $3.95, $4.98, or $7.99. This is called **psychological pricing**. The assumption here is that a customer sees a $3.98 price as significantly lower than $4.00 so that the store will sell more at 2¢ less. Few studies have been made to test the accuracy of this belief. Those that have been done tend to suggest that customers are more rational than psychological pricing assumes. How often have you "translated" $4.99 into an even $5.00? Also, consumers are usually aware that sales taxes, where they exist, raise the price of an item.

Another theory of why so many prices fall just below the next full-dollar figure is based on more practical considerations. It is certainly more likely that a person will pay for a 98-cent item with a one-dollar bill than with the exact 98-cent amount. The store clerks, having to make change, must use the cash register, which records the sale of the item. This record of sales guarantees the store manager an accurate account of business. Also, by forcing the clerks to make change, there is less likelihood of their simply pocketing the one-dollar bill.

Some manufacturers who sell consumer goods advertise their merchandise at **suggested retail prices**. They may even stamp such a price on a product at the factory. Retailers have the choice of selling the goods at the suggested price or of selling for less and creating the impression that they are offering a bargain.

Finally, there are a number of different types of *discounts* which a company may offer, depending on the type of customer and the type of item being offered. We survey these discounts in the box on this page.

BUILDING YOUR BUSINESS VOCABULARY

TYPES OF DISCOUNTS

Some suppliers have discount policies that allow certain customers a reduced price for goods. **Trade discounts** are discounts offered to middlemen. For example, the retail price of a shirt may be $10; the manufacturer may sell it to the retailer at a 40 percent discount from this price, or $6. Trade discounts permit the middleman to make a profit by performing his special marketing functions.

Quantity discounts encourage customers to buy in large amounts. A hardware dealer who buys a truckload of lawn mowers will pay a lower price per lawn mower than the dealer who buys only a few machines. Some firms offer **cumulative quantity discounts.** These permit a customer to total up consecutive orders to qualify for a discount. For example, let us assume that an order of forty typewriters qualified for a 10 percent discount. An office equipment store might order twenty-five, then ten, and then another five. Since the cumulative total was forty, the store would be entitled to take 10 percent off its entire bill.

Cash discounts are given in order to encourage prompt payment. Cash discount terms are stated on the bill that accompanies the merchandise. For example, "two/ten, net 30" means that a customer who pays within ten days of receiving the merchandise can take 2 percent off the bill. The customer has the choice of paying in ten days and taking the discount, or waiting the full thirty days and paying the net, or full, amount of the bill.

Seasonal discounts are sometimes given by firms that sell seasonal items like air conditioners or ski equipment. A company that installs central home air conditioning may offer customers a 10 percent discount on work done in the fall and winter. A ski shop may give discounts on equipment purchased during the summer. Companies offer seasonal discounts to spread out their sales into those times of the year when business is slow.

CHAPTER REVIEW

One of the major responsibilities of the market manager is to determine the product mix, or list of products, that the manufacturer will sell. This product mix may consist of a single product line, or a group of products with similar physical characteristics or uses, or several product lines. Having a single product line is economical and efficient; on the other hand, having several product lines may provide a company with protection in case business conditions change.

New products are essential to a company's success because its established products are likely to go through a life cycle that includes a final period of decline in sales. Whether a product is considered new or simply improved depends on how it is perceived by the public; either type of product can help keep sales up. A new product may be developed by the manufacturer or brought in by outsiders.

A company may decide to sell its goods under a brand name, with or without a brand symbol. The brand name may be a national brand, established by a national manufacturer, or a private brand, introduced by a middleman.

Another decision involves the packaging of a product. Many people believe that overpackaging is common in American industry. Packaging does, however, serve several significant functions, including promotion, convenience, and protection of the product.

The label is an important part of the package. For many common supermarket and textile goods, government regulations specify what must be stated on the label.

Pricing policy is another key marketing decision. A company may choose to price above the market, below the market, or with the market. Special problems are involved with the introduction of a new product, and to solve these problems companies often choose the methods of skimming or of penetration pricing. An important pricing technique is markup, which may vary a great deal depending on the type of merchandise and the turnover rate. Other pricing considerations include discount policies, policies affecting transportation costs, and such selling policies as price-lining, psychological pricing, and the use of suggested retail prices.

KEY WORD REVIEW

product mix
product line
product life cycle
brand
brand name
trademark
national brands
private brands
pricing above the market
pricing below the market
pricing with the market
price leader
skimming
penetration pricing
markup
markup percentage
average markup
turnover
trade discounts
quantity discounts
cumulative quantity discounts
cash discounts
seasonal discounts
FOB (free on board) basis
uniform delivery policy
zone pricing
price-lining
psychological pricing
suggested retail prices

REVIEW QUESTIONS

1. What are some of the factors to consider in determining whether to offer a single product line or several product lines?

2. What are the eight steps in the development of a new product?

3. Describe the four phases in the life cycle of a typical new product.

4. What are the advantages offered by a successful brand name?

5. What are the functions of packaging? Why are environmentalists concerned about it?

6. What are the three main pricing policies? Give an example for each case.

7. Why would a company make use of an average markup? Why does an average markup vary widely?

CASE 1

WHAT THE WORLD NEEDS NOW . . . ?

Many companies are constantly dreaming up new products to sell to the public, but these firms do not have a monopoly on inspiration. *Advertising Age*, a leading publication in the advertising field, publishes a column called "The Idea Marketplace" in which ordinary folk, inventors, and small businesses can unveil their own new product or promotion ideas (and possibly find people or companies willing to back them). A sampling from a recent column:

A California inventor has hit on a way to use bingo to get TV viewers to watch commercials. Just before or right after a word from the sponsor, a number is flashed on the screen. Viewers at home, who get their bingo cards by sending a postcard to the TV station, match the numbers on the screen with those on their cards—for cash prizes. In addition to gaining the undivided attention of the home audience, advertisers who use the "Video Bingo" strategy could presumably also learn how many viewers they reach per advertising dollar.

The bristles of a toothbrush, a Philadelphia woman has noticed, wear out, whereas the handle does not. Her idea: sell a package that contains one handle and six attachable bristle units. Or how about a no-handle toothbrush? A man in Canada has designed a bristle unit that attaches directly to the toothpaste tube, and that can be modified with a special chamber feed-in to squirt toothpaste onto the brush.

The multimillion dollar success of bottled water has given a New York ad agency an idea for launching a product in the powdered drink or Kool-Aid category. The manufacturer of the new drink mix introduces the product with a coupon that gives the consumer a 25 percent discount on any brand of bottled water, and the following slick explanation: "Because this beverage mix is just too good to mix with plain old tap water."

Finally, from a man in Brooklyn, N.Y., comes a breakthrough in the frozen food department. It's called the Frozen Lunch Box, and that's exactly what it is: a drink, a main course (or sandwich), and a dessert, all frozen and packed into a carton in the shape of—you guessed it—a lunch box with a fold-down handle. Just take it out of the freezer in the morning, keep it at room temperature, and it will be thawed out by noon.[9]

1. Which item do you believe has the least chance of success?

2. What are the flaws in each?

CASE 2

A PRICE WAR AMONG SMOKE-DETECTOR MANUFACTURERS

You can get Captain Kelly to help you—cheap. Gillette Company, manufacturer of the smoke detector with the fireman's name, recently cut both the wholesale and suggested retail prices of the device. This means that the store-owner as well as the customer can get the Gillette smoke detector for about 40 percent less than its original asking price. Why did Gillette suddenly decide to sell its smoke detector for less? The answer can be found with the competition.

The market for home smoke detectors is estimated at about $200 million, with approximately 10 percent of all homes currently equipped with at least one such device. In 1978, unit sales were expected to top 10 million. Gillette, apparently on to a good thing, spent some $8 million in advertising in the fall of 1977 to promote its unique photoelectric early-warning system—one that the company claims is superior to those of its competitors.

The public, however, didn't buy that expensive story. What's more, at the same time that Gillette came out with Captain Kelly, other companies were quick to see that money was to to be made in the home fire-detection business. Such giants as Honeywell, General Electric, and Sears entered the field of competition, and soon the shelves were glutted with an assortment of devices. Gillette, superior early-warning system or no, had little choice but to cut the price of its product simply to get it moving off the shelves.

As usual when such a price war occurs, it's the party on the sidelines—the consumer—who benefits most.[10]

1. Considering that each home can have only so many smoke detectors, do you think that the market for them is likely to become saturated? If so, what would happen to the price of the detectors?

2. Do you think that Gillette's ambitious advertising campaign helped its competitors in any way?

3. The idea behind purchasing a detector is to save lives, and Gillette advertised Captain Kelly as a superior model. Why do you suppose people were unwilling to pay more for it?

CHAPTER NINE

PROMOTION

It's everywhere—on television and radio, in newspapers and magazines, plastered on billboards and buses, even written across the sky on sunny days. It's advertising, and no aspect of American business is a more visible or pervasive part of our lives. Everyone sees advertising, and most people have strong opinions about it. Whatever your opinions may be, there is no question that advertising has come to occupy a vital position in our economic system.

Advertising is a form of promotion—the process of informing potential customers about products or services that the producer wants to sell. In this chapter we will look at the different types of advertising, the strategies involved, and the mechanics of getting a company's message across to consumers as persuasively as possible. We will also look at the three other types of activity—personal selling, sales promotion, and publicity—that are included in the marketing function of promotion.

WHAT WILL THIS CHAPTER FOCUS ON?

After reading the material in this chapter, you will understand and be able to discuss:

■ the four basic categories of promotion—advertising, personal selling, sales promotion, and publicity

■ the three main types of advertising—primary demand advertising; selective, or brand, advertising; and institutional advertising

■ the advantages and disadvantages of advertising in the various media, including newspapers, magazines, radio, and television

■ how an advertising agency functions

■ the roles of personal selling, sales promotion, and publicity

■ the attitude of the American public toward advertising

■ the various ways advertising is regulated by the government and by the industry itself

 P. T. Barnum, a born promoter if ever there was one, liked to say there was only one liquid a man could use in excessive quantities without being swallowed up by it, and that was printer's ink. He was talking about the importance of letting people know about something you have to sell—an activity he was as good at as anyone on earth. What Barnum had to sell was tickets to his traveling circus, and he brought to the task an energy and imagination that had no limits. He once publicized the arrival of his circus on a huge scale, organizing a spectacular torchlight parade through the city that was seen by more than half a million people. The parade vehicles were drawn by elephants, camels, zebras, and other animals. Four brass bands, a calliope, an organ, bagpipes, and more performed for the crowd. And at his own expense Barnum brought in almost a hundred newspaper editors for the occasion from around the Northeast. "A very costly piece of advertising," Barnum later recalled, "which yet yielded us a magnificent return in the enthusiastic editorial endorsements of so many papers."[1]

ASPECTS OF THE MARKETING MIX: PROMOTION

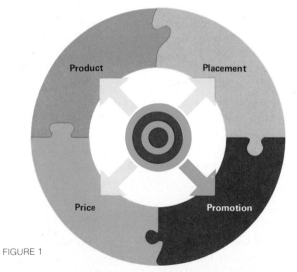

FIGURE 1

Developing an effective promotional approach is a tough challenge for the marketer. The right promotional approach depends on the needs and interests of the target market—as do all other aspects of the marketing mix.

Barnum understood a basic truth about business that has become even truer in our larger, more complex society—that building a better mousetrap is not enough. The producer must also see to it that information about the superior mousetrap is brought to the attention of potential customers. This process of communication between seller and buyer is called promotion. Many business leaders agree that it is the most important of the four Ps of marketing.

Promotion can be defined as *any communication aimed at informing, persuading, or influencing the target market.* More specifically, it can be divided into four basic methods or categories: advertising, personal selling, publicity, and sales promotion. These four methods, usually referred to together as the *promotional mix,* provide the tools with which a company's market manager seeks to communicate persuasively with the target market. In this chapter we will take a close look at all four of these methods; we will look first at advertising, which is probably the most important.

ADVERTISING

Advertising is usually defined as *any paid form of nonpersonal sales or promotional efforts made on behalf of goods, services, or ideas by an identified sponsor.* This definition may be a bit wordy, but it emphasizes the differences between advertising and the other forms of promotion. Advertising is paid for—in contrast to publicity, which seeks to attract attention in the news media and elsewhere without making any direct payment (though the indirect costs can be quite high indeed, as with Barnum's hospitality to the newspaper editors). Advertising is also "nonpersonal," in that it is done through television, newspapers, and so on, in contrast to the face-to-face contact that takes place in personal selling. It is different, too, from sales promotion, which as we shall see comprises a variety of activities that do not involve direct payment. What advertising has in common with other forms of promotion is that it can be used not only to sell goods like soap or automobiles, but also to promote services such as banking or insurance. It can even sell ideas that may not be concerned with profit at all—drug-abuse prevention, for instance, or population control.

For many companies, advertising is the most practical and effective means of getting a message out

FIGURE 2

Advertising: Here, a company or institution pays to promote a product or idea through the media. Advertising is nonpersonal selling; it reaches mass audiences.

Publicity: Publicity is nonpaid information about a company, a product, or an institution that appears in the media. Publicity is a powerful form of promotion: a single news article can generate more interest—and more sales—than pages of paid advertising.

Personal selling: In personal selling, the salesperson deals with the customer on a one-to-one basis. The salesperson can tailor the sales pitch or presentation to the individual customer, increasing the likelihood of a sale. Moreover, the salesperson can close the sale on the spot.

THE PROMOTIONAL MIX: THE FOUR BASIC WAYS TO SELL A PRODUCT

Sales promotion: Sales promotion includes any other marketing activity you can think of that's aimed at stimulating sales.

to the public. The great advantage of advertising over other types of promotion is its ability to reach mass audiences quickly at a low cost per person reached. A one-minute TV commercial during the 1978 Super Bowl may have cost a record $350,000, but it was seen by an audience of 86 million people—working out to a thrifty $40.69 for every 10,000 viewers.[2] (By comparison, imagine the cost of trying to contact 10,000 people through personal selling.)

That ability to reach mass audiences quickly is particularly important when a company wants to introduce a new product nationwide. This is true whether the company is attempting to break into a market already crowded with competition, as with Gillette's Atra razor blade recently, or to create interest in an innovative product like Sony's Betamax TV-videotape system. Advertising can also breathe new life into an older product whose sales have grown sluggish, as illustrated by the memorable ad campaign for Dr. Pepper in the early 1970s. Describing it sympathetically as "America's most misunderstood soft drink," the ads aroused enough curiosity to boost Dr. Pepper's sales 91 percent in four years.[3]

Little wonder, then, that businesses of all kinds have devoted larger and larger amounts of money to their advertising budgets, spending a record total of $37 billion in 1977.[4]

THREE TYPES OF ADVERTISING

Advertising can be classified in three main categories: *primary-demand advertising; selective,* or *brand, advertising;* and *institutional advertising.* The three categories differ in what they try to accomplish.

Primary-demand advertising *tries to increase the total demand for products without distinguishing between brands.* The Wool Bureau has attempted to get purchasers of apparel to select wool goods rather than synthetics. The California Prune Growers Association has tried to popularize prunes by running radio commercials praising the virtues of "the funny fruit." Such advertising is generally sponsored by trade associations, touting the value of everything from milk and orange juice to savings-bank life insurance and regular eye checkups. Sometimes an industry-wide union will also advertise. For example, the Plasterers Union, in an attempt to discourage the use of wallboard in construction, has run full-page ads calling on New Yorkers to "keep New York plastered." And, fittingly enough, politicians also lend their persuasive skills to appropriate causes. The governors of Idaho and Maine, for instance, have both made TV commercials praising the potatoes grown in their states.

Selective, or **brand, advertising** *aims at getting purchasers to use a particular branded product,* for example, Del Monte prunes or Hart Schaffner & Marx suits. This type of promotion accounts for the largest share of money spent on advertising. Selective advertising directed at the consumer market is generally found on TV and in newspapers and magazines. Selective advertising intended for the industrial market may be limited to trade magazines.

Institutional advertising *is designed to create goodwill for a company rather than to sell specific goods.* Since the gasoline shortage of 1973 and 1974, oil companies have spent large sums of money on newspaper

and TV advertising to suggest ways to conserve gasoline. They have hoped to create an image of themselves as public-spirited organizations, using such slogans as "We're working to keep your trust." Likewise, U.S. Steel has run a series of "We're involved" ads illustrating various energy-saving projects, some not even related to steel production. Other institutional advertising is even more subtle. Mobil Oil has sponsored "Masterpiece Theatre" on the Public Broadcasting System (PBS). Xerox has financed hour-long shows on controversial issues. Local department stores sometimes run ads supporting the United Fund. In every case, the objective is to improve the company's image and to create an aura of good feeling about the company—either among potential customers or such people as legislators, journalists, and other opinion leaders.

The political importance of institutional advertising is especially clear in the case of privately owned utility companies. These utilities, operating under government-granted monopolies, are regulated by state or local agencies that must ultimately answer to public opinion. Thus an electric company that wants permission to raise its rates or build a nuclear generating plant will be well advised to promote a responsible, public-spirited image. An example is Con Edison's "Save a Watt" campaign in New York. Such messages are directed at the public not only as consumers—Con Ed's "Save a Watt" ads actually encourage people to use *less* of its product—but also as voters.

ADVERTISING MEDIA

As used in promotion, **media** refers to *all the different means by which advertising reaches its audience.* Each medium has both good and bad features for an advertiser. The percentage of advertising dollars spent in the various media is shown in Figure 3. Newspapers account for most of the expenditures; magazines, radio, television, and direct mail account for most of the remaining outlays.

Newspapers

This medium offers certain advantages that cannot be matched by any of the other media. The most important advantage is that the lag between the time an advertisement is ordered and the time it appears in a

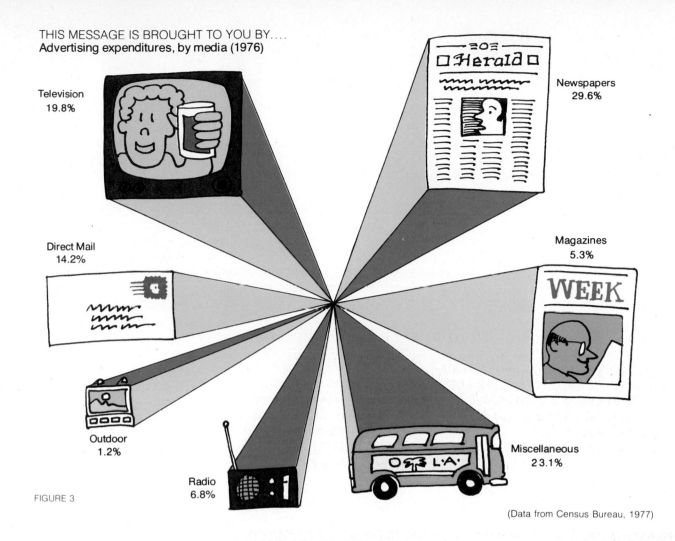

THIS MESSAGE IS BROUGHT TO YOU BY....
Advertising expenditures, by media (1976)

Television
19.8%

Newspapers
29.6%

Direct Mail
14.2%

Magazines
5.3%

Outdoor
1.2%

Miscellaneous
23.1%

Radio
6.8%

FIGURE 3

(Data from Census Bureau, 1977)

newspaper is the shortest of any of the media. An advertiser can change an ad overnight when dealing with a local paper. This means that an advertiser in a newspaper has great flexibility. If there is a blizzard in the afternoon, the local department store can feature snow shovels and boots in the next day's ad.

Another advantage is that in many communities the local newspaper will reach almost every home in the area. An advertiser can therefore be confident that the message will be seen by the entire potential market. In addition, advertising dollars are not being wasted on people who are not potential customers. For example, compare an ad placed in the Chicago newspapers by the Chicago department store Marshall Field with one placed in a national magazine like *Vogue*. The *Vogue* ad will certainly not be seen by the majority of Chicago residents if most of them do not subscribe to *Vogue*. Moreover, it will be seen by thousands of non-Chicago residents who will never shop at Marshall Field. A store like Marshall Field might still

consider it advantageous to advertise in *Vogue* for prestige reasons. Clearly, however, economy and efficiency would be sacrificed.

Newspaper advertising can also be particularly effective in selling certain types of goods and services. A few years ago, for instance, Evelyn Wood Reading Dynamic was spending only about 5 percent of its advertising budget on newspapers, the rest going to TV and radio commercials. Then, when the book and movie versions of *Jaws* were at a peak of popularity, the company ran newspaper ads stating that "Evelyn Wood graduates can read *Jaws* in just 41 minutes!" The ads drew such a heavy response—perhaps because newspaper readers have an above-average interest in speed-reading—that Evelyn Wood soon tripled its newspaper advertising.[5]

Newspaper advertising is placed both by local and national advertisers; the former are far more important than the latter. Local advertisers are usually merchants operating stores in the area served by the newspaper or they are people running classified ads. National advertisers use newspapers to publicize such brand-name items as liquor, automobiles, and gasoline. The rates for national advertising can be roughly 60 percent higher than those for local advertising. Newspapers justify rate differences by pointing out that their local customers are more frequent advertisers. Also, they say, there are cost savings because local ads are placed directly.

Occasionally *national advertisers team up with local merchants to buy advertising in local papers.* This is called **cooperative advertising**; it involves sharing the total cost. One survey of a group of Pennsylvania department stores examined the role of cooperating manufacturers. It showed that the manufacturers paid almost two-thirds of the advertising costs for major appliances and one-third of the costs for toys and games. Manufacturers support co-op advertising because it helps to sell more of their goods, not only by promoting products but also by telling consumers where they can be purchased. It also provides patronage identification. For example, when Helena Rubenstein purchases co-op advertising with the New York store B. Altman for a new line of makeup, Helena Rubenstein immediately obtains the benefit of Altman's fashionable image. For this reason, such cooperative advertising might prove to be more effective than advertising placed directly by Helena Rubenstein alone.

Magazines

Magazines were the first medium to carry national advertising, having done so since 1870. Despite the increased competition from other media they still offer important advantages for some advertisers. Unlike newspapers, which are usually thrown out after a day, magazines may remain around the house for weeks, giving the ads they carry a better chance of being read and remembered. Magazines also provide a good medium for effective photography and artwork, an important factor for those who wish to show their products accurately or to create a quality image with visually attractive ads.

In the early 1970s magazines temporarily declined in overall circulation and in the percentage of total advertising dollars they attracted. This decline was caused by competition from television, which proved

to be a more effective medium for reaching mass audiences. Thus the disappearance of the old weeklies *Life* and *Look* can be attributed at least in part to the fact that people would no longer buy weekly general-interest picture magazines when they could see the same kind of material nightly, and free, on TV. Furthermore, advertisers objected to the lack of flexibility in magazines. Color pictures for magazine ads must often be supplied two months ahead of the publication date, making last-minute changes impossible. Many advertisers also felt that magazines were not selective enough because they reached hundred of thousands of readers not interested in the product. Consider *Glamour,* for example, which sells over 1.8 million copies a month.[6] At first glance, these readers might be considered to have fairly similar tastes and in erests. In fact, though, about half of them are college students and half young working women. Consequently, an advertiser with a product like college review notes, directed exclusively at the college market, finds half its advertising money wasted.

Since 1975, however, the magazine industry has staged an impressive comeback, largely by dealing with this problem directly. Realizing they cannot hope to match television as a medium for mass advertising, magazine publishers have been concentrating on improving their selectivity. Most leading magazines no longer come out in a single nationwide edition, but instead publish several **geographic and demographic editions** *aimed at narrower audiences on the basis of region and occupation. Time* magazine, for example, offers some 228 different editions each week, including separate demographic editions that go only to doctors, or educators, or college students. Advertisers can thus buy space only in those editions that suit their purposes, reaching a more receptive audience and saving money at the same time.

There has also been a surge of growth among **special-interest magazines**, established ones and newcomers alike, which are designed to appeal to certain groups of people. These magazines offer advertisers even greater selectivity in reaching certain segments of the population. Some of these publications focus on specific subjects—amateur photography, automobiles, tennis, sewing, and even such specialized activities as snowmobiling and hang-gliding. Others deal with a somewhat broader range of subject matter, but gear their style and viewpoint to specific readerships which can be accurately profiled according to age, sex, income, marital status, where they live, and so forth. *Playboy, Rolling Stone,* and *Ms.* magazine appeal (not too surprisingly) to distinct and very different audiences. The East/West Network Company, which publishes several in-flight magazines for airlines, has the advantage of knowing not only who reads its publications but *when.*

In addition, while television may have killed off the old general-interest magazines like the old weekly *Life,* it has given an unintended boost to many of the newer ones. Commercial rates for network TV have risen so sharply in recent years—more than 30 percent between 1976 and 1978 alone[7]—that advertisers have been forced to make more use of the alternatives, especially magazines, whose rates have risen less than those of any other medium.

Radio

Radio suffered a sharp drop in advertising revenue when television first became popular in the 1950s. Since 1960, however, radio has increased its share of the advertising dollar as advertisers have begun to appreciate its unique capabilities. One important advantage is that more people have access to radio than to any other medium. There are more than 336 million sets in the United States, about five per household. And radio can go everywhere: outside, in the car, to the beach. Radio offers another advantage: it is relatively inexpensive. Some small stations offer weekly plans that provide twenty one-minute time slots for as little as $55 a week. Such costs are significantly lower than any of the other media in terms of the number of potential customers reached. They make radio an especially attractive buy for local advertisers.

However, the primary reason for the pickup in radio advertising is the broadcasters' decision to spe-

---

had annual billings of $800,000. Lasker left with a fortune put at $45 million and an agency that billed $50 million in peak years. Foote, Cone & Belding, the successor to Lord & Thomas, has huge billings today. Some of its more famous slogans: "Does she or doesn't she?" "Aren't you glad you use Dial?" and "Which twin has the Toni?" Lasker and Kennedy would be proud.

Another big go-go agency, Ted Bates & Company, is consistently one of the hotter operations in the business. At the very core of most Bates ads is the principle called USP, the "unique selling proposition." This technique relies on finding an angle, or a benefit of the product that is unique, and presenting it to consumers. Bates combined the USP approach with the Lasker/Kennedy slogan theory and came up with "Only your dentist gives a better fluoride treatment," to advertise Colgate Dental Cream, along with "Mrs. Marsh" breaking a piece of chalk to show how fluoride penetrates tooth enamel.

Sources: Joe Cappo, "The Man Who 'Invented' the Ad," *Chicago Daily News*, April 27, 1973, pp. 5–6; and "The New Hot Agency: Ted Bates Again," *Business Week*, July 19, 1976, pp. 56–58.

cialize. Many stations now devote the major part of their day to one type of broadcasting: news, rock music, sports, talk shows, or ethnic programs. By specializing, each station creates a certain kind of audience. A station concentrating on rock music will have a large teen-age audience. One featuring news and traffic reports at 8:30 A.M. and 5 P.M. will attract working people who commute by automobile. As a result of this specialization, advertisers can, by combining station selection and time selection, assure themselves of the precise audience they wish to reach.

Nevertheless, there are important limitations to radio. It appeals only to one sense: hearing. This provides a certain personal impact: someone seems to be talking directly to the listener. But it also prevents radio from selling many items successfully. Manufacturers of decorative pillows or high-style costume jewelry, for example, would find it impossible to describe their merchandise over the radio. Other drawbacks arise because the radio market is so fragmented. Many areas have eight or more stations, all competing for the listener's attention. In this case, the particular share of the total audience available to any one station and its advertisers at any one time is limited.

Television

Both the newest of the media and the fastest growing for the last quarter-century, television now accounts for about 20 percent of all advertising expenditures.[8] Television may actually have reached a leveling-off point; in 1977, in fact, total TV viewing in America declined for the first time ever, about 3 percent.[9] Nevertheless, it is and will remain a uniquely important and powerful advertising medium. A look at some statistics shows why. Television is available in 96 percent of the homes in the United States, and it is kept on for an average of six hours and twenty minutes a day. Furthermore, some programs, such as the broadcast of the Super Bowl, are watched by over 80 million people. As a result, television provides the advertiser with an excellent means of reaching a very large audience in a very short period of time. Unlike other media, moreover, television appeals to both the eye and the ear, so that selling messages have additional impact. Television is flexible in terms of geographic area. If an advertiser distributes products nationally, the firm can buy **network time**, which *guarantees broadcasts of a*

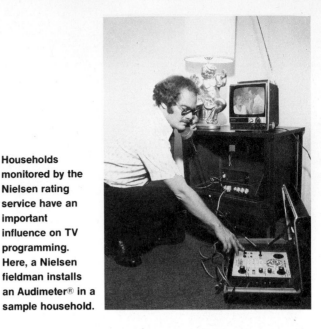

Households monitored by the Nielsen rating service have an important influence on TV programming. Here, a Nielsen fieldman installs an Audimeter® in a sample household.

message by hundreds of stations across the nation. If it is a local business, **local time** *on a single station will cover a single geographic area.* Finally, television offers selective markets in terms of age, sex, income, and occupation. A breakfast-food company can buy time on children's cartoon shows. A razor-blade company can sponsor sports events. A manufacturer of household cleansers can advertise on soap operas. The advertiser also has the choice of sponsoring an entire program, either alone or with others, or of buying **spot time**, which *consists of ten-, twenty-, thirty-, or sixty-second announcements, usually made during breaks between programs.* Spots can be purchased either on network or local TV.

During the 1950s large corporations frequently sponsored and produced their own weekly TV shows such as the "Texaco Star Theater," the "U.S. Steel Hour," and Gillette's "Cavalcade of Sports." But as production costs multiplied, single sponsorship became too expensive except for occasional specials. One solution was for two or more companies to sponsor a program jointly. The more common course now, however, is for a network to produce its own programs and sell commercial time by the minute, much as a magazine sells advertising space. Even with this "magazine format," though, the ever-rising cost of network TV advertising continues to be its major disadvantage. A mere thirty seconds on the nation's top-rated series in 1977, "Happy Days," was priced as high as $100,000. Predictably, advertisers have tried to cope with the spiraling costs by sharing time, often settling for ten-

or fifteen-second spots. Many experts feel, however, that the result has only been a large increase in the number of commercials, tending to confuse or bore viewers and reducing the effectiveness of all the ads. Another disadvantage is that television is by nature a one-time, nonpermanent medium. The viewer who doesn't get the advertiser's message the first time may not have an opportunity to see it again—in contrast to newspapers and magazines, which readers can return to as many times as they wish.

Other media

Advertisers have a wide choice of other media to reach potential customers. **Business papers and trade magazines** are *publications used by firms selling to the industrial market.* A manufacturer of frozen-food cabinets, for example, would find *Supermarket News* an ideal medium because the paper is read by supermarket executives.

Outdoor advertising, including billboards, skywriting, and neon signs, has the advantage of low cost per unit. It also offers flexibility because advertisers can buy space exclusively in those areas where they do business. But outdoor advertising has its limitations. Only the briefest message can be used. And if it is employed on a national basis, the large number of units required can make it a very expensive medium. A variation of the billboard concept is the use of advertising space on trash cans or benches. Here advertisers pay for the privilege of placing their messages throughout high-traffic business areas, where they can be seen by the thousands of shoppers and workers who use the street each day. A newer addition to the outdoor category, bus-stop shelters, offers the advantage of being viewed for longer periods of time. Whereas someone walking or driving past a trash can only glance at it, someone waiting for a bus will probably have ample time to study the advertiser's message.

The most effective medium as far as selectivity is concerned is **direct mailing**, which *makes use of mailing lists to reach a business's most likely customers.* Mailing lists can be purchased for almost every conceivable category: doctors who have traveled abroad, families who have purchased a car within the last year, women who have just announced their engagements. By using direct mail addressed to such lists, businesses

that wish to sell cruises, snow tires, or sets of dishes do not waste their efforts on those who never travel, do not own cars, or have been married long enough to have their china.

Another method of securing a mailing list is to get a list of people who subscribe to a certain type of magazine. For example, if a camera manufacturer develops a new lens, he or she might approach *Popular Photography* and *Photographic Magazine* for a list of their subscribers. This list would be made up of people interested in photography and would guarantee that the direct mailing would reach an audience likely to consider buying the new lens.

Other media include catalogs, labels, store displays, and free samples of merchandise. There is also a wide variety of giveaways featuring the advertiser's name, such as match folders, calendars, and shopping bags.

Finally, for better or worse, human ingenuity continues to find new ways of encouraging people to buy things. A California-based company, Beetleboards of America, pays Volkswagen owners $20 a month to use their cars as billboards-on-wheels, repainting them and attaching advertising decals.[10] The company in turn is paid up to $175 a month per car by advertisers, who must use at least twenty-five of them for six months.[11] Another firm in Florida, Tunnel Radio of America, has a more sophisticated idea—to install special transmitters in tunnels whose signals will be picked up on car radios (no matter what station they're tuned to) as they drive through, treating motorists to a mixture of traffic-safety messages and commercials.[12] A more worrisome development is the growing use of machines that can automatically make up to 1,000 phone calls a day, deliver a prerecorded sales pitch, and then record the customer's response. Such "junk" phone calls have in fact caused enough complaints around the country to create a strong likelihood of federal regulations and limits on their use.

ADVERTISING AGENCIES

If you get out of the elevator on the fourth floor of the Prudential Building on Chicago's Michigan Avenue, you will find yourself in the home office of the Leo Burnett Company, the fourth largest advertising agency in the country. Nearly 1,500 people work here, collaborating on advertising programs for some of the best-known products in America. In one office a producer confers with film crews on how to shoot the next set of commercials the agency will produce for a famous beer. Down the hall an art director is working on several new designs for boxes of Kellogg's Corn Flakes. Around the corner a team of Burnett account managers is meeting with marketing people from the Green Giant Company and showing them a new magazine ad series. On the floor below, a team of research people are trying to determine if there will be enough public demand for a new type of insurance package that Allstate Insurance is considering.

In other offices, similar activities are taking place on behalf of other clients: Marlboro cigarettes, United Airlines, Taster's Choice coffee, Dewar's Scotch, Kentucky Fried Chicken. And in the reception area of the Burnett headquarters—as well as of every other Burnett office in the world—is a bowl of apples. Leo Burnett, a folksy fellow who started his agency in 1935, thought a bowl of apples would be a gesture of hospitality to anyone who came calling. It also came to symbolize that someone could start a business in the depths of the Depression—when people sold apples on streetcorners—and eventually become the marketing sparkplug for billions of dollars' worth of products sold.

The complex problems involved in choosing the most advantageous media and preparing the advertising material have made the **advertising agency** a key element in the nation's marketing system. *Almost all advertising in national magazines and on television networks is produced and placed by such agencies.* On the other hand, much local advertising is still created and purchased by local advertisers. Department stores, for example, usually write their own newspaper advertisements and buy space.

Today there are 583 major advertising agencies in the United States. In 1977 these agencies billed their clients for $19.4 billion of media time and space purchased on their behalf. Much of the business is concentrated in the hands of a relatively few large agencies.[13]

The traditional **full-service agency** provides a wide range of services for its clients. It does far more than merely preparing advertisements and placing them in the media. It *has facilities to handle product research and development, a full range of marketing services, account management and media research, all in addition to its creative services—*copywriting, artwork, and the various activities involved in producing TV and radio commercials. A full-service agency thus works with the client from the time the product is conceived, or even before. Wells Rich Greene, for example, was the agency responsible for the research that preceded the introduction of the Love line of cosmetics, as well as many of the subsequent marketing decisions made by the company. The agency first surveyed the market for cosmetics among young women and then decided that a light lemon scent would have appeal. Next it suggested the name and packaging for the line. Finally it wrote and placed the advertising.

The Love case may be somewhat extreme, but many agencies today are involved in similar research on products and consumer motivation, as well as in the creation of advertising materials and the purchase of media. Thus an agency for a producer of denture cleaners might be asked to help the company make several decisions. Should the product come in paste, liquid, or powder form? Should it be advertised on TV or in magazines? Which would attract more potential customers, "The Waltons" or "Monday Night Football"? Only after these decisions had been made would the agency proceed with the actual job of writing, casting, and filming the commercial, and negotiating with television stations to buy the required time.

Traditionally, advertising agencies have been paid by a commission, usually 15 percent of the dollar value of the media they purchase for their clients. For example, an agency buying $100,000 worth of time for a client on "Laverne and Shirley" would be billed for $100,000 less 15 percent, or $85,000. The agency in turn would bill the client for the full $100,000, keeping the difference, $15,000, as its compensation.

The commission system continues today. But since the 1960s, additional ways of buying advertising services have come into use. Some full-service agencies are now willing to offer clients partial services on a fee basis. For instance, they may handle only consumer research, preparation of the advertisement, or media buying. In addition, advertisers may choose from a variety of smaller agencies, sometimes called **boutique agencies**, that *specialize in a particular service.* Either way, clients have the advantage of being able to buy services à la carte (as it's referred to in the industry), ordering only the services they need, as if from a menu. One company, for instance, may do its own product research and marketing, have a creative-services agency produce a commercial, and hire a media-buying firm to handle media research and placement. Another company might feel that one of its own employees could select and buy magazine space. In this case, the company would need only an agency's copywriting services. The company would save 15 percent on media cost—the 15 percent that would otherwise go to a full-service advertising agency. Presumably, its total expenses would then be less than this 15 percent.

PERSONAL SELLING

A very successful salesperson, whose job is selling commercial time for a large radio station, tells of a foodstore-chain executive who had never advertised on radio. It didn't sell, he was convinced; no one paid any attention. Would he give it a try, the salesperson asked, if he could be persuaded that people really did pay attention? The answer was a skeptical yes. The salesperson then suggested that the station could run ten spots a day announcing that the stores were all infested with roaches! After the executive stopped laughing, he placed an order.

The anecdote says something about the impact of advertising. It says even more about the effectiveness of good person-to-person selling. According to the Census Bureau some 6 percent of the work force, or about 5 million people, are involved in some form of personal selling. The cost of this promotional activity is a major item for many producers. This cost includes the salaries and commissions paid to salespeople; the expenses involved in hiring, training, and supervising a sales force; and the money spent for travel and entertainment. Taken together, these activities involve huge amounts of money. Personal selling costs for food represent twice the advertising budget. For highly technical products—like computers and office equipment—personal selling costs can amount to ten times what is spent on advertising.[14] Needless to say, producers would hardly part with so much money if they didn't consider it a worthwhile investment.

The great advantage of personal selling over other forms of promotion, the quality that makes it so essential, is its *flexibility*. Salespeople can tailor their presentations to fit different situations, responding to questions, handling objections, and foreseeing a customer's particular needs and problems. They can also develop a personal rapport with the customer, building a feeling of trust and making it known that they are acting on the customer's behalf as well as their employer's. Finally, of course—in contrast to advertising, which can merely attract attention and stimulate desire—salespeople can actually complete the sale on the spot.

Personal selling usually falls into one of two main categories: retail selling and business selling. **Retail selling** *is direct, face-to-face selling that takes place mostly in department or specialty stores.* The people who work in these stores are among the lowest paid of all salespeople. Management claims that the pay scales are justified because most customers have been pre-sold by need or advertising so salespeople are primarily order takers. The importance of retail selling has been further downgraded in recent years with the growth of self-service stores. In this kind of store the customer finds the item desired and has only minor contact with the salesclerk at a check-out counter. Of course, there are still some items for which expert, patient, personal selling efforts are required. Such goods include automobiles, fur coats, and expensive jewelry. In these selling situations, the salespeople enjoy excellent pay and high prestige.

A special version of retail selling involves **in-store demonstrations**, which are *presentations to show how a product is used.* While less common than in the past, the practice is still used successfully by some retailers. A southern drugstore chain, for instance, has a staff of from one to three trained cosmeticians in each of its stores. Kept up to date through periodic classes held by manufacturers, as well as meetings at company headquarters, they demonstrate new products and offer personalized advice to their customers. Alternatively, in many large department stores the salespeople behind the perfume counters, for example, may be employees not of the store but of the perfume companies. They are able to speak far more knowledgeably than a salesclerk could about their products.

Another kind of retail selling is **door-to-door selling,** in which *a salesperson goes from one house or apartment to another to sell goods.* A few national firms such as Avon and Fuller Brush sell door-to-door. So do many magazine, book, and vacuum-cleaner companies. Many people, both sales personnel and customers, dislike this kind of selling because of the low ratio of sales to calls and because of the high-pressure sales methods that must be used. Recent federal and state regulations have done away with the worst abuses of this selling method. In 1974 the Federal Trade Commission issued a ruling that requires door-to-door salespeople to give customers a seventy-two-hour cooling-off period. During this time buyers can change their minds and cancel an order for certain items, even if a contract has already been signed. People who sell from door to door must also clearly announce when they ring someone's doorbell that they are doing so for the purpose of selling something. The regulations, plus the growing reluctance of people to admit strangers to their homes, have made door-to-door selling increasingly difficult today.

Another development in retail selling has been the attempt by some companies to expand and improve sales positions. The job of insurance salespeople used to be to sell as much insurance as possible. Training was limited to insurance. Today, however, many insurance companies have trained their salespeople to be financial planners who can plan a client's whole estate. Of course, the object is still to sell insurance. In the process, though, the planner may also advise on mutual funds, trusts, and stock portfolios. Frequently these salespeople write more policies and earn more money than those less well-trained.

In general, however, the best-paid kind of personal selling is **selling to businesses**, a category that covers a wide range of possibilities. It might involve selling Du Pont's chemicals to textile and plastics companies or Wrangler's blue jeans to department stores. Some of these salespeople cover huge territories, visiting hundreds of stores in several states each year. Others, like an IBM salesperson in Chicago's Loop, may cover a territory restricted to a few blocks of office buildings.

Two special kinds of business selling are **technical selling** and **missionary work.** Both support the efforts of the regular sales staff. Technical salespeople do not take orders directly and are usually scientists or engineers. *They work exclusively with the potential customer's technical staff,* attempting to convince them of the superiority of their products. The role of missionary salespeople is to *develop long-term goodwill and demand for the company's products.* People from drug companies who visit doctors regularly to leave samples and give information about new products are said to be doing missionary selling.

PUBLICITY

The third method of promotion, **publicity**, includes *any nonpaid information relating to a manufacturer or its products that appears in any medium.* Favorable publicity would be a news release about the development of a miniaturized heart pacemaker. Unfavorable publicity would be news about the recall of a pacemaker because of defects. Companies that supply products used by commercial or industrial customers hope for favorable publicity in trade magazines. A single news article in such a magazine describing a product may create more interest and sales than pages of paid advertising. Examples of consumer-goods publicity would be newspaper reports relating to boat and automobile show openings and stories about new prepared food mixes.

One of the biggest efforts of this kind is the public-relations blitz mounted each summer and fall by the major American automakers. This is the time of the auto previews—sometimes held in Detroit, but just as often in Palm Springs or Miami Beach. The automakers' goal is simple—to get as many automotive editors as they can from newspapers and magazines, as well as from the car-buff magazines, to come to the previews. These honored guests are treated to free hotel rooms, lavish meals and entertainment, and all the test-driving they want. There are also press briefings with the presidents of the companies, their chief engineers, and marketing vice-presidents, among others. Later on, after the editors have returned to their home offices, local company representatives will offer them a chance to drive one of the new cars for a few weeks. They will also be provided with extensive press kits that usually include a dozen different photos of each new model, price lists and specification sheets, and pages of editorial material. All this material is aimed at making it as easy as possible to prepare an article on the car.

A typical publicity feature might be a newspaper story on how a family used a General Motors camper on its vacation trip. Although no direct payment is made to the newspaper, it is probable that a publicist employed by GM was involved in one way or another in developing the story. The publicist may have issued a release calling the new camper to the attention of the travel editor. He or she may also have supplied pictures, cost information, and mileage statistics. The deliberate planning of publicity efforts is clearly illustrated in the publishing industry, where authors of books travel from coast to coast appearing on TV and radio talk shows and making themselves available for newspaper interviews.

SALES PROMOTION

The fourth method of promotion, **sales promotion**, is defined by the American Marketing Association as *"those marketing activities, other than personal selling, advertising, and publicity, that stimulate consumer purchasing and dealer effectiveness."* This is a very broad definition, emphasizing the fact that sales promotion covers a wide variety of activities. They extend from arranging plant tours and trade show exhibits to distributing free samples, setting up speakers' bureaus, and publishing promotional booklets.

Some sales promotion efforts are aimed at dealers. For example, General Motors holds training sessions for the salespeople who work for its franchised dealers. Other sales promotion programs are directed at the customer but channeled through the dealer. A cosmetic manufacturer may sponsor a skin-care clinic for teen-agers at a department store.

Another effective sales promotion device is the **point-of-purchase display (P.O.P.)**, *a device by which a product is displayed in such a way as to stimulate immediate sales.* This can be a fairly simple affair, such as the stacks of recipe-book coupons found in many retail outlets or the racks offering Tic-Tac mints at supermarket checkout counters. It can also be quite elaborate. The almost overnight success of Hanes' L'eggs pantyhose was due to the unique seven-foot egg-shaped display unit on which the pantyhose were displayed and sold in supermarkets and drugstores. Hoping to repeat its success in a different market, Hanes entered the crowded cosmetics field with its line of L'Aura products, which, like L'eggs, relies heavily on eye-catching point-of-purchase displays to attract customers.

Other familiar sales promotion techniques include the free gifts offered by banks to customers opening new accounts, and the wide variety of contests and sweepstakes run by companies seeking to call attention to their products or services. A newer approach that has proven very successful is the use of T-shirts bearing a company's name or emblem. In marked contrast to such traditional giveaway items as matchbooks, calendars, and pens bearing a company's name, people buy these T-shirts as they would any other apparel. Thus, in effect, customers are paying for the privilege of advertising someone's products!

Eye appeal is the key concept behind point-of-purchase displays. If you've ever given in to temptation and bought a candy bar at a supermarket checkout counter, you know how effective these displays can be.

Finally, many companies have had particular success with **couponing**, *a technique that spurs sales by offering a small discount through redeemable coupons.* Coupons can be distributed through newspapers, magazines, and direct mail, or they can be inserted in a package. Coupons offer the purchaser a few cents off the product's cost at a store. The store-owner in turn redeems the coupons from the manufacturer, who pays not just their face value but also a small bonus, usually around 3 cents, depending on the item.

The main disadvantage of couponing is that a customer will often try to redeem the coupon for a competing product not offering the discount. Some manufacturers try to protect themselves by printing on their coupon a message saying that it can be used only to buy the stated product and that any other use is fraud. Evidence shows, however, that unauthorized redemptions are widespread. Another disadvantage connected with couponing is cost. This is particularly true if a manufacturer uses direct mail, the most effec-

tive means of distributing coupons. To overcome this drawback, noncompeting companies may combine forces, sending out a single mailing that may include discount offers for laundry detergent, shampoo, salad dressing, and a magazine.

PUBLIC REACTION TO ADVERTISING

Of the four methods of promotion directed at consumers, people are most likely to be aware of advertising because it is so visible and widespread. Because it is also the most important part of selling for many firms, marketers are interested in how the public reacts to advertising and how they can counter criticisms of it.

A survey published in 1976 revealed that of those who took a definite stand one way or another, a much larger percentage (37 percent) felt favorably about ad-

DO TELEVISION COMMERCIALS HARM CHILDREN?

Certain facts are clear. In a nation where the vast majority of homes have television, children under eleven years of age are among the most constant viewers. A child who watches only a "moderate" amount sees over a thousand hours of TV a year. If most of that viewing is children's programming, the child will watch an average of twenty-two commercials an hour. These messages add up to a yearly total of 22,000 commercials. Between 55 and 85 percent of them deal with edible products. Many of these products, such as snacks, sweetened cereals, and soft drinks, have little nutritional value.

What is less clear is the effect these commercials have on their audience. The best-known consumer group involved in children's TV is Action for Children's Television (ACT), which says that the commercials are harmful: they advertise sugary foods in a country where most children suffer from tooth decay. In addition, ACT contends that children do

not have the maturity or experience to judge ads rationally.

Most advertising and media executives disagree. They argue that advertising teaches children about the workings of the free-enterprise system and about products of interest to them. Anyway, they say, the problem is not with children but with their parents, who cannot say no.

Petitions by consumer groups for stricter government regulation have been turned down by the Federal Communications Commission. Recently, however, the Federal Trade Commission (FTC) has appeared more sympathetic to the consumer groups. Citing the doctrine of "fairness" as its key responsibility, the FTC has raised serious questions about many children's advertisements, especially those promoting sugar-heavy foods. FTC members have in particular challenged the industry argument that advertising teaches kids about the free-enterprise system. New research, they say, indicates that many children have only the vaguest idea of what TV commercials are, often making no distinction between them and the regular programs. There can

vertising than unfavorably (21 percent).[15] But the growth of the consumer movement appears to have raised doubts about the usefulness of advertising and about its truthfulness and costs.

DOES ADVERTISING RAISE COSTS?

One of the chief complaints about advertising is that it adds to the cost of the products and services. A drug and cosmetics company, for example, may spend as much as 31 cents of every dollar it takes in from the sales of its drug and cosmetics products on advertising.[16] Some critics suggest that if such advertising expenditures were reduced, companies could afford to sell their products to the public at lower prices. Other critics emphasize another way in which advertising increases costs. Expensive nationwide advertising campaigns, when successful, can develop brand loy-

alty for a few brands. This loyalty can be so strong that it becomes impossible for newcomers to enter the field, especially if they are smaller companies. As a result, a few large companies can continue to dominate the market, charging higher prices than they could in a more competitive situation.

Many experts believe that these criticisms are unjustified. They claim that advertising stimulates demand so that higher levels of production are possible. As a result, the unit cost is reduced. Thus, they conclude, even though spending for advertising may increase the price in the short run, it has the opposite effect in the long run because of its impact on production costs.

DOES ADVERTISING INFORM?

Almost everyone agrees that advertising performs useful informational functions. By advertising, a seller can inform a potential buyer of his existence, line of goods, and prices. Such advertising can reduce the time and effort spent by consumers in seeking out goods and services. It lets them know in advance what is available and where it can be bought.

There is a side benefit related to the informational nature of advertising: The dollars spent by advertisers are used to subsidize the media we rely on for information and entertainment. One estimate is that 60 percent of the cost of periodicals, 70 percent of the cost of newspapers, and 100 percent of the cost of commercial radio and TV broadcasting are paid for by advertising.

IS ADVERTISING WASTEFUL?

It is obvious that not all advertising is informative, designed to help consumers find the products they need. Nor does it always serve to increase total demand. Instead, many advertisements are tug-of-war efforts. What they really do is shift sales among firms. Another complaint is that some advertisements do indeed create additional demand, but it is undesirable demand. Do we need electric bean pots or heated shaving lather? Some people feel that demands for such products are fulfilled at the expense of greater

---

hardly be any fairness, FTC members conclude, in a contest between young viewers like these and the sophisticated techniques of professional advertisers.

Broadcasters have sought to put off criticism by voluntarily reducing the maximum time allowed for children's commercials. They have only cut them back by two minutes an hour, though. They argue that further reductions would take away needed financial support for children's programs—and that ACT's proposed ban on all candy advertising would kill the programs off entirely. Whatever the outcome of the controversy, it will probably take several years to make its way through various levels of government hearings and court cases. In the meantime, of course, children will continue to watch, while their parents continue to worry.

Sources: Robert Choate, "How Television Grabs Kids for Fun and Profit," *Business and Society Review/Innovation*, August 1973, pp. 20–25; Joan Barthel, "Boston Mothers Against Kidvid," *New York Times Magazine*, January 5, 1974, pp. 14 ff.; and "FTC Could Restrain Children's TV Ads, Chairman Hints; Sugared Items Stressed," *The Wall Street Journal*, November 9, 1977, p. 5.

REGULATIONS CONCERNING ADVERTISING

Which federal agency is most important in the regulation of advertising? Federal government control of advertising is primarily in the hands of the Federal Trade Commission (FTC). This control dates back to 1914, when the Federal Trade Commission Act was passed by Congress. The object of the original act was to prevent "unfair methods of competition" among businesses. The commission tried to outlaw misleading advertising as a particular kind of unfair competition. The commission's role was expanded in 1938 through passage of the Wheeler-Lea Act. This act gave the FTC specific authority to control false or misleading advertisements by most food, drug, health, and cosmetic companies.

What are the FTC's laws? Operating under this authority, the FTC has developed ground rules for advertisers. *All statements of fact must be supported by evidence.* This includes words ("Bounty soaks up more than the next leading brand") and demonstrations. Thus advertisers cannot use whipped cream in a shaving-cream commercial to create an impression of a firm heavy lather. Furthermore, *advertisers not only must avoid specific language that is untrue, but they also must not create an overall impression that is incorrect.* In other words, they are prohibited from claiming that doctors recommend a product if they do not. Nor can they present an actor who delivers the message dressed in a doctor's white jacket.

During the 1970s FTC enforcement of advertising regulation became much stricter. Earlier, advertisers found guilty of sponsoring untruthful ads were merely required to sign a decree in which they consented to stop running the ads. Now, however, such advertisers may be forced to run **corrective advertising,** *notifying the public of their past errors.* Of course, the mere threat of such an FTC requirement serves to keep most advertisers in line. In 1978, though, an FTC decision held that ads for STP motor oil treatment, claiming that it reduced motor oil use by 20 percent, were false. Levying the highest penalty on record, the FTC ordered the company to run $200,000 worth of corrective newspaper ads and pay a $500,000 fine.

The FTC has also removed earlier prohibitions

---

social needs and the result is that our society's resources are misused.

Again there is disagreement. The defenders of advertising claim that such judgments are based on the personal values of those who make them. In a democratic society, they say, consumers should be left to decide for themselves what is good and what they should buy.

IS ADVERTISING TRUTHFUL?

In 1929 one issue of the best-selling *Liberty* magazine carried nineteen different product endorsements from a leading actress of the day, Mabel Normand. Could anybody believe that the lady honestly meant her praise for all these different brands of merchandise? Today many people argue that much advertising contains similar untruths or half-truths. One airline has advertised that it is the fastest to New Orleans. Investigation showed that it is the only line flying that route. Thus the advertisement was true—as far as it went.

Advertising people attempt to distinguish between untruths and **puffery**. They define the latter as *legitimate artistic license, which,* they claim, *is accepted by the public as such.* Nobody really believes, they say, that the "friendly skies of United" are any different from the skies where TWA or American fly. Nobody honestly imagines that the "Pepsi generation" consists of soda drinkers who are more lively and more naturally charming than those who drink different brands. But are all consumers this sophisticated? Advertisements for children's toys and dry cereals are probably accepted as completely factual by many young viewers. It is possible, too, that a generation of homemakers has accepted, consciously or unconsciously, the industry's verdict that "ring around the collar" can break up an otherwise satisfactory marriage.

against "comparative advertising"—ads that identify the competition by name, a technique that makes them more informative to the consumer and spurs greater competition in a variety of areas. That action, and the apparent effectiveness of brand-name comparisons, have led to a steady increase in their use. An estimated one of every ten TV commercials now involves competitive product demonstrations. The practice has stirred up a heated debate among advertising people, some of whom complain that it is damaging to the industry as a whole. So far, however, the success rate of comparative advertising seems to have created more converts than critics.

FTC officials have also recently raised a more far-reaching issue: whether advertisements, even factually accurate ones, are lawful if they encourage shoppers to make unwise purchases. One area of concern is energy conservation. Are electric hairdryers, for instance, dangerously wasteful of energy? Another area of concern has to do with certain groups of people who for one reason or another are apt to be harmfully influenced by advertising. One official asks, for example, whether the high rate of obesity among poor women is a result of constant encouragement by advertisers to buy calorie-laden foods. Such questions will not be easily resolved, especially since the Supreme Court has held that advertising falls within the First Amendment's protection of free speech. Nevertheless, advertisers are being more careful than ever before about the tone and content of their messages.

Other government agencies that regulate advertising The federal Food, Drug, and Cosmetic Act (1938) also regulates advertising. By this act, the Food and Drug Administration (FDA) was given authority over the labeling and branding of foods, drugs, and many health products and cosmetics. The FDA now watches over both the accuracy of the ingredient list on the labels and the form of the labels themselves.

State regulation of advertising is exercised by forty-four states that have passed the Printer's Ink Model Statute, drawn up in 1911 by the trade newspaper of the advertising industry. The statute provides punishment for "untrue, deceptive or misleading" advertising. In addition, most states have laws regulating advertising practices for individual industries such as liquor stores, stock brokerages, employment agencies, and small loan companies.

MEDIA AND SELF-REGULATION

There are federal and state regulations guaranteeing "truth in advertising" (see "Know These Laws" on these pages). Also, the media themselves exercise control over the advertising they carry. Newspapers often require proof before they will accept an advertisement claiming that a given product is "the lowest priced." Magazines are particularly sensitive on the matter of taste. *Ms.* magazine, for instance, turns down ads it believes are offensive to women. The National Association of Broadcasters, a trade organization for TV and radio stations, has established voluntary codes that are followed by many TV and radio stations. The codes regulate the kind of advertising that may be accepted and the nature of this advertising. For example, advertisements for hard liquor are forbidden. Even beer and wine ads on television cannot show the models actually drinking the product.

Self-regulation by advertisers provides still another vehicle for the restraint of false and misleading ads. The National Advertising Review Board has members from among advertisers, agencies, and the general public. Its full-time professional staff investigates complaints of deceptive advertising. If the complaint appears justified, the board will try to get the offending company to stop, using both its moral power and the threat of referral to governmental agencies. The individual advertiser and its agency also practice self-regulation in many cases.

In sum, many people connected with advertising are highly sensitive to the ethical questions it raises, and have responded to them in a careful and thoughtful manner. We talk more about business and ethics in Chapter 14.

CHAPTER REVIEW

The promotion portion of the marketing mix includes four methods: advertising, personal selling, sales promotion, and publicity.

Most promotion expenditures are devoted to advertising. Advertising can be subdivided into three categories. Primary-demand advertising tries to increase total demand for a product without distinguishing among brands. Selective, or brand, advertising aims at getting customers to buy a particular brand. Institutional advertising is designed to create goodwill for a company rather than sell specific products. Of the amount of advertising dollars spent on media, the highest percentage goes to newspapers. Next come television, direct mail, radio, magazines, business papers, and others. Each medium has its own special advantages and drawbacks.

Somewhat more than half of all advertising expenditures are made through advertising agencies. The traditional full-service agency provides a wide range of services for its clients. It is usually paid on a commission basis. Some clients, however, prefer to buy individual services on a fee basis from standard agencies or from specialized boutique agencies.

Personal selling involves both retail selling, in stores or door-to-door, and selling to business. Compensation may be by straight salary, commission, or a combination of the two. Sales promotion, aimed at stimulating dealer effectiveness and consumer purchasing, can encompass anything from plant tours to training sessions, from point-of-purchase displays to discount coupons.

Publicity is nonpaid information about a company or its products in any of the media. Companies try to get favorable publicity both in trade publications and in consumer-oriented media.

Public attitudes toward advertising, generally favorable, may be changing. Questions are raised about its cost, informational value, wastefulness, and honesty. One response to the many criticisms of advertising has been the growth of government regulation. In addition, the media exert considerable control over advertising, and the advertisers themselves try to enforce standards of truthfulness and good taste.

KEY WORD REVIEW

promotion
advertising
primary-demand advertising
selective (brand) advertising
institutional advertising
media
cooperative advertising
geographic and demographic editions
special-interest magazines
network time
local time
spot time
business papers and trade magazines
outdoor advertising
direct mailing
advertising agency
full-service agency
boutique agencies
retail selling
in-store demonstrations
door-to-door selling
selling to businesses
technical selling
missionary work
publicity
sales promotion
point-of-purchase display (P.O.P.)
couponing
puffery
corrective advertising

REVIEW QUESTIONS

1. What types of industry are particularly interested in institutional advertising? Why?

2. What are the advantages of local newspapers to an advertiser compared with network TV or national magazines?

3. What are the primary advantages and disadvantages of magazines to advertisers?

4. What are the good features of radio as an advertising medium? What are its limitations?

5. How does the commission system for paying advertising agencies work? What other methods of buying advertising services have come into use?

6. What is the main drawback of couponing? How have companies tried to overcome it?

7. List the arguments made by those who believe that advertising adds to the price paid by the consumer. What is said by those who disagree?

8. How do the media and advertisers attempt to regulate advertising?

CASE 1

DRIVING HOME THE POINT: NEW STRATEGIES FOR AUTO SALESPEOPLE

The need to conserve energy has made smaller cars seem like a good idea, but U.S. auto companies have found that the big-car habit is tough to kick—not only for the people who buy those cars, but also for the people who sell them. General Motors, in fact, came to the conclusion that the people selling its Chevrolet subcompacts, the Monza and the Chevette, were so hooked on the big models that they had never bothered to learn about the smaller ones. So GM decided to teach them, and in a matter of months rushed more than 5,000 salespeople through a special crash course.

In lectures, salespeople heard detailed discussions of how Chevette and Monza compared to their competition—imported cars like Toyota and Volkswagen—in everything from gas mileage and price to variable-rate coil springs. They watched films on the quality control procedures used at the Chevette assembly plant. Some salespeople spent a day at a speedway, test-driving Chevettes, Monzas, and a number of Japanese imports.

The point of the crash courses was to change the salespeople's selling strategy. GM had discovered that in their efforts to sell small cars, Chevrolet salespeople were concentrating almost exclusively on price. But the typical small-car buyer, GM suspected, was interested in more than

that. And young educated buyers in particular appeared to believe that small cars from Detroit were cheaply made. They thus preferred the imports because they seemed like better products. By emphasizing the quality of the Chevette and the Monza, GM hoped to make its salespeople see that—as one Chevrolet sales manager put it—"price alone doesn't sell small cars."[17]

1. How does it help a salesperson to be familiar with competing products?

2. If you were a small-car salesperson, how would you deal with a customer who believed that small cars made in Detroit were not high-quality products? What is your own impression of American subcompacts?

3. Why do you suppose General Motors chose to promote the product to its sales force, rather than to the general public through advertising or some other form of promotion?

CASE 2

A NEW ADVERTISING MEDIUM

The theater darkens and you sit back in your seat to watch the film. But instead of a movie on the screen, you see, in living color, a commercial for a Seiko watch. After three minutes of advertising, the movie finally comes on.

Ads in movie houses have been common in Europe for years, but not until recently did commercial messages begin to appear on U.S. screens—and it took a Frenchman to put them there. Along with some partners, Roger Hatchuel, general manager of a French firm that sells

movie-house advertising to clients in Europe, started a U.S. subsidiary called Screenvision, Inc. and set out to create a new national advertising medium. Others had tried and failed in the past, but Hatchuel had at least one point in his favor. With Hollywood's annual movie output decreasing, film distributors were charging higher prices to the exhibitors who rent the films to show in their theaters. As a result, exhibitors were anxious to supplement their income without raising their ticket prices. To get exhibitors to show his ads, Hatchuel promised to share with them one-third of Screenvision's net revenues. He was not as generous, however, with the advertisers themselves: he charged them $17 per 1,000 admissions—which hardly compared favorably with the typical TV advertising cost of $4 per 1,000 viewers. But the expense is worth it, Hatchuel argued, because of the select nature of the movie-going audience, which tends to be youthful, relatively well-off, and not in the habit of watching a lot of television.[18]

1. What are some of the advantages of advertising a product in a movie theater (aside from the obvious fact that the viewer can't change the station), and what are the drawbacks?

2. Do you agree with Hollywood film distributors who say that the absence of commercials is one of the major factors that makes people leave their homes to see a movie?

3. What products or services might be especially well-suited to movie-house advertising?

10

WHOLESALING, RETAILING, AND DISTRIBUTION

Somewhere in Massachusetts a firm of skilled artisans produces a small volume of handsome, high-quality silverware. And somewhere in Arizona, as it happens, the parents of a bride-to-be are looking for just the right set of silverware as a wedding present. Clearly, they're made for each other. Only one problem presents itself—how to get the goods from producer to buyer.

The same problem, of course, presents itself in countless other forms every day, and how well it's solved has a great deal to do with how well every one of us lives. The following chapter will look into this subject, examining the complex, continually busy system of distribution—wholesaling, retailing, and transportation—that makes billions of products and services available to millions of consumers across the country.

WHAT WILL THIS CHAPTER FOCUS ON?

After reading the material in this chapter, you will understand and be able to discuss:

■ the marketing routes—called channels of distribution—along which goods travel from the manufacturer to the consumer

■ the functions wholesalers perform for maufacturers and retailers

■ the main types of retail outlets

■ changes in department stores since World War II

■ problems currently faced by supermarkets

■ the physical distribution of goods, particularly their transportation

■ the advantages and disadvantages of the basic modes of transportation—trucks, railroads, planes, ships, and pipelines

■ how the federal government is involved in transportation

 The preceding chapters have looked at the first three Ps of marketing—product, price, and promotion. We've followed the development of products from the idea stage through their life cycles on the open market, considering the factors involved in pricing them and the various means of promotion. In the present chapter we'll discuss the fourth P in the marketing mix: placement, or distribution. Placement is, in a sense, the nuts-and-bolts side of marketing; without it all the rest would be futile, because it deals with the supremely practical question of how a manufacturer actually gets its product into the hands of a consumer. We shall look first at the channels of distribution, the marketing routes along which goods and services travel from producer to consumer. We'll then examine the functions of the two types of middlemen, wholesalers and retailers, involved in the distribution of most products. Finally, we'll consider the physical distribution of products, discussing the advantages and drawbacks of each major mode of transportation and the role of government in regulating them all.

ASPECTS OF THE MARKETING
MIX: PLACEMENT

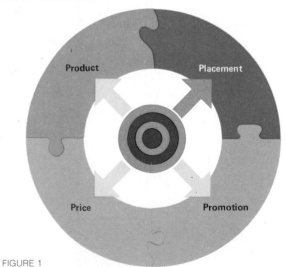

FIGURE 1

Part of the marketer's job is to choose the most effective channels of distribution for a product or service. The decision depends on the nature of the target market.

CHANNELS OF DISTRIBUTION

A **channel of distribution** can be defined as *the sequence of marketing institutions (such as wholesalers and retailers) through which a product passes on its way from the producer to the final user*. Let's look at some of the various types of channels that manufacturers use.

THE MOST DIRECT CHANNEL: MANUFACTURER TO CONSUMER

The most direct way to market a product, of course, is for the manufacturer to sell directly to the consumer. Artisans who sell their leather goods or jewelry at crafts fairs or on the street are using this simple distribution channel. Fuller Brush, Avon, and various other firms also sell directly to the consumer. Sometimes a manufacturer who normally uses more elaborate channels of distribution will sell surplus or damaged goods through an outlet or factory store. Pepperidge Farm markets day-old bread in this way.

The main problem with this direct form of distribution is that it forces a manufacturer to assume all the functions that are normally performed by middlemen. This can be quite costly for the manufacturer. Most producers therefore call on the services of middlemen to help them move their goods toward the intended customers.

THE ALTERNATIVE: CHANNELING GOODS AND SERVICES THROUGH MIDDLEMEN

Middlemen, whose duties can include a wide variety of specialized tasks, fall into two general categories—wholesalers and retailers. The **wholesaler** *sells products to others who buy them either for resale or for industrial use*. The **retailer**, in contrast, *sells directly to the public*.

The number of middlemen involved in the channel of distribution—also known as a trade channel or marketing channel—depends on the kind of product and the marketing practices of a particular industry. There are also important differences between the channels of distribution for consumer goods and those for industrial products. The basic types of marketing channels are illustrated in Figure 2 (page 254).

Manufacturer to consumer: the most direct marketing channel. In the marketplace in Guanajuato, Mexico, potters sell their own wares.

WHOLESALERS: THE FIRST CATEGORY OF MIDDLEMEN

Most wholesalers are middlemen who purchase products for their own accounts from manufacturers. They take **title** to, or *legal possession* of, the merchandise. Then they resell the merchandise to retailers or industrial users. Wholesalers usually own warehouses to receive and store merchandise; from there it is later reshipped to customers. (They may, however, ship goods directly from the manufacturer to customers.) Some wholesalers, called **agents** or **brokers**, operate somewhat differently. They *act as middlemen, but never actually take title to the products they resell.*

Wholesalers perform important functions both for the manufacturers who make the products and the retailers or industrial users who buy the goods.

WHOLESALER AND MANUFACTURER

Wholesalers serve four important functions for the manufacturer.

1. *Providing a sales force.* Many manufacturers find it expensive and inefficient to supply their own salespeople to visit the many retailers who carry their products. Instead, they use wholesalers to perform this function. For example, a stationery wholesaler will send his own salespeople to visit dozens of small stores, selling notebooks, pencils, rulers, and typewriter ribbons from a variety of manufacturers. Each manufacturer could not afford a sales force large enough to contact all the potential outlets.

2. *Carrying stock.* Most wholesalers maintain an inventory of merchandise, which they buy from a manufacturer in anticipation of sales to retailers or industrial customers. Without the wholesaler, a manufacturer would have to provide storage space until goods were ordered and would have to wait for payment until then. For example, Christmas card wholesalers receive shipments from manufacturers in late spring and pay for them within thirty to sixty days. But

CHANNELS OF DISTRIBUTION: ROUTES GOODS
FOLLOW FROM PRODUCER TO CONSUMER

FIGURE 2

Distribution channels for consumer goods

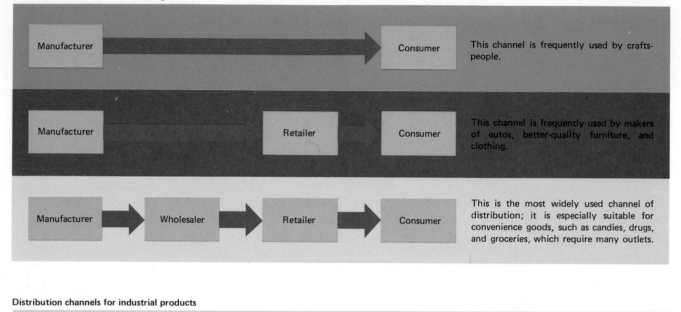

Distribution channels for industrial products

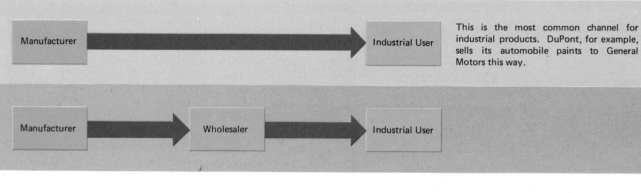

their customers, the retail stores, do not want delivery of the cards until September or October. Without wholesalers, manufacturers would have to supply storage space for three additional months—space they could use for their Valentine and Mother's Day lines. In addition, if these manufacturers sold directly to retailers, making sales in September, they would not receive payment until October or November. By dealing through wholesalers, they have their money months earlier.

3. *Assuming credit risks.* By dealing with a few wholesalers rather than many small stores, the manufacturer reduces chances for bad-debt losses. A firm also avoids the time and bother of running credit checks on hundreds of small accounts. It checks on the credit standing of only a few large wholesalers.

4. *Providing market information.* Wholesalers deal with hundreds of retailers, selling dozens of competing or complementary lines. Thus they are in an ideal position to provide manufacturers with useful

marketing information. A stationery wholesaler may be able to tell a notebook manufacturer that pencils with a Snoopy motif are very popular. With this knowledge the notebook company could investigate similar product tie-ins for its merchandise.

A good illustration of a wholesaler's usefulness to manufacturers can be seen in the Chas. Levy Circulating Company, the country's largest distributor of paperback books. Handling titles produced by all major publishers, Levy's sales force deals with some 8,500 individual retail outlets—from the big bookstore chains to the smallest newsstand and drugstore displays—a task no publishing house could possibly carry out on its own. Publishers have benefited in particular from Levy's success in tapping major outlets for paperback sales through a computer-coordinated program. Supermarket chains, discount stores, and retailing giants as Sears, J. C. Penney, and S. S. Kresge are some of Levy's newer sales targets. The publishers profit also from Levy's ability to monitor sales in every outlet on a week-to-week basis; the wholesaler thus provides a flow of timely information that enables them to order additional printings of "hot" titles while the demand is still strong. Levy's has, in addition, developed a very successful program of "media tie-ins" to promote books like *Jaws, Roots,* and others that have been made into movies or television shows. Irwin Shaw's novel

Rich Man, Poor Man, for example, had already been a best seller before being adapted for television, with some 1.3 million paperback copies sold; but during the eight weeks that it was serialized on ABC almost 4 million *more* copies were sold—thanks partly to Levy's carefully planned, coast-to-coast tie-in operation.[1]

WHOLESALER AND CUSTOMERS

As middlemen, wholesalers are useful not only to manufacturers but also to those on the receiving end of the distribution channel, retailers or industrial customers. Wholesalers provide some of the same services for customers as they do for suppliers.

1. *Anticipating needs.* The wholesaler's ability to forecast future consumer demand can be very valuable to retailers. Christmas card wholesalers must decide fairly early in the year whether to stock up more heavily on religious Christmas cards or on humorous Christmas cards. They anticipate the product line that retailers will eventually require. Unless wholesalers gauge correctly, they will be unable to supply customers' needs.

2. *Shipping convenient units.* Often manufacturers cannot be bothered with small orders. Yet retail stores cannot handle large volume. Wholesalers help here by breaking large shipments into more convenient units. An appliance wholesaler may order a truckload of TV sets and then deliver half a dozen to a single appliance dealer. In many cases the wholesaler will enjoy quantity discounts and transportation savings because of buying in large amounts. Ideally some of these savings will be passed on to customers.

3. *Delivering.* Prompt and reliable delivery is important to retailers. A service station may need same-day delivery of a starter motor or a bumper to complete a repair job. Only a nearby wholesaler can provide what is needed. On occasion, a wholesaler may even deliver the goods directly to the retailer's customer, who has merely seen a sample in the retailer's store. This is true for many appliance wholesalers who sell stoves and refrigerators.

4. *Offering credit.* Credit terms offered by wholesalers to their customers are often much more satisfactory than those available directly from a manufacturer. Wholesalers sometimes allow retail or industrial customers several months to pay. Many of the whole-

Paperback wholesaler Charles Levy has helped sell millions of copies through imaginative promotional campaigns.

Kinds of Wholesalers

Many different kinds of wholesale operations have developed in response to the special needs of various industries. The major types are merchant wholesalers, manufacturers' sales branches, and merchandise agents or brokers.

Merchant wholesalers *Businesspeople who buy goods from manufacturers and then resell to others* are known as **merchant wholesalers**. In most cases, but not all, they accept delivery, store the goods, and then reship them from their warehouses to their customers. They are the largest group, accounting for about two-thirds of all wholesale operations and handling about half of all wholesale sales. Such wholesalers are found in the electrical, plumbing, cosmetic, and drug industries.

In certain fields, the activities of merchant wholesalers have become quite specialized. **Truck**, or **wagon**, **wholesalers** drive around and *sell merchandise to retailers directly from a truck*. These wholesalers handle perishable items like tobacco, candy, and potato chips. The **mail-order wholesalers** *use a catalog*. From it retailers select the jewelry, sporting goods, or hardware items they need. The **rack jobbers** *provide the retailer with a wire rack, and keep it filled* with such merchandise as sewing goods, brushes, or toys.

Manufacturers' sales offices or branches

Local business establishments, physically separated from the home office of the manufacturer but owned and operated by the manufacturer, are called **manufacturers' sales offices** or **branches.** In some cases they may include warehouse facilities. In others, they merely sell the merchandise from samples or catalogs, with shipment coming directly from the manufacturer. Such branches now account for nearly a third of all wholesale business.

Merchandise agents (brokers)

Wholesalers who do not have title to the merchandise they sell are called **merchandise agents,** or **brokers.** They merely handle the selling function for the manufacturer and receive their income from commissions or fees paid by the manufacturer. In most cases, these middlemen do not carry stock.

salers' customers may be small, new firms. Such customers might well be unable to obtain credit on any terms from manufacturers.

5. *Buying.* Wholesalers who call on retail stores are relieving retailers of part of the buying responsibility. This saves retailers the trouble and expense of having to go out and find sources of supply.

6. *Providing marketing information.* Wholesalers have numerous contacts with both manufacturers and other retailers. They are thus in a good position to keep retail customers up to date on the latest technical and marketing developments. They may suggest new and better methods of inventory control to a storekeeper. Or they may report on trends they have noted in window dressing, store hours, or display.

Here again, the Levy book-distributing operation serves to illustrate some of the ways in which a wholesaler's efforts can directly benefit its customers—in this case, retail booksellers. Just as it monitors book sales to help publishers schedule extra printing runs, Levy also finds out in advance what new paperbacks (along with movie and TV spinoffs) are scheduled for release and advises its retail customers which ones are likely to be the most profitable. It then estimates how many copies each outlet will probably need—based on computerized records of the store's past sales. It delivers them quickly and suggests how they can best be displayed and promoted. Where large-scale media tie-ins are concerned, as with *Jaws* and the others, Levy becomes even more active, setting up complete promotional programs that include special display stands, point-of-purchase signs, and window posters—even specially designed bookmarks. All this, of course, benefits retailers in the form of higher sales. This holds not only for the particular tie-in paperbacks but for others displayed nearby that simply catch the customers' attention once they've gone over to the book section.

RETAILERS: THE SECOND CATEGORY OF MIDDLEMEN

Retailers, of course, are also middlemen: they buy merchandise from manufacturers or wholesalers and then resell the goods to consumers. But they are fundamentally different from other middlemen. The

THE RIGHT CHANNEL: IS THERE ALWAYS ONLY ONE?

Magazine publishers sell their publications at news-stands; clothes are sold in clothing stores; automobiles are bought through dealers; and paper supplies are normally purchased at stationers. Food manufacturers, naturally, market their products through supermarkets. Yet there are exceptions to all of these typical marketing procedures, many that have proved quite successful.

One company that does it differently is Lance, Incorporated, a snack-food company based in Charlotte, North Carolina. Lance started out with peanut-butter crackers; and although it has branched out into cookies and other crackers, peanut-butter snacks are still the mainstay of its business. What is unusual about Lance, however, is that it shuns the traditional marketing channels for its products. Lance snack foods are sold in gas stations, commercial offices, industrial plants, convenience stores, and soda shops, everywhere except supermarkets. Unusual? Yes. Profitable? Definitely.

Once a family business run by a Mr. Philip Lance, his wife, daughter, and son-in-law, Lance, Incorporated is now a highly profitable company with sales in excess of $151 million. Profits have increased nearly every year along with dividends.

While the cookie-and-cracker business grew an estimated 5 percent in 1976, Lance's growth was more than double that rate. Obviously, Lance's unorthodox marketing techniques pay off handsomely.

Lance does some other things in a manner unusual for the industry. Giant companies like Nabisco sell snack foods through large distributors who handle many different product lines. Not Lance. Instead Lance maintains a sales force of some 1,700 people who are actually independent businessmen. They have their own trucks, maintain their separate inventories, and distribute to customers as well as collect. Thus 65 percent of Lance's customers pay cash, which almost makes it possible for Lance to buy raw materials, make its products, sell them, and collect the money before an invoice for the raw materials is received.

Vending-machine sales account for nearly 30 percent of Lance's total gross. Lance leases and services these machines through its customers.

Lance's profitability has allowed the company to diversify into other areas, food and nonfood—all of which goes to show how an unconventional marketing program, when well planned, can reap profits from peanuts.

Source: "Gargling with Peanut Butter," *Forbes*, October 15, 1977, p. 114.

country's 1.7 million retail stores[2] represent the front line of business, the only direct contact most consumers have with the countless channels of distribution that make up the national economy. They are thus the final testing ground where the effectiveness of an entire marketing program must prove itself. In effect, the buck stops here: in a typical year Americans spend over 6.5 billion dollars, or over one-half of their after-tax income, in retail stores.[3] Figure 3 shows the six largest groups of retailers in terms of their dollar sales for 1977.

Although a few large stores account for a significant share of total retail sales, most of the retail establishments are small single units operated by one owner. Over half a million of these stores have annual sales of under $30,000.[4] This means that they sell an average of only $100 of merchandise a day. Why does retailing attract businesspeople? Because it is easy to enter. In many cases a person can start a small business with as little capital as $10,000. There are few legal or educational requirements, and experience, though helpful, is not absolutely necessary. Because retailing is easy to enter, it is extremely competitive. The failure rate for small businesses is high. In 1976 4,139 retail businesses were forced to close, of which 3,050 stores did less than $100,000 annually.[5]

The chain reduces costs in many other ways as well. One is through centralized record-keeping and accounting. In addition, advertising costs may be small in comparison with those of individually owned stores. If Sears runs an ad for washing machines in the Dallas newspapers, the cost of the ad can be spread out among all the Sears stores in the area; an independent retailer would not have this advantage.

Chain stores are multiplying even in such traditionally independent fields as drugs and hardware. Can the independent store compete? It is true that chains do offer consumers many advantages. But independent merchants provide many services that chains do not. People who run small grocery stores may take a personal interest in their customers. They may stay open longer hours, on holidays, weekends, or at night. They may cash checks, offer credit, take phone orders, and make deliveries. Furthermore, because the independent store is a local business, its owner may be able to observe trends and react to them more quickly than a chain, which depends on centralized buying. A small dress shop, for example, can order a sampling of a new longer-length skirt that it feels may appeal to its clientele. It then waits for customer reaction before stock-

Retail stores are the testing ground where the manufacturer's marketing program must prove itself.

CHAIN STORES, INDEPENDENTS, AND FRANCHISES

The ten largest retailers in the United States are **chain stores**. That is, they *consist of a group of stores centrally owned and managed that sell similar goods.* Chain stores now account for about 30 percent of all retail sales. They are particularly important in the general merchandise field, where companies like Sears and J. C. Penney operate. They are also important in the sale of food, accounting for about half of the grocery sales.

Because a chain of stores is a larger operation than an independent store, it can often operate more efficiently, lower the costs, and pass on savings to the customers. The chain practices **centralized buying**, which permits it to *hire specialists for each kind of merchandise and to receive quantity discounts.* Sears, for example, has a buyer who purchases only blankets. This buyer's job is to survey the entire market for blankets, comparing the quality and price of competing products, and to encourage the manufacturer to offer the blankets at a lower cost in exchange for Sears's large orders. A large chain also has the resources to acquire and promote private brands of merchandise, as with the line of appliances manufactured by Whirlpool under the Kenmore name exclusively for Sears.

SELLING TO AMERICA: MAJOR TYPES OF RETAILERS AND THEIR SALES IN 1976

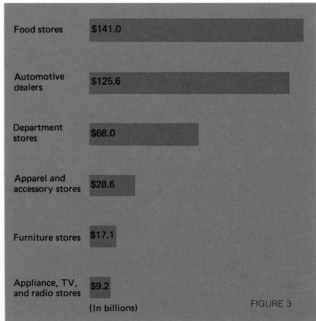

Food stores	$141.0
Automotive dealers	$125.6
Department stores	$68.0
Apparel and accessory stores	$28.6
Furniture stores	$17.1
Appliance, TV, and radio stores	$9.2

(In billions)

FIGURE 3

(Data from Census Bureau, 1977)

Table 1 Department Stores with Largest Sales in 1977

Company	Volume[1]
1. Hudson's, Detroit	$575.1
2. Macy's, New York	575
3. Broadway, Los Angeles	535
4. Bamberger's, New Jersey	525
5. May Company, California	500
6. Marshall Field, Chicago	460
7. Abraham & Straus, Brooklyn	445
8. Bloomingdale's, New York	430
9. Bullock's, Los Angeles	425
10. Korvettes Metro, New York	420

[1]in millions of dollars
Source: *Stores*, July 1978, pp. 12–13.

ing up. J. C. Penney, on the other hand, is forced to limit itself to merchandise with a potential national market because of its centralized buying. Moreover, since it must buy in volume, it has to order large amounts in advance. Rather than run the risk of stocking unsalable goods, a chain may decide not to sell what it regards as fads or high-fashion merchandise. Customers who want such goods may therefore prefer an independent store.

Finally, retailing in recent years has seen something of a revolution in the form of **franchising**. A compromise of sorts between the efficiency of chains and the virtues of independent ownership, franchising *offers local businesspeople the opportunity to buy and operate their own stores under the emblem of a larger company*. In return for an initial purchase fee and a percentage of the profits, individual proprietors receive all the essential facilities, training, and subsequent supplies they need to launch and maintain a local business—not as employees but as owners. The best known examples are probably the fast-food outlets—Burger King, McDonald's, Kentucky Fried Chicken, and the like—that have sprung up across the country in the last decade. Other familiar names, however, have been operating as franchises for a much longer period—Allied Van Lines, Martinizing dry cleaners, Midas Muffler shops, and Rexall Drug Stores, to name a few. Increasingly, then, while the mom-and-pop store on the corner may still be owned by Mom and

Pop, they have the advantage now of professional marketing, national advertising, cooperative buying, and other benefits not normally available to an independent owner.

TYPES OF RETAIL OUTLETS

Retail outlets can be divided into various categories. The most important are department stores, supermarkets, and discount stores. Others include specialty shops, variety stores, and mail-order firms.

Department stores

Department stores are *large retail establishments that bring together under one roof a vast variety of merchandise.* Before World War II most department stores were located only in downtown shopping areas. Indeed, many big cities in the United States can still be identified readily by the names of their department stores—Macy's and Gimbels in New York, Marshall Field in Chicago, Wanamaker's in Philadelphia, J. L. Hudson in Detroit. Sears, J. C. Penney, and the other national chains may have more branches and do more business, but none of them commands the kind of local feeling and customer loyalty that these stores continue to have in their respective cities. Christmas at Marshall Field, for instance, has remained an annual occasion in the Chicago area. Every year the store decorates its dozens of street-level windows with elaborate Christmas scenes, and suburban parents by the thousands bring their children into town to see them.

Elsewhere local traditions of the same sort manage to survive year after year. The rivalry between Macy's and Gimbels in New York is legendary, and the Christmas catalog from Nieman-Marcus in Dallas is always anticipated by customers eager to see what outlandish items will be sprinkled among the regular merchandise—say a $20,000 computer to run your kitchen with.

At the same time, it is equally clear that the trend in retailing is away from such venerable downtown institutions. In the last twenty-five years department stores have added more and more branches in the suburbs, especially in shopping centers. This development occurred because many of the stores' prime customers, middle-income families, moved out of the city to the

SEARS: A RETAILING GIANT

There are people who long for the old days of going from shop to shop, picking up shoes here, hats there, tires another place, and paint in yet another store. But that modern-day invention, the department store and department-store chain, is a convenience that's here to stay. Just how entrenched are these stores in the national psyche and economy? The answer is—Very.

Sears Roebuck, the largest of them all, is living proof. Occupying the world's tallest building, the 110-story Sears Tower in Chicago, the company looks out on a domain that sells more than $44 million of merchandise on a typical day, or about $15 billion a year. If that doesn't sound like much, consider this: $15 billion represents 1 percent of the gross national product, an almost unbelievable amount for one company.

Sears, if you've never been to one, has it all, including its share of problems. In recent years the company has undergone some management shuffles and rethinking of its marketing emphasis. What brought this all on was a decline in Sears's stock that began in 1974. That year, the company wound up with a very slight sales gain of 6.5 percent during a period of 12.2 percent inflation. After the recession, operating profit margins stayed down. In 1973 they were 10 cents on the dollar; in 1976 they were only 8.4 cents. This is more dramatic than it first appears. Every one-penny change in operating profit margins translates into $150 million. Today, however, Sears is on the rebound and is as important to the economy as ever.

Source: Phyllis Berman, "Too Big for Miracles," *Forbes*, June 15, 1977, pp. 26–28.

suburbs. In the suburbs, cars replaced public transportation. Shopping centers, with plenty of parking space, became the preferred retail store site.

THE BROAD SCOPE OF DEPARTMENT STORES Department stores have become the dominant retailer for general merchandise because they are uniquely equipped to serve the needs of the middle-class woman, who does most of the consumer buying in the United States. A typical department store carries a broad line of merchandise. It sells not only apparel but also staples, like sheets and kitchen utensils, and hard goods, such as furniture and appliances. In addition, this merchandise is carried in several different price ranges.

There are other reasons why department stores attract so many customers.

1. They offer many services, including credit, delivery, and the right to return merchandise.
2. They spend more money for advertising than any other type of retail outlet.

3. They are usually located in key locations both in the downtown area and in shopping centers.
4. They are the fashion leaders in many cities, that is, the first retailers to carry large assortments of the newest merchandise.

DEPARTMENT STORES IN A CHANGING ENVIRONMENT Several new developments in department-store operations illustrate their attempts to deal with the increasing complexity of modern retailing.

The greatly increased number of branches has forced stores to adopt new methods of maintaining and keeping track of inventory. Many have stopped keeping inventory records by hand and instead use automated, computerized cash registers (see our Enrichment Chapter on Computers and Data Processing). Customers at J. C. Penney's, among other retailers, have grown accustomed to the sight of checkout clerks wielding OCR (Optical Character Recognition) wands that electronically "read" and total up price tags (which can also be read by people). Indeed, a whole new generation of Electronic Point-of-Sale equipment

(EPOS, for short) is gradually taking over a wide variety of functions—instantly verifying sales by charge account or check, changing prices when indicated, producing sales reports at a moment's notice, and continuously keeping track of the store's inventory. While some retailers have worried that their customers might be mistrustful of such futuristic gadgets, experience thus far indicates that customers accept them readily enough once they realize that the new devices make for fewer errors and faster checkouts.

Another consequence of the increase in the number of branches has been a need for more professional managers. Most large stores now have formal recruiting and training programs with a heavy emphasis on bringing college and junior-college graduates into management. Many of them, however, still hold to the philosophy of promoting only from within the company, bringing everyone up through the ranks. Anyone joining the management training program at Sears, for example, has to start by working in a Sears branch. He or she will eventually become a department manager, then a store manager, and may later move up into corporate management. In other words, the company does not hire anybody at middle management or above, and all would-be Sears executives must therefore start out on the retail floor and work their way up.

Department stores increasingly have taken to expanding the variety of goods and services they sell. (Table 2 gives you an idea of the kinds of merchandise that sell best in department stores.) Some place an emphasis on providing goods that their customers cannot buy elsewhere. This approach is often used in the apparel field, which has seen a steady increase in imports and the development of private-label fashion designs. Other stores may offer the convenience of one-stop shopping for such diverse services as car rental, a travel bureau, and interior-decorating advice. An early pioneer in this trend, the Oregon-based Fred Meyer food and merchandise chain, offers an array of goods and services ranging from groceries and garden supplies to clothing departments, pharmacies, and travel bureaus in its sixty-plus stores. It has also established a major savings-and-loan business, installing minibanks in more than twenty of its branches. The underlying value of diversification is aptly summed up by Fred Meyer himself: "There are three basic things man has needed since he was civilized. He had to have

food, clothing, and a place to live. . . . Well, we're in the food business, the clothing business, and now we have the mortgages on the homes."[6]

Another change is the increasing use of nontraditional advertising media. Many stores now depend heavily on network and local TV commercials to supplement their direct-mail and newspaper advertising. A particular new emphasis is also being placed on the catalogs mailed out by stores to past and potential customers. The trend is toward more frequent mailings and a glossier, magazine-like appearance, carefully designed and edited, with high-quality photography and such extra features as contests and recipes. The new catalogs are expensive to produce (indeed, some stores have carried the magazine idea to the

Table 2 A Store Sales Directory: Departments that Performed Best and Worst in 1976

BEST DEPARTMENTS	% Sales Increase in 1976
1. Men's suits and formal wear	19.9
2. Television	18.4
3. Men's coats	16.7
4. Vacuums, floor polishers	16.0
5. Luggage	14.9
6. Small leather goods	14.3
7. Women's gloves	13.9
8. Christmas decorations	13.6
9. Men's sports shirts	12.5
10. Blankets, comforters, and bed pillows	11.6

WORST DEPARTMENTS	% Sales Decrease in 1976
1. Office equipment and wrapping supplies	23.6
2. Tobacco and smoking goods	15.0
3. Daytime utility dresses, uniforms, aprons	13.7
4. Apparel fabrics	13.1
5. Hardware, tools, and electrical equipment	10.4
6. Musical instruments, records and sheet music	10.0
7. Sewing fabrics, notions, patterns and machines	9.5
8. Sporting goods	9.1
9. Umbrellas and folding rain accessories	8.1
10. Men's ties	5.4

Source: "NRMA's Annual Merchandising and Operating Results: 1976 Analyzed," by Edward S. Dubbs, in *Stores*, Sept. 1977, pp. 32–39.

point of selling them by subscription). Most stores agree, however, that they justify the cost with increased sales, especially if they succeed in projecting a distinctive "lifestyle" image that appeals to the store's target market.

Supermarkets

The *large food stores* known as **supermarkets** vary in size from those with annual sales of less than half a million dollars to giant block-long stores with annual sales of several million dollars. They carry both nationally branded merchandise and private brands. Self-service is an important characteristic. Some, however, may have separate delicatessen or bakery departments where attendants wait on customers.

In recent years competitive pressures have forced supermarkets to adopt many changes. These include expanding the product lines to include a wide variety of nonfood items ranging from children's pajamas to small TV sets. The reasons are simple and persuasive: one recent survey estimated that an average supermarket makes 16.1 percent pretax profit on nonfood merchandise, as opposed to a scant 1.3 percent on food sales.[7] Obviously, a store that relied on grocery sales alone would be hard pressed just to break even against inflation, much less turn a profit. Some supermarkets are also trying to fight back against the fast-food industry, which has had a very damaging effect. Their approach is "if you can't lick 'em, join 'em." One California chain has introduced eat-in delicatessen sections in its stores, and a group of food-and-department stores in Arizona now offers its customers in-store cocktail lounges. Other supermarkets have sought to increase sales volume and lower prices by expanding their business hours (in some cases to twenty-four hours a day), eliminating frills like trading stamps, and selling merchandise straight from the carton to save the labor cost of shelving it. A newer idea in the same vein, similar to a recent trend in the drug industry, is selling "no-brand" food products. These goods are labeled generically—that is, simply with the name of the food—and there is no brand name on the can or box. The products can be sold at low prices chiefly because of cost savings from simpler labeling, limited promotion, and fewer variations in package sizes. Stores that have introduced no-brand foods are hoping that initial

consumer reluctance to try them will be overcome by the lower prices—10 to 35 percent less than nationally advertised brands—as well as by the government grading and nutritional information that do appear on the labels.

Discount stores

Discount stores developed after World War II. Their distinguishing feature is that they *sell a variety of goods at cut-rate prices.* The first discounters—Korvette, Lechmere Sales, Polk Brothers—confined their merchandise to brand-name appliances and durable goods. They sold these at low prices in out-of-the-way warehouse-type facilities. Later they expanded their lines to include unbranded goods, particularly inexpensive nonfashion items like children's wear or men's shirts, often imported from Hong Kong, Taiwan, or Japan.

HOW DO MANUFACTURERS GET THEIR PRODUCTS DISPLAYED IN SUPERMARKETS?

Nothing should be easier for a manufacturer than getting its product on a supermarket shelf, right? Wrong. A salesperson discussing the merits of his or her product with a store manager is a bit like a jockey maneuvering his mount into good position in a field of thirty thoroughbreds. The competition is fierce.

A quick walk through a large supermarket reveals some of the problems. Notice how certain products are battling each other not only for shelf space but for attention. Paper products are good examples. Once just a bland white, tissues, napkins, toilet paper, and paper towels now sell in a rainbow of colors. Competing for shelf space and the shopper's loyalty, some makers have even begun marketing "designer" napkins, following the recent trend in bath towels and linens. Pet foods, too, compete ferociously with one another, and the shopper sees ever more elaborate packaging and displays.

Today many discount stores carry broad lines of both nationally advertised and private-brand goods. The success of such discounters as King and Zayre encouraged conventional retailers to enter the discount business too. Kresge now operates more than 1,200 K-Mart stores across the country. Woolworth owns the Woolco stores.

Convenience stores

An increasingly significant factor in the food-retailing business, **convenience stores** are, in a sense, the rebirth of the traditional mom-and-pop store. As the name implies, they are *food stores whose chief stock in trade is convenience.* They are typically open from early in the morning until late at night, seven days a week. In return, they can control expenses by carrying only a limited selection of brands and sizes, and charge

How does one win in this war for shelf space? Ultimately the store manager or buyer has the final word. The salesperson's challenge is to convince the manager that his product is a hot item. This is not an easy job. In most cases the manager sets aside certain hours of certain days during which he will see salespeople, sometimes giving them just five minutes apiece to make their pitches. In that short time the salesperson must convince the store manager that the product interests consumers, that it occupies only limited shelf space, and that turnover will be high. The salesperson must emphasize that in return for good shelf placement, the store receives a display allowance from the manufacturer and backup advertising money for mention of the product in the store's advertising.

Compounding already difficult circumstances, the product is often competing against the store's own brand name, which normally sells for a few pennies less than nationally advertised brands. Persuading a store manager that your product deserves as prominent a display as the store's brand requires a real selling job.

higher prices to their customers—who may be too late to get to the supermarket or may simply want to pick up some cigarettes or soft drinks or beer without standing in a long checkout line.

Other types of retail stores

Three other types of retail stores are important in terms of their familiarity and numbers.

SPECIALTY STORES **Specialty stores**, so called because they *carry only particular types of goods,* are among the most common small businesses. A particularly successful example (though not so small anymore) is the Ohio-based chain of apparel stores called The Limited, which has grown from 1 location in 1963 to 207 today. The company started by choosing a very specific target market—young, relatively affluent working women—and offered a limited range of fashions (hence its name) suited to their tastes. The merchandise was restricted to well-tailored, moderately conservative styles and was priced significantly higher than similar clothes at nearby stores. The reasoning was simple, and it worked: The Limited's intended customers were only a fraction of all the women from eighteen to thirty-five, but they had enough money to care less about price than about having a certain fashion look. And from hats to shoes, the handsomely designed Limited stores offered them virtually everything they needed to achieve that look.[8] A recent and even more specialized entry in this category is a company called Solar Energy Centers, which has begun to franchise stores that sell only solar-powered devices, ranging from cigarette lighters and wristwatches to complete home heating systems.

VARIETY STORES **Variety stores**, the old-fashioned five-and-tens, *sell a wide array of small items at low prices.* They have long been a familiar fixture of American life. Gradual changes in retail merchandising and consumer buying habits, however, have led them to the brink of extinction. In 1975 W. T. Grant went out of business after a long ailment, leaving its one-time archrival Woolworth in the uncertain position of being the last national variety-store chain. To be sure, Woolworth is not yet face to face with disaster; it remains, in fact, the country's fourth largest merchant. That is due in large part, though, to its chain of

RUBBER CHECKS AND PHONY GREENBACKS

THE LOOMING PROBLEM OF RETAIL CRIME

It was Christmas time, a booming period of the year for most stores, yet in 1975 merchants throughout the northeast United States were in a fright. Counterfeit $100 bills were floating all over, many of them going undetected until someone got stung. This happens time after time, not just at holidays. The Secret Service estimated that in 1975 some $3.6 million in phony bills was passed. And merchants, it seems, were usually on the receiving end.

Crime, by many methods, not simply counterfeiting, costs stores plenty each year. Total retail losses in 1976, according to the Bureau of Domestic Commerce of the United States Department of Commerce, hit $7.2 billion, an astounding sum. Just for general merchandise and apparel stores, the crime quotient was a whopping $4.3 billion in the same year. Unfortunately, retail establishments are easy prey for all kinds of schemes to cheat them out of money.

What are some methods people use to get away with the goods? Sad but true, for one, is the fact that retail establishments can expect to be burgled and robbed more frequently than any other kind of business. Shoplifting is another popular method, accounting for 28 percent of all store losses. (Sources claim, in fact, that only one in thirty-five shoplifters is caught.) Bounced checks, too, are a big headache for retail merchandisers. Retailers, both food and general merchandise, cash more checks in a year than banks; and in 1977, when some 29 billion checks were written by the public, a $7.3 billion loss was suffered due to bad checks. In the same league, and perhaps more terrifying, is credit-card fraud. Buying with plastic is for many people a "buy now, pay never" arrangement. Counterfeit cards,

Woolco discount stores, which have enjoyed stable if not spectacular profits. The company nonetheless has serious problems: its foreign stores, which account for about half of its profits, have recently dropped in earnings, and domestic profits have risen only slowly. Hopes for putting new life into the variety-store business rest chiefly on a series of planned innovations, including a new computer system to improve inventory control and sales reporting, and more centralized coordination of the company's vast buying, advertising, and distribution operations. The management also intends to promote a more sharply defined public image, emphasizing the differences it sees in convenience, service, and merchandise between its variety stores and rival discount stores.[9]

MAIL-ORDER FIRMS **Mail-order firms** *provide customers with a wide variety of goods ordered from catalogs and shipped by mail.* Like variety stores, they too are an old-fashioned type of retailer. Unlike the former, however, they seem to be booming. Spiegel sells only through mail orders. Other familiar mail-order names are Sears, Montgomery Ward, and Penney, which also run department-store outlets. A smaller but steadily growing mail-order firm is the outdoor-clothing producer, L. L. Bean. With only one small store in Freeport, Maine, L. L. Bean has developed into a $60-million-a-year operation on the strength of a boom in outdoor recreation, a solid reputation for quality, and an efficient, computerized merchandising system. All the while, the longtime retail leader in the field, Abercrombie & Fitch, was gradually going out of business; the end for Abercrombie's finally came in late 1977.[10]

One reason why the mail-order business is so prosperous is that consumers, more interested in spending money on services like travel, are less willing to shop around for goods. In the future, high prices for gasoline may further stimulate catalog shopping.

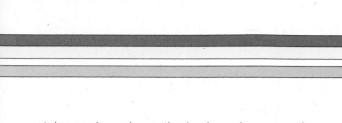

stolen cards, and unauthorized purchases are the bane of every store's existence.

A lot of money is being spent on anticrime and detection programs—$4.5 billion a year goes toward crime prevention. One nine-chain discounter spent $3 million on shortage prevention in one year—an amount that almost matched its $3.1-million after-tax profit on gross sales of $192 million! Many stores invest large sums in technological devices, such as plastic tags attached to goods that sound buzzers if not removed by clerks. However, there are also other approaches to the problem. Some stores, for example, hold store managers responsible for inventory levels; when this was done, shrinkage dropped from 5.3 percent to around 1 percent in a number of stores. And some stores are even offering employees a $50 bonus for blowing the whistle on co-workers who are stealing. In the end, this may be one of the most effective deterrents of all.

Source: From a series entitled "Retail Crime," which appeared in *Stores*, January, February, March, and April, 1978.

PHYSICAL DISTRIBUTION

Whatever channel of distribution a manufacturer has chosen, a second basic issue remains to be dealt with. Before that new pancake mix or three-speed hairdryer ever reaches the consumer's waiting hands, the very practical, sometimes formidable question of physical distribution must be decided on. For a producer with goods to move out, there is a great deal more involved here than loading cartons onto a truck and waving goodbye. As a business term, **physical distribution** encompasses *all the activities required to move finished products efficiently from the producer to the consumer*. In addition to transportation, they include such matters as warehousing, materials handling, packaging, inventory control, order processing, and customer service (see Figure 4).

Two of the essential questions that have to be answered, of course, are where the products will be stored at each stage in the distribution process, and how many will be kept at each location. Here, we will focus our attention on the third essential question: What kind of transportation should be used to transfer the goods from one location to another? If you're RCA, how will you get a shipment of television sets to your wholesaler for the New England area? How will they then be delivered to individual retailers, and from there to customers?

THE IMPORTANCE OF THE TRANSPORTATION DECISION

The cost of transportation is normally the largest single item in the overall cost of physical distribution. It doesn't necessarily follow, though, that a manufacturer should simply pick the cheapest available form of transportation. Air freight, for instance, may be much more expensive than railroads, but for a national manufacturer it might make it possible to ship everything from a single warehouse and so avoid the greater expense of maintaining several regional warehouses. The point, of course, is that the choice of transportation has to be made in conjunction with a company's other marketing concerns—storage, financing, sales, inventory size, and the like. Transportation, in fact, can be an especially important sales tool. The firm that can supply its customers' needs more quickly and reliably than the competition has a vital advantage and may find it more profitable in the long run to pay

Table 3   Agencies that Regulate Transportation

Department of Transportation (DOT)   Establishes national transportation policies to provide the country with fast, safe, efficient transportation.

Interstate Commerce Commission (ICC)   Regulates rates, services, routes, and bills of lading for water and motor carriers, freight forwarders, and railroads.

Civil Aeronautics Board (CAB)   Handles economic questions connected with domestic airways; helps to develop international air transportation.

Federal Aviation Agency (FAA)   A division of DOT (the Department of Transportation); it is responsible for inspecting and rating civilian aircraft and crews.

higher transportation costs rather than risk losing future sales. As well, the nature of some industries makes the speed of delivery a crucial factor. For a clothing manufacturer sending seasonal high-fashion dresses from New York to Denver, the promptness of air freight may be all-important, while slower (and cheaper) truck or rail transport is perfectly satisfactory for more everyday apparel. Likewise, a good transportation system may well pay for itself through greater specialization and efficiency by enabling a manufacturer to bring together a variety of resources at one plant site.

Let us now take a closer look at each of the major modes of transportation open to the shipper. We compare these modes in Figure 5.

TRUCKS Trucks rank high in meeting the needs of most manufacturers. They are usually the cheapest form of transportation for two reasons: they offer door-to-door delivery from the manufacturer to the customer with no intermediate unloading; and they operate on public highways that do not require an expensive terminal or right-of-way like an airline or a railroad. The main drawback of trucks is that they are somewhat limited in the type of cargo they can carry easily. Federal regulations limit weight loads and truck dimensions, so that trucks cannot haul heavy, bulky commodities like steel or coal economically. Also, certain types of cargoes, such as gases, are difficult to handle by truck.

RAILROADS Railroads are the most important mode of transportation in terms of total amount of goods carried. They can carry heavier and more diversified cargoes than any other kind of transportation. But they have disadvantages. They can seldom deliver directly to the customer, but must usually rely on trucking companies to make the final delivery.

PLANES Although air transport is the fastest form of transportation, it too has many disadvantages. Many areas of the country are still not served by conveniently located airports. Planes can carry only certain types of cargo because of size and shape limitations. Furthermore, planes are the least dependable form of transportation. Weather can cause airlines to cancel flights, and even minor repairs can lead to serious delays. Finally, air transport is expensive.

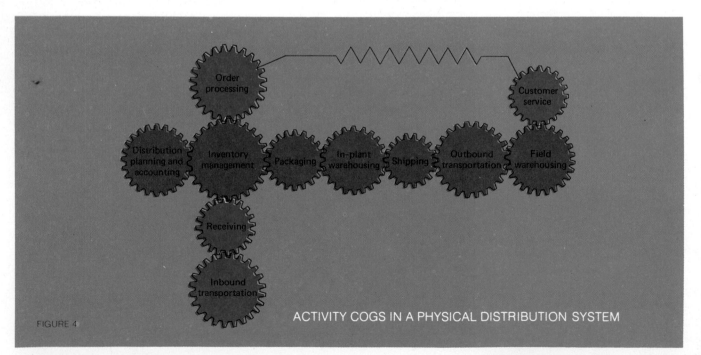

FIGURE 4

ACTIVITY COGS IN A PHYSICAL DISTRIBUTION SYSTEM

(Courtesy American Marketing Association)

FIGURE 5

COMPARING THE FIVE BASIC FORMS OF TRANSPORTATION:
WHAT'S THE BEST WAY TO DELIVER THE GOODS?

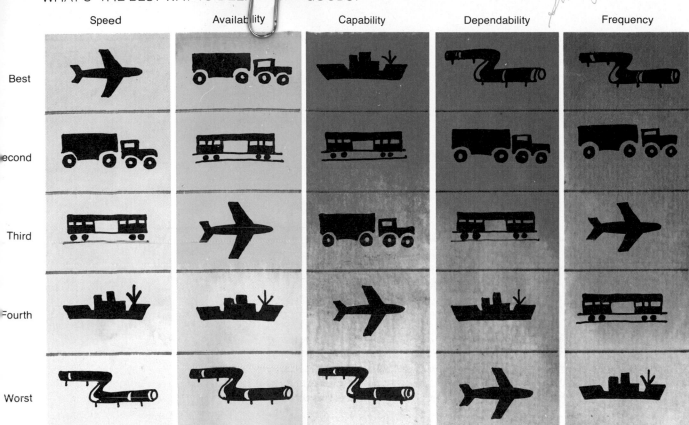

	Speed	Availability	Capability	Dependability	Frequency
Best	plane	truck	ship	pipeline	pipeline
Second	truck	train	train	truck	truck
Third	train	plane	truck	train	plane
Fourth	ship	ship	plane	ship	train
Worst	pipeline	pipeline	pipeline	plane	ship

Despite these limitations, air transport has become absolutely essential for certain industries. California growers ship their strawberries to the East Coast by plane. Without air service, perishable items like this simply could not be marketed in Boston or Philadelphia.

SHIPS Shipment by water is the cheapest form of transportation. Thus, it is widely used for low-cost bulk items like oil, coal, ore, cotton, and lumber. But the disadvantages of water transport make it unsuitable for most businesses. Ships are slow, and service to any given location is infrequent. If goods miss the boat sailing this week from Hoboken to Marseilles, there may not be another one for two weeks. Furthermore, it is usually necessary to use another form of transportation to complete delivery. Such reloading may add substantial costs because of theft, extra handling, and spoilage caused by weather.

PIPELINES Pipelines are used exclusively for the shipment of liquids and gases, and so are of little use to most manufacturers. They do provide dependable, continuous delivery for oil and natural gas (though in some cases it may cost less to ship oil by water). For this reason the Alaska pipeline has been selected as the means of bringing the vast oil deposits of the far north to the industrialized parts of this country.

COORDINATED SYSTEMS OF TRANSPORTATION Various combinations of transportation have been developed to utilize the advantages of each. These consist of **piggyback**, *a combination truck and rail service;* **fishyback**, *a truck and water service;* and **birdyback**, *a truck and air service.* Each method is tied to the growth of **containerization**, *the use of large, standard-sized, sealed containers for shipping goods.* Containers are packed and sealed at the factory. Next they are loaded on trucks and then reloaded on railroad flatcars, ships, or planes.

Containerization cuts down handling time and effort when merchandise is shifted from one form of transportation to another. It also eliminates stealing or loss of small individual items.

CHAPTER REVIEW

Placement, or distribution, involves getting goods from the manufacturer to the consumer. A manufacturer must first consider the channels of distribution, routes that merchandise takes as it moves on its way. For consumer goods there are three main channels of distribution: from manufacturer to consumer, from manufacturer to retailer to consumer, and from manufacturer to wholesaler to retailer to consumer. For industrial products, the route is from the manufacturer to one or more wholesalers to the eventual user.

Wholesalers are middlemen who function between the manufacturer and either the retailer or the consumer. For manufacturers, wholesalers provide a selling force, carry stock, assume credit risks, and provide market information. The wholesaler serves the retailer or industrial customer by anticipating needs, making shipping more convenient, delivering merchandise, and offering credit. Wholesalers also perform some buying functions and keep the retailers informed about the market.

Retailers buy goods from manufacturers or wholesalers and resell them to consumers. Most retail establishments are small and owner-operated, though a significant percentage of retail sales are made by a few large retailers, usually chain stores. There are many different types of retailing outlets, including department stores, supermarkets, discount stores, convenience stores, specialty stores, variety stores, and mail-order firms.

Businesses have a wide choice of transportation modes to ship their goods. Price is not the only consideration involved in the decision. Warehousing, selling, and financing policies must also be considered. The most popular forms of transportation are trucks, railroads, planes, ships, and pipelines. Each has advantages and disadvantages, and a business must select the mode that best suits its product and customers. Coordinated systems have been developed combining the advantages of different modes of transportation; this development is tied to the growth of containerization.

KEY WORD REVIEW

channel of distribution
wholesaler
retailer
title
agents (brokers)
chain stores
centralized buying
franchising
department stores
supermarkets
discount stores
convenience stores
specialty stores
variety stores
mail-order firms
physical distribution
piggyback
fishyback
birdyback
containerization

REVIEW QUESTIONS

1. What are the major channels of distribution used for consumer goods and for industrial goods?

2. What are the main disadvantages associated with the channel of distribution that involves only the manufacturer and the consumer?

3. List four of the services performed by wholesalers for the manufacturer.

4. List some of the services performed by wholesalers for the retail customer.

5. Explain the role of the proprietor in a franchise.

6. What competitive advantages do chain stores have over individually owned stores? Why have some individually owned stores managed to flourish despite these advantages?

7. Describe the changes that have taken place in discount stores since the end of World War II.

8. Compare and contrast the advantages and disadvantages of truck and rail transportation to a manufacturer. How do you explain the rapid growth of truck transportation during the past few years?

CASE 1

BLIND BIDDING: A PROBLEM FOR MOVIE MIDDLEMEN

How do motion picture companies choose the theaters where their latest films will play? Major distributors in particular rely on a kind of auction procedure aptly known as "blind bidding." Each movie theater owner, or exhibitor, is asked to submit a bid that indicates the amount of money a new film is guaranteed to make if it plays in his or her movie house. The highest bidders get the film. The reason this kind of bidding is called "blind" is that the exhibitors do not get to see the film before they bid on it.

Blind bidding has been kicking around the movie industry for at least three decades. But it has become widely used only recently, chiefly because the decline in Hollywood's new film output has led to greater demand and more competition among exhibitors for first-rate pictures. By 1978, at least half of the movies from major companies were being marketed this way. For the studios, the system is ideal: they can use the money they get from the winning bidders to finance the final production stages of their films. And they can also make sure that their movies will be shown in prime markets during times of peak attendance.

The exhibitors, though, have begun to bitterly resent blind bidding, which gives them little leeway in their role as middlemen between movie producers and consumers. In fact, owners have begun lobbying in several state legislatures to make the practice illegal. They complain that blind bidding leaves them defenseless against "turkeys"—bad films. Exhibit A in their brief is a film called *The Heretic,* the unsuccessful sequel to *The Exorcist.* "If we'd seen *The Heretic,*" says a man who books films for twenty theaters in the Southeast, "nobody would have ever bid for it." The studios defend blind bidding on the grounds that it has become an in-

tegral part of the way films are produced these days. Besides, films are usually not ready to be shown until just before they open, studios say, and if they had to show them to exhibitors before setting up definite theater engagements, they would miss the peak attendance periods.[11]

1. What rights do you think exhibitors should be accorded as far as inspecting the merchandise prior to purchase goes?

2. How might a ban on blind bidding change the wholesaler-retailer relationship between movie producers and exhibitors?

3. Would the consumer be likely to benefit more from leaving blind bidding in effect, or from making it illegal?

CASE 2

DISTRIBUTING A COSMETICS LINE: HANES TRIES AN INNOVATIVE APPROACH

It was unusual enough when the Hanes Corporation decided to launch an entire eighty-item cosmetics line in one fell swoop. Usually, a cosmetics company will introduce just one or two products, and then extend the line gradually. But what was even more unusual about the bold move is the fact that Hanes was not a cosmetics company at all, but an apparel manufacturer.

In 1971 Hanes shot to the top of the $1.2 billion women's hosiery market when it came up with the idea of marketing and distributing high-quality pantyhose, called L'eggs, in supermarkets and drugstores. Since those outlets had been ignored by most of the cosmetics industry giants

like Revlon, Avon, and Chesebrough-Pond's—just as they had been bypassed by high-quality hosiery manufacturers—Hanes executives figured that a L'eggs-type marketing and distribution strategy applied to cosmetics would be a good gamble. If the cosmetics line takes off, it could turn into a $50 million business for Hanes.

The chief elements of the strategy for Hanes cosmetics—the original name for the line, L'Aura, had to be scrapped because it too closely resembled another company's trademark—include the following:

☐ The cosmetics will be distinctively packaged. As opposed to most cosmetic products sold in supermarkets and drugstores, which are usually sealed in a plastic blister-pack, Hanes cosmetics will be packaged in burgundy-colored boxes with plastic windows that allow shoppers to see the contents of the box.

☐ The cosmetics will be sold from handsome open displays that are geared to attract the impulse shopper. Hanes' plan calls for those displays to be placed as near as possible to the checkout counter.

☐ Rather than use middlemen to keep the displays neat and well-stocked, Hanes will use its own sales force to serve retailers directly.

☐ Hanes will spend heavily to advertise its new product.[12]

1. Why would Hanes choose to use its own sales force to look after its cosmetics displays rather than using middlemen?

2. How would you explain the fact that most cosmetics industry giants have chosen *not* to sell their products in supermarkets and drugstores?

CONSUMER BEHAVIOR

Most of us would undoubtedly rather think of people as individuals than as statistics—as unique personalities, not types or profiles or segments of somebody's market. But if your business is selling a product or service to large numbers of people, you need to have some idea of who's most likely to buy it and how you can encourage them to do so. And since you can't meet millions of people personally, the next best course is to study facts and figures about them—how many of them are out there, where they live, how big their families are, how much money they have to spend, and so on—and use that information in deciding what to sell and how to sell it. In this chapter we will look at the increasingly sophisticated array of scientific knowledge—in the fields of demography, sociology, and psychology—available to business today to help it sell its goods and services to the most appropriate markets.

WHAT WILL THIS CHAPTER FOCUS ON?

After reading the material in this chapter, you will understand and be able to discuss:

■ how businesses find out about their target markets

■ the population statistics that are most important to marketers: statistics concerning the number of consumers in a target market, their place of residence, their age, their education level, their earnings, and their spending patterns

■ major factors in the psychology of buying: the rational and emotional motives that affect people's buying habits

■ the four most important patronage motives

■ major factors in the sociology of buying: the effects of group membership on consumer behavior, especially the effects of social class

■ the major characteristics of the industrial market

Though they may sometimes dream of it, the men and women who sell their companies' products know they can't really expect to market their goods to all the consumers in the United States. Instead, marketing and salespeople have to single out smaller, more homogeneous groups—target markets—within the total market and produce goods and services that will specifically appeal to those markets. And for this reason, a marketing manager needs certain information about the target market.

First, what are the facts about the market? Does it actually exist? Are there people who might buy the item—and if so, how many, where do they live, how old are they, how well-educated are they, how much do they earn, and how do they spend their money? Such facts are the subject of the science of **demography**—*the study of population*—an area of research that is one of the marketing manager's basic tools.

Second, what are the reasons *why* the consumers in this market behave the way they do? For example,

ASPECTS OF THE MARKETING MIX: THE TARGET MARKET

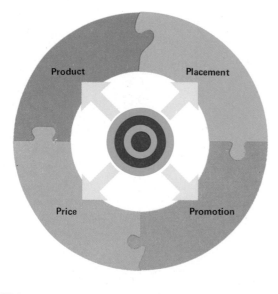

FIGURE 1

Marketers must study their target market carefully—for the target market determines the rest of the marketing mix.

why would a college professor and a crane operator who both make $25,000, live in the same city, and have the same size families tend to buy different types of automobiles or prefer different types of food? To answer questions of this sort, marketing managers turn to **psychology**—*the study of individual behavior*—and **sociology**—*the study of group behavior*. These behavioral sciences offer valuable insights into the motivations and preferences of consumers.

A business planner's understanding of any consumer market is thus based on a combination of demographic and behavioral research. Such research can be vital in helping a company decide whether it should increase or decrease production, continue or discontinue a product, or develop an altogether new product. General Motors spends hundreds of millions of dollars creating a new car and building the factories to produce it. Before the company planners spend that kind of money, they want to make sure there are people who will buy the car. They also want to know, if possible, whether in the near future that potential market will grow, shrink, or remain the same.

Likewise, demographic, psychological, and sociological research is important in shaping promotional campaigns. It is hardly by chance, for instance, that the promotional campaigns for Chevrolet and Gillette—among others—include heavy advertising on television sports programs. The marketing people are well aware that Sunday afternoon football is watched mainly by men, who happen to be the most likely customers for cars and razor blades. By the same token, Procter & Gamble is the king of advertisers on daytime TV, for the very good reason that the daytime viewers—predominantly housewives—are also the principal buyers of soap, shampoo, detergent, and the like. And think about these questions for a moment. General Motors makes other cars besides Chevrolets; how does it decide which ones to advertise on which sports programs? Is it possible, for instance, that football fans and tennis buffs tend to buy different types of cars? Would two identical commercials—one for Cadillac, one for Buick—be equally effective, or would it be better for each to have its own music and visual background and sales approach? Such details, trivial as they may seem, can have a decisive effect on a product's success in a competitive market, and business leaders have learned to take them very seriously indeed.

In this chapter we're going to take a look at some facts about the United States population and its sub-populations that have proved to be very important to marketers, and also at some aspects of consumer behavior of which marketers need to be constantly aware. As we'll see, some interesting new trends have begun to emerge in both these areas.

THE BASIC QUESTIONS IN CONSUMER DEMOGRAPHY

HOW MANY CONSUMERS ARE THERE?

For any business enterprise to succeed, there obviously must be enough people available to buy what it wants to sell. Likewise, for the business community as a whole to grow and prosper, the overall population must increase at a fast enough rate to consume the increasing variety of goods and services—as well as to provide a sufficient labor force.

What then is the status of the population of the United States at this time? Throughout American history the population trend has been an upward one. Every ten years since 1790 the census has revealed that population has grown; and between 1920 and 1970 the population of the United States nearly doubled from 106 million people to 203 million.[1] This population increase has helped stimulate prosperity. Companies have been able to expand production on the assumption that the population would continue to grow.

Today, however, more people have become concerned about overpopulation, the environment, and possible shortages of food and oil. As a result, the **population growth rate**, that is, *the rate at which the number of people increases,* has declined. This does not mean, however, that population growth will stop completely. The population is already large, and many people who were born during the baby boom after World War II are now of child-bearing age. So even if the rate of population growth declines further, the population will probably continue to grow by at least 16 million people a decade. According to the Census Bureau, the minimum likely population in 1985 is about 229 million people, and the maximum is about 239 million.[2]

Businesses, whose long-range plans generally cover a ten- to twenty-year period, will continue to make plans on the basis of a general increase in population. But different businesses will make different plans, depending on such other population factors as where growth is taking place or what the average age of the people is. We'll look at these factors in the sections that follow.

WHERE DO CONSUMERS LIVE?

The United States has always been a nation of wanderers. During the peak immigration years, 1881–1930, over 27 million people came here from other lands to join and build this country.[3] No other nation in modern times has had as much voluntary migration as ours. It is therefore as important for market researchers to know *where* our population is growing as it is to know by how much.

Throughout our history the dominant movement of people has been westward, and that trend continues today: over a third of the people live west of the Mississippi River (see Figure 2). But since World War II, there have been two other equally important population movements in the United States.

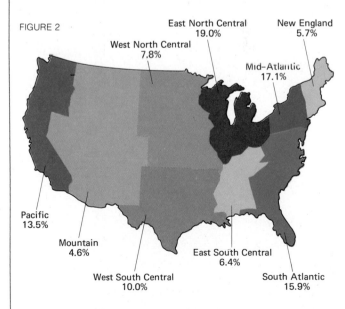

FIGURE 2

East North Central 19.0%

New England 5.7%

West North Central 7.8%

Mid-Atlantic 17.1%

Pacific 13.5%

Mountain 4.6%

West South Central 10.0%

East South Central 6.4%

South Atlantic 15.9%

U.S. POPULATION BY REGION, 1977

The move to the Sunbelt

First, there has been a movement away from the old population centers of the Northeast and upper Midwest. A large number of people have resettled in the "Sunbelt," the lower section of the United States that runs from Virginia south to Florida and west all the way to California. During the first half of the 1970s the greatest gains were registered in California and Florida. More recently the growth rates rose markedly in the major oil-producing states—Texas, Louisiana, and Oklahoma. Though the trend seems to have slowed since 1975, the Sunbelt states have continued to grow by an average of 2 percent a year (twice the national average) while populations in the Northeast and north central states have remained more or less static.[4] Market researchers, of course, must consider these movements in making their plans. Leaving aside differences in such matters as tax rates and labor costs, a company is more likely to build a new product distribution center in Texas, where the population is growing steadily, than in Massachusetts, where it is not.

The movement to the Sunbelt, with its warmer climates, has inevitably benefited some industries more than others. Makers of such things as air conditioners, power boats, mobile homes, casual apparel, and (logically enough) suntan lotion are among the businesses that have profited from this demographic shift. Another reflection of this redistribution of people is the increase in circulation and advertising in such regional magazines as *Sunset* (in the Far West) and *Southern Living.* Published since 1966 in Birmingham, Alabama, and aimed at a fifteen-state area, *Southern Living* has tapped such a receptive—and growing—regional audience that its circulation has surpassed that of many national publications. Its astounding profit margins, an estimated 30 percent, are the highest of any magazine in the country.[5]

The move to the suburbs

In addition to the migration to the Sunbelt, there has been a movement in every part of the country away from both rural areas and central cities to the suburbs. Only one out of five Americans lived in suburbs back in 1940; by 1985, however, more than 50 percent are expected to be suburbanites. The movement to the suburbs benefits, among others, housing and shop-

ping-center developers, automobile manufacturers, and makers of garden equipment and outdoor furniture. For example, the growth in popularity of the Volkswagen probably arose from the need for a second car to make commuting easier. In addition to aiding the sale of some products, the move to the suburbs has changed the nature of advertising. Television and radio are the great suburban advertising media because they reach people directly in their homes or in their cars on the way to work or shop. Television and radio, in fact, have grown far more rapidly as advertising media than have newspapers and general-circulation magazines. Moreover, while big-city newspaper circulations have leveled off, and in some cases dropped sharply, there has been a great increase in the number of suburban newspapers—which in turn has spurred many metropolitan dailies to add new regional sections carrying local news and advertising.

HOW OLD ARE CONSUMERS?

The average age of people in the United States is rising and will continue to rise in the near future (see Figure 3). This fact will profoundly affect the plans of certain industries. It means, among other things, that the purchasing power of teen-agers is leveling off and that of older people is increasing.

During the 1960s, market planners were youth-conscious to a remarkable degree. But the number of teen-agers will level off within twenty years after the number of babies levels off. In the 1970s and 1980s the teen-agers of the 1960s will be between thirty and fifty years old—traditionally the years of greatest purchasing power.

Eighteen to thirty-four: the big spenders

At present the "hottest" consumer category is the eighteen to thirty-four-age group, the now grown-up members of the postwar baby-boom generation. These are the young marrieds who buy houses, cars, appliances, and all the lesser goods needed to run a household and raise a family. Increasingly, it turns out, they are also the young *un*marrieds, a group that has grown steadily as an economic and social force. One- and two-person households now outnumber larger domestic units, the Census Bureau tells us; in 1976,

THE CHANGING AGE MIX OF AMERICANS: POPULATION CHANGES MEAN CHANGES IN MARKETS

FIGURE 3

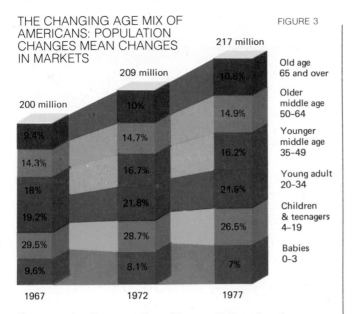

By comparing the proportion of the population of each age group in 1967 with its proportion in 1972 and again in 1977, you can trace the growth and decline in numbers of several important market segments. In 1967, for instance, there were 19,168,000 babies in the country. Just ten years later, there were only 15,236,000. What would this decline have meant in the baby food, infant toy and disposable diaper industries? On the other hand, as you can see from the chart, the number of young adults swelled from 38,264,000 to 53,222,000, as the generation that started with the post–World War II baby boom came of age. What industries would benefit most from this increase?

moreover, singles setting up new households outnumbered couples (with or without children) three to one. The reasons for this are embedded in basic social changes that have occurred during the last generation. Americans are staying single longer than they used to, and young adults who once would have lived with their parents until they married are now setting up housekeeping on their own. As well, the divorce rate has risen to such an extent that one out of every three married persons, the Census Bureau estimates, will be divorced between the ages of twenty-five and thirty-five.[6]

Clearly, these young singles represent a formidable amount of buying power, and the way they live directly affects the way they dispose of their money. People living alone spend more on entertainment and on travel than families do, for instance, but quite a bit less on major appliances like refrigerators and wash-

ing machines. They're also more likely to buy small rather than big cars, and they spend almost twice as much per person in restaurants as do their married counterparts. One noteworthy outgrowth of this bustling new market has been the appearance of such magazines as *Apartment Life* and *Your Place*, which are aimed largely at affluent, unmarried readers between eighteen and thirty-four. These magazines offer articles not only on decorating and the like but on a whole range of "life-style" topics—from advice for single parents to dating tips for the insecure.

The geriatric boom

In 1971 "The Lawrence Welk Show," one of the most popular and longest-running programs on television, was taken off the air nationally. The reason: surveys showed that its audience consisted of many older people and relatively few teen-agers or viewers between the ages of thirty and fifty. The sponsors were not willing to pay for an audience of old folks because the elderly were not considered to be big-spending consumers. Were the sponsors right about this? Not necessarily. During the 1960s American marketers concentrated on the youth culture and the thirty- to fifty-year-olds, the groups that spent most of the nation's income. This marketing outlook began to change in the 1970s, though. Demographers and others realized that those groups were leveling off in number and Americans over sixty-five were becoming the nation's fastest-growing age group. In 1950 there were only 12.4 million in the country above age sixty-five; by 1976 there were 22.9 million, and their numbers continue to increase.[7]

Moreover, the economics of old age have been changing. Improved Social Security benefits and pension plans have given old people more money to spend than was true in earlier periods. And while many of them are restricted to fixed incomes, they nevertheless represent a growing market for a wide range of low-cost goods, generic or store-brand foods, movie-theater discounts, and the like. (The combined purchasing power of older people is estimated at more than $60 billion a year and growing. By contrast, the purchasing power of the youth market of the 1960s was never more than $45 billion annually.)

Increasingly, therefore, marketers have been learning the wisdom of directing special appeals to older consumers. Real-estate developers were among the first to notice the boom in this market after World War II, designing condominiums in Florida and whole retirement communities in the Southwest to meet the needs of senior citizens. In the mid-1960s insurance companies began offering health insurance plans tailored specifically for old people who were also covered by the then new Medicare program. The trend has since continued, with increased marketing activities for everything from Geritol and Polident to senior-citizens' dating services and vacation resorts. And without question the over-sixty-five boom can be expected to persist well into the twenty-first century, as the postwar babies ripen in due course into their own golden years.

Changing age patterns: their impact on markets

Naturally, businesses selling to specific age groups are most affected by changing age patterns. For example, those industries that specialize in the needs of babies are already shifting gears. Johnson & Johnson "baby powder," while still called "baby powder," is now marketed as "talcum powder" that can be used by people of all ages. Gerber Products, well-known for its baby food, is developing a line of food for old people, who frequently have chewing problems. Certain industries grew with the teen-age market in the 1960s: transistor radios, sports cars, popular music records and tapes, electric guitars, and surfboards. It is not yet known which of these industries will level off and which will continue to appeal to people in their thirties. But one prominent beneficiary of the sixties youth market, Levi Strauss, has adapted to changing times by promoting a new line of jeans and other sportswear sized for the heftier physiques of their many customers who will never see nineteen again. In a different area, increasing numbers of colleges and universities, looking ahead to a shrinking pool of high-school students from which to draw, have greatly expanded their adult-education programs to help make up the difference.

HOW EDUCATED ARE CONSUMERS?

Americans have always placed great faith in education. They attend school longer, on the average, than

BLACK CONSUMERS: AN IMPORTANT MARKET

Even the most casual television viewer must have noticed something new during the past decade or so—the appearance of black men, women, and children in TV commercials. The reason is simple: there is now a large, visible black middle class in America, with more money to spend on consumer goods. Advertisers are consequently directing more of their messages toward them, both through the general media and through the growing number of black-oriented publications and radio stations.

But just how well are black families doing in the United States? A fair answer might be that they started way behind but have done a great deal of catching up since the early 1960s. In 1960, for instance, black families were making only half as much as white families. By 1976 they were making over 64 percent of what white families made, the av-

the people of other countries. Since World War II, "GI bills," providing for subsidized tuition and living expenses, have encouraged a generation of veterans to attend colleges and vocational schools. Thus while in 1940 only one adult in four had finished high school, today the proportion is over three out of five. Likewise, in 1940 less than one in twenty finished college; today the figure is over one in seven and will continue to grow.[8]

The rise in education levels is significant to market researchers for two reasons. First, educated people make more money. In 1976, according to a United States Commerce Department survey, the average male college graduate earned $19,338 a year, while a high-school graduate earned $14,295 a year, and an elementary-school graduate earned less than $11,312 a year.[9]

Second, people with different levels of education have different tastes in consumer goods and services. Not only do college graduates have more money to spend, but they also tend to spend it on things that less

erage income among black households having risen to over $11,000 a year. A study several years later showed that in the North and West, younger black families (with heads-of-household under thirty-five years of age) in which both husband and wife worked actually had a slight edge in income over comparable white families.

The 1960s were exceptional years for blacks for two main reasons. First, the decade was one of high employment, higher wages, and greater economic and social expectations for black and white families alike. Second, a series of civil rights laws opened the way for major political, economic, and social breakthroughs by blacks. Affirmative-action programs were launched on the federal and local levels to recruit blacks and other minorities for higher education and better-paying jobs.

Since 1970 economic growth has slowed for both white and black Americans, but a large black middle class and effective black political leadership now

exist. Furthermore, the percentage of blacks entering college has doubled since 1965, while the percentage of whites has remained the same. One important result of this, from a business point of view, is the increasing significance of the black consumer market: from $67 billion in the early 1970s up to an estimated $92 billion in 1977. This growth, combined with the fact that blacks spend more on personal consumption items than whites, has persuaded markets to abandon their long-held view of the black population as a uniform—and secondary—market. Black consumers, they have discovered, are becoming as diverse a group as the rest of the population, comprising the same variety of submarkets that must be identified and targeted in different ways. Hence the growing importance to marketers of black-oriented publications and radio stations: as the impact of the black consumer dollar increases, so does the need for advertising that speaks directly and convincingly to the black shopper.

Sources: *Statistical Abstract,* p. 447; and Barbara Proctor, "Black, It's Beautiful!" *Media Decisions,* April 1977, pp. 73–75, 124.

well-educated people would ignore, even if they had the money—for instance, foreign travel, hard-cover books, and imported cars. Market planners have taken advantage of all of these tendencies during the past fifteen years. The parking lots of college campuses are dotted with Datsuns. Foreign travel boomed in the 1960s, helped by the jet airplane.

HOW MUCH DO CONSUMERS EARN?

The total personal income of Americans increased more than six times during the past twenty-six years. In 1950, 72 million persons with income took in less than $175 billion; in 1976, by contrast, nearly 136 million persons had a total income of over $1.1 trillion.[10] There are three main reasons for this growth in income. First, the productivity of workers has increased, largely because of improved technology. Second, the

labor force has grown, mainly because of a sharp rise in the number of married women who work outside the home, from 5 million in 1940 to over 23 million in 1976.[11] Third, inflation has accounted for some of the rise in income, especially with the upsurge of prices during the late 1960s and early 1970s.

As a result of the economic boom of recent decades, millions of families have risen from poverty into the middle class. In 1955 only 35 percent of the families earned over $10,000 a year and 14 percent earned less than $3,000. By 1974 over 64 percent of the families earned more than $10,000 a year and under 6 percent earned less than $3,000.[12] Thus, from a marketing point of view, there are now more middle-class consumers, and it is to them that marketing campaigns are directed. The consumer-product boom of the past thirty years has been a middle-class boom. Suburban homes, college educations for children, and second cars have all been successfully marketed to this growing middle class, whose smaller family size has permitted greater financial freedom.

HOW DO CONSUMERS SPEND MONEY?

The *personal income that a family is free to spend after taxes* is called **disposable personal income.** All families must spend a certain percentage of their disposable personal income on necessities such as food, clothing, and shelter. But the higher a family's income, the more **discretionary income** it has—*income that can be spent on nonessentials.* Discretionary income includes money spent on entertainment, vacation travel, weekend homes, restaurant dining, and all luxury consumer items and it is a very important income category from a market researcher's point of view. As income after taxes has increased, so has the amount of discretionary purchasing power: such discretionary items as recreation and personal care have come to account for a larger share of consumer expenditures (see Figure 4). For this reason most of the recent increase in marketing activities has

involved competition for the family's discretionary income. Perhaps surprisingly, relatively little of this competition has concerned high-priced luxury items: the market for these is limited and stable enough that few manufacturers consider it necessary to wage intensive marketing battles to push these items. The real competition occurs among makers of far more commonplace products—aspirin, gasoline, toothpaste and the like—which are fundamentally similar to one another and so must fight all the harder to establish brand identification and encourage consumer loyalty.

It may be that a long period of inflation, as the United States experienced in the 1970s, will reverse the trend and force families to spend less on luxuries and more on necessities. But as of now, market planners still assume that the upward trend in discretionary income will continue.

ANALYZING CONSUMERS' MOTIVES

Statistics can tell market researchers about the nature of the potential market. But statistics alone cannot help Ford compete with Chrysler. The market manager must know *why* the consumer might choose one product over another and must then tailor the marketing campaign accordingly. If demography helps answer the question, Who buys?, the behavioral sciences help answer the question, Why do they buy? As we said before, the science of psychology investigates individual behavior: how a person thinks and feels and what motivates him or her to act. And the science of sociology deals with group behavior: how groups are formed and how they function. We'll look at some important findings of these two disciplines in the sections that follow.

THE PSYCHOLOGY OF BUYING

Generally speaking, there are two principal types of motives that influence *what* people buy: rational motives and emotional motives. There is, in addition, a third category of motives that influence *where* people buy: these are called patronage motives. All three are worth discussing in some detail.

WHERE THE CONSUMER'S MONEY GOES: CHANGES IN PERSONAL CONSUMPTION EXPENDITURES AS PERCENT OF INCOME, 1950–1975

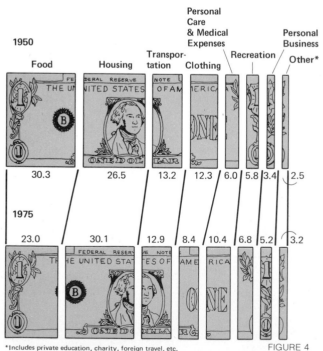

*Includes private education, charity, foreign travel, etc.

FIGURE 4

Rational motives

Imagine that you are standing at a store counter buying a wool scarf. If a stranger armed with a notebook and pencil approached you and asked you why you were buying it, you would probably answer that you needed something to keep your neck warm in cold weather. This would be a **rational motive**, that is, *one prompted by reason* and what might be called good sense. Marketers often appeal to rational motives in selling goods. Such motives are largely related to cost, dependability, and usefulness.

Cost frequently determines what product consumers buy. If a one-pound can of Hills Brothers coffee is on sale for $3.19 and Maxwell House cost $3.99, you might try the can of Hills Brothers. If you already drink Hills Brothers, you might take advantage of the sale to buy several cans. The cost-conscious customer also buys in quantities when such quantities lead to lower unit costs. Retail stores cut their prices at the end of a buying season, selling Christmas cards in January and bathing suits in July. The stores want to clear their shelves for new merchandise, and many cost-conscious customers wait for those sales.

Dependability is frequently important to upper-middle-class customers who can afford to pay more for a product that will work better and last longer. Maytag washing machines are more expensive than those of competitors, but they are successfully sold on the basis of dependability.

Usefulness appeals to customers who buy a product because they need it for a particular job. (Your wool scarf is an example.) Skilled marketers frequently help the sales of a product by finding new uses for it. For example, sales of Arm & Hammer baking soda had gone down because fewer people were doing their own baking. The market manager discovered new uses for baking soda, and the company is now successfully selling it as a household deodorant and cleanser.

Emotional motives

Now imagine that you are at a counter buying some expensive cologne. If the inquisitive stranger approached you at this point and asked your reason for buying, you might have trouble answering. It could well be that you are acting from an **emotional motive**, that is, *one having to do with feelings* rather than

reasons. Let's look at some of the emotions that sometimes affect consumers' choices.

Satisfaction of the senses—taste, touch, smell, sight, and hearing—is the most basic of emotional motives. (Your cologne would fit into this category.) Attractive men and women arouse and satisfy the senses of other men and women. Thus advertisements use attractive models to sell a wide range of consumer products. Advertisers urge you to "taste and compare" Winston cigarettes or to use Pond's cold cream for "the skin you love to touch."

Fear is the emotion arising from the instinct of self-preservation. It is a useful emotion because it helps people to avoid unnecessary risks and to take care of themselves. Marketers often appeal to it when they sell life and health insurance, fire and theft insurance, health foods, and safety devices for cars and homes. Following commercial marketers' lead, the American Heart Association has sponsored an anticigarette campaign that appeals to this same emotion.

Pride in one's position in life, home, family, or good looks can be appealed to in selling a wide range of products that enhance personal appearance or confirm wealth and good taste. Rolls-Royce automobiles and Dom Perignon champagne appeal to pride of ownership.

Sociability is the desire to be with other people in an attractive setting. Pepsi-Cola is sold to "the Pepsi generation," often depicted as a group of people at a beach party. Beer, soft drinks, restaurants, resorts, and trips on cruise ships are sold to individual customers as items that will make them part of attractive groups of people.

Emulation—the desire to imitate others—is an emotional motive marketers often appeal to. It is based on the fact that many people want to follow leaders or imitate famous people such as movie stars. Athletes help sell "Wheaties, the breakfast of champions"; movie stars are sometimes employed in beer commercials.

Overlapping motives

Of course, rational and emotional motives can overlap. A consumer frequently has more than one motive for selecting a given brand. Your scarf may not only keep you warm but also appeal to your senses of touch and sight. The television ads for Geritol in which a husband says warmly, "This is my wife . . . I think I'll keep

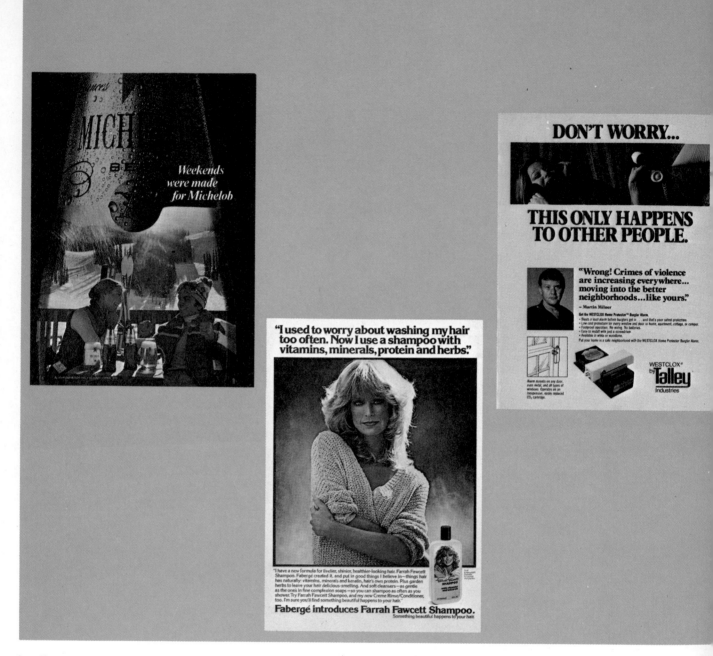

her," manage to associate love, pride, protectiveness, and good health—and identify them all with one product. In just this manner a marketing manager seeks to blend a number of elements—the advertising copy, the artwork, the choice of media, and so on—to create an effect that will appeal to a range of different motives in the mind of the consumer.

Patronage motives

Rational and emotional motives combine to influence what consumers buy. But the decision-making process doesn't end there: once a consumer has decided to purchase something, there remains the question of where to buy it. This is the point at which **patronage motives** come into play—*the factors that influence which company, which store, which seller a consumer chooses to patronize.* Among the wide variety of possible patronage motives, the four most important ones are *reputation, convenience, service,* and the *variety* of products offered.

Reputation for quality and integrity is especially important whenever services or nonbranded products are involved. A fresh sirloin steak or a diamond neck-

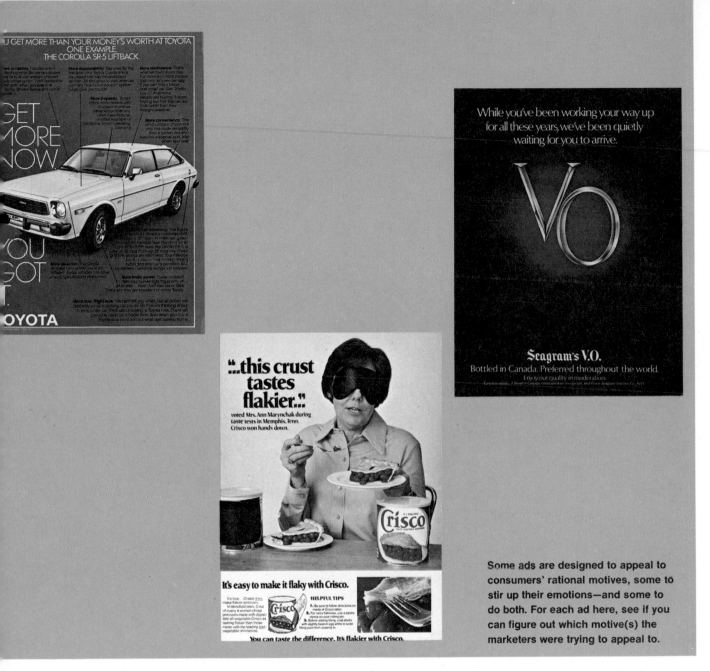

Some ads are designed to appeal to consumers' rational motives, some to stir up their emotions—and some to do both. For each ad here, see if you can figure out which motive(s) the marketers were trying to appeal to.

lace is bought on the basis not of a brand name but on the reputation of the establishment selling it. By the same token, a consumer with a TV or a pair of shoes to be repaired will, if there's a choice, most likely go to the place that's built the best reputation over the years.

Convenience, of course, is an obvious patronage motive: people are usually grateful for a store that's nearby or open late at night, even if it means paying slightly higher prices.

Good service, in the form of courteous sales people, charge accounts, free delivery, and the like, provides another strong motive for patronizing a particular

store regularly, be it Neiman-Marcus or the local grocery.

Variety of products again offers a strong incentive to customers, whether in a department store or a shopping mall, by giving them a good chance of finding everything they're looking for without having to trek all over town.

THE SOCIOLOGY OF BUYING

While psychology helps marketing planners understand consumers as individuals, sociology views con-

SOCIAL CLASSES IN THE UNITED STATES

About twenty-five years ago, the social anthropologist W. Lloyd Warner defined six social classes in the United States. His categories, which have become accepted as standard, are as follows.

The *upper-upper class* represents "old" inherited wealth. The highest-paid people in the merchant, financial, and professional fields, as well as millionaire collectors of rents, interest, and dividends, are members of the upper-upper class. Fund raisers concentrate their efforts on the upper-upper class because its members are the biggest supporters of the arts, private hospitals and universities, charities, and civic associations. Members of this class buy at the best stores and are little concerned with price. They can be appealed to on the basis of quality and pride of ownership.

The *lower-upper class* is also wealthy, but generally represents "new" money, no more than one or two generations old. The highest levels of business executives and political leaders belong to this class. The most important characteristic of this class is what the economist Thorstein Veblen called "conspicuous consumption." Its members buy expensive goods in order to display their wealth. The Neiman-Marcus department store in Dallas appeals to the lower-upper class with such items as his-and-her matching airplanes.

The *upper-middle class* is composed of doctors, lawyers, professors, and other business and professional people. They are concerned with social status, career advancement, and the further accumulation of wealth. This class, like the two upper classes, plans for the future. Its members are more likely to save, buy life insurance, and invest in securities and real estate than are members of the lower classes.

The *lower-middle class* is the second largest class in the United States. One out of every three Americans is a member. The lower-middle class comprises small business people, teachers, office workers, and skilled factory workers. Its members value work, personal achievement, respectability,

sumers as members of larger groups and studies the effects of group membership on individuals' purchasing decisions. In sociological terms, the most important group to which an individual belongs is the **social class** he or she is part of. The term "social class" is by nature an imprecise one but we can define it loosely as *a group or category of people who are in the same income bracket and who also, to some extent, share a common set of outlooks, values, and goals in life.*

Social classes provide useful categories for market managers simply because research and experience have shown that different classes tend to spend their money on different goods and services. Thus the market manager for a particular product will probably do a better job if he or she is familiar with the class whose members are that product's principal consumers. Understanding what these consumers' values and goals are—what interests them, or bores them, or makes them laugh—will give the manager valuable clues in planning a marketing program. If it's known, say, that pickup trucks are bought mainly by men in their thirties who work outdoors and like football, a manufacturer might want to make a commercial showing a thirty-six-year-old quarterback hauling fertilizer to his farm in his pickup truck. Alternately, if a Swedish car maker finds that its typical customers are well-educated professional people, it may decide to run ads mentioning that its customers are better educated than the owners of any other car.

INDUSTRIAL BUYERS: A DIFFERENT BREED

In Chapter 7 we noted that there are two major markets: the consumer market and the business market. Most of this chapter has been devoted to individual consumers because of their diverse characteristics and wide range of buying motives. But industrial buyers in

tradition, family, religion, and social and financial security. This class is the chief supporter of savings banks in America. Its members seek attractiveness and value for money when they shop.

The *upper-lower class* is the largest class in the country. Two out of every five Americans are members. Its members are primarily semiskilled workers. It is separated from the lower-middle class by the attitude of its members toward debt. The lower-middle class saves for the future and shops carefully. The upper-lower class borrows for the present; members often buy furniture, household appliances, expensive cars, and vacations on the installment plan.

The *lower-lower class* comprises unskilled workers, migrants, and the chronically unemployed. Its members have the least amount of money to spend and tend to shop in variety stores like Woolworth. The lower-lower class frequently has to buy household appliances from retail stores on credit at the highest interest rate allowed by law, generally 18 percent a year. Such purchases are often repossessed for nonpayment, and payments already made are forfeited to the store.

the business market are equally important to the economy, so we shall discuss them briefly now.

Procter & Gamble and Colgate-Palmolive compete to sell their products to millions of individual consumers. But U.S. Steel and Alcoa compete to sell their products to only a few hundred major industrial buyers. They compete, for example, to sell materials that go into automobiles or office buildings.

Let us assume that Commonwealth Edison, which supplies electricity in the Chicago area, announces that it is going to construct a large tank to store liquid natural gas for the use of its customers. Alcoa wants Commonwealth Edison to construct the tank of aluminum. U.S. Steel wants the tank to be made of steel. Alcoa and U.S. Steel are competing to sell their product to Commonwealth Edison, an industrial buyer. Marketing such a product is vastly different from selling a consumer product; let's see how.

The *motivation* for making the purchase is almost always rational and based on the product's usefulness to the buyer. The industrial buyer rarely buys a product unless there is a need for it, especially if the product is a $30-million gas tank. Emotional motives do not provide much guidance to the marketer of an industrial product.

The *product* itself is generally sold for its function rather than for its attractiveness or brand name. An industrial product is often expensive and is frequently custom-made for the buyer.

The *salesperson* of an industrial product is frequently an engineer or technician first, and a marketing person second. The salesperson must be able to sell the cost-reliability benefits of the product on a rational basis.

The *customer* is a business firm. Its purchasing agent is an expert on the product being discussed. In the case of Commonwealth Edison, the agent is able to weigh the comparative advantages of a steel versus an aluminum tank.

The *purchase time* is generally a long one, requiring several months in the offices and factories of the companies involved. Clearly, impulse buying plays little role in industrial marketing.

The industrial buyer has skills in negotiating with the industrial marketer that the ordinary consumer lacks. Rational and technical considerations predominate. The purchasing agent is committing his company to a huge investment. He needs assurance that the marketer understands the purchaser's needs and wants. The marketer must provide this assurance; he must convince the buyer that the marketer's company can build the tank on schedule at the price agreed on and that the tank will be serviced quickly and competently if anything goes wrong.

Industrial buying is a rational situation, but the personal relationship between buyer and seller can influence an industrial sale as surely as it influences the sale of consumer products. Creating and maintaining such a relationship is part of the marketing person's job.

CHAPTER REVIEW

Population statistics are a basic tool in finding out who consumers are. These statistics can tell with reasonable accuracy how many people there are, where they live, how old they are, how well-educated they are, how much they earn, and what they spend their money on. Market researchers use these statistics to define and measure the potential markets for a company's products. The company then discontinues certain products, expands others, or develops altogether new ones.

Market researchers use the behavioral sciences of psychology and sociology to help discover why consumers buy. Psychology, the study of individual behavior, is the most important behavioral science for the marketer. Psychology helps define the motives that cause consumers to purchase particular products. Marketers often play on the rational motives of cost, dependability, and usefulness. But they also have to pay attention to the emotional motives of satisfaction of the senses, fear, pride, sociability, and emulation. Frequently these motives overlap. Patronage motives have an influence in determining where consumers buy their products.

Sociology helps market researchers understand how group behavior influences consumers. Americans are divided into social classes. Members of each class are in the same income brackets and share common values, outlooks, and goals. Marketers need to know which groups the products will appeal to in order to sell.

Industrial buyers form a different market from that of individual consumers. This market varies in every respect from the consumer market—in motivation, product, sales personnel, customer, and purchase time. Technical and rational considerations predominate with industrial buyers, but they need assurances from the marketer that the company will do the job it promises.

KEY WORD REVIEW

demography
psychology
sociology
population growth rate
disposable personal income
discretionary income
rational motive
emotional motive
patronage motives
social class

REVIEW QUESTIONS

1. Why has the population of the United States grown more slowly in recent years? Why will the total figure continue to increase?

2. What has been the dominant trend in the movement of people in the United States? What two additional trends have become apparent since 1945?

3. Why is the population of the United States becoming older? What types of industries are affected by this change?

4. How does the rise in education level affect marketers?

5. What are the reasons behind the tremendous growth in personal income since 1940?

6. Why have marketing activities in recent years involved competition for discretionary income?

7. What products are most likely to be bought because of rational motives? What products are most likely to be bought because of emotional motives?

8. What are the four most important patronage motives?

9. What marketing services does the industrial buyer need? How are they comparable to the needs of the individual buyer?

CASE 1

THE QUBE TUBE: A NEW INFORMATION SOURCE FOR MARKETERS

Ever since companies started advertising their products on television, marketing managers have longed for a way to precisely measure the size of the audience that sees an ad, as well as for some means of gauging the ad's appeal (or lack thereof). Up until now, the only information available in these areas has come from direct interviews with TV-watchers—which rarely give an idea of a viewer's immediate response to an ad—or from "ratings" based on mechanical measurements of how many sets are tuned to a given station at a given time. A new kind of cable television system, however, may change all that. First put into use in early 1978 on an experimental basis, the system is called QUBE (pronounced "cube"). Owned and developed by Warner Communications Incorporated, QUBE allows viewers to "talk back" to their television sets.

Most cable or pay-TV systems use a one-way cable; QUBE's, by contrast, is two-way. It carries programming to subscribers, and it carries back to a central computer information that viewers relay by punching buttons on a control box about the size of a calculator. The QUBE system could allow viewers at home to bid on items in a TV auction, for instance, or to vote for or against participants in a "Gong Show" talent contest. What has marketing managers excited, of course, is the system's potential for tallying instant reactions to ads, new products, and the like. This capability, once fully developed, could easily revolutionize market research.

It could also provide valuable information to TV programming executives on the still-muddled question of what viewers really like to watch. That's because the QUBE system charges subscribers according to the programs they select. Unlike the typical cable pay-TV set-up, in which subscribers pay a flat monthly rate for a pre-selected amount of programming, QUBE-watchers pay a $10.95 installation charge and can then select from a wide variety of offerings in different price ranges. An opera, for example, may cost $2.50, a Frank Sinatra concert $2.00, an old movie $1.50, and so on. At the end of the month subscribers receive something like a telephone bill that itemizes the selections that were made and totals the charges. Ironically, the QUBE system, so potentially rich in demographic information, has practically no such data on which to base its own marketing strategy. Al-

though one out of every five American homes is wired for cable TV, Warner executives were unsure as they launched QUBE whether the $12-million system's pay-as-you-watch format would catch on or not. "We don't know what people will buy," said Warner Cable Corporation chairman Gustave M. Hauser. "We'll only learn by doing."[14]

1. What are the chief differences between QUBE and traditional cable TV systems?

2. How would you design a QUBE-based demographic survey to measure the popularity of a product that's been around for a while; to gauge the effectiveness of an ad; to "test the water" for a new product?

3. Why is an instant response to an ad or product so important to marketing managers?

CASE 2

A GADGET AND ITS MARKET

The mellow little tone of electronic "beeper" devices is growing louder throughout the United States as more and more people snap them on a belt or tuck them into purses and pockets. A beeper is a lightweight paging device that is activated by a specific radio signal. When the beeper goes off—and they go off everywhere, from theaters and golf courses to bedrooms and dinner parties—the tone alerts the wearer to call his or her office or home. These devices are not especially new: doc-

tors started using them in the 1950s. Suddenly, though, beepers have been booming, with the number in use growing from some 53,000 units in 1970 to 500,000 in 1976; projections show more than 3 million in circulation by 1985.

Who uses them? In the late 1960s the market began to grow when service businesses like plumbing and appliance-repair companies began handing beepers out to their work crews to speed them efficiently from job to job. Then business executives started wearing them. They are standard equipment for at least fifty members of the White House staff. One of the fastest-growing new markets for beepers is heavy industry, where they are used to track down foremen or managers in a large plant. But the uses of beepers are not limited strictly to business situations. Undoubtedly, some people wear them just for the status that a beep can confer on the user at a social gathering. A Wisconsin dairy farmer hangs one around the neck of his herd's lead cow—a kind of cowbell in reverse. Parents use them to remind their teen-age kids that it's time to get home.

1. If you were trying to market beepers, what kinds of basic demographic information would you want to have at hand?

2. How would you go about determining the right advertising media to use; the right price to charge; the features and extra services to highlight?

3. Which of the consumer's buying motives would you appeal to—rational ones like cost and usefulness, or emotional ones like pride or emulation—and how would your decision influence your advertising copy?

Adapted from "The Big Buzz in Beepers," November 1977 DUN'S REVIEW.

INTERNATIONAL BUSINESS

There is an unquestionable aura of glamor and excitement attached to the idea of international business. It conjures up images of huge multinational corporations, of executives jetting off to meetings in Europe or South America or the Far East, of ships bringing in valuable cargoes from distant ports. But there is, of course, a great deal more to it.

International trade is an enormously important field, not only to the companies but also to the economic health and political stability of virtually every nation. It entails a complex set of problems concerning currency values, balances of payment, tariff policies, regulations, and other questions for which there are no simple answers. This chapter presents a survey of the international business scene; it examines the major issues that arise in the area, and the means that are available to deal with them.

WHAT WILL THIS CHAPTER FOCUS ON?

After reading the material in this chapter, you will understand and be able to discuss:

- the ways businesses carry on international trade

- the theory of comparative advantage

- the specific reasons why companies find international trade profitable

- the restrictions that governments place on international trade

- key issues in international finance, including the problems connected with the balance of trade and the balance of payments

- the reasons why the United States has an unfavorable balance of trade and an unfavorable balance of payments

- the problems companies face when they operate in foreign countries

- the nature of multinational corporations

Foreign trade is the Yamaha motorbikes more and more people are riding these days, the French jeans that have become fashionable in many parts of the country, the Datsuns crowding American highways, even the bananas and coffee we consume every day—all the many items we use or buy that originate in other countries. And it's also the many items made or grown here for sale abroad. If you come from a farm area, or a region that produces parts for automobiles, chances are that much of your area's livelihood depends on selling produce or products that ultimately end up abroad.

Foreign trade is very big business indeed, and it's getting bigger every year. Since 1970 trade among the nations of the world has increased so that it now amounts to over $2.08 trillion per year.[1] Of this, $980 billion, a surprisingly large proportion, represents exports from comparatively small countries like West Germany (which sold $118 billion in goods to foreign countries in 1977) or Japan (which exported $67 billion).[2] But much of it represents United States imports and exports. Our exports are small for our size ($115 billion), but our imports ($147 billion) are considerable.

WHY COUNTRIES TRADE: THE THEORY OF COMPARATIVE ADVANTAGE

Why should we in the United States, a country with productive resources far outweighing those of any other nation, have to worry about foreign trade? The fact is, there are many things we do not have—and few that we can or will do without. Coffee, for instance, would be completely unavailable were it not imported from South America and Africa. So would diamonds. But even for those items that we can and do produce, foreign trade may still offer advantages. When trade among nations exists, each nation has the opportunity to specialize in producing those goods for which it's best suited. For example, Taiwan and Hong Kong are big exporters of shirts and other clothing because of their abundant—and cheap—labor supply. Japan's superior lens-grinding expertise has made Japanese cameras popular all over the world. Land-rich Austra-

Table 1 The Importance of Exports to the Major Industrial Nations

Country	Exports (in billions)	GNP (in billions)	Exports as Percent of GNP
United States	$115	$1,692	6.8
Japan	67	191	35.1
France	57	391	14.6
Italy	36	190	18.9
United Kingdom	46	119	38.6
West Germany	118	140	67.3
Canada	38	150	25.7

Source: International Economic Report of the President, 1978.

lia is, as you'd expect, a heavy exporter of agricultural products, particularly woolen goods. And South Africa, with rich and comparatively easy-to-work gold mines, is a far more efficient producer of that most basic of resources than the United States.

Such specialization leads to greater efficiency. It only follows then that *if each nation specializes in goods it can produce most readily and cheaply and trades those goods for others that foreign countries can produce most cheaply, there will be more goods available at lower prices for everybody involved.* That's the essence of the **comparative advantage theory** of foreign trade.

FOREIGN IMPORTS: THE PROBLEM OF COMPETITION WITH DOMESTIC INDUSTRY

Foreign trade offers definite advantages. But it often meets with understandable resistance as well. Some observers argue that *imports represent an additional source of competition for home markets.* This is known as the **home-industry argument**. Furthermore, some observers cite the **infant-industry argument**, claiming that *foreign imports may threaten a country's new industries,* snatching the market before the new companies have developed the skilled labor, technology, and large-scale operations needed to make a go of it against their more mature foreign competitors. And still another argument used against unlimited foreign competition is the **military-preparedness argu-**

ment, which maintains that *certain industries, crucial to the national defense, should be protected in case of war.*

Types of government protection against foreign competition

To help cope with some of the adverse effects of foreign trade, the governments of various countries have for centuries maintained certain types of barriers to protect home markets against competition by imports. Two frequently used barriers have been **tariffs**—*taxes on imported goods*—and **quotas**—*limits on the amounts of a particular item that can legally be imported.* In some instances governments have gone so far as to directly ban some items from import. Sometimes they have discouraged imports by setting up complex and costly customs procedures; or limited the amount of money citizens may use to buy goods made in another country; or given an entire domestic industry, or specific companies suffering from foreign competition, subsidies or other forms of financial assistance. Recently, for example, the French government set up a program to help C. H. Honeywell Bull (CHB), a French subsidiary of the American company, challenge IBM as a competitor in the French minicomputer market. Just after CHB was formed in 1976 for the express purpose of challenging IBM, the government funneled $100 million in subsidies into the company and backed this up with $180 million in orders.[3]

Arguments against protectionist measures

Critics of trade barriers—who are also known as **free-traders**—have some forceful arguments of their own. If a domestic industry needs protection, they counter, then perhaps it shouldn't be operating at all under the principles of free enterprise. The problems of an industry that can't compete in its own market, they add, are probably self-imposed. For example, consider the United States shoe manufacturers who have been the underdogs in competition with the more fashion-aware West German and Japanese shoe companies. There has recently been a boom in jogging shoes, but it hasn't helped the American shoe manufacturers; in 1977 almost half of the shoes sold in this country came from abroad. Pleading the home-industry argument, United States shoe makers have asked the federal government to shield their markets against the attacking imports. Accordingly, the government, naturally concerned about the situation, sent management consultants to find out what was ailing the American shoe industry. And what did these consultants report? That many of the industry's biggest

1.686 billion dollars' worth of imported shoes are sold in the United States each year—amounting to 38.3% of the 4.4 billion dollars' worth of shoes purchased nationally.

IMPORTED SHOES IN THE UNITED STATES: PERCENT OF SHOES SOLD ANNUALLY THAT COME FROM ABROAD

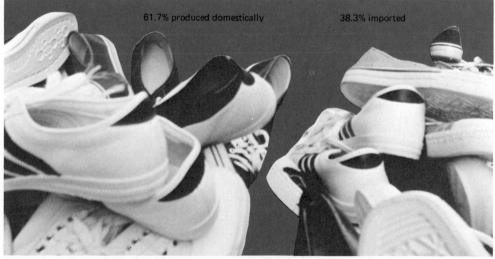

61.7% produced domestically   38.3% imported

FIGURE 1

The imports come rolling along—despite outcries from U.S. manufacturers.

problems arose from its own poor management. According to the consultants, the shoe makers had a lot of out-of-date plants and equipment and were dragging their feet on replacing them.[4]

And there's another important free-trader argument against protectionism: namely, that protectionism tends to feed inflation. Protectionism takes away from the consumer the choice between cheap imports and more expensive domestic goods; so consumers end up paying higher prices. Furthermore, as free-traders point out, there is always the danger that foreign trading partners may retaliate (strike back) against protectionist legislation by raising their own barriers in the forms of tariffs and quotas.

RECENT DIFFICULTIES WITH FOREIGN COMPETITION

Today, as faster transportation brings markets closer than ever before, the problem of competition with outsiders is becoming ever more difficult. Public and industry sentiment has grown in favor of government protection against some specific imports.

In the last few years there have also been particularly loud protests against **dumping**, the practice in which *another country sells its goods here or in other foreign markets at prices well below cost.* (The dumping country makes up the difference by selling the same goods at higher prices in its domestic markets.) In 1978, for example, the Japanese companies Matsushita

(Panasonic) and Sony were accused of dumping cut-rate televisions in the United States; whether or not the accusations were justified, the Japanese companies did compete so intensely in the American television market that they forced one domestic company, Zenith, to lay off 5,600 workers in this country and increase production at plants in Mexico and Taiwan, where labor is cheaper.[5] Similarly, some United States steel producers have charged that foreign steel makers were underselling them in this country with the help of subsidies from their own governments.

There was much heated debate over these questions in 1977; but despite the growing furor over rising imports, the Carter administration didn't clamp down hard on America's foreign trading partners. For intance, during that period the domestic steel producers sought government protection from cheaper Japanese steel after many dramatic plant closings, such as a shutdown in Youngstown, Ohio, that cost 5,000 jobs—a full 12 percent of the area's work force. However, the Council on Wage and Price Stability issued a report rejecting the sought-after steel-import quotas because they would have only a minor effect on total steel output and jobs. For the time being, the United States government took a moderate line, stating that it would only favor setting tariffs or quotas in cases of proved dumping. The administration began to work out *voluntary quota systems* (sometimes referred to as **orderly marketing agreements**, or **OMA**) in which various foreign trading partners agreed to limit their imports into the United States on their own. Not with-

FOREIGN IMPORTS: WHAT ARE THEY DOING TO THE AMERICAN CLOTHING INDUSTRY?

If the American apparel and textile industries were to adopt a slogan today, it might well be: "The imports are killing us." Combined, the two industries have the highest dollar volume and employment total in the United States. In 1976, according to United States Department of Commerce statistics, wholesale apparel and textile sales amounted to an estimated $74.6 billion; and with a total of some 2.3 million workers, the two industries account for one out of every eight of the nation's manufacturing jobs. But if some of the arguments being advanced by manufacturers and unions are true, both the American clothing industry and its workers are on their way to becoming—as one manufacturer puts it—an "endangered species."

The economics of the situation are plain enough. To American retailers, textiles and apparel (collectively known as soft goods) made in foreign countries where wages range from 14 cents to thirty-five cents an hour are far more attractive than goods made in the United States, where wages are more likely to be between $5 and $6 an hour. Reason: The lower the wholesale cost, the higher the retailer's profit will be. What is not plain, however, is the precise impact of these low-priced imports on the manufacturers and workers in the clothing industry. How big a market share do imports take? Retailers that import soft goods in high volume like J. C. Penney, Sears Roebuck, and Montgomery Ward say that imports account for only a small part of the merchandise they sell—less than 15 percent in most cases—and that the amount of merchandise imported is not growing larger.

But an expert for a large industry group, the Knitted Textile Association, had a different story to tell at a recent convention. He reported that in some categories, imports far outnumber domestic products, taking an 82 percent share of the market in women's knitted sweaters, for instance, a 70 percent share of the boys' and men's coats market, and 54 percent of the wool suit market. Before long,

argue the home-industry supporters, competition like this would amount to a death warrant for American manufacturers—some industry giants have already been forced into bankruptcy—and their employees. Retailers acknowledge that imports can hurt manufacturers but claim nevertheless that imports have become a commercial necessity and are in many instances preferred by consumers.

That's because the consumer doesn't understand the impact of imports on jobs, say major industry unions like Amalgamated Clothing Workers (500,000 members) and the International Ladies Garment Workers Union, or ILGWU (350,000 members). These unions, along with some industry groups, are sponsoring "Buy American" advertising campaigns to alert consumers to the danger that imports hold for domestic industry. Imports, the campaign points out, reduce income, lead to the loss of tax revenues in manufacturing and mill towns, and put hundreds of thousands of Americans out of their jobs. If imports continue unabated, warns ILGWU President Chaikin, "we will be out of business." Neither the unions nor the manufacturers support a total boycott of imported goods—they prefer to speak of "safeguards." But if the clothing industry disappears, says a spokesman for the Amalgamated Clothing Workers, dispossessed industry workers will choke the unemployment and welfare rolls—and taxpayers will have to foot the bill.

Source: Gay Pauley, "Union Label?" *Atlanta Journal and Constitution*, March 26, 1978, p. 5-H.

LAWS, AGENCIES, AND AGREEMENTS THAT FACILITATE INTERNATIONAL TRADE

How governments aid international trade

Despite the continued existence of many trade barriers like tariffs and quotas, almost all governments have tried to expand world trade since World War II. Various groups of nations have established international agreements and institutions to regulate and encourage international trade. Their immediate objectives are to reduce tariffs, provide loans to finance trade, and limit currency fluctuations. Their long-term objectives are to increase the volume of trade among nations. Among the most important of these agreements and institutions:

1. **The General Agreement on Tariffs and Trade (GATT)**, instituted in 1947 and since signed by the United States and about a hundred leading trading nations, *has as its object the reduction of tariffs*. A key provision, the **most-favored-nation clause**, *specifies that an agreement to cut tariffs between any two GATT members must be extended to all other members*.

2. **The International Monetary Fund (IMF)** was established by the United Nations in 1944 *to curb price fluctuations of world currencies*.

3. **The World Bank** (also called the International Bank for Reconstruction and Redevelopment) was founded in 1944 *to provide long-term loans at low interest rates to underdeveloped nations*.

4. Important encouragement for the sale and licensing of technology abroad should come from the **Patent Cooperation Treaty**, which went into effect in early 1978. The agreement *should make it easier for U.S. companies and other member countries to protect their patents abroad*. Through the treaty, paperwork involved in patent applications on the same invention for different countries has been pared down to a single international application with a standard format that is filed in as many Treaty-member nations as desired. The Treaty also permits an applicant to file in the patent office of his own country in an "agreed language," such as English in the case of Americans. And it also provides other important benefits. It enables developing nations, which do not have the resources to keep up with technological advances all over the world, to get advice on how new their own patents are, and how applicable they are to industry.

Regional economic integration

In addition, certain groups of nations have worked out special agreements among themselves, pulling down trade barriers so that trading back and forth is easier. Some of these agreements are formed because the member nations are close to each other geographically; others, because the nations have close political or historical ties.

The three major patterns of economic integration that have emerged are free-trade areas, common markets, and economic unions. *In a free-trade area tariffs are banned between members, although each member has the right to put up tariff barriers against nonmembers*. The oldest free-trade area,

out some pressure, Japan, Taiwan, and Korea signed voluntary pacts to limit their exports to America of shoes, color televisions, and certain steel products.[6]

MARKETING AMERICAN PRODUCTS OVERSEAS

Of the nearly 4 billion people in the free world, fewer than 6 percent live in the United States.[7] The remaining 94 percent represent a huge potential market for American business. Moreover, because the standard of living in the rest of the world has been rising steadily, these billions of people are able to buy more American goods because they now have more money to spend. While American exports still primarily consist of grain, heavy machinery, chemicals, manufactured goods, and transportation equipment, United States manufacturers are exporting increasing amounts of consumer goods. For example, the American fast-food

established in 1960, is the Latin American Free Trade Association (LAFTA) whose members are Argentina, Bolivia, Brazil, Chile, Colombia, Ecuador, Mexico, Paraguay, Peru, Uruguay, and Venezuela. A broader group, the Latin American Economic System (SELA in Spanish), was created in 1975 to incorporate all the Western Hemisphere nations except the Bahamas, Canada, and the United States.

A **common market** also *does away with tariffs and customs restrictions* to allow complete freedom of movement between members for economic purposes (for example, workers may move freely back and forth across borders in search of work). As a group, members may raise a common external tariff against nonmembers. The European Common Market, also called the European Economic Community or EEC, is made up of nine Western European nations which have eliminated trade barriers among themselves, but have raised tariffs on some U.S. goods. The goal of the EEC is **economic union**: its planners seek to *harmonize the national economic policies of members so that they can work together as a unit*.

Agencies that protect U.S. companies against business risks abroad

When businesses engaging in international trade make arrangements and agreements with foreign companies or countries which are not bound by our civil laws, they face the risk that the agreements will not be honored. To encourage companies to engage in foreign trade, Congress has set up various agencies and programs to minimize the risk. The

Export-Import Bank (Eximbank), set up in the early 1930s, now *mainly assists U.S. exporters by providing credit to overseas purchasers*. Eximbank may make direct loans to foreign buyers, guarantee that loans from private lenders will be repaid, or lend funds to private banks for financing exports. Eximbank loans are not, of course, available to all comers; they are only made when purchasers have a good credit rating and are likely to repay. Yet despite this limitation they do play an important part in facilitating international trade.

And there are other agencies that encourage international trade as well. The **Foreign Credit Insurance Association (FCIA)**, *a voluntary group of private insurance companies, insures overseas commercial credit risks* that individual companies would not be able to insure alone. By being able to purchase such insurance, the U.S. firm can make sales abroad that it might otherwise ignore. Likewise, the **Overseas Private Investment Corporation (OPIC)**, which began operation in 1971, *provides risk insurance for U.S. companies wishing to directly invest capital in the developing world*. In 1976, for example, OPIC insured a $360,000 Avis safari lodge in Kenya and a $44,000 Avis car rental service in Malaysia. And the same year Congress established the **Domestic International Sales Corporation (DISC)** program *to spur exports by giving companies tax deferral incentives*. This program, which is under the direction of the Department of Commerce, is designed to be especially attractive to firms just beginning to export overseas. Each of these congressional efforts, of course, is subject to change depending on the government's current foreign trade policy.

---

industry has taken a big bite out of Japan's restaurant market. From a small McDonald's on a main street in Tokyo in 1973, American fast-food interests in Japan have grown to account for more than half of the industry's $515 million in total sales in Japan last year.[8]

American companies have begun to seek such foreign trade enthusiastically because they're aware of the tremendous market opportunities that await them overseas. These opportunities are particularly important in light of the fact that many domestic markets

are becoming saturated. If a company is unable to grow at home, it can go to outside markets, including developing Third World countries, in order to fulfill its objectives.

The United States government has encouraged this move for its own reasons as well. Foreign trade helps ease world tensions because it brings nations together as trading partners in a mutual quest for economic benefits. For example, trade treaties with China and Cuba have been encouraged recently in the belief that nations that trade with each other will put their common economic interests (or greed) above their political differences.[9] And the Soviet Union, which has been hit with consistently poor wheat harvests, has been an eager and big buyer of American wheat and corn. In 1972 Russian purchases were so large and put such a drain on this country's supplies that food prices here went sky-high. Because of the outcry at the time, the Russians and large United States grain companies now tend to make their deals in secret, and American-Soviet agreements currently stipulate that the Russians can't buy more than 15 million tons of grain without notifying the federal government. But trade with the Soviets is still an important aspect of American agribusiness.[10]

FORMS OF INTERNATIONAL TRADE

Direct exporting, which involves *seeking orders from foreigners for goods that are made in this country and then shipped abroad,* is only one of the ways in which businesses can participate in foreign markets. In this section we'll briefly look at a number of the other methods used in selling to foreign customers.

Foreign licensing

Most people who've traveled in a foreign country have been pleasantly surprised to find that they can get a bottle of Coke almost anywhere. What they probably don't realize, however, is that the bottle of Coke they're so gratefully sipping hasn't come from the United States at all. Instead, Coca-Cola **licenses**, or *gives rights to* companies in foreign countries all over the world to bottle Coke for them. Every foreign licensee, in turn, pays Coca-Cola a fee. Such **foreign licensing**, in which *a firm permits a foreign company to produce and sell its products in a foreign market for a fee,* is generally used for goods with established brand names.

Foreign licensing may be the only way for an American company to enter certain foreign markets. This is true when other countries restrict imports, when transportation costs from this country are high, or when labor costs here are much higher than those in

the country in question. All of these circumstances exist in the case of Japan, and thus licensing has proved the most effective method for many American companies that want to sell in the profitable Japanese market. Petrocelli suits and Manhattan shirts are now available in Japan as a result of such licensing arrangements; similarly, Playboy has licensed one Japanese company to operate a Playboy Club and another to publish a Japanese-language edition of the magazine.[11]

Not every country, however, is in favor of licensing arrangements. In certain developing countries, such as India, licensing is becoming increasingly difficult. Many people in these nations feel that such arrangements are a holdover from the days of colonialism, and they reject the idea of paying fees simply for the right to make a product.

Foreign manufacturing

An American company can also get foreign business by **foreign manufacturing**. In this type of arrangement, *companies directly control the production and sales of their goods instead of licensing a foreign firm to do so.* Sometimes the American company builds its own plants in the foreign country. In other cases it may buy out a foreign company and operate its plants. General Motors manufactures the Opel, for instance, in plants it has constructed in Germany;[12] while Gillette simply bought out the French company that made Cricket lighters.[13]

Joint ventures

To divide profits more evenly between a United States company and its foreign counterparts, a growing number of companies are making **joint-venture** agreements—*business undertakings in which a foreign company and a domestic one agree to act on an equal footing.* Developing nations are favoring this system because, although they need foreign countries' technical know-how and capital, they are wary of business activities that seem reminiscent of a more imperialist era. This preference, furthermore, isn't confined to developing nations. Even the more industrialized economies are sometimes against foreign takeovers, which they view as inroads on their territory. Brazil, for example, one of the most highly developed nations in Latin America, is making it more difficult for foreigners to simply buy up companies without retaining Brazilian interests in them. When Hydreco, a U.S. company that makes hydraulic pumps, valves, and motors, wanted a foothold in Brazil to supply Brazilian affiliates of its customers in the United States, it heeded advice and went the joint-venture route with two local partners. This strategy helped clear away the red tape with government agencies and enabled Hydreco to take advantage of local financing and government tax incentives available only to Brazilian-owned companies. It also gave Hydreco the psychological selling edge of being the only foreign producer of hydraulic systems to be majority-owned by Brazilians.[14]

PROBLEM AREAS IN FOREIGN OPERATIONS

Why do businesses bother with overseas operations? The answer is simple: growth rates and profits are often much higher in foreign countries. But establishing and managing such operations can be complicated. Linguistic, monetary, legal, and political differences between the home country and each foreign nation must constantly be considered. And understanding and making allowances for foreign customs is a daily necessity.

CULTURAL DIFFERENCES

When a company operates in a foreign nation, managers must recognize that they will encounter differences in customs and manners at every level of their operation. For example, Americans tend to speak in a louder tone of voice when they want to emphasize something—while in China, a loud voice almost always indicates anger. Likewise, ethical differences can create confusions with grave implications: reasonably small gifts are expected in Japan, for instance, but are regarded as bribes in the Soviet Union. The more sophisticated the executive, the more he or she is likely to be sensitive to these matters.

Businesspeople abroad must sharpen their sensitivity to cultural differences.

LEGAL DIFFERENCES

Business people who assume that legal principles are the same all over the world are often shocked to find that they are not. Most countries have stringent laws regulating such matters as land ownership, building permits, export and import documents, and business licenses. Copyright and brand-name protection, by contrast, are often quite weak abroad; for instance, "pirating" of American books by copy machines is widespread and apparently legal in Taiwan.[15]

THE PROBLEMS OF INTERNATIONAL FINANCE

Though international trade may have appeal, paying for it can be an expensive proposition. In theory, for instance, a country should import to whatever degree necessary the products that it can't manufacture efficiently at home. In practice, however, a country must first determine whether it has earned enough in its dealings with other nations to pay for those imports.

KEY CONCEPTS IN INTERNATIONAL FINANCE

When we consider the problems involved in financing international trade, we must keep in mind two separate but related items: a country's balance of trade and its balance of payments.

Balance of trade

One of the reasons why governments impose tariffs, quotas, and other trade barriers is their desire to keep from developing an unfavorable balance of trade. A **balance of trade** is *the difference between the value of a nation's exports and the value of its imports.* A **favorable balance of trade** exists when *exports are greater than imports.* (West Germany, for one, had a favorable balance of trade in 1976, when it exported almost $14 billion more in goods than it imported.) An **unfavorable balance of trade** exists when *imports exceed exports.* Ideally, nations want their balance of trade to do exactly that: stay in balance.

Balance of payments

The balance of trade, then, is the net result of export-import transactions. However, exporting and importing are not the only kinds of transactions that take place among nations. Others include loans, long-term investments made abroad by businesses, gifts the American government makes to foreign nations, and money that foreign individuals deposit in or withdraw on a short-term basis from United States banks and financial institutions.

As a result, there is a second important balance, the balance of payments, which refers to the net sum of both the balance of trade and all those other transactions. In other words, the **balance of payments** is the *difference between a nation's total payments to foreign countries and its receipts from foreign countries.*

RECENT BALANCE-OF-PAYMENTS DIFFICULTIES IN THE UNITED STATES

The United States enjoyed a favorable balance of trade every year from 1893 through 1970. Since 1950, however, deficits resulting from nontrade factors such as foreign aid, travel, and military spending have been substantial enough to produce an unfavorable balance of payments in almost every year. Moreover, since 1973 the situation has worsened, with the balance of trade itself remaining persistently unfavorable (see Figure 2). In 1977 it reached a deficit five times its previous record.[16]

Why did this change take place? The reasons are complex. One major factor, however, was the rapid

THE BALANCE OF TRADE PROBLEM: THE U.S. TRADE DEFICIT HAS WORSENED IN RECENT YEARS

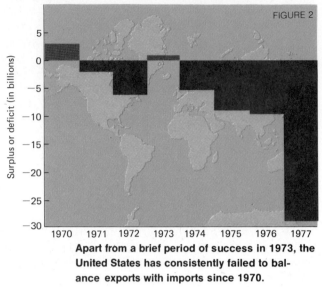

FIGURE 2

Apart from a brief period of success in 1973, the United States has consistently failed to balance exports with imports since 1970.

industrialization of Japan and Western Europe after World War II. These countries' new plants and equipment (ironically, financed in part with American foreign aid), plus their lower labor costs, enabled them to underprice this country both here and abroad. And since 1974 there have been other major reasons as well. For one thing, there has been a staggering increase in the price of foreign oil. Oil import costs in the United States soared from $7.8 billion in 1973 to $45 billion in 1977, and some experts have stated that this increase has accounted for fully 40 percent of the trade deficit's expansion.[17] Other major factors have included an economic recovery in the United States that attracted imports from major trading partners at a time when their own domestic economies were sluggish, and therefore could not absorb American imports. Also, unlike other countries, the United States has never before *had* to depend on exports to support its economy. As a nation it has not given exports much thought. Even today many American companies, instead of exporting their products, would rather enter foreign markets from within those countries. They find it more efficient to own businesses or plants abroad. While this may be good business logic, the trend has taken its toll on our trade balance, for revenues from foreign operations of American companies are usually spent overseas. (We'll discuss this point in more detail below.)

Currency difficulties

Until August 1971, balance-of-payments differences between nations were generally settled by the transfer of gold from the nation with the deficit (unfavorable balance) to the nation with the surplus (favorable balance). Gold was then valued at $35 an ounce. Suppose, for example, that German merchants accumulated extra dollars because Americans purchased more German goods than Germans bought American goods. To make up that difference, German merchants, through their banks, could exchange the dollars they held for gold.

By 1971, however, the accumulated payments deficits exceeded the amount of gold held by the United States. At that point President Nixon announced that the United States could no longer redeem dollars for gold at the unrealistic price of $35 an ounce. The American government took the dollar off the gold standard—and in effect overturned the entire international monetary system. Until 1971, because the dollar had a fixed value based on gold, the dollar had been the pivotal world currency against which all other currencies valued their own. But today international finance operates on a new system of **floating currencies**, which is still in the process of being fully worked out. *The value of a given currency is now determined in foreign exchange markets where the currency varies in price*—much the same as a corporation's stock—*depending on what the market is willing to pay for it.* There is, in effect, a shifting **foreign exchange rate**—*the number of pounds or lire or any other foreign currency that must be exchanged for one dollar.* Consequently, the German merchants we discussed would exchange their dollars for marks or any other currency rather than for gold. Similarly, because of fluctuation, an American could get about 235 yen for one dollar in early 1978. This is low compared to the 303 yen that a dollar would have brought two years earlier, when United States currency was in greater demand.

Currencies fluctuate in this way for many of the same complicated reasons that stock prices go up and down. The value the market places on a nation's currency reflects the market's evaluation of that country's economic health and stability. How are these intangible factors measured? In a number of ways. The nation's productivity is an important consideration; so are its rate of inflation, its balance of payments, and its politics.

Overseas earnings and foreign exchange

Such changes in the rate of exchange can influence not only the size of the profits a foreign operation sends home, but also any financing that a company does abroad. R. J. Reynolds, for instance, borrowed $185 million in German marks in 1972 and 1973 to build several container ships for a subsidiary. When Reynolds borrowed that sum, the German mark was valued at 3.2 to the United States dollar. Reynolds subsequently paid back $59 million. But by 1977 its debt was $151 million, instead of the remaining $126 million you might have thought. Why? By 1977 the value of the dollar had plunged 40 percent against the mark from its 1972 relationship.[18]

Conversely, when McDonald's sells a Big Mac in Japan, it receives payment in yen. However, at some point McDonald's or any other American company doing business abroad will want to take at least a portion of its earnings home. To do this, it will have to exchange the local currency it earned for United States dollars. But under the present system of floating currencies, this foreign exchange rate may fluctuate greatly—so McDonald's profits will fluctuate too.

And complicating still further the movement of money from foreign subsidiaries to home offices is the existence of **exchange controls**. Where these controls are the law, *the host nation limits or bans entirely the flow of local currency into dollars.* This limitation, of course, prevents the subsidiary from sending its profits home in that form—so it must find some way to use its earnings overseas, or turn them into items of value it is permitted to ship out of the country.

THE MULTINATIONAL CORPORATION

In reading the preceding discussion, you might have asked yourself what an American company like Reynolds or McDonald's was doing abroad in the first place. These companies, and countless others like them, are known as **multinationals**—*businesses whose operations, in addition to their sales, cross international boundaries.* General Electric, for example, owns operations in thirty-two different countries. And Nestlé, which you might have thought was an all-American chocolate maker, is actually a Swiss-based multinational with more than 200 subsidiaries in over thirty-nine countries. Figure 3 shows the subsidiaries of another famous multinational.

Among the largest multinationals are the major automobile companies, which provide an excellent example of the corporate benefits of leaping international borders. Ford, for instance, makes the engines for its American Pinto in its German plant but puts together the Pinto transmission in the more cost-effective British plant. At the same time, Ford has found it worth its while to make the Pinto's electrical system in the company's Canadian plant. Finally, all the parts are assembled in the United States, where the Pinto is sold.

Such tactics may benefit the multinational, but they have not had entirely good effects on the American economy. One of the underlying reasons for the country's currently unfavorable balance of trade has been this entrance of the multinationals into the international business picture. As we've seen, those American companies that participated in foreign sales used to do so mostly by exporting products made here; and they helped our balance-of-trade position through these sales. Today, however, companies such as Ford operate through foreign plants and sometimes have management, marketing, and finance divisions overseas as well. For reasons we've mentioned in our discussion of international finance, not all the revenues from such operations are reflected directly in the United States balance-of-trade figures.

MULTINATIONAL VERSUS HOST COUNTRY: A STRAINED RELATIONSHIP

A multinational may have a competitive edge over purely native operations and may even attain a domi-

From its headquarters in New York, Colgate-Palmolive directs operations in facilities as far afield as Argentina and Zambia, the United Kingdom and Fiji. The dots on the map represent Colgate-Palmolive locations worldwide.

Headquarters

FIGURE 3

WORLD OPERATIONS OF A TYPICAL MULTINATIONAL COMPANY: COLGATE-PALMOLIVE AND ITS BRANCHES

nant market position. This doesn't tend to endear the multinational to its local competitors. In fact, foreign ownership of a domestic industry is in some cases viewed as an insult to national pride, particularly if the foreign operation has tried to impose its own social and cultural practices on the host population. Hostility toward multinationals can be even more intense in developing nations, where people fear what might happen in the event of a foreign company's retreat to its homeland. A major employer that did retreat this way would leave behind it a disastrous economic void.

Multinationals are often viewed and feared as powerful organizations with little, if any, social responsibility to temper the effects of the power they wield. That fear has proven to be justified in certain instances when multinationals have abused their position to influence local politics. (In 1970, for example, International Telephone & Telegraph contributed money to opposing parties in Chile to bring down the existing democratically elected Marxist government.[19]) Multinationals are also seen as threatening because of their potential ability to control prices and markets throughout the world. Most countries, like the United States, have antitrust laws that protect competition by preventing companies from monopolizing markets and inflating prices. The multinationals, however, have, for the most part, been able to dodge the antitrust laws, especially since there are few international watchdogs to oversee their activities.

Occasionally a multinational's monopolistic practices come under sharp public scrutiny. In 1975, for example, the European Economic Community (EEC) challenged the pricing system of a huge and powerful multinational—United Brands, which supplies 35 percent of the world's bananas. The European commission accused the company of abusing its leading market position by unfair and excessively high pricing; according to EEC experts, it had sold bananas of the same quality and brand name to distributors in six nations (Germany, Holland, Belgium, Luxembourg, Denmark, and Ireland) at prices that varied as much as 50 percent. United Brands contended that these differences in prices simply reflected as much as possible anticipated market prices in each country for the following week, based on weather, price of competitive

fruits, and risk of wastage. The European court, however, said that United Brands was simply charging whatever the market would bear. And this meant that the company was taking advantage of national boundaries—despite the fact that there might be no more costs to the company in one country than in another.[20]

Partly as a result of similarly perceived corporate misbehavior and partly, perhaps, because of rising nationalism, multinationals by their very nature tend to be suspect. When such feelings of distrust run particularly high, a multinational faces the very real risk of **expropriation**, or *government takeover*.

THE OTHER SIDE OF THE PICTURE: BENEFITS OFFERED BY MULTINATIONALS

Clearly, the nature of the multinational is such that it can contribute to international tensions—especially if managers lack sensitivity to social needs in host countries. Yet the multinational also has great potential to expand world trade and promote business efficiency. With their enormous pools of capital, multinationals can be highly effective in bringing technical know-how from countries with advanced technologies to countries that are still developing. And they can also create vast numbers of new jobs, which contribute to prosperity. Nor do all the benefits flow to the host country alone; for the more industrially advanced homeland, the multinational brings new investment opportunities and new foreign customers.

How do all these pros and cons balance out? Are multinationals ultimately dangerous to world peace and the integrity of national economies, or are they basically a stabilizing force? There is probably no one answer to this question. Instead it is more useful to view each multinational as a unique entity, with its own history and policies, its own goals, and its own relationships with the host country and the countries around it. And it is important to remember that multinationals are changing rapidly; in only a few years they may play a quite different role in the world economy.

CHAPTER REVIEW

Foreign trade is a very big business, and it's growing every year. The value of United States exports is $115 billion, and the value of its imports is $147 billion. According to the theory of comparative advantage, foreign trade is helpful to all nations because it allows each to concentrate on producing those items it can manufacture most efficiently.

Some observers claim that foreign imports should not be allowed to compete with domestic industry. Their arguments in favor of government protection against foreign imports include the home-industry argument, the infant-industry argument, and the military-preparedness argument. The government does protect domestic industry through two frequently used barriers—tariffs and quotas—and on occasion may ban foreign goods altogether. The free-traders' argument supports importing foreign goods, claiming that protectionism goes against the principles of free enterprise, feeds inflation, and restricts the choices available to consumers, who thereby end up paying higher prices.

Foreign markets represent a special challenge to the United States because 94 percent of the people of the free world live outside its borders. Increases in American companies' income and levels of sophistication promise more sales for them. Among the forms of international trade are direct exporting, foreign licensing, foreign manufacturing, and joint ventures. Problems in foreign operations include differences in culture, ethics, language, regulatory mechanisms, and legal matters.

International finance involves such questions as a nation's balance of trade and balance of payments. Since the early 1950s the United States' balance of payments has been unfavorable. The trade balance has been in a similar condition since 1973. One result was this country's 1971 announcement that it would no longer exchange dollars for gold but instead allow the dollar to float. In effect, floating the dollar means that its value will vary relative to that of other currencies, depending on the market conditions that prevail.

Multinationals are businesses whose operations cross international boundaries. Host countries may view the multinational as an insult to national pride and may fear the potential ability of the multinational to control prices and markets. Multinationals run the risk of expropriation, or government takeover. Nevertheless, multinationals may also help expand world trade, promote business efficiency, bring technical expertise to developing nations, and create new jobs, new investment opportunities, and new foreign customers.

KEY WORD REVIEW

comparative advantage theory
home-industry argument
infant-industry argument
military-preparedness argument
tariffs
quotas
free-traders
dumping
orderly marketing agreements (OMA)
direct exporting
licenses
foreign licensing
foreign manufacturing
joint venture
balance of trade
favorable balance of trade
unfavorable balance of trade
balance of payments
floating currencies
foreign exchange rate
exchange controls
multinationals
expropriation

REVIEW QUESTIONS

1. What is the theory of comparative advantage?

2. What are some of the arguments against international trade? What restrictions does the government place on it?

3. What are some of the arguments in support of importing foreign goods?

4. Explain the difference between the balance of trade and the balance of payments.

5. How has the United States tried to improve its unfavorable balance-of-trade and balance-of-payments positions?

6. Under a system of floating currencies, what determines the number of marks or yen that can be obtained for $1?

7. What are some of the problems a business faces when it operates in a foreign country?

8. How do multinationals affect the United States' balance of trade?

9. What are some of the positive and negative ways in which a multinational may affect its host country?

CASE 1

PEPSI GOES OVERSEAS

As Pepsi executives know, there really is a "Pepsi generation." The core market for the soft drink consists of people in the thirteen- to twenty-four-age bracket, and these Pepsi drinkers empty, on the average, 823 cans of soda apiece every year. The problem is that the Pepsi generation's members are not only drinking almost all the soda they can swallow, they are also growing older. So, in search of

young and thirsty new customers, Pepsi has lately been accelerating its expansion into international markets. Since Coca-Cola, which outsells Pepsi by a two-to-one margin, has dominated Western Europe since the 1930s, Pepsi was forced, at first, to seek markets behind the Iron Curtain. And it has succeeded, particularly in the Soviet Union. As long ago as 1959, Pepsi had designs on Russia. In that year Donald Kendall, then president of Pepsi's international division and now chairman of the company, took a trade exhibition to the USSR and succeeded in accomplishing his one and only goal—getting a bottle of Pepsi into the hands of Nikita Khrushchev. The results were hardly instantaneous, but in 1974 Pepsi finally won permission to sell its soda in Russia—which Coke has yet to do. By 1978 Pepsi was operating two plants, readying to open as many as eight more and was selling 144 million twelve-ounce bottles a year. Eventually Pepsi plans to sell 72 billion bottles a year in Russia, where Chairman Kendall sees a great pent-up demand for consumer goods.

Pepsi's other target markets include developing nations in Africa and Latin America, and in the Middle East. Demographics explain why Pepsi and other soda manufacturers should enjoy growth in those markets for decades to come: the birth rate is high, per-capita income is rising steadily, and the consumption of soft drinks is low. Compared to the United States, where the average American drinks 480 eight-ounce bottles of soda a year, per-capita consumption in international markets averages 100 bottles annually. Richest of all the international markets is the Middle East, where per-capita consumption of soda has already

reached 280 bottles a year. Coke was expelled from the area in 1967 for political reasons, and Pepsi has taken advantage of the situation by opening no fewer than forty-eight bottling plants in the region. Coke will no doubt return to the Middle East soon, but rather than see it as a threat, Pepsi executives expect the renewed competition to broaden the already burgeoning market.

To keep up with the aging Pepsi generation, Pepsi has also begun to map out an international expansion plan for its two fast-food chains, Taco Bell and Pizza Hut. Pepsi plans to take Taco Bell into Central America (and also into new United States markets) and to scatter Pizza Huts all over the globe. Within ten years Pepsi plans to have 1,500 Pizza Huts in locations outside the United States, a sizeable increase over the 175 "international" Pizza Huts—all of them in Canada—that Pepsi was operating in 1978.[21]

1. Why are the demographics of international markets so encouraging to Pepsi and other soft-drink bottlers?

2. What was the point of arranging for Khrushchev to be seen with a bottle of Pepsi in his hand?

3. Some people criticize Coke and Pepsi for aggressively marketing their soft drinks in areas (like developing nations) where people should be encouraged to spend their hard-earned dollars on nourishing products rather than on sugary treats that have no nutritional value. What is your response to this argument?

PERSPECTIVES ON SMALL BUSINESS

MARKETING ASPECTS

While the function of marketing in any business is to create and satisfy customer demand, a significant difference exists between marketing in the smaller firm and marketing in the large corporation. Part of that difference is due to money. Small businesses simply have less of it to spend on such things as market research, public relations, advertising, high-caliber salespeople, large-scale sales promotions, and the many functions performed by a marketing department. The small business entrepreneur is usually sales manager, marketing manager, advertising directer, and head of market research—all rolled into one.

There is an old saying in advertising, "You waste half of your advertising dollar, but you don't know which half, so you spend it all." This is fine for a large corporation, but the small business owner simply cannot afford to waste dollars. Limited funds require immediate profitability, so each marketing program must be cost-effective. That is, every incoming and outgoing dollar must be spent in the most effective way possible for success. In the following pages, we will discuss some major areas of marketing which can help any small business to maximize sales. These include effective pricing, analyzing the marketplace, and selling. To illustrate these aspects of marketing, we will use examples from retailing, wholesaling, and service businesses, because there are so many small firms in these areas.

APPROACHES TO PRICING

Effective small business marketing should begin with careful consideration of the selling price of each product or service the business offers for sale. There are several things to

think about when you establish prices:

1. What is the competition charging?

2. Do you offer features or benefits that the competition does not provide, and that would allow you to charge a higher price or earn a greater profit margin?

3. Is your major competitor well entrenched and a recognized price leader in the market? If the answer to this question is "yes," the upper limits of your price range may already be established. Even if your product is better, you may still be forced to sell for less, or at the same price.

4. How close are you to major urban centers? Geographic isolation may allow you to charge a higher price without complaints from customers. The key question here is how much more inconvenient and expensive it would be for the customer to buy from a more distant competitor.

5. Who pays the cost of shipping?

6. How much profit will you need to make? You will need sufficient profit margin to cover overhead, plus an adequate return on your investment.

Let's consider various profit margins essential in retail and wholesale, plus some ideas on handling costs in a service business.

Retail markup

The basic markup: while there will be minor variations throughout the United States, a markup of 35 to 40 percent is considered essential for success in a retail business. For example, let's consider a product for which the wholesaler charges the retailer $6.00. Most experts say that the retailer should add on about 40 percent of the final price to pay for rent, utilities, insurance, taxes, employee salaries, and the costs of inventory and advertising, and to provide some profit for himself. So the final price is $10.00: the retailer added

$4.00, or 40 percent of $10.00, to the wholesaler's price.

You must also think about whether your price will cover the cost of shipping. Some publishers, for example, offer a discount of 40 percent and don't charge for shipping; others offer their books to retail outlets throughout the country at a 45 percent discount but add a charge for shipping. Both methods are considered normal and acceptable in the industry.

Certain types of business (television and appliance sales and office equipment, for example) must maintain service departments to perform warranty work. For such a business, it is essential that the retail markup be large enough to cover the extra costs involved in maintaining the service function. A minimum of 5 percent extra markup is recommended to prevent an unnecessary profit squeeze in businesses of this kind.

Finally, specially large margins must be planned if the business sells products that go in and out of fashion; the large margins serve as a hedge against style and seasonal changes. Prices must cover the costs of the large inventories required to satisfy varied customer tastes, and must allow for the large discounts used in selling out-of-season and out-of-style goods. Typically, margins in these fields are twice as large as normal retail margins. One word of caution, however: the size of the potential profit is meaningless unless the product sells! Poor judgment in purchasing can bankrupt a small store.

High-volume retailing or increased inventory turnover
An entirely different set of pricing considerations is involved if your business sells in high volume. The aim here is to lower your prices in the hope of attracting more customers. But before you do this, there are several things to consider:

1. Will the lower price increase sales enough to compensate for the profit loss?

2. What is your competition's pricing policy?

If after considering these questions you still believe low prices are right for your business, you can decide on an overall margin to aim at. Ordinary retail stores, as we've mentioned, mark up their merchandise about 35 to 40 percent. Yours, however, is a high-volume enterprise; let's assume that you will use an average markup of only 20 percent.

Wholesale markup
The wholesaler is the middleman between the retailer and the manufacturer. His job is to provide storage facilities, a sales force, and feedback to the manufacturer on new trends and popular products, and to assume the risks of credit. Any small firm offering these services to a manufacturer will need a minimum markup of 20 % of the retail selling price. (A lesser percent can be tolerated if the rate of inventory turnover is especially high.) Some small wholesalers, which operate only as manufacturers' representatives, have margins that are reduced to approximately 11%. Since they neither provide storage facilities nor assume the risks of credit, these lower percentages are adequate.

Here's how the wholesaler's and the retailer's markups relate to the retail price and the price charged by the manufacturer, for an item priced at $10.00 in the retail outlet.

Suggested retail selling price	$10.00
40% retailer discount or markup	−4.00 (40% of $10.00)
20% wholesaler discount or markup	−2.00 (20% of $10.00)
Price charged by manufacturer	$4.00 (40% of $10.00)

Incidentally, we should note here that specialized wholesaling offers good small-business opportunities. For example, a small wholesale distributor catering to the stationery-store industry might choose to market only felt-tip pens, offering the retailer a wider selection and faster delivery of felt-tip pens than his larger general-purpose distributor competitors.

Service business pricing
If yours is a service business, your prices will depend on your competition, the quality of your service, and any special or unique service you offer. If your service is office machines or computer maintenance, the prices are established by the price leaders in the industry like IBM, Xerox, Monroe, Burroughs, and other major office equipment manufacturers, and you will not be able to increase profits by raising prices; the growth of your service business will depend on the quality of your service. On the other hand, if you are a well-regarded artist, designer, or consultant, you will be able to command an hourly rate in direct relationship to your value to your clients, without concern for the current going rate.

STUDYING THE MARKETPLACE

Once you have established a realistic and competitive pricing policy, you must determine the potential acceptability of your product or service to the consumer or end user via the product life cycle concept.

Product life cycle

This is the multiphase sequence of growth and decline in sales and earnings which most products go through. Effective use of this concept hinges on the entrepreneur's ability to perceive where in the cycle a particular product might be located. An error in judgment at this point could easily mark the difference between success or failure. A closer look will clarify our statement.

Introduction: The primary achievement of small business has always been the introduction of new ideas, new products, and the creation of entire new industries, and thus a small business's product is likely to be in the introduction phase of the life cycle. While this introductory phase offers maximum returns on initial investments, the risks are high, and success is not guaranteed. How can you cut the odds in your favor? Here are some simple rules:

a) Test your market: you can sample your potential customers on the phone or by personal visit. Develop a short series of questions to provide feedback on your new venture, and seek the opinions of fifty to 100 well-chosen people. Your main cost will be time.

b) Seek advice: fellow business associates, bankers, accountants, local political figures, and librarians can provide advice and counsel to help reduce your risks.

c) Update your education: seminars, trade journals, college classes, and special books and magazines geared to new business ideas can increase your awareness of potential new marketplaces.

Growth: if your product is in the second, or growth, phase of the cycle, you may have a good chance for success since the high risks are no longer a factor. But good management is especially important for a growth-phase product, since you must compete with others for your share of the product's growing market.

Maturity: In this phase, as demand for the product continues to grow, more and more competitors enter the market. Large corporations begin to show interest, and the profit squeeze begins. This concept holds true not only for products and services, but also for geographic areas. For example, let's look at a typical medium-sized town in suburbia (pop. 30,000), forty to fifty miles from a major metropolitan area. The vast majority of retail stores in the area have developed with the growth of the town, and the distance from the city has caused the average consumer to purchase locally. As the area develops, each new growth spurt entices the large chains to reevaluate this somewhat isolated area. Finally, a major chain like Sears or K-Mart opens a large store, and their variety, selection, convenience, and lower prices attract many new customers. Now the profit and sales squeeze is a reality.

What to do? You can lessen the impact of this phase through long-term planning and product specialization.

Large chains are geared to the mass market and generally do not cater to the unique and special needs of the consumer. Thus if you have a local shoe store, for example, offering an excellent selection of extra-wide and extra-narrow shoes, you may be able to develop a loyal clientele, impenetrable to mass merchandisers.

Decline: Unless you have a penchant for failure, the final phase of obsolescence and dropout is to be avoided. And avoiding it is tricky: spotting the end of a product's usefulness requires experience, good advice, and common sense. A sense of timing is critical at this point.

While no reliable statistics exist, it is believed that approximately 500,000 new businesses form each year and approximately 450,000 fail each year. The high failure rate is partially due to entrepreneurs' failure to recognize that their product has reached the final stages of the life style.

THE SELLING PHASE

The only reason any business exists is to sell its products or services. All other business functions are secondary to this critical phase. We can break this area down into four categories: advertising, sales promotion, publicity, and personal sales.

Advertising

Small businesses use four main advertising methods or forms of media: newspapers, magazines, radio, and direct mail. There are certain basic rules to follow in all these areas.

1. Effective advertising is costly in the short run, but cost-effective in the long run.

2. Unless you're lucky, shoddy advertising is rarely effective.

3. One-shot advertising is a waste of money.

4. The greater the frequency of the exposure in a variety of media, the greater the success.

5. Consistency of advertising format is very important. That is, your ad should have an identifiable design that gains the reader's attention.

Newspapers: This unique form of advertising offers the small business-person several advantages. First, newspapers reach a specific geographic area—frequently the very area covered by the small entrepreneur. And second, newspapers have a high degree of readership, since they supply local news. This is especially true of local newspapers published outside the larger metropolitan areas.

By advertising in a newspaper, local businesspeople can contact a large percentage of their potential customers. Naturally, the rates (or costs) are geared to the circulation of the paper (number of paid readers) and the size of the ad. The success of the ad will depend on several factors:

1. Size: The bigger the ad, the more likely readers are to look at it.

2. Uniqueness: If your ad looks like the rest of the paper, your readership drops. Eye appeal is important. Use lead-in captions such as "LOWEST PRICE EVER," "20% DISCOUNT," "$10 OFF," "ONLY SIX DAYS LEFT," "FIRST TIME EVER." The reader scans each page for only a second—so you must grab the reader's attention.

3. Repetition: It may take three or four exposures of the same or slightly different ads to reach your potential customers. Consumers of any type need prodding to break their old familiar buying habits.

Magazines: Magazine ads offer some unique advantages to small businesses that are specialized in nature. A firm that produces booklets for the savings and loan industry could reach that marketplace via trade magazines read by savings and loan personnel. Likewise, real-estate professionals can be easily contacted through publications geared to their marketplace. For about $1,000, a firm could display a full-page ad in the *California Real Estate Magazine,* and have its product exposed to 100,000 real-estate people. No other form of advertising media could directly contact that many interested realtors, over such a large area as California, at so low a cost. Truly cost-effective!

Magazine advertising is cost-effective for any specialized small business whose potential customers are not necessarily local, but are related by interests (such as gambling), occupations (such as banking), hobbies (such as sailing), politics, and so on. Every unique special-interest group maintains a newsletter and/or magazine that makes them readily accessible at a low cost per-person exposure.

Radio: "Lowest cost per person reached"—that's the claim of the radio industry. The reason is simple: radio audiences have increased in the last decade, while newspaper and magazine readership has decreased in the same period. The cost for the preparation of simple commercials is normally included in the price of the air time. In short, radio is very cost-effective when the area served by the radio station is the area covered by your business.

Direct mail
This unique form of selling actually completes the sale for you. The mail piece must include all the ingredients for purchase: order form, complete descriptive literature, and a reply envelope. Expected response to any given mailer will vary between 1 and 3 percent of the total number of people who receive mailing pieces, and the profitability of each direct mail campaign will depend upon the profit generated from each scale. Figure your potential profit at a response rate of 2 percent before you begin the campaign. If the profit is small per sale, direct mail is not for you.

How does direct mailing work? You may purchase or rent mail lists, or develop them using membership files, phone directories, and industrial journals. We should note here that there's one problem you face with all lists: high addressee mobility causes 15 to 20 percent of the mailers to reach the wastebasket.

Direct mail is another form of advertising media that suits the specialized nature of small firms. Many specialized marketplaces have easily identifiable potential customers: for example, if your business is geared to banks, you can obtain the several catalogues published that list every bank in the U.S. (including all officers), and prepare your mail list from this source. The key is to do carefully selected mailings, not mass-mailing.

Another excellent method in any type of small business is to send special mailings to current and past customers. Advance-sale announcements and new products can be offered to these people via well-timed mailing. This method is a low-cost way of stimulating new sales results.

Lists of past and current customers are easy to compile using one or more of the following:

1. Guest-book sign-ins at the cash register.

2. Free gift-certificate raffles. The raffle tickets become an ideal source of customers' names and addresses.

3. Handwritten customer sales receipts.

For maximum success, think about careful use of both direct mail and magazine advertising. One form reinforces the other, and you get even greater sales results.

Sales promotion

This more subtle approach is not a direct attempt to sell, but is an attempt to provide a service which may ultimately lead to a sale. For example, a model and hobby shop could sponsor a model-airplane contest, which would attract hobbyists who usually deal with large chains or your competitors. This way you break potential customers' old habit patterns, and sales may follow. Another promotion device is handsome window displays of new products, which will increase foot traffic.

Publicity: This nonpaid promotional approach works through articles in newspapers or newsletters and promotions on talk shows. Local interest and/or the uniqueness of the product sometimes prompts free coverage in the papers, and editors and program directors are constantly seeking newsworthy events that will generate audience interest.

Personal sales

The retailer must have informed, helpful, and courteous salespeople to compete with the lower prices and greater selections of the larger chains. Frequently, a small business's main appeal is the specialized expertise of its salespeople. A salesperson in a small hardware store, for example, can help the customer to understand wiring designs, plumbing requirements, and other similar information—a service not usually available from salespeople in the large, impersonal chains.

TRENDS IN THE JOB MARKET

The old adage that a good salesman can always get a job remains true and will continue to be true for the marketing major; and with the increasing demand for new products, new merchandising methods, new advertising concepts, and market research, there will be no shortage of job opportunities in this field. But this doesn't mean that finding a good job in marketing will be easy. Each year a substantial supply of graduates enter this field, so competition for the better jobs will be high. And you should note one more key point: mobility is a strong factor when selecting a career in marketing, and graduates who choose a marketing career should be prepared to move from place to place frequently if they are also going to move up the ladder of success.

KEY AREAS

■ Most of the opportunities in marketing will be in direct sales or sales promotion, and this is the best training ground for future sales management positions.

■ Marketing research openings are limited and require strong quantitative skills and frequently an MBA.

THE OUTLOOK FOR MINORITIES AND WOMEN

Many firms have special programs to recruit women and minorities for their marketing departments, and where women have taken traditionally male marketing positions they have been very successful.

THE SALARY PICTURE

Though most marketing graduates do not like to work on a commission basis, usually the best remuneration comes from those jobs paid by commission. College graduates often start on a straight salary basis and are given on-the-job training about the product, the organization, and the competition. Once the employee has the basic knowledge, a good manager tries to set up a salary arrangement that has bonuses or some commission/salary combination that rewards successful efforts. The average starting salary for someone with a Bachelor's degree in marketing is $11,900 per year. Two-year marketing graduates can expect $8,500 per year to start; and an MBA can expect $15,500 per year for a nontechnical undergraduate degree or $17,500 per year for a technical undergraduate degree.

WOMEN IN THE BUSINESS WORLD

When your mother was your age, she probably had a pretty good idea of what her future role would be. Chances are she imagined herself as a wife and mother. She might have worked, but probably only if the family's finances required it. Very few of your mothers, or other women in their generation, took full-time jobs after they had children. And if they did work, it was usually in one of the traditional "female occupations"— teacher, nurse, secretary, bookkeeper, salesperson, or waitress.

A lot has changed since your mother was your age, including the way women think about their futures. Since 1950, 20 million women have entered the work force, and by 1985, it is estimated that 50 million women will be working. That accounts for 65 percent of the adult female population.

Not only have women been seeking jobs, but more and more have been seeking jobs in the fields that, until recently, were considered open to men only. The lady lawyer and the female physician are no longer rarities, and if business-school enrollments are any indication, the businesswoman too may soon be commonplace. At Emory University, 40 percent of business-school students are women, and at the Wharton School of Economics, enrollment of women has increased from 4 percent in the early 1970s to 25 percent in the late '70s. What has happened at these two schools is not unusual: in fact, claims Emory's Dean, the growing number of women in business schools is "a national trend." *

What becomes of these female business-school graduates? Do they, as many men believe, work only until they marry or have children? Not any more. Between 1900 and 1960

* Fred T. Ferguson, "More Women Enter Top-Level Management," *The Wall Street Journal,* February 22, 1977, pp. 14C, 17C.

CAREERS IN MARKETING

Title	Job description	Requirements	Salary* and advancement prospects	Outlook through 1985	Comments
TWO-YEAR PROGRAM					
Media specialist	Keeps records of clients' advertising for ad agency and computes costs. Records media used. Determines cost of advertising space in competing areas, factoring in size and population of city, space rates, and frequency of publication.	Two-year Associate degree in Marketing minimum. Part-time or summer work experience in newspaper, radio or TV.	$8,000 to $9,000 Account representative	Good	High competitive career path, with outstanding financial rewards for those who make it.
Assistant buyer—retailing	With buyer, selects and orders merchandise from showings of manufacturing representatives for resale. Checks invoices and return of merchandise, and authorizes payment for merchandise. Sets prices for merchandise.	Two-year Associate degree in Marketing, plus co-op or part-time experience in retail store.	$8,500 to $9,800 Buyer	Very good	
Sales manager trainee	Trainee for supervision of retailing department. Displays, advertises, and sells items such as furniture, clothing, and hardware. Maintains inventory control and requisitions merchandise as needed.	Two-year Associate degree desirable, plus ability to supervise part-time and full-time employees.	$8,500 to $11,000 Department manager to store manager	Very good	With larger chain organizations, willingness to make frequent geographic moves is necessary for continued success.
Travel agency representative	Arranges travel and tours for leisure and company business; coordinates and sometimes accompanies tours. Extensive telephone communication.	Two-year Associate degree desirable.	$8,000 to $9,600 Tourist bureau manager or ownership of travel agency	Excellent	A good way to combine interest in travel with job. It's not all glamour, however.
Sales—real estate	Lists, sells, and sometimes rents property. Solicits property listings and sells to clients. Draws up contracts such as deeds or leases, and negotiates selling price, loans, and mortgages.	Two-year Associate degree in Marketing, plus aggressive and persistent personality.	Commission Sales manager or broker	Very good	Requires great tenacity. Those who are successful do very well financially. Supplemental real-estate courses helpful.
Sales—insurance	Sells insurance to new and present clients, recommending amount and type of coverage. Develops contact lists and explains features of policies based on needs of client.	Two-year Associate degree, preferably in Marketing, plus desire to succeed in nontangible sales (considered by many to be difficult).	Commission (or salary plus commission for training program) Sales manager to agency manager	Very good	Professional life insurance salesperson should get a C.L.U. (Certified Life Insurance Underwriter) certificate.
Sales—automotive	Sells motor vehicles, tires, and parts; uses advertising, sales, and promotion techniques in advising dealers about increasing sales volume. Analyzes dealers' records to help improve sales records.	Two-year Associate degree in Marketing, plus dynamic personality and interest in motor vehicles. Considerable travel involved.	$9,000 to $13,000 Usually starts with smaller dealers, and advances to working larger accounts	Very good	Additional courses and knowledge in accounting and advertising helpful.
Traffic agent	Sells tickets, i.e., air, railroad, bus; supervises cargo handling. Handles customer complaints.	Two-year Associate degree.	$8,000 to $9,000 Traffic manager	Good	Good starting position for career in transportation.
FOUR-YEAR PROGRAM					
Market researcher —interviewer —editor —statistician —analyst	Performs one or several of the following duties: secures information from consumers; writes and proofreads survey material; analyzes and interprets data; collects secondary data for compilation of final report on project.	Four-year college degree, with emphasis on Marketing or Advertising.	$9,500 to $17,000 Field supervisor; project supervisor	Good	Mathematical aptitude helpful.
Salesperson—retailing trainee	Sells apparel, appliances, cosmetics, tools, etc. Answers questions pertaining to goods for sale. Arranges displays. May coordinate advertising and inventory control. Resolves customer complaints.	Four-year college degree in Marketing desired.	$10,800 to $15,000 Department manager	Very good	Excellent training ground for management position.

* Represents *starting salary* range

Title	Job description	Requirements	Salary and advancement prospects	Outlook through 1985	Comments
Salesperson —computer —food products —pharmaceutical —petroleum —chemicals	Sells appliances, computers, clothing, etc. to individuals, businesses, or government agencies. Demonstrates items, and prepares estimates, credit terms, and trade-in. May collect payments.	Four-year college degree in Marketing desirable. Specialist training in product line necessary and usually available in training program.	$9,800 to $15,600 (commission sometimes part of total income) District sales manager	Very good	Aggressive, highly motivated, and "self-starting" persons usually do well in this field.
Salesperson—securities	Provides clients with information on stocks, bonds, and market conditions, and history and prospects of corporations. Transmits buy and sell orders to trading division as customers wish. Develops portfolios for clients.	Four-year college degree in Marketing preferred. Strong academic background in economics helpful. Lengthy training required.	$11,000 to $14,000 Manager, partner	Very good	Unlimited opportunities for persistent, personable, knowledgable person.
Public relations	Produces publicity or information services for organizations through the media, such as radio, TV, etc. Writes news releases and scripts, and takes ad photos. Participates in community and civic programs.	Four-year college degree in Marketing desired but not necessary. Ability to communicate via the written and spoken word essential.	$8,500 to $13,000 Supervisor, manager, or director of public relations, depending upon size of firm.	Good	Entry-level jobs difficult to find in this field. Best access is through utilization of writing or verbal skills.
Media analyst	Keeps records for clients on media, computing cost of space used and ad program. Determines costs of various media, factoring in size and population of city, space rates, and kind and frequency of publication.	Four-year college degree in Marketing Supplemental courses in advertising desirable.	$8,500 to $13,000 Account executive	Good	Job involves routine work in early stages, but is one of best ways to enter this field. Highly competitive.
Methods analyst	Develops new systems for effectively applying electronic equipment to existing office procedures. Investigates work done, size of staff, working conditions, etc. Recommends changes based on investigation.	Four-year college degree in Business, specializing in Marketing. Requires alert thinker who can "sell" ideas for change.	$12,000 to $17,760 Manager	Very good	Excellent position for demonstrating one's abilities; enables one to directly affect cost/benefits to employer or client.
Account executive trainee	In ad agency, the account executive represents the agency to the client; within the agency, he is the client's spokesman. Must have excellent selling abilities; must know client's business and market	Four-year college degree in Marketing or Advertising.	$12,000 to $15,000 Account executive	Good	

MBA PROGRAM

Title	Job description	Requirements	Salary and advancement prospects	Outlook through 1985	Comments
Technical sales	Sells highly technical equipment such as generators, computers, jet engines, turbines, structural materials, etc. to customers, usually involving high dollar volume.	MBA in Marketing, with Engineering undergraduate degree.	$17,000 to $24,000 Sales manager	Excellent	A combination of non-technical (sales) and technical (engineering) abilities required.
Traffic manager	Supervises shipments of cargo and passengers; establishes schedules and coordinates all activities associated with scheduling, movement of cargo and passengers; supervises traffic agents and clerks.	MBA desired, specializing in Marketing or Transportation.	$15,000 to $22,000 Director or vice president of traffic	Good	There is a shortage of highly qualified personnel in this field; it will experience rapid change in near future.
Assistant advertising manager	Under the direction of the manager, may work in any or all of the following: 1. Research 2. Production 3. Writing 4. Layout 5. Media sales	MBA specializing in Marketing or Advertising.	$14,500 to $21,000 Advertising manager	Fair	Competition keen for most jobs. Great potential for those who can make it.
Assistant marketing manager	Under the direction of the manager, supervises all phases of the marketing of a product, from its conception to market design to advertising to sales.	MBA specializing in Marketing.	$14,500 to $21,000 Marketing manager	Good	Statistical and analytical aptitude beneficial.

the number of years a woman worked tripled, and the higher up a woman goes, the more likely she is to stay on at her job. As one young woman explained it, "it costs $20,000, including living expenses, to attend two years of graduate business school. To throw that away would be absurd."*

FINDING A MANAGEMENT JOB

Even with a solid business education and strong motivation, women often have trouble landing management jobs. There is no sure route to finding such jobs, but there are several avenues women may consider.

First, there are the classic methods, such as the campus interview. This interview is important: before the interview the candidate should find out something about the company she is applying to, and she should prepare to tell the interviewer what her own interests and goals are. It is helpful, too, to discuss business-related experience, including summer jobs, campus activities, and internships. Other classic methods include applying directly to companies by sending a letter and résumé to the personnel department, and looking in professional journals for information about job openings. Last but not least, there is the time-honored "grapevine": friends often tell each other of opportunities in their company, and this is a good way to gain information about an organization's "style" and policies.

* Ibid.

Recently, another route has opened for women seeking management-level jobs. In 1964 a Civil Rights Act declared it illegal for an employer to refuse to hire or discriminate against someone based on his or her sex. Since that time many companies have decided that ending discrimination against women wasn't enough; what was needed was a positive plan for giving qualified women an edge. Such plans are known as "affirmative action." What this means is that qualified women may actually have an advantage over qualified men as companies try to end sex discrimination. The best opportunities for women are still in retailing, utilities, banks, and public services, particularly in jobs like advertising and marketing, and even in sales management positions.

SALARIES

Once the new women graduates are hired, how do their salaries compare with those of their male counterparts? Very well. "For qualified newcomers," reports *Business Week*, "the days when companies automatically offered men 25 percent more than they offered women . . . are definitely over."*

WOMEN AND THEIR CO-WORKERS

Women still face some psychological difficulties on the job. Many men dislike reporting to a woman, which means that even when a woman is promoted to a supervisory job, she often has to cope with staff members who are not only resentful but skeptical as well. As one female executive explained: "The men challenge just about everything—your ability, your authority, everything they can. You

* "A Double Standard for Women Manager's Pay," *Business Week*, November 28, 1977, p. 61.

have to prove yourself a third, fourth, and fifth time, almost on a daily basis. This was probably the hardest thing I had to overcome."*

A woman manager may have a particularly difficult time if she has been promoted primarily to fill an affirmative-action quota. Men will be doubly resentful of a female supervisor who lacks confidence and managerial experience. To succeed, a woman manager must have the full support of higher management.

WOMEN IN SALES

One field in which women have been particularly successful is sales. Women consistently rank among their companies' top sales representatives, and sales provides a good route for promotion into management jobs. One reason why women are so successful in sales is the money: a $25,000-a-year sales job represents a major opportunity to women who still have lower income expectations than men, and a woman is likely to be proud of such a salary and to work hard at proving she deserves it.

ADDING IT ALL UP

All in all, women business students have a good future waiting for them. Despite the obstacles that still exist, they can hope to find jobs in business, do well in them, and receive good pay—and most of all, enjoy their experiences in the business world.

* Niles Howard, "Sales Jobs Open Up for Women," *Dun's Review,* March 1978, pp. 86, 88.

FINANCE

In the entertainment industry, 1977 will long be remembered as the year of **Star Wars,** the movie which broke all domestic box-office records. And at Twentieth Century-Fox, where **Star Wars** was produced, 1977 will go down as the year when revenues were good enough for the company to start investing in other industries. But that didn't mean that all of the company's money problems were automatically solved. Since no business wants to use all its resources for acquisitions, Fox had to borrow money, and the managers had to figure out the best way to do this. Likewise, once they had the funds, they had to figure out the best way to put them to use.[1]

Even success, in short, meant a need for good financial management—the management of the inflow and outflow of funds. Of course, good financial management is also crucial for businesses that aren't expanding—small ones as well as large. In Part 4 we'll discuss some key aspects of this important business area.

☐ Chapter 11, **Short-Term Finance,** discusses basic financial concepts and the sources of short-term capital.

☐ In Chapter 12, **Long-Term Finance,** you'll read about the major sources of long-term capital.

☐ The Enrichment Chapter on the **Money and Banking System** focuses on the Federal Reserve System and other financial institutions.

☐ The Enrichment Chapter on the **Stock Market** tells you all about this fascinating and sometimes mysterious segment of the American economy.

☐ In the Enrichment Chapter on **Risk Management and Insurance,** you'll read about the reasons why risks are inevitable in business—and the ways they can be minimized.

SHORT-TERM FINANCE

As you've probably noticed, money seldom stays in your pocket for very long; but then, it never stays in any one place for very long. If you deposit it in a bank it's sent right back out in the form of loans, investments, and the like. If you spend it in a store it moves on to pay employees, wholesalers, and anyone else who's owed money by the proprietor.

It's the nature of money to circulate through the economy, and business managers must make sure it circulates through *their* part of the economy as efficiently as possible. In this chapter and the chapter that follows, we'll look at some of the tough questions involved in finance—the management area that deals with the inflow and outflow of money. Here we see how managers handle financial questions that arise within a one-year time frame. In Chapter 12, we'll see how they handle such questions over longer periods of time.

WHAT WILL THIS CHAPTER FOCUS ON?

After reading the material in this chapter, you will understand and be able to discuss:

- how financial managers handle the outflow and the inflow of money
- two basic concepts in finance—assets and liabilities
- the various ways businesses obtain short-term capital
- the three major sources of short-term financing
- the various ways businesses extend trade credit—through open-book accounts, promissory notes, and trade drafts and acceptances
- the role of financial institutions in making loans
- the difference between unsecured and secured bank loans

In the late 1970s the auto manufacturers of America were in the process of spending big to think small. In response to pressures from both the government and society, the Big Three automakers were planning to reduce the size and increase the fuel efficiency of the gigantic gas guzzlers that they had put out for decades. A retooling of plants and machinery does not come cheap, however. In 1977 General Motors alone spent $3.5 billion on downsizing its range of products. Even the relatively small Chrysler Corporation spent over $700 million. It was estimated that in order to make the changeover to smaller, safer, more fuel-economical cars, the industry would have to spend more than $50 billion by 1985. That's more than twice what the nation spent on the Apollo project to land a man on the moon![1]

Not all companies pay out sums of this size every year, of course, for their projects. But almost every company has to spend relatively large amounts of money at least periodically. It can cost thousands, sometimes millions, of dollars to start up an operation, expand it, or rework the product line. And meanwhile, large projects are not the only drain on company funds. There are also smaller but equally important day-to-day expenses on items such as rents, salaries, advertising, insurance, and raw materials. Even coffee for the coffee machine costs money—and it can add up.

WHAT IS FINANCE AND WHY IS IT NECESSARY?

Where is the money for all these business expenses to come from? Some of these needs can be met with **revenues**, *money a company makes through sales, rental of its property, and so on.* On every medium-sized Cadillac GM sells in 1979, for instance, a few dollars will go to designing a new smaller version for the future. Several more dollars will help meet GM's bills for salaries, rents, and the like. Some of the money needed by a company may be borrowed. Some may come from the sale of **stock**—*shares of ownership*—in the company. And in some instances, the company can simply get **credit** from the companies it owes money to—*arrange to put off paying them for a time.* But whatever method

or combination of methods the company employs, management must make sure the money is obtained and used as efficiently as possible. The area of management that includes dealing with expenses is known as finance.

Finance involves handling the outflow and inflow of money. Management experts define **finance** as *the management function of effectively obtaining and using money.* It's such a complex area that in all but the smallest businesses, there is at least one person, and sometimes even a whole department, whose sole responsibility is to keep tabs on the flow of funds and to plan the best way to get and make use of them. Good financial management is basic to the success of any business, whether it's the corner newsstand or GM itself.

ASSETS AND LIABILITIES: TWO BASIC CONCEPTS IN FINANCE

Managing a company's finances means thinking in terms of two opposite categories: assets and liabilities. **Assets** are the *items of value the company owns* (including money itself). **Liabilities** are *debts, the sums the company owes to other businesses or individuals.* If you subtract your liabilities from your assets, you know exactly where you stand financially—and that's one of the essential ways to judge a business's health.

But, as we'll see, there are different kinds of assets and liabilities, each with its own advantages and disadvantages. One company may have the same dollar amount of assets and liabilities as another company, yet be in better shape to face the future because of the *nature* of its holdings and its debts. For example, it may own a piece of undeveloped real estate that would skyrocket in value if buildings were put up on it. Or it may have the greater part of its debts in long-term loans that could be paid back over a ten-year period, rather than in the next year. In sum, the dollar amount of a company's assets and liabilities is not the financial manager's only concern.

In this chapter we're going to take a look at some of the details of business finance, including the various kinds of assets and liabilities a business may have. As you might imagine, the financial manager's problems are different when he or she is looking for money to take care of next month's payroll than when he or she is thinking of developing a uranium mine that will be open in five years' time. For this reason, we'll look at finance in terms of two different time periods. This chapter will focus on **short-term finance**, *finance involving a time span of one year or less*. The chapter that follows will discuss **long-term finance**, *finance involving time spans of more than a year*. (Some experts in finance use "intermediate-term" to describe financing that pertains to periods between one and ten years, but we will use "long-term" for this category.)

SHORT-TERM FINANCE: ASSETS AND LIABILITIES

One of the biggest problems in short-term finance is that a company's revenues don't always come in at exactly the same rate that bills have to be paid. Though GM may expect to raise enough cash on the sale of its current models to meet payroll or advertising expenses, there are often short-term gaps involved. And what's true for General Motors is true for every other business: there are often gaps between incoming and outgoing cash. But these gaps can be dealt with if the financial manager has an effective strategy for figuring out *which kinds of assets,* and *which kinds of liabilities,* are going to offer the company the most advantages. Let's look at the kinds of assets and liabilities a company can have on a short-term basis.

SHORT-TERM ASSETS

Short-term assets, often termed **current assets**, are defined as *those resources that can be turned back into cash within one year*. A bin of raw materials like steel, cotton, or flax, or a warehouse full of jeans ready to be shipped to stores across the country is a short-term asset. Cash itself is a short-term asset. So are **time deposits**—*savings accounts at financial institutions and United States government bonds*. Other short-term assets are a company's **accounts receivable**, *the money that is owed to the company for items or services it has sold*. A factory, on the other hand, is not an easy item to convert into cash and so isn't included in any list of short-term assets.

Short-term assets are generally highly liquid. *The faster any asset can be changed into money, the higher its* **liquidity**. Cash, of course, is the most liquid of all assets.

SHORT-TERM LIABILITIES

Borrowed money that must be returned within one year is a prime example of a short-term liability, or debt. Other short-term liabilities include unpaid bills for short-term assets such as raw materials, and such liabilities as rent, salaries, and insurance premiums.

COMMON PROBLEMS IN SHORT-TERM FINANCING

Short-term finance calls for a balancing of all these short-term incomings and outgoings to get the most out of the business dollar. The task is neither an easy nor a simple one. It involves posing and then answering a variety of difficult financial policy questions, and a question wrongly answered can mean ruin.

For instance, how liberal should a business be in extending credit to other companies and individuals? How big should its accounts receivable be? On the one hand, liberal credit policies may attract more customers. On the other hand, a company may risk not having enough ready cash to cover its immediate expenses if it allows too much leeway to people and businesses that owe it money.

Or take another typical short-term financing problem: how large an inventory of finished goods should a company stockpile? Will the large cash investment in this inventory be offset by a high demand for the goods?

Or consider another short-term headache: what's to be done with whatever excess cash the company has on hand? Should the company lend it out to earn interest, or use it to build up extra inventory, or spend it on new promotion schemes? These are just a few of the short-term financing questions the financial manager has to deal with.

Ongoing short-term needs

For some businesses, short-term finance is more than a stopgap measure, it's a regular way of doing business.

SHORT-TERM FINANCING CYCLES IN THREE SEASONAL INDUSTRIES   FIGURE 1

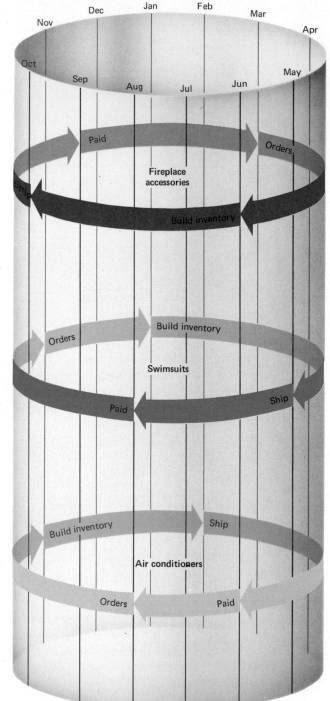

In each of these industries, how many months elapse between the time orders are received for the merchandise and the time the company receives payment?

In fact, entire industries are often dependent on the concept of short-term financing. The toy industry is a case in point.

A toy company such as Mattel may take orders from stores as early as March; its factory hums during the spring and summer months, and its products are shipped to the stores in the fall. But since stores don't immediately pay for these toys, Mattel must borrow short-term capital to pay for the raw materials, labor, and office expenses incurred while producing the Christmas line. (Note that when we're discussing financing, the term **capital** simply means *money*.) The company will then repay this short-term capital when the stores that have purchased the line pay the company.

Or, take the case of short-term financing that is used by auto dealers on a regular, year-round basis. Your local Chevy showroom doesn't just happen to have all those gleaming new models to tempt you. The dealer had to borrow the money to get that racy little yellow number or that ice-blue coupe on the showroom floor. Without such samples—and as many of them as he or she can afford—the dealer would have little chance of making any sales at all. As every salesperson knows, people aren't likely to buy what they can't see. Naturally, your dealer can't afford to lay out all the cash needed to buy a dozen or so cars at a time—and that's where short-term finance meets the dealer's needs. The dealer borrows the money to purchase the vehicles on display in the showroom and pays the money back soon after the cars have been sold.

Is such dependence on borrowing poor business practice? Hardly. There was a time perhaps when it was considered unwise for businesses to owe large sums; but those times are long gone. Today it's a common and well-respected business practice to borrow money in order to make money.

How much short-term capital should a business borrow?

Just how much a business should borrow to meet its short-term needs and how long it should obtain that credit for depends, first, on the nature of the business. Large tobacco farmers use short-term capital to pay bills for seed, fertilizer, and labor during the time between planting and harvesting. This period can be six months. Other businesses, such as restaurants, that

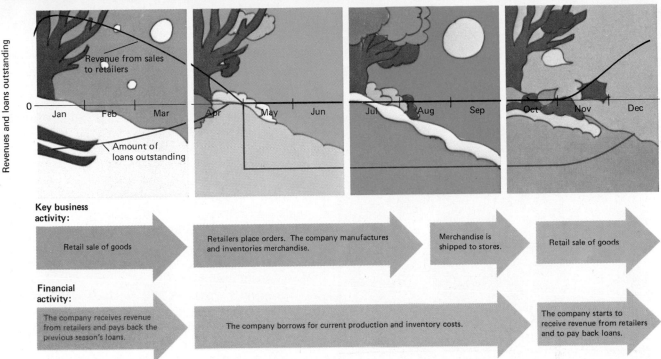

Revenues and loans outstanding

Revenue from sales to retailers

Amount of loans outstanding

Jan Feb Mar Apr May Jun Jul Aug Sep Oct Nov Dec

Key business activity:

Retail sale of goods

Retailers place orders. The company manufactures and inventories merchandise.

Merchandise is shipped to stores.

Retail sale of goods

Financial activity:

The company receives revenue from retailers and pays back the previous season's loans.

The company borrows for current production and inventory costs.

The company starts to receive revenue from retailers and to pay back loans.

What relationships do you see between short-term debts and revenues as the year progresses?

operate on shorter time cycles, may have only a very short lag—a month, perhaps—between the time they acquire their inventory and the time they sell it. Figure 1 shows how long the manufacturers of three types of seasonal products must wait for payment for their goods.

The second factor that determines short-term needs is the size of the business. IBM won't depend on short-term loans as much as will the little ski repair shop on the corner. And these two factors—the nature of the business and its size—will also be crucial in determining which of the numerous different *sources* of short-term financing would be best to use. We'll look more closely at these different sources in the section that follows.

THE THREE MAJOR SOURCES OF SHORT-TERM FINANCING

How does a small housewares manufacturing company finance operations during the production season? It may do so by purchasing plastics on credit from du Pont, or perhaps by borrowing from a local bank to meet the payroll. By contrast, how does a huge company such as General Motors Acceptance Corporation

(GMAC) meet its short-term needs? Usually through loans from nonbanking sources. Broadly viewed, businesses have three major sources of short-term financing, which are as follows: (1) They can get credit from their suppliers. (2) They can borrow from a commercial bank or some other type of short-term lending institution. (3) If they are among a few large companies, they can borrow from outside investors or other businesses. Table 1 (page 319) gives an overview of all three sources. Here we'll examine them in some detail.

TRADE CREDIT

On one notably shabby block of West 47th Street in midtown Manhattan, it's estimated that half of the world's supply of diamonds can be found at one time or another. This in itself is a remarkable fact. But more remarkable still is the way in which these stones are bought and sold. So close a commercial community is the New York diamond market that, more often than not, stones worth the ransom of a whole gathering of kings are consigned on credit. No more than a handshake and mumbled good wishes seal the deal. That's an example of trade credit at its most breathtakingly simple.

In no more time than it takes to shake a colleague's hand, a deal worth tens of thousands of dollars can be transacted on the sidewalk in New York's diamond district.

Though rarely transacted on so grand a scale as that, **trade credit** is the most widespread source of short-term financing for business. It means that rather than borrowing money to pay for goods or supplies, *the purchaser gets credit directly from the supplier.* The degree of formality in such arrangements can run the range from the diamond-district handshake to relatively iron-bound written agreements. However, most examples of trade credit fall within one of three specific types: open-book accounts, promissory notes, and trade acceptances.

Open-book credit

More than 85 percent of all business transactions involving merchandise are financed through **open-book credit**, *informal arrangements whereby purchasers may obtain goods from suppliers and pay for them later.* Open-book credit, one of the oldest of credit systems, dates back to those primitive days before credit cards when store-owners usually knew their clientele well enough to allow purchases "on the book." It still exists in this form today, for example, in many a corner grocery store. You can see it if you go into one of New York's *bodegas,* or Puerto Rican grocery stores. When the customer (who is probably a neighbor) needs a quart of milk but hasn't the cash, the shopkeeper simply lets her have it and adds it to her bill. To keep track of such transactions, the shopkeeper keeps a ledger, or book, with the amount owed by all of the store's credit customers.

Open-book credit is still common between purchasers and suppliers in numerous larger-scale industries—advertising, for example. Ad agencies keep open-book accounts for clients who need their goods or services but lack the cash to pay for them on delivery.

HOW IT'S ACTUALLY DONE

OPEN-BOOK CREDIT

Companies using the open-book credit system indicate credit or repayment terms to the customer on the bill that accompanies delivery. Such terms vary with the industry. In the paperboard box industry, for instance, open-book credit is usually extended for thirty days. Customers are expected to pay their bills by the end of this period. However, many businesses try to pay before the end of the credit period because suppliers, in order to encourage speedy repayments, offer special discounts for early payments. In the box industry, terms are 1/10 net 30, which means that bills are payable either with a 1 percent discount in ten days or in full in thirty days. A customer who buys $10,000 worth of boxes on June 15 is not required to pay for them until July 15. But if he pays the bill by June 25 (ten days after the purchase), he can subtract 1 percent, or $100, from the amount he owes the manufacturer.

Study.

TABLE 1 Major Sources of Short-Term Financing

Arrangement	Description
TRADE CREDIT	
Open-book account	Smith's grocery store buys display racks from Jones to be paid in full in 30 days or with a discount in 10 days.
Promissory note	Smith signs a note promising payment in 30 days.
Trade acceptance	Jones orders Smith to pay either in 30 days or immediately.
LOANS FROM FINANCIAL INSTITUTIONS	
Unsecured bank loan	Smith borrows from First National Bank on his good name and repays with interest.
Secured loan	
pledge of accounts receivable	Smith borrows from First National on the bills owed him and repays with interest.
pledge of inventory	Smith borrows from First National on his marketable groceries and repays with interest.
pledge of other property	Smith borrows from First National on his delivery truck and repays with interest.
Sales of accounts receivable	Smith sells what is owed him for less than the amount owed.
LOANS FROM INVESTORS	
Commercial paper	Smith, Inc., becomes so large that it can borrow money from First National and Jones, Inc., at a lower interest rate on the promise to repay alone.

A soft-drink manufacturer may hire an ad agency to create an advertising campaign and put it on nationwide television. The agency contacts the network and orders ten commercials a day to be played on the air in prime time. The station sends a bill, but the agency doesn't pay it immediately because it has to wait for the soft-drink manufacturer to pay its bill plus commission. As a result of this practice, ad agencies are often 90 to 120 days behind in paying their broadcast bills. If the agency is lucky, the client will only be 60 to 90 days late in paying. Sometimes, however, the client is even later. Perhaps it has money tied up in high-interest-bearing bank accounts, and it wants to earn all it can before paying any bills. Or maybe the client is defaulting on the bills. When that happens, ad agencies can and do go out of business because of their inability to pay TV-station bills.

Open-book credit plays an important role for many businesses. Without its aid in financing their inventories many small firms would find it impossible to start a business or keep it going. Most of them are not overly supplied with cash from their own resources. Relatively stiff bank requirements mean that such customers often have nowhere to turn for credit except open-book arrangements.

This is not to say, however, that by allowing open-book credit a supplier can be regarded as an easy mark for any fly-by-night operation. Most sellers investigate the credit rating of any new customer before extending credit. A supplier can check a potential customer's credit by asking the customer to show a financial statement and by contacting the customer's bank for information. Or, if necessary or more convenient, a supplier may use the services of a **credit-rating agency** such as Dun and Bradstreet, which *maintains its own staff of investigators and keeps records of the paying abilities of tens of thousands of firms.*

In addition to being of use to the customer, open-book credit is also important to suppliers themselves. Liberal credit policies serve as an attraction to customers. A printer, for example, may offer retail customers 60 days to pay their bills. Although the general industry practice is to require payment in full in 30 days, a 60-day policy may bring in more business.

Promissory notes

Not all business people or even all industries are always comfortable with the relative informality of open-book credit. They prefer the security of a written agreement to repay, signed in advance by the customer they're supplying. One such agreement is a **promissory note**, *an unconditional written commitment drawn up by the customer in which the customer promises a supplier a fixed sum of money on a specified future date in return for immediate delivery of goods.* (See Figure 3.) Often, there is an interest rate on promissory notes that is indicated on the face of the note itself.

Promissory notes provide a means of extending credit to customers who might otherwise not qualify for it because of the extraordinarily high value of the goods received (furs, for instance). Or the customers may have poor credit ratings or a history of having fallen behind in paying open-book accounts. A promis-

---

HOW IT'S ACTUALLY DONE

PROMISSORY NOTES

The mechanics of a promissory note are simple. The customer who draws up the note, signs it, and so promises to pay is called the **maker** of the note. The **payee** is the person or firm who receives the money at the designated time in the future. Shown below is a promissory note for $5,000 signed by John Simpson, the maker of the note, to the Gray Manufacturing Company, the payee.

What if the supplier needs the money right away, before the due date on the note? Should the supplier (that is, the payee) have need of immediate repayment, the money can be obtained in advance without breaking the written terms of the agreement. The payee need only *sign the note on the back (endorse it) and take it to the bank. The bank then pays the face value of the note, minus a fee for this service.* This procedure is called **discounting** a promis-

sory note. The bank goes on to collect the full amount on the note for itself when the note falls due.

For example, the $5,000 note shown in Figure 3 matures on September 1. If Gray Manufacturing Company discounts the note at its bank on July 1, the bank may give Gray $4,950. The $50 discount is the bank's interest charge to Gray for advancing funds to the company. In effect, the bank has advanced Gray the money for the two months between July 1 and September 1, using Simpson's promise to pay as the basis for the loan. The dollar amount of the discount depends on the rate of interest the bank is currently charging. In this example, a 6 percent rate is assumed; 6 percent of $5,000 is $300 per year, or $50 for two months (one-sixth of a year). The dollar amount of the discount would have been different, of course, if the bank used a different interest rate.

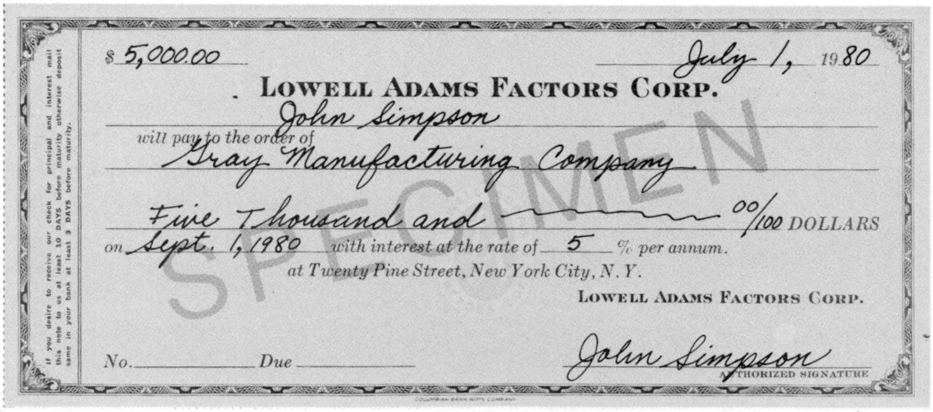

$ 5,000.00   July 1, 1980

LOWELL ADAMS FACTORS CORP.

John Simpson

will pay to the order of

Gray Manufacturing Company

Five Thousand and ⸻⸻ 00/100 DOLLARS

on *Sept. 1, 1980* with interest at the rate of __5__ % per annum. at Twenty Pine Street, New York City, N.Y.

LOWELL ADAMS FACTORS CORP.

John Simpson
AUTHORIZED SIGNATURE

No. _____ Due _____

SPECIMEN

An example of a promissory note

FIGURE 3

HOW IT'S ACTUALLY DONE

TRADE DRAFTS

There are two kinds of drafts: sight drafts and time drafts. A **sight draft** *is payable on demand (or on sight).* The customer must pay the sight draft as soon as the drawer presents it for payment. (The draft in Figure 4, for example, is a sight draft drawn up by Acme Refrigeration Company on July 1 and payable by Ace Appliances on demand.) A **time draft** *specifies a particular date in the future on which the draft must be paid.*

What happens after a draft is accepted by a customer? Once a sight draft is back in the hands of its drawer, it can be presented for immediate payment. With a time draft, the drawer has the option of holding on to the draft until the designated payment date or, more commonly, the supplier gets money for the draft at once by discounting the time draft at a bank in much the same way that a promissory note is discounted.

An example of a trade draft

FIGURE 4

sory note from a customer provides the supplier with relative peace of mind about the payment of the bill. This holds particularly true when, as in most cases, the supplier's bank, as a service, "takes up" the note when payment is due—that is, the bank serves as its client's collector. The persuasive power of a bank is generally more powerful than that of the business's own credit department. When collected by a bank, promissory notes are often repaid without any problems whatsoever.

Trade drafts and acceptances

The third category of trade credit is drafts and acceptances. Drafts and acceptances give the supplier a way of combining the attractions of open-book credit with the relative security of payment that promissory notes afford. Drafts and acceptances can be particularly use-

ful when the merchant is dealing with poor or unknown credit ratings, or with foreign customers whose credit position is difficult to find out about.

A draft, or trade draft, is like a promissory note in that it is a piece of paper exchanged between the supplier and the customer, binding the customer to pay for goods or services. But whereas a promissory note is initiated by the customer, who as we have seen is the maker of the note, a draft is initiated by the supplier. A **trade draft**, then, is *an order to pay, drawn up by the person or company* (the **drawer**) *who is to receive the money.* When the Acme Refrigeration Company, for instance, sends a shipment of refrigerators to a customer, Ace Appliances, it attaches to *the shipping document* (the **bill of lading**) a second document, the **trade draft**. This draft is *an order* for Ace (the **drawee**) *to pay a stated amount of money within a certain number of days.* Ace must sign, or "accept," the draft in order to receive the merchandise. By signing the draft, Ace agrees to pay the designated sum for the refrigerators. The *signed trade draft,* which is now a **trade acceptance**, is returned to Acme. Figure 4 shows a draft for $5,000 drawn up by the Acme Refrigeration Company and duly signed, or accepted, by Ace Appliances.

LOANS FROM BANKS AND OTHER FINANCIAL INSTITUTIONS

As important as trade credit may be to the operation (and often even the survival) of a business, there may come a time when the business has needs that trade credit cannot fill. Perhaps the business finds itself unable to pay its own debts because the customers haven't yet paid theirs. Or the managers of the business may wish to make a purchase for which they have to pay cash. At this point, the business may turn to a bank or other financial institution for short-term credit.

In what were known as the "go-go" years of the 1960s, banks and other financial institutions were inspired by the same drive to expand that took hold of other parts of the economy. They were so eager to get their money out there earning interest for them that traditionally straitlaced bankers took risks, both short-term and long-term, that would have shocked their predecessors. By the early 1970s, however, when the go-go years had ended and the economy was in a recession, financial institutions found that they were forced to write off huge sums as uncollectable debts. In New York, for instance, the Franklin National Bank, the nation's twentieth largest, with 103 branches and well over half a million depositors, found itself owing the Federal Reserve Bank of New York $1.7 billion. Not too surprisingly, the Franklin National Bank is no longer in existence.

After the banking crisis of the mid-1970s banks became a good deal more cautious—as subsequent loan applicants have discovered. Today when a financial institution makes a substantial loan, it's apt to demand—and get—an important say in the running of the borrower's business. Even the all-American sport of baseball isn't immune from the current suspicions of

---

BUILDING YOUR BUSINESS VOCABULARY

THE ABCs OF SHORT-TERM BANK LOANS

If a business needs a short-term bank loan, it can get one or the other of the following two kinds of loans:

■ A **secured loan**—*a loan that is backed by collateral.*

What's **collateral**? *Any valuable item or items that a bank can seize if a business fails to repay a loan.*

What kinds of items can a business use as collateral? Here are some:

The business's **accounts receivable**—*the amounts that are owed to it by customers who have open-book accounts.* A two-person sportswear manufacturing company, for example, may have as much as 33 percent of its assets in accounts receivable—a fairly sizable sum.

The business's **inventories**—in this case, *finished items that are ready to be sold.* For example, the small sportswear company may have 38 percent of its assets in finished goods on hand. (Note that in general, the term *inventory* can also refer to raw materials. But banks prefer to use finished-goods inventory as collateral for loans.)

Other property—*vehicles, machines, buildings, and many other types of property.* A twelve-ton dump truck, for example, may be worth $35,000; a bank loan officer may be quite willing to accept it as collateral.

■ An **unsecured loan**—*a loan that requires no collateral.* An unsecured loan may be an appealing alternative. But it has one disadvantage: the business may be required to keep part of the borrowed sum on deposit at the bank. The borrower can't use this money, yet it has to pay full interest on it.

Of course, banks are not the only possible source of loans. A business may also get a loan from a private individual. Or it may get one from another business (not a bank). We discuss these other ways of obtaining loans in the text.

Though they haven't yet started dictating on-field strategies, some banks that finance baseball teams have insisted on a say in personnel policies. Banks often review the operating procedures of other companies seeking loans as well.

banks. When State Street Bank of Boston discussed the financing of the Boston Red Sox, for example, its loan officers spoke of putting a ceiling on the total player payroll and sharply limiting players' annual pay increases—all to protect the bank's potential investment.

Despite such restrictions, however, businesses continue to rely on banks for much of their short-term capital. The loans businesses arrange with banks are of two types—secured loans and unsecured loans.

Secured bank loans

Secured loans are *loans backed by a pledge of some specific valuable item or items,* known as **collateral**, *which can be seized by the lender should the borrower fail to repay the loan.* The three main types of collateral for bank loans are accounts receivable, inventories, and other property.

PLEDGING ACCOUNTS RECEIVABLE One way of obtaining a secured loan is by pledging **accounts receivable**, which are *the amounts due the business from customers with open-book accounts.* The procedure is this: Suppose the Global Gadget Company has sold

$100,000 worth of corkscrews to various customers on open-book credit. Global can then go to a bank or commercial finance company and borrow about $75,000 against the promise that the lender will get all the payments received from these customers until Global pays off the loan. This sort of arrangement is usually handled on a **nonnotification plan**, meaning that Global's *customers are not told that their accounts have been pledged.* They continue to send their checks directly to the manufacturer of their corkscrews, and Global then forwards them to the bank or finance company.

FACTORING ACCOUNTS RECEIVABLE A less attractive alternative, for most businesses, is the *actual selling of accounts receivable to a financial institution.* This procedure is known as **factoring accounts receivable**. It leads to a **notification plan** in which *customers are informed of the situation and directed to pay their bills directly to the financial institution.* Such an arrangement means that a business's financial weakness will probably become apparent to customers and others in the field.

Raising money by either pledging or selling accounts receivable to a financial institution is an expensive proposition, almost always more costly than obtaining an ordinary unsecured bank loan. In many cases, the financial institution charges a commission of 2 percent for each open-book account handled, plus an interest rate considerably higher than the charge for a straight loan. As a result, the practice of pledging or factoring accounts receivable can run up a business's interest costs to more than 20 percent. The high cost of the money thus received, combined with the poor reputation that, in factoring, may come with it, makes many firms reluctant to use this method of raising short-term capital.

Interestingly enough, however, in the textile and apparel industries factoring is not considered as dire a recourse as in other businesses. Instead, it's seen as an acceptable means of coping with the large time gaps between the manufacture of a bolt of cloth or a dress and its sale sometime during a subsequent fashion season.

The sale, or factoring, of accounts receivable has a great impact on a supplier's customers as well as on the company itself. Consequently, **factors**, the *financial institutions that buy accounts receivable from suppliers,* can control the destinies of even the largest retail outfits. The case of the W. T. Grant collapse provides a particularly striking illustration. By late 1975 W. T. Grant, one of the country's major retail chains, was some half a billion dollars in debt. Much depended on how well the chain would do during the Christmas season. Grant decided to make a last-ditch attempt to get much-needed merchandise shipped in time for the holidays. It called a meeting of its manufacturers in September to try to persuade them to extend credit for the merchandise. But the attempt failed, because of the influence of the factors. Since the factors weren't optimistic about Grant's prospects, the suppliers expected that they would refuse to purchase receivable Grant accounts from the chain's suppliers. The suppliers counted on getting early cash transfusions from their factors, and they were forced to call off all deals with W. T. Grant. Grant went into bankruptcy soon thereafter.

PLEDGING INVENTORIES What's in store for that field of golden corn rustling in the breeze? More often than not, a few months after it's harvested it will be found in some warehouse—cooked, canned, and looked on as collateral by its packer and by the bank or lending institution that has advanced the packing company a short-term loan.

In some businesses it's common to borrow by pledging inventories as the security for a loan. If a firm has an excellent credit rating and valuable inventories, then its bank or finance company may simply accept the firm's signed statement that the inventories are pledged to the lender in the event of nonpayment. It's more usual, though, for the lender to insist that the borrower place the inventory in a warehouse, as we implied in predicting what might happen to a field of corn. *The warehouse in which the goods are stored gives the company a receipt,* called a **trust receipt**, *which the borrowing company then signs over to the bank in exchange for the loan.* Since the warehouse is not supposed to release any inventory without a trust receipt, the company must pay off its loan and get its trust receipt back in order to reclaim its inventory from the warehouse. If the company defaults on its loan, the bank can get its money back by selling the inventory.

Obviously, though, not all goods are as suitable for inventory financing as cans of corn. Highly perishable fruits and vegetables or high-fashion merchandise will lose most if not all of their value if they remain month after month in a warehouse. Financial institutions will not, therefore, make loans against trust receipts for such goods.

It should be noted that for the lending institutions, even trust receipts are not always a guarantee against fraud. Despite the fact that the warehouse is supposed to guarantee the existence of the pledged inventory, lenders have occasionally been cheated. A pledged-inventory caper on a grand scale was the Great Salad Oil Swindle of 1963. A group of banks and other financial institutions made loans against warehouse trust receipts for 161 million pounds of vegetable oils. The oils were supposedly stored in huge tanks on the Bayonne waterfront in New Jersey. When the tanks were eventually opened, it was discovered that they did indeed contain some salad oil, but only 7 million pounds of it. Considering what should have been there, one might say there was little more than enough for a side order of salad. In the end, the lenders lost $150 million.

PLEDGING OTHER PROPERTY Other forms of collateral against which loans are made are almost infinitely varied. If something has value, chances are some bank or finance institution will lend on it. The most common loans are those made against movable property, in-

FIGURE 5

An example of commercial paper

cluding automobiles, trucks, and agricultural machines. In fact, the loans are most often taken out to buy such items. When a loan is made for that purpose, the bank or finance company will sometimes require that the borrower sign a **chattel mortgage** agreement in addition to a loan agreement. Under the terms of the chattel mortgage *the movable property, along with the risk of loss, belongs to the borrower.* However, *the lender has a legal right to take possession of the property if payments are not made as specified in the loan agreement.*

Unsecured bank loans

An **unsecured loan** is one that *requires no collateral, or security.* In this type of loan the bank relies on the general credit record of the borrower. To protect themselves from defaults, most banks insist that the borrower maintain some minimum amount of money at the bank while the loan is outstanding. Such a deposit—called a **compensating balance**—means that while a borrower pays interest on the full amount of a loan, *a substantial portion of that loan is kept on deposit in the bank.*

For example, if the Hibernian National Bank requires a 20 percent compensating balance, and Ed Vogel borrows $10,000, no less than $2,000 of that amount must be kept on deposit in Vogel's account at Hibernian. In other words, although Vogel has borrowed $10,000 and is being charged interest on that amount, he has only $8,000 to actually use. More important from the bank's point of view, it has only $8,000 actually at risk. The compensating balance also has the effect of raising the real interest rate Vogel is obliged to pay. Though on paper a loan of $10,000 that requires an interest payment of $600 carries a 6 percent interest rate, Vogel is paying $600 for the use of only $8,000. That means he's really paying 7½ percent interest. Moreover, the bank is retaining use of the

$2,000 he has on deposit. Hibernian—which incidentally is one of the survivors of the banking crisis of the 60s—is thus eating its cake and having it too. Of course, should Hibernian or any other bank be taking too big a bite in demanding compensating balances, it runs the risk of dropping out of competition with other institutions. If Vogel can get his money for a lower interest rate and a smaller compensating balance, Hibernian has lost a customer.

Another important type of arrangement often made with unsecured loans is the line of credit. To eliminate the need to negotiate with the bank each time a business finds itself in need of a loan, both bank and business often get together and establish the *maximum amount of money that the bank is willing to lend the business during a specific period of time*—usually a year. The amount they decide upon is called the **line of credit**. Once it has been established, the business can automatically obtain unsecured loans for any amount up to that limit.

UNSECURED LOANS FROM OTHER BUSINESSES AND INVESTORS

When it comes to raising money, many businesses—particularly large corporations—can look much further afield than their own suppliers or even banks and lending institutions. Other businesses may have spare money, and they are often looking for a temporary spot to put it where it can increase and multiply. The company looking to borrow can take such cash in for a time; of course, it must pay to do so.

One way larger businesses borrow short-term capital from other businesses is by selling commercial paper. **Commercial paper** is *a company's promise to pay back a stated amount of money on a stated date.* Commercial paper is unsecured; behind it stands only the good credit of the business itself.

For example, a $1-million offering of General Motors Acceptance Corporation (GMAC) commercial paper is a promise by GMAC to repay $1 million to the holder of the paper ninety days from its original date. The buyer would pay a price somewhat less than $1 million. The difference between the purchase price and $1 million is the interest earned by the holder during the ninety days. Figure 5 shows an example of this form of corporate IOU.

Why doesn't GMAC simply go to a bank for the money? Its managers prefer not to, since the interest rate they must pay on commercial paper is, at the time, lower than that charged by banks for unsecured loans. Using commercial paper also saves the corporation from the compensating balance required by banks which, as we saw, makes the effective interest rate the banks charge even higher. At the time of this writing, for instance, the prime lending rate at large New York banks is 9 percent, compared to commercial-paper interest rates that are hovering between 7¾ and 8½ per-

cent. The exact rate depends on the issuer and the maturity date of the paper, which can vary anywhere from a few days to a year or even longer. Since commercial paper is generally sold in units of $100,000 or more (although occasionally it is available in lots as small as $15,000), these fraction-of-a-percent differences in the interest rate are of great significance to the borrower. (On the basis of the rates just cited, for example, the difference in interest could be $1,250 for each unit of $100,000.) What's more, commercial paper is a means of raising cash that can be relied on when banks are short of money. Such a situation occurred in 1974, when even good customers were often unable to obtain bank funds.

Who lends money to corporations by buying commercial paper? Virtually any company or individual with the necessary amounts of excess cash. The traditional purchasers are other business corporations who find themselves with a great deal of money on hand for the moment. For example, department stores are often

DIPPING INTO FLUID CASH

What if a company can't—or doesn't want to—borrow on a short-term basis? There is another source of cash, which more and more companies are indulging in as the cost of credit soars. These firms get funds by tapping **fluid cash,** *the money that companies temporarily gather in the course of their business.* It is an attractively cheap alternative to short-term financing. Some ways of using it are perfectly legal and permissible; some are in a "gray area," ethically speaking; and some are illegal and unethical.

These tactics are legal:

Take possession of cash as quickly as you can. This is the chief principle of the fluid-cash concept. To get their money as soon as they're entitled to it, many corporations have established a network of so-called **lockboxes,** which are simply *post-office boxes in strategically selected locales with good mail deliveries.* Companies instruct customers to mail their remittances to such addresses and

then arrange with a local bank to pick up and deposit those checks to the corporation's credit. In this way companies can make immediate use of cash that might otherwise have taken days of "mail-float" time to arrive at headquarters. One major Midwestern metals company established six lockboxes across the country. Its available cash was thereby increased by $2.5 million, which the company used to pay off some short-term debts.*

Put off paying bills as long as possible. This is simply the converse of the first principle of fluid-cash management. Just as a corporation can take advantage of good mail service, it can also rely on the shortcomings of the postal service in certain areas to make certain that outgoing checks go out as slowly as they possibly can. On the premise that what's not yet anyone else's is still your own, corporations have hunted out the most inaccessible of banks on which to draw checks for paying bills and debts. One West Coast food company has in-

* "Companies Gain Funds by Speeding Intakes and Slowing Outgoes," *Wall Street Journal,* July 31, 1974, p. 1.

flush with cash for a few weeks in January and February, after their customers have paid their Christmas bills and before the department store's own bills to suppliers for Easter merchandise fall due. In order to make some money on these excess funds, the stores will use them to buy one- or two-month commercial paper. Other investors include pension funds and bank trust departments, which occasionally purchase commercial paper because it's a safe investment with a high return. In that uneasy year of 1974, for example, the interest rate paid on commercial paper was a whopping 12 percent.

All in all, commercial paper is a convenient and thrifty vehicle for money-raising. But there are definite legal limitations to its use. According to government regulations, for instance, commercial paper cannot be used to finance long-term projects. The reason behind such a rule is obvious: If a corporation attempted to use commercial paper to finance anything other than current transactions—to build a new plant, for example—it could soon find itself issuing paper to cover the repayment of previous papers. Then it might issue newer papers still to cover those until, eventually, the whole shaky paper structure could be blown away in one puff by a recession.

Purchasers must be wary, too, of commercial paper issued by corporations that are not as stable as they may seem. Investors in the commercial paper issued by the Penn Central Railroad still look back on the transaction with a shudder. Given the size and importance of the corporation, commercial-paper investment had seemed a sure thing. Then, in 1974, Penn Central unexpectedly started bankruptcy proceedings in one of the largest such cases in history. Four years later the court disputes were still going on. As a result of its bankruptcy, Penn Central defaulted on its outstanding paper. Several banks that had, as third parties, guaranteed the paper might have collapsed along with the railroad if the government had not stepped in to save the situation.

creased its available cash by some $7 million by using a bank in Richmond, Virginia—a city with "horrendous" airline schedules that delay the dispatch of mail.

Of course, the simplest way to increase available cash is to pay bills only at the very last minute. According to harried credit managers, that's just what more and more businesses are doing. The money game has reached the point at which bills in **arrears** *(late in payment)* for sixty days are becoming the rule rather than the exception.

These tactics are unethical and in some cases illegal:

"Kite" a check. Even when bills are paid, there's a way some companies still manage to cling to the cash for just a bit longer. By **kiting checks**—*writing drafts on nonexistent funds and then covering them with deposits drawn on other overdrawn accounts*—some companies are able to float massive short-term loans before bringing their accounts back to earth with a cash infusion. There are, however, serious drawbacks to check-kiting. For instance, TI

Corporation, the nation's largest title insurer, was charged some years ago with mail and wire fraud after it had generated fictitious balances of more than $100 million. What went wrong? A courier took an unexpected day off, and so one of TI's overdrawn checks didn't arrive in time to cover another overdraft and the whole scheme collapsed around the company's head.*

Use the "cheapest money in town." A common, but absolutely illegal and inadvisable, business ploy is to bilk the United States government out of the income tax and Social Security money deducted from employees' paychecks. By hanging on to and using that cash until the last possible moment when it must be turned over to the government (sometimes up to four or five months after the deductions are made), a business has the use of a considerable sum without paying any interest on it at all. To repeat, however, this *is* an illegal practice, and the number of convictions for the fraud is increasing.

*"Top U.S. Title Insurer, TI Corp., Indicted for Fraud in Huge Check-Kiting Scheme," *Wall Street Journal*, January 15, 1976, p. 6.

CHAPTER REVIEW

Management experts define finance as the management function of effectively obtaining and using money. Two basic concepts in financing are assets and liabilities. Assets are the items of value that the company owns. Short-term assets, sometimes called current assets, are resources that a company can turn into cash within a year. Short-term assets include raw materials, money that is owed by other firms, time deposits, accounts receivable, and cash on hand. The faster an asset can be converted into cash, the higher its liquidity. Liabilities are debts which the company owes to other businesses or to individuals. Short-term liabilities include unpaid bills for short-term assets such as raw materials, and such liabilities as rent, salaries, and insurance premiums.

Trade credit given by one business to another is the most important source of short-term capital. Most of this credit is extended on an open-book credit basis, but some is provided through promissory notes and trade drafts.

Short-term capital can also be obtained through banks and other financial institutions. Banks make unsecured loans to many customers, usually on the basis of a prearranged line of credit. In addition, banks and commercial lending companies loan money on a secured basis against accounts receivable (which may be pledged or sold), inventories, or other property.

Some large companies raise short-term capital through the sale of commercial paper. This may be a good investment for businesses with a temporary excess of funds.

REVIEW QUESTIONS

1. What is financing? How important is financing to a company?

2. Explain short-term financing. What are the three major sources of short-term financing?

3. If two companies have the same dollar amount of assets and liabilities, how might one company be financially better off than the other?

4. What are short-term assets? Give some examples.

5. What are four problems that are basic to short-term financing?

6. Why do suppliers require promissory notes or draft acceptances from some customers?

7. Why do many businesses prefer to obtain funds by pledging accounts receivable rather than by selling them outright to a bank or other financial institution?

8. What advantages does commercial paper offer as a source of short-term capital?

KEY WORD REVIEW

revenues
stock
credit
finance
assets
liabilities
short-term finance
long-term finance
short-term (current) assets
time deposits
accounts receivable
liquidity
capital
trade credit
open-book credit
credit-rating agency
promissory note
trade draft
drawer
bill of lading
trade draft
drawee
trade acceptance
unsecured loan
compensating balance
line of credit
secured loans
collateral
accounts receivable
inventories
other property
nonnotification plan
factoring accounts receivable
notification plan
factors
trust receipt
chattel mortgage
commercial paper
fluid cash
lockboxes
arrears
kiting checks
maker
payee
discounting
sight draft
time draft

CASE 1

FINANCING A COUNTRY INN

It was circumstance more than intention that led Rodney Williams and his wife Ione into the venerable and demanding business of keeping a country inn. Back in 1967, on a skiing trip to Vermont, the Williamses bought a ramshackle farmhouse and barn sitting on thirty-seven hilly acres for $75,000. They immediately had to spend an additional $75,000 to renovate their property. To ease the financial strain, they began taking in paying guests who had come to the area to ski or, in the summer, to attend an annual music festival nearby.

Business proved steady, so Rodney—an architect by training—and Ione—an interior designer—began plowing their profits into further improvements on what had by then become the Inn at Sawmill Farm. They spent $30,000 to turn an old cider shed into a four-room guest house. Then they added a trout pond, a swimming pool, a tennis court, a garage, and an office; they extended the dining room; and they installed a three-room guest suite in the farmhouse. With most of the $70,000 profit that they made in 1977, the Williamses put in a new kitchen. The following year they took out a $200,000 mortgage from a bank, and with the loan they added four rooms to the nine in the barn. By that time, the Inn's professional staff had grown to twenty-four—with the Williamses' twenty-nine year old son serving as head chef, Rodney as host, bartender, and wine steward, and Ione as pastry maker, head housekeeper, bookkeeper, and payroll clerk.

Needless to say, the Williamses were having no trouble attracting guests.

On occasion, they have had to turn away as many as 250 customers on a Saturday night. To spend a night or more at Sawmill Farm, some people make reservations a year in advance, and then pay $80 to $100 a day for a country breakfast, an unhurried, fresh-cooked dinner, and comfortably rustic lodgings. As for the Williamses, they say they're not interested in making a lot of money from their inn. But their hard work has transformed a bunch of lonely farm buildings into a well-groomed $625,000 property that grosses in excess of $500,000 a year.

1. Which of the Williamses' assets can be described as long-term, and which as short-term?

2. Similarly, which of the Williamses' liabilities are long-term, and which are short-term?

3. What sources of short-term credit are available to innkeepers like the Williamses?

CASE 2

THE SHORT-TERM CREDIT STRATEGY OF ONE BUSINESS

Murray Siegel, a fifty-eight-year-old New Yorker who sports a neatly trimmed Vandyke beard, used to be a door-to-door egg salesman in Virginia. Today, he, his wife, and their son-in-law run a profitable clothing store that specializes in styles for "huskies" and "chubbies"—clothing-trade slang for fat boys and girls, respectively. In between Siegel's two careers came a struggle for capital and credit that most would-be merchants encounter—but that few survive.

When the egg business went bust, Siegel came back to New York and

started selling children's clothing at farmers' markets. After a lot of hard work, he managed to pull together an inventory worth about $1,000 and to sock away $1,700 in a savings account. Siegel's next move was to buy a defunct business in a seedy neighborhood for $600. But with only $1,100 in cash, Murray and his wife Gertrude were having a tough time building up an inventory for their store, which they named Murray's Outlet. Then, however, the Siegels made an important discovery: they found that on small orders, many suppliers were willing to extend credit. So rather than place large orders with just a few sources, the Siegels did the opposite. That is, they ordered a few items from a dozen or so wholesalers and were able to obtain small amounts of credit—less than $100—from each.

That tactic proved helpful enough to give Murray's Outlet the start it needed: it grossed $56,000 in its first year, $76,000 the next year. Still, it took a full decade for the store to gross $500,000, which made it possible for the Siegels to borrow more than $10,000. That milestone was passed in 1962, and many others have followed. Murray's Outlet grossed more than $1.5 million in 1978, and Murray and Gertrude were by then running not only the original store, but eleven others as well.

1. What is the importance of short-term credit to a clothing retailer? Why is it so necessary?

2. How did placing small orders with many suppliers—rather than buying in bulk from just a few sources—help Murray's Outlet get started?

3. How could Murray Siegel have used his inventory to obtain financing? What were the risks involved?

12

LONG-TERM FINANCE

Money is a rare commodity. Everyone wants it; no one has enough. If you've ever been a couple of dollars short just when you've seen the perfect sweater or that album you've been wanting, you know the feeling.

Businesses need and want money as much as you do—and that holds true for even the biggest businesses. But business has an advantage over individuals in raising money. They can offer the investor or lender a chance for large profits, and thus they can raise sums that are comparatively large—and sometimes truly gigantic. In this chapter we'll look at some of the ways businesses raise money over long periods of time, and some of the long-term choices financial managers face.

WHAT WILL THIS CHAPTER FOCUS ON?

After reading the material in this chapter, you will understand and be able to discuss:

■ the two major methods of long-term financing—obtaining debt capital and obtaining equity capital

■ the advantages and disadvantages of stocks and bonds

■ the ways in which common and preferred stocks differ

■ the three major considerations that go into making a financing decision—the advantages and disadvantages of the various modes of obtaining capital, the needs of the particular company, and the state of the stock and bond markets

■ the types of situation in which short-term investments are more appropriate than long-term investments, and vice versa

■ the various types of tong-term financing institutions

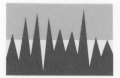 It takes a great deal of money to build a fifty-story building, or set up an automobile assembly line, or drill for oil from an offshore rig. Few businesses—including those that are among the largest in the world—have immediate access to the amounts of cash necessary for such undertakings. How then do they raise the money for the kind of structures and projects vital to their futures? In the last chapter, we saw that there is a variety of ways in which businesses can tide themselves over financially for the short term. Similarly, there is a range of different ways companies go about the problem of filling long-term needs.

As we mentioned in Chapter 11, some corporations are so successful that they can tap *profits earned and accumulated in previous years,* or **undistributed profits**. Such profits really belong to the owners of the company, the shareholders, but are left in the business for future needs. In 1977, for example, IBM earned about $2.7 billion after taxes, but it distributed only some $1.5 billion of this to its shareholders. The remainder, or $1.2 billion of undistributed profits, was kept to pay for new laboratories and factories.[1]

IBM, however, is pretty much in a class of its own. It has a far greater capacity for financing its operations from internal sources than most companies do. Most businesses must fill at least a part of their long-term financial needs by obtaining capital from outside sources. They may obtain long-term loans from private investors, selling a form of corporate IOU known as bonds. (*The capital obtained by selling bonds* is known as **debt capital**.) Or they may sell stock—shares of ownership in the company. (*The funds derived from selling stocks* are known as **equity capital**.) Sometimes a company will do both; managers must decide on the proportion of debt capital to equity capital that suits the company's needs.

An interesting example of long-term financing for a huge project—one of the biggest ever, in fact—is the story behind the building of the Alaska pipeline. Imagine a structure crossing the state of Alaska from the oil-rich North Slope south to the port of Valdez, 800 miles away. Spanning hills and valleys across miles of frozen tundra, such a pipeline would make available some 9.4 billion barrels of oil worth roughly $122 billion. It would be daring and innovative in its concep-

tion and construction. And it would be costly in the extreme—about $9.3 billion. For such an undertaking long-term finance would be the only solution.

Under direction of a central operating company stationed in Alaska, various oil companies agreed to finance a percentage of the pipeline construction for the same percentage of ownership in the completed pipeline. Atlantic-Richfield took on 21 percent of the financing burden, Exxon 20 percent, and four other companies a much smaller percent. But the biggest buyer was a relatively small company—Standard Oil of Ohio (Sohio)—that in partnership with British Petroleum (BP) pitched in 49 percent. (As part of the arrangement, BP now controls 51 percent of Sohio's stock.) Ranking twenty-third in its field before the completion of the pipeline, Sohio will catapult into third place in terms of domestic oil production as the oil begins flowing. It is also in the enviable position of owning bigger reserves of domestic oil than any of its larger competitors. But how did this fairly small company manage to contribute its share in this vast Arctic venture?

From the start, Sohio's management knew that the company's own cash resources couldn't begin to cover the expense of such a project. Looking elsewhere, they were only able to raise several hundred million dollars through short-term arrangements—revolving credit agreements and the sale of commercial paper. Meanwhile, pipeline construction was costing them $4 million *per day,* and the days were flying by. Arguments with regulatory agencies, protests by environmentalists, and technical obstacles that came up in connection with untried construction methods all delayed the project and cost Sohio more money at the same time. A new source of money for the job had to be found—and quickly, if Sohio were to survive.

After a series of frantic negotiations, the company managed to arrange for some long-term financing at almost the last minute. First, the company issued and sold over one million shares of common stock in the project. Then it located a number of investors willing to make $1.75 billion worth of long-term loans to the company. Just six weeks before the company's capital was due to run dry, Sohio managed to raise sufficient cash to complete the project. Of course, today the company is very much in debt, having borrowed a total of some $4.5 billion. Profits, however, more than offset

the debt obligations that Sohio must meet every year.[2]

Long-term financing is a major part of the United States economy. In February 1978, for example, it accounted for fully 20 percent of the country's entire gross national product.[3] In this chapter we'll take a look at some of the most important aspects of long-term financing, including debt and equity capital and the way each is obtained. We'll discuss the pros and cons of each, and the factors financial managers must consider when deciding how to raise capital for long-term needs.

BONDS: BASIC CONCEPTS

WHAT IS A BOND?

A **bond** is *a certificate indicating that its issuer has borrowed a set sum of money from the bondholder.*

San Francisco's Golden Gate Bridge is more than a magnificent piece of engineering; it's a prime example of long-term finance put to good use. The bridge was built from the proceeds of a $35 million bond sale in 1932, plus bond issues every year thereafter until 1971, when the last construction issue was retired. Investors received a total of $38,821,307 in interest.

When a corporation raises money by selling an issue of bonds, it usually sells parts of the issue, or individual bonds, to many different buyers. For instance, an issue of $300 million AT&T bonds may consist of thousands of individual bonds. Each of these bonds has a **denomination**, *the amount of the loan represented by one bond.* Bonds sold by corporations are usually available in $1,000 denominations. More expensive bonds are in denominations of $5,000, $10,000, $50,000, and $100,000.

A bond usually shows the date when *the full amount of the bond,* the **principal**, must be repaid. That date is called the **maturity date**. A bond is is-

An example of a bond

Table 1 Types of Secured and Unsecured Bonds

Type	Backing	Example
SECURED		
First Mortgage	Real estate	$25 million Iowa Electric Light and Power Company first mortgage bonds due December 1, 2007. Proceeds used to repay outstanding commercial paper used primarily for construction. Rated "A."
Equipment Trust	Capital equipment	$40 million Union Tank Car Company equipment trust certificates due December 1, 1987. Certificates secured by equipment costing $53.3 million. Proceeds used to retire $33.2 million of indebtedness and to buy 267 rail cars. Rated "A."
Mortgage-backed	First mortgages on residential real estate	$100 million Home Savings and Loan Association mortgage-backed bonds. Due November 15, 1983. Secured by mortgage notes, which must be secured by mortgages constituting first liens on one-to-four residential dwelling units. Rated "AAA."
UNSECURED		
Debenture	Faith and credit of borrower	Leading corporations such as AT&T, Dow Chemical, and U.S. Steel.

sued for a fairly long period, usually for ten years or more. Many large corporations sell bonds whose maturity dates are thirty-five or forty years.

A bond provides for **interest**, *payment that the issuer makes to the bondholder in return for the use of the borrowed money.* Thus, the bondholder of a $1,000 denomination 8 percent bond that pays interest on January 15 and July 15 could expect to receive $40 on each of these dates.

WHAT BACKS A BOND ISSUE?

If you want to borrow money from a local bank, your banker will require **collateral** for the loan—*a valuable item or items that can be seized if you fail to repay the loan.* The car you purchase with the loan is the collateral behind the typical automobile loan. If you do not make the payments as they are due, the bank will repossess the car. Occasionally, however, banks make personal loans to individuals with good credit standings without specific collateral, merely on their signatures.

Similar arrangements exist for issuing bonds.

Some issues, called **secured bonds**, *offer bondholders specific backing for their bonds.* This backing, or security, consists of property of one kind or another that will pass to the bondholders if the issuer does not live up to the terms of the agreement. The security can be a mortgage on a piece of real estate or a claim to other assets, such as freight cars, airplanes, or plant equipment owned by a company. Other issues, called **unsecured bonds**, are *not backed by any specific collateral, but only by the general good name of the issuing company.* If the bond-issuing company fails, the bondholders have a claim on the assets, but only after creditors with specific collateral have been paid.

At first glance, *unsecured bonds,* or **debentures**, may appear to be riskier than secured bonds. However, many unsecured bonds are issued by the best-known borrowers. Their **credit rating**, or *ability to get loans based on their past financial record*, is so good that they need not offer specific security to get investors to buy their bonds. American Telephone & Telegraph, Dow Chemical, and U.S. Steel are among major corporations in the United States that issue only debentures. Examples of secured and unsecured bonds are shown in Table 1.

CLIPPING FOR FUN AND PROFIT

In films and novels from the 1920s and 1930s a strange breed of little old ladies swathed in lavender and furs and rakish playboys in checkered tweeds were often referred to—usually in sneering terms—as "coupon clippers." This definitely did *not* mean they collected the supermarket coupons with which we're all so familiar. Instead, these people were the owners of **coupon bonds**. Such bonds *indicated that they were payable upon maturity "to the bearer."* The bonds were called coupon bonds because they came with a strip of attached coupons, each of which represented one interest payment. On each interest payment date, the holder of the bond would cut the appropriate coupon and use it to collect the interest due. The phrase "clipping coupons" thus refers to the practice of cutting off

and submitting those valuable little scraps of paper.

The major drawback of coupon bonds is that the corporation that issues them has no record of who owns the bonds and, therefore, must assume that they belong to the persons holding them.

In recent years registered bonds have become more popular than coupon bonds. **Registered bonds** *bear the name of the owner, who is also registered with the issuer of the bond.* Interest checks are mailed to the bondholder when they are due, making coupons unnecessary.

Today, many corporations will supply bonds to purchasers in either coupon or registered form. Holders of registered bonds benefit in case of loss or theft. Coupon bonds, on the other hand, require less paperwork if the bondholder decides to sell them. They are also fun, as the coupon clippers of the old days would probably attest.

HOW ARE INTEREST RATES ON BONDS SET?

A look at the financial section of any newspaper will show that some corporations are selling new bonds at an interest rate of two or three percentage points higher than other companies. Yet the terms of the bonds they are offering seem similar. In early 1978 most high-quality corporate bonds of industrial companies were yielding about 8 to $8\frac{1}{2}$ percent. Lower-grade industrial bonds were yielding up to 10 percent. Tax-exempt bonds—on which no tax is paid on income from the interest earned—were yielding about 6 percent.

How can we explain these different interest rates? What determines the interest rate that an issuer will have to pay at a given time to persuade investors to buy bonds? Basically, the answer is this: The bonds of a borrower (that is, a company issuing the bond) that is in a strong financial position naturally represent less risk to the investor (the buyer of the bond) than those of a weak company. As a result, a corporation with excellent prospects of earning enough money in future years to pay both the interest on the bonds and the principal at maturity can afford to offer bonds at a relatively low interest rate. A risky, weak issuer of bonds has to offer higher interest rates to attract buyers.

Are bonds a good risk or a bad one?

It would be almost impossible for any one investor to be able to judge the financial health of the thousands of corporations that issue bonds every year. Fortunately, there are experts to supply that evaluation. Several private independent rating services, including Moody's and Standard & Poor's, rate bonds for the amount of risk they offer. Moody's ratings vary from Aaa to C and Standard & Poor's from AAA to D. In both rating systems the highest rating is naturally given to bonds issued by companies with earnings sufficiently high and stable to provide exceptional protection for interest and principal. The lowest rating is assigned to bonds issued by companies that may very well default. Between these two extremes are bonds that—because their companies' earnings are less reliable than the triple-A group—present a slight, moderate, or considerable risk.

Such differences in rating have proved to be of increasing importance in recent years. Income from the interest on bonds, for example, is often affected by inflation. A drop in the purchasing power of the dollar can mean hardship for people—such as those living on pensions—whose daily comfort depends on the wise investment of their capital. (In our chapter on personnel management we have already seen something of the care that, thanks to ERISA, is devoted to the investment of retirement funds.) These effects of inflation, combined with a general tightening of credit in recent years, have probably benefited no one more than the rating organizations themselves. The demand for their services is at its highest level ever: in the three years from 1974 to 1977 Moody's corporate debt staff increased by more than 65 percent.[4]

The ratings services have become so influential that it's now common for their opinions to either make or break a bond issue. The case of a recent municipal bond that Moody's didn't favor illustrates the point. In 1976 Moody's determined that New York City bonds issued by the Municipal Assistance Corporation (MAC) rated only a B. In other words, Moody's was telling the investment world that MAC bonds "lacked characteristics of a desirable investment." Not surprisingly, investors heeded Moody's warning and stayed away from the bond issue. The city's financial guardians were so angered at what they termed Moody's improper and false rating that they threatened to take the rating service to court. Moody's, however, stood firm and refused to change the rating, adding considerably to the city's fiscal woes.[5]

CHANGES IN INTEREST RATES FROM YEAR TO YEAR

In the 1940s AT&T sold bond issues with interest rates of $2\frac{3}{4}$ percent. But in the 1970s bond issues from the same company paid 9 percent or more. What caused this striking increase? Interest rates are influenced not only by inflation but also by overall business conditions—including how much money is required at the moment in the economy for housing, business expansion, and government borrowing. In the 1940s bank interest rates were very low: home mortgages were available at 4 percent and savings accounts were paying less than 3 percent. Thus it was possible then to sell

Aaa corporate bonds with relatively low interest, such as AT&T was offering. In the 1970s, however, home mortgages had risen to 9 or 10 percent, and savings accounts earned as much as $7\frac{1}{2}$ percent. Consequently, even triple-A companies were forced to pay as much as 9 percent simply to get investors to buy their bonds.

HOW IS THE PRINCIPAL PAID BACK?

A corporation that sells bonds must repay its bondholders. The simplest arrangement is to repay the bonds at maturity date. Some issues consist of **term bonds**, in which *all the bonds mature at the same time.* The $100-million Southwest Bell Telephone $4\frac{3}{4}$ percent bonds of 1992 will all come due in 1992. Another type of issue consists of **serial bonds**, which *mature at different times.* In 1974, for example, the Philadelphia Parking Authority issued $5.6 million worth of serial bonds to help pay for the building of an airport parking facility. Of these bonds, $175,000 will mature in 1978, $190,000 in 1979, $200,000 in 1980, and additional amounts each year through 1994.

Serial bonds provide issuers with a convenient schedule of repayment that relieves them of the need to pay off an entire issue in any one year. Another way of accomplishing this objective is through a **sinking fund**. When a corporation issues a bond payable by a sinking fund, it must *set aside a certain sum of money each year to "sink," or pay off, the debt.* This money is either used to buy in and retire a few bonds each year from investors, or it is set aside to accumulate until the issue matures.

Calling and converting

With some bond issues *a corporation retains the right to pay off the bonds before maturity.* Bonds containing this condition are known as **callable**, or **redeemable**, **bonds**. Why would a business want to pay off its debts before it must? The answer is, to save money. As we have seen, bond interest rates rise and fall. If a corporation issues bonds when interest rates are high and then finds that interest rates have fallen, it may want to call in its high-interest bonds and pay them off by selling a new issue at a lower interest rate.

For example, ITT Financial Corporation recently sold a $100-million issue of bonds at $8\frac{1}{2}$ percent, maturing in 2002. The bonds are callable after 1987. If interest rates should decline to $5\frac{1}{2}$ percent by 1987, ITT could call in the issue. To obtain the funds to repay the bondholders, they could sell a new issue of bonds at $5\frac{1}{2}$ percent. Thus ITT would save three percentage points each year on the interest on $100 million, or $3 million a year. For the fifteen years from 1987 to 2002 the total savings would be $45 million.[6]

Occasionally when a fall in the interest rate is particularly spectacular, a company will try to get its bondholders to part with the bonds even before the date at which the bonds are callable. To do so, companies have to offer their bondholders a premium on the price of the bond. For instance, when interest rates fell in 1977, Mountain State Telephone & Telegraph, part of the Bell System, offered to pay a tempting $112.84 for $100 bonds it had issued at $9\frac{3}{4}$ percent, due in 2012. This was done well before the call date of August 1, 1979, when the redemption price was to be $107.78. From Mountain's point of view the deal was worth making, since it would relieve the company from paying the high $9\frac{3}{4}$ percent interest rate for the two years left until the call date.[7]

Another way for a corporation to pay off bonds is to repay them with stock rather than with money. *Bonds that may be paid off with stock* are called **convertible bonds**. The actual decision to accept stock or money is left up to the bondholder. For example, several years ago Philip Morris sold an issue of $1,000, 6 percent bonds due in 1994. A purchaser would receive $60 a year and get back the original $1,000 loan in 1994. The bonds were convertible, so that the bondholder could exchange each bond for approximately seventy-two shares of common stock in Philip Morris. When the bonds were first issued, the common stock was selling at about $12 per share. The price of the stock went up to $50 per share in a few years. At that point, a bondholder might well have decided to convert a bond into seventy-two shares, which could then be sold for $3,600.

Convertible bonds are popular with borrowing companies and investors alike. They make a bond issue easier to sell because they give the investors an opportunity to share potential profits. Because convertibles are considered desirable by investors, they can be sold at lower interest rates. Of course, the issuers of the bonds like this. In addition, convertible bonds may be used by a corporation to sell stock at prices higher than they currently command on the open market. The corporation sets the conversion price a percentage above the market price, which, of course, means that fewer shares are issued at conversion.

Finally, the cash obtained through issuing convertible bonds is generally inexpensive to the issuer. AT&T, for example, issued $4.2 billion in convertible debentures during the course of a decade in the 1940s and 1950s. The money raised was used to upgrade the corporation's facilities. With improved facilities AT&T stock became more desirable than ever. Consequently, about 80 percent of the bondholders converted their bonds, thereby canceling the debts. AT&T thus raised money almost free of charge, without having to make the unwise move of throwing a huge block of its shares on the market and thereby decreasing their value. Of course, had AT&T not prospered, the holders of its bonds could simply have gone on collecting their regular interest payments until the maturity date of the issue and the return of the principal.[8]

TAX-FREE BONDS

There are certain bonds, known as **tax-free bonds**, which *enable an investor to earn an income that is legally exempt from federal income taxes*. This feature is an extremely attractive one: a tax-free yield of 6 percent may be the equivalent of a 10 percent yield, or more depending on the investor's income bracket, from a regular corporate bond on which income tax must be paid. Investors in high tax brackets benefit particularly from buying tax-free bonds. And with inflation increasing, more and more Americans are finding themselves in relatively high tax brackets.

The most traditional tax-free source of investment income is the **municipal bond**. *It is issued by a town, city, state, port authority, territory, or the like and used to finance new public services such as housing, schools, roads, or power plants.* Municipal bonds' most important characteristic is that the interest they pay to bondholders is exempt from federal income taxes—something *not* true of federal bonds or savings certificates. The market in municipal bonds has grown rapidly. In 1970, for instance, long-term municipal debts

outstanding totaled just over $144 billion. Six years later, the figure was almost $249 billion.[9]

An interesting variation on the municipal bond theme is **industrial-revenue bonds**. These bonds are something of a cross between corporation bonds and those issued for purely municipal purposes; they are *sold by cities and states to finance* private *industrial development in their own localities*. The idea behind such financing is that growth in industry is for the local good, particularly in terms of jobs and tax revenue. The federal government limits bonds of this type to issues of no more than $5 million.

A more recent alternative open to investors is a category of tax-free bonds actually issued by corporations themselves—**pollution-control bonds**, *authorized by the Congress in 1968 to help companies keep up to date in environmental technology*. In 1974, for example, Exxon Corporation sold $110 million worth of tax-free bonds at 5.9 percent to help pay for pollution-control facilities at its Baton Rouge operation. Bondholders of that issue thus enjoy a generous tax-free return on their investments, and Exxon has been able to meet pollution-control standards without using its own capital.[10]

STOCKS: BASIC CONCEPTS

WHAT ARE STOCKS?

Stocks are, simply, *shares of ownership in a company*. Thus a *purchaser of stock* (or **stockholder**) is also a **shareholder**—in other words, a *part-owner of the business*. The **stock certificate** that a shareholder receives is *evidence of that ownership*. Each certificate shows the name of the shareholder, the number of shares of stock owned, and the special characteristics of the stock.

The number of shares of stock that a corporation can sell is specified in its original corporate charter. This number is based on the amount of equity capital (capital obtained through the sale of stock) the corporation will require and on the price of each share that it sells. For instance, if an infant corporation decides that it needs $1 million in equity capital, it might

A certificate of common stock

divide itself into one million shares, each of which will be sold for $1. The *maximum number of shares into which a business can be divided* is called the **authorized stock**. In theory, all of these shares may be sold at once. What often happens, however, is that the corporation will sell only part of its authorized stock. *The part sold and held by stockholders* is called **issued stock**; *as yet unsold stock* is referred to as **unissued stock**. In 1977, for example, IBM had 162.5 million shares authorized. Of this total, 147.5 million shares were issued and about 15 million remained unissued.[11]

Many stock certificates show a *stated amount*, or **par value**. To illustrate, a stock certificate might show a par value of $5, determined by dividing the total capital of the company ($5 million) by the number of authorized shares (1 million). A stock that *does not carry a printed dollar amount on the certificate* is called **no-par stock**. Many companies *distribute part of their profits to their shareholders;* these distributions are called **dividends**.

PREFERRED STOCK

There are two types of stock that a corporation may issue. *Preferred stock,* as the name implies, refers to a class of stock that gives its holders certain preferences or special privileges. Holders of *common stock* do not have these privileges. Preferences vary from one corporation to another. In general, all **preferred stocks** *have preference over common stock in at least two areas:*

1. *They are preferred as to dividends.* Dividends on preferred stocks must be paid before any dividends are paid on common shares.

This announcement is neither an offer to sell nor a solicitation of an offer to buy any of these Securities. The offer is made only by the Prospectus.

Not a New Issue

1,500,000 Shares

Avon Products, Inc.

Capital Stock
(par value $.50)

Price $61⅝ a Share

Copies of the Prospectus may be obtained in any State from only such of the undersigned as may legally offer these Securities in compliance with the securities laws of such State.

MORGAN STANLEY & CO. *Incorporated*	E. F. HUTTON & COMPANY INC.
THE FIRST BOSTON CORPORATION	MERRILL LYNCH WHITE WELD CAPITAL MARKETS GROUP *Merrill Lynch, Pierce, Fenner & Smith Incorporated*
DEAN WITTER REYNOLDS INC.	BACHE HALSEY STUART SHIELDS *Incorporated*
BLYTH EASTMAN DILLON & CO. *Incorporated* DILLON, READ & CO. INC.	DONALDSON, LUFKIN & JENRETTE *Securities Corporation*
DREXEL BURNHAM LAMBERT *Incorporated* KIDDER, PEABODY & CO. *Incorporated*	LAZARD FRERES & CO.
LEHMAN BROTHERS KUHN LOEB *Incorporated*	PAINE, WEBBER, JACKSON & CURTIS *Incorporated*
SMITH BARNEY, HARRIS UPHAM & CO. *Incorporated*	WERTHEIM & CO., INC.
BEAR, STEARNS & CO.	SHEARSON HAYDEN STONE INC.

August 10, 1978

"Tombstone" advertisement for a stock offering

2. *They are preferred as to assets.* If a corporation fails, preferred stockholders have the right to receive their share of whatever assets are left (after the corporation's debts have been paid) before common stockholders receive anything.

How are dividends paid?

The amount of the dividend on a preferred stock is usually specified in its name. It can be stated either as a percentage or as a dollar amount. Where the dividend is stated as a percentage, this refers to a percentage of the par value given on the face of the certificate. For example, Koppers Company has a $100 par value 4 percent preferred stock. Each share of this stock pays a dividend of 4 percent of $100, $4 a year. Where the name of the issue carries a dollar amount, this is the annual dividend on the preferred stock. Thus General Motors $5 preferred pays an annual dividend of $5 a share.

Most preferred stock is **cumulative preferred**. This means that *if a corporation does not pay the designated dividend in one period, the unpaid dividends accumulate.* The company must pay this accumulation before it can pay any dividends on its common stock. For example, the General Motors $5 preferred is cumulative. Let us assume that GM omitted paying the $5 dividend in 1980 and 1981. The company would not be able to pay any common dividends in those two years. It also could not pay any common dividends in 1982 until it paid $15 in dividends on preferred stock ($10 accumulation plus $5 current).

What if a company booms?

A small number of preferred stocks include special provisions that will benefit the preferred shareholder if the company booms. As we have seen, the dividend on most preferred stocks is limited to the stated amount.

STOCKS AND BONDS COMPARED

Stocks differ from bonds in several important ways. The differences may be explained as follows:

1. *Stocks show ownership; bonds show debt.* A stockholder buys part ownership in the company, whereas a bondholder lends money to the company.

2. *No principal is repaid with stocks; principal is repaid upon maturity with bonds.* Stock represents ownership, which continues indefinitely. When a company sells stock, it does not have to refund money to the shareholder at any future time. Bonds, on the other hand, reach a date of maturity. At this time the company is required to return funds to the bondholder.

After this has been paid and the dividends have been paid on common stock, whatever money is left over is retained by the company. **Participating preferreds**, however, *allow the holder to receive a further dividend if there is still money left.*

Convertible preferreds offer another way for the preferred shareholder to benefit if the corporation profits. The conversion feature is similar to that of convertible bonds. *A holder of convertible preferred stocks has the option to convert preferred into common stock of the corporation.* Conversion is desirable if the value of the common stock rises above the value of the preferred. From the corporation's point of view, inclusion of a convertibility clause makes a preferred issue more attractive to prospective buyers.

What are the voting rights of shareholders?

Generally it is the common shareholders who exercise control over the management of the company. Preferred shareholders have much less control. In some companies, preferred shareholders have no voting power at all. More commonly, however, they receive limited voting privileges. These usually involve matters that directly concern their rights, such as a decision to sell off a major part of the company or to change a provision of the charter that involves the preferred stock.

COMMON STOCK

Like preferred stock, common stock represents equity in, or ownership of, a corporation. Unlike preferred shareholders, however, common stockholders enjoy no special privileges as far as dividends or assets are concerned. **Common stock** is *stock that has last claim on distributed profits.* It never carries a stated dividend and its dividends are never cumulative.

What determines dividends on common stock?

Fundamentally, dividends are determined simply by the preferences of the board of directors in charge of the company. There is nothing in any law that states a corporation must distribute to its shareholders any

---

3. *Shareholders may receive dividends; bondholders must receive interest.* A shareholder is not legally entitled to any regular payments. It is true that many companies distribute part of their profits to their shareholders. These distributions are called *dividends.* The board of directors of the company decides whether dividend payments will be made. Generally the board cannot be sued if it does not pay a dividend as it can if it misses an interest payment on a bond. Because bonds represent debt, a company has a legal obligation to pay the stated interest on them at regular intervals.

4. *Dividends are paid, if at all, after taxes; interest on bonds is paid out before taxes.* Under the present tax laws of the United States, the money that a company pays out in stock dividends is treated quite differently from the interest payments on its bonds. Dividends are paid out of whatever money is left after the payment of income taxes. Say a corporation earns $2 million in a year. Given the current corporate federal income tax rate, 46 percent for earning over $100,000, the corporation would have only about $1 million available for dividend payments. Interest on bonds, however, is paid out before a corporation pays its income tax. A corporation earning $2 million a year would have this entire amount available for interest payments.

5. *Stockholders have a say in running the company; bondholders do not.* Under most circumstances, as long as bond interest and other requirements are being met, bondholders have no management rights. They do not participate in the election of boards of directors. The management of a corporation is the right of the owners or stockholders. They exercise this right by voting for the board of directors.

THE BUNNY GOES WITHOUT

Throughout the 1960s Hugh Hefner's Playboy Enterprises was one of the most glamorous of glamor stocks. Based on a best-selling magazine for men, the company had expanded into clubs, restaurants, merchandising, and hotels. There seemed to be no end in sight for ever-increasing profits.

Just a few short years later, however, the Playboy bubble had burst. Sales of the magazine were down, as was its advertising revenue. And many of the company's diversifications—including its movie ventures—were fairly dismal failures. Profits in fact dipped so sharply that at one point they were lower than the already declared per-share dividend. To make up for this sad state of affairs and to ensure that Playboy's shareholders would get their dividends, chairman and founder Hefner—who also owned a substantial block of the Playboy stock—declined to accept his own dividends.

It was the Playboy Philosopher's finest hour.

percentage at all of its cash on hand during the normal course of business. At ABC, for example, despite recent earnings of $6 per share (up from little more than $1 per share not too long ago) the dividend paid was only 75 cents per share.[12] There is nothing that says the stockholders are entitled to share the wealth in the form of dividends, much as they would like to.

Companies often have legitimate reasons for failing to declare a dividend, or keeping the size of dividends down to a minimum. In the case of a small, young company, for instance, it's only natural to put all the profits back into the business. By so doing, the company can build and grow while keeping expensive outside financing down to the lowest possible amounts. It's usually not until a company is fairly well established that it will declare any dividends at all. Control Data Corporation, for example, was for years one of the most successful new companies anywhere. It only recently decided to declare its first dividend, a 15-cent-per-share initial annual payment.[13] Caution in the paying out of profits can do much to build up a com-

pany. On a national scale, such a policy can help the economy as well: business expansion ultimately puts more money in circulation. In fact, in times of recession the federal government has been known to set limits on the dividends corporations can pay. (This happened, for example, in 1971, when the economy was in recession.)

Stock splits

A dividend is not, however, the only thing a corporation can offer its shareholders. An increasingly popular alternative is a **stock split**, a procedure whereby the *company doubles (or triples, or whatever) each share in the business that each stock certificate represents* (see Figure 1). For instance, an investor holding fifty shares of Blue Bell, a work-clothes manufacturer, suddenly became the possessor of one hundred shares instead when Blue Bell split its stock in 1972. While the split had no immediate effect on the shareholders (since dividends, and market price, were split as well), its impact on the future was tremendous. Following the Blue Bell split, the market price of one new, split share rose from $35 to $43.[14] By selling some or all of the split shares, the investor could realize a handsome profit.

Moreover, splits benefit the companies themselves, since the more shares a company has outstanding, the less affected they are by the ups and downs of the market. Splits, too, have the advantage of making undesirable power plays or mergers that much more difficult. The more shares outstanding, the tougher it is for any one individual or group to accumulate a controlling interest in the company. In sum, share-

When a stock split occurs, the number of shares represented by each stock certificate multiplies. For example, when a company splits its shares in half, each old share is worth two new shares. A block of one hundred old shares becomes two hundred new shares, and if each of the original shares was worth $2, each new share will be worth $1 initially.

FIGURE 1

holders and directors alike tend to be happy with stock splits.

Why does common stock attract investors?

Common-stock dividends are far from being as sure a thing as either bond interest or preferred dividends. The opportunities they offer for financial gain, however, make common stocks attractive to many investors. Common shareholders have the **residual right** to company earnings. That is, *when the prior claims of the bondholders and preferred shareholders have all been met, the remaining, or residual, earnings are available for the common shareholders.* Though the actual dividend payments from these earnings depend on the vote of the board of directors, over the years shareholders in many companies with growing earnings have seen the dividends on their stock soar—and the value of the stocks themselves grow tremendously as well.

Unfortunately for investors, this residual right to earnings works both ways. If a company's earnings decline, bondholders and preferred shareholders are at the front of the line in collecting their rights. They have first claim to whatever earnings there may be. Dividends on common stock may be reduced or eliminated entirely, and the price of the common stock will probably fall. In such cases, the common shareholders suffer the greatest losses. For example, consider the

unfortunate situation of an investor who started 1977 as the owner of $10,000 worth of shares in Eastman Kodak, when the stock was selling at almost $87 per share. Although the company had done well over a long period of time, the year 1977 was not an especially good time for the camera maker and film processor. It was being challenged by low-priced competing products, both American and Japanese, and it was also being sued for violations of antitrust regulations. Investors' confidence in the company decreased, the demand for its stock fell off, and stock prices fell as well—to a low of just under $49. By the year's end the worth of the block of shares had fallen about 40 percent; an investment originally worth $10,000 was now worth $6,000.[15]

While such spectacular losses are always possible with common stock, so are spectacular gains. And it's for this reason that many investors are drawn to common shares rather than preferred shares. They are also attracted because common-stock ownership guarantees the investors at least some voice in company affairs. Usually, the investors' voice is heard on such business-related subjects as the choice of company management, when the stockholders hold their annual election of the board of directors. Occasionally, however, stockholders deal with more dramatic issues. On one highly publicized occasion in 1977 the shareholders of the Kennecott Copper Corporation, who didn't approve of their director's plan to acquire the Carborundum Company, brought suit against their own management to halt the acquisition. According to the shareholders, Kennecott's offer for Carborundum's stock was "imprudent," "reckless," and due in part to the managers' own wish to keep themselves in office.[16] Nonetheless, the acquisition took place.

The stockholders of a corporation can help keep other corporations from grabbing their own company. Such was the case when Foremost-McKesson was threatened with a takeover bid by an industrialist famed for his raids on smaller companies. In an attempt to prevent the takeover, Foremost-McKesson management dug into the financial background of the raider. Some of what the management found appeared in full-page ads in *The Wall Street Journal* as a warning to stockholders not to sell out. The damaging information persuaded the stockholders to foil the takeover bid.[17]

In recent years stock ownership has even become

WHAT HAPPENS IN
A STOCK SPLIT?

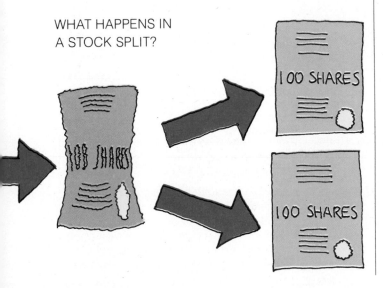

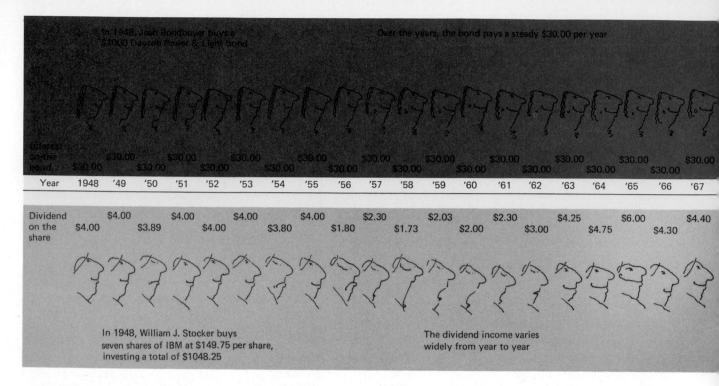

In 1948, Jean Bondbuyer buys a $1000 Dayton Power & Light bond

Over the years, the bond pays a steady $30.00 per year

Year	1948	'49	'50	'51	'52	'53	'54	'55	'56	'57	'58	'59	'60	'61	'62	'63	'64	'65	'66	'67
Interest on the bond	$30.00	$30.00	$30.00	$30.00	$30.00	$30.00	$30.00	$30.00	$30.00	$30.00	$30.00	$30.00	$30.00	$30.00	$30.00	$30.00	$30.00	$30.00	$30.00	$30.00
Dividend on the share	$4.00	$4.00	$3.89	$4.00	$4.00	$3.80	$4.00	$1.80	$2.30	$1.73	$2.03	$2.00	$2.30	$3.00	$4.25	$4.75	$6.00	$4.30	$4.40	

In 1948, William J. Stocker buys seven shares of IBM at $149.75 per share, investing a total of $1048.25

The dividend income varies widely from year to year

a platform from which stockholders can speak out on important social issues. During the Vietnam war, for example, shareholders in Dow Chemical, a producer of napalm, sought to halt the company's involvement in making war materials. And in the past few years activist stockholders have brought their companies to task on such issues as political corruption, destruction of the environment, and investment in apartheid-ruled South Africa. Today numerous religious organizations and other socially conscious groups are among the large investors at the stockholders' meeting. More than ever before, management is often obliged to be responsive to stockholders on a variety of social issues.

MAKING CHOICES IN LONG-TERM FINANCE

As we have seen, when a corporation decides it's in need of long-term finance, there are three major roads it can take: it can sell bonds, preferred stock, or common stock. Of course, these alternatives are not mutually exclusive. Sohio, for instance, when it needed money to build its Alaska pipeline, chose to sell common stocks as well as bonds.

But often the company must devote its major efforts to only one out of the three, and so it must weigh its choices carefully. There are three factors that a corporation must keep in mind if its money-raising schemes are to prove a success. One involves the general advantages and disadvantages of bonds, preferred stock, and common stock. A second is the nature of the

TELLING STOCKHOLDERS THE WORST

There's only one sight uglier in the business world than a stockholder who doesn't get an expected dividend. And that's a roomful of such people. The management of New York's Consolidated Edison power company recently faced such a mob after the company had declared a halt in its dividend payments.

"I never saw so many angry people in one place," said one only slightly harried survivor of the meeting at which Con Ed discussed its economy measure.

More than 5,000 shareholders, many of them retirees of the company, attended the disorderly meeting, but Con Ed had provided seating for only 4,000. As a result, late arrivals struggled to get past guards and into the meeting room. Others engaged in brawls while attempting to get microphones to ask

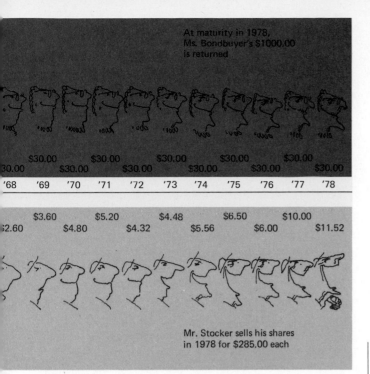

At maturity in 1978, Ms. Bondbuyer's $1000.00 is returned

$30.00 | $30.00 | $30.00 | $30.00 | $30.00 | $30.00 | $30.00 | $30.00 | $30.00 | $30.00 | $30.00

'68 '69 '70 '71 '72 '73 '74 '75 '76 '77 '78

$2.60 | $3.60 | $4.80 | $5.20 | $4.32 | $4.48 | $5.56 | $6.50 | $6.00 | $10.00 | $11.52

Mr. Stocker sells his shares in 1978 for $285.00 each

business in question—which methods are the most appropriate for its needs. And finally, when the corporation launches its long-term financing plan, it must keep an eye on the state of the stock and bond market.

questions of Con Ed chairman Charles Luce. It was Luce's job to explain to the irate crowd just why its investment wasn't paying off for at least the time being. Blaming the company's financial troubles on the energy crisis, unpaid customers' bills, and a one-third cut in its requested rate increase, Luce was defensive.

"We are not a Penn Central," he told the audience, referring to the bankrupt railroad. "We have a forward-looking modernization program. The decision to suspend the dividend was an agonizing move."

The only popular move of the meeting came from a shareholder from Wisconsin. Loud cheers echoed through the hall when he put forward the motion that no executive salaries be paid until the dividend payment was restored. Needless to say, management didn't go for the idea.

Source: "Uproar at Con Ed Meet," *Chicago Daily News*. May 21, 1974.

BONDS: PROS AND CONS

Given a choice, many managers would prefer to raise money through the sale of bonds. Bonds have a number of advantages. First, they represent the cheapest way of financing. Because bond interest comes out of pretax dollars, the company does not have to earn nearly as much to pay interest on bonds as it would to pay the same amount in stock dividends. Second, when bonds are sold, there is no loss of control because bondholders do not have any voice in management. And finally, the sale of bonds has no effect on the original stockholders' rights to residual earnings. Once the interest on the bonds has been paid, common stockholders do not have to share any future earnings of the company with new bondholders. Against these advantages, the company must weigh the one major disadvantage of bonds: their high risk factor. A company that finances by selling stock may survive a few bad years; it will simply omit its dividends. But the same company, financed with bonds and unable to meet interest payments, could be forced into bankruptcy by its bondholders.

PREFERRED STOCK: PROS AND CONS

The sale of preferred stock is an attractive way of financing. It generally leaves control in the hands of the common shareholders and preserves their right to residual earnings. It is also much less risky than the sale of bonds. Dividend payments to preferred share-holders are not a legal obligation, and, unlike bond-holders, preferred stockholders do not have to be repaid at some future date. On the other hand, preferred stock is a relatively expensive way of raising money because dividends are paid with dollars that remain after the company has paid its federal income taxes.

COMMON STOCK: PROS AND CONS

What about financing through common stock? This method carries some of the same advantages and disadvantages as financing through preferreds. On the one hand, it is riskless; on the other hand, it is expensive. There are two additional disadvantages to raising new money through the sale of common stock. When new common stock is sold, the original stockholders are forced to share both their control of the company and their rights to future residual earnings with the new owners.

THE EFFECT OF MARKET CONDITIONS

At any given time, the choices available to a company seeking long-term capital are limited by the state of the stock and bond market and the general economic climate. If business is slipping and investors are nervous, selling stock can be very difficult. Investors may be willing to buy only "safe" bonds in order to insure their future incomes. But in an economic climate in which everyone is optimistic, common stocks' potential for future earnings is very attractive to investors.

In the mid-1960s the sale of common stocks was the major long-term financing technique in many companies. But in the buying frenzy of those years the prices of stock were artificially inflated and many investors were seriously hurt. Today many investors (particularly small investors) have not forgotten the pain of those losses, and confidence in the market fluctuates between high and low. Companies in need of capital are paying the consequences; the issuing of new stocks for long-term capital has fallen off drastically. In 1976 there were only fifty new stock issues—

an unbelievably small number compared with the almost 1,300 new issues of stock in 1969. Further contributing to the up and down performance of the stock market has been the caution of money managers for institutions. Institutional investors, who are responsible for a major sector (some 70 percent) of all investing capital, are difficult people to convince—and no wonder. Due to increasing government regulations such as ERISA, institutions must be particularly careful about what they do with the funds in their charge. As dictated by the government, "prudence" (that is, caution) must win out in any move institutional investors make.

Some companies, of course, are so well known for their excellent management and the technological innovations of their products that they can get away with issuing new stock. Data Resources is a case in point. It recently went public with an offer of 300,000 shares at $11.50 each. They were quickly snapped up and, just a few months after the issue, demand had driven the price of Data Resources' shares as high as $21. But companies whose stock sells as well as Data Resources' are rare. In the late 1970s most corporations must think very carefully before trying to finance long-term capital through a stock issue.

LONG-TERM VERSUS SHORT-TERM FINANCING: WHAT'S APPROPRIATE WHEN?

At first glance, the differences in use between long-term and short-term financing might seem to be cut and dried. If a business needs to build a factory, it clearly needs long-term financing. For a project of so long a duration, long-term loans would provide the only way for a manufacturer to be assured of having all the money necessary and at a fixed rate of interest. Nothing could be worse than having to negotiate a new loan—probably at a greater interest rate—when a half-completed factory stands open to the sky. On the other hand, if a business needs cash merely to purchase its inventory, there's no reason why it should commit itself to debt for several years at a time. In other words, permanent assets (such as factories) should be financed with long-term capital; temporary assets (such as inventories), with short-term credit.

study.

LONG-TERM FINANCING INSTITUTIONS

When we speak of the institutional investors who so heavily influence the course of the securities market, we are referring primarily to six distinct types of organizations:

Life-insurance companies With funds collected from the sale of insurance, these companies purchase stocks and bonds—the income from which is used to meet the company's obligations to policyholders. Among the most influential of investors, insurance companies accounted for nearly $155 billion in stocks and bonds in 1976.

Trust institutions Trust companies, and the trust departments of banks, have staffs of professional money managers who, for a fee, handle the property of trust beneficiaries.

Savings and loan companies Though these safekeepers of family savings accounts invest mainly in home and commercial mortgages, some of the interest they pay depositors is earned via investment in stocks and bonds.

Pension funds Also known as retirement funds, these are the fastest growing of all financial institutions. Public pension funds, which manage retirement funds for teachers, firemen, and other public servants are, generally speaking, invested conservatively in government and corporate bonds. Private funds are usually invested in stocks. The combined assets of public and private pension funds in 1976 were $412.6 billion.

Investment banks Devoted solely to long-term finance, these institutions (which neither receive deposits nor make short-term loans) *underwrite* or buy entire issues of stocks and bonds from their issuers. The investment banks then sell these bonds or shares to other buyers. The *spread*, that is, the difference between the price the investment bank pays for such bonds or certificates and the public offering price, is the profit the bank makes.

Brokerage firms Brokers act as middlemen, charging their customers a commission for the buying and selling of stocks and bonds. When brokers pool their talents, a brokerage firm comes into being. Such a firm encourages long-term financing because investors will more readily buy stocks and bonds when they know that there will be a market for them at a brokerage firm should they choose to sell.

Sources: *Moody's Bank and Finance Manual*, 1978, pp. a14–a15; *Pension Facts* (Washington, D.C.: American Council of Life Insurance, 1977), p. 23.

There is, however, a broad middle ground between the two needs—one spanning a number of different situations that do not clearly call for either long-term or short-term financing. In such cases, it's the difficult task of management to decide which financing route to take.

For example, one of the traditional advantages of short-term credit has been the comparatively low interest rates that are charged on loans of about one year or less. In a business environment in which short-term interest rates are decreasing, the money manager may thus decide, whenever possible, to finance longer-term projects with short-term cash. Of course, the project must be secure enough that it will merit a loan renewal at the same or lower rate of interest at the time of the loan's expiration.

Conversely, there are times when the cheapest money around is available only in the long-term category. In that case, it's worth a company's while to consider both its current and future loan needs and perhaps then opt for a large long-term loan at a lower interest rate to meet them all.

The trick of successful financing is in following the rise and fall of interest rates, and determining what, if any, pattern occurs. When there's a pattern, there's a chance future trends can be predicted. Then, and only then, can the differences in long-term and short-term interest rates be made use of profitably.

CHAPTER REVIEW

Corporations raise long-term capital from outside sources. Such capital can be either debt capital in the form of bonds or equity capital in the form of stock.

A bond is evidence of a debt. The corporation issuing the bond has borrowed money from the bondholder.

Corporations also handle long-term financing by selling stocks, which represent ownership.

Preferred shareholders have preference over common shareholders in the payment of dividends and access to assets. The voting power of preferred shareholders is generally limited.

Common shareholders normally have the sole right to manage the company by electing the board of directors. Their right to the residual income of the corporation is their most important right. It offers potential for high earnings.

KEY WORD REVIEW

undistributed profits
debt capital
equity capital
bond
denomination
principal
maturity date
interest

collateral
secured bonds
unsecured bonds
debentures
credit rating
term bonds
serial bonds
sinking fund
callable (redeemable) bonds
convertible bonds
tax-free bonds
municipal bond
industrial-revenue bonds
pollution-control bonds
stocks
stockholder
shareholder
stock certificate
authorized stock
issued stock
unissued stock
par value
no-par stock
dividends
preferred stocks
cumulative preferred
participating preferreds
convertible preferreds
common stock
stock split
residual right
coupon bonds
registered bonds

REVIEW QUESTIONS

1. What are the sources of long-term debt capital available to a corporation? What are the sources of long-term equity capital available to a corporation?

2. What is the difference between secured and unsecured bonds? What is the backing for each? Which is the safer investment?

3. Under what circumstances does the cumulative feature of preferred stock take on importance?

4. How does the residual right of common shareholders make it possible for them to reap large profits on their holdings?

5. For a corporation interested in long-term financing, what are the advantages of issuing bonds? Of selling stocks?

CASE 1

CLEARED FOR TAKEOFF: THE LONG-TERM PROSPECTS OF THE AIRLINE INDUSTRY

The general business outlook for the airline industry has grown increasingly bright during the late 1970s. One of the most promising signs is the increase in demand for air travel on the part of Americans. In mid-1978, the percentage of available seats filled was up to 60 percent, its highest altitude since 1967. One contributing factor is the widespread use of discount fares; even more important is the fact that rising employment has expanded the amount of money that Americans can spend on travel. To cash in on the boom, the airlines have begun increasing the seating capacity of their planes by tearing out cocktail lounges and putting in more seats.

Even so, profit margins have not increased significantly, largely because of the two factors that make the airline business one of the costliest in the U.S. These are labor, which accounts for about 40 percent of a carrier's operating costs, and fuel—which burns up 20 cents of every revenue dollar. Added costs lie ahead: the airlines will soon be spending a sky-high $60 billion or so to replace about 75 percent of their aging commercial fleet.

Still, airlines spent comparatively little on new jets during the 1970s, which helped to reduce long-term debt. Solid-looking balance sheets and projections that the increase in demand for air travel will not plummet abruptly as it has done in the past have enabled the airlines to do something they have been unable to do for years—raise money. Recently, Braniff pulled in $240 million from a common-stock sale and bank loans, while American Airlines sold $95 million worth of preferred stock. And industry experts expected that airlines would be able to tap other sources for long-term finance, such as insurance companies.

Adapted from "The Airlines: Flying High," July 1978 DUN'S REVIEW

1. What are some of the factors that have made it possible for airlines to come by long-term financing once again?

2. As an investor, what questions would you ask before buying (a) common stock, (b) preferred stock, or (c) a convertible bond offered by an airline?

CASE 2

STATE OF SIEGE: HOW DOES A MERGER THREAT AFFECT A COMPANY'S FINANCING?

Executives of Leeds & Northrup Company, an electronic instruments manufacturer in Philadelphia, were feeling optimistic in the fall of 1976. Earnings were strong, and the company was trying to decide which of a dozen businesses it should acquire in order to expand into new markets. Suddenly, though, there was trouble, and it was serious: Tyco Laboratories, Incorporated, an electronics firm based in New Hampshire, had launched an all-out effort at a takeover of L&N.

What followed was a nineteen-month state of siege during which L&N's president, general counsel, and chief financial officer met twice daily—at 7 A.M. and again late at night—to devise new tactics for keeping hungry Tyco at bay. Immediately, L&N had to scrap its expansion plans and cancel a common-stock offering (because there would be no way to prevent Tyco from gobbling up those shares). L&N had to renegotiate its bank loans and spend heavily on legal advice. In an attempt to find a way to keep Tyco from buying enough stock to gain control, L&N's harried executives consulted one investment banker after another. Some bankers suggested that the company buy a sprinkler or wire-and-cable company to create antitrust problems for Tyco, which was in both of those businesses. And almost all of the bankers, sniffing with sharklike instincts the possibility of a huge fee for arranging a deal, advised L&N to sell out to a company other than Tyco.

But L&N followed neither of those suggestions. Instead, it doubled its outstanding stock shares (to 4 million) in a 3-for-2 split, and paid a 10 percent dividend in order to boost the market value of L&N stock and make it too expensive for Tyco to buy. In January of 1977, in fact, Tyco appeared to surrender by selling its 22.5 percent of L&N stock to another company, Cutler-Hammer, Incorporated. But that was temporary: since Cutler-Hammer had only 5.8 million shares of stock outstanding, Tyco started buying that company. L&N alertly worked out a deal in which Cutler-Hammer sold its L&N stock to General Signal Corporations, whose 19.8 million outstanding shares put it beyond Tyco's reach.

In the meantime, L&N worked hard to reassure its customers that the company would survive. And to its loyal stockholders, 30 percent of whom were L&N employees or retirees and their families, the company sent eighteen letters, often with handwritten notes from the president, and five dividend increases (the payout rose from thirty to eighty cents a year) over the space of eighteen months. Remarkably, during the takeover try, L&N's annual earnings jumped from $4.2 million to $10.2 million, and the market value of its outstanding shares rose from $36 million to $148 million. Finally, in the summer of 1978, Tyco backed off. Was L&N out of the woods? The company was safe from Tyco, L&N's president said. "But every time it gets quiet, it's like the calm before the storm. So the quieter it gets, the more nervous I become."[18]

1. What was the point of L&N's raising its dividend so often?

2. Why was it important for L&N to negotiate an extended loan agreement with the bank?

THE MONEY AND BANKING SYSTEM

The book you are reading is about business; and business, trimmed down to the essentials, is about money. It would be as difficult to over-state the importance of money as it would be to say anything about it that hasn't been said before. One often-made obser-vation is that money functions in society much as blood does in the human body, flowing continually, carrying life-giving nourishment to every fiber. Clearly, a steady and adequate circulation of money is essential to the health of any eco-nomic system, and in a society as complex as ours even the slightest hitch in that circulation can have far-reaching effects. In this chapter we will look at the network of banks and other institutions through which the money supply is channeled, with special emphasis on the Federal Reserve System and its role in monitoring and regulating the money flow.

WHAT WILL THIS CHAPTER FOCUS ON?

After reading the material in this chapter, you will understand and be able to discuss:

- demand deposits and how they work
- the basic functions of the Federal Reserve System
- the four principal economic tools of the Federal Reserve System—changing reserve requirements, carrying out open-market operations, changing the rediscount rate, and exercising selective credit controls
- the four primary categories of financial institutions
- the basics of electronic funds

From your earliest days, when you scrounged nickels and dimes for bits of candy, to today, when your purchases are of a somewhat larger and more varied nature, you come into contact with money daily. Yet how much do you really know about money—other than the fact that you never seem to have enough? For instance, answer true or false: The government is the only institution that's allowed to create money in this country. True, you say? Try again. Of course, none of us is allowed to keep a convenient press and print a few dollars ourselves, but the fact is, the government is *not* the only institution in this country allowed to create money.

How money is created is one of the things we'll talk about in this brief look at money and banking. So far, we've discussed money from the point of view of businesses: why they need it, how they get it, and what they do with it. But we've never actually determined what money is. In this chapter we'll look at the basic definition of money, and we'll also examine the special institutions created to handle money.

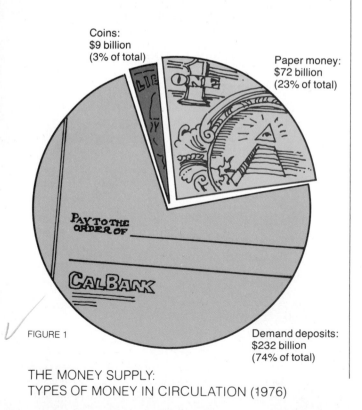

Coins:
$9 billion
(3% of total)

Paper money:
$72 billion
(23% of total)

PAY TO THE ORDER OF

CALBANK

FIGURE 1

Demand deposits:
$232 billion
(74% of total)

THE MONEY SUPPLY:
TYPES OF MONEY IN CIRCULATION (1976)

WHAT IS MONEY?

Money is *anything that is generally accepted as a means of paying for goods and services.* By anything, we mean any substance or item at all—from the shells American Indians used for wampum to the bricks of tea used by the ancient Chinese. Salt has been used as currency in some cultures—and in fact the word "salary" comes from the Latin for salt. In parts of Africa, cattle are still used as a form of money. And, of course, that definition of money includes the coins and paper bills that are more familiar to us.

Checks are another form of money with which we're equally, if not more, familiar. They are, in essence, promises from a bank that it will pay you or someone else specific sums of money on demand. *When a bank establishes a checking account for you, it sets aside a sum of money known as a* **demand deposit**. (Anyone with a check from you can present this check at the bank and *demand* cash in the amount written on the check—hence the name *demand deposit*.) The money that exists in the form of demand deposits far outweighs currency in use and importance; we'll see this as we take a look at the country's money supply.

THE MONEY SUPPLY

The money supply of the United States includes the change you have in your pocket at this moment. It also includes the cash in the supermarket till, the stacks of bills in the bank vault, and whatever millions might be stored away in mattresses across the country. As of April 1976, the total currency in circulation amounted to $81 billion.[1]

In addition to that sum, however, there's the even larger amount of money that exists as demand deposits. In April 1976 that figure came to $232 billion. In other words, demand deposits constituted almost 75 percent of the total money supply (see Figure 1).[2]

THE CREATION OF DEMAND DEPOSITS

How do demand deposits originate? The way you're probably most familiar with involves a trip to the bank and the handing over of a specific sum, in coins and

WHAT MAKES MONEY WORK?

The next time you slap a dollar down on a restaurant counter to pay for a cheeseburger and an order of French fries, why not take a moment to reflect on how that bit of green paper differs from any other bit of paper you might just toss away. Aside from an impressive print job, the dollar—and every other denomination of American currency—carries with it several fundamental characteristics. Let's examine each of these qualities one by one.

DIVISIBILITY If the price of your snack comes to 92 cents, you can be certain that you'll receive 8 cents change from your dollar. That's what we mean by divisibility, and it's one of the most important characteristics of money. Think what problems you'd have in getting change if you were, say, a Masai warrior who counted wealth in cattle. A burger costing one two-hundredth of a cow would be ludicrous at best.

PORTABILITY You can hardly say you're weighted down if you have $12 in your pocket. For that matter, $12,000 or even $12 million in large currency denominations wouldn't be that difficult to transport. In fact, it would easily fit in a suitcase, if you were in a lucky enough position to have that much to carry around in the first place. That is the advantage of portability.

DURABILITY Admittedly,a flimsy dollar bill won't last an eternity. In fact, the average life of a one-dollar bill is eighteen months. Nevertheless, that's a respectable time span for a piece of paper that's handled so often. Try to imagine what life would be like if our currency were physically unable to last that long. A monetary system based on dead fish, for instance, would have a great many drawbacks—not the least of which would be the smell. Durability of currency simply means that if you were to put away $1 today, it would be in the same physical condition next time you wanted to spend it.

STABILITY Not only is it important that money remain in the same physical state for a respectable period of time, but it has to be worth the same amount as well. That's what we mean by stability. If $1 at noon today bought only half as much as $1 would buy at nine o'clock this morning, the currency would not be stable.

LEGITIMACY One of the reasons that money is valuable is its scarcity. If everyone could make as much money as he or she wanted, then money wouldn't be worth much to anyone. For that reason, money is designed and produced so that it's difficult to copy or counterfeit. The small bits of silk thread you can see when you hold a dollar up to the light, for example, were placed there to help differentiate official money from the sort illegally turned out on some criminal's basement printing press.

LIQUIDITY If you were to liquidate your assets—meaning sell everything you own—you would be temporarily storing your wealth in the form of money. In doing so, you'd be confident that you could, at any time, reconvert that wealth back into goods and property. Money is thus the most fluid asset, because it can be converted instantaneously into other forms of wealth. Though diamonds, real estate, antiques, and art work all have their advantages, they can't surpass the benefits of money pure and simple.

paper money or in check form. It's then understood between you (the depositor) and the bank that the bank will hold on to that money for safekeeping until you issue a demand (in the form of a check) for some or all of the money on deposit.

But that is only one way in which demand deposits come into being. A demand deposit can also be set up when a bank makes a loan. Say you apply to your local bank for a loan of $1,000. If the bank grants you the loan, it's essentially permitting you to write checks against your account for money that you have not put into the account. Where did the bank get this money? Though banks *do* borrow, in such a case it's unlikely that the bank is lending you money it has borrowed itself. Instead the bank is simply exercising the right granted it by the federal government to set up demand

CAN THERE BE TWO KINDS OF MONEY IN ONE COUNTRY?

The economy of communist Rumania is tightly controlled. In an effort to build up the society, the government has severely cut down on production of consumer goods and focused on reinvesting the bulk of the national income in industry. Since the desirable consumer goods are consequently no longer officially available, Rumanian currency isn't much good to Rumanians any more except for certain necessities. When it comes to the niceties (which consumers *can* buy, but only on the black market), a new form of money has come into being: American cigarettes. You can't buy a silk scarf, for instance, with Rumanian currency, but one would be available for a few packs of Marlboros. If you want to have a tooth fixed on the spur of the moment by the best dentist in Bucharest, it will cost you exactly two cartons of the 100-millimeter-size Kents. Not only that, but cigarettes can be used to compare values. A bottle of perfume, for example, might be worth eight packs of cigarettes. And a box of chocolates might cost you four packs. The perfume is thus more expensive than the chocolates.

Obviously, cigarettes don't meet the five criteria of an official currency. Though a pack may be divisible, portable, and hard to counterfeit, you could hardly call cigarettes either durable or stable. It just goes to show, however, that when the need for money develops in an economic system—even an "unofficial" economic system—*some* form of money will appear.

Source: "U.S. Cigarettes Serve as Hard Currency in Rumania," *New York Times,* December 11, 1977, p. 14.

deposits—within certain limits—*without* obtaining backup cash to fill those deposits. In other words, banks can and do create money out of thin air. This money is then used in check form.

Safeguarding demand deposits

By now you may be wondering what would happen if, by some fluke, everyone in possession of a check suddenly demanded that the bank on which it was issued pay out the equivalent amount in paper currency and change. Of course, this never happens, but should a tremendous run on currency occur, the banks are prepared up to a point, thanks to regulations on demand deposits established by the federal government.

As part of the regulations governing them, banks are required to retain certain levels of currency reserves. Parts of these reserves—the smaller part—are kept in a bank's own vaults. The greater part of these cash reserves, however, remains on deposit in the federal government's own banks. In effect, the government is banker to the banks.

The combined total of a bank's reserves on hand and those reserves it has on deposit with the government banks determines how much the bank can create in the way of demand deposits unsupported by actual cash deposits. The government requires the bank always to have a certain amount of reserves to back up its demand deposits. This amount is expressed as a percentage of the total demand deposits the bank is permitted to set up. For instance, if a 20 percent reserve is required, a bank can only write demand deposits for up to five times the amount it has on reserve deposit. If it has $10 million, it can only write $50 million worth of demand deposits. From time to time, the government changes its requirements for the proportion of demand deposits which banks must maintain as reserves. Changing the proportion is part of the way the government controls the money supply.

If all of this sounds like a fairly delicate financial balance, that's because it is. When a country's monetary system goes haywire, the result can be disaster. In Germany, for instance, after World War I the money supply got so far out of hand that the purchase of a loaf of bread required a wheelbarrowful of paper currency. Even today in Italy the system has faltered to the extent that it's often impossible to make change for simple transactions. Instead shopkeepers are obliged to hand over to their customers bits of candy or the like in place of coins.

Let's take a look at the system that helps prevent such occurrences in the United States.

THE FEDERAL RESERVE SYSTEM

As we've seen in our chapters on short-term and long-term finance, commercial banks—the banks at which

Baskets full of devalued currency: a common sight in Germany in the early 1920s. Enormous sums of the virtually worthless German Mark were needed for even the most trifling transactions.

you can open a checking account—affect businesses directly because they are a source of so much of the money that businesses need to operate. They also affect businesses indirectly, since a good deal of the money that companies borrow from finance companies and other sources comes originally from commercial banks in the form of the demand deposits they're empowered to create. Banks are thus crucially important to the country's economy and must at all times be carefully regulated by the federal government. The *government's bank regulating system* is known as the **Federal Reserve System**—or, familiarly, the Fed.

This system exists to do two things. First, it makes certain that enough money and credit are available to allow the economy to expand—thus giving the country an ever-increasing supply of goods, services, and jobs. But at the same time, the system is designed to ensure that there is never too much money and credit available at any one period. If that were to happen, as it did in Germany, suppliers would charge increasingly high prices for their goods and so every dollar would pur-

chase less. When a dollar purchases less, it's worth less. That's the essence of inflation. In sum, the Federal Reserve System acts as a safeguard to keep just the right amount of money available in the country.

The Federal Reserve System encompasses all federally chartered banks and many state chartered banks; and the Federal Reserve Board, which oversees operations of the almost 6,000 member banks, is the most important banking regulatory agency in the country. The system is so named because it governs the amount of reserves member banks are required to keep on deposit when they create demand deposits. We show the Federal Reserve districts in Figure 2 (next page).

THE REGULATING FUNCTION OF THE FED

As we've discussed, the prime objective of the Fed is to stimulate economic growth and a high level of employment while keeping inflation to a minimum. To do this, the Fed has four basic tools at its disposal. It can *change reserve requirements,* it can carry out *open-market operations,* it can *change the rediscount rate,* and it can exercise *selective credit controls.* Figure 3 (page 357) gives you an overview of the way these tools work; here we'll discuss them in some detail.

Changing reserve requirements

All member banks of the Fed are required to set aside *sums of money equal to a certain percentage of their deposits.* These amounts are called **reserves**, and *the percentage* is called the **reserve requirement**. The reserve requirement is the Fed's primary way of controlling the money supply. If the Fed believes that consumers and business are buying too much and that inflation—that is, rising prices—is threatening, it will increase reserve requirements. When that happens, banks are not able to create demand deposits in as large sums as before. Thus there is less money for banks to lend to their customers. Conversely, if the Fed's economists feel that the country would benefit if business were stimulated, it will reduce reserve requirements. By doing so, it hopes to encourage banks to make more loans to businesses and consumers so that they, in turn, will buy more. The result, in theory, is more sales for business and more jobs for everyone.

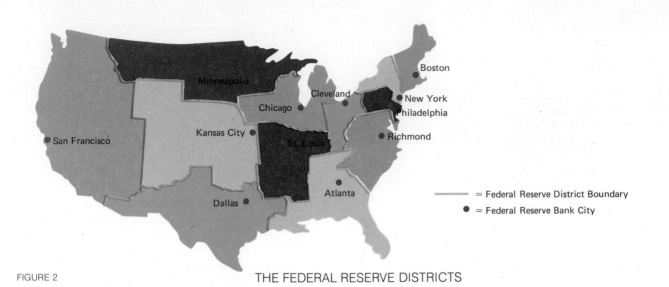

FIGURE 2

THE FEDERAL RESERVE DISTRICTS

Open-market operations ✓

The Fed can also control the amount of money in the hands of businesses and consumers through **open-market operations**. This term refers to *purchases and sales of government bonds on the open market by the Federal Reserve System.* If the Fed is concerned about inflation and so wants to reduce the amount of money available, it will sell government bonds to the public and to banks. When the public and the banks pay for the bonds—which, of course, are attractive purchases since they earn interest—the money paid for them is immediately out of circulation. Conversely, when the Fed wants to get the economy moving again, the government will buy back its bonds, thus putting additional cash back into the economy.

Changing the rediscount rate ✓

One of the ways that banks obtain extra funds to lend to their customers is by borrowing from the Federal Reserve Bank, which, as we've said, is banker to the banks. Often, when banks borrow from the Fed, they use as collateral promissory notes that they have discounted for their customers. (We discussed the discounting procedure in Chapter 11.) *Just as the bank discounted its customers' promissory notes, the Federal Reserve Bank now discounts them once again.* That is, the Fed lends the member bank the value of the notes, less a fee for services. This process is called **redis-**

counting, and the *rate that the Fed charges banks for such loans* is called the **rediscount rate**. It clearly follows, then, that rediscounting is most attractive to commercial banks if they can charge their own customers a substantially higher rate for discounting than the rediscount rate they themselves must pay the Fed. Here again is a way in which the Fed can control the economy. If it wishes to encourage member banks to make loans to customers, it will lower the rediscount rate. On the other hand, if it wants to discourage loans, it will raise the rediscount rate. This, in turn, will cause banks to raise the **prime interest rate**—the *lowest rate at which they will make loans to their most credit-worthy business customers.*

Selective credit controls

The Fed has the *power to set credit terms on various kinds of loans.* By exercising this power, known as **selective credit controls**, it can exert a great deal of influence on business activity. For example, it sets **margin requirements** that *limit the amounts of money stockbrokers and banks can lend customers for the purpose of buying stocks.* As of this writing, the Fed margin requirement is 50 percent of the loan—that is, if a stock buyer wants to borrow $1,000 from a brokerage house to buy securities, he or she must pledge $500 worth of stock to the brokerage house or deposit $500 in cash with the brokerage. If pledged stock is used as backing for the loan, and the stock suffers a setback on the stockmarket and drops in value—say to $400—a **margin call** will be issued by the brokerage house. *A margin call warns the stock buyer that he or she no longer meets the margin requirement.* The stock buyer then must purchase enough stock to regain the backing necessary for the loan. In this case, the stock buyer would have to purchase $100 worth of stock more to meet the required $500 backing on the $1,000 loan.

The power of setting margin requirements comes in handy when the government's economists feel that there is too much stock-market speculation for the economy's good. When that happens, the Fed simply sets margin requirements at a level that is high enough to prevent financial institutions from lending very much money for stock purchases. Selective credit controls mean that the Fed can limit the size and duration of consumer loans as well. At the beginning of the Korean War in 1950, for instance, there was a great surge of appliance buying as consumers stocked up in fear of a repetition of World War II shortages. As a result of this buying frenzy, prices rose dramatically. In an attempt to control this inflation, the Fed raised the requirements for consumer down payments for appliance purchases made on time and limited the period of time over which consumers could stretch their payments.

Another selective credit control, instituted by the federal government around the time of the Depression, goes by the name of Regulation Q. This legislation allows savings and loan institutions and mutual savings banks to pay higher interest rates on deposits than commercial savings banks. The purpose of Regulation Q is to encourage thrift and to make funds for mortgages more readily available.

In short, the Fed keeps its hand on the pulse of the country's economy. When that pulse turns sluggish or speeds up alarmingly, the Federal Reserve System steps in with one or more of the four prescriptions we've just discussed.

FIGURE 3

HOW THE FED REGULATES THE MONEY SUPPLY

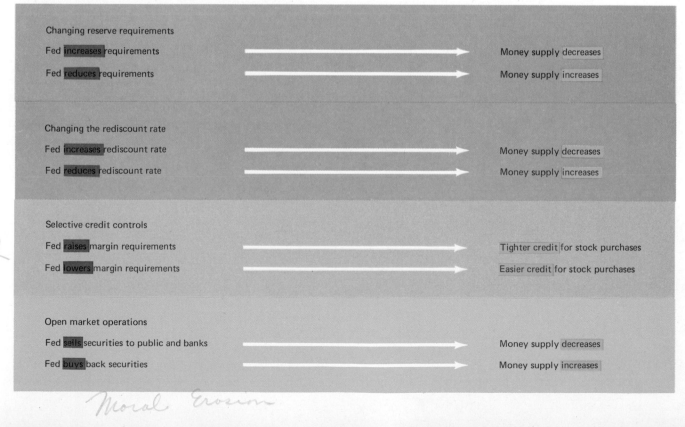

Changing reserve requirements

Fed increases requirements → Money supply decreases

Fed reduces requirements → Money supply increases

Changing the rediscount rate

Fed increases rediscount rate → Money supply decreases

Fed reduces rediscount rate → Money supply increases

Selective credit controls

Fed raises margin requirements → Tighter credit for stock purchases

Fed lowers margin requirements → Easier credit for stock purchases

Open market operations

Fed sells securities to public and banks → Money supply decreases

Fed buys back securities → Money supply increases

HOW A CHECK MOVES
THROUGH THE FEDERAL RESERVE SYSTEM

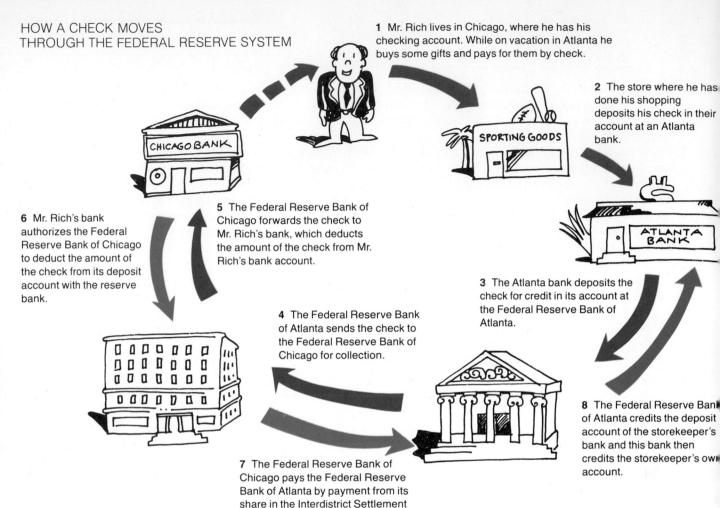

1 Mr. Rich lives in Chicago, where he has his checking account. While on vacation in Atlanta he buys some gifts and pays for them by check.

2 The store where he has done his shopping deposits his check in their account at an Atlanta bank.

3 The Atlanta bank deposits the check for credit in its account at the Federal Reserve Bank of Atlanta.

4 The Federal Reserve Bank of Atlanta sends the check to the Federal Reserve Bank of Chicago for collection.

5 The Federal Reserve Bank of Chicago forwards the check to Mr. Rich's bank, which deducts the amount of the check from Mr. Rich's bank account.

6 Mr. Rich's bank authorizes the Federal Reserve Bank of Chicago to deduct the amount of the check from its deposit account with the reserve bank.

7 The Federal Reserve Bank of Chicago pays the Federal Reserve Bank of Atlanta by payment from its share in the Interdistrict Settlement Fund.

8 The Federal Reserve Bank of Atlanta credits the deposit account of the storekeeper's bank and this bank then credits the storekeeper's own account.

FIGURE 4

CLEARING CHECKS THROUGH THE FED

A major objective of federal banking regulation is to ensure that the mechanics of the entire banking system function smoothly. For example, a check written against an account in a Chicago bank may be deposited in a bank in Atlanta. Funds in this transaction must be collected and credited promptly and—above all—accurately. Doing so is a major responsibility of the twelve Federal Reserve Banks. Checks drawn on various commercial banks within the same Federal Reserve district are sent to that district's Federal Reserve Bank, where each commercial bank maintains an account. Every day all the checks are totaled, the final balances are added to or subtracted from each bank's accounts, and the checks are returned to the banks on which they were drawn.

Let's use an example of the Sixth District Federal Reserve Bank in Atlanta. On a given day, customers of the Tallahassee National Bank may have written checks on their accounts for a total of $550, checks that have been deposited by recipients in accounts at the First Miami Bank. At the same time, the Sixth District Bank notes that depositors of First Miami have written $400 worth of checks, which have been deposited at Tallahassee. The reserve bank will balance out the difference, crediting the Miami bank's account with $150 and subtracting the same amount from Tallahassee's account. The reserve bank will also return the checks to Miami and Tallahassee, so that each bank can add or subtract the appropriate amounts from its customers' balances. This example is extremely simplified, since, in reality, the checks written by the customers of Tallahassee National and First Miami are actually deposited in banks all over the district during the normal course of business. In actuality, *all* the debits and credits from all the banks in the district have to be added up before the proper amounts can be added to or subtracted from Tallahassee National's and First Miami's accounts with the district bank.

For another example, see Figure 4, which shows how one check would flow through the Federal Reserve System.

A similar process handles the clearing of checks that are written on banks in the different Federal Reserve districts. Each year, the Federal Reserve System clears about 8 billion checks, involving nearly $4 trillion.

THE FDIC AND THE FSLIC

Both state and nationally chartered banks that offer savings accounts are required to participate in the Federal Deposit Insurance Corporation (FDIC). The FDIC insures depositors for up to $40,000 per account if their bank should fail. If a member bank is on the brink of closing, the FDIC will help keep it open; it will reopen banks that have closed. The FDIC also sets guidelines for safe banking policies and sees that those guidelines are followed. And where does the money come from to fund these FDIC functions? Each of the nearly 15,000 member banks pays the FDIC a percentage of its deposits. If for some reason—say, the closing of too many banks—the fees of FDIC members do not cover the expenses of paying insurance, the FDIC may call on the United States Treasury for assistance.

And what agency protects depositors in federal savings and loans institutions? The Federal Savings and Loan Insurance Corporation (FSLIC) provides the same services for its members as the FDIC provides for banks that fall under its protection.

SUPPLYING CURRENCY

Last, the individual Federal Reserve banks are also responsible for providing member banks with adequate amounts of currency. The demand for coins and paper money is a seasonal one. For instance, as you might expect, the Christmas shopping season is a time when many people withdraw their savings from banks in the form of cash. The Federal Reserve has to supply the currency that banks need at such times.

COMMERCIAL BANKS AND OTHER FINANCING INSTITUTIONS

Now that we've surveyed these federal regulations and procedures, it's time to take a closer look at the commercial banks themselves. It's the primary business of banks and other financing institutions to provide money to individuals and businesses when they run short of funds. We've already seen the importance of these institutions in making cash or credit available to companies and individuals needing them. However, the services of banks and financing institutions go beyond filling only those fairly simple needs. Today they fulfill a variety of complex but useful functions for customers who know how to take advantage of them.

For our purposes, there are four principal categories of financial institutions: commercial banks, commercial finance companies, factors, and commercial paper houses. And there is also a fifth category, credit unions, which are fast growing in popularity.

COMMERCIAL BANKS

Commercial banks are sometimes confused with savings banks or with savings and loan associations because they all accept savings accounts and some make mortgage loans. However, those are generally the only areas in which the two types of institutions offer overlapping services. For the most part, only **commercial banks** can *provide checking accounts*—demand deposits—for their customers *and make short-term business and personal loans.*

In White Plains, New York, for example, you can open a savings account or get a mortgage at either the Home Savings Bank (a savings bank) or the First National Bank of Westchester (a commercial bank). However, if you want a checking account, an unsecured business loan, or a personal loan to finance a new car or your college education, you must choose the commercial bank, which, incidentally, will have been chartered for those purposes by either the state or the federal government.

In addition to these services, commercial banks assist businesses by collecting promissory notes or drafts the banks hold for customers. They also serve as an excellent source of credit information about prospective customers and of general business advice. They can, for instance, help a business that operates in foreign countries because they buy and sell foreign currencies and can arrange for credit and collections abroad. What's more, many banks help their customers to select and manage their stock and bond investments, and some even prepare payrolls for customers and rent them time on the bank computers.

Bank checks

It would be difficult to imagine the business environment without the convenience of checks as a substitute for the clumsiness of cash. As we've seen, the checking account is an arrangement by which a customer deposits money in an account and is given a book of checks to be drawn against that account. Each **check** the customer writes and signs is, in effect, *an order to the bank to release the amount of money specified on the check* to the **payee**, *the business or person indicated.* (Of course, the bank may not honor the check if the account is overdrawn—that is, if the customer's account lacks sufficient funds.)

In addition to customers' checks, banks also sell cashier's checks, money orders, and traveler's checks. They can be purchased from a bank for their face value plus, usually, a small additional fee. The main difference between these checks and a customer's checks is that checks purchased from a bank are payable from the funds of the bank itself rather than from an individual's account. As such they are usually acceptable as a form of payment in situations in which the individual isn't personally known.

NOW accounts

In recent years the distinction between commercial banks and other institutions has been blurred in the area of checking accounts. In New England, for instance, **NOW accounts** *permit individuals to write checks on interest-bearing accounts, even those deposited in savings banks.* (The initials NOW stand for Negotiable Orders of Withdrawal.) The NOW system has proved to be a popular innovation, and the Federal Reserve is preparing to ask Congress to consider nationwide NOW legislation. If the legislation goes through, commercial banks will eventually be forced to pay interest on all consumer checking accounts simply in order to remain competitive.

COMMERCIAL FINANCE COMPANIES

Commercial finance companies, such as CIT, Commercial Credit, and Talcott National, provide an alternative to commercial banks for the customer requiring short-term finance. These institutions (not to be confused with personal finance companies or small loan companies like Household Finance, which lend primarily to individuals) supply funds for business through secured loans backed by inventories, accounts receivable, fixtures, or heavy equipment. In most cases the businesses that seek short-term funds from commercial finance companies are those that cannot, for one reason or another, borrow from banks. They may have reached the limit their own banks are willing to lend them, or they may be new businesses or troubled firms that don't meet the lending standards of the banks. In any case, because such loans involve greater risks, commercial finance companies tend to charge higher interest rates than commercial banks.

FACTORS

In Chapter 11 we discussed how businesses can raise short-term capital from specialized financial institutions called **factors**, which *buy accounts receivable from businesses.* Here we'll raise one more point. What happens if customers refuse to pay their bills after the factor has taken over the accounts? Most often the factor according to the terms of the agreement would be forced to take the loss if the customer doesn't eventually come through with payment. For that reason, a factor must be particularly careful about the accounts it buys—and so it will usually insist on the right to prior approval before its client extends credit to any particular customer. The potential power of the factors is thus awesome.

COMMERCIAL PAPER HOUSES

The commercial paper with which large corporations raise short-term unsecured loans is distributed by commercial paper houses all across the country (see p. 325). In some cases, commercial paper houses buy the paper outright from the issuing businesses. In others, they act merely as intermediaries between the issuer and the purchaser and make their profit by taking a commission on the sale. Buyers who wish to purchase commercial paper can contact the commercial paper house directly. More commonly, however, buyers will arrange such purchases through their banks. The banks, in turn, ask a commercial paper house to find paper for the amount and maturity desired.

CREDIT UNIONS

Credit unions are essentially banking co-ops, whose members are people linked by a common bond of employment, religion, or even hobby. Members must purchase at least one share in the credit union. This enables them to borrow money the credit union has on hand through the sale of shares at an interest rate that is relatively lower than that available at banks. Credit unions also offer members savings plans.

NEW DIRECTIONS IN BANKING: ELECTRONIC FUNDS

Both currency and checks—the two forms of money we've discussed at some length—have been on the business scene for quite a long time. We're now well into the age of computers, however, and those machines have brought with them what some experts consider to be a third kind of money: electronic funds. Since electronic funds could very well prove to be the dominant form of money in the future, it is worth our while to examine how they came about and where they are today.

ELECTRONIC FUNDS TRANSFER (EFT)

Electronic banking got its first large-scale sendoff in 1974 when a bank in Lincoln, Nebraska, teamed up with the Hinky Dinky supermarket chain. What the bank did was to set up a network of satellite computer terminals in the stores and link these to a central computer in the bank's head office. A store customer who happened to be a bank client could then buy groceries and have the check-out clerk electronically withdraw the necessary funds from his or her bank account—plus maybe a bit extra for pocket money. In computer banking terms, the transaction would be described as an EFT (electronic funds transfer) at a POS (point-of-sale) terminal located in a retail outlet.[3]

Even before that, however, different types of electronic funds-transferring systems were in existence, and today they're used more than ever before by consumers, banks, stores, and even the federal government. These fragmented systems, though, are not by any means hooked up into a greater whole; there is not any type of national network or megasystem, despite the predictions that followed in the wake of the famed Hinky Dinky EFT experiment. Why not? To answer that question, let's first see some of the different components of the system now in operation. Then, perhaps, we can get a clearer idea of what some of the advantages of a megasystem might be and also some of the obstacles that stand in the way of national EFT development.

Components of electronic funds transfer systems

CREDIT CARDS The most familiar device used for non-check fund transfer is undoubtedly the credit card. There are two major bank credit cards, Visa and Master Charge. The next time you use either one of them, bear in mind that the card shows the merchant from whom you're buying that a line of credit has been established in your name by the bank that issued you the card and that the sales draft being submitted by the merchant will be purchased by that bank. (Sales drafts, or trade drafts, you'll recall from Chapter 11, are promises to pay that are drawn up by a merchant and signed by a customer.) When you use the card, there is no mechanism that *instantaneously* withdraws funds from your account. Such a card, which would authorize instantaneous withdrawal, would be what experts term a *debit card*. There aren't any widespread debit-card systems in operation—yet.

Among other credit cards are those issued by American Express and by individual stores. However, the latter have often proved to be so expensive for the enterprises involved that recently major stores have turned to banks that custom-tailor credit programs to their needs. With these programs, stores no longer have to extend costly credit to their customers. Instead, they maintain the prestige of having their own names on customer cards, while allowing the bank to handle the collecting end of the job.

There's no such thing as bankers' hours or a bank holiday for the Automated Teller Machine. ATMs have made round-the-clock banking a reality for millions of depositors.

POINT-OF-SALE TERMINALS POS computer terminals placed by banks in participating retail enterprises are increasingly popular. However, despite their potential as seen in the Hinky Dinky episode, most POS terminals are now used merely to verify checks. In department stores that have their own POS terminals, the terminals are mainly used for quick credit verification.

AUTOMATED TELLER MACHINES ATMs are the mechanical equivalent of miniature bank branches. When activated by a depositor's specially coded computer card, they can dispense cash, accept deposits, and report balances.

AUTOMATED CLEARINGHOUSES ACHs are a means by which big companies can transfer large-volume funds. For example, instead of laboriously making out hundreds of payroll checks, a major corporation can take advantage of an ACH to transfer salaries directly to employees' bank accounts.

BIG BANK WIRES These are transfer arrangements on a grand scale. The bank wire is used on a national basis by some large banks to shift funds to one another. The Federal Reserve Wire, the government version of this innovation, handles large transactions among banks that are members of the Fed.

Why isn't there a nationwide hookup now?

As we've pointed out, none of these fund transfer components has merged into anything approaching a nationwide megasystem, despite the apparent convenience such a system would offer. Probably the foremost among the obstacles to the creation of such a network is the cost. Some estimates have put the possible figure at $10 billion for just a basic system designed to replace cash transactions only—not even the greater number of check transactions.

Another hard-to-surmount obstacle in the way of a national EFT system is consumer resistance. While the banks have been attempting to revolutionize the industry with the latest technology, their customers have tended to let the revolution carry on without them. Though checks may be viewed by banks as expensive-to-process nuisances, the fact is, most consumers like to rely on those handy little stubs as their own foolproof way of keeping track of what the bank is doing with their money. Moreover, checks give people and businesses who write them a period of **float time** until the checks are cleared. That means that *when you write a check, you don't have to worry about having the money drained from your account for at least a few days.* Until then, the money is still yours. With instantaneous automatic debiting, however, the money would be gone immediately. As for having salaries paid directly into their accounts by means of ACHs, consumers have tended to be more dubious still. People just don't trust computers. This, combined with fears of invasion of privacy, has meant that the marketing efforts of the banks have thus far failed on the whole.

Merchants, too, are not always thrilled at the prospect of a national EFT system. Instead they like the flexibility that their own credit systems and the options of using various private credit lines can give them. Some prefer to deal in cash or checks exclusively. Where would they be if a national EFT went into effect?

The trend toward a widening network

Despite the obstacles we have discussed, moves toward a widening of the EFT network and perhaps even a nationwide system seem inevitable. When will the first moves happen? They have already begun. In New England, as we've seen, there is already a trend toward NOW checking accounts. If this innovation should spread to other parts of the nation—and the chances are it will—banks will have no choice but to start charging more for check cashing, if only to make up for the interest expenses they're forced to pay on the accounts. When that happens, customers may very well lose their loyalty to the check payment system and switch to a system that would be less costly for them—namely, some form of EFT.

And there's another sequence of events that may help the trend toward a nationwide EFT system. Once large merchandisers in an area start hooking up to a bank-operated credit verification system, the bad-check pushers will take their patronage to smaller merchandisers who aren't yet connected to the system or who have no intention of getting involved with a bank in that way. However, the concentration of bad checks that such merchants would be likely to receive would soon make those retailers see the error of their ways. Tired of checks bouncing all around them, they too will join the parade to closer bank-retail ties.

Even public distaste for computer banking might well be on the wane. In Atlanta, for instance, All-Time Tillie, an amusing red-and-yellow-painted ATM serving as the computer banking outlet of the First National Bank, has become something of a popular folk figure. In New York, Citibank has spent some $175 million on a series of twenty-four-hour computer banking centers. The chatty machines installed there—they're even programmed to light up with an "Oops!" when a mistake is made—have done much to break down consumer resistance to dealing with hardware rather than people. At least machines are never in a bad mood.[4]

An unresolved problem: EFT and monopoly

Some of the problems standing in the way of the development of a nationwide EFT system have to do with the fact that the more banks use EFT, the more they tend—in some cases—toward monopolistic practices that are illegal. In Illinois, for instance, branch banks are illegal because they were originally seen as a threat to bank competition. And what is the status of a supermarket POS when its function goes beyond credit verification to accepting deposits and making withdrawals? Doesn't it become a minibranch of the bank to which it's connected? The courts in Illinois, for one, think that it does. Recently in Chicago one satellite terminal had its plug pulled with considerable publicity because a court had decided that it was the thin end of the wedge to a bank monopoly.[5]

And there is another way in which the development of a nationwide EFT system could lead to monopoly. Because the start-up costs would be so extraordinarily high, many smaller banks might be frozen out of a national network. Others would tend to band together and share facilities, and such coziness among former competitors could lead to charges of monopoly. There *is* the possibility that such cooperation would be viewed as a natural monopoly and therefore beyond antitrust laws; but it will be up to the courts to decide.

CHAPTER REVIEW

Money is anything generally accepted as a means of paying for goods and services. The money supply of a country consists of two kinds of money: currency and demand deposits (checking accounts). The federal government requires banks to back up demand deposits by keeping a certain percentage of them as a reserve. This reserve may be stored in the bank's own vaults and in government banks.

The system that regulates banking is the Federal Reserve System (the Fed). All nationally and many state-chartered banks are controlled by the Fed. The Fed performs two basic functions—making sure that there is enough money and credit available, and guarding against inflation. The Fed regulates the money supply through four basic procedures: changing reserve requirements, carrying out open-market operations, changing the rediscount rate, and setting selective credit controls.

In addition to the Fed, there are four other basic types of financing institutions. Commercial banks provide checking accounts and make short-term business and personal loans. Commercial finance companies provide short-term finance for business by making secured loans. Factors buy accounts receivable from businesses. Commercial paper houses buy and sell commercial paper, and they also act as intermediaries between issuers of commercial paper and prospective buyers.

The age of computers has made electronic funds transfer (EFT) an impor-

tant aspect of banking. Devices facilitating electronic funds transfer, including credit cards and automated teller machines, are being used widely. Some observers have suggested that there may eventually develop a nationwide electronic banking network, which would let consumers plug in to any bank across the nation. Though there are obstacles to the creation of such a network, including its cost, resistance from consumers and merchants, and the threat of monopoly, some trends suggest that the nationwide network may indeed become a reality some day.

KEY WORD REVIEW

money
demand deposit
Federal Reserve System
reserves
reserve requirement
open-market operations
rediscounting
rediscount rate
prime interest rate
selective credit controls
margin requirements
margin call
commercial banks
check
payee
NOW accounts
factors
float time

REVIEW QUESTIONS

1. Explain the importance of demand deposits. In what way does the federal government regulate them?

2. What are the basic functions of the Federal Reserve System? Explain them in detail.

3. How does the Federal Reserve System make sure that checks drawn on various commercial banks are cleared smoothly?

4. Other than the Federal Reserve System, what are the four principal categories of financial institutions?

5. Explain the advantages and disadvantages in using electronic funds. Give examples of some of the new devices used in electronic banking.

CASE 1

HOUSE OF CARDS

During the past few years the increasing use of credit cards by Americans has sparked fierce competition between the companies that dominate the burgeoning credit-card industry. The two international bank-card systems, Visa and Master Charge, are engaged in a close and high-stakes race for a greater share of the already huge bank-card market. And these two giants are at the same time embroiled in conflict with the three largest "travel and entertainment" card companies: American Express, Diners Club, and Carte

Blanche. According to recent reports from the credit-card battlefront, both Master Charge and Diners Club were planning to move into the traveler's-check market, a lucrative territory long dominated by American Express; and Citibank, second largest bank in the nation, was preparing to acquire Carte Blanche.

The current battle between the big card companies dates back to 1976, when the United States Supreme Court ruled that individual banks could issue more than one kind of card to a customer. That decision pushed Master Charge, formally known as the Interbank Card Association, and Visa International (once known as BankAmericard) into close-quarters combat for more customers. Although Interbank (Master Charge) is a nonprofit organization whose 9,600 members share operating costs and revenues, while Visa International is a profit-seeking outfit owned by about 10,000 banks, both groups work in basically the same way. When a New Yorker uses his or her Bankers Trust Company Visa (or Master Charge) card to buy something in Chicago, for example, the Chicago store sends a copy of the charge slip to its bank, which gives the store a credit for the amount of the purchase minus the merchant's discount rate. That Chicago bank then sends the purchase slip to Bankers Trust in New York, which bills the cardholder. The two big card companies are also similar where market share is concerned: in the United States, as of 1978, Master Charge had 47.6 million cards in circulation, Visa had 44 million; worldwide, Master Charge leads Visa by a hair, 59.3 million to 58.7 million.

If the spread of credit cards creates rich opportunities for the card com-

panies, it also raises troubling questions for consumer groups and members of Congress who feel that the industry should be more closely regulated than it is. These groups question the way credit-card companies set their finance charges, for instance, and they argue that the use of mailing lists to solicit new customers is an invasion of consumer privacy. The card companies contend that cardholders are using only about 20 percent of the credit available to them and that delinquent payments have never been lower. But consumer groups and members of Congress worry that too much credit has already been extended and that, as the sudden appearance of counseling services for debtors suggests, many consumers are simply unable to handle large credit allowances.

Just as worrisome to Congress as the credit card is the debit card. The debit card is not used to finance purchases, but to withdraw cash from a bank, to transfer funds from one account to another, or, increasingly, to pay bills at electronic banking terminals. Concerned by signs that the credit industry is readying a major effort to mass-market debit cards to the public, Congress has been debating legislation that would establish strong controls over the use of debit cards. One of Congress's main fears is that a boom in debit card use would expose millions of dollars in deposits to electronic robbery. Lawmakers suspect that a debit card could be used as easily as a forged check to remove funds from an account. All a thief would need was the card itself and the secret identification number that a bank or store customer must use with the card to start a transaction. One solution that Congress has considered is to protect cardholders by requiring their explicit assent before a debit card issuer could assign them a secret number.

Other features of Congress's regulatory plan include limiting customer liability in the case of a lost or stolen card to $50; tightening up error-correction practices (by requiring, for instance, that mistakes be cleared up within ten days); and specifying that debit-card companies use the "country-club billing" method, in which all transactions must be documented with receipts. Credit-industry executives have resisted regulation so far, and they especially object to country-club billing. Such a procedure, they say, would make electronic funds transfer (EFT) networks too expensive to operate profitably. At the same time, though, bankers and other members of the credit industry acknowledge that the regulatory measures being considered by Congress only formalize practices that the debit-card industry already follows. And there is one issue on which both supporters and opponents of strong controls agree: consumer abuses have been few—so far. But as the number of cards in use multiplies—one member of Congress puts the number already in circulation at 40 million—the likelihood of abuse is almost certain to increase as well.

Adapted from "Clash of the Credit Cards," June 1978 DUN'S REVIEW

1. What kinds of regulatory practices or controls should be required by law in the credit- and debit-card industry?

2. What are some of the chief threats against which consumers who use either credit or debit cards need protection?

3. Describe some of the invasion-of-privacy issues that are involved in the marketing and use of credit and debit cards.

THE STOCK MARKET

Wall Street: The name signifies not only a place but an institution, a philosophy, an entire way of life. It is the nerve center of the world's capitalist economies, where billions of dollars continually change hands and control of giant corporations can be bought and sold with a few telephone calls. It is also a place that can exert a considerable influence on you, both as a member of the work force and as a private individual—whether or not you ever buy a single share of stock.

This chapter provides an introduction to the workings of the New York Stock Exchange and other security markets here and abroad. It focuses on investment strategies, sources of information, the principal types of stock-market transaction, and the ground rules under which the entire system operates.

WHAT WILL THIS CHAPTER FOCUS ON?

After reading the material in this chapter, you will understand and be able to discuss:

- the importance of security markets
- how the stock exchanges and the over-the-counter market function
- the way securities are bought and sold
- the various kinds of stock-market transactions
- the way the government regulates security trading
- the way information concerning securities is given in the newspapers
- the importance of other sources of information in making investment decisions

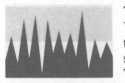

The economy of much of the Western world is centered in a temple-like building on a narrow street in downtown New York. The street, of course, is Wall Street, and the building is the home of the New York Stock Exchange.

Far from being the hushed, calm, and stately type of place an outsider may imagine, the New York Stock Exchange (NYSE) is as loud and confusing as a bargain basement sale on Washington's birthday. From the safety of the visitors' gallery you can see hundreds of men and women running back and forth at top speed. They gesture wildly, shouting and waving wads of paper clutched in their fists. These people are engaged in the important job of buying and selling—and getting the best prices for—shares of the country's leading businesses.

Whether an investor wants to buy or sell one share of a major stock or one million; whether the order comes from a wall phone in a retiree's kitchen or by way of a panelled boardroom, chances are that it will end up and be executed by one of those harried people on the floor of the New York Stock Exchange. On a typical day upward of twenty million shares may change hands, and they'd be worth a total of about half a billion dollars. On occasion the number of shares—or the volume—traded in one day has topped 60 million.

All shares traded on the New York Stock Exchange are sold "secondhand." As we learned in Chapter 12, corporations raise capital by selling shares of ownership to investors. But this is far from the only time these shares change hands. Most investors don't plan to keep their stocks indefinitely; they expect to sell them at some point. And this is why **security markets**, such as the NYSE, are needed. They *provide investors with a convenient means of disposing of their stocks and purchasing new ones.*

The ease with which stocks can be bought and sold in a security market is of prime importance to business, since many businesses depend on issuing stocks to survive. The NYSE, for example, boasts that it can take as little as one minute to dispose of a stock such as AT&T once the sell order is placed. Contrast this with an investment in real estate—which can take months or years to dispose of—and the handiness of stocks is readily apparent.

Securities markets are also important because they supply an investment outlet for excess funds, both funds held by corporations and funds belonging to private individuals. Thus these markets are vital to the overall growth of the nation's economy. Purchases in a securities market help provide the capital that United States industry needs in order to expand, to create additional jobs, and to supply the general population with new products and services.

The most important marketplaces for the stocks of the largest corporations in the United States are the stock exchanges. A **stock exchange** is an *organization whose members join together and provide a trading room where members can meet to buy and sell securities for their customers.*

But there is also another very important kind of marketplace for stocks and other securities—the **over-the-counter market**. In this market there is no single trading floor where transactions occur. Instead, the market consists of *a network of about four thousand stock and bond dealers scattered across the country, who trade with each other by telephone or teletype.* Generally speaking, the over-the-counter market deals with stocks of smaller companies. In addition, although there is some bond trading on the stock exchanges, most of the buying and selling of corporate and government bonds takes place in the over-the-counter market. According to estimates, the securities of 30,000 companies are traded in the over-the-counter market. In 1977 this amounted to almost $2.5 billion in trading.[1]

Table 1 The Ten American Corporations with the Largest Number of Stockholders

Company	Stockholders (1977)
American Telephone & Telegraph	2,891,000
General Motors	1,254,000
Exxon Corporation	684,000
International Business Machines	577,000
General Electric	555,000
General Telephone & Electronics	509,000
Texaco	404,000
Gulf Oil	357,000
Ford Motor	334,000
RCA Corporation	295,000

Source: *Information Please Almanac 1978* (New York: Information Please Publishing, Inc., 1977), p. 54.

in their areas. For example, the stock of Checker Motors, which makes Checker autos and owns a few taxi companies, trades on the Midwest Exchange; Pacific Gas Transmission trades on the Pacific Coast Exchange. There are also some stocks that are traded on a national exchange and on several regional exchanges as well. U.S. Steel stock, for example, is traded primarily on the New York Stock Exchange, but it's also available on the Boston, Cincinnati, Midwest, Philadelphia, and Pacific Coast stock exchanges.

A centralized stock exchange?

In 1975, Congress mandated the establishment of a national securities market which would link together all the stock exchanges in the country. Such an exchange would have an obvious advantage: by increasing competition among buyers and sellers, it would help make prices more favorable for all investors. But Congress didn't say what kind of national market it would be, or how it would be set up.

What if a brokerage house goes bust?

It's been known to happen. In fact, during the late 1960s several major stockbrokerage firms were forced out of business because of financial trouble. The NYSE was obliged to step in to prevent as many losses as possible to the customers of those troubled firms. Clearly, steps needed to be taken to retain the faith of the nation's investors. To cope with such collapses in the future, Congress passed in 1970 the Securities Investor Protection Act. This act established the Securities Investor Protection Corporation (SIPC), which provides up to $50,000 worth of federal insurance for each investor who buys and leaves securities for safekeeping with a brokerage house, and up to $20,000 of insurance for cash left with a brokerage house. SIPC does not, of course, guarantee investors against losses from declines in the price of their securities. That would take all the fun out of the game. It merely insures them against losses resulting from fraud or bankruptcy in the brokerage house itself.

How can an investor be sure that speculative information is accurate?

Until 1933 when Congress passed the Securities Act (also known as the Truth in Securities Act), an investor couldn't be at all sure that stock information was correct. There was no way for an investor contemplating the purchase of a new issue of stock or bonds to be certain that the issuers weren't lying through their teeth. After the federal regulations came into force, however, there were some big changes made in financial disclosures. Any company offering stock, for instance, must give data on its earnings, its financial condition, its product lines, and the qualifications and salaries of its officers. Every potential buyer of the new issue must be furnished with *a summary of this registration statement*, called a **prospectus**, before buying the securities in question. If at a later date the information given in the prospectus is found to be inadequate or false, the officers, directors, lawyers, and accountants of the issuing company can be sued by investors and can also be open to criminal prosecution.

Similarly, municipalities and other issuers of bonds are also required to be both full and accurate in their disclosures to prospective investors. Nevertheless, this doesn't take the risk out of investing. In 1974 and 1975, for example, New York City sold $4 billion worth of notes. According to the Securities Exchange Commission, the city's chief financial officers knew full well at that time that New York was hovering on the brink of bankruptcy. Nevertheless, an SEC report says, they gave "unwarranted reassurances" about the safety of the investments, issued misleading statements, and deflected attention from New York's true financial situation by attributing the city's troubles to the national economy. By SEC standards, the city was thus in violation by selling the notes as good investments. Whether or not any civil or criminal action will be taken against those who handled the city's finances at the time—including former Mayor Abraham Beame—is not that important. What we should note is that such charges *can* be brought against anyone misleading potential investors in such a way.

To date, the nation's exchanges have not worked out a master plan for the SEC to approve. The New York Stock Exchange has, however, come up with a pilot system of its own: the Intermarket Trading System (ITS), an electronic network intended to link the NYSE with stock exchanges in Philadelphia, Boston, and the Pacific region across the continent, as well as with the American Exchange down the street. ITS has had some success, but some critics have claimed that it is biased in the NYSE's favor. Thus, the SEC will probably continue to push for the development of a truly national network.

FOREIGN EXCHANGES

There are stock exchanges in all the major cities of the world, including London, Paris, Hamburg, Tokyo, and Toronto. Amsterdam boasts the world's oldest stock exchange, one founded in 1611 when the Dutch East India Company first sold its shares to the public. Each of these foreign exchanges concentrates on trading the securities of its national companies. However, some companies in the United States, particularly those with worldwide sales and plants, have become interested in attracting foreign buyers for their securities, and their stocks now trade on these foreign exchanges. The stock of IBM, for example, is traded on the Tokyo and London exchanges. On the London exchange it's recently become a favorite of the biggest investors of them all—the newly rich Arabs. So active has IBM been on the London Exchange that rumors of an Arab acquisition of the giant corporation have driven the price of its stock very high at certain times.

INVESTING IN STOCKS

The old image of the "fat cat" stockholder—a portly old man in a silk top hat, frock coat, and striped trousers, chomping on an expensive cigar—is out of fashion in our time. Today **institutional investors**—that is, *companies that invest money entrusted to them by others*—make up the most important segment of stockholders in the United States, accounting for an ever-increasing percentage of the shares traded in recent years. This is not to say that the individual has been shunted out of the picture, but today many individuals become stockholders indirectly *through* institutional investors. You can become a stockholder indirectly merely by putting money into an insurance policy or a pension fund. That money will be invested in securities by the insurance company or pension fund, both of which are institutional investors.

Over 25 million Americans—more than one out of every ten people in the United States—are direct owners of stock.[2] Since so many people have become stockholders, it's wise to know something about the investing process.

THE PROCESS OF INVESTING

An investor's first step is to open an account with a brokerage house. The brokerage house may be a large multimillion-dollar enterprise with thousands of employees like Merrill Lynch, or a small two-person office handling a few accounts. After selecting a firm, the investor signs a few simple papers authorizing the house to trade. Depending on the investor's credit rating, a small deposit may also be necessary. Next the investor chooses, or is assigned, an account executive. This person is known as a **stockbroker**, or **registered representative (RR)**. He or she *has passed a test on investment practices and has been registered with an exchange for the purpose of buying and selling stocks.* The most important stockbrokers are registered with many exchanges—sometimes all nine.

A customer who wishes to buy or sell a stock on the New York Stock Exchange must give his stockbroker specific instructions. He can place a **market order**. This means that *the broker will instruct the member on the floor to make the trade almost immediately at the best price that can be negotiated at the moment.* Or the customer can place a **limit order**. This means he *specifies the highest price he is willing to pay if he is buying the stock or the lowest price he will accept if he is selling.* For example, if you enter a limit order to buy 100 shares of AT&T at 60, the member on the floor is not permitted to pay more than $60 a share. If the stock is selling at 60¼ ($60.25 per share) when you place your order, he or she will be unable to buy it for you. It is possible, however, that the stock may later become available at the lower price. Your order will then be executed.

Unless otherwise specified, limit orders are en-

TWO TYPES OF STOCKHOLDERS?

Depending on who is doing the describing, a purchaser of stock may be called by one of two different names—investor or speculator. What's the difference between the two? Broadly speaking, an **investor** *buys stock in a company in the hopes that its earnings and value will increase gradually over the long term.* A **speculator**, on the other hand, *buys stocks with the goal of making a quick profit by reselling them at a higher price.* For instance, he or she may try to buy stock at a point shortly before the company announces a new contract or an increase in its dividend. The speculator will plan to sell that stock soon after and make a handsome profit. A speculator, in other words, is often thought of as a "wheeler-dealer," an investor as a careful businessperson. Of course, the distinction between the two is not always clear-cut; one person's "risk" is often another person's "sensible move."

tered for one day only. The brokerage house will try to buy the stock for you at your limit price all during that particular day, but your order will expire at the end of the day. If you wish, you can enter an **open order**, which *instructs your stockbroker to leave your order in on subsequent days until you cancel it.*

A customer with special confidence in the stockbroker's ability to judge the trend of market prices may place a **discretionary order**. Such an order *gives the stockbroker the right to judge whether to have the order executed at once or wait for a better price.* In some cases, discretionary orders will save the customer money. If the stockbroker's judgment proves wrong, however, and the customer ends up paying more on a purchase or getting less on a sale, the broker cannot be held responsible.

SPECIAL KINDS OF STOCK MARKET TRANSACTIONS

Many people go into the stock market to "make a quick killing." For them, certain types of stock market deals are of special interest.

Margin trading

In **margin trading**, *customers do not pay for stock in full. Instead, they borrow money from their stockbrokers.* They pay interest on the amount of money borrowed and leave stock with the brokers as collateral for the loan. Margin requirements (that is, the percentage of the cost that the customer can borrow) are set by the Federal Reserve Board and are changed periodically. Short-term speculators find margin trading attractive because it permits them to buy more shares than they could otherwise afford. For example, a speculator could buy only fifty shares of the stock if he or she paid for it in full, but he or she could buy 100 shares under a 50 percent margin requirement. For more detail on this subject, see our Enrichment Chapter on the Money and Banking System.

Short selling

Short selling involves *selling stock the customer does not own in the hope of buying it back later at a lower price.* Thus if a speculator recognized in early 1974 that Polaroid, then selling at $88 a share, was about to have difficulties in marketing its new SX-70 camera, she might have sold 100 shares of Polaroid short for $8,800. Her stockbroker would have borrowed the stock for her to deliver to the purchaser. Then, several months later, when the stock declined to $15 a share, the speculator could have bought 100 shares for only $1,500, using it to replace the stock she had borrowed. Her profit on the transaction would have been $7,300. This figure represents the difference between the cost of the 100 shares she bought ($1,500) and the money she received for the 100 shares she sold ($8,800).

There are risks in selling short. If Polaroid had not declined but had gone up sharply, the speculator would have been forced eventually to buy 100 shares at some higher price. She would then incur a loss on the trade amounting to the difference between her selling price of $8,800 and the price she finally had to pay to repurchase the stock.

Options trading

A **stock option** is the *purchased right to buy a specified number of shares (often 100) of a stock at a prede-*

HOW IT'S ACTUALLY DONE

MAKING A STOCK PURCHASE

Let us assume that Nancy Richards, who lives in Chattanooga, wants to buy some shares of General Motors common stock. She has read the listing of New York Stock Exchange transactions that appears daily in her Chattanooga newspaper and knows that GM is now selling at around $65 a share. She calls her local stock brokerage firm, Jones & Company, and talks to her broker. Ms. Richards enters a market order to buy 100 shares of GM.

The order is telephoned to the Jones & Company clerk on the floor of the New York Stock Exchange. The clerk hands it to the New York Stock Exchange member who is a partner in Jones & Company. This member goes to the GM **trading post**, *the specific location on the floor where a particular stock is traded,* and calls out, "How's Motors?" A specialist in GM stock answers, "65 to a quarter." This means that someone is currently bidding $65 a share for 100 shares (or more) of the stock, and that someone else is willing to sell at $65.25. The Jones & Company member could buy the stock immediately for Nancy Richards at $65.25 a share, because hers was a market order. More likely, however, the member will bid $65\frac{1}{8}$ for a few minutes, hoping to save a little money.

Meanwhile Doug Andrews, in Palo Alto, California, has decided to sell his 100 shares of GM in order to pay his son's college bills for the year. He has phoned his broker, giving him an order to sell 100 GM at $65\frac{1}{8}$. The Exchange member representing Andrews's brokerage firm reaches the trading post in time to hear the interchange between the GM specialist and the Jones & Company member. He hears the Jones member bid $65\frac{1}{8}$ for the stock and shouts out, "Sold at $65\frac{1}{8}$." The two members initial each other's order slips. *A stock exchange employee called a* **reporter** *makes a note of the trade.* Within minutes the transaction is reported back to the brokerage houses and to the two customers.

The transactions just described involve listed securities. If Nancy Richards wanted to buy over-the-counter stocks, the procedure would differ. Say

Key moments in a trade: first, a member-firm clerk signals to relay the customer's market order from the booth to the floor partner.
▼

▲
The floor partner walks through the crowd to the post where the specific stock is traded, and makes the trade with another member who has a market order to buy the stock.

The members hand-signal the execution of their orders to their respective booth clerks. Then the sale is recorded on a "mark-sense" card, which is inserted into an electronic card reader for transmittal to ticker tape.
▼

she wanted to buy 100 shares of American Express, an unlisted stock. Her stockbroker would work through the over-the-counter department of the brokerage. A clerk there would check to see which brokers trade in this stock. Then calls would be placed to several of them, and the clerk would buy the shares at the lowest price quoted. Once the transaction was completed, Ms. Richards would be billed for this price, plus commission.

In addition to commissions, there are small costs involved in buying or selling **odd lots**, deals that involve *fewer than 100 shares of stock*. The odd-lot buyer pays $\frac{1}{8}$ of a point (or 12.5¢) more for each share of stock bought. The odd-lot seller receives $\frac{1}{8}$ of a point less for each share sold below $55 on the New York Stock Exchange. (The fee goes up to $\frac{1}{4}$ of a point for each share selling above $55.) Thus if a customer were buying ten shares of GM at the same time the Richards/Andrews transaction occurred, he would pay 65\frac{1}{4}$ per share for the stock. The customer selling forty-four shares at that moment would receive only $65 per share.

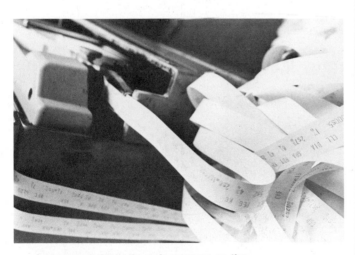

Just seconds later, the sale appears on the ticker tape.

termined price during a specified period of time. Here we'll discuss two kinds of options.

A **call option** works this way: *the option buyer, placing money on what's known as a **call**, is betting that the price of the stock will rise during the option period.* If it does, then the owner of the option can either buy the shares (which are thus obtained at a bargain price) or sell the option to someone else at a profit.

A **put option** works the opposite way: it *gives its purchaser the right to sell to (or "put to") another investor a block of shares at a fixed price within a specified period of time.* The purchaser of the option is betting that the value of the shares will fall below the specified amount during the option period. If it does, the right of sale can be exercised, allowing the purchaser of the option to get rid of the shares at a price higher than their market value.

CAN INVESTORS BEAT THE ODDS?

The stock market is often compared to a giant casino in which the stakes are very large. As in casinos, every other player seems to have not only *a* system, but *the* system with which to unlock the complexities of the game and win a fortune. Some investors' systems have been based on the phases of the moon; others call for investments to be made in tune with the speculator's biorhythms. But there are schemes based on somewhat more concrete data.

Ed Thorp, for instance, is a mathematician who has put his skills with numbers to work in the stock market. As he puts it, "From a mathematical standpoint, the market is far more interesting than other forms of gambling because of the enormous number of variables and imponderables it encompasses. Besides, the bulk of the past thinking about the market is nothing but alchemy and astrology." His system, he claims, is a mathematically based stock-trading technique and is supposed to yield profits no matter what direction the market takes. How does Thorp do it? He applies some very complex personal formulas to stocks and bonds in a state of flux. To be specific, he takes advantage of situations in which convertible bonds can be had for prices well below those of the stocks for which they can eventually be exchanged.[3]

For the more fainthearted, there are a variety of

Many investors seek systems for beating the odds on the stock market.

systems that have been developed to soften up—if not actually beat—the odds against the investor. One highly favored method, **hedging**, involves *spreading speculation among several moves.* It works like this: suppose an investor thinks the price of a given stock is going to go down. He sells some of the stock short to make a profit when it falls; but at the time, to protect himself ("hedge") against the possibility that the stock may go up in price instead, he will buy some shares of the same stock.

Another approach, **dollar averaging,** is based on the fact that stock prices tend to go up and down in a fairly regular pattern: *the investor sets aside a certain sum of money for stocks to be purchased when they are at the low part of their fluctuating cycle.* Perhaps the safest of all, however, is the **indexing** approach, in which *the investor studies Standard & Poor's Index (p. 378), notes the proportion in which various stocks are represented, and then tries to accumulate a portfolio in exactly these proportions.*

INTERPRETING THE FINANCIAL NEWS

There's no such thing as "happy ignorance" when it comes to investing. Only an informed investor has anything approaching an even chance to succeed. For-

tunately, a great deal of investment information is readily available, and it's not difficult for investors to obtain the basic background knowledge they need.

The media are full of financial news. General, though often scanty, information is available on television news programs. More information is carried by *The Wall Street Journal,* a financial newspaper published every business day and on sale throughout the country. Weekly magazines such as *Barron's* or *Business Week* can provide valuable insights into the state of the market. And in addition, there are economic, industrial, and company surveys available from leading banks, from financial service companies such as Moody's, Standard & Poor's, or Value Line, and from individual brokerage houses.

Probably the most convenient source of financial information for the average investor, however, is the local newspaper. It provides statistics of various kinds, including stock quotations and prices of bonds, mutual funds, and commodities. Securities listed are both those sold on the national exchanges and those of local interest. The information is in condensed form, but it is not difficult to read once you know how.

READING STATISTICAL DATA IN NEWSPAPERS

Stocks traded on a stock exchange

Following the day's activities, a listing of trading is prepared by each stock exchange. Most newspapers carry the New York and American stock exchange reports. Many papers also provide a report from a regional exchange.

A sample from a daily newspaper listing and an explanation of how to read it is shown in Figure 2. For any given stock, the information begins with the high and low prices to date, proceeds through the number of shares traded, and ends with the net change from the closing price of the day before.

THE PRICE-EARNINGS RATIO One item of information included is the **price-earnings ratio** (also known as the **price-earnings multiple**). This is *the relationship between a stock's market price and its earnings per share.* It is computed by dividing a stock's market price by its earnings per share. Say that Acme stock sold for

HOW TO READ A NEWSPAPER STOCK QUOTATION

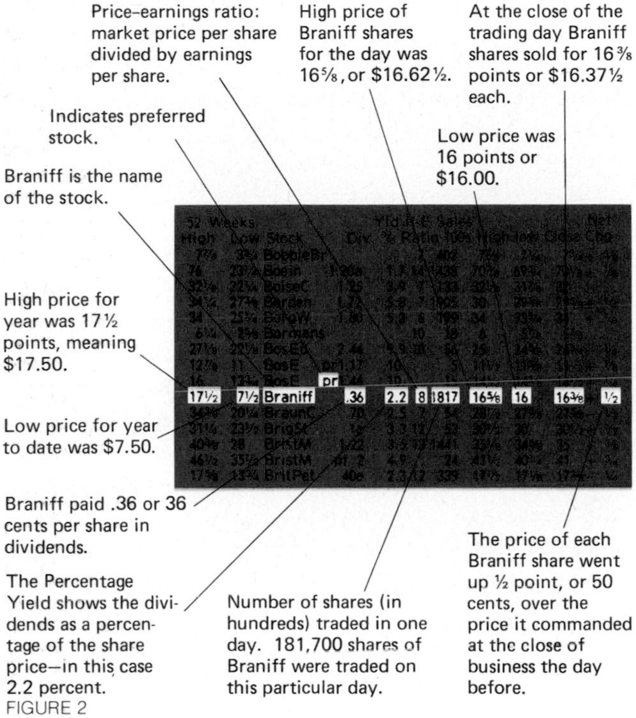

Price–earnings ratio: market price per share divided by earnings per share.

High price of Braniff shares for the day was 16⅝, or $16.62½.

At the close of the trading day Braniff shares sold for 16⅜ points or $16.37½ each.

Indicates preferred stock.

Braniff is the name of the stock.

Low price was 16 points or $16.00.

High price for year was 17½ points, meaning $17.50.

Low price for year to date was $7.50.

Braniff paid .36 or 36 cents per share in dividends.

The Percentage Yield shows the dividends as a percentage of the share price—in this case 2.2 percent.
FIGURE 2

Number of shares (in hundreds) traded in one day. 181,700 shares of Braniff were traded on this particular day.

The price of each Braniff share went up ½ point, or 50 cents, over the price it commanded at the close of business the day before.

$20 a share last year and earned a dividend of $2 per share. The price-earnings ratio is 10:

$$\frac{\$20 \text{ market price}}{\$2 \text{ earnings per share}} = 10$$

If Central stock cost $20 but earned $4 per share, the price-earnings ratio would be 5:

$$\frac{\$20 \text{ market price}}{\$4 \text{ earnings per share}} = 5$$

Clearly, Central is preferable to Acme, since the stock costs the same but pays higher earnings. Therefore the lower the price-earnings ratio, the better the value. (This ratio also indicates the number of years necessary to recoup the investment, assuming that earnings remain the same. For example, at the rate of $2 per year for Acme stock it would take ten years to earn back the original investment of $20.)

Bond prices

Many newspapers also carry a report of trading that occurred in bonds listed on the major exchanges, as shown in Figure 3. In reading bond prices, remember that the price given in the newspaper must always be multiplied by 10 in order to arrive at the dollar price. For example, a bond shown as closing at 65 actually sold at $650.

Prices for over-the-counter stocks

Prices for over-the-counter stocks are reported somewhat differently from prices for securities listed on a stock exchange. Trading in these securities takes place among thousands of scattered dealers who communicate by telephone or teletype. Thus it is often impossible to keep a record of the exact prices at which the shares trade. The opening and closing prices, or daily highs and lows, are difficult to compile. So, shortly before the close of trading each day the National Quotation Bureau contacts a few leading dealers in each stock. It obtains the *prices at which these dealers were willing to buy the stock,* the **bid price**, or *sell the stock,* the **offer price**, at that time. This information is then printed in the newspaper, as indicated in Figure 4, under the headings "bid" and "asked." However, there is a difference between the price information for stocks

FIGURE 3

HOW TO READ A NEWSPAPER BOND QUOTATION

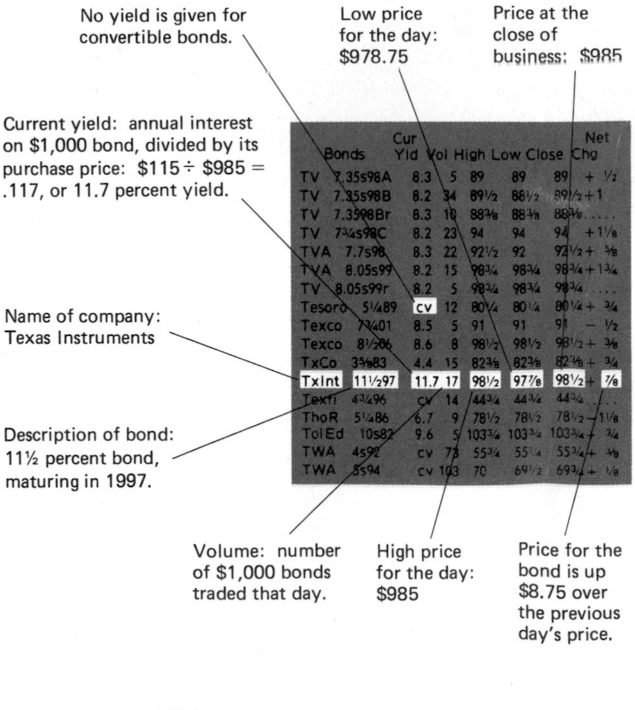

No yield is given for convertible bonds.

Low price for the day: $978.75

Price at the close of business: $985

Current yield: annual interest on $1,000 bond, divided by its purchase price: $115 ÷ $985 = .117, or 11.7 percent yield.

Name of company: Texas Instruments

Description of bond: 11½ percent bond, maturing in 1997.

Volume: number of $1,000 bonds traded that day.

High price for the day: $985

Price for the bond is up $8.75 over the previous day's price.

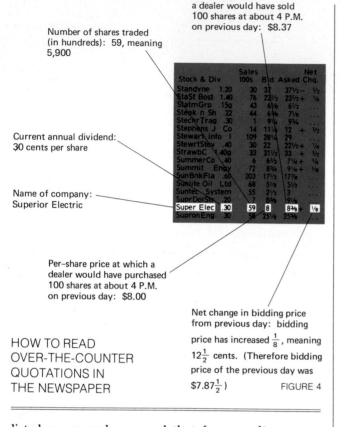

Number of shares traded (in hundreds): 59, meaning 5,900

Per–share price at which a dealer would have sold 100 shares at about 4 P.M. on previous day: $8.37

Current annual dividend: 30 cents per share

Name of company: Superior Electric

Per–share price at which a dealer would have purchased 100 shares at about 4 P.M. on previous day: $8.00

Net change in bidding price from previous day: bidding price has increased $\frac{1}{8}$, meaning $12\frac{1}{2}$ cents. (Therefore bidding price of the previous day was 7.87\frac{1}{2}$)

HOW TO READ OVER-THE-COUNTER QUOTATIONS IN THE NEWSPAPER

FIGURE 4

listed on an exchange and that for over-the-counter stocks. The former represents actual trades, while the latter is merely the price bid and asked at one particular moment.

Stock averages

In order to provide a quick summary of the general stock market trends, investors often use **stock averages**, which *describe the overall action of stock market prices*. For example, the Dow Jones Industrial Average dropped from over 1,000 to under 600 between January 1973 and January 1975. This is a shorthand way of saying that the prices of most stocks declined badly during this period. Averages are derived by adding the closing prices of selected stocks and dividing by a complex number that is not the exact number of stocks selected.

THE DOW JONES AVERAGES The oldest of the averages are the four prepared by Dow Jones. The best known is

the Dow Jones Industrial, an average of thirty leading industrial stocks, including U.S. Steel, General Electric, Eastman Kodak, and Du Pont. There is also a Dow Jones Utility, an average of fifteen utility stocks; a Dow Jones Transportation, an average of twenty transportation stocks; and a Dow Jones Composite, an average of the sixty-five stocks in all three of the preceding averages.

OTHER AVERAGES Many people prefer to use two other averages that include more stocks. These are the Standard & Poor's 500 Stock Average and the New York Stock Exchange Index, which covers all of the roughly 2,550 common stocks listed on the Exchange. Figure 5 shows the behavior of the Dow Jones Industrial and the Standard & Poor's Index over the period from 1965 to 1978. Note that their peaks and declines are parallel.

When the trend of the stock market is up—say, at the peak shown in the middle of 1976—we speak of a **bull market**. *When it is down,* as in early 1975, we speak of a **bear market**. (The origin of these terms is uncertain, but you can remember which is which by recalling that a bull tosses an attacker upward off his horns, while a bear wrestles his downward to the ground.)

Mutual fund prices

About 8 million people in the United States participate in stock and bond markets by owning shares of mutual funds rather than by owning their own securities.[4] A **mutual fund** (or **investment company**) is *a company in which many investors pool their money to buy securities*. The fund buys various stocks and/or bonds. Each shareholder in the fund owns a proportionate piece of these securities.

Mutual funds are particularly suitable for small investors and for those who lack the knowledge or the time to investigate and choose securities on their own. For example, an investor with $1,000 worth of a mutual fund has an ownership interest in perhaps fifty different securities that have been selected and watched continually by professionals in the investment business. Clearly, that person could not get such professional management, diversification, or convenience by investing the $1,000 directly.

The *price of a mutual fund,* called the **net asset value per share**, is determined daily by adding up

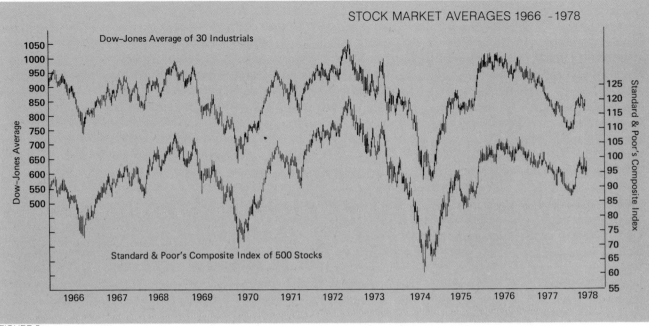

STOCK MARKET AVERAGES 1966 - 1978

Dow–Jones Average of 30 Industrials

Standard & Poor's Composite Index of 500 Stocks

FIGURE 5

the value of all the securities the fund owns and dividing by the number of shares. **Load funds**, which are sold by salespeople—usually stockbrokers—*require a sales charge (load) on top of the net asset value.* **No-load funds**, which *do not employ salespeople, have no sales charges.* Since the two types of funds tend to do equally well for investors, no-load funds are naturally the more popular.

Daily prices for the larger mutual funds are printed in many newspapers. The number in the first column is the price a fundholder would receive by selling shares on a particular day, that is, the net asset value per share of the fund. The second column lists the price an investor would have to pay to buy a share of the fund. It is the net asset value of the fund plus a load, if any. In Figure 6, the funds with a difference between the "sell" and "buy" price are obviously load funds. The initials "N.L." in the buy column indicate a no-load fund. (In some newspapers, a no-load fund is identifiable because there is no difference between the sell and buy listings.) The third number in Figure 6 represents the change in net asset value from the preceding day.

In recent years the mutual fund concept has gone well beyond its simple origins. Today a wide variety of **equity funds**—*mutual funds for stocks*—are available to meet every investor's need. Part of the success of mutual funds can be attributed to the aggressive mar-

keting techniques that have made their sales soar. Mutual funds today are backed up by consumer research that would do a company such as Procter & Gamble proud. Fund purchasers are studied, segmented, and tested just the way potential buyers for a new detergent are. The aim is to create the right fund package and then successfully promote it. Newspaper financial sections and pages of such magazines as *Forbes* and *Business Week* are crowded with ads for different kinds of funds.

Many funds have even gone so far as to set up toll-free phone numbers so that fundholders and po-

HOW TO READ A NEWSPAPER MUTUAL FUND QUOTATION   FIGURE 6

Change between the present buy price and the last buy price

Indicates a "no load" fund—i.e., there is no sales charge

Name of mutual fund

Net asset value per share (N.A.V.), i.e., the nominal value of one share

Price per share, including sales charge

	NAV	Offer NAV Price	Chg.
Acorn Fnd	20.62	N.L.+	.09
Adv Invest	11.22	N.L. +	.05
Afuture Fd	12.62	N.L. +	.13
AGE Fund	4.71	4.81+	.02
Allstate	9.95	N.L. +	.02
Alpha Fnd	12.67	N.L. +	.03
Am Birthrt	10.32	11.28+	.02
American Funds Group:			
Am Bal	x8.58	9.38 −	.09
Amcap F	8.92	9.75+	.06
Am Mutl	11.11	12.14+	.08
An Daily	1.00	N.L.	...
An Gwth	7.55	8.25+	.01
An Spect	4.79	5.02+	.20

tential buyers may discuss the status of the fund in general or their accounts in particular. This system enables the funds to keep in close contact with their shareholders and arrange for over-the-phone dividend transfers and redemptions. To get down to the grass-roots investors, some funds, such as T. Rowe Price, send their executives on cross-country coffee-klatch tours, while others, such as Funds, Incorporated, set up regional seminars for advice on taxes, estate planning, and the like.

Among the many different kinds of mutual funds are aggressive growth funds and conservative growth funds; funds for new businesses and funds for older businesses. Mutual funds for bonds have also seen much collective investor action. Particularly popular are tax-free municipal bond funds, which allow investors in relatively high tax brackets to enjoy the same tax benefits they would have if they purchased municipal bonds on their own. Other popular forms of mutual funds include those dealing in mass purchases of corporate paper and corporate bonds.

Commodity prices

Many business people are interested in the prices of raw materials. A pot-and-pan manufacturer, for exam-ple, wants to know about the daily fluctuations in the price of copper. A breakfast-cereal producer must keep track of trends in the prices of wheat, rye, oats, and sugar. *These raw materials,* known as **commodities**, *are traded on* **commodity exchanges**. Figure 7 shows a report of spot prices for a partial list of commodities.

The commodity exchanges operate somewhat like stock exchanges—though on a larger scale. Among the better-known commodity exchanges in the United States are the Chicago Board of Trade and the New York Mercantile Exchange. Both of these facilities surpass the NYSE in physical size. This isn't surprising when one realizes that in the mid-1970s commodity trading grew in volume more than twice as fast as the NYSE—and this is in addition to the active trading in copper, sugar, coffee, and cocoa on various London exchanges and elsewhere throughout the world.

Some commodity trading is *done for immediate delivery* and is called **spot trading**, or **cash trading**. In other cases, the *buying and selling is negotiated for future delivery,* often for dates a year or more distant. This is called **futures trading**. (See our Enrichment Chapter on Risk Management and Insurance for a case concerning the actual procedures involved in futures trading.)

As is the case with the securities market, there is a move to consolidate the country's six commodities or futures markets. The Chicago Board of Trade and the New York Mercantile Exchange have already begun discussions aimed at combining their clearing operations. One of the results of such a move would be the leveling off of the charges exacted for one trade—which now range from five cents to as high as $1.50 per trade. Industry experts predict that if all the exchanges can agree to consolidation terms, the work could be done in three years.

GENERAL NEWS AND THE STOCK MARKET

Interesting as the latest commodity or stock prices may be, there's more to following the market than being able to read the financial pages. It's also vital to understand the *reason behind* a shift in the price of a

NEWSPAPER LISTING OF CASH-TRADING PRICES ON THE COMMODITIES MARKET

GRAINS AND FEEDS
Thursday, August 24, 1978
(Quotations as of 4 p.m. Eastern time)

	Thurs.	Wed.	Yr. Ago
Wheat, No. 2 ord hard KC bu	3.22½	3.19	2.32½
Wht,No.1 dk Nthn 14%-pro Mpls	3.20½	3.16½	z
Wheat, No. 2 soft red Chgo bu	n3.41½	3.38	2.06¾
Milo, No. 2 KC cwt	3.71	3.63	3.03
Corn, No. 2 yellow Chgo. bu ..	h2.23½	2.22¾	1.78¼
Oats, No. 2 milling, Mpls bu	1.30	1.29	z
Rye, No. 2 Mpls bu	2.35	2.35	1.90
Barley, top-qlty, Mpls bu	2.35	2.35	2.10
Soybeans, No. 1 yellow Chgo bu	n6.68	6.62¼	5.32
Flaxseed, Mpls bu	5.85	5.55	z
Bran, KC ton	72.00	71.00	59.00
Linseed Meal, Mpls ton	133.00	133.00	110.00
Cottonseed Meal, Memphis ton	152.50	152.50	122.50
Soybean Meal, Decatur, Ill. ton	170.00	167.50	139.50
Corn Gluten Feed, Chgo ton ..	92.00	92.00	78.00
Hominy Feed, Ill. ton	64.50	64.50	49.00
Meat-Bonemeal 50%-pro, Ill.ton	207.50	203.75	165.00
Brewer's Grains, Milw ton	78.00	76.00	80.00
Alfalfa Pellets, dehy, Neb., ton	65.00	65.00	51.00

Type of commodity: top quality

Commodity: barley

Location of commodities market: Minneapolis

Unit of price: bushel

Price per bushel on Thursday, August 24, 1978: $2.35

Price on preceding trading day, Wednesday, August 23, 1978: $2.35

Price same date a year ago: $2.10

FIGURE 7

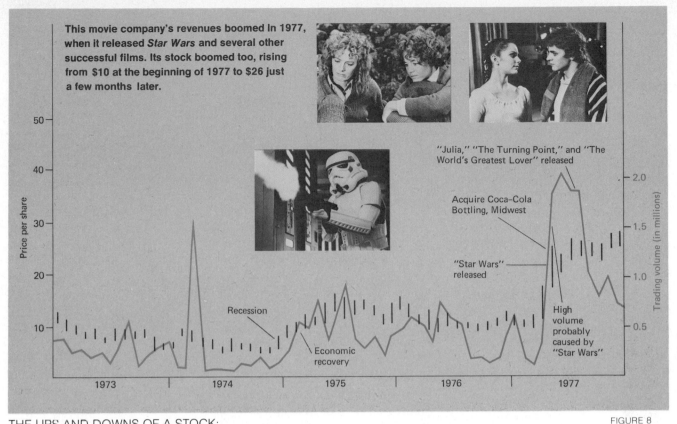

This movie company's revenues boomed In 1977, when it released *Star Wars* and several other successful films. Its stock boomed too, rising from $10 at the beginning of 1977 to $26 just a few months later.

"Julia," "The Turning Point," and "The World's Greatest Lover" released

Acquire Coca-Cola Bottling, Midwest

"Star Wars" released

Recession

Economic recovery

High volume probably caused by "Star Wars"

Price per share

Trading volume (in millions)

1973   1974   1975   1976   1977

THE UPS AND DOWNS OF A STOCK:
TWENTIETH-CENTURY FOX, 1973-1977

FIGURE 8

company's stock. Well before the price of a stock moves up or down, an astute investor can often get a hint of what's to come by reading about changes in top management, new products, or expansion plans. Likewise, it's particularly important to keep up to date on the quarterly sales and earnings statements that all listed companies and many over-the-counter companies report to the financial press. The trend of dividend payments is also significant. These trends, which are often reported in the press, can also be learned about by reading the investment newsletters that some brokerage houses produce.

In addition to news about individual companies, the press and other media give excellent coverage to news about the market in general, the economy as a whole, the nation, and even the state of the world—all of which can be involved in causing price fluctuations of even the most unlikely shares or commodities. Elements as diverse as unemployment figures, housing starts, retail sales, an act of Congress, a court decision, an administrative order, the fall of the British pound, the actions of a pack of terrorists, weather conditions,

and the state of the wheat crop in Russia—all can trigger the psychological impulses that are at the root of many swings in investments. Even the entertainment pages of the daily newspaper can hold important clues to the next moves of a particular stock or market. In late 1977, for instance, Columbia Pictures gambled $19 million on its production of *Close Encounters of the Third Kind.* The reviews after a sneak preview in Dallas were lukewarm, at best. Word got out, and soon film critics throughout the country were besieged for their opinions on the film by investors and analysts who wanted a head start on the rise or fall of Columbia shares. The film, it turned out, was a success, and Columbia stock rose accordingly. (In Figure 8, we show how the stock of another movie company has fluctuated.)

In short, following the securities market doesn't mean endlessly studying balance sheets and price lists while ignoring the world outside the office. On the contrary, it can mean getting a new and much deeper understanding of the diverse events that affect the entire business picture.

The two kinds of marketplaces in which securities can be bought and sold are stock exchanges and over-the-counter markets. The most important stock exchanges in the United States are the two national exchanges, the New York Stock Exchange and the American Stock Exchange. There are also seven regional exchanges and numerous foreign exchanges.

In placing an order to buy or sell stock, a customer can indicate the price basis for the transaction by entering a market, limit, open, or discretionary order. Customers who buy or sell less than 100 shares of one stock at one time are called odd-lot customers. They pay an additional fee on each share they buy and receive less on each share they sell. Market procedures of special interest to speculators are margin trading, short selling, and options trading.

Reports of daily trading on specific stocks and bonds are given in most newspapers. These also publish other statistical data, including stock averages and mutual fund and commodity price information. Astute businesspeople and investors will also carefully follow other news that may have a bearing on the market, including the general state of the economy.

securities markets
stock exchange
over-the-counter market
national exchanges
regional exchanges
institutional investors
stockbroker
registered representative (RR)
market order
limit order
open order
discretionary order
margin trading
short selling
stock option
call option
call
put option
hedging
volatile stocks
dollar averaging
indexing
price-earnings ratio (multiple)
bid price
offer price
stock averages
bull market
bear market
mutual fund (investment company)
net asset value per share
load funds
no-load funds
equity funds
commodities
commodity exchanges
spot (cash) trading
futures trading
investor
speculator
trading post
reporter
odd lots
blue-sky laws
prospectus

1. Compare trading on a stock exchange with trading in the over-the-counter market.

2. What are the basic steps in a transaction to buy or sell stock?

3. What are the additional costs imposed in buying or selling odd lots?

4. Why may a speculator prefer to buy stock on margin?

5. What happens to a speculator who sells stock short if the stock rises in price?

6. Explain the differences between newspaper price information regarding listed securities and that given for over-the-counter stock.

7. What kinds of financial news other than daily reports of transactions may be helpful in understanding the market?

INVESTING IN SOLAR ENERGY STOCKS: A RISKY VENTURE

Solar energy, according to Wall Street wisdom of the late 1970s, is not an industry for the casual investor. But for the person with $10,000 or so to spare, it's about the most exciting stock game in town. Indeed, since the price of fossil fuel began to multiply following the Arab oil embargo, solar energy stocks—most of them traded over the counter—have climbed high into the sky, offering the chance for large profits—and have also fallen back down to earth, taking investors' dollars with them.

Both the advantage and the danger of solar energy as an investment is the fact that the industry is so new. As one of the few alternative energy sources now undergoing serious development, solar power has attracted government funding and political support from a number of the nation's leaders. On the other hand, solar energy stocks are extremely vulnerable to shifts in the economic and political climate. When President Carter gave his energy message in 1977, for instance, one stock was trading as high as seventy cents—seven times its initial price. When Carter's energy program got slowed down in Congress, that same stock fell to a dreary fourteen cents.

Most of the solar energy devices on the market today are designed for such home uses as heating water or air; the basic element is the solar collector, a sheet of black metal enclosed in heat-trapping glass or plastic. Sales of these solar heaters (and other, yet-to-be-developed devices) are expected to exceed $1 billion by the early 1980s, in contrast to 1977 sales of $150 million. And hundreds of firms, lured by the uncomplicated nature of solar energy technology, have begun jockeying for their own places in the sun. But only a handful of these companies offer stock to the public, and even fewer investment analysts are following the industry on a full-time basis.

For investors, then, obtaining information or advice on solar energy is, at this point, difficult. John Sauter, member of a Denver-based firm that trades solar stocks, counsels investors to follow a cautious strategy. He says that with $20,000 or so, he would invest in four or five different companies—"and stay ready to move." Anthony Adler, the only full-time solar analyst in the United

States in 1978, also advises investors to split their risks, not only among solar energy companies but also among various sectors of the industry. Investing in a company whose only business is solar energy, Adler notes, offers the greatest opportunities, but also the greatest risk of painful loss. So his ideal portfolio consists of some "pure" solar companies, some others that are only 5 to 50 percent solar, and still others—like Exxon, Shell, and Motorola—that are less than 5 percent solar. Of course, the advice given by Sauter and Adler is not the last word on the matter. One journalist in the solar energy field tells of some Oklahoma dirt farmers who bought more than 30,000 shares in a "pure" solar company at the dirt-cheap price of ten cents a share. Recently, that same stock was selling at a sunny $2.13.

Adapted from "The Cloudy Dawn of Solar Stocks," MONEY Magazine, April 1978, by special permission; © 1978, Time Inc. All rights reserved.

1. What makes the solar energy industry seem like a good bet, and what makes it so risky?

2. Why does Sauter advise investing in several different companies, rather than just one?

3. Why does Adler suggest splitting the risks among various sectors of the industry?

CASE 2

JET-AGE TRADER: ANOTHER KIND OF EXCHANGE

Maps of the world and the United States and clocks showing the time in more than half a dozen capital cities scattered around the globe line

one wall of a unique exchange in Washington, D.C. Known as the OMNI International Jet Trading Floor, this is where people go when they want to buy, sell, or trade any model, make, or size of jet aircraft. Finding potential clients is no problem for Wayne J. Hilmer, OMNI's thirty-six-year-old owner, because every country keeps lists of registered aircraft. Once a week, Hilmer uses his telex machines and the mail to send reports of available aircraft to the people on those lists; then he waits for buyers to materialize.

The deals that Hilmer sets up range from the exotic to the extremely lucrative. Recently, for instance, Hilmer found buyers for two jets that had belonged to the late Elvis Presley, sold another jet to a Saudi Arabian prince, and accepted Frank Sinatra's private plane as part of a trade. But Hilmer does most of his dealing in the $1-billion executive jet market, which keeps hopping because companies can reduce their tax bills by trading in rather than selling their jets. Typically, OMNI itself provides the financing on these trade-ins, and then sells the planes to other buyers, wherever they may be. Trading activity on the OMNI Exchange will probably never become a regular report on the "Six O'Clock News," but for Hilmer there are compensations. In 1978, he planned to sell 100 jets for a total in excess of $100 million—which would earn him more than $3 million in commissions.[5]

1. In what ways is the OMNI Trading Floor similar to the New York Stock Exchange?

2. What services does OMNI provide—aside from handling jets—that other exchanges do not?

RISK MANAGEMENT AND INSURANCE

A secretary hurts her arm at an office softball game: is her employer liable for the injury? A warehouse is insured against fire but not against "acts of God": what happens if it's destroyed by a fire started by lightning? Risk, of course, is built into the free enterprise system. Any business venture is something of a gamble, and along with the hope of profit is the ever-present possibility of loss. While a good manager does everything possible to minimize that possibility, there are some risks that are inherently difficult to guard against—from natural disasters and freak accidents to strikes, lawsuits, and so on. It will be the purpose of this chapter to examine such risks and to discuss the means that have been developed to deal with them. We will look first at the categories of risk that can and cannot be insured against, and then at the various types of insurance available for the mutual protection of businesses and their employees.

WHAT WILL THIS CHAPTER FOCUS ON?

After reading the material in this chapter, you will understand and be able to discuss:

■ the reasons why risks are inevitable in business

■ the three types of risks—insurable, absorbable, and uninsurable

■ the four kinds of risks covered by business insurance—loss of property, legal liability, loss of earning power, and loss due to dishonesty or nonperformance

■ the ways businesspeople can insure their property and assets against losses due to fire, natural disasters, theft, and other causes

■ the three important categories of insurance through which employers protect their employees—health insurance, life insurance, and retirement insurance (pension plans)

■ the reasons why businesses must provide unemployment insurance, and the way unemployment insurance works

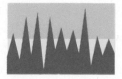

Disasters have a way of happening to every sort of business. A toy shop crammed with its pre-Christmas inventory burns to the ground in mid-November. A ship-owner hears that his largest supertanker has broken up, fully loaded, in Boston harbor, and he's responsible for cleaning up the mess. A jeweler opens the store one morning to discover that a thief has left behind only the crumbs of a hasty midnight snack.

Such things do happen. *Risk* is the possibility that such an event will occur and cause a business to lose money.

TYPES OF RISKS

INSURABLE RISKS

Some risks are easier to foresee than others. It's unlikely, for instance, that a meteorite will plunge through the ceiling of the room in which you're reading this chapter. In fact, it would be next to impossible to calculate the odds against so remote a possibility. Far more likely is the risk of fire. Therefore it would be sensible to insure against that calamity. This means that you or someone in business (the insuree) pays a company (the insurer) for protection against damage by fire. Should a fire occur according to conditions stated in your agreement (the insurance policy), the insurer would be obliged to reimburse you (pay you back) for the losses caused by the fire.

Of course, an insurance company doesn't make any profits through such one-on-one transactions. To make a profit, the insurance company requires a pool of insurees, each of whom is paying for a policy but only a few of whom will ever collect against a policy. The deal the insurance company makes with each insuree is like a bet. The insuree bets that he or she will have a fire; the insurance company bets that he or she will not. The insurance company wins *most* of its bets with insurees. Occasionally it loses a bet—an insuree has a fire. The insurance company can't pay for the damages out of the **premium** *(the fee that the insuree pays to the insurer for coverage)* it has received from that one insuree. But it can pay for the damages by drawing some money out of the pool of premiums it has received from all its insurees.

The risk of fire is a good example of what is known as an **insurable risk**—*a risk for which it is possible to buy insurance from some insurance company.* Insurance companies will offer insurance against fire because they have tremendous amounts of statistical data telling them exactly how frequently fires occur, under what conditions, and how much the damages they cause generally cost. Using this information, the company can calculate exactly how much it must charge each policyholder in order to be able to pay for fire damages when they occur and still make a profit (assuming they also know approximately how many policyholders they will have). The company also knows exactly what conditions must be stipulated in the policy in order to keep all claims within the range of what the company considers to be "typical" fires—not freak occurrences whose frequency would be im-

WHAT RISKS WILL AN INSURANCE COMPANY ACCEPT?

An insurable risk must meet the following requirements:

1. *The peril insured against must not be under the control of the insured.* A building cannot be insured against the possibility that its owner will burn it down. Losses caused by faulty judgment or careless planning are not insurable because such matters result from the actions of management.

2. *There must be a large number of cases subject to the same peril.* For example, fire is a common danger that threatens virtually all buildings. Most insurance is based on the law of averages. According to that law, only a certain number of losses will occur out of a great number of similar risks. However, the law of averages cannot be applied to unusual risks, those that threaten only a small number of subjects. For example, the possibility that a baseball pitcher might injure his throwing arm and miss an important game is an unusual risk. There are not that many pitchers. Consequently, most in-

possible to predict. Other types of insurable risks are theft, automobile collision, illness, and—of course—death. (Life insurance essentially represents a bet that an individual's life will—or will not—end within a certain period of time.)

Since an insurance company would prefer that its policyholders lead safe and notably calamity-free existences, it tries to spread its risks as thinly as possible. Consider, for example, what would have been the position of an insurer who wrote fire policies for many of the buildings in downtown Chicago a little more than one hundred years ago. The great fire of 1871 that swept the center of the city would have destroyed not only those structures, but the business of the foolhardy insurance company as well. It's for that reason that insurers like to have as shallow a pool of insurees as possible, spread across a wide range of risks.

ABSORBABLE RISKS

A second category of risk is known as **absorbable risks**. Absorbable risks *can be covered by insurance, but for one reason or another they're assumed or absorbed by a business itself.* This doesn't necessarily mean that a company that absorbs its risks is asking for trouble. Instead, it is simply *arranging to insure itself, rather than buy insurance from another company.* This form of protection is called **self-insurance**. For example, a huge corporation with one thousand factories might put aside a certain amount of money each year to cover possible fire losses. During the years in which there are no losses by fire, the self-insurance fund grows. If a factory should burn down, the company consequently has enough money on hand to either rebuild or replace it. Since it's unlikely that more

surance companies would not consider this an acceptable risk. A famous exception is Lloyd's of London, which is actually not an insurance company but an association through which members buy and sell insurance risks. Lloyd's is best known for arranging insurance for risks not covered by conventional insurance companies—injury to a singer's voice, for example.

3. *Losses must be calculable, and the cost of insuring must be economically feasible.* Insurance companies must have data on the frequency of losses caused by a given peril. This information should cover a long period of time and be based on a large number of cases. The insurance company can usually predict quite accurately how many losses will occur in the future with this information. For example, the number of people who will die each year in the United States has been calculated with great precision. Insurance companies know the death rate and life expectancy for Americans of different ages. They use such figures to estimate life insurance losses in various age groups. Once losses have been calculated, the insurance company decides whether expected losses from a given peril can be covered by the policyholders' payments.

Sometimes an uninsurable risk becomes insurable after a time. When airplanes were a new invention there were not enough data to calculate losses in air transportation. The risks also appeared to be very high. Flying, therefore, was considered an uninsurable risk. Then technical improvements gradually reduced risks. At the same time, information accumulated to the point where insurance companies could estimate losses. Insurance thus became economically feasible. Today low-cost flight insurance is available in nearly every airport.

4. *The peril must be unlikely to affect all insured simultaneously.* An insurance company should spread its coverage over large geographic areas. A single tornado might force an insurance company to pay out on all its policies at once. Similarly, a fire insurance company would be unwise to insure buildings in only one city. Fires like the ones that occurred in Chicago and San Francisco could destroy or damage all buildings at the same time.

5. *The possible loss must be financially serious.* An insurance company could not afford the paperwork involved in handling numerous small claims of a few dollars. As a result, most automobile insurance does not pay for minor repairs. A *deductible clause* specifies that the insurance company will pay a claim only after a certain amount has been deducted.

than one factory will burn in any given year, the company should always have a large enough fund to meet those needs. Setting aside money on a regular basis could very well be cheaper than purchasing insurance on each of a thousand factories. Moreover, the company can earn interest on the cash it has put in the fire reserves.

Of course, self-insurance is possible only on a large scale. The business with just one factory or store to its name could hardly accumulate enough money to face its loss without panic.

Self-insurance is becoming increasingly popular with companies large enough to afford it. Some must self-insure to some extent simply to cover the great size of their possible losses. Others believe that self-insurance is ultimately cheaper than the protection purchased from an insurance company. For example, Standard Oil of Indiana used to buy insurance coverage for any piece of property or equipment worth more than $1 million. Today, however, because of rising insurance costs, the company doesn't bother insuring any asset worth less than $5 million unless it's required to do so by law or contract. Potential losses under $5 million are planned to be absorbed.

UNINSURABLE RISKS

Unfortunately not every risk businesses face is always subject to protection by insurance. **Uninsurable risks** are *those that few if any insurance companies will touch*. For instance, no insurer will issue protection against business failures due to poor management or incompetence. When McDonnell Douglas aircraft produced the remarkably unsuccessful—and expensive—DC-8, it had to bear the brunt of that failure without the cushion of insurance. No insurance company in the world would have written a policy guaranteeing that the DC-8 would sell against competition that proved to be much more popular.

Other untouchable risks as far as insurers are concerned are those related to governmental actions and economic conditions. If an insurance company can't calculate the likelihood that it will be required to pay off a policy, chances are it won't write the policy. It follows, then, that things as incalculable as future legal changes and economic fluctuations are beyond the realm of risk insurance. For example, who twenty

years ago would have foreseen the government's mandate that air bags be installed in new cars as a safety device? Nevertheless, the regulation has been passed, and it will cost the automakers hundreds of millions of dollars to meet it. No insurance company would have wanted to be in the position of insuring against the passage of such a regulation, no matter how remote the possibility.

The conditions that affect our physical environment are similarly difficult to predict, as anyone stuck in an unexpected storm can attest. While businesses can purchase disaster insurance that covers hurricanes, floods, tornadoes, and the like, what about more specialized and prolonged conditions? In the winter of 1977, for example, hundreds of resort-related businesses were affected by an unusual phenomenon: a lack of snow. Hotels, restaurants, shops, discotheques, real estate agents, and rental shops across the western United States found that their usual sources of income had dried up with the snow that refused to fall. Few, if any, were insured against the eventuality of a snowless winter in the Rockies. Such a disaster without precedent is one against which insurance is difficult or unrealistically expensive to acquire, since the degree of risk involved can't be calculated.[1]

Can a business reduce its uninsurable risks?

The one certain way in which to reduce uninsurable business risks is through good management, pure and simple. A company that conducts thorough product research and then acts on that research is unlikely to turn out a product such as the DC-8. A business that keeps a close eye on governmental and social trends will rarely be caught unawares, as were the auto companies when safety became a prime concern in the early 1960s. And an enterprise that relies on more than one source for its profits is unlikely to be endangered when one of those sources can't be tapped for a time—unlike the ski-related businesses out West.

Changes in uninsurable risks

Sometimes a risk that was once uninsurable becomes insurable as times goes by. The insurance industry isn't static, though it does move with caution. In the early years of air travel, for instance, there simply wasn't enough information for insurers to know how much risk was involved. Now, however, insurance is easily available in virtually every airport lounge in the world. Or consider the case of kidnapping insurance in Europe. Just a few years ago kidnapping for high ransom was rare, and insurance against such a thing virtually unheard of. Recently kidnapping of wealthy Europeans has become relatively commonplace, and the insurance industry has responded by selling kidnapping policies (though they're illegal in some countries). With such a policy the purchaser, or insuree, is guaranteed that any ransom demands—up to the limit set in the policy—will be met in the event of his or her being kidnapped.

The details of coping with risk in a business situation bear closer examination. In the rest of this chapter we'll look at some types of risk that companies routinely cover by means of insurance.

KINDS OF INSURANCE

Most families in the United States take out two kinds of insurance. One is property insurance, which covers the house, car, and other property against the specific threats of fire and theft. The other is personal insurance, which covers life and health. In general, businesses have the same insurance needs. They have to protect the business itself, that is, the property and the assets. They must also protect the people who do the work, that is, they must insure their employees. Because businesses encounter many more kinds of risks than families, each of these two large categories of insurance can be broken down into many different types of business coverage. We can examine each of these separately.

PROPERTY AND ASSET INSURANCE

As we've pointed out, to protect itself from loss, a business has to insure its property against various kinds of damage. Furthermore, it needs to protect assets such as cash and securities from loss due to natural or human causes. Basically, insurance can cover four kinds of business losses: loss of property,

loss of earning power, loss due to liability, and loss due to dishonesty or nonperformance (see Table 1, next page).

Two of the risk categories, property and legal liability losses, are the most heavily covered by insurance. Moreover, such types of coverage are still on the increase. There are several reasons. Most important, the growth of the economy has increased the ownership of goods. When more businesses and more people own more property, there is the potential for that much more loss.

BUILDING YOUR BUSINESS VOCABULARY

The Insurance Policy. Let us assume that a business faces an insurable risk and wants to buy insurance. What actually happens? *One party, the insurer, agrees to pay another party,* the **insured** (or **insuree**), *for losses specified in a written contract,* the **insurance policy**. The policy states the amount of money the insurer will pay if the insured suffers financial loss under the conditions described in the policy. *The amount payable in the event of loss* is called the **claim**. *The insured agrees to pay the insurer a fee,* called the **premium**, the amount of which is also specified in the policy.

The amount of the premium is based mainly on the probability of loss in insuring a specific type of risk. For example, since fire is a greater risk for wooden buildings than for brick ones, insurance premiums tend to be higher on wooden structures. The insurance company must collect enough money in premiums to pay the claims of policyholders and also enough to cover its own expenses and operate at a profit.

A person employed by an insurance company to compute expected losses and calculate the cost of premiums is called an **actuary**. An actuary considers three basic factors in setting the premiums. One is the estimated loss rate—how much the insurance company expects to pay out in claims. A second is the company expenses such as taxes and salaries. A third is interest rates. Because reserve funds are invested to earn income for an insurance company, falling interest rates may force it to raise premiums.

TABLE 1 Business Risks and Protection

Risk	Protection
Loss of property	Fire insurance Disaster insurance Marine insurance
Loss from legal liability	Liability insurance Workmen's compensation
Loss of earning power	Business interruption insurance Extra expense insurance Small business and key executive life insurance
Loss from dishonesty or nonperformance	Burglary, robbery, and theft insurance Fidelity bonding Surety bonding Credit life insurance

LOSS OF PROPERTY

When a record manufacturer in California sends a shipment of discs to Chicago, the manufacturer subjects the goods to certain unavoidable risks. If the truck that is carrying them catches fire or goes over a cliff, all that would be left would be thousands of shattered or melted bits of plastic and a substantial loss. Furthermore, the record factory itself is always subject to damage by fire, flood, or, particularly in California, by earthquake. To protect against such losses, the manufacturer buys property insurance. **Property insurance** *covers the insured company or individual for physical damage to, or destruction of, property resulting from unavoidable perils.* This insurance comes in three varieties: fire insurance, natural disaster insurance, and marine insurance.

Fire insurance

Fire is of equal menace to the shoe repair shop on the corner and the most impressive corporate office tower, although the damage fire leaves behind may be more sharply felt by the small business. It's fortunate, then, that almost every kind of building and its contents can be insured against losses caused by fire. Today the definition of damage by fire has grown to include coverage against lightning damage. This was a conces-

sion that insurance companies made when they found they could rarely tell whether damage in a lightning-caused fire was due to the fire or to the initial bolt of lightning. Fire insurance policies are written on a one-, three-, or five-year basis. Premium rates vary according to the amount of risk involved. Wooden buildings, for instance, are more costly to insure than brick structures.

Insurance against natural disasters

Natural disasters are among the most spectacular in terms of property lost. In 1973 a record number of tornadoes (1,109) caused property losses in excess of $500 million. The year before, Hurricane Agnes caused property damages totaling more than $3 billion. Natural disaster insurance helps individual and business property owners cope with such losses, though not all who can do so avail themselves of the protection. Of the $3 billion in losses from Hurricane Agnes, for example, only $98 million of the damage was covered by insurance.

Less dramatic natural disasters account for millions of dollars of property damage each year. Businesses can protect themselves against these losses by purchasing extended coverage agreements—usually issued as *supplements* or **riders** to a basic insurance policy. As always, the cost of coverage is related to the amount of risk the insurance company incurs. Earthquake damage in California, for instance, would be considerably more costly than in Kansas. Riders can also be purchased to cover losses from such unnatural but potentially disastrous hazards as riots, explosions, and falling aircraft.

Marine insurance

Marine insurance, despite its title, *covers losses related to transportation on water and on land.* The term dates from the time when it was used exclusively to insure ships and cargoes at sea. There are two kinds of marine insurance. **Ocean marine insurance** *provides protection on all types of oceangoing vessels and their cargoes, be they at sea or in port.* It insures against losses from sinking, collision, fire, and so on. **Inland marine insurance** *covers domestic shipments by ship and barge on inland waterways, and by rail, truck, air-*

Wind-shattered windows fly off a Boston skyscraper, snow crushes a Long Island sportsdome, and a giant oil tanker breaks up in a storm off the coast of Brittany: as these recent examples suggest, natural disasters can mean costly property loss.

plane, and other means of inland transport. A typical inland marine insurance policy insures the holder against nearly every possible accident, including fire, collision, natural disasters, and train derailments.

LIABILITY INSURANCE

Liability insurance *covers the insured for losses arising from injury to another person or damage to the property of others.* Such liability can occur in the least likely places. On a ski slope at Stratton Mountain, Vermont, for instance, a bit of apparently harmless brush on an otherwise well-tended run turned into a liability that cost the slope's owner—or, rather, its insurer—a fortune. It happened when a skier stumbled on the stray vegetation, fell, and was permanently paralyzed. A court found that the owner of the slope was liable for the injury and awarded the plaintiff $1.5 million.[2]

More familiar is the liability insurance taken out by drivers. If a driver causes an accident, he or she is liable for damages, just as the operator of the ski slope was liable. Automobile liability insurance covers property damage and bodily injury, including death. It protects the insured against financial loss if the policy-owner is found to be negligent and so responsible for the accident.

Similarly, businesses are liable for any injury they cause to a person or to the property of others by some negligent act. What sorts of accident would make a business legally liable? Here are three common types:

- injuries received on the company's property, for example, injuries received in an elevator accident;
- injuries caused by the company's products, such as a toy that is judged unsafe or a poisonous food product;
- injuries from malpractice. Doctors and dentists are often sued for bodily injury, and lawyers and accountants may be sued for loss of assets or property.

In recent years the scope of liability has grown immensely, extending even to indirect involvement in loss, injury, or death. Recent court interpretations have stated that those who distribute goods, as well as those who manufacture them, are liable when the goods cause damage. A wholesaler of coffins, for in-

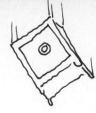

The businessperson must be aware of potential sources of liability on his premises.

stance, was held strictly liable to a pallbearer who was injured due to a defective handle—even though the wholesaler had nothing whatever to do with the manufacture of the coffin. Similarly, a telephone lineman injured in a fall caused by a shock from a defective lighting fixture successfully sued the distributor of the fixture. What was remarkable in that case was that the fixture had been shipped directly by the manufacturer. It had never even been in the possession of the distributor.

As a result of these developments, the cost of liability insurance for distributors has gone skyward. Fortunately for them as well as for other holders of liability insurance, most policies cover the insured up to the amount of the claim, or at least to the limit of the policy, when the insured is held liable by the courts.

Workmen's compensation insurance

Workmen's compensation insurance, which is required of businesses by law, *covers claims that employees make against their employers if they are injured on the job or become ill as a result of their work.* This insurance protects businesses from loss of assets due to compensation claims. It covers both full-time and part-time employees.

What's unique about workmen's compensation insurance as a form of liability protection is that negligence need not be shown. Instead, negligent or not, an employer is obligated to reimburse—usually through an insurance company—the financial losses of employees whose health is impaired because of their work.

Over the years the courts have interpreted workmen's compensation laws broadly, to say the least—often holding companies liable for injuries only indirectly related to an employee's work. Claims have been awarded for injuries as unrelated to the job as an arm broken by a lawyer at his office softball game. Topping that is the case of a bagel baker in California who was recently awarded $15,000 in workmen's compensation for construction of a fancy swimming pool to be used in a physical therapy program for a back injury.[3]

Today all fifty states require almost every employer to carry workmen's compensation insurance or to set aside enough money for self-insurance. The costs of the insurance vary depending on the hazards associated with the particular type of work. In all but nine states the weekly benefit ceilings have been set at two-thirds the average weekly wage.

Workmen's compensation insurance pays the medical bills of an employee who is hurt on the job. If the injury is serious enough to temporarily disable the employee, he or she receives weekly benefits, usually after a waiting period of a few days to two weeks, depending on the state. If the injury is fatal, dependents receive weekly payments for a specified period (frequently eight years). Workmen's compensation insurance also covers the employer if the injured employee wins a lawsuit for damages greater than those provided for in the policy.

COPING WITH THE EXPENSE OF WORKMEN'S COMPENSATION INSURANCE With the benefits from workmen's compensation rising to ever higher levels, it's hardly surprising that the cost of premiums for this type of insurance are on the upswing as well. In fact, they have doubled, on average, in the past three years. To handle these costs, businesses are seeking less expensive alternatives to traditional workmen's compensation insurance. B. F. Goodrich, for instance, has switched to a less costly and less burdensome self-insurance system, free of the bureaucratic delays of a government-supervised program. In Florida, businesses too small to set up individual plans of their own are considering banding together to form a self-insurance pool.[4]

Another way to avoid paying out high premiums is to cut down on the number of claims made by employees. The only way for a business to do that is to reduce injuries and job-related illnesses. With that aim in mind, many companies are examining their safety programs more closely. Insurance companies are naturally all for this. At least one, the Employers Mutual of Wisconsin, has a full-time staff of 200 nurses and consultants ready to give counsel on how to cut down on accidents.[5] So serious are the insurance companies about such programs that those businesses that ignore the health and safety of their workers run the risk of losing their insurance altogether.

LOSS OF EARNING POWER

A small fire in a grocery chain's warehouse obviously results in the loss of a certain amount of property. There is another loss as well: the fire could put the chain's stores out of business for several days because of a lack of stock. Fire insurance would cover the damages at the warehouse, of course, but not the loss of income in the stores. That loss, however, would probably be the more serious of the two. A prolonged interruption of business could even cause bankruptcy. For this reason, many companies carry insurance protection over and above coverage for mere loss of property. Types of policy in this area include **business interruption insurance**, which *protects the insured when a fire or other disaster causes a company to temporarily shut down;* **extra-expense insurance**, which *pays the additional costs of maintaining operations in temporary quarters;* and **key executive insurance**,

Tennis is much more than a game for stars like Jimmy Connors—a fact that is reflected in the costly and comprehensive insurance coverage major sports figures are obliged to carry.

FIGURE 1

The special multiperil policy (SMP) is a comprehensive policy that includes mandatory property and liability coverage, plus optional coverage for theft and other perils.

life insurance that *protects a company from financial loss resulting from the death of a major executive.*

LOSS DUE TO DISHONESTY OR NONPERFORMANCE

Dishonest employees and criminals outside the company pose yet another threat to business property and assets. There are various ways of dealing with this problem. A business owner can obtain a **fidelity bond**, which *protects the insured against dishonest acts*—such as embezzlement, forgery, and theft—*committed by employees.* Likewise, he or she can obtain a **surety bond**—*a three-party contract in which one party agrees to be responsible to a second party for the obligations of a third party.* Another form of insurance against loss due to nonperformance is **credit life insurance**, which *guarantees repayment of the amount due on a loan or an installment contract if the borrower dies;* yet another is **crime insurance**, which *covers loss from theft of any kind;* whether it is burglary (forc-ible entry into the premises) or robbery (taking property from another person by violence or the threat of violence).

COMPREHENSIVE POLICIES

As you can see, insuring a business properly is quite a complex undertaking. (Above, we have discussed only some of the many policies available to protect business property and assets.) The expense and time involved in managing insurance policies and keeping them up to date can be burdensome. To avoid some of this burden, a business may buy comprehensive insurance policies that cover virtually all perils in a single package contract (see Figure 1).

EMPLOYEE INSURANCE

In addition to insuring property and assets, a business is concerned with insurance protection for the employees. It is required by federal law to pay half the Social Security taxes on employees. In most states, companies also finance state unemployment insurance programs. And, as already mentioned, all fifty states require businesses to buy workmen's compensation insurance. Most businesses provide substantial additional protection for their employees as well (see Figure 2). This coverage is offered not only because most union contracts require it, but also because it helps attract and keep employees.

Generally, companies are interested in three kinds of employee protection: health insurance, life insurance, and pension plans. These are usually provided through group policies, which are sold to the company by the insurer. In some cases, the employer pays for the insurance in full; in other cases, employees pay part or all of the cost through a payroll deduction plan.

HEALTH INSURANCE

According to the Health Insurance Institute, Americans received $37.29 billion in private health benefits in 1976. Insurance companies paid $18.21 billion of this, and Blue Cross–Blue Shield, a nonprofit organization, paid $19.08 billion.[6]

Kinds of health insurance

The coverage provided by these payments falls into four general areas:

HOSPITALIZATION INSURANCE **Hospitalization insurance** *pays for the major portion of a hospital stay.* Coverage varies depending on the policy, but most policies pay all or part of the cost of a semiprivate room and all the cost of drugs and services while the insured is in a hospital. Blue Cross is the best-known hospitalization plan.

SURGICAL AND MEDICAL INSURANCE *The costs of surgery and of physicians' in-hospital care are paid for by* **surgical and medical insurance**. Policies usually specify a maximum for each surgical procedure covered. For example, a policy may pay $75 in benefits for the removal of a cyst, $150 for an appendectomy, and so on. The range of procedures covered and the benefits paid each vary with the policy. Blue Shield is the best-known plan.

MAJOR MEDICAL INSURANCE *Medical expenses that fall outside the coverage limits of the two basic plans just discussed are covered by* **major medical insurance**. Benefits are usually limited to a percentage (often 80 percent) of medical expenses, and frequently the insured must pay the first $100. A typical major medical policy may pay 80 percent of all medical expenses up to $20,000 that are not covered by hospitalization or surgical and medical insurance, less $100.

DISABILITY INCOME INSURANCE *The worker is protected from loss of income while disabled or partially disabled because of illness or accident by* **disability income insurance**. The insured receives monthly payments while disabled, usually after a specified waiting period. Benefits normally depend on the extent of disability: whether it is partial or total, temporary or permanent. Some policies will pay lifetime benefits, but most state a maximum number of years for benefit payments. Many policies continue partial payments after the insured returns to work.

Covering the increasing costs of medical care

As medical technology becomes more sophisticated, the cost of medical care increases as well. To help employees cope with costs above and beyond the scope of traditional health insurance policies, some employers have either included new types of policies in their insurance packages or offered their workers the option of paying for extra coverage through payroll deductions. Dental insurance, for example, is an increasingly common addition to company benefits. More innovative still are the special cancer insurance policies that help cancer sufferers and their families deal with the extraordinary expenses associated with that disease. It's estimated that about 14 million Americans currently hold cancer insurance.

A health insurance alternative

One way in which more and more companies are avoiding the ever-increasing expenses of employee

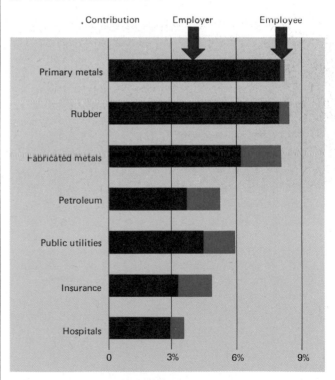

LOOKING OUT FOR EMPLOYEES: INSURANCE CONTRIBUTIONS AS A PERCENTAGE OF TOTAL PAYROLL IN 1975   FIGURE 2

Contributions by employers tend to be proportionately larger in the manufacturing sector. One possible reason: the higher levels of unionization in these industries.

health insurance is through the use of **health maintenance organizations (HMOs)**. HMOs are *prepaid medical plans that entitle policyholders to the unlimited use of complete medical centers.* Whatever the needs of a patient—hospitalization, X-rays, tests, doctors' consultations—they're covered in just one monthly tab. The cost is usually shared by employer and employee. HMOs depend on a large and steady stream of subscribers who pay for the service regularly (even though they may use it only a few times each year). The organizations are thus able to offer medical services at prices well below those found in standard private medical practices and ordinary hospitals. Some

large companies, such as R. J. Reynolds Tobacco Company, have even set up their own HMOs, exclusively for the use of employees.[7]

LIFE INSURANCE

Businesses generally buy insurance to cover the lives of their employees. Of the approximately $2.583 billion of life insurance in force in the United States in 1977, approximately $1.289 billion was bought on an individual basis to cover individuals. (Most of it was bought by the individuals themselves, although some

---

HOW IT'S ACTUALLY DONE

LIFE INSURANCE

All life insurance sold falls into one of three classes: term, whole life, or endowment. The three differ in how long payments must be made, if (and under what conditions) repayments are made to the insured, and if the policy can be cashed in.

Term life insurance

Term life insurance (often called **straight term**) *pays stated benefits to the* **beneficiary**, *the person specified by the policyholder to receive the benefits, if the holder dies within the period covered by the policy.* Individuals usually buy five-year, ten-year, or twenty-year policies. If the insured is still alive at the end of that period, the policy expires, and all premiums that the policyholder has paid belong to the insurance company. In other words, the policy has no accumulated cash value.

The premiums for term insurance are based on the age of the insured. Fewer people die at the age of twenty than at the age of fifty, as common sense tells us and the mortality rates demonstrate. Therefore the younger you are, the cheaper your term insurance will be because the life insurance company is assuming a smaller risk. Term insurance provides the maximum insurance protection at the lowest cost for young people.

Most term policies sold today are renewable and convertible. The **renewable** feature *allows the insured to take out another term policy before the*

first one expires. The **convertible** feature *allows the purchase of another type of insurance before the term insurance policy expires.* Renewing or converting a term policy does not require a medical exam. This feature is attractive to many. Obviously those who renew or convert term insurance are older than when they first took out the policy, and thus likely to be less healthy than they were earlier. Insurance companies make up for the greater risk involved in renewable and convertible policies by charging higher premiums.

Because of its low cost, term insurance is widely favored by businesses buying group life insurance for their employees. In 1977 the amount of group term insurance in force was $1.107 trillion. The policies are usually one-year renewable, requiring no medical examination. The employer typically pays some or all of the premiums, which are lower than for individual policies.

Whole life insurance

Whole life insurance *provides coverage for the entire life of the insured.* The face value of the policy (the amount of insurance coverage purchased) is paid to the beneficiary when the insured dies. Besides providing protection for dependents of the insured, whole life policies can be cashed in at any time. If the insured cancels (surrenders) the policy, he or she receives the amount already paid in. Also, the insured can usually borrow the cash value of the policy from the insurance company. Although

was purchased by companies through key executive insurance.) Another $1,002 billion was bought in the form of group policies, generally taken out by companies for their employees. The remainder was bought in the form of credit life insurance.[8]

PENSION PLANS

Few working people are able to save enough money in the course of their working years to be financially independent when they retire. Although nearly all workers are covered by Social Security, they can hardly rely on it to support more than a minimal standard of living once they've retired. The average monthly payment to retired workers in June of 1978 was $260.21.[9] Therefore pension plans have grown rapidly over the past decades as a way of providing retirement security. In 1940 only slightly more than 4 million people were covered by pension plans; by 1975 the figure had increased to almost 30 million (see Figure 3), and enrollment is still growing.[10]

Employers are not required by law to provide pensions for their employees. Many choose to do so, however, as an incentive to attract and keep good workers. Under some company pension plans, retired

premiums on whole life policies are higher than on term policies, individuals favor whole life insurance over term insurance because of its more extensive coverage and because of its accumulated cash value.

Whole life insurance is divided into two categories by method of payment.

1. **Straight life policies** *require the insured to pay premiums until death or until age ninety-nine.* Premiums are based on the insured's age when taking out the policy. Since straight life provides the cheapest *permanent* protection, it is the most widely sold form of individual life insurance.

2. **Limited-payment policies**, as the name implies, *require payment only for a specified number of years,* frequently twenty. After this period the policy is considered paid up. The insurance continues in force, but no more payments are required. However, just as with straight life, the insurance company will pay the full face value of the policy only to the beneficiary when the insured dies. (It can be cashed in for less than face value.) Premiums are based on the insured's age and the length of time set for payment. They are higher than for straight life, and consequently the cash value of the policy builds up more quickly.

Endowment life insurance

Endowment life insurance *pays the whole value of the policy to the beneficiary if the insured dies within a specified length of time. If the insured is alive at the end of that period, however, he or she collects the face value of the policy.* Most endowment policies are written for periods ranging between ten and thirty years. They are frequently arranged to mature when the holder is sixty-five, so as to provide funds for retirement. Premiums, which reflect the insured's age and the term of the policy, are higher than for any other form of life insurance. But for those who can afford them, endowment policies combine the advantages of insurance protection and guaranteed savings.

The table below shows a comparison of the typical annual cost of a five-year renewable convertible term policy, a straight life policy, and a twenty-year endowment policy. These are average annual premiums currently paid by males for a $10,000 policy. As you can see, the difference in cost among the three types is considerable. The greater the coverage, the greater the premium.

Typical Annual Premium for Males on a $10,000 Life Insurance Policy

Age	Five-year convertible term	Straight life	Twenty-year endowment
20	$53.80	$125.40	$432.00
30	56.80	166.00	436.80
40	79.60	233.20	452.00
50	142.10	345.10	489.10

Source: Health Insurance Institute.

RETIRING WITH MORE THAN A GOLD WATCH:
WHAT PERCENT OF AMERICANS WERE ENROLLED IN
CORPORATE PENSION PLANS IN 1975?

46% covered   54% not covered   FIGURE 3

Out of a working population of 65.5 million, 30 million employees were enrolled in corporate pension plans in 1975. The rest, on retirement, may have to get along on Social Security—which is barely adequate at best.

employees are paid out of the business's current income. More often pension plans are funded, that is, money is set aside on a regular basis to provide retirement benefits.

Pension guarantees

Even with their pensions, retirees are often in fairly tight economic circumstances. But the threat of a failed pension plan—one in which their company closes or goes bankrupt or, simply, a plan in which the money runs out—is no longer something to worry about. In the Employee Retirement Income Security Act of 1974 the United States Congress created a federal agency, the Pension Benefit Guaranty Corporation, to insure the assets of pension plans. (All provisions of the 1974 act did not become effective immediately; they were staggered to take effect between January 1, 1974, and January 1, 1981.) This act guarantees that retirement benefits will be paid no matter what happens to the company or the plan itself. The act also sets standards for managing pension funds and requires public disclosure of a plan's operations.

While this law has meant a new degree of security for retirees, it's also meant potential trouble for companies with pension plans. Salary rates are increasing, and people are tending to live longer than ever after retirement. As a result, many companies are finding that their pensions claims for the foreseeable future have grown nearly as large as their total assets. Dur-

ing the 1970s pension contributions have increased an average of 15 percent while profits before taxes and pension expenses have risen only about 7 percent. The pension obligations of the Lockheed aircraft corporation, for instance, totaled $1.3 billion in 1976, or 82 percent of the resources that the company owned. The unfunded portion of those liabilities—the amount that had not yet been set aside in a pension trust fund—came to $276 million. Other companies show even more startling figures relating to the as-yet unfunded portions of their pension plans. Chrysler, for instance, has amassed unfunded pension liabilities equal to the last twenty-seven years of its pretax profits.[11]

What would happen in the unlikely event of a pension plan collapse? The first to feel the crunch would be the shareholders of the company involved. Before any profits could be taken from the company, it's likely that surplus funds would have to be milked to feed the pension fund. If there was still a gap between what was in the company's pension fund and what was demanded of it, the "plan-termination insurance" policy set up by the 1974 legislation would go into effect. Whatever guaranteed benefits were left uncovered would be picked up by all the other companies in the government-established insurance scheme. Consequently, shareholders are now at risk not only for the pension activities of their own company, but also for those of all other corporations as well.

Vesting

The most controversial issue surrounding payment of retirement benefits is how much employees are enti-

WHO HANDLES INSURANCE?

NONGOVERNMENT INSURERS

Stock companies are profit-making insurance companies owned by stockholders who have invested in the business. Stock companies earn profits by:

- charging premiums that exceed the cost of paying claims and operating the company; and
- investing their assets and surplus premium income in other companies.

Mutual insurance companies are nonprofit insurance companies owned by the policyholders.

Some of these companies charge relatively low premiums, but if losses exceed income, policyholders are assessed an additional amount to make up the deficit.

GOVERNMENT INSURERS

Federal government programs include:
- Social Security
  old age and survivor's insurance
  disability insurance
  health insurance (Medicare and Medicaid)

- Government retirement plans (such as those for railroad workers and federal civilian employees)

- Federal Deposit Insurance Corporation (for discussion of the FDIC, see our Enrichment Chapter on Money and Banking)

- Pension plan assets insurance

- Crime insurance (for business in high-crime areas)

State government programs include:
- Unemployment insurance
- Legislation requiring workmen's compensation insurance (state agencies sell this insurance in some states)
- Disability income programs (in some states)
- Hail insurance (in a few agricultural states)

tled to receive if they leave a company before retiring. When this occurs, the employees have always been assured of getting back their contribution (if any) to the plan. But what about the employer's contribution? **Vesting** refers to *the employee's claim on the employer's contribution to his pension plan.* Some firms give employees vesting rights immediately upon participation in their pension plans; others require a period of service first. Under the 1974 act, employers with pension plans must give employees vesting rights. However, employers have several options on how this is to be done, and they may still require five to ten years' service before vesting begins.

Another provision of the 1974 act concerns the pension benefits of workers who change jobs. A worker with pension rights who leaves a company and then returns to it would be eligible for the benefits accumulated previously. However, a worker cannot transfer pension rights from one company to another without the approval of the companies involved. In the future, extension of the vesting privilege to cover transfer of pension rights is expected to be an important goal of labor.

UNEMPLOYMENT INSURANCE

Business responsibility to an employee doesn't end when the job is over. According to laws in all fifty states—and based on a federal mandate—employers finance special unemployment insurance to benefit workers who are laid off or, to a lesser extent, those who quit their jobs. The tax paid by each employer is related to the number of people from the business who have been on the unemployment rolls previously.

Also included in unemployment insurance benefits are job counseling and placement services, in which the government acts as an employment agency for the out-of-work.

CHAPTER REVIEW

Businesses face three main types of risks: uninsurable, absorbable, and insurable. Uninsurable risks usually result from poor management, environmental conditions, economic fluctuations, or governmental actions. Self-insurance enables companies to absorb risks themselves. Insurable risks must meet certain requirements. If they do, insurer and insured agree on terms through an insurance policy.

Businesses protect themselves by two chief kinds of insurance coverage. They want to insure their property and assets. To do so, they take out insurance against property loss due to fire, natural disasters, or accidents occurring in transit. This category also includes protection against liability suits, loss of earning power, and loss due to the dishonesty or nonperformance of others. Businesses also want to insure their employees. They do so through health insurance, life insurance, and pension plans. Although pension plans are subject to government regulations, they still vary in payments and benefits.

KEY WORD REVIEW

premium
insurable risk
absorbable risks

self-insurance
uninsurable risks
property insurance
riders
marine insurance
ocean marine insurance
inland marine insurance
liability insurance
workmen's compensation
  insurance
business interruption insurance
extra-expense insurance
key executive insurance
fidelity bond
surety bond
credit life insurance
crime insurance
hospitalization insurance
surgical and medical insurance
major medical insurance
disability income insurance
health maintenance organizations
  (HMOs)
vesting
insurer
insured or insuree
insurance policy
claim
actuary
term life insurance (straight
  term)
beneficiary
renewable
convertible
whole life insurance
straight life policies
limited-payment policies
endowment life insurance

REVIEW QUESTIONS

1. Explain how insurance companies make a profit and why they try to spread their risks as thinly as possible.

2. How does self-insurance work, and what are its advantages?

3. How can a business protect itself against uninsurable risks?

4. What does marine insurance cover besides ships at sea and their cargoes?

5. Why is liability insurance important for a business?

6. What are the three types of insurance that cover a business against loss of earning power?

7. How does major medical insurance operate?

8. In the category of whole life insurance, explain the difference between straight life and limited-payment policies.

CASE 1

THE COMPANY THAT CAN'T SAY NO

Some things can't be insured. That's the theory, anyway. In practice, however, just about anything is insurable, provided an insurance company is willing to take the risk. A company that seems much more willing than most is the Continental Casualty Company.

No fly-by-night organization, Continental is one of the country's largest financial institutions, ranking eleventh among diversified product insurance companies. And it prides itself on taking on clients and risks that other companies can't or won't handle.

In recent years Continental has insured

- every NASA astronaut

- everyone connected with the Indianapolis 500 automobile race

- the United Nations peacekeeping force at Suez

- actors Paul Newman and Robert Wagner during the filming of their sports car racing movie *Winning*

- a Texas rattlesnake hunt

- participants in the Rose Bowl parade

- a plumbers' training class

- test pilots for the Boeing 747

- an occasional flagpole sitter

Of course, when it comes to risks like these, Continental's policies don't come cheap. What's remarkable is that they're available at all.[12]

1. Why wouldn't *most* insurance companies be willing to insure the items insured by Continental?

2. What kinds of facts do you think Continental would have to gather in order to insure the actors in a movie about sports-car racing?

3. Suppose you were forming a small movie company. What kinds of insurance would you have to buy? What kinds do you think you could do without?

CASE 2

HEDGING YOUR BETS

The world of "what if's" goes well beyond insurance itself to include even the most basic transactions. As we have seen, many raw materials are bought and sold on commodity exchanges, where two types of contracts are available: spot, or cash, contracts for immediate delivery; and futures contracts, which guarantee delivery at a later date. The latter provide one way for businesses to cope with the uninsurable—fluctuating prices.

Industries that use large quantities of raw materials, such as manufacturers of foodstuffs or metals, are especially subject to the ups and downs of pricing for the commodities they require. To guard against price increases, they can sign long-term contracts with suppliers. Utilities, for example, often have such contracts with coal producers.

A more complex means of combating fluctuating prices is the practice known as **hedging**. Suppose that a chain of bakeries anticipates a drastic increase in sugar prices. *The business can guard,* or "hedge," *against the increase in price by signing a futures contract.* If sugar is selling for seven cents per pound when the contract is signed and that's the agreed-upon price one year hence, no matter how much the real price of sugar goes up in that year, the supplier is obliged to let the baker have the amount ordered at the price specified. Thus in a year's time sugar may be at nine cents per pound, but the baker gets delivery at the seven cents price agreed upon one year earlier. Of course, had sugar gone down in price during the time of the con-

tract, the bakery would then have been stuck with paying more than the going price of sugar.

Hedging can also be used merely to offset price increases rather than avoid them altogether. Suppose that the same bakery business knows six months in advance that it will require 500 pounds of sugar by June 15, but it can't take delivery until June 1. To protect itself against a possible rise in price, the business buys a futures contract for sugar at the current price of nine cents per pound. By June 1 the price of sugar, as expected, has gone up, this time to eleven cents per pound. The baker, however, wants to be sure of having good, fresh sugar and so buys a supply at the current high price with a cash contract. Although the business is paying more, it can offset that loss by selling its now more valuable futures contract, which offers sugar at the less expensive price. Since spot and futures prices tend to parallel each other, rising and falling at the same time, a company that loses money on one contract usually makes approximately the same amount on the other.[13]

1. List three types of industry in which hedging would be an important technique.

2. Suppose the price of the desired commodity goes down, rather than up, between the time the contract is signed and the delivery date. What are the direct effects, if any, on the company that has signed the futures contract? Can you think of some indirect effects?

PERSPECTIVES ON SMALL BUSINESS

FINANCIAL ASPECTS

THE SMALL BUSINESS AS A LOAN RISK

Many people will tell you that small businesses have a high failure rate, but few reliable statistics on the success rate of small firms are available. Every year, it is pointed out, approximately 500,000 new businesses are formed, and every year 450,000 businesses fail: a failure rate of 90 percent. But another look at the same figure for failures reveals quite a different picture. Some 5,900,000 small businesses are estimated to be in existence today. If only 450,000 fail, the annual failure rate is only 7.6 percent of the total number of businesses. So, depending on your point of view, small firms may be a poor or an excellent risk.

The shakiness of the small firm does create concern among bankers. It is fair to say that any small business will have difficulty in obtaining funds for any purpose except by taking out a collateral loan, that is, a loan for which property or equipment with a recognized resale value is used as security. But numerous ways still exist for small entrepreneurs to borrow funds for daily operations, inventory requirements, new equipment, and other necessary expenses.

APPROACHES TO FINANCING

Listed below are the various financing approaches open to the entrepreneur:

1. Trade credit
2. Short-term bank loans
3. Long- and short-term leasing
4. Outside investors
5. Home mortgage
6. Accounts-receivable financing
7. Lines of credit
8. The Small Business Administration (SBA) (the lender of last resort)

Below, we'll take a closer look at the first seven of these categories. For information on the SBA, see pages 528–530.

Trade credit

To obtain trade credit, the owner must establish a credit standing with the manufacturers or wholesalers who can provide the needed goods. If he or she succeeds in doing so, the suppliers will allow the firm to delay payments on goods received rather than requiring cash on delivery (COD).

It is very difficult for new firms to obtain trade credit. Few vendors (manufacturers and wholesalers offering goods for sale to businesses) are willing to risk selling their products to a small business; any firm without a "track record" of paying its bills is considered too high a risk. Even large firms rely on prompt payment of their invoices—in fact, any large corporation will have a credit department whose sole function is to reduce credit risks. How, then, does the small operator effectively arrange his or her credit relationships? Here are some steps you may wish to follow.

First, obtain fixed assets through a collateral loan. Any new business must have sufficient capital to buy or rent the basic fixed assets that are necessary to begin operation; without such essential items—typewriters, office furniture, and other necessary tools or pieces of equipment—no business could ever start. Rarely can money be borrowed to finance the basic start-up costs without collateral.

Next, it's a good idea for a new business to negotiate a special arrangement with a few of its new customers. Goods ordered can be shipped COD in exchange for a reduced price, and the cash thus obtained from the customer will allow the new entrepreneur to obtain goods from vendors. In this manner, you can begin to establish a credit relationship with several vendors. Once you have demonstrated your ability to pay bills and remain in business for three to six months, most vendors will begin to issue you a line of credit, enabling you to purchase a maximum dollar amount of goods on a minimum of thirty days' credit. With proper money management, by the end of one year your firm will have developed a track record good enough to permit you to qualify for extensive credit.

The larger and better established manufacturers and wholesalers will frequently extend more liberal terms to a small business after it has become established. While vendors normally expect their bills to be paid within 30 days, these more liberal terms extend the repayment term to as long as 90 to 120 days. This arrangement is especially useful to a retailer who needs a large inventory to display the available product lines effectively; and to such seasonal businesses as toy stores, which must have most of their sales inventory available for only a brief portion of the year. Without these special terms, vast sums of capital would be required.

It is most important to realize that your small business will greatly benefit from the prompt payment of all vendors' bills. Every sacrifice should be made to pay bills when they come due or earlier. Avoid past-due notices! The reason is simple: business success is frequently based on servicing customers on occasional difficult problems. Help customers when they most need it and you develop loyalty. Your prompt payment of vendor invoices will increase your leverage, allowing you to expect favors for your customers when necessary. You may need a speedy delivery of a certain order or an extended warranty period for a persistent maintenance problem. Business is a two-way street: if you have proved your value as a customer, your vendors will want to demonstrate their value to you.

If a small firm is slow in paying bills, special favors will be impossible. In fact, the overall quality of your service in every area may drop. Large firms can be slow to pay and still demand special concessions because their large purchases are profitable; the small operator lacks this advantage.

Short-term bank loans

Banks, it is often said, are happy to lend you money if you can prove you don't need it. Under the right conditions, though, banks are excellent sources of money. In dealing with small firms, banks generally like to limit their loans to those that are completely repaid in less than a year (short-term loans). Small businesses are not considered solid risks for long-term dollar commitments unless they have collateral equal in value to the amount of the loan. Loans that are not repaid will go against the bank manager's record, so few will accept even moderate risks.

Typically, short-term loans fit into the small business situation quite well, since small businesses frequently have short-term needs—to finance seasonal inventory, say; or to meet an unusually large payroll in order to complete a contract; or to purchase inventory to fill an order from a large firm that is typically slow to pay; or to make a volume purchase of goods at a reduced price. (If you show a dollar savings to the bank, you will probably get the loan.)

If your business is in need of short-term money, here are some approaches that are effective with a bank.

1. Maintain a healthy bank balance. A portion of the money a bank lends comes from funds kept in checking and savings accounts. You must have a balance in the bank before it will consider your loan application. (Incidentally, you should always have at least two checking accounts. When you need funds, one may be low but you may have funds in the other. The second account gives you a safety factor.)

2. Always contact the manager or branch manager first. This officer's approval is essential, so why not start there?

3. Apply at two banks simultaneously for the same loan. As long as you don't attempt to borrow twice on the same collateral, this procedure is neither illegal nor unethical. Since one may deny you your loan, it's safer to have a second option. It would be more difficult to go to the second bank after you were refused by the first. It is also possible that each bank would grant you a portion of the loan. You might even let them know they are competing for your business; this tactic might enhance your position.

4. Present a sound business reason for wanting the money. Have detailed facts and figures ready. Be sure to stress that the loan is for the improvement of the firm, not for its survival.

5. Submit complete financial statements to the bank. This step is important to establish the financial stability of your company and to indicate that your business is receiving professional accounting supervision.

Lines of credit

Every small business should consider establishing a line of credit with several banks. By doing so you establish the maximum amount of money your business can borrow at any given time. Knowing the limits of your credit is essential for your long- and short-term planning.

Long- and short-term leasing

Leasing is a form of financing; instead of buying a piece of equipment outright, the business owner pays a monthly rental charge for a fixed period of time, say twelve or twenty-four months. Leasing has proved to be an excellent method of acquiring necessary capital equipment without bank financing. You have the use of the equipment for the period of the lease; at its expiration you can either return the equipment to the leasing company or renew the lease at a greatly reduced monthly rate for an additional period.

One great advantage of a lease is the low initial cash investment necessary. The purchase of a $10,000 piece of equipment through a bank loan would require a down payment of 25 to 35 percent. For a standard twenty-four-month lease, in contrast, the only cash required is the first and last months' rent or an amount equal to 10 percent of the purchase price. Even more attractive terms are available for leases on more expensive equipment.

Some leases offer buy-out agreements; however, any such lease will be questioned by the IRS. The special tax status of a lease allows the entire monthly rental to be deducted from income as a regular monthly business expense. Outright purchase at the end of the lease period can affect the tax treatment of these lease payments. Purchasing leased equipment is a very touchy subject that requires your accountant's attention.

Outside investors

One way for a small business to raise capital is by attracting individuals to invest money in the firm. This dollar investment buys the investor an ownership position in the business and an opportunity to participate in its profits and losses. While this idea has definite merit, the real problem is attracting people willing to invest money. Here are some alternatives available to you:

1. The first and most obvious place to look for investors is among your own employees. We don't suggest offering ownership in the business to all employees, though. This practice could represent a threat to your control: any employee graduated to the status of part-owner would probably want to participate in management decisions. Key employees, however, might well be offered the opportunity to invest in the company.

2. Seek the advice of your CPA, lawyer, business associates, or a recognized consultant. They might know people who are interested in investing in a small firm. Try every angle; you never know what door an investor sits behind until you knock.

3. Newspapers, trade journals, and newsletters can be good places to advertise for potential investors.

When advertising, a number of points must be considered. Give as many details as possible without revealing the identity of your company; indicate the expected rate of return and the risk factor involved. Receive all leads and information at the newspaper or at a location not traceable to your company. You don't want to be bothered by salespeople, money brokers, or other opportunists. Furthermore, you can't afford to waste your time with endless and fruitless meetings. Time is too valuable. Your only contact should be with investors, not with agents who represent investors.

Once you have arranged a meeting with a potential investor, be ready with your financial statements neatly and professionally prepared for presentation and a clear statement of your financial needs arranged in logical steps. An investor will want to see a concrete program of action.

Don't expect an investor to fund executive salaries or luxuries such as cars or plush furniture.

Reduce any possible areas of fear. Allow the investor to bail out at any time. You're not trying to trap anyone; you want someone who will be willing to help your business grow in exchange for a better-than-average return on his investment.

Don't deal with anyone who needs the income from this investment for living expenses. The risk is too great for this type of investor, and in the event of any problems, members of this group may sue.

Expect to have several meetings before any serious commitments are made. Don't rush investors. Let them rush you. A reluctant person who is pushed into a deal may cause you

endless problems—even a lawsuit.

Impress the investor with your knowledge of the industry or marketplace. Give details. Who are your competitors? What are their strengths and weaknesses? Indicate the relative size of each competing firm. A display of knowledge of this sort will create an atmosphere of trust and enhance your chances of success.

Home mortgage

One of the means most commonly used to obtain funds for small business development is borrowing money against the equity in your home. Your equity—the difference between the market value of your home and the amount of money you owe on the existing mortgage—can be turned into cash for any worthwhile purpose. With the rapidly appreciating values of real estate, equity in a home is an excellent source of funds. As a homeowner you have two options:

1. You can refinance your present home loan and obtain a new, larger loan. The amount of cash you gain is tax-free. In many states this is the only type of real-estate loan available to the consumer.

2. Some states, such as California and Florida, allow a homeowner to obtain a second mortgage on a home without refinancing the first one. This is the preferred method if the interest rate on the existing mortgage is lower than the interest rate on any potential new first mortgage.

This method also enables you to avoid any prepayment penalties when the existing loan is canceled.

Most homes are jointly owned by a husband and wife. If both agree, borrowing against the home is generally an acceptable risk, especially if both are involved in the business. Of course, the risk of losing the home if the business fails is a serious disadvantage.

Accounts-receivable financing

It is not uncommon for many of the small businessperson's larger customers to pay their bills slowly. The elaborate accounting procedures of the large corporations require forty-five to ninety days before a check can be issued. Since the small entrepreneur requires both prompt payments and the business of the larger firms, what solutions are available?

The first option is to sell the accounts receivable to a firm that specializes in the purchase of such accounts at a discount. The small firm receives immediate cash, and the firm purchasing the bills keeps the cash it collects. Usually this service is available only when the firms owing money have high Dun and Bradstreet ratings.

You can also borrow money at the bank to cover late bills, either occasionally or on a regular basis. You might consider increasing prices to those companies that are regularly slow to pay, in order to cover the cost of the interest you have to pay for the loan.

INSURANCE

As you have already learned in our Enrichment Chapter on Risk Management and Insurance, insurance is a necessary item in any business regardless of size, because it wards off the adverse effects of property and personal liability losses. Frequently, however, small operators feel they can't afford to insure their businesses fully. This type of cost cutting can be disastrous.

Low-cost medical and dental insurance is a major problem for most small entrepreneurs and their employees. It costs insurance companies more to service small businesses than large ones, so medical coverage for a small business owner is expensive. Some insurance organizations have formed trusts that are available to small firms. The rates are still high and the benefits low, but they cut the costs somewhat.

One area of insurance that offers some unique advantages and opportunities to small business is life insurance. Because it creates instant money upon the death of an insured owner, life insurance has helped solve many sticky business problems.

One of the most serious problems that can befall a sole proprietorship is the death of the owner. Usually the business dies, taking with it the careers of its employees and the survivors' income. Life insurance can be used to solve this problem. If one or more of the employees wishes to buy the business at the owner's death, this is how it works:

A life insurance policy is purchased on the life of the owner in an amount equal to the value of the business. The employees who wish to buy the business pay the premiums on the policy. If the owner dies, the face value of the policy is paid to the owner's heirs or estate and the business is transferred to the policyholders. The insurance money has provided the funds for the transfer of ownership. An attorney must provide the legal documents necessary for the transfer at death.

All small businesses have one or two key people whose contribution to the firm is critical to its survival. Their lives can be insured. In the event of the death of one of these key people, the face amount of the policy becomes available to hire a replacement. The company still must go through a critical period, but the insurance money should enable it to survive.

As we mentioned earlier, life insurance can be used as a means of funding buy/sell agreements for partnerships and corporations. Few small firms have enough capital to pay a dead owner's heirs the full dollar value of the share of the business they have inherited. Life insurance provides that needed money.

Finally, life insurance can be used to provide a death benefit in a company retirement plan. The death of one of the members of the plan, especially in the early stages, could easily bankrupt the program. The instant money from life insurance can solve this problem.

TRENDS IN THE JOB MARKET

If you are majoring in financial administration, you can look forward to one of the most promising career paths in the world of business. This field has been strong in recent years and will continue to be in high demand in the next five years. What kinds of background are required? Summer work experience with a banking, securities, or investment firm or government agency is a good background; it should be coupled with a sound academic foundation.

KEY AREAS

■ Most of the job openings in financial administration are in analysis, planning, and long-range projections.

■ Opportunities in financial institutions, especially banking, look exceedingly good, and if you acquire an MBA, your prospects will be even better—especially with the more established financial institutions.

■ A recent trend in government, business, industry, and education toward more emphasis on cost and financial analysis also translates into more job opportunities.

THE OUTLOOK FOR MINORITIES AND WOMEN

Financial administration organizations traditionally are more conservative than most other businesses, but more of them now have set up special programs to hire minorities and women. Most report marked success with these new employees.

THE SALARY PICTURE

Salaries for two-year finance graduates will average $9,500 per year. Four-year graduates can expect an average salary of approximately $12,000 per year, and MBAs will average approximately $17,800 with a nontechnical undergraduate degree. Those having a technical undergraduate degree can expect to start at about $19,100 per year.

AN INTERVIEW WITH A RECENT BUSINESS GRADUATE

Ron Kaiser is a 1977 graduate of Michigan State University who is now working as a public accountant with a well-known accounting firm. Although he chose the field of accounting, his approach to selecting a career and finding a job would have worked just as well for any other business-related area.

RON'S BACKGROUND

Before he even decided on a major, Ron made an even more basic decision about his education. He knew that once he left college, he would meet many kinds of people, both socially and professionally, so he wanted to get as broad an education as possible. Ron took specialized courses in his major field, but he decided to select his remaining courses from a wide range of subjects. And he made one special point about this: he urges everyone to take a speaking course, especially if you feel shy about speaking to groups of people.

Ron's choice of a career was not automatic. As he considered various fields, he analyzed his abilities and objectives by asking himself the following questions:

1. Do I prefer to work alone, or primarily with others?

2. How much technological knowledge do I wish to acquire?

3. What kind of an organizational structure do I prefer? A small business? A large company?

4. How well do I work under pressure? Would I prefer a slower pace?

The closer you can come to answering these questions while you're in college, the better are your chances of choosing a satisfying career and working environment.

During his years in college, Ron held several jobs with accounting firms. And this is something you should consider: even if you cannot find a part-time or summer job that is directly related to your major

CAREERS IN FINANCE

Title	Job description	Requirements	Salary* and advancement prospects	Outlook through 1985	Comments
TWO-YEAR PROGRAM					
Insurance (claims adjuster)	Investigates claims for loss or damages filed with insurance companies. Interviews parties involved. Inspects accident areas and property damaged; negotiates settlements; attends legal hearings.	Community-college degree minimum. Four-year degree desired. Usually requires some travel.	$9,500 to $10,500 Head, claims department; district claims manager	Fair	No-fault insurance has seriously curtailed this activity.
General clerk	In governmental agency, writes and types bills, statements, etc. Answers inquiries; compiles reports. May supervise part-time employees. Usually specializes in one function, such as processing passports, licensing automobiles, etc.	High-school diploma minimum. Community-college degree desired. General clerical skills required, plus aptitude for office work.	$7,000 to $8,000 Clerk-supervisor	Good	Entry into government. Good starting point for learning and growing in a stable occupation.
Junior auditor (county government)	Under county auditor. Records deeds and similar legal instruments, keeps records of county accounts, compiles and transfers fiscal records as directed, prepares financial statements.	Minimum of two-year Associate degree in Finance or Accounting	$7,500 to $10,500 Auditor	Very good	Responsibilities vary greatly, depending upon size of government office.
Credit authorizer	Authorizes credit charges against customer accounts. Verifies or denies credit requests. Prepares credit cards or charge-account plates.	Two-year Associate degree in Finance or Accounting	$8,000 to $10,000 Credit supervisor	Very good	
Bank clerk	May: 1. Sort checks, etc. 2. Post and process accounts 3. Keep interest files 4. Handle mortgages; maintain tax records and insurance on customers' property	Two-year Associate degree in Finance or Accounting.	$8,000 to $12,000 Various bank supervisory positions, usually in loans, mortgages, personnel, etc.	Good	Good entry-level position for career in banking.
Loan counselor	Analyzes loan contracts and attempts to obtain overdue installments; receives and records payments; prepares reports on delinquent accounts; answers loan inquiries. May represent employer in legal proceedings.	Two-year Associate degree minimum, specializing in Finance or Accounting	$8,500 to $12,500 Branch manager	Very good	
Bank teller	Cashes customer checks; handles deposits and withdrawals; receives and issues receipts; issues and collects cash, checks, and other notes.	Two-year Associate degree in Finance or Accounting. Courses in banking helpful.	$8,000 to $11,000 Chief teller	Good	Ability to handle precise, detailed work necessary.
Securities salesperson	Contacts client for purchase and sale of securities; executes orders for clients; furnishes information on investments to clients; encourages sales.	Minimum of Associate degree. Additional courses in banking, finance, and economics helpful.	$8,000 to $15,000 (commission sales common) Branch manager	Good	Licensing by state required.
FOUR-YEAR PROGRAM					
Finance specialist (credit)	Analyzes credit data to estimate degree of risk involved in extending credit or lending money to individuals or firms; visits firms to determine condition of facilities; prepares reports and suggests credit limitations.	Four-year college degree in Finance or Accounting. Internship desirable.	$12,000 to $15,000 Manager, credit department	Excellent	
Senior credit analyst	Analyzes financial data, provides credit information on customers. Transcribes balance sheets into reports. Writes credit reports on customers, providing information on operating, depository, and borrowing figures, etc.	Four-year college degree with major in Finance or Accounting. Internship in accounting is desirable.	$12,000 to $16,000 Chief credit analyst	Excellent	

* Represents *starting* salary range

Title	Job description	Requirements	Salary and advancement prospects	Outlook through 1985	Comments
Accountant (public)	Provides a variety of accounting services to clients either as an individual or a member of a firm. Employees with public accounting firms generally seek Certified Public Accountant status while employed.	Four-year college degree in Accounting or Finance. Entry-level employees usually seek a CPA while working.	$12,000 to $16,000 Senior accountant and then to partner	Very good	Affords opportunity for highly diversified experience with many organizations.
Accountant (industrial)	Installs and maintains accounting system. Handles bookkeeping. Maintains accounting controls over inventories and purchases. Audits contracts, orders, and vouchers. Prepares tax returns.	Four-year college degree in Accounting or Finance. Additional courses in computers, tax, and economics highly desirable.	$9,600 to $17,000 Assistant comptroller	Excellent	Excellent opportunity for career path to top management in organization.
Credit reporter	Investigates history and credit status of individuals and businesses applying for credit, insurance, and jobs. Contacts trade and credit associations, banks, employers, and personal references to verify data.	Four-year college degree in Finance or Accounting desired.	$11,000 to $13,000 Credit manager	Very good	
Operations research analyst	Conducts logical analyses of management problems, and formulates mathematical models of problems for solution by computer. Develops proposals to afford maximum probability of profit in relation to risk.	Four-year college degree in Finance or Operations Research.	$12,000 to $15,000 Project leader, operations research	Very good	
Insurance examiner (state government)	Evaluates policyholder complaints and conformity of insurance companies and agents with standards set by state regulatory commission through research and interviews.	Four-year college degree in Finance desirable.	$10,000 to $13,500 Supervisor, insurance examiner department	Good	
Financial economist (U.S. government)	As part of a government unit, studies money, credit and credit instruments, and operation of banks and other financial institutions to develop monetary policies and forecast financial activity.	Four-year college degree in Finance or Economics minimum.	$12,500 to $13,800 Project leader	Good	Federal Civil Service examination required.

MBA PROGRAM

Title	Job description	Requirements	Salary and advancement prospects	Outlook through 1985	Comments
Actuary	Examines problems in health, life, casualty, and social insurance, annuities, and pensions. Determines mortality, accident, sickness, disability, and retirement rates. Constructs probability tables; calculates premiums.	MBA in Finance or Statistics with undergraduate degree in Mathematics desired.	$14,000 to $21,000 Manager	Excellent	
Financial analyst —computers —sports —retailing —insurance	Analyzes investment program for businesses. Interprets data concerning investments, their price, yield, and stability trends. Sets forth current and long-range trends in investment risks and measurable economic influences.	MBA in Finance desired.	$13,000 to $20,000 Director of investments	Very good	
Stockbroker	Gives data to clients on stocks, bonds, market conditions, history and prospects of companies or government bonds. Transmits buy and sell orders on stocks and bonds for clients. Develops portfolio of selected investments for client.	MBA in Finance desired, but not necessary.	$13,000 to $21,000 (commission sales) Manager, branch office	Very good	Must have broker's license for state in which person works.
Commercial loan analyst	Evaluates applications for commercial lines of credit in banking organization. Analyzes customers' financial status, credit, history of payment on other credit, and property evaluation to determine feasibility of making loans.	MBA in Finance.	$14,000 to $21,000 Mortgage loan officer	Excellent	

field, it is a good idea to get some work experience. Employers like to know that you can work within a structure and that you can handle responsibility. Whatever employment you've had will show that you can.

Ron also saw the importance of campus activities. As a member of an honorary accounting fraternity, he made many contacts, including an initial meeting with his present employer. Not everyone can join an honor society, of course, but all students can join groups that interest them and that increase their contacts with other people.

WRITING A RÉSUMÉ: RON'S ADVICE

With all your courses, part-time jobs, and campus activities behind you, the first real step toward finding a job is writing your résumé. Remember that a résumé has one purpose—to get you an interview. It is essential, therefore, that you describe yourself in a way that shows your suitability for the job in question. In addition to your educational background, you must describe your work experience, extracurricular activities, and interests.

Ron's advice, and ours as well, is to show how you relate to the job you seek. Point out the experiences and traits you have that make you right for the opening. Another point: include personal references with your résumé. Ask people who know you well enough to describe you, both personally and as an employee.

HOW RON CONTACTED HIS EMPLOYER

Ron made his first contact with his employer through the honorary accounting fraternity. You may not have access to such a society, but you do have access to a campus placement office. Check with your instructors, too, and don't be shy about asking them to help you make contacts with the business community.

SOME DOWN-TO-EARTH POINTS ABOUT INTERVIEWING

Ron's experience with the interviewing process can give you a good idea of what to expect. He found that first interviews were of the "getting to know you" sort, but that later interviews with various levels of management probed quite deeply into his goals and abilities. You should be prepared, then, to discuss your assets as well as your career expectations. And be prepared to evaluate your prospective employer. Remember, the interviewing process works both ways—so ask questions about working conditions, opportunities for advancement, salary scales, and anything else about a job that is important to you. Then, when you receive a job offer, you'll have the information you need to decide whether or not to accept it.

ADDING IT ALL UP

For Ron Kaiser, launching his career has been a very positive experience. He is very satisfied with both his occupation and his employer. Ron's satisfaction comes not from luck, but from a carefully thought-out career plan that began in college and is still developing.

QUANTITATIVE TOOLS

Ten years ago they rarely got to see the top managers. Today they may **be** the top managers. Who are they? The controllers—top members of companies' accounting staffs. In the past, when companies stressed growth first and worried about debts later, controllers weren't too visible; but now, many companies have turned to their controllers for advice, and some controllers have risen to become their companies' chief executive officers.[1]

Of course, controllers and other accountants are not the only group involved in the quantitative—that is, number— oriented—aspects of business. The field of market research involves highly complex mathematical methods; so do personnel administration, production management, and numerous other areas of management and marketing. And in the past two decades an entire industry has grown up around computers. Part 5 surveys several of the quantitative areas of business, and allows you to try out some basic quantitative skills.

☐ In Chapter 13, **Basic Accounting Principles,** you'll learn some basic facts about the methods accountants use.
☐ The Enrichment Chapter on **Computers and Data Processing** discusses the way computers work and the uses of computers in business today.
☐ In the Enrichment Chapter on **Research, Statistical Analysis, and Reports,** you'll read about sampling methods and statistical techniques, and about the ways reports, tables, and graphs are used to present information.

13

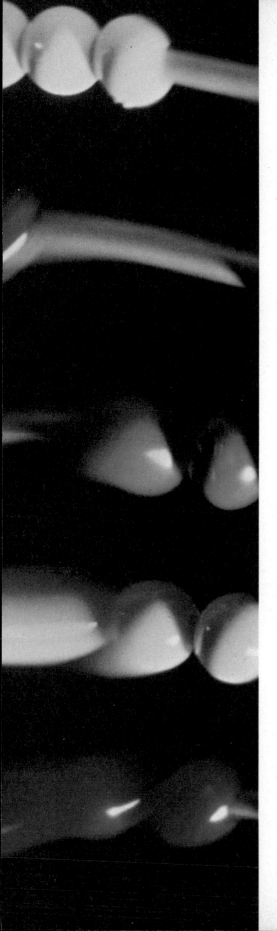

BASIC ACCOUNTING PRINCIPLES

If you have ever been at a restaurant with a half-dozen friends and had to figure out afterwards who owed what—or if you've ever tried to live within a tight budget, or simply balance an uncooperative checkbook—you have had a small taste of what accounting is all about. Perhaps you have a flair for working with figures; if so, accounting may offer you a promising career opportunity. If not, however, you will still find the following chapter to be one of the most important in this book.

Accounting deals with an essential business problem. The goal of every company is to make more money than it spends, and the purpose of accounting is to determine whether that's happening—and if not, why. Here, we'll study the basic principles of accounting, and see how they are applied in various situations.

WHAT WILL THIS CHAPTER FOCUS ON?

After reading the material in this chapter, you will understand and be able to discuss:

- the nature of accounting and its importance to managers, investors, and creditors

- the difference between private and public accountants

- the accounting equation and the double-entry bookkeeping system

- the balance sheet and the major categories of information it contains: assets, liabilities, and owners' equity

- the income statement and the major types of information in it: revenues, expenses, and profits

- the major ratios used in assessing the condition of a business

- what goes into a budget, and how management uses budgets to estimate and control business performance

- how zero-base budgeting works

In 1977 Harvey Kapnik made more than $410,000; Walter M. Baird, who earned just over $300,000, didn't do badly either. Nor, for that matter, did Sara Lou Brown, who, at the age of 34, scraped along at $50,000 per year.[1] No doubt you have never heard of these people, and that's not surprising. Yet they're among the ranks of the busiest and most powerful individuals in American industry today. They're accountants.

For decades accountants have suffered from having a backroom image. They were considered mere bookkeepers: jugglers of figures, people whose lack of imagination was made up for by a weird skill with numbers. If any of those ideas were once true of accountants, they're valid no longer.

The figures bear that out. People are fighting to get into the profession. In 1977 universities awarded almost 45,000 undergraduate degrees in accounting and an additional 5,500 graduate degrees—more than double the number for just seven years before.[2]

Why all the fuss about pushing numbers around on a balance sheet? That's still a part of accounting, of course, but as we've seen, modern business is an ever more complex way of making money. For a number of reasons, including the movements of the economy and the volumes of government regulations that now affect every step a business takes, the role of the accountant has grown tremendously. It's the accountant's job to stay on top of the financial situation. In recognition of this importance, today's accountants are generously rewarded both in salaries and in job excitement.

THE ROLE OF THE ACCOUNTANT

Traditionally the job of the accountant has been to give management the financial information and controls it needs to run a profitable business. And even in those cases in which profit doesn't enter the picture, the accountant must still ensure that the organization is efficiently run. **Accounting** is *a system of principles and techniques that permits bookkeepers or computers to record, classify, and accumulate sales, purchases, and other transactions.* And in addition to providing ways of recording data, accounting also provides ways to

present and interpret this information so that past performance, present condition, and future planning can be clearly and efficiently evaluated.

Such information is crucial for business management; it is the basis for all important decisions affecting a company's future. **Accounting statements—** *records of business operations during a given time period*—trace the money-flow of the business. Through these statements, accountants help managers see that customers are billed for sales of goods and services; that **receivables**—*money owed to the business*—are collected; and that cash is put to work. Likewise, accounting helps management keep track of wages, taxes, and other **payables**, or *money the business owes.* And furthermore, in addition to keeping management informed, accountants have also traditionally kept others less immediately involved with the business aware of its true financial state. Stockholders, investors, creditors, and the government, for instance, have to rely on accountants for the fiscal picture of almost any business.

Today none of that has changed. What has changed, however, is the depth in which the accountant performs these tasks and the power he or she wields in doing so. Some accountants rise to the position of controller in their firms, exercising a firm financial hand over virtually every phase of a company's operations. The controller of a medium-to-large corporation monitors and cross-checks every aspect of financial data, usually making use of a computer to pinpoint the company's financial health at any given point in the past, the present, or the future. More than that, however, the controller is charged with making certain that a company employs all of its assets to the

1925

Accounting is a booming field. Today, there are thirty times as many accountants as there were fifty years ago.

6,000

fullest and acquires new assets that will increase the company's earning power even further. The controller of American Can, for example, is directly in charge of corporate planning, mergers, and acquisitions for the packaging giant.

The importance of controllers can't be overestimated. In fact, it's borne out by the number of their ranks who have risen to the very top of the nation's largest companies. The current heads of Singer and General Motors, for instance, once were controllers.[3]

Even at lower levels the role of the modern accountant can be exciting. In New York City, for one, auditors or city accountants can be found not only at their desks but high above the East River, determining the effectiveness of the maintenance rate on the city's bridges.[4] Accountants have even penetrated the secretive ranks of the Federal Bureau of Investigation. As criminals have become more sophisticated in their financial operations, the FBI has recruited more and more accountants to help trap interstate swindlers and con artists at their own games.[5]

WHAT ARE THE MAJOR TYPES OF ACCOUNTANTS?

With the diversity of opportunity that accountancy presents, it's not surprising that there is a whole range of types of accountants. Accountants can be divided into two basic groups: public and private.

Public accountants

Public accountants *operate in a service capacity; they are independent of the businesses and other organizations they serve.* Their position of detachment permits them to submit honest and, when necessary, critical reports on the financial statements of a business. They are of great value to anyone (and everyone) who must have an accurate picture of the financial workings of a particular business; their clients include creditors, stockholders, investors, and even government agencies. Objectivity is a public accountant's stock in trade, and he or she can be sued for issuing financial information that doesn't accurately reveal a business's condition and income.

Public accountants fall into several categories. Those who *meet a state's requirements for education and experience and pass an examination prepared by the American Institute of Public Accountants* become **certified public accountants (CPAs)**. It's estimated that every year another 10,000 accountants are certified. In 1977 there were about 180,000 CPAs in the country, or one for every two lawyers.

A MULTIPLICITY OF ACCOUNTANTS: TRACING THE GROWTH OF THE PROFESSION SINCE 1925

1977

1964

1939

18,757　　　　　**87,890**　　　　　**180,000**　　FIGURE 1

Private accountants

Private accountants are *those in the employ of one business or individual,* supervising the accounting system and the bookkeeping staff. They're responsible for both the flow of financial reports and their interpretation. They usually specialize in one of the areas listed in Table 1.

About half of the CPAs in the United States are in private practice, spread across no fewer than 23,500 accounting firms. Four hundred of those firms are large, having about fifty partners each and hundreds of lesser, salaried accountants. There are thirty-five giant nationwide and multinational firms with more than fifty partners each. And finally, there are those eight firms at the top, universally known as the Big Eight of accounting. Harvey Kapnik, with whom we began this look at accounting, is at the head of Arthur Andersen & Company, one of the largest of the eight. It has more than 1,000 partners, each of whom *averages* almost $100,000 per year in pay.[6]

KEY CONCEPTS IN ACCOUNTING

Let's examine how accountants go about earning such large salaries. To begin, an examination of the accounting equation and double-entry bookkeeping is in order.

BIGGEST OF THE BIG EIGHT

Peat Marwick Mitchell & Company isn't exactly a household name, yet in 1977 it earned more than half a billion dollars in fees from clients. These clients included more than one out of ten of the top companies in the country. PMM & Company is the largest of the so-called Big Eight accountancy firms that dominate the industry in the United States and around the world.

In 1977 some 1,700 partners benefited directly from the company's position at the top. That same year 1,300 eager young graduates were recruited (out of 20,000 college students who were interviewed). If that seems like a great number of new people to hire in any one year, consider the demands of some of the company's clients: one client alone requires the services of 400 professionals in thirty-seven United States offices and thirty-six foreign locations.

What does PMM & Company do? Naturally, an operation of that size does more than merely keep the books. Though accounting for its clients is one of the basic services the firm offers, it's only one of many.

First, as we've seen, government requires corporations of any significant size to be audited (have its financial records examined) by an independent outsider for its report to the shareholders. PMM & Company is one of the nation's leading auditors.

Second, PMM & Company, for a fee, handles the most intricate tax problems its clients must solve. (Corporate clients of the caliber that deal with the firm naturally have tax problems that surpass filling out a 1040 form once a year.) In addition, the firm's expertise in tax matters can help a client plan to anticipate and legally avoid crushing tax bills.

Finally, the leader of the Big Eight can help its clients manage all of their business affairs more efficiently by means of a special management consulting service. This includes participation in any or all phases of management, encompassing internal accounting and operating controls, financial planning, manufacturing and marketing, employee benefits, executive compensation, and recruitment. Moreover, through the years, PMM & Company has developed particular knowledge in several specialized industries, including banking, education, health, transportation, public utilities, TV, and motion pictures, to name a few. Once again, for a fee, the firm will make this knowledge available to its clients. In short, PMM & Company, along with the other accountancy firms in its class, has become an all-around business advisor.

Source: *Annual Report 1977 Peat, Marwick, Mitchell & Co. in the United States*, 1978.

TABLE 1 Areas of Specialization for Private Accountants

Area	Job Responsibilities
General accounting	Records all business transactions and prepares reports and financial statements
Controlling (management) accounting	Uses reported data to help managers plan operations, price new products, select alternative methods of financing, and make other decisions
Internal auditing	Checks the accuracy of company's records and accounting methods; polices errors and possible larceny of employees
Cost accounting	Controls the cost of manufactured products and their distribution; helps management estimate future costs
Accounting systems installation	Designs systems for recording and reporting financial data that include cross-checks on the record keeping

THE ACCOUNTING EQUATION

For thousands of years businesses and governments have kept records of their **assets**—*valuable things they owned,* like gold and wheat—and of their **liabilities**—*what they owed,* like loans. When it was said of ancient princes that they were as "rich as Croesus" (a wealthy king of Lydia), it was not just because they had stored away much gold and grain. It was because they owned these treasures almost outright and had few debts or creditors' claims on their assets.

The wealth of a person or a business is not measured by assets alone. It is what remains after you deduct liabilities from the assets. And that remainder is called **owners' equity**, which is the *owners' claim on the assets.*

$$\begin{aligned} \textbf{Assets} &= \$100{,}000 \\ \textbf{— Liabilities} &= \underline{\quad 30{,}000} \\ \textbf{Owners' Equity} &= \underline{\$\ 70{,}000} \end{aligned}$$

This rather ordinary observation is the basis for the all-important **accounting equation**:

Assets = Liabilities + Owners' Equity
$100,000 = $30,000 + $70,000

The liabilities are placed before the owners' equity because creditors have first claim on the assets. After liabilities are paid, anything left over belongs to the owners or, in the case of a corporation, the stockholders. However, if you want to emphasize the amount of owners' equity, you might write the same equation as:

Assets — Liabilities = Owners' Equity
$100,000 — $30,000 = $70,000

Whichever form you use, the relationship between assets, liabilities, and owners' equity remains in balance, that is, one side of the equation equals the other side. This is important in understanding the double-entry system of keeping records.

DOUBLE-ENTRY BOOKKEEPING

Like many other useful discoveries, the double-entry system of bookkeeping surfaced here and there for centuries before anyone took a careful look at it. The Greeks flirted with it, and it certainly was used for a while in Italy around 1340. But it was not until just after Columbus landed in America that a practical monk wrote down the first clear and systematic description of double-entry bookkeeping. This man was Fra Luca Pacioli. His system immediately caught the attention of the merchants and princes of his day.

Pacioli explained that every transaction—a sale, a payment, a collection—had two sides or two monetary effects. Every transaction led to changes in parts of the accounting equation. But no matter what kinds of transactions were made, the accounting equation remained in balance if the transactions were properly recorded. **Double-entry bookkeeping** *requires two entries for every transaction.* The accounting equation is kept in balance by offsetting any change in one part of the equation with a change in another part.

Transactions using the double-entry principle

Let us say that you go into business, investing $12,000 in cash. The accounting equation of your business would show:

$$\text{Assets} = \text{Liabilities} + \text{Owners' equity}$$

(cash) $12,000 = 0 + $12,000

In other words, $12,000 in cash is equal to your owners' equity of $12,000. As yet, your business has no liabilities.

Next, your business borrows $5,000 from a bank.

| | | Owners' |
| Assets = | Liabilities + | equity |

(cash) $12,000 = *(bank loan)* $5,000 + $12,000
+ 5,000
(total cash) $17,000

The same amount ($5,000) is added to cash and to bank loans. Your accounting equation is still in balance.

Now your business has enough cash to buy $13,000 worth of inventory.

| | | Owners' |
| Assets = | Liabilities + | equity |

(cash) $12,000 = *(bank loan)* $5,000 + $12,000
+ 5,000 =
− 13,000 =
(total cash) $ 4,000 =
(inventory) + $13,000 =

Total assets = Liabilities + Owner's equity
$17,000 = $5,000 + $12,000

The meaning of double-entry transactions

Each of the transactions of your business was recorded to show what happened in dollar terms. Your initial investment in the business increased cash by $12,000. At the same time it increased owners' equity by the same amount, showing that the owner had a claim on the business equal to the full amount of the assets (cash).

If you had recorded the second transaction (the bank loan) merely by increasing cash by the $5,000 borrowed, your records would have been out of balance. More important, the other side of the transaction (the $5,000 bank loan) would have caught you by surprise when the loan came due. One of the beauties of the double-entry system is that errors of omission (such as neglecting to record half a transaction) throw the accounting equation out of balance. This gives warning that an error was made.

The third transaction demonstrates the changing of one asset for another. The $13,000 in cash is exchanged for $13,000 in inventory. Cash is decreased by $13,000 while inventory is increased by the same amount. Subtraction and addition on the "Assets" side keep the accounting equation in balance.

Obviously, after a few months, the transactions recorded by a bookkeeper can pile up. Management would need weeks to sort through all of them for the information it needed. To save time, accountants prepare summary reports. Let's take a look now at the two most common reports: the balance sheet and the income statement.

THE BALANCE SHEET

The Grizzly Bear camping equipment store (a fictitious enterprise) has a new idea for an all-in-one trail pack that includes featherweight sleeping bag and tent, solar-powered cookstove and freeze-dried French and Chinese food. However, retailing this trail pack calls for new inventory and a new advertising and promotion campaign. As we've seen in previous chapters, the company can get the money for those expanding needs through both short- and long-term finance. In order to get that cash, however, it has to persuade potential lenders that it's a worthy credit risk. That's where balance sheets come into the picture.

The **balance sheet**, sometimes referred to as the **statement of financial condition**, *includes both the accounting equation and the details of financial transactions that back it up.* The balance sheet thus reveals the kind and amounts of assets, liabilities, and owners' equity at a specific moment in time. Using the information on the balance sheet, potential creditors can determine whether a company can cover its present and future debts.

Of course, no business can hold still for someone who is examining its financial condition. Even during a holiday, office fixtures grow older and interest on a savings account accumulates. Yet the accountant must set up a balance sheet to show the condition of a

Grizzly Bear Camping Equipment, Inc.

Balance Sheet
as of December 31, 1978

ASSETS

Current Assets

Cash		$15,000	
Marketable Securities		5,000	
Accounts Receivable	$54,000		
Less: Allowance for Doubtful Accounts	3,000	51,000	
Notes Receivable		15,000	
Merchandise Inventory		37,000	
Prepaid Insurance		4,000	
Total Current Assets			$127,000

Fixed Assets

Store Equipment	$20,000		
Less: Accumulated Depreciation	6,000	$14,000	
Furniture & Fixtures	$10,000		
Less: Accumulated Depreciation	3,000	7,000	
Total Fixed Assets			21,000

Intangible Assets

Goodwill		$8,000	
Total Intangible Assets			8,000
Total Assets			$156,000

LIABILITIES AND OWNERS' EQUITY

Current Liabilities

Accounts Payable	$16,000		
Notes Payable	10,000		
Accrued Wages Payable	3,000		
Income Taxes Payable	4,000		
Total Current Liabilities		$33,000	

Long-Term Liabilities

Long-Term Notes Payable	$ 4,000		
Bonds Payable	20,000	24,000	
Total Liabilities			$ 57,000

Owners' Equity

Common Stock		$65,000	
Retained Earnings		34,000	
Total Owners' Equity			99,000
Total Liabilities and Owners' Equity			$156,000

FIGURE 2

business *at one moment in time*. The status of the business, through the accountant's technical know-how, is rendered in a kind of stop-motion photograph while the business itself goes on.

At least once a year, every company, including Grizzly Bear, prepares its balance sheet. This is most often done at the end of the year. The year is most often the **calendar year,** *January 1 to December 31*. However, many business and government bodies use a **fiscal year,** which may be *any twelve consecutive months*. For example, a business may choose a fiscal year from June 1 to May 31 because its peak selling season is over in May. Such a fiscal year would then include its full manufacturing and selling cycle.

Some companies require a balance sheet more often than once a year, for example, at the end of each month or quarter. Thus every balance sheet is dated to tell you when the financial "snapshot" was taken.

Figure 2 shows a typical balance sheet. Most detailed balance sheets use similar categories to classify income and expenditures. A closer look at these categories will help you understand other balance-sheet reports you may come across.

ASSETS

Most often, the asset section of the balance sheet is divided into three groups—current, fixed, and intangible—listed in the order in which they can be turned into cash.

Current assets

These assets are always listed first. Included in this group are cash and inventory that will or can become cash within the following year.

The term **cash** includes *cash on hand, in checking accounts, and in savings accounts*. Not included are funds in special deposits or in any other form not readily available for use.

Marketable securities are *stocks, bonds, and other investments that can be quickly turned into cash when needed*. Such investments are temporary and not important to the business as a means of long-term control over the company in which it invested.

"Accounts receivable" and "notes receivable" are accounting terms for the short-term financial instruments you learned about in Chapter 11. *Amounts due from customers* are known as **accounts receivable**. Often accountants immediately deduct from accounts receivable an allowance for doubtful accounts. This deduction notifies creditors and stockholders that not all of the receivables are considered collectible. **Notes receivable** differ from accounts receivable in that they *are signed and written promises to pay a definite sum, usually on a certain date and at a certain place*. As noted in Chapter 11, they are generally collected routinely through the customers' banks.

Inventories are usually *merchandise on hand*. Manufacturing companies, however, may have inventories of *raw materials, goods in process, and finished goods ready for sale* as well.

Supplies on hand and services paid for but not yet used are known as **prepaid expenses**. An example is prepaid insurance, the unexpired portion of insurance purchased by a business. It is classified as a current asset because it can be turned into cash if canceled, or it will be used and thus reduce cash outlay in the next year.

Fixed assets

Fixed assets, sometimes called **plant assets**, are *permanent investments in buildings, equipment, furniture and fixtures, transportation equipment, land, and any other tangible property used in running a business*. They have a useful life of more than one year and are not expected to be converted into cash. With the exception of land, they depreciate over the years.

Depreciation is *the loss of value or usefulness of an asset during the period of its life*. An asset like a machine or a truck loses value day by day through age or use. This loss of value may not be noticeable, but it occurs nevertheless, like the gradual deterioration of a favorite record album played every day on the stereo. In the ordinary course of business, no transaction is recorded to show this depreciation. At the time the balance sheet is prepared, however, the accountant will record the depreciation to date. Depreciating a fixed asset has the effect of spreading the cost of that asset over a number of years (see Figure 3).

Intangible assets

Intangible assets include *patents on a process or invention, copyrights to written or reproducible material, and trademarks*. They can be valuable even though

HOW TO ACCOUNT FOR AN ELEPHANT

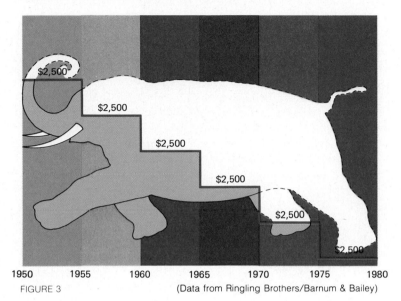

$2,500
$2,500
$2,500
$2,500
$2,500
$2,500

1950   1955   1960   1965   1970   1975   1980

FIGURE 3   (Data from Ringling Brothers/Barnum & Bailey)

An elephant is one of a circus's most important assets—and like any other asset, it depreciates. An elephant costs approximately $15,000, and it has an average lifespan of thirty years and no salvage value after death. Circus accountants will generally figure its depreciation at $500 a year.

they are not solid, physical properties like a chair or a desk, because they can be licensed or sold outright to others.

Least tangible of all but no less valuable an asset is goodwill. **Goodwill** is a resource that consists mainly of a *company's reputation, especially in its relations with its customers.* Goodwill is not entered as an asset in a company's books unless the business is purchased. In that case, there are specific guidelines used in determining the amount of goodwill to be recorded, and its value may be put at anything from one dollar to several millions.

LIABILITIES

Liabilities, the debts a business owes, represent claims against the assets and come next on the balance sheet. Liabilities may be current or long-term, and they are listed in the order in which they will come due.

Current liabilities

Debts that will have to be paid within a year of the date of the balance sheet are known as **current liabilities**. The items considered current liabilities are, as we have said, listed in the order in which they are expected to come due.

Because they are generally *due in thirty days,* **accounts payable** are listed first. Generally they result from goods or services bought on credit.

Notes payable, like the notes receivable mentioned in the assets section, are *written and signed promises to pay a certain sum at a definite time and place.* In this case, however, it is money owed rather than money coming. These notes may come due after a much longer time than accounts payable.

When the balance sheet is prepared, certain expenses, such as purchases, may have been *incurred for which bills have not yet been received and recorded.* Labor, interest, and taxes may also be payable in the near future. Such payable—but unrecorded—items are known as **accrued expenses**. If such expenses were not recorded, the financial statements of the business would be both incorrect and misleading.

Long-term liabilities

Debts that fall due in a year or more after the date of the balance sheet are **long-term liabilities**. They are similar to owners' equity in that they are claims on the business that may remain unpaid for a long time. Usually, however, the claims of the long-term creditors are paid before those of the owners when a company goes out of business.

Other items that may fall in the long-term category are **mortgages**, *agreements conveying land, buildings, machines, or other property owned by a business to creditors as security.* If a business can't pay a mortgage as it comes due, the lender has the right to seize the property and sell it. If some of the mortgage payments are due within a year, they are classified under current liabilities. However, the larger part of the mortgage will most likely extend over a period of decades.

OWNERS' EQUITY

The investment of the owners of a business is listed under owners' equity. Listings here vary with the form of business organization. Sole proprietorships list owners' equity under the owner's name, with the amount (assets minus liabilities). Partnerships list each owner's share of the business separately. Since our balance sheet is for a corporation, it gives the amount of common stock that is outstanding—meaning the amount in the hands of shareholders. The amount listed is the investment paid into the corporation by the stockholders when the stock was issued. (Preferred stock would be listed separately.)

The **retained earnings** of a corporation are *the total earnings of all previous periods, including the current period, reduced by amounts distributed as dividends.*

WHAT THE BALANCE SHEET REVEALS

Though a balance sheet may at first glance seem a rather boring document, it can tell you a great deal about corporate plans, aspirations, and attitudes.

How much cash does the company have on hand—and why?

For example, recent balance sheets of many of the top corporations have tended to show enormous accumulations of cash. The reason is that there has been a trend toward liquidity, or keeping assets in an easily disposable form. In early 1978, for instance, Gulf Oil's balance sheets showed more than $2 billion on hand, a

$400-million increase in four years. At the same time, General Electric had more than $1.7 billion in cash and marketable securities, compared with only $753 million in 1976 and $477 million in 1975. Why are major corporations holding onto these big sums of money? According to William E. Simon, former Secretary of the Treasury, such cash build-ups are the result of a relatively healthy economy combined with some uncertainty about the future. Ordinarily, cash in such imposing quantities would go toward capital investment programs. These, however, are being postponed because of what Simon sees as "the uncertainty and deep-seated fear of inflation that exists in our economy."[7]

Companies do various things with these piled-up liquid assets. Some, such as Avon, are taking the opportunity to increase their dividends: during the early part of 1977 cash dividends by 500 top corporations increased 16.6 percent. Meanwhile, other companies, like IBM, are using their cash to buy back their own stock. With more than $6 billion on hand, IBM has been "eating itself alive," thereby channeling the returns on its investment back to itself. Additional savings accumulated will be used in the future to cope with unforeseen competition. Still other rich corporations are using their cash to buy up other companies, on the principle that buying is cheaper than building.

What are the effects of inflation on the company?

Another insight to be gained from the study of a company's balance sheet is the impact that inflation has had on its operations. As we've discussed, assets depreciate—they gradually lose value through normal wear and tear. No truck, for example, is likely to improve its performance with age. Consequently, a company can write off the purchase of a $10,000 truck over the course of several years; say $2,000 per year for five years or $1,000 per year for ten. At the end of those ten years, however, a new truck to replace the old one might very well cost $20,000 due to the effects of inflation. Is it accurate, then, to show depreciation only up to the original cost of the truck? The government thinks not, and so it now requires the largest companies to disclose the *current* replacement costs of their inventories, plants, and equipment, and compute the effects that replacement would have on depreciation costs in particular and the company as a whole. The results can appear disastrous on paper. For U.S. Steel, for example, depreciation on a replacement-cost basis rather than on a historical-cost basis turns fairly healthy profits into horrifying losses. In 1973, using traditional methods of figuring depreciation, the company reported earnings of $367 million after taxes. Replacement-cost accounting, however, would have shown the company *losing* $374 million. Both figures are equally accurate—and also equally misleading, depending on the accounting point of view. The latter figure, though, would not be apt to please current shareholders of U.S. Steel or potential investors.[8]

THE INCOME STATEMENT

From the point of view of the investor, the glamor of a Broadway musical hit isn't always what it's cracked up to be. Take the case of *Annie.* Based on the popular Little Orphan Annie comic-strip character, *Annie* was the sensation of the season, packing them in and playing to standing-room audiences every night. Yet, as of mid-1978, *Annie* had yet to make a Daddy Warbucks (Annie's wealthy benefactor) of any of its backers or investors. (It may do so yet, of course—time will tell.)

During its run at the Alvin Theater on Broadway the show grossed $150,000 weekly. Out of that had to come built-in expenses of salaries and the like amounting to $95,000 every week, plus $10,000 to $15,000 in other weekly overhead. At those rates it would take the backers of *Annie* thirty weeks—many times longer than the average theatrical run—before they began to realize *any* profits at all from their investments. Even were the show to run for years, they couldn't realistically expect much more than a 50 to 100 percent return on their money. It's for that reason that it's so difficult to produce a Broadway show. Few people want to take such risks for so little return.[9]

How do accountants find out where *Annie*'s backers stand in terms of their investment? They use an **income statement**, which *shows how a business's revenues stack up against expenses over a given period of time.* This statement lists all the **revenues** (or sales), *the amounts received or to be received from customers for*

goods or services delivered to them. And it lists **expenses**, the costs that have arisen in generating revenues. And finally it *subtracts expenses from revenues,* to show the *actual profit or loss of a company,* a figure known as **net income**. The income statement summarizes financial transactions over a long period of time, usually a year.

Figure 4 (next page) shows a typical income statement. Let's look at its parts a little more closely.

REVENUES

The revenues of a business usually come from sales to customers, fees for services, or both. Other kinds of revenue may be rents, commissions, interest, and money paid by other firms for the use of the company's patents.

How revenues are recorded: two alternative methods

It makes no difference whether the sales are for immediate cash or are "on account" and collected later, if a company is on an **accrual basis**—meaning that *all sales revenues are recorded in the year they are made,* even if the customer pays the following year. Similarly, *expenses are reported in the year in which the associated revenue is reported*—an accounting method based on the matching concept.

A business run on a **cash basis**, however, *records revenue only when the money is actually received. Expenses are recorded when they are paid for.* Manufacturers and retailers use the accrual system. Service businesses and professionals prefer, on the whole, to operate on a cash basis.

Gross sales versus net sales

Gross sales, *the total dollar amount of goods sold,* doesn't give the entire revenue picture. In the normal course of business, there are deductions from gross sales—and these may be considerable. For example, customers are liable to return goods, for which they get refunds. Cash discounts, offered to customers to speed their payments, also reduce gross sales. *After such discounts are deducted from gross sales, the remainder is called* **net sales**.

Grizzly Bear Camping Equipment, Inc.
Income Statement
for Year Ended December 31, 1978

Revenues			
Gross Sales		$180,000	
Less: Sales Returns & Allowances	$ 3,000		
Sales Discount	2,000	5,000	
Net Sales			$175,000
Cost of Goods Sold			
Inventory, Jan. 1		$ 41,000	
Purchases during year	$86,000		
Less: Purchase Discounts	2,000		
Net Purchases		84,000	
Cost of Goods Available for Sale		$125,000	
Less: Inventory, Dec. 31		37,000	
Cost of Goods Sold			88,000
Gross Profit			$ 87,000
Operating Expenses			
Selling Expenses			
Sales Salaries	$28,000		
Advertising	5,000		
Sales Supplies	3,000		
Insurance—Sales	2,000		
Depreciation—Store Equipment	3,000		
Miscellaneous Selling Expenses	2,000		
Total Selling Expenses		$ 43,000	
General Expenses			
Office Salaries	$21,000		
Depreciation—Office Equipment	1,000		
Insurance—Office	1,000		
Miscellaneous Office Expense	4,000		
Total General Expenses		27,000	
Total Operating Expenses			70,000
Net Income from Operations			$ 17,000
Interest Expense			1,000
Net Income before Taxes			$ 16,000
Income Taxes			4,000
Net Income			$ 12,000

FIGURE 4

ACCURATE FIGURES AND "GUESSTIMATES": TWO ACCOUNTING CATEGORIES

There are a number of figures accountants can assess accurately—including cash, accounts receivable, stock, notes receivable, accounts payable, and mortgages. But there are others which can only be estimated—including goodwill; allowance for bad debts; income tax payable; and the value of buildings, raw materials, inventory, equipment, trucks, land, capital, and patents.

FIGURE 5

COSTS

Cost of goods sold

For any goods a retailer or wholesaler sells, it must pay certain costs. A manufacturer, for instance, must take into account the added expense of producing the goods. Let's see how the cost of goods sold is calculated in two kinds of businesses—manufacturing businesses and retailing and wholesaling businesses.

Retailers and wholesalers start by evaluating inventory on hand at the beginning of the year. Purchases made during the year (less discounts) are then added to this figure. These sums make up the total cost of goods available for sale. To find out the cost of goods sold, the cost of inventory still on hand at the end of the period is deducted.

Manufacturers, on the other hand, must first total the costs of producing goods, including labor, raw materials, and factory expenses. These costs are then added to the cost of inventory of finished goods on hand at the beginning of the year. The cost of inventory (finished goods not sold) at the end of the year is then subtracted, resulting in the cost of goods sold.

STEPS IN FIGURING NET INCOME

Now that we have examined revenues and costs, let's see how net income is figured.

Figuring gross profit

The first step in figuring net income is to deduct *the cost of goods sold from net sales,* to obtain a figure known as **gross profit** (or **gross margin**). This is an important figure for management to compare against previous income statements. The gross profit should be large enough to cover all operating expenses and still allow for some profit for the owners or money for reinvestment.

Figuring net operating income

The next step is to deduct from gross income a figure known as **operating expenses**—*all the costs of operations that aren't included in the category of goods sold.* The remainder is a figure known as **net operating income**.

Exactly what expenses do operating expenses include? They may be divided into selling expenses and general expenses. A firm's **selling expenses** are *incurred through marketing and distributing the products it buys or makes for sale.* Selling expenses include salaries of salespeople, advertising, sales supplies, insurance related to the sales operation, depreciation of the store or other sales equipment, and all the miscellaneous expenses of the sales department, such as utilities and maintenance. **General expenses**, on the other hand, *arise out of overall administration of a business.* They include office salaries, depreciation of office equipment, insurance covering office operations, supplies, and miscellaneous expenses.

Net income: the "bottom line"

Net income, representing the actual profit or loss of a company, sums up the results of all the company's activities. First, management usually compares this year's net operating income with that made in other years. Then, two more deductions are usually made from net operating income: money paid out in interest on loans and income tax. The resulting figure, net income, is the all-important bottom line of the income statement, showing the profit or loss in which managers, owners, creditors, and investors are vitally interested.

USING RATIOS

As we have seen, the balance sheet and the income statement reveal a good deal in themselves. But they can also be made to yield further clues to the present health and future prospects of a business, when information from them is analyzed in terms of ratios. **Ratios** are simply *arithmetical relationships between two amounts.* The ratio between 1,000 fans at a rock concert, for example, and the 100 security guards protecting the featured group is:

$$\frac{1,000}{100} = \frac{10}{1}$$

or 10 fans for every 1 guard. (The relationship can also be expressed as 10:1.)

TESTING THE PROFITABILITY OF A BUSINESS

Information from the income statement and the balance sheet can be used to set up ratios that show how profitable the business is. Potential investors are, of course, interested in the profitability of a business; and managers are particularly concerned with it, since any change in profitability means something has changed in the way the business operates, or perhaps in the market it attempts to serve.

Return on sales

One important indicator of profitability is the net income a business makes per unit of sales, which can be determined by setting up a *relationship between net income and net sales*—the **return-on-sales ratio**. Take, for example, the case of the Denim Den, a shop for jeans, which netted $12,000 in income from $175,000 in sales last year. The ratio can be set up as follows:

$$ROS = \frac{\text{Net income}}{\text{Net sales}} = \frac{\$12,000}{\$175,000} = 6.9\%$$

By dividing the $175,000 net sales into the $12,000 net income we can arrive at a percentage, 6.9 percent, which is the Denim Den's return on sales. This figure, when compared to the percentages of other companies in the same business, can give a potential investor a valuable warning of inefficiency—or reassuring knowledge that the store is doing well. In this case, the Denim Den is doing very well; most retail stores average only 2 to 5 percent.

Return on equity

Using another equation, we can determine what return the owners of the Denim Den are getting on their equity, $99,000. We set up the **return-on-equity ratio**—the *ratio between net income and total owners' equity*—using information from the balance sheet and the income statement. The ratio (again expressed as a percent) would be:

$$\frac{\text{Net income}}{\text{Owners' equity}} = \frac{\$12,000}{\$99,000} = 12.1 \text{ percent}$$

How good is this particular return? There is no agreed-upon ideal return. Clearly, however, 12.1 percent isn't bad, compared to, say, the interest of 6 or 7 percent that savings accounts return.

One might expect that a corporation would declare dividends to its stockholders based on its return on equity; if the company is making—let's say—12.1 percent of income per unit of equity, shouldn't the stockholders receive dividends right up to this amount? Not necessarily—the corporation may decide to plow back a portion of the earnings into the business, so the business can grow in future. This course of action, however, is not without benefits to the stockholders; even if a portion of the earnings does go back into the business, it still increases their equity.

TESTING THE ABILITY OF A BUSINESS TO PAY ITS DEBTS

There is always some risk involved when one business grants credit to another or when an investor buys stocks or bonds. But these risks can be minimized by using ratios based on information from the company's balance sheet and income statement.

Ratios a short-term creditor needs to know

The **current ratio**, for example, is used to test how well a company is able to pay its short-term debts. It's expressed as *current assets divided by current liabilities.* Suppose, for instance, that the Open Road, a small custom motorbike outfit in Los Angeles, has current assets of $127,000 and current liabilities of $33,000. The current ratio would be set up as follows:

Bal sheet

$$\frac{\text{Current assets}}{\text{Current liabilities}} = \frac{\$127,000}{\$33,000} = 3.8$$

This means that the business has $3.80 of current assets to meet every dollar of current liabilities. How safe is a 3.8 ratio? To answer this question, analysts will compare a company's current ratio with the average for that type of business. As a rule, though, a company with a current ratio of at least 1.5 is considered a safe risk for short-term finance.

The **acid-test ratio**, also called a **quick ratio**, *shows the ability of a company to meet its short-term debts with its cash, marketable securities, and receivables.* Some analysts consider it a better indication of a company's ability to pay its immediate debts because, unlike the current ratio, inventories are left out of the equation. The acid-test ratio for the Open Road would look like this: *Bal sheet*

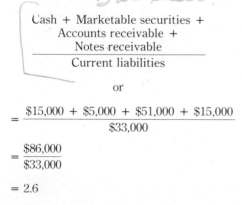

$$\frac{\text{Cash + Marketable securities +}}{\text{Current liabilities}}$$
Accounts receivable +
Notes receivable

or

$$= \frac{\$15,000 + \$5,000 + \$51,000 + \$15,000}{\$33,000}$$

$$= \frac{\$86,000}{\$33,000}$$

$$= 2.6$$

The Open Road isn't in bad shape at all, since some analysts consider a ratio of 1 to be reasonable. If the company were pressed for cash and inventory was moving sluggishly, it would still have $2.60 in quick assets to meet each dollar of current liabilities.

An inventory turnover ratio would tell potential investors how fast the inventory was turned into sales. The quicker the better is the general rule.

Using the income statement, the **inventory turnover ratio** *is computed by dividing the average inventory for a period into the cost of goods sold.* Where inventories are fairly constant, averaging the inventories for the beginning and the end of the year would be accurate enough. But if there are high and low inventory seasons not represented by the beginning and end-of-year inventories, all the month-end inventories for the year should be averaged. Since the Open Road's inventory is more or less constant, the January and December figures are used. Its turnover is:

$$\frac{\text{Cost of goods sold}}{\frac{(\text{Inventory, Jan. 1 + Inventory, Dec. 31})}{2}}$$

$$= \frac{\$88,000}{\frac{(\$41,000 + \$37,000)}{2}}$$

$$= \frac{\$88,000}{\$39,000}$$

$$= 2.3$$

This means that the average inventory was converted (turned over) into sales every 159 days (365 days divided by 2.3). As a potential investor you would be interested in this information because it tells you that the Open Road's average monthly inventory can be turned into at least $39,000 in cash and probably more, depending on the store's markup. The "ideal" turnover varies with the type of operation. A grocery store's turnover would be much faster, usually around 16.

Ratios a long-term investor needs to know

Long-term loans can be tested for their safety in much the same way. Before handing over the sort of huge amount that long-term financing entails, it's best to determine whether or not the potential debtor has put enough money into the business to act as a protective cushion for your loan.

An **owners' equity-to-debt ratio** can help answer that question. Creditors are protected by a high ratio of owners' equity to debt. Only if the business loses more than the amount of the owners' equity would the creditors suffer a loss. The owners' equity ratio of the Open Road is:

$$\frac{\text{Owners' equity}}{\text{Total liabilities}} = \frac{\$99,000}{\$57,000} = 1.7$$

This means that if the assets of the Open Road could be disposed of at the amounts recorded in its balance sheet, the shareholders' investment is $1.70 for each dollar of liabilities. If the ratio goes below 1, debts exceed equity and the business may be relying too heavily on debt.

Of course, none of these ratios is a magic formula. Investments can and do go wrong despite the cheery picture sometimes suggested by the equations. Ratios reduce risk; they don't eliminate it.

THE BUDGET

Accounting is more than taking stock of what has been happening in a business; it also entails planning for the future. That's where the **budget** comes in. It's a *financial blueprint for a given period of time* (often one year) *that structures future plans on a framework of estimated revenues and expenses.* Since working out a budget forces a company to determine how much money will be coming in and what costs will be entailed, it simultaneously becomes a controlling as well as a planning operation.

TYPES OF BUDGET

Since the budget is a guideline to what will take place over a lengthy period of time, a great deal of careful thought must go into its planning. Consequently, the master (or operating) budget, which is an overall estimate of revenues, costs, and expenses, is based on several subbudgets, including the sales budget, the production budget, and the cost-of-goods-sold budget. These are described in more detail in Table 2.

ZERO-BASE BUDGETING

An increasingly popular type of budget is one set up on a zero base, meaning that *every year each manager must justify every current and future expense.* Called **zero-base budgeting**, it eliminates the tendency, particularly widespread in government, to take current appropriations for granted and simply build future budgets on top of them. Instead, working from the lowest levels of an organization to the highest, zero-base budgeting calls for a reexamination of every expense, with estimates showing what would be done if current appropriations were cut entirely or partially and what would be done if they were increased.

According to defenders of **ZBB** (as it's often called), it's simply common sense to question every expense on a regular basis. According to others less keen on the system, ZBB can result in ruinous backlogs of needless paperwork.

TABLE 2 Breakdown of a Typical Master Budget

Type of Budget	Function	Sources of Information
Sales Budget	To estimate future sales (units to be sold and expected unit price)	Study of past sales and estimates of future business conditions (often obtained from salespeople via sales managers)
Production Budget	To estimate number of units needed to fill anticipated sales and leave inventory over at end of budget period.	Projected sales added to number of units expected to be on hand at end of period, minus number of units on hand at beginning of period
Cost-of-Goods-Sold Budget	To determine cost of goods sold	Estimates of cost of materials used in manufacture of units, cost of labor, overhead expenses (light, insurance, property taxes, etc.)

ZERO-BASE BUDGETING

Starting out with zero-base budgeting is somewhat like beginning in the dark.

Despite the controversy, however, ZBB has soared to high governmental and corporate popularity. In Washington, as of this writing, the Carter administration has begun ZBB experiments in several governmental agencies, including the Housing and Urban Development Department, the Federal Reserve Board, and the Consumer Product Safety Commission. One United States Navy facility has already saved at least $500,000 per year from a ZBB look at computer operations. There is one hitch, however: congressional appropriations are the source of all federal funds, and the Congress is hardly likely to change its traditional fund-allocation approach. For instance, when Congress decides to allocate $20 million for road safety, it only dictates what must be accomplished with that money. It doesn't set up a budget for the most efficient ways of spending the allocation. Since ZBB dictates the examination of those specifics, the success of ZBB in Washington is still an open-ended question.[10]

In business, ZBB has scored a fairly well-proved triumph. The Southern California Edison Company, for example, is saving $300,000 per year because a vehicle-maintenance manager insisted in a ZBB report that adding to staff was cheaper in the long run than farming out work, as had been done in the past. The company did get bogged down in detail at one stage of its ZBB appraisals—so much so that managers found themselves justifying costs for one-tenth of an employee. (Such quibbling is one of the pitfalls of ZBB.) Now, though, the company sets minimum discussion standards of one entire employee, or $10,000 in expenses. In general, the larger the company, the more efficient ZBB can be in cutting costs. Ford, for example, credits the system with saving it millions, and Westinghouse managed to save $4.2 million in one year from a partial attempt at ZBB.

All in all, it's still too early to tell whether ZBB is merely a fad—or a true accounting innovation.

CHAPTER REVIEW

Accounting is a system for reporting and analyzing the financial operations of an organization. Accounting reports help managers keep track of accounts receivable and payable, thereby serving a control function. They provide investors and creditors with a way of analyzing a business.

Private accountants serve a single business in one of a number of specialized areas. Public accountants operate independently of the businesses they serve and monitor their reports. Both depend upon two basic accounting concepts. One is the theoretical accounting equation:

$$\text{Assets} = \text{Liabilities} + \text{Owners' Equity}.$$

The other is the technique of double-entry bookkeeping, which keeps the accounting equation in balance by offsetting any change in one part of the equation with a change in another part.

Accounting reports usually take one of two forms. The balance sheet shows in detail the kinds and amounts of assets, liabilities, and owners' equity at a specific time. The income statement reports the accumulated revenue and expense transactions that result in either a profit or a loss over a period, generally one year.

Financial statements are analyzed and interpreted through the use of ratios, the arithmetical relationships between amounts, shown on such statements. They provide information on an organization's ability to meet short-term debt, to pay off long-term debt, and to give an adequate return on investment.

A budget is a plan that estimates the revenues and expenses of an organization for a specific period of time. The process of budgeting usually involves formulating an overall plan (or master budget) for the whole company and specialized plans for departments or other business units.

KEY WORD REVIEW

accounting
accounting statements
receivables
payables
private accountants
public accountants
certified public accountants (CPAs)
assets
liabilities
owners' equity
accounting equation
double-entry bookkeeping
balance sheet (statement of financial condition)
calendar year
fiscal year
cash
marketable securities
accounts receivable
notes receivable
inventories
prepaid expenses
fixed assets (plant assets)
depreciation
intangible assets
goodwill
current liabilities
accounts payable
notes payable
accrued expenses

long-term liabilities
mortgages
retained earnings
income statement
revenues
expenses
net income
accrual basis
cash basis
gross sales
net sales
gross profit (gross margin)
operating expenses
net operating income
selling expenses
general expenses
ratios
return-on-sales ratio
return-on-equity ratio
current ratio
acid-test (quick) ratio
inventory turnover ratio
owners' equity-to-debt ratio
budget
zero-base budgeting (ZBB)

REVIEW QUESTIONS

1. List the ways in which managers, creditors, and investors make use of accounting.

2. What kinds of fields can private accountants specialize in?

3. What are the three basic parts of the accounting equation?

4. Why is it important to keep accounting records in balance?

5. What are the three types of assets and the two types of liabilities listed on a balance sheet? In what order are they listed and why?

6. How does an income statement differ from a balance sheet?

7. Explain the difference between gross profit and net income, as reflected in the income statement.

8. Which is a better indicator of a company's ability to pay its short-term debts: the current ratio or the acid-test ratio? Why?

CASE 1

TO LEND OR NOT TO LEND: THE SIGNIFICANCE OF THE INCOME STATEMENT

You are a banker. One day, the owner of The Face Place, a discount cosmetic store, walks in with a loan request. She wants to start a cosmetic-shop chain, but to do that she must borrow a good deal of money. Being an obliging sort of banker, you decide that a chain of beauty supply shops might indeed be a good idea, but first you want to take a closer look at The Face Place's operation.

You ask to see an income statement for last year. It reads:

Revenues	$300,000
Costs	
Inventory	40,000
Net purchases	140,000
Year-end inventory	20,000

Therefore, you can determine that The Face Place sold $160,000 worth of goods ($40,000 in inventory on hand plus $140,000 in new purchases minus the $20,000 worth of inventory unsold at year's end).

However, that's not yet the complete picture. The income statement also shows that customers returned $5,000 worth of a particularly ugly shade of lip gloss. Additionally, the shop ran up the following costs:

Advertising	$10,000
Salaries	35,000
Phone	1,500
Interest	1,200
Depreciation	4,000
Insurance	1,500

1. Above is all the information the statement shows. In other words, it's incomplete. Using the information you've been given, determine net sales, gross profit, total operating expenses, and that most important item of all, the bottom line showing net income.

2. Once you've done that, compute the return-on-sales ratio for The Face Place.

3. Comparing the return-on-sales ratio for The Face Place with those of other stores of the same type will give you a good idea of how the shop is doing—and whether or not you should risk your bank's money in an expansion scheme. Suppose the ratio isn't all it could be. Perhaps you should advise the shop's owner to make a few changes before you'll make a loan. For instance, the store currently spends $10,000 a year on advertising. How do you think it would affect profits to halve that amount to $5,000 per year, provided the money were effectively spent? Or should The Face Place advertise at all? Maybe word-of-mouth is all it needs. Or, alternatively, how much more profitable do you think the store would be if it cut its payroll down from $35,000 per year to $20,000 per year? Of course that would mean fewer or less experienced sales people. Would that have a bad effect on profits? Why or why not?

CASE 2

WHITE-COLLAR CRIME: CAN ACCOUNTANTS SPOT IT?

Not everyone gets the chance to make a $50 million mistake during the course of a career. Yet that's what happened to a stock analyst a few years back when he recommended shares in Mattel to many of his clients. Instead of projected earnings of $30 million in 1973, the toymaker actually lost more than $19 million during that period.

How did the analyst get his forecast so completely fouled up? In part, it's because he was misled by Mattel's financial professionals. It is open to question whether or not these people *intentionally* misled the unfortunate analyst—who has since lost a good many clients because of the Mattel incident. There's no doubt, though, that outright management fraud has been known to happen in the past and will occur again in the future. Is there any way to stop it? [11]

1. One suggestion put forth in accounting circles is for an end to blanket "adjusting entries" to correct errors or questionable practices on company books. Would that prove anything, in your opinion?

2. When an accountant does uncover something suspicious in a client company's books, on whom is the whistle to be blown? Traditionally, a company's board of directors is told. But do you think that is sufficient? Should the Securities and Exchange Commission be told of an accountant's suspicions? And what about the exchanges on which the client company's shares regularly trade?

COMPUTERS AND DATA PROCESSING

If you've ever wondered *why* you should not fold, spindle, or mutilate your computerized course registration cards or the bill from the phone company, read on.

It should come as a surprise to no one that we live in an age of computers. They control the power that lights our cities, the routes our planes must fly, the amount of taxes we pay, and the balances in our bank accounts. Of course, no computer does this by itself; computers are controlled by people. Yet few people outside the computer field have any real understanding of how even the most simple computer works.

In the following pages you'll have an opportunity to delve into the workings of modern society's workhorse. You'll learn something about the history of computers, computer functions, the types of computer equipment, and the ways humans communicate with computers. You'll also read about some of the amazing new developments in the computer field.

WHAT WILL THIS CHAPTER FOCUS ON?

After reading the material in this chapter, you will understand and be able to discuss:

■ the ways computers affect our everyday lives

■ the four basic types of operation carried out by a computer—arithmetic, logic, memory, and following a program

■ the major milestones in the development of computers

■ the two basic types of computer equipment—the central processing unit and input and output equipment

■ the various kinds of media used for coding raw data

■ the advantages and disadvantages of the two basic ways of processing data—batch processing and on-line processing

■ the difference between computer hardware and computer software

■ recent developments in the computer field

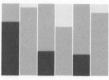Strange things have begun to happen to some of the most familiar machines and appliances that serve our daily needs: they're getting smarter. The engines in some new American cars are equipped with tiny computers that continuously monitor temperature, speed, and other factors, and then adjust the spark to get the best possible gas mileage. The wheels of commercial airliners have tiny computers of their own that can automatically release the brake if they sense a skid beginning. Plans are in the works for computer-controlled radar systems with faster-than-human reflexes to help automobiles avoid collisions. And for the countless millions who hate getting up in the morning, life may soon be a little easier thanks to household computers that will be able to make the coffee, tune in the television, or turn on the shower at just the right temperature—all while the drowsy human is still struggling out of bed.

Futuristic as such visions may seem, the future they represent is quite real and very nearly here. They are all part of what Earl G. Joseph of Sperry Univac has termed the "smart machine revolution," the arrival of a new generation of small, inexpensive computers that may well become as common as the television set.[1] The heart of this revolution is a phenomenal device called a microprocessor (which we'll discuss later in the chapter), an electronic "brain" smaller than a dime that can do as much as computers that used to take up an entire room. The advent of these "miracle chips," as they're also called, will make computer technology available for an intriguing variety of personal uses—and in the process open up major new markets for an industry that is already one of the fastest growing in the world.

As we can scarcely help noticing, computers have come to play a central role in the operations of government, business, finance, communications—indeed, in virtually every important sector of modern society. In 1951 the United States Census Bureau became the first customer for Remington Rand's UNIVAC (Universal Automatic Computer), and three years later General Electric became the first business to buy one. Today there are more than 230,000 computer installations in use by public and private institutions, and the number continues to increase. Stock exchanges use them to keep track of the more than 5 billion shares of stock traded annually in the United States. They process more than 500 million telephone calls every day. There is hardly a bank, credit-card company, department store, insurance company, or university in America that does not depend on them. Not one commercial airliner takes off or lands without their help—nor, for that matter, would man have ever set foot on the moon without them. Indeed, it is safe to say that if computers suddenly disappeared, our society would find itself in serious trouble. A recent study, for example, found that about one-third of all American jobs rely directly on electronic data processing—and one expert estimates that without computers it would take half the population between eighteen and forty-five years of age just to run the telephone system![2]

It's no surprise, then, that the computer industry has grown to impressive proportions. At present some half a million people are employed in the field; by the end of 1977 more than $52 billion worth of computer equipment was in use in the United States and in 1978 alone an estimated $38 billion more was spent on data processing—for new equipment, personnel, programming, supplies, servicing, and the like.[3]

In 1838, the British mathematician Charles Babbage conceived the idea of the program —a set of stored instructions that tells a machine how to operate. His "Analytical Engine," shown here, was the world's first digital computer. It was forgotten until 1937, when Babbage's writings were rediscovered.

The first fully automatic calculating machine of the twentieth century was Howard Aiken's room-size Mark I, built in the early 1940s.

WHAT DOES A COMPUTER DO?

Despite the amazing capabilities of today's ultrasophisticated computers, their operations still boil down to a few very basic functions—tasks no harder in principle than those performed every day by millions of schoolchildren. (The chief difference, of course, is that computers perform the tasks with superhuman speed and accuracy. Any time you hear the phrase "computer error"—when the electric company bills you for $25 million instead of $25, say—you can safely translate it to mean a computer *operator's* error.) These basic computer functions can be broken down into four categories.

First of all, computers perform **arithmetic tasks**—that is, *they add, subtract, multiply, and divide numbers.* A computer could, for example, instantly balance your checkbook—making sure the bank's figures were right, then adding any subsequent deposits, totaling all the outstanding checks, and subtracting them from the balance. You could do this too, of course, but a properly programmed computer could do it for you and everyone you know in, say, a hundredth of a second, without making a mistake.

Second, computers perform **logical tasks**—tasks requiring reasoning. This frequently involves making objective comparisons between things—determining, say, whether a given item is the same size as another item, or larger or smaller than the other item. The computer handling your checking account, for instance, would see whether the balance in your checkbook is the same amount as the one shown in your bank statement. Similarly, a computer can determine whether an item logically fits into a particular category—whether a number entered in your checking account, for example, is a withdrawal (that is, a check that's been cashed) or a deposit.

Third, a computer can follow a **program**, *a prearranged sequence of arithmetic and logic operations.* Whether the program is simple or complicated, it is carried out just one step at a time (though, again, the speed is phenomenal: new computers work at rates measured in *billionths* of a second), and what is done at each step depends on the result of the preceding step. The programming for your checkbook would instruct

Modern computer systems, which have all-electronic circuitry and miniaturized components, work far faster than earlier computers.

Today, many operations can be carried out by highly sophisticated minicomputers, which are priced so that many smaller businesses can afford them.

the computer to determine what category each entry falls into before going on to the next step: if it is a withdrawal, then the next step will be to subtract it from the balance; if it's a deposit, the computer will add it to the balance.

Fourth, a computer can keep *information stored* in its **memory**, as if in a filing cabinet, and retrieve it rapidly whenever needed. If you want to see how many checks you wrote last August or how many deposits you've made since then, the data will be readily available.

HOW THE COMPUTER DIFFERS FROM THE HUMAN BRAIN

It should always be kept in mind, of course, that a computer is different from the human brain in several important respects. From birth onward, a person learns by interacting with his or her environment, accumulating knowledge and arranging it into useful thought patterns by means of repetition, practice, trial and error, and so forth. A computer, by contrast, no matter how sophisticated, remains a machine. It depends on humans for all necessary data and programming and is incapable of original thought or self-education—much less of anything resembling inspiration. As well, a computer can process facts only in numerical form, whereas the human brain can understand not only numbers but also words, visual images, sounds, smells, and other such carriers of information. Writing, for instance, has to be translated into a numerical code—by giving a number to each letter of the alphabet, say—before being fed into a computer.

On the other hand, a computer can "learn" many types of things much more efficiently than any human could hope to do. Anyone who has ever had to memorize multiplication tables or the capitals of every state will appreciate the computer's ability to absorb such information effortlessly. It has to be told something only once, and it never forgets. By the same token, a computer can store a vastly larger number of facts in its memory than the human mind and recall them with incomparably greater speed and accuracy. Here's one example: You have probably awaited the results of an election by watching votes being tabulated on the television. If so, you may well have wondered how news commentators can predict the outcome of the election

with as little as 1 percent of the vote counted. The answer: The television networks own computers that store historical voting patterns for each of the tens of thousands of voting precincts in the United States. An enormous bank of information like this, combined with the computer's lightning speed, allows the networks to predict the outcome of an election using only a minimum sample of the total votes cast.

A BRIEF HISTORY OF THE COMPUTER

The computer is an unmistakable hallmark of the twentieth century, although—as with many other breakthroughs in modern technology—its ancestry can be traced back to the ideas and devices of earlier eras, from the abacus (which originated perhaps 5,000 years ago) to the now-old-fashioned cash register. The modern computer, however, is more than a souped-up adding machine. There are at least three basic features that set it apart from all its predecessors: stored instructions (the program), the use of binary arithmetic, and electronic rather than mechanical components.

FIGURE 1

WHEN IS A 1 NOT A 1?
A LOOK AT BINARY NUMBERS

0001   1 in this position represents 1

0010   1 in this position represents 2, since values increase by multiples of 2 as they move to the left

0100   1 in this position represents 4

1000   1 in this position represents 8

Therefore, to represent the value 3 we have the following:

0011   that is, 2 + 1 = 3

And to represent the value 13, we have:

1101   that is, 8 + 4 + 1 = 13

ELECTRONIC CIRCUITS

Unlike earlier calculating machines that used elaborate systems of gears and levers to perform their operations, computers use electrical signals that pass through a network of circuits. Essentially, when an electrical impulse reaches the end of a particular circuit, it delivers one of two messages: *On* or *Off.* If the message is *On,* a new impulse will be sent through the next circuit; if *Off,* the current will be stopped there. In effect, then, a computer operation consists of millions of On/Off decisions. These are carried out much faster than they could be in any mechanical system (electricity, after all, travels at the speed of light)—and without thousands of moving parts to break down.

THE BINARY SYSTEM

We do most of our calculating in the **decimal system**, which *uses ten numbers and combinations of them.* But because of the basic On/Off nature of electronic circuits, virtually all computers use the binary system of mathematics. The **binary system** *uses the combination of only two numbers, 0 and 1, to represent all numbers* (see Figure 1). Converting numbers from the decimal to the binary system was a breakthrough that made computer operations possible.

THE PROGRAM

Binary numbers, in effect, serve as the language with which programmers tell computers what to do. A computer program essentially contains instructions needed to carry out two types of operations (see Figure 2). First, the program establishes a sequence of tasks that have to be carried out one after the other, as we saw in the checkbook-balancing example: *first* add up all the canceled checks, *then* add up all the outstanding checks, *then* subtract that total from the balance in the checking account.

Second, the program contains a variety of points, comparable to forks in a road, at which the computer has to perform one of two possible operations, the choice depending on the outcome of the preceding operation. In some cases, the choice may be between going on to the next step in the program or making a

FIGURE 2

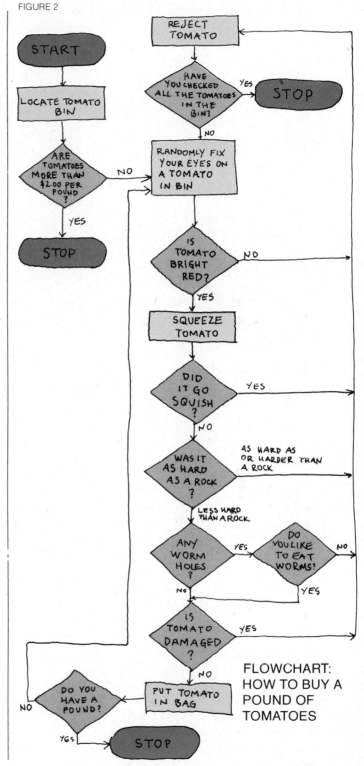

FLOWCHART: HOW TO BUY A POUND OF TOMATOES

"loop"—that is, going back to a previous point in the program.

MILESTONES IN COMPUTER DEVELOPMENT

Since the debut in 1946 of the first all-electronic computer, ENIAC (short for Electronic Numerical Integrator and Calculator), technological advances have brought about a dramatic increase in the speed and capability of computers, along with an equally drastic reduction in size and cost. Five million On/Off computations by a computer in the early 1950s, for example, took three minutes and cost the user about $42; today the same amount of electronic brainwork takes one-eightieth of a second and costs less than half a cent.[4] By most standards, such an improvement in any service—especially accompanied by such a reduction in price—would seem little short of miraculous. In this case, though, there are no miracles involved—only ingenuity, combined with an ever-more sophisticated arsenal of tools and techniques.

The transistor

The first great milestone after ENIAC was the development in 1948 of the **transistor**, *a small electronic device for controlling the flow of current.* The transistor came to replace vacuum tubes in computers just as it did in portable radios, TV sets, and most other electronic equipment. Whereas vacuum tubes were large, used lots of electricity, generated a great deal of heat, and burned out quite frequently, transistors were small, needed little electricity, and were cooler and much more reliable. Moreover, engineers soon began to find ways to make transistors smaller still, establishing a trend toward miniaturization that has characterized the field ever since.[5]

The integrated circuit

By 1960 the next milestone had been achieved in the form of the **integrated circuit (IC)**, *a network of tiny transistors and other components compressed onto a small chip of silicon.* The integrated circuit made possible a new generation of computers, smaller, needing less electricity, and faster—much faster. The earlier, bulkier computers had contained miles of copper wiring, and even an electrical impulse traveling at nearly the speed of light—about a billionth of a second per foot—had a relatively long trip to make. By contrast, an IC's wiring was so compact that it could be measured not in miles but in *inches*—resulting in a phenomenal increase in the speed of computer operations.

Large-scale integration

Even the integrated circuit had its limitations, though. An IC was designed to perform only one specific function, and depended on other components to regulate its operations. By the late 1960s, however, further advances in miniaturization opened the way for another major breakthrough: **large-scale integration (LSI)**, a range of new techniques that made it possible for *numerous separate circuits with different functions* to be *assembled on a single chip.* These chips could then be soldered together on circuit boards, which in turn could be combined like building blocks to produce an entire computer—and a very small one.

The microprocessor

The one real drawback of LSI circuitry was that it was, in computer parlance, "hard-wired"—that is, it had to be designed for a particular function and could not be used for other jobs. Thus, for example, the same computer could not handle a company's payroll and also keep track of inventory or forecast economic trends. The solution to this problem appeared in the early 1970s in the form of a truly amazing device, the **microprocessor (MPU)**. The last word (or at least the latest) in miniaturization, an MPU is *a sliver of silicon less than a quarter-inch square, containing up to 20,000 transistors and designed to perform the basic arithmetic and logic functions at the heart of all computer operations.* In effect, a single MPU no larger than a contact lens and selling for less than $15 has a calculating ability equal to that of IBM's first commercial computer, which occupied a large room, consumed huge amounts of electricity—and cost $1 million. Moreover, one of these computers-on-a-chip offers virtually limitless flexibility since its function can be changed simply by programming new instructions into its memory

The microprocessor is a silicon "chip" that can perform the arithmetic and logic functions essential to all computer operations. It is less than ¼″ square, but it contains amazingly complex circuitry.

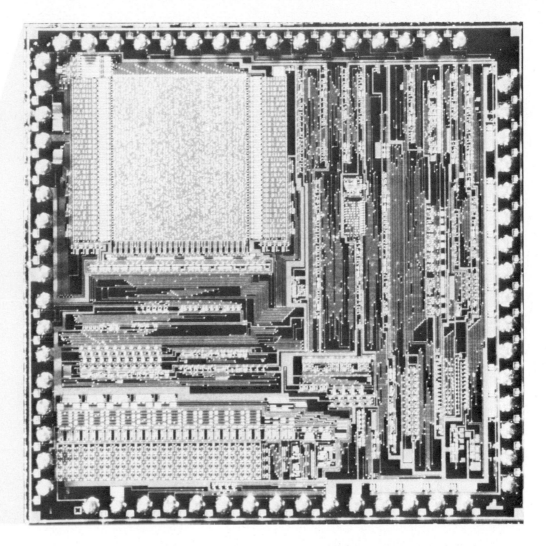

circuits. Thus, in principle, the same microprocessor could be used to play video games on your TV set or guide a spacecraft to a soft landing on Mars.

The advent of these miracle chips has had a revolutionary impact on the computer industry, an impact that will be felt in countless ways throughout society. "Computer power today is essentially free," as one expert put it; and this economic fact, combined with the minuscule size and great flexibility of the MPU, has opened a range of possibilities that has barely begun to be explored.[6] Before we turn to that subject however, we should take a closer look at the different parts of a modern computer system.

PARTS OF THE COMPUTER AND HOW THEY ARE USED

Basically, a computer is made up of two types of equipment: the **central processing unit (CPU)**, the part that *does the "thinking";* and the **peripheral**, or **secondary**, **equipment**, *the input and output devices through which a computer and its operator communicate with each other.* In principle, this system can be compared to an old-fashioned adding machine. If you want to add up a column of numbers, you punch the appropriate keys (input), the adding machine calculates the answer (processing), and the figures are typed

FIGURE 3

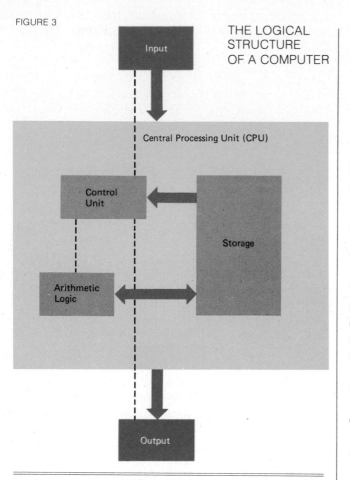

THE LOGICAL
STRUCTURE
OF A COMPUTER

2. To tell the memory unit where to put the data and when to remove them.

3. To tell the arithmetic and logic unit where to find the data, what to do with them (that is, add, subtract, compare), and where to store the results.

4. To tell the output device what data it wants produced and how and when to produce them.

All instructions for the control unit come from internally stored programs. The control unit reads these instructions one at a time until the entire program has been executed.

The arithmetic and logic unit

The **arithmetic unit** is the *place in the computer where all mathematical calculations are carried out.* It bases all its calculations on the principle of addition: subtraction is nothing more than negative addition, division is repeated subtraction, and multiplication is repeated addition. All these operations, of course, are performed at extremely fast speeds.

The **logic unit** *compares a piece of data with another and can determine whether the two are equal or unequal and, if unequal, which is higher.* Nonnumerical data, such as names, can be compared for likeness.

The memory unit

After the computer has translated input data into binary language, the data can then be stored. The **memory unit** of a computer is *where items are stored and called for when needed.* Many of today's computers use magnetic cores for storage. **Magnetic cores** are like tiny doughnuts that can be *magnetized either clockwise or counterclockwise.* The binary *0* is represented by one direction, and the binary *1* by the other.

All data processed by the computer pass through memory, where they are either stored permanently or on a temporary basis to be recalled as needed. The **access time** for this information, *the amount of time that elapses from the moment the data are asked for until the moment they appear,* is what determines the speed of the computer, its efficiency, and its capability.

Magnetic-core storage has many advantages. The equipment is easily magnetized, does not wear out, and has much faster access time than most other media. It is, however, more costly than other media and provides only a limited amount of storage.

out on paper tape (output). A computer likewise receives input, processes it, and gives out the result. The computer's electronic equipment, of course, is considerably more sophisticated, and each function is carried out by a different component. Figure 3 illustrates the **hardware**—as the *electronic components of computers* are known collectively—involved in a central processing unit and the route by which information flows.

THE CENTRAL PROCESSING UNIT

The control unit

The **control unit** is *the supervisor of the whole computing operation.* It has four main functions:

1. To tell the input devices to put certain data into storage. It lets the input device know what data the computer wants and in what order to record them.

For these reasons, most computer systems often use a secondary, **external storage unit**, along with the core storage. While external storage units are *not an integral part of the computer, they are always attached to the system so that they are immediately accessible to the CPU.* Tapes or discs can be used for storage.

A major innovation likely to come into widespread use is the magnetic-bubble memory, a thin multilayered chip within which thousands of microscopic "bubbles"—tiny magnetized pockets—move along precisely designed pathways. Propelled and guided by external magnets, the bubbles carry information in binary code—each bubble representing an individual **bit**, or *binary-system digit*—and pass by sensors that pick up the coded message and relay it to the control unit. The great advantage of the bubble memory, as with other advanced components, lies in its speed and extremely small size. An experimental bubble chip one-quarter of an inch square containing 250,000 bits of information—vastly more than earlier devices—has already been produced; and in the foreseeable future, chips of the same size will be able to store the contents of an entire encyclopedia.

INPUT-OUTPUT EQUIPMENT

Input equipment and output equipment (also called I/O devices) are normally treated together because they use the same media—punched cards, tapes, and the like—and because some units can be used to handle both input and output functions.

The most common input devices are card readers, magnetic tape drives for larger jobs, and console typewriters for individual questions. The most commonly used output devices are high-speed printers, though cathode-ray tubes, used in teaching machines and airline reservation systems, are also becoming common.

The choice of I/O devices must be based on two factors: the user's particular needs, and the nature of the media that feed I/O equipment raw data and produce processed information. Let's take a closer look at these.

Punched cards

This is the workhorse of the computer industry. The most commonly used punched card has eighty conse-

cutively numbered vertical columns, each column having twelve punching positions, or rows. The computer reads a punched hole as 1, or On, or 0, or Off.

A punched card system can be used generally for any information that can be stored in files. Punched cards are very economical because they are easy to transport and store. They are easy to correct because there is one full record per card.

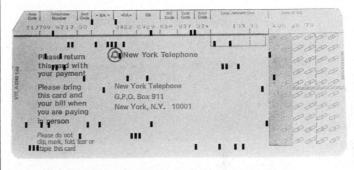

This telephone bill serves as a communication to both the customer and the computer. The computer "reads" the holes punched in the card.

Magnetic tape

Magnetic tape is actually a strip of plastic coated with a substance that can be magnetized. A tiny magnetized area on the tape represents 1, or On; an unmagnetized area represents 0, or Off. A 2,400-foot reel of one-inch magnetic tape has a total storage capacity equivalent to 250,000 punched cards and can transmit data at very high speeds.

Magnetic tape is used for large file storage, especially data in **sequential storage**—*beginning with an item numbered "1" and continuing in order up through the numbering system.* In preparing payroll checks, for example, a company may use a spool of tape containing all the basic employee data—Social Security number, rate of pay, name, and address—that remain fairly constant from week to week.

Magnetic discs

A magnetic disc looks like a long-playing record. Discs are stacked about an inch apart in packs. Unlike magnetic tape, on which records are stored sequentially, magnetic discs provide **random-access storage**, with *no particular regard to sequence.* Random-access storage is often preferable to sequential storage because the computer can go right to the record it is looking for without having to spin through a whole spool of tape. Another advantage is that discs can transmit information at a rate more than double that of tapes.

Disc packs are most commonly used in business situations requiring immediate responses, especially from very large files. Their random-access characteristic enables them to update and retrieve information quickly.

Newer I/O devices

Additionally, a number of innovative I/O devices have appeared recently, all with the goal of making it

A MAN AND HIS PET

You may have been noticing ads in magazines and elsewhere for a variety of new "personal" computers—some preprogrammed to play chess or video games, others meant to be used as general-purpose home computers. Well, so did a fellow named Peter Bird Martin, an editor at *Money* magazine, who decided to try one out for a few months as research for an article. He also had an imaginative angle—instead of writing about his experiences living with a home computer, he thought he'd program it to write (well, at least print out) an article about its experiences living with him. What he discovered, though, is that the old saying about the best-laid plans of mice and men often going astray is just as true in the computer age as it's ever been.

For $795 Martin purchased a Commodore Pet 2001-8, a desktop computer with a display screen, a keyboard, and a tape deck for programmed cassettes—a very handsome machine. There were, however, one or two small problems. The regular instruction manual wasn't ready yet, it turned out, and a pamphlet that came with the Pet neglected to mention how to turn the thing on—a problem, since there was no on-off switch in sight. A phone call to the Commodore people in California finally cleared that up—it was a black lever at the back of the machine—but couldn't help much with the next problem. What should he do after he turned it on? Without the instruction book, and with no knowledge of BASIC—the computer language used to program most home machines—Martin and his Pet had very little to say to each other.

The first movement in the logjam occurred when Martin's son, Bill, came home from college for Christmas vacation. Bill had belonged to a computer club in high school, and with obvious delight he sat down at the keyboard and began operating the machine like an old pro. At least it was possible. The elder Martin was duly impressed, of course, but he declined Bill's offer of a little coaching—resolving to meet this challenge on his own or not at all.

Finally, some weeks later, the freshly minted instruction book arrived and Martin set about learning the strange language of computer programming. (WAIT, for instance, was an instruction explained this way in the manual: "Stops execution of BASIC until contents of A, ANDed with B and exclusive ORed with C, is not equal to zero. C is optional and defaults to zero." Child's play.) At length, Martin took the plunge and began typing his first program into the Pet, copying it word for word, comma for comma, from an example in the book. It took half an hour, but the results filled him with space-age pride: stick-figure rockets shooting upward across the screen in an endless series. Not an event to call a press conference about, perhaps, but a beginning. Martin also found the game his son had programmed into the Pet's tape recorder, a computerized sea battle that—after first inadvertently bombing some of his own ships—he played happily into the night.

The thrill of victory began to fade all too quickly, though. Any way he looked at it, $795 was a rather steep price for two games—one of which he hadn't even programmed himself. Clearly, more programming was needed—including some of a practical nature—but from where? The instruction book boasted of "easy access to a library of BASIC programs, either created by you or purchased from the extensive Commodore library." When Martin telephoned for information about this extensive library, however, he discovered that it was still, alas, only a gleam in Commodore's eye.

simpler for people to communicate with computers. At present the most common alternative to the standard typewriter-style keypunch system is the optical scanner, which can read printed characters at a very high speed. Another promising device is the "Datapad," which can receive instructions handwritten on a special pad. Sensors underneath the pad recognize numbers and letters and translate them into the computer's binary code. A further step toward closing the gap between human and machine is a new system that allows computer operators to type instructions in standard English (or whatever their native tongue happens to be), rather than in one of the various code languages that have generally been required. And finally, a related system currently being marketed—to the delight, no doubt, of science-fiction buffs—activates the computer by voice command, permitting the operator not only to use plain English but literally to tell the machine what to do.

At the output end of the computer process there have likewise been a number of ingenious and very useful new developments. One of the most important involves a marriage of data-processing and microfilm technologies, resulting in *computer systems that print out data on microfilm rolls or cards* (rather than large, cumbersome sheets of paper) that can be read with a small desktop viewer. This **computer output microfilm (COM)** equipment not only cuts down drastically on the need for storage space but also prints out information five to ten times faster than conventional printers—and does it for one-quarter of the cost or less. Another innovation worth mentioning here is the "talking computer," a new audio-response system that enables a user not only to give verbal instructions but also to get a verbal response put together from the computer's prerecorded vocabulary. The audio-response system offers particular benefits for organizations with a high volume of telephone business—for instance, companies whose salespeople phone in a large number of orders from around the country.

He would have to go it alone, then. Undaunted, Martin bought a bunch of books on programming in BASIC—and gradually came to realize how complicated computers actually are. The only thing to do, he decided, was to repeat what he had done to begin with—simply transfer a program letter by letter from the book into the computer, without trying to understand how it worked. This he did, successfully programming the Pet to balance his checkbook against the monthly bank statements. Satisfying, to be sure—but more so on principle than as a practical achievement: with a $795 machine and three hours of work, Martin had done what normally took five minutes with a $10 pocket calculator.

So it went for the next several weeks as Martin experimented, with varying degrees of success, with other programs, until he arrived at the sensible conclusion that home computers will not win over the general public until they're cheaper, easier to use, and capable of such services as income-tax preparation and family budgeting. "Which is what I told my son Bill in March," Martin recalls, "when he came home for his mid-term vacation. He thereupon sat down at Pet's keyboard and, in about four hours, prepared me a Schedule A income-tax program that itemized all my tax deductions, listed them according to the categories and subcategories that appear on the IRS form, calculated the permissible deductions for medical insurance, subtotaled each category, and gave an overall total."

The experience led Martin, humbled but still quick-witted, to see an alternate way to make home computers more practical for America's millions: just have a programmer in the house!

Adapted from "My Pet and I" by Peter Bird Martin, MONEY Magazine, May 1978, by special permission; © 1978, Time Inc. All rights reserved.

THE SCHEDULING OF DATA PROCESSING

Basically, there are two different ways to process data: batch processing and on-line processing. A variation of the latter is time sharing. The method used depends on cost and how quickly the information is needed.

BATCH PROCESSING

In **batch processing**, *data are collected over a fixed interval of time* (a day, a week, a month) *before they are* *processed.* For example, at the end of every day a company might process invoices for the orders it received that day. *The daily group of invoices* is referred to as a **batch**. Batch processing is used for keeping historical records and producing output on a regular basis.

ON-LINE PROCESSING

Sometimes immediate feedback is needed in order to make urgent business decisions. Then a computer user will utilize **on-line processing**, *a direct computer connection for instant input and data retrieval.* The term "on-line" refers to the fact that all peripheral equipment is hooked directly into the central processing unit. This equipment could be on the premises or hundreds of miles away, linked through special telephone circuits.

On-line systems require the use of random-access equipment. As discussed earlier, random-access equipment stores records randomly, with no particular reference to sequence. The records that are stored can be retrieved immediately without searching an entire file for them.

Because of the computer's sophistication and high speed, random-access processing can be mixed with the processing of regularly batched data. For example, at the same time the accounting department is using the computer to run the weekly payroll, the marketing department can be querying the computer about the current status of sales in Oklahoma.

Time-sharing systems

Time sharing is *the virtually simultaneous use of an on-line computer by many users,* some with many terminals in a single location, and all with a different program or set of programs. In time-sharing systems, all users communicate with the main computer via remote terminals. These terminals can be next door or two hundred miles away. A computer may spend two picoseconds on one user, then five on another, and then three on a third. (A picosecond is one-trillionth of a second.) Because the speed of such transactions is so fast, the users have what appears to be continuous and exclusive access to the central processor. Time-sharing systems are generally useful for monitoring pro-

---

HOW IT'S ACTUALLY DONE

BATCH PROCESSING

Let us examine one specific application of batch processing, the payroll.

A payroll system is called upon to perform a variety of functions. First, there are usually several categories of payroll: biweekly salaried employees, weekly hourly-wage employees, and monthly-commission employees. Second, for every paycheck, a number of calculations must be performed: withholding tax, Social Security payments, hospitalization insurance premiums, and so forth. Third, in addition to the primary output of a payroll system, the paycheck and individual earnings statement, the computer is usually asked to produce a variety of managerial reports. These may include a record of current and cumulative wages paid and deductions taken, quarterly and annual governmental reports, and such special information as excessive overtime or absenteeism.

---

duction lines and keeping management information up to date. Time sharing is expensive, but it can increase productivity. Also, users pay only for the time they actually use the computer, as opposed to rental, where they pay whether or not the system is in use.

MAINFRAMES AND MINICOMPUTERS

The advent of the microprocessor and other miniaturized hardware has given businesses a far greater choice in matching the type of computer service they need with the amount of money they can afford to spend on it. Previously the only real choice was between a huge, multi-million-dollar "mainframe" computer and a much less powerful minicomputer that was still beyond the financial reach of many smaller companies. Today, however, the new technology has created a new breed of minicomputers, much less expensive than their predecessors and considerably more sophisticated. The resulting benefits have been shared by smaller companies, whose routine needs are well within the capacity of the minis, and by larger ones for whom the minis offer a way to upgrade their mainframe systems at a relatively modest cost. A minicomputer at a bank branch, for example, can readily be tied in with the central computer to give or receive information as needed and can also function independently when the mainframe is needed for higher-priority tasks. As well, the mini enables a large user to incorporate the latest technology into its system without the huge expense that would be needed to replace a mainframe computer.

COMPUTER SOFTWARE: PROGRAMS AND PEOPLE

Years ago, the term "computer" meant the machine itself, the hardware. But in recent years people have recognized that the machine is only as good as the procedures given it for solving problems. Therefore, the definition of computer has been altered to include both the machine and its programs, both the hardware and the software. **Software** includes *the materials and procedures used with computers.* It's a category which covers checklists, forms, programs, and written diagrams and instructions.

The collection of information and eventual communication of it by means of computer to people who can use it is known as **electronic data processing (EDP)**. Four categories of personnel work in EDP·

1. input personnel (keypunchers and so on)
2. computer operating staff
3. systems analysts
4. programmers

Input personnel are concerned chiefly with transferring data to whatever medium the I/O equipment uses. For instance, a keypuncher may "translate" wage and salary figures into punches on cards. The computer operating staff, as the name indicates, is responsible for the actual operation of equipment—manipulating buttons and switches and correcting malfunctions, if possible. We will devote more attention to systems analysts and programmers because they are directly responsible for computer software.

SYSTEMS ANALYSTS: ESTABLISHING AN OPERATION

The key to any successful computer system lies in the thoroughness and logic brought to analyzing the problem at hand. The **systems analyst** *investigates the problem and acts as a link* between those in need of a computerized solution and those who will write the programs that make the solution work. Because the analyst oversees the work of the programmer, he or she must know the programmer's job. In fact, analysts often train as programmers.

A good example of creative—and profitable—programming can be seen at American Airlines, one of the most thoroughly computerized companies in any business field. Computer management has proved especially helpful in the area of fuel consumption—a vital consideration for an enterprise that uses 1.25 billion gallons each year of a commodity that jumped some 230 percent in price between 1973 and 1977. American's flight planning system, for instance, not only charts an aircraft's route—computing wind, payload weight, and other data in the process—but also supplies continuous weather information that enables the pilot to avoid storms and headwinds that would reduce fuel mileage. Meanwhile, a separate fuel management system keeps track of supplies and prices in different areas, advising the flight crew where it can take on fuel at the lowest cost. Computers even monitor the jet's takeoff, constantly adjusting engine thrust and wing flaps to get the plane airborne without wasting fuel.[7]

Virtually every other aspect of the airline's operations is likewise aided by computer. One system organizes maintenance schedules for American's entire fleet, so that an individualized checklist can be printed out for every plane before it takes off from any airport. There are also countless details related to passenger service that only an advanced computer network could handle, from reservations and connections to hotel and car rentals—even ticket prices in foreign currencies for any other airline. All these services are available on a moment's notice through the computer terminals at every ticket counter.

HOW IT'S ACTUALLY DONE

STEPS IN COMPUTER SYSTEMS ANALYSIS

The first thing the systems analyst must do is define the problem. For example, in one company the volume of incoming bills may have grown so large that the accounting department wants to investigate the possibility of computerizing all its billing. The analyst must learn the present billing system thoroughly: how it is done, the information the billing form records (or should record), the volume handled, and so forth.

After digesting this basic information, the analyst goes to work. He or she meets with other depart-

ments to see where the accounting department's computerization could help them too. For example, the new computer system might produce a daily sales report for the marketing department as well as a record of billings for the accounting department.

Once the analyst has all this information, he or she must answer the questions: Is computerization financially justifiable? What kind of hardware will be necessary for the proposed system? Should the equipment be bought or leased? What will the total cost be? How many new employees will be needed? What would they do? What present jobs, if any, should be phased out?

PROGRAMMERS: TALKING TO COMPUTERS

Since most computers do not understand English, it is the job of the **programmer** to *write instructions in a language the computer does understand.* This machine language is the binary system discussed earlier.

At the beginning, all programs were written out in full in the binary system of numbers. This was not only difficult to learn but time-consuming as well. As a result, *short-cut computer vocabulary systems* known as **symbolic languages** were created. When symbolic languages are used, it is not necessary to write a program in binary arithmetic. Words and symbols are used instead. Using a built-in "decoder," the computer automatically translates the symbols into machine language. For example, in machine language, the command for adding two quantities may be 110001. Using symbolic language, the programmer issues the simple command ADD, and the computer automatically translates that command into 110001.

SOFTWARE PACKAGES

Software packages are *prewritten routines that can be bought from computer firms to assist in writing and*

running specialized programs. At first, before software packages were available, users of data-processing equipment had to develop their own programs for even the most routine tasks. All that the manufacturers provided was the hardware.

Today many companies in the data-processing field are marketing a variety of software packages. For example, you can buy one package containing all of the 1970 census data; another is available with a complete accounts-receivable system. These packages are highly attractive to computer users because they allow maximum use of electronic processing equipment.

Other companies go a step further and offer complete computer services—software and hardware both—tailored to the needs of their customers. One firm provides computer analysis of complex engineering and architectural problems for a large-scale construction project, furnishing in hours answers that would have taken months to find by conventional means. Another coordinates the large inventory of an aerospace manufacturer with customer inquiries from around the world, processing orders, verifying shipments, and keeping track of inventory levels. The biggest independent computer-service company, Automatic Data Processing (ADP), earns the lion's share of its $245 million yearly revenues by providing basic payroll and accounting services for thousands of busi-

Assuming that computerization is feasible, the analyst next designs a flowchart, showing each step that will make up the overall computer system. (We show a flowchart on page 437.) Using a flowchart to outline the steps helps the programmer break the problem down into units of manageable size. He or she can minimize errors while making sure that everything is done logically and in order.

After designing the flowchart and handing it over to the programmers, the analyst draws up a plan for bringing about computerization. Finally, the analyst will usually act as a general overseer until the system is running smoothly.

nesses that lack the resources or inclination to handle such chores themselves. Backed up by a nationwide computer network, ADP also offers its clients more specialized programs, for jobs ranging from high-volume paperwork for Wall Street stock brokerage firms to inventory control for liquor stores and auto-parts suppliers.[8]

COMPUTERS AND THE FUTURE

From the standpoint of both business and technology, the computer's future has virtually no limits in sight. Even such miniaturized marvels as the microprocessor and the bubble-memory chip do not represent the end of the line by any means. Another new microscopic memory system, the charge-coupled device (CCD), will soon be coming into commercial use, storing information in chains of distinct electrical impulses that can be moved around like records in a jukebox. Further, a technique now being developed to design circuitry with ultraprecise electron beams will likely produce devices that make even today's miracle chips look large and clumsy.

As for the business uses of the new technology, the possibilities seem endless. One of the fastest-growing applications at the moment is the new breed of word-processing systems offered by IBM, Xerox, and a host of smaller manufacturers. These computerized "thinking typewriters" enable an operator to type out a letter or any other document on a video display, make simple corrections or complex revisions, then press a button, sit back, and watch the machine type up a perfect copy in seconds. Further, the document can be stored on a magnetic tape cartridge or "floppy disk" and reproduced whenever it's needed—with individualized addresses in the case of form letters—either in the same office or on a similar machine thousands of miles away.

A related development coming into widespread use is high-speed facsimile equipment that can transmit exact copies of documents through telephone lines much faster, and often more cheaply, than if they were sent by mail or messenger. The same system is even being used to hold "conferences" over a period of days or weeks for people in different locations, saving the expense of travel and, assuming quick decisions don't have to be made, allowing the participants time to gather needed information and give careful thought to the subject under discussion.

Professional estimates of future sales in computers point to full-speed-ahead growth. Word-processing equipment sales are expected to jump at an average yearly rate of 16.7 percent between 1977 and 1981.[9] Moreover, total revenue for the computer industry is expected to blossom 17.7 percent a year from 1977 to 1981, lifting sales to a lofty $30.5 billion.[10] And personal computer sales will also climb, from $100 million in 1978 to the $1-billion plateau in 1985.[11] Inconceivable? Wait a few years—even these figures may look like conservative estimates.

CHAPTER REVIEW

Three breakthroughs—the development of programming, the use of binary arithmetic, and the application of electronics—made modern computers possible. Since the appearance of the first all-electronic computer in 1946, four major technological advances—the transistor, the integrated circuit, large-scale integration, and the microprocessor—have made the computer much more sophisticated.

All computers consist of two types of equipment: a central processing unit (made up of a control unit, an arithmetic and logic unit, and a memory unit) and input and output devices, or peripheral equipment. Data are fed to computers through a variety of media, including punched cards, magnetic tape, and magnetic discs.

To make efficient use of computer time, many users process data in batches. This is usually done with material that is not urgent and can be scheduled in advance. When information is needed instantaneously, the user will prefer an on-line system, where equipment is hooked into the central processor at all times. In time-sharing systems, users share a central computer with others, each having individual programs and communicating terminals.

Computers depend not only on hardware but also on software, particularly programs. The personnel chiefly responsible for producing software are systems analysts and programmers. The latter "talk" to computers through symbolic languages. Software packages supplied by computer firms may make their tasks easier.

KEY WORD REVIEW

arithmetic tasks
logical tasks
program
memory
decimal system
binary system
transistor
integrated circuit (IC)
large-scale integration (LSI)
microprocessor (MPU)
central processing unit (CPU)
peripheral (secondary)
  equipment
hardware
control unit
arithmetic unit
logic unit
memory unit
magnetic cores
access time
external storage unit
bit
sequential storage
random-access storage
computer output microfilm
  (COM)
batch processing
batch
on-line processing
time sharing
software
electronic data processing
  (EDP)
systems analyst
programmer
symbolic languages
software packages

REVIEW QUESTIONS

1. What are the four basic functions of a computer?

2. What are the four major innovations in the field of computers since 1946?

3. What are the basic components of a computer system? How are they related?

4. What are the major uses of the four basic types of I/O media? What are some of the new I/O devices?

5. When would batch processing be used? When would on-line processing be used?

6. What is software? What is a software package?

CASE 1

COMPUTERS IN MODERN WARFARE: MOVES AND COUNTERMOVES

The mind-boggling rate at which computer technology is advancing is nowhere more apparent than in the area of electronic warfare. Electronics serve military purposes by allowing ground radar stations, aircraft, ships, tanks, and helicopters to detect the presence, say, of an enemy missile, to determine what kind of missile it is, and to instantly prepare a countermeasure. This may involve "jamming" or scrambling a radar signal so that a radar system on the ground would be rendered incapable of guiding the missile to its target. One of the newest of these so-called electronic countermeasure (ECM) systems allows ships to detect and "confuse" an enemy missile within ninety seconds—which is how long it takes a missile to reach a ship after first appearing on the horizon. Electronics can also be used for spying by allowing computers to precisely track the movements of troops, or to eavesdrop on radio transmissions or other signals coming from weapons tests.

At the heart of electronic warfare is the microcomputer, a thin sliver of silicon coated with thousands of transistors. Small computers and microcomputers are often combined into sophisticated systems—known as "distributed intelligence"—that can filter through tens or hundreds of thousands of signals to detect, analyze, and jam an enemy radar in microseconds (millionths of seconds). The first of the computer ECM systems relied chiefly on hardware, or permanently programmed computers. The problem with these "black boxes" was that advances in technology on the enemy's side often made the ECM system useless. In the first

week of the 1973 Yom Kippur war, for example, Israel lost more than 100 of the most advanced American planes because the ECM hardware they carried could not jam the radar guidance system of the new Soviet surface-to-air missiles that the Arabs were using.

Since 1973 the United States has turned increasingly to software-programmable ECM systems. These are microcomputer-aided minicomputers that can be quickly reprogrammed to recognize a new signal. In addition to being flexible, these systems have other advantages. Because they are small, they can do much more while taking up much less space than hardware—meaning, for instance, that their power to jam enemy radar or detect enemy signals is much greater. Improvements in technology have made the microcomputer much less expensive to use than older technologies like the large-scale integrated circuit (LSI chip).

The lower costs mean that ECM systems no longer need to be restricted exclusively to planes; where ECM protection once cost almost as much as a helicopter, it now represents only about 5 percent of a helicopter's cost. Distributed intelligence systems in airplanes can now perform functions that used to require a computer too large for a plane to carry. And the software-programmable systems can add years to a plane's life because the systems can be updated whenever necessary, allowing the plane to remain in use.

For the select handful of companies that build this complicated and usually top-secret equipment for the government, ECM spells profits and stability. In 1978 the government spent $1.4 billion on ECM equipment—an increase of 166 percent over the previous year—and an addi-

tional $2 billion on highly classified electronic intelligence (ELINT) devices. Technology companies like Northrop Corporation and Raytheon Company were recording sales of $50 million or more. And one firm, Loral Corporation, hadn't even finished building its new system for the F-15 fighter jet when the government gave it more money to update the system. Indeed, new developments are appearing so quickly in the ECM field—both in the United States and abroad—that companies like Loral are constantly busy either designing new systems or bringing old ones already in use up to date. It is, in short, a cat-and-mouse game: if the United States develops a new missile, the Soviet Union must spend billions on a radar system capable of knocking the missile down. Then the Americans can equip their missile with ECM gear. Then the Soviets would need an electronic counter-countermeasure (ECCM), and the United States could retaliate with an ECCCM—and computer companies would be kept very busy for a long time to come.[12]

1. What are some of the advantages of using microcomputers in electronic warfare?

2. What is the difference between hardware and software, and what type of software is involved in this particular case?

3. How might the computer industry in general be affected by the microcomputer revolution taking place in the arms race?

RESEARCH, STATISTICAL ANALYSIS, AND REPORTS

What do baseball games, pantyhose, and television shows have in common? For one thing, all are potential money-makers in the business world. And whatever earns money is worthy of study. Thus, marketers have done intensive investigations of all three—using sophisticated information-gathering methods and interpretation techniques that allow them to get a clear view of the size of the market, the costs involved, and many other factors.

Without such research, manufacturers would find themselves making some very costly errors. What if McDonald's, for instance, decided to come out with a special seafood burger made primarily of octopus? Even if the marketers gave it a catchy name like Octo-Mac, the product wouldn't sell if there were no demand. But if the company took a long, serious, and scientific look at the fast-food market, it could determine beforehand whether or not to proceed in cornering the octopus market, and it could save itself a lot of time, effort and money. In this chapter we'll take a look at some of the basic techniques marketers use to conduct studies of this sort, and we'll discuss some of the mathematical tools they use in interpreting their data.

WHAT WILL THIS CHAPTER FOCUS ON?

After reading the material in this chapter, you will understand and be able to discuss:

- types of data—internal and external, primary and secondary
- the way sampling is done
- some of the most important statistical techniques
- the meaning of correlation
- ways of presenting information, including reports, tables, and graphs

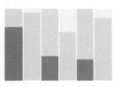

Just how good a player is all-star first baseman Rod Carew? Ask a dozen baseball fans and you'll probably get as many answers. One thing that no one can quibble with, however, is Carew's .388 batting average for 1977, an average so high that it hadn't been achieved since 1957, by Ted Williams. On the basis of that .388 average, the team management can assess Carew's value to the ball club and determine his salary accordingly.

Rod Carew's .388 average is a **statistic**—*an item of factual information expressed as a number.* If you follow sports in the newspapers, you've undoubtedly seen other important types of baseball statistics too— the number of no-hitters various stars have pitched, the number of RBIs players have hit, and so on. And we use statistics in countless areas outside of sports. For example, the National Safety Council tells us that according to statistics it has compiled, it's a good deal more risky to travel by car (1.34 passenger deaths per 100 million passenger miles) than by airplane, the death rate for which is so small that it can barely be measured at all. Perhaps more surprising is that the average American consumer drank no fewer than 36.3 gallons of soft drinks in 1977. That's a statistic. So is much of what we hear on the evening news: we hear, for example, that the rise in the cost of living is 0.8 percent this month, or that the popularity of the President has dipped to 25 percent. All these are types of

In 1978, Volkswagen based a promotional campaign on the findings of a fuel-consumption study by the Environmental Protection Agency.

FIGURE 1

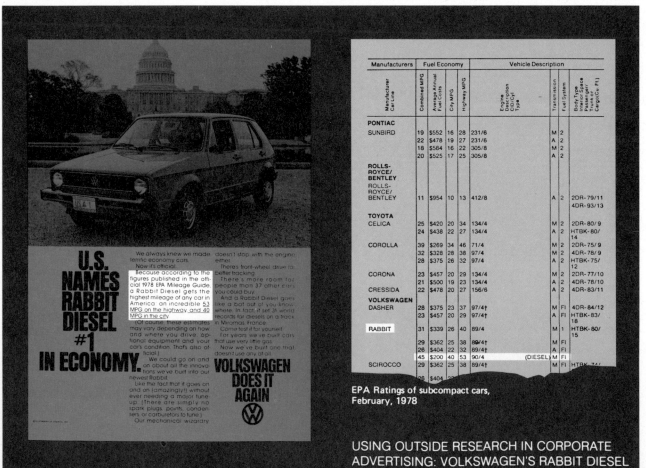

EPA Ratings of subcompact cars, February, 1978

USING OUTSIDE RESEARCH IN CORPORATE ADVERTISING: VOLKSWAGEN'S RABBIT DIESEL CAMPAIGN

data (*factual information*) which we're accustomed to receiving in statistical form.

The word **statistics**, however, can mean more than just items of numerical information. It also refers to a mathematical discipline concerned with *methods of collecting, analyzing, interpreting, and presenting numerical information.* Statistics is a theoretical field, but it has many practical applications. Business managers use statistics frequently to deal with questions relating to production output, market characteristics, and many other areas. For example, one of the most frequently asked questions in many businesses is "What is our market and in what ways is it changing?" Once that question is answered, other questions on how best to accommodate and sell to that market fall into place, together with their appropriate answers. Lipton Soup, for instance, analyzed figures concerning their soup market and noted that the number of people living alone was increasing. Just a small step of logic dictated development of the quick and easy small-portion instant soup called "Cup-a-Soup." Similarly, *Reader's Digest*, on discovering that many of its readers were over fifty-five, began to use larger type to make reading easier for those with weak eyesight. A statistical approach can even help solve problems involving the name of a product. Bic, for example, came out with a line of pantyhose a few years back that they cleverly dubbed "Fannyhose." A catchy name, and Bic thought it would help the product sell; but strangely enough, few women were buying the new hose. Why? Statistical research showed that women tended to assume the product was exclusively for the overweight—and few women wanted to count themselves among that category. Bic changed the product's name to merely "Pantyhose."

Statistical studies can also help out in a variety of other business areas. In personnel management, for example, statistical data are vital in complying (and showing proof of compliance) with the EEO requirements that we discussed in Chapter 5. Or, in the field of production operations, a manufacturer of children's toys might run time-and-motion studies to improve efficiency and discover that it's cheaper to pay overtime (something most manufacturers hate to do) than to hire and train new workers during busy periods. Statistical studies can also be used to make long-range plans. A company that manufactures insulating materials, for example, might trace the rise in costs of fuel oil in certain locations and then decide to concentrate its sales efforts in those areas, perhaps even expanding production.

Using statistics, then, is a vital skill for managers in all phases of business, and managers must be familiar with a broad range of statistical methods. In the sections that follow, we'll survey some of the statistical approaches managers use most frequently. First we'll look at methods of doing research—that is, methods of obtaining basic information about the questions under study. And then we'll look at some of the basic mathematical techniques that are used in summarizing, analyzing, and interpreting this information.

BASIC RESEARCH METHODS: WHAT ARE THE MAJOR SOURCES OF DATA?

The Pizza Tower, a small Italian snack bar, is leaning heavily toward bankruptcy. Its owner, Julia, decides that she needs help. She needs to know more about the costs most pizza parlors incur, and then she needs to figure out why her own costs are so high and why she is having so much trouble meeting expenses. Where does she turn? Where can she get the information that she needs quickly? And what type of information should she look for?

There are two main ways to classify the information that managers such as Julia need for decision making. One way is to group information according to the places where it can be located. The other, more common method is to classify it according to the reason it was gathered. Since businesspeople often refer to both types of data, it's useful to look at both classes of information.

DATA GROUPED BY LOCATION

Data grouped according to location can be either internal data or external data. **Internal data** consists of *information that is obtained directly from the records of the company's own invoices, purchase orders, personnel files, and the like.* In the case of Julia's Pizza Tower, internal data Julia might gather includes receipts, canceled checks, and records of pizzas sold, to enable her to find out how much it costs to produce each pie. This internal data might show that the cost of labor, materials, and rent comes to $3.89 for each pizza. When Julia compares this figure with what she gets for each pie–$4.00–she can readily see she's making a profit of only eleven cents per pizza.

External data consists of *information obtained from sources outside the records of the business itself.* These sources could include government census figures and other information from Washington, plus such nongovernment sources as trade periodicals. For example, Julia might consult the Pizza Manufacturers' Association of America, of which she's a member. By calling the organization's information office, she might find out that the average cost of making pizza throughout the industry was only $3.01 for a pie selling at $4.00. She would see, then, that she'd better cut her costs to survive.

DATA GROUPED BY PURPOSE

Data grouped by purpose can be either primary or secondary. **Primary data** consists of *information gathered specially for the study of the problem at hand.* The information Julia gathered on the production costs per pie at the Pizza Tower, for instance, was primary data. **Secondary data** consists of *information previously produced or collected for a purpose other than that of the moment.* The government and such trade organizations as the Pizza Manufacturers' Association are the major sources of secondary data.

Choosing between primary and secondary data

When would a businessperson choose to use secondary data? Of course, the term "secondary" as used here in no way means "inferior." As a matter of fact, businesspeople usually examine such information first, because secondary data usually has three advantages over primary data:

1. *Speed.* Neither the Pizza Tower nor any other business can wait until a solution to a problem just happens to come along. Secondary data sources, such as *A Guide to Consumer Markets*, put out by the Conference Board, provide needed information at a moment's notice.

How does a marketer go about studying a community? There are so many families in this one that it would be impossible to find out the needs and wants of each. It is possible, however, to get a fairly accurate impression by taking a sample.

2. *Cost.* Collecting fresh data can be an expensive process. On the other hand, for the cost of a membership in an organization such as the Pizza Manufacturers' Association, a business can have all the group's research work at its disposal.

3. *Availability.* The troubled owner of the Pizza Tower can hardly expect the owner of the Pie in the Sky Parlor down the street to make his information available to a competitor. Trade associations and the government, on the other hand, are in the business of collecting information from all and making it available impartially to everyone.

Secondary data does have some drawbacks, however. Before relying on it, users must examine it cautiously. The information may be out of date—or it may not be as relevant as it first seems. And there is the possibility that the company or agency that collected the data may not be so impartial as it should be. For example, a study showing that people favor tacos as a snack food might be somewhat biased if it had been conducted by an association representing the Mexican restaurants of America. (The same study done by the Small Business Administration would probably be more impartial.) Furthermore, the organization that produces the study may lack expertise: the survey may not have been broad enough to cover the targeted geographic or income group, or questions may have been phrased in a way that "telegraphed" answers to the respondents.

HOW PRIMARY DATA IS OBTAINED

As we saw, Julia of the Pizza Tower compiled data to determine the actual cost of producing every pie. This was primary data; it involved original research. Many larger companies do exactly the same thing—on an enormous scale—to acquire additional information that has a specific bearing on a problem under study.

"Well, if you *did* have a dog what dog food would you prefer?"

Let's take a look at some of the techniques used in accumulating primary data.

SAMPLING

It's 8:30 on a rainy Monday night. You're curled up in front of the television, and the telephone rings. "This is the Inquire Corporation, a research company, and we're calling to find out what TV program you're watching." That's probably the most widely known and publicized form of sampling. It's also one of the most efficient.

A **sample** is *a small part of a large group—of people or other items.* (In statistical language, *the group from which a sample is drawn* is known as a **population** or **universe**.) The idea behind sampling is simple. By properly selecting and then using a small sample, you can reach some conclusions or make forecasts about the population from which the sample was drawn. For instance, if ten of the hundred people sampled by the Inquire Corporation on Monday night are watching a specific program, then it will probably be safe to assume that 10 percent of the whole TV-watching population in this geographical area are watching that program—provided that the sample has been selected to represent the population fairly.

How do you go about selecting a sample? The most common method is called random sampling. According to this method, a large group of items or indi-

PROBABILITY: THE PRINCIPLE BEHIND RANDOM SAMPLING

Probability is *the likelihood, over the long run, that a certain event will occur in one way rather than in another way.* We know how likely the event is to occur in that way because of the nature of what we're dealing with. For example, we know that if we flip a coin, the likelihood of throwing "heads" is $\frac{1}{2}$ or 50 percent—because a coin only has two sides—and the likelihood of throwing "tails" is also 50 percent. Similarly, we know that if there are ten drugstores in town, the likelihood of picking any one of them at random is $\frac{1}{10}$ or 10 percent; if there are 234 sportswear shops, the probability of picking any one of them at random is $\frac{1}{234}$ or 0.43 percent. Each one has an equal chance of being picked.

How does a businessperson use probability in everyday business operations? Here's a simple example. You recall what we have said about flipping a coin: the probability of throwing "heads" is 50 percent—so in a series of tosses, let's say ten tosses, you would expect to throw "heads" about five times out of the ten. Throwing ten "heads" *could* happen—but it's very unlikely. More likely, if the coin comes up "heads" ten times, it has two heads!

Similarly, let's say the sales manager of a department store finds that out of 1,000 letters from customers, about 50 letters, or 5 percent, are complaints. On any date, then, if he receives 100 letters from customers, he expects that about five of them will be complaints; the *probability* of receiving complaints is about 5 percent, given this store, this town, and these customers. What if complaint letters suddenly increase to 20 or 30 percent? The new rate is way above the probability the store manager has come to expect from experience. Something is fishy. One, or both, of the following two things has happened: someone is fooling with the customer correspondence file, or something has gone wrong in the store's operations and the customers don't like it. In either case, the sales manager must investigate further. And there's a high probability he'll have to take drastic action.

viduals is fixed upon and numbered. The items or individuals are chosen from this group in a way that gives each an equal chance of being selected. (The simplest method of giving each an equal chance of being chosen is to draw it at random—"out of a hat," as we often say.)

Sampling is useful in a number of business situations. For instance, let's say that the bookstore at State College has ordered 1,000 T-shirts imprinted with the school's name, from Tyrone's T-Shirt Company. It occurs to Tyrone that he may be onto a good thing. Since he has to make up one batch of shirts anyway, he wonders if the men's and women's clothing stores in town would like to stock the local college T-shirts also. How can he determine if his idea is a good one before making all those extra shirts? He decides to ask all the stores by calling them individually. A glance at the Yellow Pages, though, shows him that 234 stores carry his kind of merchandise, and it's impossible (or, at any rate, impractical) to call them all. So Tyrone figures he can get a good idea of what stores will be interested in stocking his goods if he calls up the first ten men's

shops, and also the first ten women's shops. Taking the first ten in the phone book is very much like picking the names out of a hat, since the order in which they appear is determined only by the letters with which their names begin—not by their size, their location, their type of customer, or any other factor that might affect their interest in buying Tyrone's T-shirts. He finds out that only one in ten men's stores is interested in the merchandise. Eight out of ten of the women's stores he called are interested, however—and he can plan accordingly. Tyrone has just made a sampling of the market and so saved himself a good deal of time and effort.

The major limitation of the sampling method is that the population to be sampled has to be small enough and concentrated geographically so that a list of all the names or items it includes either is available or can easily be made. It's obvious that if you wanted to draw your sample from all the clothing stores in the United States you'd be faced with much too large and expensive a task. But there are other sampling techniques to handle this problem. It's sufficient for our purposes to note that random sampling is a very effective technique when used with limited populations.

OBSERVATION

The next time you're driving along and you see an inconspicuous cable stretched across the road, don't panic. It may not be a speed trap. Instead, it may simply mean that you're about to be included in a study.

Face-to-face interviewing can be expensive, but it may yield valuable market information.

Every time a car passes over one of those lines in the street, a counting mechanism records it, and a compilation of those records gives city planners help in assessing where to put street lights and stop signs. The method being used here is **observation**—*watching or otherwise monitoring all incidents of the particular sort the investigator wants to study.*

Other forms of observation—usually aided by cameras and videotape—are used to study the way in which employees do their work. In time-and-motion studies, for example, production experts study the exact number of movements each assembly-line worker makes to complete a job and the amount of time taken for each movement.

SURVEY

Businesses must often know *why* employees or potential customers behave the way they do. The simplest way to find out is to ask them, and that's where surveys come in. Often the investigator will use a **questionnaire** or *list of questions,* either mailing the questionnaire to the **respondents** (*the people who are answering the questions*) or getting their answers via face-to-face or telephone interviews. Respondents may be questioned once or a number of times.

EXPERIMENT

In an **experiment**, the investigator tries to *find out how one set of conditions will affect another set of conditions, by setting up a situation in which all factors and events involved can be carefully measured.* Experiment differs from ordinary observation in that the experimenter can deliberately change any aspect of the situation he wants to, and then see what effects the changes have. Experiments are often done in laboratories, where even such tiny factors as air temperature and lighting can be changed at will by the investigator; for example, a scientist studying the effects of crowding on animals might set up a cage of mice in a laboratory, where he could control the size of the cage, the number of mice in it, the amount of food the mice received, and so on. But some experiments can be done in an ordinary social setting such as a classroom or a street; for example, a professor might carry out an experiment to see whether a relaxed classroom atmosphere helped students learn better by changing the arrangement of the furniture in the classroom, encouraging more open-ended discussion, and so on.

In many cases, an experimenter tries to observe or survey two separate but similar groups, which are controlled so that one group is exposed to the specific factor or situation of interest and the other is not. (*The group that is not exposed to the factor being studied in an experiment* is called the **control group**.) Suppose your professor decided to find out whether being allowed to get up and stretch made it easier for students to do well on tests. The professor could divide the class in half, and allow one half to go out in the corridor one by one during tests but require the other half to stay seated at all times. At the end of the term, he or she could compare the test scores of those students who were allowed to move around with those who had to stay seated. If the group allowed to leave the room at will did better, one might argue that this approach helped students keep their minds clear and work in a relaxed manner. But if the group that had to stay seated did better, or if the two groups did equally well, one might argue that stretching and relaxing weren't helpful.

ANALYZING DATA: KEY NUMBERS TO WATCH

Suppose you have obtained a body of numerical data, through one of the methods we have just described. As you go about the task of analyzing this data, what types of numerical information might you look for—or develop—that would be particularly useful to you? We'll look at some answers to this question in the section that follows.

AVERAGES

One way to take data and present it in a simple, easily understood way is to find the average. The **average** is *a number typical of a group of numbers or quantities*. Averages are often used in business. For example, a personnel manager may want to know the average wage of workers in each labor classification, in order to present the officers of the corporation with a forecast of future labor costs when changes in production occur or a new union contract is negotiated. Or a marketing manager may want to know the average age of potential consumers of a new product, in order to slant advertising and other promotion toward that age group. The most widely used averages are the mean, the median, and the mode.

The mean

The term most often thought of as the average is the **mean**, *the sum of all the items in a group, divided by the number of items in the group*. It is invaluable when comparing one item or individual with a group. For example, if the sales manager of Jersey Nuts and Bolts Company wants to compare the performance of the salespeople during a certain week, the mean would give a simple figure for comparison.

To find the mean, he first lists the members of his sales staff together with their sales for the week:

Salesperson	Sales	
Wilson	$ 3,000	
Green	5,000	
Carrick	6,000	
Wimper	7,000	*Mean*
Keeble	7,500	*Median*
Kemble	8,500	
O'Toole	8,500	*Mode*
Mannix	8,500	
Caruso	9,000	
Total	$63,000	

After totaling sales, he divides by the number of salespeople, so that the mean is

$$\frac{\$63,000}{9} = \$7,000 \text{ in sales}$$

The advantages of the mean are ease of comprehension and speed of computation. One great disadvantage of the mean, however, is that it can be distorted by an extreme value at the high or the low end. For instance, in the above example, if Caruso's sales for the week were $27,000, the mean for the nine salespeople would be $9,000 ($81,000 divided by 9), clearly a distortion, as eight of the nine salespeople would have sold less than the mean. Obviously, additional methods of summarizing data are necessary.

The median

When items or numbers are arranged from lowest to highest, the **median** *is the midpoint, or point at which half the numbers are above, half below.* If the number of items is odd, the figure can be arrived at by inspection. In the sales manager's quest for average sales in the example above, the median is $7,500. There are four figures above it and four below. If there had been an even number, ten salespeople instead of nine, the midpoint would be the mean of the two central figures.

The median is easy to find and a great time-saver when items that are difficult to measure can be arranged in order of size. It also avoids the distortion caused by extreme values and is thus more typical of the data. In the study of salespeople's performances, if Caruso's sales total was $27,000 instead of $9,000, the median would not be affected.

The chief disadvantage of the median is that many people do not understand what it means. Moreover, it can sometimes be cumbersome to arrange items in order of size when there are many of them.

In business, however, the median is a useful measure, especially when management needs an average that is not affected by inclusion of the largest producers or spenders in a given category. For example, if it is necessary to know the average spent on advertising by retail grocers, the figure used would probably be the median. Thus, the amounts spent by the big chains would not distort the average.

The mode

The **mode** *is the number that occurs most often in any series of data or observations.* The mode answers the question: "How frequently?" or "What is the usual size or amount?" In the sales manager's study above, the most frequent amount, the mode, is $8,500.

One important use of modes is to supply marketing people with information about common sizes of shoes and clothing. If you were the owner of a shoe store, you would *not* want to stock four pairs of every shoe size in each style. You might find, perhaps, that for every forty pairs of size eight sold, only two of size twelve were sold.

As with the median, an advantage of the mode is that extreme values do not influence the average. The mode, however, should not be used when the total number of observations is small or when a large group is spread over many small classifications. In such cases, a significantly repeated observation value may not exist. There is no mode if a number does not appear more than once.

INDEX NUMBERS

In business, it is often important to know how the sales or industrial production of one period of time compares with that of another, and to have a convenient expression of this comparison. In this case, an index number is used. An **index number** is *a percentage usually used to compare such figures as prices or costs at one period of time with those figures at a base or standard period.*

Let us say that the Reedy Oil Company wants to keep an index on the number of workers it employs. It chooses as a base year 1976, when it employed 5,000 workers. In 1977 employment slipped to only 4,900 workers. In 1978, it surged ahead to 5,300 workers.

The index numbers for the years 1977 and 1978 are obtained by dividing the base-year figure into the current-year figure and then multiplying by 100 to change the resulting decimal into a percent.

$$\frac{\text{Current-year employment (1977)}}{\text{Base-year employment}} = \frac{4,900}{5,000} = 0.98$$

$$= 98\%$$

$$\frac{\text{Current-year employment (1978)}}{\text{Base-year employment}} = \frac{5,300}{5,000} = 1.06$$

$$= 106\%$$

The figures tell us that employment was off 2 percent in 1977 but up 6 percent in 1978.

One of the best-known index numbers is that represented by the Consumer Price Index, used by economists in tracking inflation. Others include the Dow Jones Industrial Average, the Index of Industrial Production, and the Wholesale Price Index.

WHEN FIGURES DO LIE

We Americans rely heavily on statistics, and because of this, we are easily exploited. If statistics really spoke for themselves, there would be no problem. But, in fact, there are many ways that statistics can be deceptive.

One is to play with averages. Say that you and two partners have just had a good year in the bumper-sticker business. You paid ninety employees a total of $720,000 in wages and allotted yourselves salaries of $20,000 each. You have an additional $75,000 in profits to divide up among yourselves. Your totals can look like this:

mean wage of employees	$ 8,000.00
mean salary and profit of owners	45,000.00

This tabulation might not look very good on the company bulletin board. So you and your partners can each take a $20,000 bonus (not reportable as profit or wages), lump your salaries together with those of your employees, and then list your totals this way:

mean wage or salary	$8,387.09
mean profit of owners	5,000.00

Another statistical trick is the so-called "semiattached figure." The more precise, the better. Your advertising agency can claim that a half ounce of Pastorene antiseptic killed 31,108 germs in a test tube in eleven seconds. But what does this mean? Does an antiseptic that kills germs in a test tube work in the human body? What kinds of germs bit the dust? Were they harmful? Maybe there are so many thousands of germs in a comparable portion of the human anatomy that 31,108 is a drop in the bucket.

Beware, too, of the shifting base. Say that a store offers $10 Christmas gifts and urges you to buy them in October to "save 100 percent." Management isn't giving anything away. The price will go up to $15, so your saving is 100 percent of the markup, not of the present price. In other words, the base on which the percentage was figured has shifted.

The next time someone tries to persuade you with a neat average, a suspiciously precise "result," or an almost unbelievable discount offer, think twice. The statistics you save could be reflected in your own personal income statement.

Source: Darrell Huff, *How to Lie with Statistics* (New York: W. W. Norton, 1954).

TIME-SERIES ANALYSIS

Executives must often consider what caused the changes in their business activity that the statistics point to. Suppose, for instance, that a department store's monthly index of sales shows an increase of 6 percent for December. Before the sales manager can decide whether or not to increase the sales force, inventory, and advertising budget, the manager must know what underlies the change. Time-series analysis can help uncover the reasons.

A **time-series** (or **trend**) **analysis** is *the examination of data over a sufficiently long period of time so that regularities and relationships can be detected, interpreted, and made the basis for forecasts of future business activity.* The analysis generally explains change in terms of three factors: seasonal variations, cyclical variations, and secular (or long-term) trends in business growth (see box).

INTERPRETING DATA: STUDYING CAUSE AND EFFECT

What happened to the stock market when William Howard Taft was elected President of the United States in 1908? Much the same thing that happened when Richard Nixon was elected sixty years later—namely, it dropped startlingly. Exactly why the elec-

BUILDING YOUR BUSINESS VOCABULARY

TRENDS REVEALED BY TIME-SERIES ANALYSIS

Seasonal variations In January of 1977, dairy manufacturers produced more than 51 million gallons of ice cream. Of course, that's enough ice cream for a great many ice cream cones, but that figure is nothing compared to the 83 million gallons produced in August of the same year.* As you might expect, the demand for ice cream is higher in August than in December, and so the supply is proportionately greater as well. Such *regular annual changes* in sales or other items are called **seasonal variations**. Other examples are increased department store sales before Christmas and the increased sale of snow tires when cold weather sets in.

Time-series analysis sometimes uncovers seasonal variations where none was known or foreseen before. Makers of tea, for example, discovered a trend toward heavy consumption in winter and a marked falloff thereafter. This finding disturbed management because they wanted to keep a constant manufacturing and sales force rather than look for extra workers in peak season or lay off workers when times were slow. To combat this seasonal trend, the tea manufacturers waged a successful promotion campaign for iced tea, to keep sales—and thus production—more evenly distributed throughout the year.

Cyclical variations Over a period of several years (often four years), the economy goes through a period of fluctuation known as the **business cycle**, which is a familiar form of *medium-term cyclical variation.* The business cycle begins with **prosperity**, *a period of high income and employment,* in which businesses grow and there is a large amount of construction. (The year 1972 was one such period.) Then follows **recession**, during which *income, employment, and production all fall.* (This happened in 1973.) If sufficient corrective measures aren't taken—usually by government regulation—then de-

pression sets in. **Depression** is *a radical drop in business activity with consequent high unemployment and frequent business failures.* (In 1974, recession became so severe that we approached true depression.) Generally, depression is followed by **recovery**, characterized by *a rise in production, construction, and employment,* such as that which occurred in 1975. And the cycle is then usually ready to repeat itself. Government spending, wars, and inflation may temporarily disrupt the pattern, but eventually the cycle's phases are likely to progress again.

Secular trends A **secular** or **long-term trend** is *a pattern of growth or decline in a particular business, and industry, or an economy as a whole over a lengthy period,* usually twenty to thirty years. Secular trends may develop because of population growth, availability of capital, new inventions and production methods, changes in consumer habits and spending patterns, or any of a number of other causes. One familiar secular trend has been the decline in the demand for rail travel with the development of the automobile and airplane. Another is the upward trend the drug companies have been riding, due to increasing interest in good medical care. And that interest in health care may, in turn, have had some connection with a recent reduction in the death rate. In any case, coincidental with it is a decline in the funeral industry. For one funeral conglomerate, it's meant a drop in the price of its shares from $25 to as low as $2 in the past ten years.

Managers study the secular trends for their industry and the national economy so that they can plan for the future, compare their growth with that of other firms in the same industry, and set up standards for their own performance. Investors also use secular trends to select stocks with potential for long-term gain.

* Crop Rotating Board, U. S. Department of Agriculture, "Production of Dairy Products, United States, 1975–1977" (Washington, D.C.: Government Printing Office, 1978).

tion of these two disparate political figures was associated with a drop in the market no one can say for certain, but there did seem to be some relationship between the two sets of *changeable factors,* or **variables** (as statisticians would call them).[1]

A connection of this sort is known as a **correlation**—*a relationship between two or more variables.* When data show that changes in one variable (such as the election of a particular President) appear to be accompanied by changes in another variable (such as the stock market), we may presume that some correlation exists. Each election in this case would be called the **independent variable**, since it is *an event that is controlled by outside factors* (here, by the voters). The health of the stock market would be called the **dependent variable**, because it *changes as the independent variable changes.* Correlations of independent and dependent variables can be positive or negative. In the Presidential elections, the correlation was *negative* because the election of each President seemed to trigger a *drop* in stock prices the following year. Had stocks gone *up,* as they did in the years following the elections of Franklin D. Roosevelt and John F. Kennedy, the correlation would have been a *positive* one.

WHAT IS THE SIGNIFICANCE OF A CORRELATION?

Does finding a correlation mean that one can predict or even control future events? Not exactly. A correlation just means that variables change at the same time; it does *not* mean that change in one is actually the cause of change in the other. Even though the stock market plunged when Nixon was elected, there was no evidence that Nixon's election *caused* the market to drop.

There's a danger in relying upon an apparent relationship between variables to predict business activity. For example, a large department store discovered that its sales were positively correlated with the Dow Jones Industrial Average: an increase in the stock price index (say, 5 percent) was regularly followed by a similar increase in the store's sales. After several years, however, the correlation suddenly turned negative: when the price index went up, the store's sales

inexplicably went down. What had happened? Statisticians soon found the reason. The Dow Jones Industrial Average and the store sales were both dependent variables related to yet a third variable, the state of the economy as a whole. When the economy started to decline, the correlation of the economy with store sales remained strong (both went down). But the economy's correlation with stock prices somehow weakened and became capricious and subject to time lags and stock prices even temporarily rose at certain points during the period of low prosperity. So the store managers realized that watching stock prices would not help them predict how well their business would do; there was no real cause-and-effect relationship between the two.

PRESENTING DATA

Even the most carefully thought out and painstakingly executed research and statistical exercise can prove to be a total waste of time if the information is poorly presented. It's of prime importance to present data in effective, easy-to-understand form. Written reports highlighting key research results must be clear and easy to follow (see box). And it's often very helpful to use a good number of tables and graphs; such visual aids can be crucial in helping managers get a clear picture of the situation. In a recent article on management consulting firms, for example, *Business Week* reported that such firms "lean heavily on visual aids to lay out problems for their clients. They use series of charts and graphs that plot such things as inventory levels, product pricing, and profitability."

One manager in a firm that relies on consulting firms' services said:

> From the graphs you can see the dynamics of the business [that you cannot spot] when looking at pieces of paper.... The graphs save me from having to study reams and reams of computer printouts to discover that my inventory level has been unnecessarily creeping upward for three months.[2]

It's essential to learn how to use these presentation methods to their best advantage.

THE PROPER REPORT FORM

Time, we're often told, is money. It's only natural, then, that the organization of a report should be determined by the limited time that the reader can devote to it. Not many executives have either the hours or the inclination to sift through hundreds of pages of research. It's up to the writer to do a good deal of that sifting for the reader, and this task is best accomplished by careful attention to the way a report is organized.

A good report has six basic parts:

1. *Title.* A brief description of what follows, rather than a catchy headline, is the best beginning. The names of the report's preparers and the date should also be included at the start.

2. *Introduction.* This is where executives must be told what the report is about and why it was prepared. The reader must also be told here the purpose of the report, how it came to be ordered, and what research procedures were followed in its preparation. The specific problem to be solved should be stated.

3. *Conclusions.* Without going into many details, the writer should state the conclusions next. Busy executives want to know the answers to the problem stated in the previous section.

4. *Recommendations.* After the conclusions, a reader naturally wants to know what the company should do. Suggestions should be pointed and practical, and should follow from conclusions.

5. *Body of the report.* Here is presented the data to back up the conclusions and recommendations. Executives may merely skim this section, but it's important that it be complete. In that way the researcher can defend any point made previously.

6. *Appendixes, sources, and notes.* Less important material or data less directly related to the problem at hand should go into an appendix. Sources detailing where information was obtained follow.

Writing a good report may seem like common sense. In many ways it is. In practice, however, common sense is difficult to achieve consistently. Similarly, good reports are hard to prepare. They should, however, be easy to read. That's the essence of skill in communications, one of the most important abilities for top management to achieve.

TABLES

Tables are commonly used to present data when there is a large amount of precise numerical information to convey. They can at first appear frightening because they're tightly packed with information. Once the form of a table is understood, however, the meaning can be deciphered with a little background information. The concise quality of a table then becomes a real advantage. Figure 2 breaks the table down into its important parts.

The title at the top gives a brief description of the contents in the main body of the table. Sometimes a unit of measure, such as "millions of dollars" or "thousands of tons," is placed below the title. In the main body, information is arranged horizontally in rows and vertically in columns. The rows are described on the left, in the stub. The columns are described at the top, in the column heads. At the bottom are the source note and sometimes footnotes on individual items in the table.

A table is useful mainly to present concisely precise numerical data that support a conclusion. Where precision is less important than giving a general idea, graphs are a more useful tool.

GRAPHS

A graph or chart is usually a diagram or picture showing the relationship of one set of data to another. For example, it may present the way the production of corn varies with the amount of rainfall.

A TYPICAL TABLE

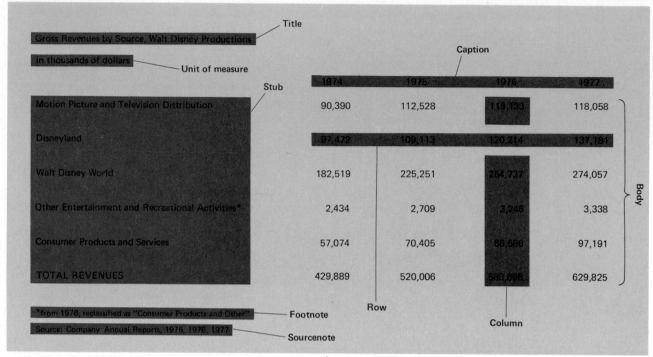

FIGURE 2

The graph fulfills an important intention of the statistician: presenting information in the clearest, most easily understandable way. Comparisons of data need not be studied laboriously. The graph presents them instantly, at a glance. Thus, it is very useful for presenting data to a group of people or to a single reader.

Depending on the data, the needs of the reader, and the kind of impact desired, the data may be presented in at least five different forms:

1. A **line graph**. The graph is *a line connecting points*, as shown in Figure 3a. Each point records vertical data (amounts in dollars, in this case) at each variation of the horizontal data (years from 1967 to 1977, in our example). Line graphs clearly show trends, such as an increase in profits.

2. A **bar chart**. This chart *uses either vertical or horizontal bars to compare information*. Figure 3b shows the number of CB radios sold over the past five years. Because of its simplicity, the bar chart is often used; it may be made fairly accurate by the use of graph paper.

3. A **pictograph**. This chart is *a variation of the bar chart, in which pictures representing the data are substituted for the bars*. The information in Figure 3b could have been shown by substituting drawings of radios representing CBs. If each figure represented 1,000,000 radios, a number lower than 1,000,000 would be shown by an incomplete figure. Pictographs are good attention-getters, but some accuracy is sacrificed.

4. A **circle chart**. This chart, commonly referred to as a **pie chart**, often takes the form of *a pie or a coin divided into slices*, as shown in Figure 3c. The circle shows the relationship of slices as percentages of the whole pie, or 100 percent. A circle chart provides a vivid picture of the relationships shown, but it is not good for very precise data. Budgets of the government of other organizations are often represented in this manner.

5. A **statistical map**. The map *shows quantities by variations in color, texture, or shading, or by the concentration of dots*. In Figure 3d, each dot represents a specific unit of sales. The heavier the concentration of dots, the greater the sales.

TYPES OF GRAPHS

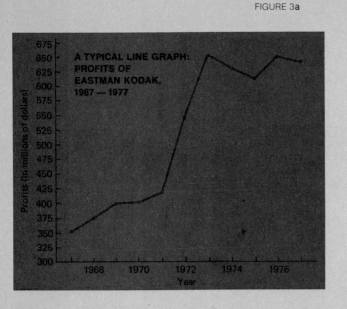

FIGURE 3a

A TYPICAL LINE GRAPH:
PROFITS OF
EASTMAN KODAK,
1967 — 1977

The line graph is a line connecting points. Line graphs clearly show trends, such as an increase in profits.

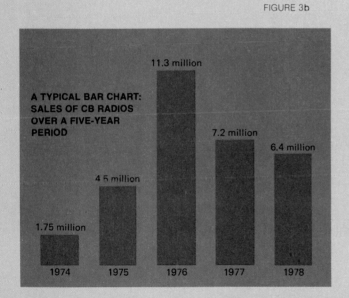

FIGURE 3b

A TYPICAL BAR CHART:
SALES OF CB RADIOS
OVER A FIVE-YEAR
PERIOD

The bar chart uses either vertical or horizontal bars to compare information. Because of its simplicity, the bar chart is often used; it may be made fairly accurate by the use of graph paper.

The pictograph is a variation of the bar chart, in which pictures representing the data are substituted for the bars. Pictographs are good attention-getters, but some accuracy is sacrificed.

A TYPICAL PIE CHART:
HOW GENERAL MOTORS
SPENT ITS ADVERTISING
DOLLAR IN 1978

FIGURE 3c

Network TV
$27,285,500

Newspaper
Supplements
$460,900

Outdoor
$696,700

Network Radio
$805,100

Spot TV
$6,262,900

Magazines
$15,587,000

The circle chart, commonly referred to as a pie chart, often takes the form of a pie or a coin divided into slices. The circle shows the relationship of slices as percentages of the whole circle, or 100 percent. A circle chart provides a vivid picture of the relationships shown, but it is not good for very precise data.

FIGURE 3d

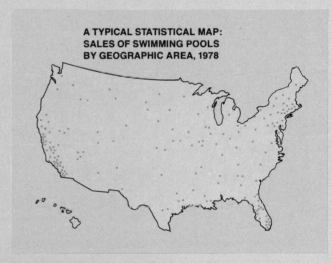

A TYPICAL STATISTICAL MAP:
SALES OF SWIMMING POOLS
BY GEOGRAPHIC AREA, 1978

The statistical map shows quantities by variations in color, texture, or shading, or by the concentration of dots. Here, each dot represents a specific unit of sales. The heavier the concentration of dots, the greater the sales.

An important part of an executive's job is making decisions. One aid to making the right decisions is statistics, which involves collecting, analyzing, interpreting, and presenting numerical data.

The data collected may be internal or external, depending on the source, and primary or secondary, depending on whether they are gathered for the specific project at hand. Secondary data are usually quickly gathered, cost relatively little, and contain information not always available from private sources. Much secondary data can be obtained from reports published by the government, especially the Bureau of the Census. Private sources include trade associations and various periodicals that can be located through indexes.

Collecting primary data can be expensive, so choosing a sample is important. Random sampling, the main sampling method, is based on probability. After a sampling has been carried out, further information may be obtained from the items in the sample by observation, surveys, or experiments.

After data are collected, statistical methods can be used to summarize and interpret them. Some of the methods are averages (the mean, the median, and the mode), indexes, time-series analyses, and correlations. Each of these techniques refines the mass of collected data into a few figures that tell management what it wants to know about market-ing and other functions of business. Averages simplify data. Indexes give sample figures that permit managers to make comparisons and note changes. Time-series analysis seeks to isolate the various influences underlying changes in business activity. And correlation is used to find relationships between varying factors or events.

Just as important as analyzing information is its presentation in report form. Here the refined data are presented in a way that best conveys their message. This is done with statistical tables, graphs, and written reports.

KEY WORD REVIEW

statistic
data
statistics
internal data
external data
primary data
secondary data
sample
population (universe)
observation
questionnaire
respondents
experiment
control group
average
mean
median
mode
index number
time-series (trend) analysis
variables
correlation
independent variable
dependent variable
bar chart
pictograph
line graph
circle chart (pie chart)
statistical map
probability
seasonal variations
business cycle
prosperity
recession
depression
recovery
secular (long-term) trend

REVIEW QUESTIONS

1. What are the major sources of data? What are the advantages and disadvantages of each type of source?

2. What is a sample, and why is it so useful?

3. Explain the uses of observation, survey, and experiment.

4. What are the advantages and disadvantages of using the mean, the median, and the mode?

5. Why are index numbers useful? Show how a specific, commonly used index demonstrates this.

6. What is a correlation, and why is it useful?

7. What three types of trends influence business activity?

8. What drawback is there in using correlation analysis?

9. When might you use a bar chart? A line graph?

10. In what order should the parts of a report be presented?

CASE 1

SELLING HARDWARE: SOME UNEXPECTED FINDINGS

Who buys tools? What tools? Where? Why? When? The answers to all of those questions may not make fascinating reading for most people, but to owners of hardware, houseware, and home-improvement stores, nothing could be more riveting. To find out about the market for these products, *Hardware Age,* a trade magazine, commissioned a telephone-interview study of a random sampling of U.S. households. The result: some intriguing information for readers in the hardware trade.

For example, the researchers found that women play an important role in building-materials selection. Though the study found that only about one-third of the female heads of households or wives were in the store when the most recent building materials purchase was made, nearly half were involved in the choice of style, color, brand, or place of purchase. In other words, the home-improvement center owner who aims at winning over only male customers can lose out on half the potential market. Instead, he or she should make a special effort to attract women customers—or at least their buying influence. This, the study points out, can be done by means of special promotions.

The *Hardware Age* report also discusses the consumer's reason for choosing a store for buying hand tools. Price, for instance, was the reason most often given for the choice of store—it was cited by 31.7 percent of hand-tools purchasers. However, cost was nearly nosed out by convenience: a store's location was the deciding factor for 30.2 percent of those questioned. The third most prevalent reason for choosing a particular store was good display. "Twenty-seven percent of the consumers who bought hand tools said either they needed it and happened to be in the store, or they saw it on display and bought it. Hand tools, it seems, are more of an impulse purchase than most retailers suspect," the report says. Such research information can be translated into dollars and cents for the clever business person.[3]

1. If you were a hardware-store owner, what would be the easiest way to increase your sales of hand tools?

2. How would you organize your own study to supplement *Hardware Age*'s information? What questions would you ask of consumers in *your* area that would be particularly helpful to *your* business?

3. Is the *Hardware Age* report an example of primary or secondary research data? Would you classify it as internal or external data?

CASE 2

RECORD-SPINNING IN THE RECORDING INDUSTRY

The recording industry is as exciting as the latest disco hit—especially to marketers trying to cash in on its swiftly changing trends.

The following are some nuggets of information about the industry. As you read each one, try to visualize the form of presentation you think would be most appropriate to it—bar chart, pictograph, line graph, circle chart, or statistical map. List the form you choose and tell why you believe it is the most suitable.[4]

1. In January 1976, eleven albums became gold; in February, eight albums became gold; in March, thirteen; and in April, twelve.

2. Record sales totaled $2.7 billion in 1976. It is interesting to compare this with movie ticket sales for the same year—which amounted to $2 billion.

3. Classical records accounted for 25 percent of all record sales in 1947, the first year in which long-playing records became available. That year, domestic sales of records totaled $224 million. In 1976, however, classical records represented only 5 percent of the total $2.7 billion worth of records sold.

4. Sales of 8-track tape cartridges have blossomed with the record industry. The 100.2 million 8-tracks, 282 million LPs, and 164 million singles total 546.2 million tape and disc sales for 1975.

PERSPECTIVES ON SMALL BUSINESS

USING QUANTITATIVE TOOLS

Every small firm is inevitably involved with the manipulation of numbers. Reports are needed on dollars invested, returns on investment, sales, payroll expenses, inventory, and countless other items. Few self-employed people have any expertise or formal schooling in accounting, business mathematics, or the use of computers. "I'll never get involved in the records," the small entrepreneur is frequently heard to say. "That's what I have an accountant for." This attitude has certain merits but it leaves two questions unanswered. Is your accountant the best person for your particular company? And are you making the most effective use of your accountant's services? Let's explore some ideas that help answer these questions.

RECORDS AND THEIR KEEPERS

Speak your accountant's language

You'll need to become familiar with the accounting terminology presented in Chapter 13 of this text. Without this knowledge, you cannot develop a working relationship with accounting professionals. You need to speak their language. Develop an understanding of accounting principles through books and education. The better you bridge the gap between you and your accountant, the greater your chance of receiving good, timely advice.

Choose well and ask questions

Choose an accountant who is knowledgeable in your business area. Ask a few pointed questions: "How many small businesses do you handle? How many in my particular line of work?" The more experience the accountant has in *your* marketplace, the more meaningful the advice you will receive. If the accountant has a basic familiarity with your problems, you will save many dollars in unnecessary research costs.

But no accountant, even an expert in your field, has all the answers, and many are too busy to provide extensive preventative planning. This is where your knowledge can be of great assistance. Asking questions is the key. "Why can't we depreciate this asset over five years instead of seven?" "One of my associates used the ten percent investment tax credit. Why can't we do that?" Keep the accountant on his toes. Make it clear that you expect the best from him. Develop a relationship that allows you to phone the accountant every day, if you have to, to get answers to your problems as they arise. (But expect to pay for this service, too.) To make the best tax and business decisions, you need timely information. If you wait, the problem will grow and erode your profits.

Hire a problem-solver

Your accountant should be a problem solver, not a problem *finder*. Almost anyone can locate a problem area, but not everyone is able to formulate a set of procedures or organize a plan of action that will solve the problem. Your accountant should also be willing to consult a specialist if a unique problem arises.

Share basic attitudes

Find an accountant who shares your attitude on the interpretations of the law. Many government agents cannot agree on the meaning and application of the law; approaches vary widely. But one word of caution: if you are not a fighter, don't choose a professional who is just aching for a battle with the IRS.

Accounting services

Finally, we need to look at the various kinds of accountants and accounting services that are available to the small businessperson. There are five categories:

1. Certified Public Accountants (CPAs) who are also attorneys.
2. CPAs and Public Accountants (PAs)
3. Persons enrolled to practice with the IRS
4. Bookkeeping services
5. Tax specialists operating only during the tax season.

Let's take a close look at each category.

Certified public accountants who are also attorneys: The CPA-attorney is a highly qualified specialist in complex areas of estate planning, corporate taxations, and numerous other areas. This is an expensive person—$100 an hour minimum. He or she should be consulted on a small business matter only as a specialist, on the advice of another accountant.

Certified public accountants and public accountants: CPAs and PAs are licensed by the state to practice the profession of accounting. They prepare, analyze, and report the financial aspects of any business in a manner acceptable to the government. Most states require both the CPA and the PA to attend classes in accredited schools of accounting, a specified number of hours per year.

There are two basic differences between the CPA and the PA: (1) the CPA is usually younger than the PA because most states (and likely all in the near future) no longer issue the designation of public accountant; (2) a CPA is required to pass a difficult examination in all phases of accounting; a PA generally has received only basic college-level training. It would be advisable, however, to check with your state society of accountants to determine the state requirements for each group.

Persons enrolled to practice with the IRS: People who are enrolled to practice with the IRS have passed rigorous tax exams that neither lawyers nor CPAs are required to take. They are not required to continue their education after they have passed the exam, however, so you have to take on faith their desire to remain in touch with new legislation and new ideas. But remember too that people in this group charge less than CPAs, and their work may be excellent. A CPA title is no guarantee of quality.

Bookkeeping services: Bookkeeping services post business transactions to accounts and produce monthly financial statements. People who run such services need not have a college education in accounting, nor are they required to pass an exam to show competency or to enroll in courses to expand their knowledge. A person in this group *may* provide valuable services, at a cost far lower than a CPA would charge. Some bookkeeping services have clients who recommend them highly. They are not equipped, however, to provide sophisticated management planning services.

Many small businesses have solved the problem of accounting services by engaging a reputable bookkeeping service to perform the weekly posting to the accounts, and a CPA or qualified accountant to prepare the monthly financial statements. They thus have the best of both worlds: the knowledgeable advice of a qualified professional and the competent but less costly services of bookkeepers to handle the routine posting to accounts.

Tax specialists operating only during the tax season: Tax specialists who operate only during the tax season offer no advantages to a small business owner. Where are they when you need their advice? You are in business 365 days a year, and you need specialists who are there when you are. Deal only with qualified, full-time people.

YOUR ACCOUNTING RECORDS

What are accounting records and financial statements designed to accomplish? They indicate the financial health of the business. Your firm's profit-and-loss statement, if properly prepared in a timely manner (monthly), will indicate the exact ratio of sales to expenses. This ratio indicates whether the business is meeting its financial goals. A small business must carry its own weight from the very beginning. If there is nothing left on the bottom line for the owner, how long can the business survive?

The profit-and-loss statement and the balance sheet are thus of critical importance as business barometers. It is not uncommon for a small business to begin operation without any financial statement during the initial start-up period of three to six months. This is an almost certain invitation to failure. Financial statements must be used from the beginning and on a regular basis. Once a month is the accepted frequency for any new business and during any critical growth period. The regular financial statement is your primary means of monitoring the progress of your business. If you see a problem area developing, you can make adjustments to put the business back on the track.

Special accounting reports

Besides the standard financial statement, numerous other reports can be generated by your accounting service or automatically produced by computer or computerized cash registers. These reports can become valuable tools in the management of your business.

Aging of accounts receivable: While your balance sheet may indicate the dollar amount of your accounts receivable, this is only a small part of the necessary information. How long have these bills been outstanding? Most bills are due in 30 days; you need a report designed to indicate the length of time each account is overdue and the amounts of money overdue 60 days, 90 days, and 120 days. Such reports, known as aging

reports, must be used properly if their benefits are to be realized.

Other types of aging reports indicate aging by product line and aging by market area. If you need to increase your cash flow, this kind of report will indicate the areas to attack first.

Sales analysis: A sales analysis breaks down total sales into specific categories—product line, salesperson, market area—indicating strengths and weaknesses as they begin to develop. It also enables you to compare the current period's performance with performance in any previous period, so you can calculate the percentage of increase or decrease.

Let's look at an example to see how we make that calculation.

Suppose your firm had sales of $5,275 in January and $6,133 in February. First, find the difference between current sales and those in the previous period.

$6,133 Current period
− 5,275 Previous period
$ 858 Increase in sales

Then divide this difference by the sales in the current period.

$$\frac{\$858}{\$6,133} = 0.139, \text{ or a 14 percent increase in sales.}$$

Or, take another example. Let's use a period in which sales decreased from $9,275 in March to $8,125 in April. We find the difference between current sales and those in the previous period:

$8,125 Current period
− 9,275 Previous period
−$1,150 Decrease in sales

Next we divide this difference by current sales:

$$\frac{\$1,150}{\$8,125} = 0.141, \text{ or a 14 percent decrease in sales.}$$

Why are these calculations necessary? You need to know the significance of your problem. A 2 percent increase or decrease would be of little concern; a 14 percent decrease, however, would demand your immediate attention.

BUSINESS MATHEMATICS

As an entrepreneur, you need a good grasp of business mathematics in order to know whether you're making enough profit to pay the bills. Study the subject! There are many simplified texts on the market, and numerous low-cost calculators that can help you.

One of the most common problems facing the small business owner is calculating the percentage of profit on a sale. Say you sell a radio for $29.95 and your cost was $19.50. What percentage of profit did you earn? To find the answer, first subtract the cost from the selling price, and then divide the difference by the selling price.

$29.95
− 19.50
$10.45 profit

$$\frac{\$10.45}{\$29.95} = 0.349, \text{ or a 35 percent profit margin.}$$

USING COMPUTERS

The first so-called computers were accounting machines, and only a small selection of products was offered. Now dozens of manufacturers offer hundreds of low-cost, sophisticated computers suitable for use by small businesses. With the ever-decreasing cost of computer hardware, more and more entrepreneurs have started to use computers to cut labor costs and control the various aspects of their operations. The question for the small business is not whether to buy one but when. Before a final decision is made, a very careful analysis should be undertaken. Let's discuss the necessary steps in this decision-making process.

Where will you use them?

First, review the areas of your business for possible computerization or automation.

Suppose you own a manufacturing company that employs twenty-five operators on a piecework basis. Calculating the payroll is a complex business, and errors are made from time to time. Such a situation is bound to create unhappiness among the employees, affecting their morale and their productivity. Under the circumstances, the payroll would seem to be an ideal place to start a computerization analysis.

Determine the cost

The most realistic way to justify the expense of a computer is to calculate the dollars and cents it will save. The computer must carry its own weight in the company. If it is simply an ego trip for the owner, it may cost him a great deal of profit and possibly the business.

How much does it cost you to process your payroll now? This question must be answered. Since you need to know the precise amount of your current costs, you have to calculate the time it takes to figure the piecework payroll checks manually.

Let's say it takes two full days per week of your office manager's time. Her hourly rate is $5.50. Two full days is 16 hours. Therefore we multiply $5.50 by 16 hours and arrive at $88.00. We add a 25 percent burden to cover overhead and fringe benefits, and arrive at a figure of $110.00 per week. We multiply the $110.00 by 52 weeks and divide the answer by 12 months to arrive at a monthly cost of $476.67. Now we need to calculate the work necessary to compute the quarterly government reports. We estimate the approximate time per quarter to be four days, or 32 hours of our office manager's time; 32 times $5.50 equals $176, to which we again add 25 percent: a quarterly cost of $220. We divide this figure by the three months in the quarter to arrive at a monthly cost factor of $73.33. We now have a monthly cost of $550.00 ($476.67 plus $73.33) under your current system.

Now we want to determine how much it will cost you to calculate the same information with a computer. Since the piecework payroll requires complex calculation, it would be safe to say that a computer could easily master this job in 20 percent of the time. The old job required a total monthly cost of $550. If we take 20 percent of $550, we arrive at $110. This figure represents an estimate of the actual cost involved for the computer and the person operating it to complete the entire payroll. The difference between $550 and $110 is $440. The computer, then, would save you $440 a month. If your computer system costs $600.00 a month, including maintenance, you are well

on your way to being able to justify its cost.

Two additional points remain:

1. What is your office manager going to do with her extra time? If she has nothing else to do with it, you can forget the time saving involved. But there may well be other jobs in the company that she could handle, such as the collection of past-due accounts. Either use the time saved or reevaluate the problem.

2. How much would it cost to write the computer program to compute this unique piecework payroll? We estimate that $2,400 would be a realistic figure for such a program. If you spread that cost of $2,400 over 12 months, you would add an additional $200 to your actual monthly computer costs. Your real cost, then, is $800 a month, not $600. The computer must pay its way. Unexpected costs can and will seriously hamper the overall success of the business.

Set up a list of priorities

What other procedures might you want to computerize? You should select two or three additional areas and make the same cost comparisons for them as you did for your payroll. You must be able to prove a cost savings in reduced labor and other hard expenses. When choosing an area, don't inform your employees any sooner than you have to. They're bound to fear that their jobs will be eliminated. Unfortunately, there is a general feeling that computers reduce the number of jobs available. This is not necessarily so. If computer programs are designed properly, they frequently enable a firm to increase its efficiency and thus to handle more business. The increase in business will usually support more employees, not fewer.

We repeat: do not attempt to justify the use of a computer by relying in any major way on such intangible benefits as improved employee morale, reduced employee turnover, or improved customer relations. And be very sure the time saved by the computer can be used in other areas or to cover the requirements of future growth. It's not always possible to lay off employees, and those who are busy are likely to resent a fellow employee with time to spare. It's better to computerize in order to grow and to improve your control over costs than to try to eliminate a certain percentage of your employees. An employee lawsuit over termination would be costly.

In analyzing the potential cost savings offered by a computer, never use a time frame of more than five years. The computer must prove itself in that length of time because new technology will provide improved products within that period. And once you bite the bullet and purchase your first computer, every computer marketing organization in the country will rush to tell you why you need to upgrade to the newest generation of equipment. Eventually, you'll weaken.

Choosing a vendor

Before you sign a contract with any vendor, be sure of two things: the vendor's reputation and the availability of service for both the hardware and the computer program. If the computer and the program come from different vendors, make sure all parties are clear on their obligations to your firm and that these obligations have been spelled out in writing.

Require your potential vendor to submit the following information and perform the following tasks:

1. Submit a detailed proposal outlining all specifications of both hardware and programs.

2. Provide an actual demonstration of the computer performing the job you want done or a very similar one. You need to acquire a feel for the operation of the computer and see how easy it will be to perform the various tasks you will be required to do.

3. Indicate in writing all technical and training support that will be provided and all costs and responsibilities of the parties involved. As a business owner, you are making a major purchase; the vendor must make a commitment too.

4. Provide the names, addresses, and phone numbers of people who are using the equipment you are considering. Call them and get their opinion of the equipment and the vendor's services.

If a vendor refuses or hedges on any of these requirements, drop him immediately. None of these requests is unreasonable; each would be considered a normal requirement by any knowledgeable computer manager in a large firm.

TRENDS IN THE JOB MARKET

The fields of accounting and data processing offer some of the most promising opportunities for college graduates in the field of business. These fields have been strong in the past and will continue to be in high demand for many years to come. Regarding background, internships, co-op programs, and summer employment are particularly valuable when coupled with a sound academic foundation, and employers look at this experience as a definite asset when they hire for entry-level positions.

KEY AREAS

■ We are still in the early years of the computer age, and the demand for experts in this field can only increase. This is particularly true for those who have a computer-science academic background.

■ In the area of accounting, the demand will increase, but so will the number of business graduates, so public accounting firms will continue to compete for the top accounting graduates. Some predictions say that the demand is falling off, but for the past five years the reverse has been true.

■ The best accounting graduates usually work for public accounting firms rather than for business, industry, and government. Thus, a highly skilled accountant can move rapidly to the top in business, industry, and government—mainly because the competition is not as tough as it is in the public accounting field. This is not, of course, to discourage you from looking into public accounting. Many people prefer to join a public accounting firm upon graduation, get some experience, and *then* take a job in business, industry, or government.

THE OUTLOOK FOR MINORITIES AND WOMEN

Minorities and women have exceptional opportunities in the data-processing and accounting fields, and this trend will continue for some time to come. In fact, because of the shortage of women and minorities in these fields, their starting salaries are sometimes higher than those for other graduates. This goes back to the supply-and-demand ratio, and the special efforts employers are making to hire more women and minorities.

THE SALARY PICTURE

Starting salaries for two-year graduates in these fields will average $10,000 per year. Four-year graduates can expect an average salary of approximately $13,500 per year, and MBAs will average approximately $18,000 with a nontechnical undergraduate degree. Those having a technical undergraduate degree can expect to start at $19,200 per year.

INTERNSHIPS AND COOPERATIVE EDUCATION PROGRAMS

A college degree will certainly help you when looking for a job in business, but in today's highly competitive job market, a degree alone is often not enough. Many employers like to see that an applicant already has some experience related to the kind of work he wants to do after graduation. You can get such experience while you're in college through cooperative education programs, internships, and part-time and summer employment. These show students how the subjects they've been studying in the classroom are actually applied in the business world, and they can help students decide what kinds of job they will be most interested in once they graduate.

HOW THE PROGRAMS WORK

Cooperative education programs are offered by about 500 colleges and universities. These programs combine classroom work with practical experience. Students alternate full-time attendence at college with periods of full-time employment in business, industry, government, or service-type work. Students are paid while they work, but because they

CAREERS IN COMPUTERS AND DATA PROCESSING

Title	Job description	Requirements	Salary* and advancement prospects	Outlook through 1985	Comments
TWO-YEAR PROGRAM					
Procedures analyst (data processing)	Analyzes requirements for information, evaluates the existing system, and designs new or improved data-processing procedures. Outlines the system and prepares specifications that guide programmer.	Two-year Associate degree minimum, with four-year degree in Business desired.	$8,500 to $13,000 Team leader, or supervisor, data processing	Excellent	For persons wishing to follow a career path in this field, additional education above the two years is highly recommended.
Programmer (data processing)	Charts the logic of the computer programs specified by the systems analyst. Programmer also codes the logic in the language of the computer, debugs the resulting program, and prepares program documentation.	Minimum of two-year Associate degree in Data Processing or Business. Aptitude for math desirable.	$8,500 to $12,000 Systems analyst	Excellent	Additional education recommended for advancement in Data Processing career path.
Unit record equipment operator	In a relatively uncomplicated computer, may operate the following: 1. Tabulating equipment 2. Sorter 3. Collator 4. Reproducer 5. Accounting machine 6. Keypunching	Two-year Associate degree in Data Processing or Business preferred.	$7,800 to $12,500 Supervisor	Very good	
Computer operator	Beginning level for entry into the computer field. Operates the computer according to operating procedures set forth in the computer operator instructions, which are relatively uncomplicated.	Two-year Associate degree in Data Processing.	$7,800 to $12,500 Programmer	Excellent	
Forms designer	Designs, drafts, and prepares master copy for new or modified forms and prepares instructions for their use. Records information concerning form origin, function usage, cost, and inventory.	Two-year Associate degree in Data Processing or Business desired. Some knowledge of business procedures and systems preferred.	$8,500 to $12,000 Forms analyst or supervisor	Good	Some sales ability desired, as person in this position must work with clients in designing forms.
Systems analyst	Analyzes business procedures and problems to refine data and convert to a programmable form for processing. Studies data-handling systems to evaluate effectiveness and designs new systems.	Two-year Associate degree minimum with four-year degree preferred in Data Processing. Part-time work in Data Processing helpful.	$10,000 to $14,000 Team leader or supervisor	Excellent	
Reports analyst trainee	Under supervision, examines and evaluates purpose and content of business reports to develop new or improve existing reports. Works as a kind of efficiency expert.	Two-year Associate degree minimum with four-year degree preferred. Good analytical mind required.	$8,500 to $12,500 Report analyst	Excellent	Good way to learn a lot about an organization for future career growth.
FOUR-YEAR PROGRAM					
Associate systems programmer	Under direction of software supervisor, performs detailed software design, coding, debugging, and start-up on industrial control and monitoring systems and writes compatible process control programs.	Four-year college degree in Computer Science, Accounting, Math, Statistics, or Operations Research.	$12,500 to $16,000 Systems programmer	Excellent	
Technical writer	Generates use-oriented software documentation. Reviews, proofreads, and coordinates production of documentation, assists writers in running programming examples, and coordinates various service groups.	Four-year college degree in Computer Science, Statistics, or Math. Programming experience desirable.	$12,500 to $14,800 Supervisor	Very good	
Scientific programmer	Develops mathematical methods for use in solving design problems, analyzes mathematical and statistical systems, and develops various computer techniques.	Four-year college degree in Computer Science, Math, or Statistics.	$14,500 to $18,000 Senior scientific analyst	Excellent	

* Represents *starting salary* range

Title	Job description	Requirements	Salary and advancement prospects	Outlook through 1985	Comments
Information systems specialist	Helps develop computer systems for corporations. Designs and implements computer systems, working closely with professionals in engineering, construction, finance, and administration areas.	Four-year college degree in Computer Science, Business Administration, or Engineering.	$13,000 to $17,500 Project leader or supervisor	Excellent	
Statistician (Bureau of Census)	Assists in planning, processing, analyzing, evaluating, and publishing results of large censuses and smaller current and special surveys.	Four-year degree in Statistics, Operations Research, or Mathematics. Twenty-four semester hours of Statistics or fifteen of Mathematics and six of Statistics.	$9,500 to $13,500 Supervisor	Very good	Contact the Civil Service Commission Federal Job Center in your area if interested.
Applications analyst	Supports marketing activity. Responsible for software system installations and maintenance, programmer consultation, and liaison between customer and various in-house software groups.	Four-year college degree in Business, Statistics, Data Processing, or Math.	$12,500 to $16,800 Sales representative or senior analyst	Excellent	Special courses by company at home office are a usual part of training program.
Programmer	Assignments may include: coding, modification or maintenance of computer program to meet program/system specifications; correcting program malfunctions; testing and debugging programs to insure correct logic.	Four-year college degree in Computer Science, Statistics, or Math. Programming experience helpful. Courses in programming important.	$12,500 to $16,000 Various levels of programmer and then to supervisor	Excellent	
Systems analyst	Prepares systems through: system/program flowcharts; code structures and search arguments; file design and report formats, etc. Works on system documentation, file conversion, and parallel testing.	Four-year college degree in Computer Science preferred. Statistics or Math degree may be acceptable.	$12,500 to $16,500 Various levels of systems analyst and supervisor	Excellent	
Computer systems software specialist	Functions as a problem-solver, providing the operating systems, compilers, and utility programs. Job includes the installation and maintenance of highly complex software provided by outside sources.	Four-year college degree in Computer Science, Math, Statistics, or Accounting.	$12,500 to $16,500 Various levels of software specialist and supervisor	Excellent	

MBA PROGRAM

Title	Job description	Requirements	Salary and advancement prospects	Outlook through 1985	Comments
Applications engineer	Performs general micro-computer applications work, including support of specialized application areas, writing application notes, assisting customers with problems, and doing product planning.	MBA plus Electrical Engineering or Computer Science undergraduate degree, with emphasis on logic/circuit design (hardware).	$16,500 to $21,000 Supervisor of operating unit	Excellent	
Product marketing engineer	Responsible for market and account penetration for manufacturer of semiconductor memories and micro-computers. Works with sales and support groups in setting pricing, products, product mix, and timing.	MBA plus undergraduate degree in Electrical Engineering, Computer Science, or related field.	$16,500 to $21,500 Supervisor of operating unit	Excellent	
Applications analyst (sales)	Provides sales information for marketing. Begins in post-sales analyses, and is responsible for software installations and maintenance, programmer consultation, and liaison with customer and employer software groups.	MBA plus BS in Computer Science, Math/Statistics, or Engineering.	$15,500 to $20,000 Branch manager or supervisor of technical unit.	Excellent	
Computer applications engineer	Formulates mathematical models of systems, and controls analog or hybrid computer system to solve scientific and engineering problems. Prepares reports for staff and articles for publication.	MBA plus undergraduate degree in Math, Computer Science, or Electrical Engineering. Experience with computer mandatory.	$16,000 to $20,000 Project leader	Excellent	High aptitude for solving mathematical engineering, or science problems necessary.

are spending time away from the classroom, cooperative education programs lengthen the time it takes to complete a degree. Internships are a bit different. They tend to be unpaid, and since students generally participate during the summer, an internship won't add any time on to your stay at college.

WHAT ARE THE POINTS IN FAVOR?
Both cooperative education programs and internships are attractive to potential employers for a number of reasons. They signal a highly motivated student who is also likely to be a highly motivated employee. In addition, students who have participated in such programs usually require less on-the-job-training than new employees who have had no work-related experience. One manager with the 3M Company reported that 70 percent of the cooperative students in his company were offered jobs after graduation. *

ARE THERE ANY DRAWBACKS?
There are some drawbacks to work-related programs, which you should be aware of before you decide to take part in one. First of all, any part-time employment during the school year will reduce the time you will have for studying or for on-campus activities. Also important: transportation to your job will mean additional expense—and note that if you are in a nonpaying internship, you will lose the chance to work at a job that would pay.

* D. C. Hunt, "50 Views of Cooperative Education," University of Detroit.

HOW DO I FIND A WORK-RELATED PROGRAM?
If you agree that the benefits of work-related experience outweigh the disadvantages, we have a few suggestions. Employment offices, both private and government-run, are good places to look for part-time or summer jobs; faculty members and relatives may also be helpful. You can also contact your college placement and financial aid offices for information about cooperative education programs and internships.

The companies listed below are just a few of the many which sponsor cooperative and internship programs:

*Employers Sponsoring
Co-op Programs*

Burroughs Corp.
Diamond Shamrock Corp.
Dow Chemical Co.
Eaton Corp.
Ford Motor Co.
General Motors Corp.

*Employers Sponsoring
Internships*

Arthur Young and Co.
Coopers and Lybrand
Ernst & Ernst
Peat, Marwick, Mitchell and Company
Price Waterhouse and Co.
Touche Ross and Co.

PART 6

THE ENVIRONMENT OF BUSINESS

"What do I care about the law? Hain't I got the power?" Commodore Vanderbilt knew what he was talking about.[1] By the end of the nineteenth century he and a few other men who held monopolies in steel, oil, the railroads, and finance so dominated American industry that they were indeed above the law. The right to profit was all that mattered and, as one younger Vanderbilt put it, "The public be damned."[2] But by the time Theodore Roosevelt won the election of 1904, partly on a promise of fighting the "Robber Barons," a good part of the public saw things differently. And today, though business and government are still battling over trusts and monopolies, most businesses are complying with a wide range of regulations established for the public benefit.

Of course, not all laws and regulations represent obstacles in business's path. On the contrary, some help to protect business; and some make it easier to carry on daily business operations by ensuring a predictable, orderly social setting. There are several sides to the relationship between business and its legal, governmental, and social environment. You'll read about them in Part 6.

☐ Chapter 14, **Business Law and Ethics,** reviews the legal and ethical considerations business people must keep in mind.
☐ In Chapter 15 you'll read about the complex interaction of **Government and Business.**
☐ The Enrichment Chapter on **Technology, Business, and the Future** looks at the ways business's social environment may have evolved by the year 2000, and makes some interesting predictions about the ways business may change.

BUSINESS LAW AND ETHICS

Can a cookie company be held responsible when one of its salesmen roughs up an uncooperative grocery store owner? Can a novelty manufacturer market a canvas bag that looks just like the one an expensive luggage maker produces? If your favorite candy bar is discovered to contain rodent hairs among the raisins, is the president of the company that produces the rodent-hair surprise violating the law? And what happens when a giant corporation backs down on a seemingly ironclad agreement that's been made with its customers?

These are some of the questions we discuss in this chapter. Though, as you'll learn, there is no special law for business, the public nature of private enterprise often leads to issues that can best be resolved by legal precedent or written law. It also leads to tough ethical problems; we'll look at these as well.

WHAT WILL THIS CHAPTER FOCUS ON?

After reading the material in this chapter, you will understand and be able to discuss:

- the overall scope and purpose of common law, statutory law, public and private law, and the Uniform Commercial Code

- the requirements for making a contract, and what happens if a contract is broken

- the powers and duties of business agents

- the way in which property, real and personal, is transferred

- the legal procedures involved in declaring bankruptcy

- the scope of business ethics, and how business codes help promote them

A few years ago, Westinghouse came up with an attractive plan to encourage utility companies to buy its big nuclear reactors: a guaranteed long-term supply of uranium fuel at a prearranged price. What seemed like a good idea at the time, however, turned into a financial nightmare as uranium prices began to skyrocket shortly after the contracts were signed. Before long, the uranium Westinghouse planned to buy for about $700 million had risen in cost to almost $3 billion—an amount larger than the giant company's total assets. The manufacturer thus found itself in an impossible bind: it had a legal obligation to supply the uranium, but to do so would amount to corporate suicide. Given such a choice—one that involved, among other things, the jobs of thousands of employees—Westinghouse saw no course but to back out of the agreements.

Not surprisingly, it was soon hit by a wave of lawsuits for breach of contract, the utilities demanding payment equal to the value of the undelivered uranium. The issue turned out to be less open-and-shut than it seemed, however. Westinghouse based its defense on a particular section of the Uniform Commercial Code, a massive compilation of business-related laws drawn up by experts in 1957 and since adopted by forty-nine states. This section of the code permits a party to be released from contractual obligations if "commercial impracticability" can be established—that is, if the party can show that an obligation has become impossible to fulfill for reasons beyond its control. Westinghouse argued that the sharp rise in uranium prices had been brought about by an international cartel of producers—much like OPEC, the cartel of oil-producing countries—and that its initial assumptions about uranium prices (assumptions shared by the utilities) had thus been made invalid through no fault of its own. This argument, backed up by evidence, was so persuasive that one lawsuit after another ended in an out-of-court compromise that allowed Westinghouse to settle with the utilities for about 25 cents on the dollar—or roughly the same amount it would have spent for the uranium at the original prices.[1]

The Westinghouse case illustrates only one of the several types of legal issues that will be discussed in this chapter—issues centering around the types of activities businesses are permitted by law to carry out in our society. All businesses, just like all individuals, must obey the **law**—*the rules made by elected legislators and by judicial decisions which the society enforces to assure its existence and to function smoothly.* The law protects businesses against those who act against society's interests, and it spells out accepted ways of performing many essential business functions—along with the penalties for failure to comply. Thus the law promotes the survival of business but will allow no individual business to operate except within legal boundaries.

The law is complex, and at times it may seem unpredictable. But, as we've seen in the Westinghouse case, it owes much of its complexity to the need to deal with a huge variety of problems in which the right and the wrong are not clear-cut. Indeed, not all the choices businesspeople face are within the sphere of law at all; they raise ethical or moral questions that become the focus of much uncertainty and disagreement. In this chapter we'll look at some of the major legal guidelines that businesspeople must follow, and also at some of the crucial ethical issues that come up in the course of business activity. Our first focus will be on the types of law that exist in the American legal system.

TYPES OF LAW

There is no business law per se, only laws applying to all of society, including many that concern commerce and industry. Business is therefore affected by both of the two major kinds of law: common law and statutory law.

COMMON LAW

Common law is sometimes called the "unwritten law" because it does not appear in legislative acts. Instead it is *based on the precedents established by judges' decisions.* A new decision may be based on a previous judicial ruling; or, through a new interpretation, another precedent may be set for future judges to follow.

Common law began in England many centuries ago and was brought to America by the colonists. The continuity of common law was, and still is, guaranteed by the doctrine of **stare decisis** (Latin for *"decided* *matters"*). What the stare decisis doctrine means is that judges' decisions establish a precedent for deciding future cases of a similar nature.

STATUTORY LAW

A good deal of the common law eventually finds its way into **statutory law**, *laws created by government statutes.* (A **statute** is *a law that is written and passed by a local, state, or federal legislature.)* So much of the common law has been incorporated into statutory law that today the difference is often indistinguishable. We take for granted, for instance, that the products we buy from reputable companies contain what the labels say they contain. If you bought a Rolling Stones record and then found out when you got home that it was actually a record made by an unknown group imitating the Stones, you could sue the record company for misrepresentation. While this is an old concept in common law, it has also been incorporated in more specific forms in our body of statutory laws—for instance, the various rules on fraudulent and misleading advertising that are enforced by the Federal Trade Commission.

What happens if there is a conflict between common law and statutory law? In this situation, statutory law prevails.

THE UNIFORM COMMERCIAL CODE

As we know, laws often vary widely from state to state; such variation could make things very difficult for companies doing business in more than one state. It was to ease this problem that the Uniform Commercial Code (UCC), which figured so prominently in the Westinghouse case, was developed. The UCC covers a number of areas of commercial law, including laws concerning sales contracts and warranties.

PUBLIC LAW AND PRIVATE LAW

Both common law and statutory law can be further classified as either public law or private law. **Public law** *covers wrongs to society;* **private law**, by contrast, *concerns itself with wrongs to individuals.* In the following discussions we shall concentrate on private law, both common and statutory. We shall emphasize the areas of major importance to business: tort law and the laws of contracts, agency, property, and bankruptcy.

CONTRACTS

In the Westinghouse case, as we saw, the central issue was the company's failure to live up to the terms of its contracts with the various utilities. What exactly is a contract? A **contract** can be broadly defined as an *exchange of promises enforceable by law.* Few people realize how many business and personal transactions involve contracts. Contracts are so fundamental to business practice that even 5,000 years ago the Egyptians and Mesopotamians knew and enforced them. The contracts with which you are probably familiar—insurance policies, leases, installment buying agreements—are only a few of the many forms. They are visible and recognizable as contracts because of their pages of legal jargon. But a contract can be formed without even an exchange of spoken words.

REQUIREMENTS FOR CONTRACTS

A large portion of the law of contracts concerns itself with identifying the exchanges that constitute contracts. In the United States all of the conditions below must be met for a promise to be considered a valid and binding contract:

1. *An offer must be made.* One party must propose that an agreement be entered into by both parties. (*Each person or group of persons forming a contract* is referred to as a **party**.) The offer can be oral or written: A salesperson telephones or writes a prospective client, telling the client he can purchase materials at a certain price. Or it can be in the form of an act: The telephone company offers to provide service by the act of placing a pay phone on a street corner. In any case, the offer must be specific enough to make clear the intention of the offering party.

An advertisement is not considered an offer. The placement of merchandise in a store window, therefore, is not considered by contractual law as an offer to

ELEMENTS OF A CONTRACT

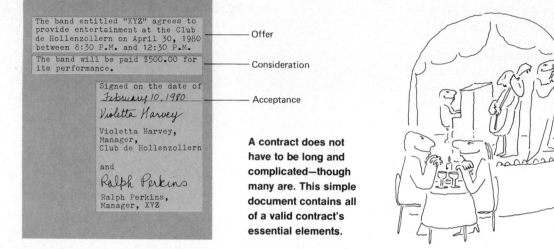

The band entitled "XYZ" agrees to provide entertainment at the Club de Hollenzollern on April 30, 1980 between 8:30 P.M. and 12:30 P.M. ——— Offer

The band will be paid $500.00 for its performance. ——— Consideration

Signed on the date of
February 10, 1980 ——— Acceptance
Violetta Harvey

Violetta Harvey,
Manager,
Club de Hollenzollern

and

Ralph Perkins

Ralph Perkins,
Manager, XYZ

A contract does not have to be long and complicated—though many are. This simple document contains all of a valid contract's essential elements.

FIGURE 1

sell that merchandise. But when a store places merchandise on the shelf and marks it with a price tag, this is considered a legal offer.

2. *Acceptance of the offer must be voluntary.* Don Corleone, the Godfather of film and novel, frequently made people "an offer they couldn't refuse." Luckily for him, he did not depend on the law to enforce the promises gained by these offers, for an ability to refuse is a prerequisite for a valid contract. *The courts will not uphold a contract if either the offer or the acceptance was obtained through what is termed "duress or undue influence."*

This rule is referred to as the **principle of mutual acceptance**. A counteroffer implies rejection of the offer. If, for example, someone offered to sell you a car for $1,000 but you refused to pay more than $880, there would be no contract. But if the seller handed you the keys after your counteroffer, this act would be considered voluntary acceptance, and a contract would be made.

3. *Both parties must give consideration.* A promise binds legally only when each party gives something of value to the other. This *item of value,* or **consideration**, may be money, goods, services, or the forbearance (giving up) of a legal right. The central idea behind this requirement is that bargaining should take place and that each party should get something for giving something.

The relative value of each party's consideration does not matter to the courts. If people make what seems to be a bad bargain, that is their affair. Consideration is legally sufficient when both parties receive what they thought was sufficient when making the agreement. In a famous 1888 Maryland decision (*Devecmon* v. *Shaw*) a man had promised that if his nephew took a trip to Europe, he would fully reimburse him for expenses. The uncle attempted to avoid payment, but the courts ruled in favor of the nephew. The nephew was under no previous obligation to make the trip. By giving up his legal right to stay at home, he gave sufficient consideration. Thus, even though the bargain was very much to the nephew's advantage, the contract was legal.

4. *Both parties must be competent.* The law gives to certain classes of people only a limited capacity to enter into contracts. These are minors, the insane, and the intoxicated. In most states, people so classified can make agreements only for the necessities of life: food, clothing, shelter, and medical care.

If a store sells an insane man a television set on credit, the installment purchase agreement is not a valid contract and the store must bear any losses incurred. A hospital that gives this same person emergency treatment on credit, however, is entitled to payment.

There is little variation among the states on the

matter of contracts with the drunk or insane, but minors are a special category. The age of majority is established by state law. It is usually 18 or 21, with the trend being to lower the age to 18. In addition, many states have adopted the Uniform Minor Student Capacity to Borrow Act. This law allows a lender to enforce an educational loan made to a minor, provided that the lender has in his possession a statement indicating that the borrower has been accepted for enrollment at a specific school.

5. *The contract must be legal.* The law will not enforce a promise that involves an illegal act. Some illegal situations are obvious: A gangster cannot get help from the courts to enforce a contract to deliver illegal drugs at a prearranged price. Less obvious is the case of the man who signs a promissory note to repay a gambling debt: The note is not an enforceable contract if state law prohibits gambling. Even on a loan that is otherwise legal, if the lender asks more interest that state law allows, the courts will allow him to collect only the principal, not the interest.

6. *The contract must be in proper form.* Although many contracts can be made orally, by an act, or by a casually written document, in certain situations the law requires that a prescribed form must be followed for a promise to be considered a valid contract. Usually a written contract is required for the transfer of certain kinds of property above a fixed value (often $500). The written form may also be required for contracts that cannot be fulfilled within one year, such as installment purchase agreements. When the law requires a written document, any change in the agreement must also be written.

A contract need not be long; all the elements of a contract can be contained in a simple document, as shown in Figure 1.

WHAT IF A CONTRACT IS BROKEN?

The great majority of valid contracts are adhered to by both parties. Each does what was promised, and the contract is dissolved by being carried out. Sometimes a contract will not be fulfilled because both parties agree to end it. Occasionally the law will excuse one party from meeting an agreement. (For example, bankruptcy frees a person from credit agreements, and

death or serious illness is a valid excuse for not fulfilling a contract for personal services.) But *where one party has no legal excuse for failure to live up to the terms of a contract,* the situation is called **breach of contract**.

The essence of a contract is that the law will enforce the promise made. Three enforcement alternatives—discharge, damages, and specific performance—are open to a person whose contract has been breached by the other party. We can illustrate the protection afforded by law with a hypothetical example. Nick Santo, a builder, contracts to buy 2,000 feet of pine board from the Zeller Lumberyard. The contract stipulates that the price for the board is to be $2 per foot and that delivery must be made by January 25. But on January 10 the lumberyard calls Santo and tells him that another contractor has offered to buy all of the yard's lumber at $2.50 per foot. Zeller tells Santo that he must pay the higher price or wait until February 15 for delivery. The builder has the following options:

1. *Discharge.* When one party violates the terms of the agreement, the other party is under no obligation to continue with his or her end of the contract. In other words, the second party is discharged from the contract. Santo is free to buy his wood from another lumberyard. If Zeller goes ahead and delivers the wood at the later date, Santo does not have to accept it.

2. *Damages.* A party has the right to sue in court for damages that result from the other party's failure to fulfill a contract. The damages awarded usually reflect the direct loss of profit resulting from the nonperformance. If Santo had to pay another yard a higher price to get lumber, he would be entitled to collect the difference from Zeller, plus court costs. If Zeller's failure to deliver the wood as contracted caused Santo to lose a large contract or a good customer, the court might force Zeller to pay damages far exceeding the value of the wood itself.

3. *Specific performance.* A party can be compelled to live up to the terms of the contract if money damages would not be adequate. If, for instance, Zeller had agreed to sell not pine board but one-of-a-kind wood paneling from a sixteenth-century Spanish castle, Santo could demand specific performance of the contract. Since the wood paneling was unique and could not be purchased elsewhere, the only satisfactory remedy would be to order Zeller to go through with the deal.

AGENCY

During the more than twenty years that Elvis Presley reigned as the king of the pop-music world, virtually every professional move he made—recording new songs, giving concerts, making movies—was actually dictated by another man, Tom Parker. Parker liked to use the honorary title "Colonel" in front of his name, but the title that really counted was that of manager. Elvis did the performing, but just about everything else—all the nuts-and-bolts business matters, from scheduling tours and negotiating contracts down to selling souvenir photos—was taken care of by Parker, who engineered Presley's career with a flair that would have made P. T. Barnum envious. Of course, Parker himself did quite well in the process: for his managerial services he received 25 percent of Elvis's earnings, which made him considerably richer than most rock stars.[2]

While hardly a typical pair of business associates, Presley and Parker illustrated a common legal relationship known as **agency**, which *exists when one party, known as the principal, authorizes another party, known as the agent, to act in his or her behalf.* The principal usually creates this relationship by explicit authorization, either orally or in writing. If, for instance, you telephone a stockbroker and ask her to buy stock for you, she is then empowered to act as your agent. In some cases—where a transfer of property is involved, for example—the *authorization* must be *written in the form of a document* called **power of attorney**. In some situations agency can be created simply by conduct. When someone allows someone else to act in his behalf, he can't subsequently deny that an agency relationship existed, even though no oral or written authorization was ever actually expressed.

Agency is of critical importance to business because it allows delegation of the authority to enter into a contract. Under the law, the principal is liable for any contracts made by an agent so long as the agent is acting within the scope of his authority. Equally important, the principal may also be held liable for wrongdoing on the part of an agent. In a 1973 case, for instance, the manager of a small grocery store in Minnesota sued the National Biscuit Company because one of its agents, a salesman named Lynch, had assaulted him. Lynch's aggressive conduct had already been the subject of complaints from several stores, in particular his practice of stocking Nabisco products on shelf space reserved for other brands. On the occasion in question he got into a furious argument about his behavior with the store manager, named Lange, who finally told him to leave. Lynch challenged the manager to fight; when Lange refused, Lynch attacked him—in full view of the customers—and beat him up.

In the subsequent lawsuit, Nabisco based its defense on the argument that the assault resulted from personal antagonism, not from anything legitimately related to business, and therefore the company should not be held responsible. The court concluded, however, that since the assault not only occurred while Lynch was officially on duty but also stemmed from a dispute clearly related to his job as an agent for Nabisco, the company was indeed liable for the harm done to Lange.[3]

The range of possible agency relationships is nearly limitless. An agent can perform any act the principal could legally perform except vote, execute an affidavit, give sworn testimony in court, and make a will. Almost every executive of a company acts as the company's agent in some capacity. A purchasing manager is authorized to make agreement to buy ma-

CORPORATE VIOLATIONS: WHO BEARS THE BLAME?

In November 1971, agents of the Food and Drug Administration inspected the Baltimore warehouse of Acme Markets, a national retail food chain. The inspectors found unsanitary conditions, including rodent contamination. A second inspection showed little improvement. Subsequently, both the corporation and its president, John R. Park, were charged with violating the Food, Drug, and Cosmetic Act of 1938.

Why was Park himself charged? The government did not suggest that Park had purposely violated the law, but it pointed to his awareness of conditions in the warehouse and his overall responsibility for the company. Park defended himself by claiming that one of his corporate executives was responsible for

terials. A salesperson may be authorized to draw up sales contracts. The treasurer can dispense the company's money.

An agent must serve the principal loyally. The agent should not use authority for personal interests and is bound to follow instructions. Just as a company can be sued for wrongdoing by one of its agents, an agent can be sued for abuses of authority. Thus a purchasing agent who buys only from a brother-in-law, causing added expenses for the company, can be held liable. At the same time, of course, an agent also has basic rights. He or she is entitled to compensation for services, and the principal cannot interfere with an agent's efforts.

✓ TORT LAW

It happens all the time. A group of people set up a real estate company and buy thousands of acres of cheap, undeveloped land. Then, through mail and telephone solicitations, they claim to be selling highly desirable tracts, excellent for homesites or investments. Many people are convinced and spend thousands of dollars for this worthless land. While getting rich, these real estate salesmen have not only done something immoral but have also broken the law—in this case, a law which belongs in the category known as torts.

A **tort** is *an act, not involving a contract or an agency relationship, that results in injury to another person's body, property, or reputation, and for which that other person is legally entitled to compensation.* Tort law covers both intentional and unintentional acts. The real estate fraud we described was clearly intentional; so are **libel**—*defamation of another person's character*—and the infringement of patents and copyrights. You cannot, for example, claim that your competitor in the home-appliance business refuses to make service calls if in fact he does make them. You cannot manufacture the Never-Slip Can Opener without having an agreement with its patent holder. Nor can you use another company's trademark: the names Xerox, IBM, and Coca-Cola, for example, may be used only on products made by those companies. Even using a name that *sounds* like a registered trademark may be a violation of tort law. (In one recent lawsuit, a leather-goods manufacturer, Gucci, known for its high prices and

---

correcting the violations. But in his instructions to the jury, the judge noted that to be liable, Park did not consciously have to do wrong. The issue was one of authority: "Though he need not have personally participated in the situation, he must have had a responsible relationship to the issue." The jury found Park guilty. The Court of Appeals reversed Park's conviction, but a later decision by the Supreme Court reaffirmed his guilt. The Court ruled that "Park had responsibility and authority either to prevent violations in the first instance or to promptly take steps to seek out and correct them once they were discovered."

A corporate officer, then, cannot simply leave the job of obeying the Food and Drug Act to others—he must personally make sure that no violations occur. And the principles of the Park case go far beyond the food and drug industry. They could also apply to violations under the jurisdiction of the Environ-

mental Protection Agency, the Consumer Product Safety Commission, and the Occupational Safety and Health Administration. To prevent charges of personal liability and to avoid infractions in the first place, many companies are trying to tighten their quality controls; some are trying to reduce the risks of delegating authority by increasing centralized control. At General Electric, scientists may go to a company ombudsman if they detect a danger in a product's design.

What all of these companies are responding to is not just the decision in the Park case. The mood of the times seems to have shifted from "buyer beware" to "manufacturer beware," and no company wants to be subject to both stiff financial penalties and personal liability among its executives.

Source: Tony McAdams and Robert C. Miljus, "Growing Criminal Liability of Executives," *Harvard Business Review*, March-April 1977, pp. 36–37, 40, 164, 166.

tricolor trademark, sued the maker of a canvas bag that sported a "Goochy" trademark.) Even if your use of patented or otherwise protected material was unintentional, you could be sued—so do some research before you go ahead.

Your own negligence, even if it is unintentional, may make you liable under tort laws. If, for example, a customer in your store injures himself after tripping over a misplaced carton, you can be sued. And a manufacturer is liable for injuries caused by his product even if he does not know that the product is dangerous. A judge recently ruled that liability exists "as long as existing technology suggests the *possibility* of an accident."[4] (We discussed product liability in more detail in our Enrichment Chapter on Risk Management and Insurance.)

PROPERTY

It's important for anyone interested in business to know the basics of property law. **Property** is *anything of value that can be owned.* The law recognizes two types of property, real and personal. **Real property** is *land or anything more or less permanently attached to land.* **Personal property** is *anything that can be owned other than land.* A strip of marble in the earth is real property. When it is cut and sold as a block, it becomes personal property. When the block is made part of a building, it again becomes real property.

The law concerns itself with many aspects of property. Here we shall concentrate on the transfer of interest in property.

TRANSFERRING REAL PROPERTY

Two types of document are important in the transfer of real property: deeds and leases.

Deeds are important to businesspeople who must buy land or buildings for factory, office, or store space. A **deed** is *a legal document by which an owner gives an interest in real property to a new owner.* A deed is not a contract and requires no consideration to be valid.

A **lease** is *a document used for a temporary transfer of interest in property. The party that owns the property* is commonly called the **landlord**. *The party*

that occupies or gains the right to occupy the property is the **tenant**. A lease is granted for a specific period of time, during which the tenant pays rent to the landlord in periodic installments. There is no limit on the length of time for which a lease may be granted; ninety-nine-year leases are not uncommon. A long lease allows a business that lacks sufficient capital to buy real property to enjoy the stability normally associated with ownership.

TRANSFERRING PERSONAL PROPERTY

A transfer of personal property, such as a TV set or a check, is technically a transfer of **title**, or *legal possession of the property and the right to use it.* Sometimes the property transferred is something intangible, like a check, which is transferred by endorsement (see Figure 2). In other instances the property transferred is a tangible item, which is transferred via sale.

When does a sale occur?

The question may sound like an easy one, but in a legal sense it is sometimes difficult to determine. Legally, a sale involves the transfer of title by the *owner,* or **vendor**, in exchange for consideration from the buyer. A sale is therefore a contract, and may be subject to some interpretation.

The issue that needs interpretation is the exact time when title passes from the vendor to the buyer. Sometimes the time of transfer is easily established. In the typical cash register sale, for example, title passes when the clerk accepts the customer's money and hands over the goods. Any loss before the transaction is the seller's, and any loss afterward is the buyer's. In certain situations, however, the transfer does not take place immediately, and this small legal detail can make a big financial difference. Let's look at a few such situations:

WHEN DOES TITLE PASS ON AN FOB SHIPMENT? A sales contract may call for goods to be shipped FOB (free on board) point of origin. In this case, title passes when the property arrives at the shipping point in sound condition. Thus if you buy a Chevrolet from a dealer FOB Detroit, you will have title when the auto is

TRANSFERRING OWNERSHIP IN A CHECK:
FORMS OF CHECK ENDORSEMENT

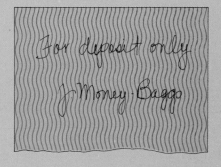

Blank endorsement is the most common form of endorsement. To make a blank endorsement, you sign your name and place no restrictions on payment. The instrument can then be exchanged for cash by anyone. Losing such a check is equivalent to losing cash, so you should use a blank endorsement only at the time of actual transfer.

If you wish to specify the purpose of the endorsement, you use a *restrictive endorsement,* such as "For Deposit Only" of "For Deposit to the Account of _____." A restrictive endorsement gives you strong protection, because the check can be transferred only to a bank account.

A special endorsement specifies the party to whom you transfer the check. If you receive a check and wish to turn the money over to your friend Sarah Smith, you can make a special endorsement by signing your name on the back along with the words, "Pay to the order of Sarah Smith." You are thus protected against loss, and Sarah Smith can endorse the check as she wishes. Businesses frequently make use of a special endorsement. It allows them the convenience of rubber-stamping checks (with an endorsement) instead of having an authorized agent like the president or treasurer personally sign each check.

If you receive a check in payment and, in turn, give it to someone else in payment, you should use a *qualified endorsement.* This would relieve you of any responsibility if the check "bounces," that is, if it is not backed by sufficient funds. The most common form of qualified endorsement is a signature and the words "Without Recourse." A qualified endorsement is often used by a person such as a lawyer who was given a check for endorsement to a third party contingent upon some action of the third party (as in the purchase of real estate). The lawyer is only providing a service and does not want to be held responsible if the writer of the check should stop payment or if the check is returned marked "Insufficient Funds."

FIGURE 2

In an FOB agreement, title passes to the customer at the shipping point—and the dealer is not responsible for subsequent damages. In the situation shown here, would the dealer have been responsible if the shipment were COD? What if the car had been purchased on installment?

FIGURE 3

"Here's your new Zowie 500, FOB Detroit, Sir—just sign here and you can drive it away."

placed on a train or truck in Detroit. Damage to the car en route to its destination is your responsibility.

WHEN DOES TITLE PASS IN A COD SHIPMENT? When property is purchased COD, title is not transferred until the buyer receives the goods. Before you pay for the dress or suit that is delivered to your door, it is a good idea to inspect it for damage. After payment, the loss will be yours.

WHEN DOES TITLE PASS IN AN INSTALLMENT PURCHASE? When property is purchased on installment, title passes when the buyer takes possession of the property. If, for example, you buy a stereo set on credit, you must pay the full purchase price after delivery, even if the set is stolen or damaged before you've finished paying for it.

You'll find it useful to think over these distinctions carefully. After you do so, you might enjoy testing yourself on the situation shown in Figure 3.

BANKRUPTCY

At the end of 1977 one of the country's oldest and most prestigious retailers, Abercrombie & Fitch, closed its doors for good. After eighty-seven years in business—and ten years of operating at a loss—the famed sport-ing-goods chain finally collapsed into bankruptcy after the failure of a last-ditch effort to turn things around. Abercrombie had actually filed a court petition in mid-1976 to reorganize under a section of the federal bankruptcy act, which gave it protection from creditors' lawsuits while it looked for ways to pay off its debts. It subsequently managed to obtain more than $7 million in loans to cover operating expenses, but the hoped-for upturn in business simply didn't materialize, leaving Abercrombie owing more than the total value of its assets. A federal bankruptcy court finally turned control of the company over to the First National Bank of Chicago—which had issued most of the loans—authorizing it to sell off as much of the merchandise as it could and close down the remaining stores whenever it was ready.[5]

Bankruptcy is *the legal procedure by which a person or a business, unable to meet its financial obligations, is relieved of debt by having the court divide the assets among the creditors.* The Constitution provides for a federal bankruptcy law, which is outlined in the Bankruptcy Act of 1898 and the Chandler Act of 1938. Here we'll discuss a few key points of this law.

Sometimes, bankruptcy proceedings are *initiated by the creditors;* this type of bankruptcy is called **involuntary bankruptcy**. Or, far more commonly, *the debtor himself begins the proceedings in court;* this process is call **voluntary bankruptcy**. Except for municipal, railroad, banking, insurance, and building and loan corporations, any business or individual can go into voluntary bankruptcy if liabilities exceed assets and total debt is over $1,000. And with the additional exceptions of farmers, nonprofit corporations, and wage earners making less than $1,500 a year, any business or individual can be forced into involuntary bankruptcy, provided that certain other legal standards are met. Involuntary bankruptcy is rare because creditors seldom are able to recover all of their debt from the bankrupt's assets; whereas if bankruptcy is not declared, the debtor continues to owe the money and some chance of recovery remains.

Another reason that involuntary bankruptcy is uncommon is that the debtor often owes money to a number of sources, and the federal law establishes a priority system of payment that is unfavorable to most creditors. Before most of the creditors can be paid, other debts of the bankrupt must be settled. These debts include court costs associated with the proceedings, unpaid employee wages (up to $600 for each employee), taxes, and other government debts. Then come creditors with secured claims, such as a bank holding a mortgage. The remaining assets are then divided among other creditors in proportion to the amount each is owed.

Both the House of Representatives and the Senate are currently taking steps to overhaul the bankruptcy laws. Under the proposed revisions, the amount awarded unpaid employees would at least triple (to $2,000 per employee). Also, reimbursement to consumers who have put money down on an item but do not receive it because the company has gone bankrupt would be given priority.

THE SCOPE OF BUSINESS ETHICS

So far we have focused on some of the ways businesspeople are required by law to conduct business. But what about rules of conduct that are not embodied in laws, but which many people in our society nevertheless feel they should observe? Our standards for what is *morally right* or **ethical**—honesty, fair dealing, concern for other people's well-being—often create hard choices for businesspeople. Often the most ethical course of action is not the most profitable.

THE MEANING OF ETHICS

"Ethics" is a word with many meanings. In one sense, **ethics** can be defined as *a branch of philosophy that concerns itself with the moral concept of right and wrong.* Ethics attempts to determine whether, in a given instance, the end justifies the means, when the problem is viewed from the standpoint of the good of society. In another sense, ethics is *the entire body of moral values that society attaches to the actions of human beings.* Ethics can also refer to *codes or other systems for controlling means so that they serve a human end.*

Business ethics, by extension, concerns itself with *the relationship between business goals and practices and the good of society.* A businessperson behaves ethically when her or his actions are upright and serve the interests of society.

It is a bit shortsighted to argue that businesspeople behave morally only because the law forces them to do so. Law is a reflection of the ethics of society, and it always lags behind ethics. False advertising, price fixing, monopoly, and stock manipulation were considered unethical and therefore avoided by the majority of businesspeople long before the law declared such practices illegal.

SOME ETHICAL QUESTIONS

Each day people in business are faced with choices between ethical acts and unethical ones that could work to their personal advantage or increase the profits of their company. In some of these situations, the choice is clear. Then the average businessperson decides in favor of ethics even though the law provides no punishment for not doing so. Here are a few ethical questions to which most businesspeople would answer "no."

1. Should you entertain a client lavishly in the hope that the client will feel obligated to purchase from your company? The government does not allow tax deductions for lavish entertainment, but the chances for cheating are numerous. Still, the majority of companies follow a policy of only modest entertaining.

2. Should you give a client a false receipt so that the client can claim a larger tax deduction? This illegal practice is easy to get away with.

Business secrets can be as "hot" as political ones.

3. Should you promote a friend in place of someone more qualified?

4. Should you use privileged information for personal gain or to help out your friends?

5. If you're the head of a candy-bar company and chocolate prices are rising rapidly, should you simply raise the price—and risk a falloff in sales—or should you quietly make the bars smaller and hope no one notices?

6. Meat shrinks a little after it's been cut and wrapped in a display package. If you're a grocer, should you put more than the marked amount in the package so that it will be closer to the right weight when the customer buys it?

7. Should you pay an employee of a competitor to tell you trade secrets about his company?

ETHICAL QUESTIONS FOR TOMORROW

Questions of the sort listed above are specific and relatively easy to deal with. But other situations raise more complex issues that defy simple, clear-cut resolutions. Below are some of the major ethical questions that confront business today.

How should human beings be regarded?

As we mentioned in our Enrichment Chapter on Human Relations, little attention was paid to the human needs of workers until fairly recently. The prevailing attitude for generations was that business did the worker enough favors by the simple act of providing work, and practices were long accepted that are now viewed with horror.

Child labor, low pay for long hours, and grossly unsafe conditions are concerns that have long since become matters of law, not just ethics. Yet many jobs remain that are tedious, stifle creativity, and waste human talent, and few people would dispute the need to redesign and humanize such work. But what of the workers displaced by automation, which tends to make work more creative by eliminating repetition? Is a manager who phases out someone's career acting ethically, even though doing so may provide another worker with a far more attractive life?

The whole truth and nothing but the truth

Before passage of the Pure Food and Drug Act, there was a brand of candy guaranteed to induce weight loss. The candy worked, but only because each piece contained a tapeworm segment. Clearly, not informing the public of such an unpleasant fact was unethical by any standards. But what about an ice cream advertisement shown on television? If real ice cream is used, the studio lights will melt it before the scene can be filmed, so colored mashed potatoes are substituted for ice cream. Must the sponsor confess to the whole truth, even though the product may be perfectly attractive in reality, and even if telling the whole truth means that nobody will buy the product? Keep in mind that the manufacturer employs many thousands of people at the ice cream plant.

Everybody else does, why shouldn't I?

This is an argument that can apply to a host of marginally unethical or illegal practices. They include spreading unfavorable information about a competitor, pirating employees, and taking advantage of a competitor's temporary weakness to run him out of business. The ethical decision in these cases may seem glaringly clear to the general public, but to a businessperson the choice can be agonizing.

In our competitive system no enterprise operates in a vacuum. The acts of competitors are of major consequence to any business, and thus the pressure is strong to conform to actual practice in an industry—whether that practice is perfectly ethical or blatantly dishonest. This hard fact of life, with the conflicts it creates, has become especially evident in the operations of multinational corporations. Imagine, for example, that you're the head of a major aircraft company, and the finance minister of a foreign country tells you privately that for a "consultant's fee" of half a million dollars he'll see to it that you get a contract with his government worth $200 million. At first glance the issue seems as clear as day: he wants a bribe, and bribery is against the law. On second thought, though, there are other factors to weigh. Not only would the contract mean a profit for your company; it would also mean jobs for, say, 5,000 workers who might have to be laid off otherwise. On top of that, you have reason to believe that if you don't get the contract, it will go to a foreign competitor—taking much-needed tax revenues with it. Given all this—along with the knowledge that official bribery is a standard business practice in many other countries—it might seem naive to refuse on ethical grounds. The decision is a tough one.

Conflict of interest

Conflict of interest is another type of problem that has long troubled thoughtful businesspeople, particularly since it can arise in so many ways. Assume for a moment that you're the president of a management consulting firm, with a number of large corporations among your clients. Could you serve on the board of directors of one of them without a conflict of interest—could you be totally objective about the corporation's needs, for instance, if someone proposed using a rival consulting firm? If one of your top consultants recommended that a client company's president be fired, should your firm also have the responsibility—and the lucrative fee—for finding a replacement? Or if, in the course of studying a company's operations, you discover some fraudulent practices, should you "betray" your own client by going to the authorities, or treat the matter as confidential—and thereby risk becoming an accessory?

AIDS TO ETHICS: BUSINESS CODES

Many of our business leaders are seriously concerned with ethical questions, and they have developed tools to deal with them—among them have been specific **codes of ethics** for various industries. These codes, or *guides to ethical behavior,* perform a number of useful functions. Ethics deals not with things as they are but with the way they ought to be; a code thus provides a road map for desirable behavior. It can also help support the businessperson if he or she chooses an ethical but unpopular action, providing practical relief from some of the day-to-day strains of a competitive, not always ethical world. An industry code of ethics, backed by some method of enforcement, greatly reduces the advantages one company may gain by behaving unscrupulously and makes it harder to rationalize such behavior with the "everybody else does it" argument.

TYPES OF CODES

Three major varieties of codes currently exist in the American business world: professional codes for occupational groups; business association codes for companies engaged in the same line of activity; and advisory group codes, which are guidelines suggested by governmental and other agencies.

Business occupations are fighting for and slowly winning the professional status long accorded medicine and the law. The move toward professionalism is led by the various associations in each work area, such as the American Management Association, the American Marketing Association, and the American Association of Advertising Agencies. Virtually all of these organizations have adopted ethical codes that members are expected to follow. Some of these codes are general guidelines, while others encourage or prohibit certain specific practices.

There are business associations representing almost every industry, from retail drugs to dairy farming, and most have likewise adopted codes of ethics. A few inspect for adherence to the code and penalize offenders in one way or another. One well-known example is the National Association of Broadcasters (NAB), which has developed separate and highly detailed radio and television codes that prescribe standards for programming and advertising. The Television Code, for instance, has lengthy guidelines for

individual advertising categories such as nonprescription remedies, alcoholic beverages, children's advertising, even vegetable oils and margarines. More generally, it sets forth basic standards of content, taste, fairness, and the like for various types of programming. The NAB also monitors its member stations—which include most of the country's TV and radio broadcasters—to check for code violations. While adherence to the code is voluntary, there are strong incentives for compliance: the withdrawal of a station's code seal might deter potential advertisers, and could ultimately jeopardize the station's broadcasting license.

In addition to the numerous industry codes of this

There's little else that's "laid back" about the consumer movement. Many consumer groups function as active, effective critics of unethical business practices.

Table 1   Rating our institutions: the public's attitude toward business and other institutions in America. (Criteria: honesty, dependability, integrity.)

Institution	"Good" Rating
Science and Technology	41%
Supreme Court	33
Organized Religion	30
Small Business	27
Broadcast News	26
Consumer Groups	25
Environmental Groups	24
Educators	23
Legal Profession	11
Business Executives	10
Senate	9
Large Business	9
Democratic Party	8
Republican Party	7
Labor Union Leaders	5
Politicians	2

Source: *U.S. News and World Report,* "Study of American Opinion," 1978.

sort, there are two nationwide associations that concern themselves with improving the ethics and the public image of business as a whole. These are the Chamber of Commerce and the Better Business Bureau, each comprising a network of local and regional organizations. The Better Business Bureau, in particular, focuses its attention on ethical practices at the retail level, keeping extensive records on consumer complaints in each geographic area.

Finally, a wide variety of outside observers—foundations, religious organizations, civil rights groups, consumer advocates, and others—have also drawn up codes of business ethics. While businesspeople have a tendency to dismiss such advice as unrealistic or openly hostile, it can actually be quite useful to business as a barometer of public concerns—and as a forecast of what may well become law if business fails to comply voluntarily.

In fact, there is some evidence that business leaders are coming to take the opinions and expectations of outsiders more seriously. In 1977 the *Harvard Business Review* conducted a survey of its readers to see whether ethical standards in business had changed in the previous fifteen years. While there was considerable disagreement as to whether those standards had risen or declined, the readers expressed a much greater awareness of the social responsibilities of business. A large majority rejected the idea that profit is the only important measure of a company's performance, and that businesses are trapped in an economic system that gives them very little power to change social conditions. Perhaps most striking of all was the finding that this influential group of executives ranked responsibility to customers above responsibility to stockholders or employees. While the long-term importance of profits was by no means belittled, the survey provided a surprisingly strong indication that America's business leaders have begun to broaden and humanize some of their most basic views of business in relation to the society at large.[6]

CHAPTER REVIEW

Laws are the rules that society enforces in order to function properly. Common law is based on the decisions of judges. Statutory law is created by government bodies, but in the United States it is derived in large part from common law. Businesspeople are most concerned with private law, especially law dealing with contracts, agency, property, and bankruptcy.

A contract is a promise enforceable by law. To be considered valid, it must meet the following conditions: An offer must be made, acceptance must be voluntary and mutual, both parties must give consideration, the parties must be legally competent, the purpose must be legal, and the form must be correct.

Agency is a relationship whereby a principal authorizes an agent to act in his or her behalf. Agency can be created through power of attorney or by conduct.

Real property is land or anything permanently affixed to land. Personal property is everything else subject to ownership. A deed permanently transfers interest in real property; a lease conveys temporary interest. Title to personal property is transferred most often by sale or endorsement.

A business that can no longer meet its financial obligations may declare bankruptcy. Under bankruptcy proceedings, the court relieves the business of its debt by dividing its assets among its creditors. Bankruptcy proceedings begun by the business are called voluntary. Involuntary bankruptcy comes about when the creditors of a business initiate court action.

Business ethics concerns itself with the relationship between business practices and the interests of society. Ethical questions confronting the average businessperson involve the utilization of human resources, truth in advertising, and marginally unethical practices in fairly common use. Professional organizations, business associations, and advisory groups have set certain guidelines for business ethics, and are developing new guidelines for ethical problems that may come up in the future.

KEY WORD REVIEW

law
common law
stare decisis
statutory law
statute
public law
private law
contract
party
principle of mutual acceptance
consideration
breach of contract
agency
power of attorney
tort
libel
property
real property
personal property
deed
lease
landlord
tenant
title
vendor
bankruptcy
involuntary bankruptcy
voluntary bankruptcy
ethical
ethics
business ethics
codes of ethics

REVIEW QUESTIONS

1. How does law differ from ethics? Why is an understanding of both important to the businessperson?

2. List and explain the six conditions that must be met for a contract to be valid.

3. How is agency created? What can an agent not do for the principal?

4. When does title pass in an FOB sale? A COD sale? An installment sale?

5. Give seven typical ethical questions facing modern business. What four areas present more difficult problems?

6. Why is it that involuntary bankruptcy proceedings are so seldom initiated?

CASE 1

AN INJURY ON THE GRIDIRON: WHO'S TO BLAME?

A kick in the head by a 220-pound fullback during a football game can do a player a great deal of harm.

That holds true even if he's wearing a well-designed football helmet. When an Arizona ball player was injured in just such a way recently, the manufacturer of the helmet was sued for $2.5 million.

This product liability suit fell into the broad legal area known as tort law: the manufacturer was being sued because an apparent failure of his product resulted in injury to another person. Since the manufacturer knew its helmet would be worn in hazardous situations, the helmet should have been able to function effectively under such conditions. That was the position of the plaintiff in the case.

The court, however, thought otherwise. In clearing the manufacturer of liability, the court decided that the injury was the result of an uppercut to a necessarily exposed part of the face—and not from a blow to the helmet. In fact, tests showed that the helmet could protect its wearer from far more powerful blows, provided those blows were on the helmet itself. In other words, as far as the court was concerned, the helmet was free of defects and so its manufacturer was free of liability for the football player's injuries.[7]

1. Under what circumstances do you think the helmet manufacturer would have been held liable?

2. Suppose the manufacturer had fully intended to make a safe helmet, but had simply erred in his calculations. Do you think he would still be held liable?

3. The helmet maker was cleared in this suit. What other parties might have been blamed for the football player's injuries, in your opinion?

4. What other manufacturers of products supposed to protect people from injury might be subject to liability suits?

CASE 2

THICK'N'SWEET'S STORY: SOURING THE COMPETITION

Thick'n'Sweet (a fictitious company) is a manufacturer of ready-to-eat chilled desserts. Though not a giant company, it's still a force to be reckoned with in its chosen markets: for instance, it accounts for 75 percent of all sales of artificially sweetened synthetic yogurt. Profits in 1977 were some $40 million on about $360 million in sales.

All, however, is not sweetness and light with Thick'n'Sweet, as its competitors are fond of pointing out. One of the company's favorite tactics is known as "exclusive dealing," or twisting the arms of its distributors to handle Thick'n'Sweet products exclusively. Considering the large market share of Thick'n'Sweet, that's not a threat many distributors can afford to take lightly.

Of course, some Thick'n'Sweet products are more poular than others. Rather than being stuck with warehouses full of less popular flavors, the company has found it makes sense to require distributors to handle them as well. For instance, if a wholesale customer wants to buy 100 cases of the well-liked Strawberry Fluff flavor, twenty-five cases of the deadly Pumpkin Surprise must be ordered as well. If not, there's no Strawberry Fluff to be had. This form of coercion is known as a "tie-in."

Thick'n'Sweet isn't above price fixing, either. When competition is making headway, it orders its distributors to drop prices. When its products are in demand, it dictates that prices soar.

What Thick'n'Sweet can't accomplish by way of threats, it manages to do by other means. At a recent ready-to-eat foods trade show, for example, the Thick'n'Sweet booth attracted potential buyers like bees to honey. What drew the buyers most wasn't the prospect of a tasty free sample, but the scores of $500 color television sets being awarded as "prizes" to the most powerful chain-store purchasers. Less blatant bribes have taken the form of price discounts, advertising allowances, and rebates. The company has also indulged in price discrimination, in which it offers different deals to different competing customers.

Not surprisingly, Thick'n'Sweet's tactics don't endear the company to its fellow manufacturers of chilled desserts. However, short of fire-bombing the Thick'n'Sweet executive offices—which would be illegal—what can they do? Put yourself in their position.

1. Which of the company's sales practices would you consider merely unethical?

2. Which of the company's sales practices verge on the illegal? Why?

3. Which of the company's sales practices are overtly against the law? Which laws do they violate?

4. Ultimately, what effect would Thick'n'Sweet's sales practices have on the competition if they went unchecked?

5. If the company were allowed to continue its tactics, what would be the ultimate effect on the consumer?

CHAPTER FIFTEEN

GOVERNMENT AND BUSINESS

"A government that governs best is one that governs least." This has been the traditional attitude of many Americans toward the running of society. It's also a point of view that's somewhat out of date, particularly when it comes to business. For today, government is dependent on private enterprise for vital goods and services; and business, in turn, rightfully regards government as one of its best customers.

Despite this mutual dependence, however, government and private enterprise aren't always in agreement. Business doesn't always approve of the government's tax policies; the government finds some business practices unfair. In this chapter, we'll look at both sides of the business-government relationship, and highlight some areas still under dispute.

WHAT WILL THIS CHAPTER FOCUS ON?

After reading the material in this chapter, you will understand and be able to discuss:

■ the relationship between business and government, especially the federal government

■ the antitrust laws that grew up around the need to restrain monopolies

■ why the government supports some natural monopolies while exercising strict control over them

■ government's involvement in legislation aimed at regulating retail prices

■ the two major types of taxes—revenue-collecting taxes and regulatory and restrictive taxes

■ the arguments used to support the wedge theory

■ how the government protects businesses through copyrights, trademarks, and patents

Every business day of every week of every year, the federal government puts out its own newspaper, called, rather quaintly, the *Federal Register*. The *Federal Register* isn't the sort of paper you might pick up for a casual read; it's a weighty volume of at least two hundred pages of tightly packed prose tracing the most recent government rules. In 1977, the *Register* contained over 60,000 pages of regulations![1] In the last twenty years the government has increased its regulatory role a great deal.

There are almost ninety separate federal bodies that regulate American business, and one of the chief complaints raised against them—apart from the millions of worker-hours needed each year to complete the voluminous paperwork—is that often each just doesn't know what the others are doing. One meat-packing company, for instance, tried to meet Occupational Safety and Health Administration (OSHA) guidelines on noise reduction by installing new insulation in its plants. The noise was reduced, but it turned out that the insulation absorbed germs and odors at a level that violated Food and Drug Administration standards. To meet the standards of one regulatory agency, the company ran afoul of those of another; so it was breaking the law no matter what it did.[2]

Such frustrations, along with the mounting expenses created by government regulation—some estimates put the total cost to business, and ultimately to consumers, at $100 billion a year—have created a backlash that is beginning to be felt in Washington. (Whereas agencies in the past sometimes seemed to invent new regulations just for the exercise, many now make it a policy to think twice before proposing any new rule, and OSHA has already reduced its mountain of regulations by more than 10 percent.[3]) Yet it is not just the complexity of government regulations that many businesspeople find hard to accept. For many years, the American tradition has strongly favored the view that government should maintain a hands-off policy when it comes to business. Whenever Congress passes a new law to regulate trade, some critics denounce government as a needless meddler in business affairs; and whenever a new tax is proposed, a protest goes up from businesses and private citizens alike.

What are the pros and cons of this question? Are

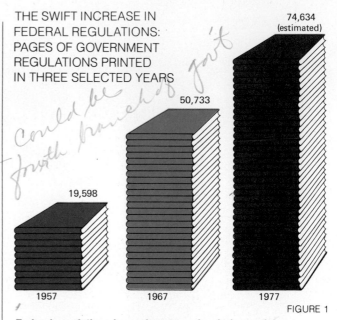

THE SWIFT INCREASE IN FEDERAL REGULATIONS: PAGES OF GOVERNMENT REGULATIONS PRINTED IN THREE SELECTED YEARS

could be fourth branch of govt

74,634 (estimated)

50,733

19,598

1957   1967   1977

FIGURE 1

Federal regulations have almost quadrupled over the past twenty years.

there arguments that justify the resentment of government that many businesspeople feel? Or is a relatively high degree of government control needed to help business and the economy operate? These are extremely complex questions, which we cannot begin to answer fully in this chapter. But we can look at some of the major issues involved, in the areas of both regulation and taxation. First, to fill in some important background, let's look at some of the ways government and business cooperate to carry out some of their key functions.

HOW BUSINESS AND GOVERNMENT WORK TOGETHER

The business-government relationship is not always one of government domination; sometimes each needs the other, as we'll see here.

govt can't produce own goods

GOVERNMENT DEPENDENCE ON BUSINESS

In the spring of every year, fishing boats in the waters off the American east coast are joined by another sort of craft, when Soviet submarines converge in the Atlantic for full-scale tactical exercises. How closely does the United States watch these Russian subs? Until recently, not too closely. By 1980, however, the Defense Department's budget for submarine surveillance should top $5 billion. And how will the government spend that money? It will turn to such familiar names as IBM, Western Electric, and Hughes Aircraft for the equipment and technology needed to protect American waters from potentially aggressive Soviet activity.[4]

GE and Hughes are producing ultrasensitive hydrophones, listening devices that can be used on shore, aboard ships, or in airplanes to detect submerged submarines with great reliability. At the same time, Western Electric has developed underwater sound detectors that are planted on the ocean floor at strategic points around the world, providing a continuous flow of data about the movements of Soviet subs. Finally, from IBM has come the new Proteus computer to tie the far-flung system together—small enough to be carried aboard

ships and airplanes but also powerful enough to handle the huge amount of information constantly coming in.

Situations such as this are good examples of the way the federal government relies on private enterprise to meet its needs and the way various industries depend on government contracts for a large portion of their revenues. State and local governments, too, frequently call on business for assistance. If a state decides to build a new office tower or a town needs new police cars, government officials must turn to private industry for the necessary products and services. On all levels, from national to local, government depends on the cooperation of business to implement laws and provide for the public well-being.

Business often works to help communities solve some of their problems. The Ford Motor Company, for example, has used its vast resources in working with governmental and other private organizations to attack urban problems in Detroit and elsewhere in the country.[5] On a somewhat less lofty level, private enterprise now has a hand in running the city of New Orleans' white elephant of a Superdome. The largest enclosed stadium in the world, the 95,000-seat Superdome proved a nightmare of mismanagement from the beginning. The construction costs, originally esti-

Ford's Detroit urban redevelopment program exemplifies business-community cooperation. Shown here, Renaissance Center, the $350-million hotel-office-retail complex that is helping to revitalize the downtown area.

mated at $35 million, mushroomed to $163 million by the time it was finished in 1975—almost three times the cost of the 75,000-seat Kingdome in Seattle, which was built around the same time. And the trouble hardly stopped there: under state management the Superdome ran up an operating loss of $5.5 million in its second year, and seemed headed for more of the same. In desperation and embarrassment, state officials turned for help to the Chicago-based Hyatt Corporation, whose Hyatt Regency Hotel is near the Superdome. Hyatt agreed to take over the stadium's operations in return for 30 percent of any reduction in its yearly deficit, and began the long-overdue task of managing it with the same efficiency and organization that are taken for granted in private business.[6]

GOVERNMENT AND BUSINESS AS EQUALS

Of course, government is not always in the position of having to plead for help when it turns to business. Very often the two cooperate as equals. The National Alliance of Businessmen, for instance, is a group of business leaders who, with limited federal financing and help, train and then aid in the placement of hard-core unemployed. The success of this cooperative venture helps to whittle away at a social problem that constantly plagues government, and at the same time it benefits businesses by providing a labor pool that they can readily tap.

A more spectacular partnership is Comsat, the Communications and Satellite Corporation, which is an international venture operated jointly by business and government. Business provides management skills; government supplies expertise and hardware in rocketry and satellite construction. The result has been an ever-growing communications network serving both government and the private sector. What's more, Comsat has been so successful that the government recently decided to experiment with a similar arrangement: getting private businesses to manage its Landsat series of earth-resource-monitoring satellites. For the time being, the government's financial and technical resources will remain essential to Landsat operations. The latest and most sophisticated of the satellites cost $360 million to develop—a prohibitive price tag for a private concern—and few if any cor-

porations could match NASA's capability for operating Landsat's network of ground receiving stations and data-processing facilities. But many observers feel that a private company could do a much better job than the government of packaging and selling Landsat services to the foreign countries and other customers who have use for them—oil and mining companies, utilities, environmental researchers, and the like.[7]

BUILDING YOUR BUSINESS VOCABULARY

COPYRIGHTS, TRADEMARKS, AND PATENTS

A special form of government assistance at the federal level comes from the laws and procedures that protect certain exclusive rights that businesses may hold. If the government did not rigidly enforce copyrights, trademarks, and patents, many businesses would be mown down by aggressive competition.

Copyrights

Copyrights protect the originators of literary, dramatic, musical, artistic, and other intellectual works. Any printed, filmed, or recorded material can be copyrighted. The **copyright** *gives its owner the exclusive right to reproduce ("copy"), sell, or adapt the work he has created.* The Registrar of Copyrights, Library of Congress, will issue a copyright upon an application from the creator or from someone deriving the right to reproduce the work directly from the creator. (A book may be copyrighted by either the author or the publisher.) Copyrights issued after 1977 are valid for the lifetime of the creator plus fifty years. The copyright laws that went into effect in 1978 also extend to seventy-five years the protection of works already copyrighted (the previous maximum was fifty-six years) and cover newer reproduction methods such as xerography, videotape, and magnetic storage.

Trademarks

A **trademark** is *any word, name, symbol, or device used to distinguish the product of one manufacturer*

GOVERNMENT ASSISTANCE TO BUSINESS

These, then, are some examples of ways in which government and business work together. But it's important also to be aware that government often *helps* business as well. If a company needs marketing information, it can obtain it from such agencies as the Census Bureau, the Small Business Administration, and the Departments of Commerce and Labor; the information is wide-ranging, up to date, and free. If the company needs advice on tax matters it can get a free steer from the Internal Revenue Service. If it is involved in a labor dispute, it can turn to federal mediators and arbitrators. And a business can get help of a more direct nature in the form of loan guarantees,

from those made by others. McDonald's golden arches are one of the most visible of modern trademarks. Others are such well-known brand names as Coca-Cola, Exxon, Polaroid, and Chevrolet. If properly registered and renewed every twenty years, a trademark under most circumstances belongs to its owner forever.

There are exceptions to that rule, however. One exception that has recently been in the news is brand names that have become so popular that they are now **generic terms** (meaning that they now *apply to a whole class of products*). There are several ways a brand name may become a generic term. The trademark may have been allowed to expire, as was the case with nylon and cellophane. Or the brand name may have been incorrectly used by its owner. For instance, the owner is not supposed to use the brand name as a noun, as a verb, or in the plural; the manufacturer should refer to Baggies plastic bags, not Baggies. Even when a trademark is well protected and properly used, however, its very success may lead to its downfall. The Formica Corporation, for example, is operating under the threat that its trademark may be canceled simply because Formica has come to be the common descriptive name for decorative laminates. Similar fates have already befallen the makers of cellophane tape, trampolines, and yo-yos.

Patents

A **patent** *protects the invention or discovery of a new and useful process, an article of manufacture, a machine, a composition of matter, or an improvement on any of these.* Issued by the U.S. Patent Office, a patent grants the owner the right to exclude others from making, using, or selling the invention for seventeen years. After that time, the patent becomes available for common use. There's a point to the seventeen-year time limit. On the one hand, it guarantees the originator the right to make use of the discovery exclusively for a relatively long period of time, thus encouraging people to devise new machines, gadgets, and processes. On the other hand, it also ensures that rights to the new item will be released eventually. Other enterprises may be able to make use of it more creatively than its originator, and the public will reap the benefit.

Because of the enormous financial value of some patents, it is hardly surprising that they have been the subject of some fierce legal battles through the years. One of the most recent had to do with the laser. A physicist named R. Gordon Gould, after years of insisting that he had originated the laser's basic design in the late 1950s, finally convinced the U.S. Patent Office in 1977 that he was right. Gould was awarded patents covering most of the lasers now in use—throwing the laser industry into confusion and anger, particularly since most manufacturers had already been paying royalties to another firm that they thought owned the basic patents. The decision, in effect, created more questions than it solved—whether laser makers have to pay retroactive royalties to Gould, for instance, and what happens to the millions already paid to the dethroned patent holder—and still more years will probably be needed to untangle these new issues in court.

Source: Thomas P. Murphy, "The Wild Card Gets Wilder," *Forbes*, September 15, 1977, pp. 204–205.

which the government makes available to businesses ranging in size from the corner pizzeria to the Penn Central Railroad.

State governments, too, provide much-needed services and advice, including free employment services and, occasionally, financial aid. Sometimes the state and federal governments—plus, occasionally, local governments—even collaborate to benefit business. Such an alliance was formed during the winter of 1977, when Colorado spent more than $1 million in state and federal money on cloud seeding in an effort to save the Rocky Mountain ski resorts from a barren season. Lack of snow the previous winter had brought financial trouble to Colorado's ski industry—and to the state's tax coffers—and public officials considered the cloud-seeding investment well justified by the need to recapture business that had been lost to eastern ski areas.[8]

And finally, on the local level, government helps business in a number of ways—providing police, fire, water, and sewer services to the enterprises in its area. It's hard to imagine businesses operating without these basic services.

GOVERNMENT REGULATION OF NONCOMPETITIVE PRACTICES

If government contracts and financial aid are clearly benefits that most businesspeople would welcome, there are plenty of other government activities about which business opinion is much more divided. A good example is the government's regulation of non-competitive practices—an extremely complex area, as we shall see. This type of regulation has developed over the course of almost one hundred years.

THE HISTORICAL BACKGROUND

As we saw in our Enrichment Chapter on Business and the American Economy, business was given a free hand in the period of rapid industrialization after the Civil War. The Roman principle of *caveat emptor,* or "let the buyer beware," dominated the American business climate during that era. Frauds, swindles, and extraordinarily untruthful advertising were commonplace. And, not surprisingly, it was in this period that some of the country's greatest fortunes were made—by such tycoons as J. P. Morgan, Cornelius Vanderbilt, Andrew Carnegie, and John D. Rockefeller, all of whom took advantage of the lack of government restriction to create strong positions of power in certain key industries.

Some of the most ruthless practices in this ruthless age took place in the railroad industry. Train schedules during the 1870s were often established on a take-it-or-leave-it basis, with no consideration for customer convenience. With this type of scheduling, a line could run all of its trains at maximum load and thereby increase profits—a plan that was good for the railroad but bad for the public. Sometimes railroads even discriminated among towns, charging higher rates in some than in others.

Because of the high visibility of these unfair practices, the railroad industry was the first to feel the force of citizens' resentment. The wealth and power of the railroads were great enough to stifle public opinion for some time, but finally an organization of midwestern farmers, the National Grange, managed to win passage of a few laws that regulated railroad practices. Though most of these laws were later found to be unconstitutional, they marked a milestone in American history. They led to the passage of a congressional act to regulate commerce in 1887, known as the **Interstate Commerce Act**. This key act *was the first U.S. law to regulate business practice.*

Aimed squarely at the railroads, the Interstate Commerce Act was hailed as a sure means to put an end to abuses by such industries for all time. The hoped-for relief did not materialize, since the law contained too many weaknesses and loopholes to be effective for long. The legislation did, however, lead to the establishment of the Interstate Commerce Commission (ICC), a federal agency that still exists—with additional powers—operating as a regulator of interstate shipping rates.

LAWS CONTROLLING MONOPOLIES

Beginning with the Interstate Commerce Act in 1887, the body of government regulation grew, expanding to control monopoly in other industries and to protect the consumer.

The Sherman Antitrust Act

The principal tool of the monopolists was the **trust**, which is established when *one company buys a controlling share of the stock of competing companies in the same industry.* (One of the most notorious trusts was Rockefeller's Standard Oil Trust, established in 1882.) In industries dominated by trusts, competition was stifled and prices and profits climbed. Because of public outrage at this situation, Congress passed the **Sherman Antitrust Act** in 1890. The new law *declared that trusts and conspiracies "in restraint of trade or commerce" were illegal.* While the intent of the law was good, however, its vaguely worded provisions once again left loopholes large enough to permit many of the offending monopolies to stay powerful. As a result, Congress had to think again in order to discover a means of combating the growth of trusts.

The Clayton Act

To eliminate the defects of the Sherman Antitrust Act and boost competition, Congress passed the Clayton Act in 1914. The **Clayton Act** *amended the Sherman Antitrust Act, clearing up wording and forbidding specific actions that Congress saw as leading to monopoly.* Among the forbidden practices were **tying contracts**—*forcing buyers to buy unwanted goods along with goods actually desired;* setting up **interlocking directorates**, where *members of the board of one firm sit on the board of a competing firm;* acquiring large blocks of competitors' stock; and establishing discriminatory prices, other than discounts made "in good faith."

With that last provision—"in good faith"—Congress once again failed to state its purposes clearly. The Clayton amendments, like the act they were designed to amend, were simply too vague to do any real damage to monopolies.

The Federal Trade Commission Act

In the light of the difficulties the lawmakers were encountering, observers believed it might be advisable to try another approach—to outlaw unfair trade practices by very general laws and then establish a powerful federal commission that would continue to look for specific abuses. In 1914 President Woodrow Wilson pressed successfully for passage of a bill incorporating this concept, which would make up for the weaknesses of the Sherman and Clayton acts. The result was the **Federal Trade Commission Act**. This act, with its deliberately vague wording, *stated that "unfair methods of competition in commerce are hereby declared illegal." In addition, it set up a five-member commission empowered to define, detect, and enforce compliance with this and the Clayton act.* The Federal Trade Commission (FTC) is still very much in evidence; it acts on complaints made by business, and also takes action on its own initiative. A violator is given thirty days to answer a charge of unfair practice. If the commission is not convinced that the violator's excuses are valid, it issues a "cease and desist" order, requiring the violator to stop the offensive practice. A significant drawback of the FTC is that its effectiveness depends on the five people running it. Consequently, over the years, the quality of enforcement has ranged from very tough to not tough enough.

The years have brought with them new provisions to strengthen the original act further. In 1938 an amendment called the **Wheeler-Lea Act** *expanded the FTC jurisdiction to include practices that injure the public generally, in addition to those that specifically harm competitors.* It also declared illegal false advertising of foods, drugs, cosmetics, and therapeutic devices. And it gave the FTC the authority to increase the fines it imposes if a cease-and-desist order isn't obeyed within sixty days.

The Celler-Kefauver Act

In 1950 the **Celler-Kefauver Act** finally closed one of the most glaring loopholes in the Clayton Act, which had prohibited anticompetitive mergers only if they were made by stock acquisition. The new act *forbade anticompetitive mergers by other means as well, including acquisition of assets.* Other provisions of the 1950 amendment *gave the FTC general authority to approve mergers before they took place.* As a result, companies that wish to merge have to describe their plan to the FTC, which then furnishes an opinion on the merger's legality.

THE FIGHT AGAINST CONGLOMERATE MERGERS

Armed with the Celler-Kefauver Act, the FTC and the Justice Department moved vigorously against mergers

Greyhound Lines
Greyhound Lines of Canada
Korea Greyhound
Texas, New Mexico & Oklahoma Coaches
American Sightseeing Tours of Miami
Atlanta Airport Transportation
Brewster Transport
California Parlor Car Tours

Royal Hawaiian Transportation
Transportation Manufacturing Corporation
Universal Coach Parts
Vermont Transit
Walters Transit

Armour Food Company
Faber Enterprises
Greyhound Food Management
Post Houses

Prophet Foods
Restaura

Greyhound Support Services
Greyhound Temporary Personnel
Nassau Air Dispatch
Pine Top Insurance
Research Information Center
Travelers Express

Carey Transportation
Gray Line of New York
Gray Line of San Francisco
Greyhound Airport Services
Greyhound World Tours
Loyal Travel Service
Motor Coach Industries
New Mexico Transportation
Red Top Sedan Service

Greyhound Leasing & Financial Corporation
Greyhound Computer Corporation
Armour-Dial
Amour International
Armour Pharmaceutical
Bucilla Company
Malina Company

Aircraft Service International
Border Brokers
Consultants & Designers
Dispatch Services
Exhibitgroup
Florida Export Group
Freeport Flight Service
Greyhound Exposition Services
Greyhound Rent-a-Car

CURRENT ISSUES IN ANTITRUST ACTIVITY

The Justice Department's antitrust division has surfaced in some unexpected places recently. A look at the supermarket cereal shelves, for instance, might convey to the average consumer the idea of almost infinite variety. Yet according to the FTC, which investigated cereal companies in 1972, only three leading companies—Kellogg, General Mills, and General Foods—accounted for 86 percent of all industry sales! Using a strategy known as brand proliferation, the companies had divided the cereal market into pieces so small that they left no room for outside companies to find entry into the market worthwhile. While the lawsuit may run into the 1980s, a possible hint of the outcome emerged when related charges against Quaker Oats, which was also named in the original suit, were thrown out by a federal judge in 1978 for insufficient evidence.

Another target of antitrust activity has been the camera industry. In 1977 a small company named Berkey Photo successfully concluded its court battle against the giant Kodak, which it had charged with monopolizing the market for film, cameras, and color print paper. Berkey won, and Kodak faced a potential damage liability of $900 million. The decision also raised the possibility that companies in other industries might be encouraged to bring private suits against larger competitors rather than wait for the federal government to take action on its own. The case was of particular interest to corporate observers because, somewhat surprisingly, the trial jury was not swayed by Kodak's excellent public image or the unquestioned quality of its products—factors on which the defense had relied heavily.

GREYHOUND, CORPORATE OMNIBUS:
A COMPANY AND ITS SUBSIDIARIES

**Many of Greyhound's subsidiaries are
travel-related—but by no means all.**

FIGURE 2

Even General Motors, the biggest manufacturing business in the country, isn't hidden from the watchful eye of the Justice Department's antitrust division. In 1977 GM produced 56 percent of all the American-made cars sold in the United States, a gain of 10 percent since 1970. And it's estimated that GM's share of the market will go even higher, thanks to the company's success in meeting federal economy and pollution standards. Ironically, as a result of its ability to meet those standards, the auto giant may find itself in antitrust trouble with the government. In 1976 the FTC began an investigation of the automakers that may very well result in a move to break up GM.

Sources: "Too Many Cereals for the FTC," *Business Week*, March 20, 1978, pp. 166, 171; "The Legal Shockwaves of the Berkey Decision," *Business Week*, February 6, 1978, p. 48; and "You're Damned If You Do . . ." *Forbes*, January 9, 1978, pp. 33–36.

within industries that tended to result in monopolies. But meanwhile, during the late 1960s, there developed a sudden increase in another type of merger—**conglomerate mergers,** *mergers between firms in unrelated industries.* (For example, a restaurant chain might merge with a mattress manufacturer; or, for another example, see Figure 2.) At first little action was taken against conglomerate mergers, in part because it was unclear to government enforcers whether mergers across industries truly lessened competition in the traditional sense. But suddenly, in 1969, the government began to go after the giant conglomerates, beginning a struggle that is still going on today.

Why did the government change its position regarding conglomerate mergers? First of all, government economists had come to believe that such mergers *did* impair competition. A conglomerate might force its subsidiaries to buy from one another (for instance, the restaurant chain we have mentioned might be acquired by a housewares manufacturer and be required to buy all its kitchen equipment from this company). Or a conglomerate might obtain needed supplies (such as, in our example, aluminum and stainless steel) by taking over companies that manufactured these materials, rather than getting them from outside sources in competition with each other. Or a conglomerate might discourage smaller firms from entering fields in which the conglomerates held sway. And second, the government was spurred by growing protests from consumers. The public felt that lack of real competition, most visible in the oil industry, was causing needless inflation. (One economist placed the cost to consumers at $80 billion for 1973 alone.)[9] Neither President Nixon nor President Ford could ignore the enormous public outcry against rising prices.

Thus the 1970s became a period of increased pressure against anticompetitive actions of all sorts. In 1974, for example, the **Antitrust Procedures and Penalties Act** *increased the fines for violation of Sherman Act provisions to $100,000 for individuals and to $10 million for corporations. On top of that, it made violation of the law a felony rather than a misdemeanor, with a maximum jail sentence of three years.* Two years later, the 1976 **Antitrust Improvements Act** *required premerger notification for companies, including conglomerates, and it also empowered attorneys general at the state level to bring suit on behalf of injured consumers in their states.*

CATCHING UP: THE RESULTS OF ANTITRUST JUDGMENTS

Through judicial decisions such as Berkey v. Kodak, smaller companies are gaining support in their fight against industry leaders' domination.

In addition, other basic attitudes toward mergers and competition changed in Washington in the 1970s. The government began to look not only at the purely economic effect of mergers but at their political and sociological effects as well. Before, government experts had tended to assume that a merger might be allowable unless it curbed competition; but now they assumed that any big corporation's acquisition of another would have a negative impact on society. It became Washington's attitude that the prospective corporate buyer would have to prove that society would, in fact, *benefit* from the proposed merger, rather than being harmed by it. In other words, the burden of proof switched from the government to business.

Ironically, the new government attitude toward large mergers developed just at the time when industries were beginning to be hurt by foreign competition, and spokesmen for many industries were claiming that mergers were necessary to keep threatened companies strong. The steel industry argued that it was obliged to arrange mergers simply in order to hold its own against foreign competition in the market. The LTV

Corporation and the Lykes Corporation, in particular, argued that since they were losing money, their joining together would actually *foster* competition by enabling them to hold their own against other companies. Even another branch of administration, the Commerce Department, publicly recommended that antitrust enforcers in the Justice Department stop blocking mergers and start finding ways for smaller steel producers to get together instead.[10] What types of antimerger action will the government take as business becomes increasingly international? At present, this question is still unanswered.

GOVERNMENT REGULATION OF NATURAL MONOPOLIES

Despite the actions that have been taken against threats to competition, the law does not consider all monopolies to be harmful to the public. In fact, in certain industries, competition may even hurt the consumer. Such businesses, called **natural monopolies**, are those that *provide services that it would be unnecessary or impractical to duplicate*. The telephone company is a natural monopoly; so are public utilities.

Consider what would happen if two electric companies were competing for business in your community. Rates would actually be higher than they are now. The reason? Often the power that produces electricity is virtually free, in the form of running water or the energy locked in the atom's nucleus. The biggest factor in the cost of electricity would be the company's investment in generators and wiring. If, instead of enforcing competition, the government allows one company to monopolize electricity production, that company can spread the cost of capital equipment over the greatest possible number of customers—and the cost to each customer can be reduced.

REGULATING COMMISSIONS

Though natural monopolies are indeed monopolies, this is not to say that they have no limits on what they can charge their customers. The government has enacted a wide range of legislation to control these businesses and others that are powerful for similar rea-

FIGURE 3

UNCLE SAM AT THE CONTROLS: GOVERNMENT AGENCIES AND THE INDUSTRIES THEY REGULATE

CAB

The Civil Aeronautics Board (CAB) fulfils regulatory functions similar to those of the ICC, but its powers are restricted to air transport. It sets rates for passenger and air mail transport, approves routes for domestic and overseas airline companies, and establishes standards of service.

FPC

The Federal Power Commission (FPC) regulates interstate electric rates. It has jurisdiction over interstate transmission lines, sale of electric utilities, and transmission of natural gas by pipeline.

ICC

The Interstate Commerce Commission (ICC) regulates the rates and trade practices of companies engaged in interstate commerce. It is concerned with transport by rail, water, and motor vehicles.

FCC

The Federal Communications Commission (FCC) regulates interstate telephone, telegraph, radio, and television communications. It sets rates for wire communication and community area television, and licenses commercial broadcasters and assigns them frequencies.

sons. Control is vested in a number of specialized public-service commissions at the federal, state, and local levels, which keep an increasingly strict eye on the pricing and planning activities of the utilities they regulate. (See Figure 3.) The public-service commissions are particularly watchful over the power companies, which are notorious for their rate-increase requests.

Nearly every state has commissions similar to those on the federal level, and these agencies control statewide natural monopolies. Local public utilities, however, are often regulated by the communities they serve.

REGULATION OF RETAIL PRICES

As we've seen, the primary goal of the Sherman, Clayton, Celler-Kefauver, and most of the FTC acts was to limit anticompetitive practices on the manufacturing end of industry. Firms that dealt directly with individual customers on the retail level were considered too small to threaten competition; thus for a time they remained unregulated by the federal government, except in matters connected with advertising. Nevertheless, as the nation struggled to free itself from the Depression of the 1930s, free competition was threatened by a new type of marketing enterprise—giant retailing businesses, such as chain merchandisers and discount houses, which could buy in huge quantities and sell cheaply to millions of customers. To protect small retailers and wholesalers against uncurbed monopoly among these marketing enterprises, Congress passed the Robinson-Patman Act in 1936.

THE ROBINSON-PATMAN ACT

The Robinson-Patman Act of 1936 amended the sections of the Clayton Act dealing with price discrimination. It aimed to outlaw discrimination against buyers as well as sellers, by providing that no seller could make a price concession—that is, mark down its prices—to any one buyer without giving all other buyers the same concession on a proportional basis. This rule applied to concessions for advertising as well as price concessions. The act also forbade suppliers to offer any quantity discounts that might tend to lessen competition. The only permissible quantity discounts were those that reflected decreased costs; and if a seller offered a discount on this basis, all purchasers of an equal quantity of goods had to receive the same discount.

How did these provisions actually affect retailing? In one case in Utah, the Robinson-Patman Act saved the day for a pie company. When the Utah Pie Company began producing its wares it had three main competitors: Pet Milk, Continental Baking, and Carnation, all giant marketers that produced their pies outside the state. Despite this formidable competition, Utah Pie began to win an increasing share of the market. In an effort to halt this growth, the three larger companies cut their prices in the Utah market while holding the prices of their pies constant in other geographic areas—and thus substantially reduced Utah Pie's market. Thanks to the Robinson-Patman Act, however, the three giants were found guilty of price discrimination in an attempt to destroy a competitor, and were obliged to discontinue their discriminatory pricing policy.[11]

TAXATION: ANOTHER GOVERNMENT ACTIVITY THAT AFFECTS BUSINESS

The people who work for the friendly folks who make Coors Beer were in for a series of shocks a few years back. Suddenly, unexpectedly, their paychecks went up substantially, some as much as 30 percent. Their checks stayed at these new high levels for two months. Then, just as suddenly, salaries apparently fell from the Rocky Mountain high levels to about a third of what they had been before the sudden increase. What had happened? The Coors management had wanted to drive a point home to its employees about the magnitude of taxes. For two months it didn't deduct any taxes from payroll checks and then, in the third month, it deducted three months' worth of taxes. Coors employees got the point: the taxes we pay are by no means inconsiderable.[12]

The Coors management believed we pay too much in taxes—and they wanted their employees to believe this too. But what are the actual facts? How *do* taxes affect individuals and businesses? Where does tax money go, and what is it used for? These are some of the points we'll discuss here.

1976, accounting for over 24 cents of every tax dollar.[14]

IF THE TAX IS ON INDIVIDUALS, HOW DOES IT AFFECT BUSINESS? The individual income tax has a strong, though indirect, effect on business practice. For one thing, the majority of small businesses are partnerships or sole proprietorships in which, for tax purposes, the profits are considered to be the personal income of the owners. For another thing, as we've seen in the Coors episode, the law requires all employers to withhold from their employees' pay a percentage of earnings equivalent to the individual income tax rate. This withheld money is periodically forwarded to the federal, state, and local tax agencies to be credited to the employees' tax accounts. Although the money so collected comes strictly from the employees, the company pays all expenses of administering the pay deductions, and these costs can be high for a large company.

Corporate income taxes

A corporation pays tax on profits similar to that paid by an individual. The federal tax rate for corporations is 17 percent of the first $25,000 in income; 20 percent of income in the $25,000–50,000 range; 30 percent of income from $50,000 to $75,000; 40 percent of income from $75,000 to $100,000; and 46 percent of income over $100,000.[15] Many state and local governments also impose corporate income taxes, but at lower rates. Corporate income taxes rank third as a source of federal revenue, providing about 15 cents of every dollar raised. For the states, these taxes constitute about 5 cents per dollar.[16]

Since most of this country's large corporations operate abroad also, they must pay income taxes in foreign countries as well. The tax system and corporate income tax rate of a country thus influences a business's decision to operate in that country. It should be noted that the U.S. government allows American corporations a **tax credit**, *an amount deducted from*

Overall, taxation has two main purposes: it is a way for the government to collect revenue to pay for government services, and it is a way for the government to impose certain trade restrictions.

REVENUE-COLLECTING TAXES

Someone has to foot the bill for government, and that is the purpose of the five major revenue-producing taxes we pay: Social Security, individual income, corporate income, property, and general sales. The revenue-collecting taxes are intended to equalize the tax burden by passing the cost of government on to those who can best afford it, or those who use government services most.

You'll recall that we discussed Social Security in Chapter 5. Here, let's look at the four other taxes and their impact on business.

Individual income taxes

Income taxes form the largest source of revenue for the federal government, accounting for over seventy-seven cents of every tax dollar collected by the United States in 1976.[13]

Several states and many cities also levy taxes on the earnings of their residents and on the earnings of persons working but not living within their boundaries. The individual income tax ranked as the fifth greatest source of general revenue at the state level in

the money on which they're taxed here, for taxes paid to a foreign government.

Sales taxes

Nearly all states and a number of city and county governments levy general sales taxes against virtually all retail sales—with the exception, in some areas, of true necessities such as food and drugs.

Sales taxes vary considerably with the area. In some states, such as New Hampshire, there is no such tax at all, while in other localities the sales tax can range all the way up to the 8 percent charged in New York City, with its combination of state and local taxes. The national average, however, is between 3 and 5 percent.[17] About 32 cents of every dollar of state money is derived from general sales taxes, while at the local level it's 9 cents per dollar.[18]

HOW DOES THE SALES TAX AFFECT BUSINESS? It should be noted that businesses don't pay a general sales tax on merchandise they buy for resale. The sales tax does affect business, however, in that it increases the prices customers have to pay, and thus it may make the mer-chandise less attractive. Also, as with personal income taxes, the business is required to collect the sales tax, and to pay the accounting expenses associated with that operation.

Property taxes

Taxes on property provide about 26 percent of the revenue that supports local governments.[19] A few states also collect property taxes; the federal government does not. Property taxes are most often based on **assessed valuation**, meaning *the taxing agency's estimate of the property's value.* In determining this valuation, emphasis can be placed either on the land itself or on the buildings and improvements on the land. The tax is computed as a fixed amount of money per thousand dollars of assessed value, or a fraction of the assessed value.

Because business is a large owner of property, it naturally pays a large portion of the property tax in communities that aren't primarily residential, particularly when the tax emphasis is on the value of buildings. A twenty-story office tower, for instance, is worth far more than a filling station. In addition, commercial

---

BUILDING YOUR BUSINESS VOCABULARY

TYPES OF REGULATORY AND RESTRICTIVE TAXES

Excise taxes

A number of items are subject to **excise taxes**—*taxes intended to help control potentially harmful practices or to help pay for services used only by certain people.* The United States imposes excise taxes on the making of gasoline, tobacco products, liquor, firearms, tires, automobiles, sugar, and fishing tackle. Excise taxes are also levied on certain services of national scope, such as air travel and telephone calls. In addition, all states levy excise taxes on gasoline and liquor, and some impose them on the sale of luxury items, such as furs and fine jewelry.

Income from federal excise taxes must be used for a purpose related to the tax. The gasoline tax, for example, goes toward funding road-building projects. Through the gasoline tax, the burden of paying for the roads is in large part borne by those who use them most.

Through taxes on cigarettes and liquor, the government tries to discourage people's use of these substances. (Needless to say, the method has not entirely succeeded.) Some excise taxes, such as those on legally produced narcotics and firearms, are so small that they're almost purely regulatory. Through the existence of these taxes, the government can place rigid controls on their manufacture and, it's hoped, their use.

Excise taxes are imposed on either the manufacturer, the retailer, or both. Ultimately, however, the consumer pays these taxes, since they are often hidden in the prices of goods. Because these hid-

property is usually taxed at a higher rate than houses and farms.

REGULATORY AND RESTRICTIVE TAXES

Regulatory and restrictive taxes produce revenue, but that is not their main purpose. Instead, some are levied because they allow government to temper potentially harmful practices; others are imposed to protect American business against foreign competition (see box).

THE WEDGE THEORY QUESTION: DO HIGH TAXES HINDER ECONOMIC GROWTH?

As the owners of Coors Beer so pointedly showed their employees, the tax bite is even bigger than most people realize. Some economists argue that high taxes are the only means of paying for the benefits and services we have come to expect in our increasingly complex soci-

den taxes are often subject to the general sales tax as well, the consumer is hit twice.

Customs duties

Goods brought into this country are subject to *import taxes*, or **customs duties.** These taxes are selective; they vary with the product and its country of origin. Designed to protect American business against foreign competition, customs duties have the effect of raising the price of imports to a level comparable to similar American-made merchandise. Congress often passes or increases customs duties in response to lobbying pressure from industry or labor.

Because of their effects on international trade, customs duties have been used with increased frequency as a weapon in foreign policy, the goods of friendly nations being taxed at rates below those of indifferent or openly hostile countries.

ety. Other economists, however, argue that when it comes to taxes, less might very well mean more.

These economists are concerned about what they call the **wedge principle**. They point out that over the years, *taxes have driven an even larger wedge between the cost of labor or investment capital and the after-tax receipts of the worker or investor.* In other words, the bigger the tax bite, the less incentive people have for working or investing. And when these incentives are destroyed or diminished, the whole economy suffers, resulting in lower tax revenues and more unemployment in the long run. If, as the wedge theorists maintain, the bigger the tax bite, the worse off the economy, then the fiscal health of our country may not be very sound.

How, you may well ask, would cutting taxes help the economy? According to the wedge theory proponents, tax cuts could save the country money in the following way: Suppose that a reduction in the rate of corporate income tax averaging 5.5 percent were to go into effect. This reduction might cost the federal government $8 billion in direct losses over the course of ten years. At the same time, however, the wedge between cost of labor or investment and after-tax receipts would be lessened as well. With more spendable and investable money in their pockets, corporations could expand during those ten years. In that time, the theorists estimate, this money could generate sufficient growth in sales, investment, and employment to account for about $17 billion in actual revenue gains. Thus, while the Treasury might be out $8 billion on the one hand, it might accumulate $17 billion on the other, and so might be a total of $9 billion ahead.[20]

Are the wedge theorists right? At the moment, no one can really be certain. If the Congress can be convinced that by lowering taxes it will actually boost the economy, you can be certain that taxes will come tumbling down during the next election year. But what to do about taxes is a political question that has yet to be answered.

One response to the tax question came in loud and clear from California, where voters dramatically endorsed Proposition 13, an amendment to the California state constitution that cuts down the state's power to tax homeowners. Whether this voter uprising will give rise to an avalanche of tax reform in other states remains to be seen. As of this writing, seven other states are considering bringing legislation similar to California's Proposition 13 up for a vote.

CHAPTER REVIEW

Much of the interaction between government and business is cooperative. The government enlists the assistance of business for certain goods and services. In some situations, business needs and seeks the support of government. Types of government assistance include loans, statistical information, and protection of copyrights, patents, and trademarks.

Congress has taken a number of steps to restrain monopoly and other noncompetitive business practices that weaken free enterprise. Important antitrust laws are the Interstate Commerce Act (1887), the Sherman Antitrust Act (1890), the Clayton Act (1914), the Federal Trade Commission Act (1914), the Wheeler-Lea Act (1938), the Celler-Kefauver Act (1950), the Antitrust Procedures and Penalties Act (1974), and the Antitrust Improvements Act (1976). In recent years the government has taken a tough stand against the noncompetitive practices of conglomerates.

Sometimes monopoly is considered to be in the public interest. Natural monopolies, such as public utilities, are regulated by commissions at the federal, state, and local levels.

In order to protect small retailers and wholesalers against marketing monopolies, Congress enacted the Robinson-Patman Act (1936) to regulate retail prices.

Government also interacts with business by exercising its taxing powers. There are two major forms of taxation: revenue-raising and regulatory. Revenue-raising taxes include Social Security, those on individual and corporate incomes, sales taxes, and property taxes. Regulatory taxes, such as excise taxes and customs duties, not only produce revenue but also serve to equalize tax burdens, restrict potentially harmful practices, and protect American business.

KEY WORD REVIEW

Interstate Commerce Act
trust
Sherman Antitrust Act
Clayton Act
tying contracts
interlocking directorates
Federal Trade Commission Act
Wheeler-Lea Act
Celler-Kefauver Act
conglomerate mergers
Antitrust Procedures and Penalties Act
Antitrust Improvements Act
natural monopolies
tax credit
assessed valuation
wedge principle
excise taxes
customs duties
copyright
trademark
generic terms
patent

REVIEW QUESTIONS

1. In what ways does business help and cooperate with government?

2. How does government help business?

3. Describe some of the monopolistic abuses that led to the passage of the Interstate Commerce Act and the Sherman Antitrust Act.

4. List the major antitrust laws and briefly describe their purposes.

5. Why must natural monopolies be regulated?

6. How does the Robinson-Patman Act help to regulate retail prices?

7. What are the revenue-collecting taxes that affect business?

8. Give an example of a regulatory tax and state how it regulates.

9. What arguments are used to support the wedge theory?

CASE 1

GOVERNMENT REGULATION AND THE INDEPENDENT TESTING LABS

Today government has become the strict guardian of consumer rights, and it can dictate to business exactly what it can and cannot do. For instance, the company that produced the paper on which this text is written spent its share of about $400 million on pollution-control devices in the past year to conform to federal standards. And airlines will have spent a total of about $3 billion by

1982 to meet federal antinoise standards. More monumental still will be the results of the new Toxic Substances Control Act, which will require the testing of more than 70,000 industrial chemicals already on the market.

How can business cope with meeting these deadlines and demands? In essence, it can't. A papermaker, an airline, or a chemical corporation has neither the time nor the manpower to ensure that federal standards are being met. Fortunately for all concerned, however, a relatively new branch of business has stepped in to fill the breach: the independent testing laboratory. Today there are an estimated 2,000 to 2,500 private testing laboratories, and their business is growing at approximately 20 percent per year—largely as a side effect of government regulations imposed on their clients.

Testing has become such a big business that specialization is now commonplace. The biggest and oldest segment of the testing laboratory industry is devoted to work on consumer and industrial hardware: everything from the blow-dryer you used on your hair this morning to the latest artificial kidney for hospital use is subject to laboratory testing for safety, performance, and reliability. Another major branch of the testing laboratory business works on soil and building-material analysis for construction of such projects as bridges, dams, and other structures. But the biggest bonanza in the testing laboratories has been in the life science testing market, which includes scrutiny of products such as chemicals, food additives, drugs, cosmetics, and tobacco. News that means trouble for manufacturers and consumers alike—the presence of

cancer-causing agents in plastics, drugs, cigarettes, and food preservatives—can spell additional profits for the laboratories engaged to test these products, and the same holds true for those laboratories specializing in environmental testing.

Yet despite the boom in the testing industry, laboratories are facing some problems. For one, the ever-increasing complexity of the tests required by the government provides a built-in limitation. The analysis of each and every product under study takes far longer today, because the elements need be examined more thoroughly than ever before. It's not uncommon for a single product to remain in a laboratory for a year or more. Likewise, the increasingly high standards called for by the government mean a greater need for skilled laboratory personnel—a need which at this moment isn't being met. A shortage of toxicologists, pathologists, and microbiologists in particular has stopped many laboratories from accepting all the work they might otherwise want. Worst of all, overheads are soaring: increasingly costly personnel, more and more sophisticated equipment, and product liability insurance costs that have quadrupled in recent years all cut into the laboratories' profit margins.

And now, ironically, the government has put forward new regulations that will regulate the testing industry itself. New governmental codes will require testing facilities to expand their staffs and revise their procedures—the aim being to improve the reliability of laboratory test data so that experiments can be duplicated, when necessary, to verify results. It's expected that compliance with the government's regulations will raise industry overhead even further—perhaps by 30 percent. That, in turn, means that laboratory fees will continue their upward spiral. In the past

five years alone, the cost of a typical two-year rat study has jumped from $60,000 to $150,000.

Is government intervention in the testing laboratory industry warranted? The FDA has had unpleasant experiences with laboratories that have kept inaccurate data and mishandled animal experiments. Conceding the tainted image associated with independent testing facilities, some industry leaders—particularly those from the larger laboratories—even welcome government intervention. For the smaller laboratories, however, which can't afford to comply with costly government codes, FDA and EPA action could mean the end of the scientific testing bonanza.

Adapted from "Heyday of the Testing Labs," August 1978 DUN'S REVIEW

1. Suppose you ran one of the life science laboratories in which personnel shortages are a constant problem. To recruit qualified scientists, you can either raid the staffs of other facilities and lure talented people with higher salaries, or you can set up college scholarships to increase the talent pool for your own firm and your competitors. Which solution would work better in the long run? Why?

2. Inflation seems to be a fact of life in the independent testing laboratory industry. What effect will this have on the future of firms both large and small?

3. Independent testing laboratories, like many other businesses, have been known to cut corners to save costs. Is this good for the industry in the long run?

4. What do increasingly high testing standards mean for consumers? Who will pay for these raised standards?

TECHNOLOGY, BUSINESS, AND THE FUTURE

Contrary to many predictions that we'd never make it this far, the twentieth century is well on its way to becoming the twenty-first. In fact, many of today's college students should be near the heights of their careers on January 1, 2001, when the new century begins. What sort of world will be in your charge on that day? One thing is certain: that world will be even less like today's than today's world is like that of the late 1950s. Of course, there may be a '70s revival, with quaint disco music and John Travolta imitators, but essentially the world will be a different place.

This chapter outlines some of the changes that may appear by the year 2000. Technological change may enable us to master space and solve the energy problem; social change may bring us new values and new ways of spending our time. All this means rapid change for business, and business planners are already getting ready to meet the challenge.

WHAT WILL THIS CHAPTER FOCUS ON?

After reading the material in this chapter, you will understand and be able to discuss:

- the speed with which our society is likely to change by 2000
- some ways in which the world economic system is likely to change
- some of the ways we may be using space in the near future
- some of the major new programs in the field of energy
- some of the new ways we may use television in the future
- current trends in family size and family income, and their implications for business in the future
- some facets of the future development of the entertainment and recreation industries

 The executive presses the button of the dictating machine built into his desk. He recites the date—April 3, 2000—then he dictates his letter to a prospective customer. Next he presses another button in the word-processing system, and his spoken words are transformed into a written letter by a computer that can "read" and process vocal impulses. Just seconds later, the letter appears on the executive's video display terminal (VDT). All he has to do is read it through to make sure there are no mistakes—and the letter is completed, without the aid of a secretary.

Sounds incredible? He'll do some other surprising things too. For one thing, he won't use the mails, because it has become far too costly and time-consuming to send a simple letter through the post office. Instead, he will merely type in the telephone number of his prospective customer, who is 2,000 miles away, and press a command button that will transmit the letter via telephone satellite to the customer. In virtually no time at all the customer's own VDT will emit a beep letting her know that a letter has been received. She will tap a key that says "incoming communications display," and the letter will appear on her screen. She'll read the letter, nod at the terms, and dictate her own letter back to the executive agreeing to the terms of the transaction. In a few minutes, without the services of secretaries or the postal service, without typewriters, paper, or pens, two people will have completed a long-distance business deal. Twenty years earlier it might have taken weeks and much expense to complete the same deal.

It may all sound like a fairy tale to those of us who are still stuck in the twentieth century. But there was a time earlier in this century when landing on the moon, electronic data processing, satellite television transmission, and supersonic jet flight all sounded like fairy tales—yet all these became reality.

THE INCREASING SPEED OF CHANGE

Our little scenario from 2000 may or may not be accurate. But the chances that we—or at least some of us—may live in a world like that are pretty good. In *Future Shock*, published in 1970, Alvin Toffler observed that change was accelerating, and "technology feeds on itself": the technological changes of the next twenty years will be far more dramatic than those of the last twenty. Toffler also pointed out that knowledge was growing at an accelerating pace. "Prior to 1500," he wrote, "by the most optimistic estimates, Europe was producing books at a rate of 1,000 titles per year . . . By 1950, four and a half centuries later, the rate had accelerated so sharply that Europe was producing 120,000 titles a year . . . And by the mid-sixties, the output of books on a world scale, Europe included, approached the prodigious figure of 1,000 titles per *day.*"[1] If we follow Toffler's reasoning, we become convinced that the world of the very near future will indeed be startlingly different from the one we know.

Exactly what will 2000 be like? No one knows for sure. Some people suspect that a nuclear holocaust will wipe out every major city by then, leaving the world networked with the smoldering ruins of weapons technology. Others believe that the East and West will join hands and march together peacefully—though with differing philosophies—into the twenty-first century. And others, no doubt, feel that the cold war will continue to linger. In this chapter, our object is not to make definite predictions. We will simply suggest some of the kinds of changes we may see—particularly those with an impact on business.

HOW IS THE WORLD ECONOMY LIKELY TO CHANGE?

Today there are thousands of experts in the field of economics who devote much of their time to trying to determine the future course of our country and our world. No one knows how many of their predictions will be correct—particularly since at any time, unforeseen technological discoveries or political events may occur that could profoundly alter the course of the future. Certain interesting changes have, however, been suggested.

One of the changes predicted by an eminent futurist is that around the year 2000 the United States economy will be surpassed by that of Japan. Herman Kahn, of the Hudson Institute, predicts in fact that the Japanese, whose economy is growing at a far greater rate than ours, will match the American per-capita income by about 1990. By 2000 Japan "may surpass the United States in total GNP, making Japan the largest economic power in the world. If not this they will at least very likely equal or pass the Soviet Union in GNP at that point, if they have not already done so earlier. In any case this will be an economic, financial and technological superstate, and probably also a military and political superpower."[2] Meanwhile, there are other economic experts who see West Germany or Brazil as the superpowers of the future. Many other smaller nations are growing faster than the United States, but it may take them a hundred years or more to start rivaling our economy.

Why is the United States losing ground economically? One factor often identified as a major, if not *the* major economic problem in the United States, is inflation. Inflation makes American-produced goods more expensive, so other countries buy fewer goods from us. Higher wages here also encourage manufacturers to move or build in foreign countries where labor is cheaper. These factors tend to slow down economic growth.

THE ECONOMIC FUTURE OF THE UNITED STATES

Inflation will probably continue to be the chief political and economic issue in the United States for the next decade at least. And inflation may stay at relatively high levels. Two financial analysts, Roger Ibbotson and Rex A. Singuefield, have projected that inflation will average 5.4 percent a year between now and the year 2000—over twice as high as the average inflation rate for the last fifty years, which has been 2.3 percent.[3] Given this rate, a gallon of gasoline in 2000 would cost about $2.70; a pound of hamburger would be $2.80; a first-class postage stamp would be about 50¢; and a Big Mac with a side order of fries and a small Coke would cost about $5.50!

But even if inflation does slow down our economic growth, this does not mean that Americans will necessarily be forced to return to simpler, more austere patterns of living. As we have noted, technological development is highly likely to continue bringing us new industrial possibilities, and new machines and systems that will make our lives easier and more pleasant. And meanwhile new social trends, already beginning to appear, are likely to direct us to new, more leisure-oriented consumption patterns. We'll look at both these areas in the sections that follow.

THE TECHNOLOGY OF THE FUTURE

It isn't all that difficult to predict some of the directions in which technology will have progressed by the year 2000. Already, intensive work is being done in two fields that are crucial for the future—energy and space.

EXPLORING SPACE—AND MAKING USE OF IT

Until now, our journeys into space have been nothing more than exploratory probes; man has had to fight space in order to conquer it. In the next few years, though, it appears that we will finally start to *use* space. Already, we have satellites that enable us to beam television and telephone signals uninterrupted across the world, but that's only a start. We'll probably take advantage of space in a number of other ways.

Some experts feel that in the 1980s we will begin to establish electrical power stations in space. And, with the aid of space shuttles already under development, we will be able to put solar power stations into orbit around the world. These stations will be above the cloud cover and in constant view of the sun, so they will be able to operate perpetually. The energy they collect will be beamed to earth via microwave, picked up by ground stations, and converted into electric power that can run your electric shaver—or be used in industry.

We may also begin to establish factories in space. Space has a couple of advantages—zero gravity and nearly perfect vacuum—that are ideal for the manufacture of certain products that need a high degree of purity and structural uniformity. Already, the technology exists to send up teams of experts into space for ninety days at a time. Under the conditions mentioned above—which do not exist on earth—it will be possible to manufacture "superquality" laser objects, diodes, switches, and other sophisticated items that can't be duplicated in an earthbound factory.

And that's not all. Though the earth will be exhausting its low-cost supplies of aluminum, silicon, ti-

Scientists planning future operations in space have predicted that a large-scale solar-power satellite may be under development by the mid- to late-1990s. (Shown here, an artist's conception.) Not long after, we may see the first residential space colonies—which will pose new challenges to enterprising marketers.

tanium, iron, nickel, and other minerals, it may be possible to extract these resources from the moon. Some theorists say that a nuclear device could be exploded on the moon, loosening the surface crust, and the ore scooped into a space barge and also shipped off into orbit around the earth. Likewise, it may be possible to obtain minerals from nearby asteroids. Michael J. Gaffey, of the Massachusetts Institute of Technology, has been quoted as saying that one cubic kilometer of a nickel-iron asteroid that is nudged into an earth orbit would be worth about $5 trillion, and could supply us with enough nickel for 200 years and enough steel for 15 years at our current rate of use.[4]

All this sounds hopeful—but there's only one problem. Before we turn space into industrial parks and the moon into a mining camp, we will have to settle something else: the legal and political aspects of it all. Who owns space? Can we put all kinds of hardware into earth orbits without coordinating our programs with other nations? Even space must have its traffic laws. And who owns the moon? We have landed there, but what if the Soviet Union or some other country sends a modern-day Columbus to plant another flag on the lunar surface? And what happens when worn-out satellites start falling from the sky? This happened in 1978 when a piece of Russian space equipment plummeted to the ground in the barren wastes of northern Canada. What if one of them falls on Paris?

All these are tough questions, and we may have a difficult time answering them. But if we can find workable solutions to such problems, we may be ready to turn space into a profitable operation—maybe even by 2000.

HOW WILL WE SOLVE THE ENERGY QUESTION?

As we have noted, it may be possible to obtain energy via solar power stations in space—sometime in the future. But meanwhile, we have pressing energy needs right now. Ever since the Arab oil boycott of the early 1970s, engineers and scientists have been looking for something to replace crude oil, and in the next twenty-five years a large portion of their efforts will be devoted to developing new energy sources on earth and finding better ways to use the sources we already have.

Oil and coal

Several companies, as well as the U.S. Department of Energy, are working on projects that will allow oil to be extracted economically from stratified rock, or shale, that abounds in the western states. Oil producers say that conventional methods allow them to recover only about one-third of the crude oil in the earth, but there may be ways of bringing far more of the oil to the surface—such as steam flooding and injecting carbon dioxide into the deep underground reservoirs. (This technology may also bring to life oil wells that have already been considered played out.) Scientists are also working on methods of exploiting America's huge reserve of coal. Technology exists for coal gasification and liquefaction, but methods need to be developed to turn coal into a clean-burning fuel at a reasonable cost.

Nuclear energy

Although there is still much controversy on the subject, experts in the American power industry—the utilities and energy companies—generally feel that nuclear energy will eventually be able to replace oil as the leading source of power. One key fight is going on over the fast breeder reactor, a nuclear plant that uses plutonium but actually creates more plutonium than it consumes. (This has created another problem that concerns environmentalists, that of developing safe sites at which nuclear waste can be stored.) Another source of nuclear energy that is just beginning to gain some attention is nuclear fusion, the same source that is present in the sun or a hydrogen bomb. Though it may sound ominous, fusion actually is safer and cleaner than conventional nuclear energy: it doesn't produce the highly radioactive elements that the currently used nuclear fission does. The United States and other countries have started pouring billions of dollars into fusion research.[5]

Solar energy

While oil, coal, and nuclear processes are the energy sources with which the government and the energy companies are concerned today, many environmentalists, such as Barry Commoner, feel that more attention should be paid to the possibility of developing solar

NEW FUELS FOR AUTOMOBILES

Someday solar or nuclear power may provide all of the electricity for our homes, schools, and offices, but neither of them is likely to be able to power our automobiles. What are we going to do about this? The question of what we shall be putting in our gas tanks for the next twenty-five years may well be answered by a newly coined word, "gasohol."

Gasohol is made up of a combination of fermentation alcohol and gasoline, in varying proportions. One such combination—gasohol containing nine parts gasoline to one part alcohol—could be used in today's automobiles without making any changes in the engines. The resulting fuel would be somewhat more expensive than the gasoline we now use, but it might produce some benefits. First, it could help the United States reduce its dependency on foreign sources of petroleum. And second, the process by which it was manufactured would produce as a by-product dried grains that could be used as high-protein animal feed. Not surprisingly, the gasohol program has received support from farm lobbies: it would greatly increase the market for grains.*

There is no question about the technology for gasohol; it is simple and it exists. (The only barriers to

energy stations on earth. "Solar energy," Commoner writes in *The Poverty of Power,* "has been largely ignored in the current debate over national energy policy—usually dismissed as only a faint, distant hope, irrelevant to current concerns over the price and availability of fuel. When the facts are known, however, it turns out that solar energy can not only replace a good deal, and eventually all, of the present consumption of conventional fuels—and eliminate that much environmental pollution—but can also reverse the trend toward escalating energy costs that is so seriously affecting the economic system."[6]

Energy: old ideas and new ones

One of the interesting facets of energy is that its future may well be determined by new, more sophisticated work in technologies and resources that really aren't new in themselves—such as shale oil, batteries, and coal, which have been used for a hundred years or more. Our future may depend not so much on our developing totally new technologies as on our learning how to get more out of what we already have.

Perhaps the best example of this can be seen in methods used to unlock the energy potential in garbage. A plant that opened in Milwaukee in 1977 is designed to turn that city's garbage dump into a source of energy. The process starts by plucking materials that can be recycled—steel, tin, aluminum, paper, and glass—from the trash. After that, much of the residue is turned into a fuel that is used to generate electricity. Sounds amusing? It is—but it's also an excellent way to conserve resources.[7]

EXPLORING THE POTENTIAL OF TELEVISION

As we think about the major fields in which science and engineering will advance in the next twenty years, it is also interesting to think about the kinds of machines we will be using. Computers, whose future applications we have discussed in our Enrichment Chap-

setting up a gasohol program are political and economic.) There is far more question about another technology that is being pushed as a means for powering autos, namely, batteries. A battery car, if it

PRE-DENTED

could be successfully developed, would offer numerous benefits—it would create no pollution, it would have a simple motor mechanism, and it would need no other fuels. Accordingly, dozens of American companies have been experimenting in recent years with autos that could be run by batteries, and they have developed numerous working models of battery-powered cars. But so far most of these cars are nothing more than glorified golf-carts—they run,

but they don't run fast enough and far enough without being recharged to make them practical.

Despite these difficulties, slow but steady progress is being made, and it appears that in ten years or so the battery-powered car may be a reality. At first, it may be the second car in the family. It will probably have a top speed of fifty miles an hour and a range of 150 miles, which would make it suitable for short jaunts to the supermarket, for delivering small items in town, and for short-distance commuting.

* U.S. Department of Agriculture, "Gasohol from Grain— The Economic Issues," January 19, 1978.

ter on Computers and Data Processing, will of course form the core of our future technology. But there will also be significant advances in the use of television— including some advances that will directly affect the consumer.

Today, television is used mainly as a mass-audience medium; but in the future, it will probably become a more specialized tool capable of appealing to smaller audiences, principally through cable television technology that already exists. There will be an increase in programming aimed at special-interest groups: physicians may be provided with reception devices that will allow them to watch advanced surgery being performed, and lawyers may be able to watch landmark decisions being handed down by courts. And there will be more utilization of the two-way capability of cable television. A supermarket may be able to broadcast its sale items on a channel, and the viewer will be able to order the items by pressing a button as they appear on the screen. The order will be totaled and charged to the consumer's credit card. Later the consumer will go to the "drive-through" supermarket

where the groceries ordered earlier will simply be packed into the car. (In many cases, this will do away with the need for supermarkets to have parking lots.)

Meanwhile, big-screen television, coupled with cable TV programming and video cassettes or video disks, will mean changes in entertainment and recreation. Arthur D. Little & Company, the research and consulting firm, has predicted that the movie theater will start to become obsolete by 1985. The company projects that big-screen television, which became available in the late 1970s, will become a standard attachment to the entertainment center in every home, and most Americans will be able to see any movie in the comfort of their own homes.[8]

And the same will happen to spectator sports. Rather than travel several miles, or fight traffic jams and tight parking, fans will be able to pay perhaps the game ticket price and see the local football team play on their big screens. This doesn't mean, of course, that stadium owners aren't going to fight these trends and continue to entice fans to fill their seats: the newer stadiums will be equipped with their own huge screens so that fans in the stadium can see the same instant replays that fans see on TV.

SOCIAL TRENDS: DIRECTIONS FOR THE FUTURE

While the technology is being developed to bring us more free time and new forms of recreation, new social attitudes and demographic trends are working to make Americans more interested in leisure and more able to afford it. Let's take a look at these.

NEW DEMOGRAPHIC TRENDS AND WHAT THEY MEAN TO BUSINESS

As we have mentioned in our Enrichment Chapter on Consumer Behavior, population growth has slowed down in the past decade. There are many more single households, and families are smaller—a trend that has already had a significant impact on business. Smaller families mean that people will buy smaller cars. (The Detroit automakers have long been criticized for taking such a long time to detect the trend toward smaller cars, which led to a greater penetration of the American auto market by foreign manufacturers.) Families will be more mobile—a married couple with a small child is more likely to hop on an airplane headed for a resort than a family with four children—and more money will be spent per person. And women will be freed more easily from maternal duties and will be able to enter or return to the work force. All of this suggests that the family of the next few decades will be far better off financially than when families were larger— which means growth for a number of different types of business.

Leisure-time growth

Virtually all Americans have more leisure time, which has led to the creation of the greatest entertainment-recreation industry the world has ever seen. Fifty years ago, the entertainment business was relatively healthy: there were nightclubs (or speakeasies), vaudeville houses, movie theaters and legitimate theaters, circuses and burlesque houses. Then, the suc-cessive shocks of the Depression, World War II, and television virtually wiped out this industry; but now entertainment is booming again.

What are some of the new trends in leisure? For one thing, people tend more and more to go out—and spend money—to be entertained. While television still provides much of the show-business type of entertainment, young Americans are also flocking to discos and singles bars for personal contact that TV doesn't offer. Families that once went for a ride in the country now hop on a plane to visit Disneyland, Great Adventure, or Six Flags. And sports too are attracting more enthusiasts: the charter airline business is flourishing, cruise ships are booked up a year or more in advance, ski resorts from Colorado to Austria are crowded with young and old Americans. Amazingly, according to an A. C. Nielsen report in the mid-1970s, the number of tennis players in the United States tripled in less than five years—and many of them became members of hundreds of indoor and outdoor tennis clubs that sprang up across the country.[9]

The convenience revolution

Yet another trend related to increased affluence is the growing American taste for convenience in all forms. We've already seen the approach of the Convenience Revolution in the convenience foods, including cake mixes, Hamburger Helper, and TV dinners in their little tinfoil pans. And in the last few years, we've seen the incredible growth of the fast-food industry. Each year, Americans eat a greater percentage of their meals away from home, and it is estimated that sometime in the 1980s more meals, overall, will be eaten away from home than in the home.[10] And convenience will be the key: while some people still look for leisurely dining for an anniversary celebration or a special date, many who go out to eat are looking for a restaurant that will serve them fast—so they can get on to other things.

Then there is what Alvin Toffler calls the "throwaway society"—the world of paper plates, disposable towels, disposable shavers, plastic utensils, throwaway cigarette lighters, and the like.[11] Even more expensive and complex items will be disposable, because it will be cheaper to manufacture them than to pay people to repair them. You don't keep what you have—you get another instead.

GOVERNMENT AND BUSINESS: THEIR FUTURE RELATIONSHIP

Above, we've outlined some far-ranging changes in the ways Americans lead their private lives, and suggested ways these changes may affect business in our country. We should also note that in the surprisingly near future there may be some major changes in our public institutions and the way business relates to them.

Today, the federal government is engaged in more far-ranging functions than ever before—witness, for example, the current debate over national health insurance. And it is becoming increasingly involved in the activities of business, overseeing employee health and safety, pricing, packaging, transportation, financing, and countless other aspects of business. Some observers even believe that government regulation may be leading to the end of corporate enterprise and toward some sort of "state capitalism," a system which would hardly fit the American free-market philosophy, but which we may be approaching faster than we think.[12] Meanwhile, business, in turn, has been taking on some of the functions of government—such as working to preserve the environment and contributing to community educational programs.

Where will all this lead? Eventually, the day may come when executives have a double allegiance—an allegiance to the corporation but also a strong allegience to consumers and the general public. Already, as Harlan Cleveland notes in *The Future Executive,* 1972, there seems to be "a blurring of public and private," and perhaps by 2000 we will no longer be aware of the differences between these two areas. It seems a little far-fetched now—but it *may* happen.[13]

BUSINESS AND *YOUR* FUTURE

As you think about the changes we've mentioned, you may feel that what's to come will have such a strong impact that it will be almost too much to cope with. Yet—as you've probably noted—there's something intriguing about the future too. Not only will it challenge and surprise us, it will also lead us to find creative solutions to new problems—and perhaps bring forth capabilities we didn't know we had. For everyone curious about his own potential, the future offers opportunities for tremendous personal growth.

If you sense the excitement of the future, then maybe business is the field for you. Why? Precisely because business, perhaps more than most other parts of society, will be faced with the necessity of adapting rapidly to change. The key to business survival is planning, which means looking constantly to the future—and as we rush toward 2000, business people will need to be more alert than ever before to new patterns in the market, the labor force, the economy, and the legal and governmental environment. Business will need people with new ideas. And if *you* are interested in new technical developments, social patterns, and political trends—*you* can be very useful to any company you work for, even if you're just starting out. Or, you may be able to make an important contribution via a business of your own. Either way, your ability to solve problems flexibly and imaginatively will be a "plus" in the business world.

Your next question may be, "Where do I begin?" Clearly, it will be important to take a broad range of courses in the various functional areas—Management, Marketing, Finance, and Accounting and Data Processing. Likewise, you may want to investigate the possibility of working part-time in a business setting, or perhaps taking a summer internship, just to get a sense of what the business environment is really like and explore areas of business you think you might be particularly interested in. In addition, you may want to talk to people who are working in various business areas. They can tell you about the kinds of training they have, the problems they faced when they started work, and the parts of their work that most excite them now. And last, take a look at the section titled "Techniques for Entering the Job Market," in the Appendix of this book. It gives you concrete suggestions for writing your résumé, preparing for interviews, and planning your career strategy.

But most of all, develop your ability to do two things: to work cooperatively with other people, and also to be a "self-starter" when the occasion requires. You'll find that these two skills are an unbeatable combination—and furthermore, they make any kind of job enjoyable. As you develop them your confidence will steadily grow, and you'll begin to experience the most significant satisfactions of working in today's business community.

CHAPTER REVIEW

Change is accelerating in all parts of our society, and technological development, in particular, is rocketing ahead faster and faster. The result may be a number of new trends in our society.

First of all, the United States may lose its front-running position in the world economy because of inflation. But continuing technological development will probably help us maintain our high standard of living.

New scientific developments will probably enable us to take advantage of space. The satellites we already use will be improved to make communication across the globe even quicker. We may mine the moon for valuable minerals that have become scarce here on earth. And space offers an ideal location for manufacturing high-precision instruments.

Energy is another area where big changes may take place. Researchers are trying to develop new techniques for extracting more coal and oil from the earth, and extensive use of nuclear and solar energy may be just around the corner. Even garbage may help provide energy: it may be recycled and converted to fuel. We may soon see cars powered by new types of fuel, or even by batteries.

TV too may change. It is likely that more specialized programming will be offered. Also, the expected growth of videocassette and videodisk sales may make home TV-watching even more important in our lives.

There may also be an increase in leisure time and wealth. People may travel more, engage in sporting activities more, and purchase more convenience items. "Throw-away" products will grow in popularity; it will be cheaper to buy new items than to have them repaired.

Last, the federal government is already expanding its sphere of interest to include a deeper involvement in business. This trend is likely to continue, leading to more and more overlap between the responsibilities of the two institutions.

REVIEW QUESTIONS

1. Explain why inflation may force the United States to assume a less important economic position in the future.

2. Explain how we may be able to *use* space to our advantage in the years to come.

3. What are some of the approaches being considered as answers to our energy problems? Which do you think is the most promising?

4. How is the role of television likely to expand?

5. How is the family of the future apt to be different from the family of today?

6. What trends may we look for in the areas of leisure time and convenience items?

7. What changes are likely to take place in the relationship between government and business?

CASE 1

A STUDY IN CHANGE: THE U.S. CONVERSION TO METRICS

Even though the world is changing rapidly, change doesn't always take place smoothly and without opposition. Instead, it's likely to be a difficult, uneven process, involving much confusion and argument. Take, for example, America's switch to the metric system—the international standard of measurement based on units of ten. This switch is breezing along by the kilometer in some sectors of U.S. industry. But in others, its progress can be measured in millimeters.

On the one hand, there has been a fairly smooth transition in some of the nation's leading corporations, which have grown used to working with the metric system thanks to a fairly long tradition of international trade. For example, you may have noticed that the new family-size bottles of soda hold two liters; that's because all of the major U.S. soft-drink companies began converting to liter packing in 1976. Similarly, most 1978 model cars were built to metric specifications. While that doesn't affect the driver very much, it does make a difference to the mechanic, who must use tools calibrated with metric measurements rather than the more familiar inches. By 1982 it's expected that IBM will have completed its shift to metrics as well. The chemical industry should complete its conversion even sooner.

But what about other industries? So far, it would seem that the typical American consumer wants as little as possible to do with those foreign measurements. According to recent surveys, opposition to metric conversion is strongest among the older, the less educated, and the less affluent. And the opposition seems to be mounting. Drivers on the nation's highways, for instance, have begun a vigorous write-in campaign against signposts measuring distance in kilometers rather than miles. It's not surprising, then, that oil companies hesitate to convert their gas pumps from gallons to liters. And imagine how difficult it might be for a dress-shop owner to convince a customer that a slender 24-inch waist converts to a whopping 61 centimeters. As a result, clothing manufacturers have strongly resisted the metrification trend. Other industries, too, are lining up in firm opposition against the decimal-based unit of measure. [14]

1. The construction trade has shown virtually no inclination toward changing building specifications to the metric system. Can you figure out why this is so? (Hint: compare the position of a locally-oriented construction firm with that of a multinational corporation such as General Motors.)

2. Given Gallup Poll findings that people who oppose metric conversion tend to be older, less well off, and less educated, can you make some predictions concerning which industries will probably have the most trouble converting to the metric system? Which industries will probably have the least trouble?

CASE 2

HIP BUSINESS

Is a new breed of entrepreneur about to transform American capitalism into a spiritually rewarding—but still very profit-oriented—way of life? Robert Schwartz, a former entrepreneur with counterculture sympathies, believes the answer is yes. And not long ago he invited two dozen men and women to his Executive Conference Center in Tarrytown, N.Y., for a three-week course (tuition: $400) in which students could figure out how to change themselves and American business for the better. The students, whose wardrobes ran the gamut from tie-dye to pin stripe, included an accountant, a restaurant owner, an artist, a solar home builder, and a granola manufacturer.

The credo of this new entrepreneur is "right livelihood." That means that work should not only provide income, but also lead to self-growth, promote friendship and cooperation between people, and make possible satisfying contact with nature. For these new entrepreneurs, enterprises are to be believed in—not just invested in. Their goal is for their business values to express their personal values. Not only individuals but corporations as well are ready for this

kind of thinking, in Schwartz' view: corporations are realizing that in a heavily regulated economy, the best way to compete is by "growing better people."

But the course run by Schwartz was more than a philosophical bull-session. Students spent long hours talking about risk-taking, marketing strategies, profit margins and other technical matters. They drew up detailed business plans, and debated various models of entrepreneurial behavior. Indeed, in his lectures to these budding "counterculture capitalists," Schwartz stressed that only by accepting the hard facts of economic reality could they hope to create a workable alternative to America's current business way of life. "Just because you believe in vegetarianism," he said, "doesn't mean your vegetarian restaurant will flourish. The more dedicated you are to the idea, the more dedicated you must be to the business." [15]

1. How does the idea of "right livelihood" strike you as a business strategy? Does it seem to be a radical departure from the American business tradition, for instance, or a reaffirmation of what business used to stand for?

2. Do you think it would be easier to be the kind of entrepreneur described above in a system of pure capitalism, or in a system of modified capitalism?

3. What changes in the social or economic environment might make "right livelihood" products appealing to consumers?

PERSPECTIVE ON SMALL BUSINESS

LEGAL AND GOVERNMENTAL ENVIRONMENT

You are a small contractor who has taken on a job for a large city. After studying the city's specifications, you determined that the work could be completed within three months, but halfway through, you find that a great deal more work is required if you are to do a competent job—so much more that your costs will be one-third more than you had estimated. The city refuses to pay you more than your original bid. If you walk away from the job, the city will sue you and, perhaps worse, never award you another contract. So you finish the job and bill the city for the rest of your fee. The city still refuses to pay you. Now what? You hire an attorney and sue the city.

THE SMALL BUSINESS AND THE LAW

Not every small business owner will take a city to court, but most will need legal advice from time to time. Large corporations have numerous attorneys, either on staff or on retainer, to provide immediate answers to the many legal questions that arise. But the small entrepreneur must sort through the maze of laws with minimal help from the legal establishment. True, lawyers are happy to provide opinions at $65 or more per hour, but how can you be sure you are receiving the best advice? It is not uncommon to receive conflicting opinions from equally competent attorneys on the same case. Ultimately, the business person must

choose among them and be willing to live with the consequences of that decision.

Finding the right lawyer

The small business owner must seek the best qualified legal help available. You could start your search by asking your CPA or fellow entrepreneurs about lawyers they have used. Their advice should certainly be an improvement over a random choice from the Yellow Pages. Still, don't overlook the advertisements that attorneys are now able to place in newspapers. Perusal of such ads may help you identify attorneys who specialize in the areas of law in which you need help. Successful business people may be able to suggest a suitable law firm, since most large companies have departments that specialize in the problems of corporation and business law. Anyone they recommended would be a specialist, and your chances of receiving a competent opinion would be enhanced.

Once you have made your initial choice, you need to ask the attorney some probing questions concerning your particular case:

"Do you regularly handle cases similar to this one?" Even a business specialist may be unfamiliar with your particular problem. You don't want yours to be the first such case he's handled. The cost is by the hour, and the learning process can be lengthy.

"Are these types of cases an important aspect of your practice?" Maybe the last time the attorney handled a case such as yours was ten years ago. You want to know whether the attorney is familiar with current aspects of your problem.

"Were you successful in the past on this type of case?" You must have someone with a successful track record in your area of interest.

These are important questions. Ask them, and any others you can think of. It's your business and your money. You deserve the facts and the best opinion available. If any attorney should deceive you concerning his qualifications, you have a perfect right to demand compensation in court. Although this is not generally known, all practicing lawyers are protected by errors-and-omissions insurance to cover their oversights.

Making the best use of your lawyer

As a small business person you will inevitably have to deal with contracts many times in your career. An attorney's primary function is to interpret and define the essential ingredients of a contract, and eventually you will need his expertise. Since most of a small business's contractual relationships are simple, however, reading and education can help you to lower your legal costs. Many trade journals, associations, and newsletters provide low-cost solutions to common legal problems. Membership in these organizations and subscriptions to these services give you access to valuable insights on current problems.

To make the best use of any attorney you hire, be prepared to discuss your problem in detail, with your ideas clearly defined. Remember, a lawyer's function is to draft business contracts that protect your interests. Lawyers are not business people, and it is not their function to suggest profitable deals. Tell your attorney what you want to do, and he or she will tell you if you can do it legally and how to protect yourself if you go ahead. The better prepared you are, the better the service you will receive and the lower its cost.

ETHICS AND YOUR BUSINESS

Does a small business have a unique need for ethics—a need not felt by large firms? Yes. We're suggesting that a very definite difference exists, which a simple example will illustrate.

Let's say the widget industry, producing an essential consumer item, is composed of three large companies that produce 80 percent of all widgets sold. Is a code of ethics essential for their success? We think not, for this reason: All three companies have high-volume production assembly lines, and most of the widgets they produce are of acceptable quality. Their emphasis on volume, however, weakens quality control. This downplay of quality control produces a relatively low but predictable percentage of inferior widgets, commonly called "lemons" or "goofs." The reason is simple: the faster the assembly line, the greater the incidence of errors. Do these goofs affect the overall sales of each company? Not really. When a consumer buys one of these poor-quality widgets, dissatisfaction forces him to switch brands on the next purchase in the hope of obtaining greater satisfaction. The odds are in the consumer's favor. Since each of the three companies will experience this brand switching in the same degree, the poor-quality items do not actually deter sales. The large corporations are aware of this fact, and they can concentrate on marketing and management to increase profits rather than on strict control of quality.

Now the question is, can a small firm operate in this manner and succeed? It cannot. Usually the existence of a small firm is due largely to the uniqueness and quality of its service or product. Most of its clientele may be composed of consumers dissatisfied with the impersonal service and mass-produced goods provided by the large firms. In fact, word-of-mouth advertising is absolutely essential to the growth of any small business. It is generally assumed that each new customer has at least five friends or associates who are influenced by each other's actions. For each new customer who is satisfied, five others will patronize your company, and you will begin to develop a loyal customer base. This building process will continue as long as customers are satisfied with your product or service—and no longer.

The reverse of this building process has a devastating effect. When you fail to stand behind your product and lose a customer, that dissatisfied former customer will spread the bad word about your company. This kind of adverse publicity can doom a small firm.

All successful small business owners attribute a major portion of their success to word-of-mouth advertising. Other forms of advertising and image building are of course essential to success, but the goodwill created by fair treatment of each customer is the basic foundation on which small firms' profits rise.

TRADEMARKS, BRAND NAMES, AND OTHER FORMS OF COMPANY IDENTIFICATION

Your brand name, company name, and other forms of company identification must project an accurate picture of your firm or product. Kool-Aid is widely advertised as a drink that will satisfy your thirst on hot days. The name suggests an aid to body cooling—excellent product identification!

In choosing a brand name, special advertising identification, and your company's name, you will need legal protection. Some advertising material must be copyrighted. Brand names and trademarks must be registered. These procedures are inexpensive and provide necessary protection. Copyright forms are available from the Library of Congress, Washington, D.C. Trademark information is contained in a booklet available from the U.S. Department of Commerce.*

* Richard H. Buskirk and Percy J. Vaughan, Jr., *Managing New Enterprises* (St. Paul, Minn.: West Publishing Co., 1976), p. 218.

Your company's name can be protected by incorporation or by statement.

Incorporation

When a business is incorporated, it is protected throughout its existence within the state in which it is incorporated. The name may also be reserved in other states if the corporation meets their individual requirements.

Statement

The name of a nonincorporated business can be protected by the county in which it is located if its owner files a statement of fictitious business name. The names of the owner and the company ("John Doe dba [doing business as] Super Squeegee Service") and your address are filed at the county seat and published for three weeks in the public notices section of the local newspaper of record. This procedure will protect a business name for five years; it may be repeated at five-year intervals as long as the business exists.

PATENTS AND NEW PRODUCTS

The purpose of a patent is to protect an inventor from having his idea or product appropriated by another firm or individual. In reality, the process is so costly and complex that the ordinary person seldom receives the protection that is theoretically available. Any inventor will need the services of an expensive patent attorney, both to obtain the patent and to defend it in court against infringements. The courts are not always favorable to the inventor.

Assuming one is granted a patent by the U.S. Patent Office two or three years after it was filed, the patent may not really mean much after all; it may be challenged in court. In a very real sense, no patent is valid until the U.S. Supreme Court says so and they don't say it often. The bulk of patent cases taken before the U.S. Supreme Court are declared to be void because they do not truly represent new inventions. The courts have rather severe tests of invention.*

As you can see, the U.S. Patent Law is an adversary law, and the courts offer the only final protection. So the small business owner must consider all the potential costs and risks involved when building a business around a product that is supposedly protected by a patent.

UNCLE SAM AND SMALL BUSINESS

All statutory and common law is generally applicable to all businesses equally. Very small businesses, however, are free from certain aspects of statutory law: companies with fewer than eight employees are not required to comply with regular reporting procedures of the Occupational Safety and Health Administration (OSHA), and companies with fewer than fifteen employees need not initiate the affirmative action programs otherwise required under the Equal Employment Opportunity Act (EEOA).

* Ibid., p. 219.

The Small Business Administration

For the small business sector, the most important of all government agencies is the Small Business Administration (SBA). The SBA was created in 1953 to assist the small firm with its unique financial requirements. Since that time, dozens of programs have been developed to provide needed services for the millions of firms classified as "small." The general SBA size standards were outlined in the "Overview of the Small Business Sector" at the end of Part 1. Let's proceed with a detailed discussion of all the SBA services.

Financial assistance: Generally speaking, the SBA provides loans to small businesses that are unable to obtain funds from conventional sources.

Surety bonds: The SBA is committed to making the bonding process accessible to small contractors who find bonding unavailable to them elsewhere. The agency is authorized to guarantee to a qualified applicant up to 90 percent of the losses incurred under the bid, payment, or performance bonds issued to contractors.

*Small Business Investment Companies (*SBICs*):* The SBICs provide venture capital and long-term financing to small firms for expansion, modernization, and other acceptable business purposes. Special consideration is given to small firms owned and managed by socially or economically disadvantaged persons, generally defined as black Americans, American Indians, Spanish-Americans, Oriental Americans, Eskimos, and Aleuts. Vietnam military service may also be considered a contributing factor in economic and social disadvantage, according to SBA publications.

While management assistance is part of the SBIC package, it is not uncommon for SBICs to accept partial equity or ownership in companies in exchange for money and assistance.

Procurement assistance: With the help of the SBA, thousands of small businesses have received as much as one-third of the total federal procurement budget. Special federal procurement specialists are available through the SBA to provide the following services to small firms:

1. Aid in preparing bids.

2. Aids and special considerations in obtaining prime contracts and subcontracts.

3. Directions to government agencies that could use their products and services.

4. Placement of small businesses on bidders' lists.

5. Provision of certificates of competency (COC) that authorize small businesses to perform contracts, following on-site inspections.

6. Making their names available, through its regional procurement source files, to large firms and government agencies attempting to locate small firms that can provide specialized services.

7. Workshops conducted throughout the country to inform small businesses of the opportunities for contract work with government agencies.

8. Many kinds of technological assistance, from technical assistance on internal problems to help in obtaining federal research and development projects.

9. Contracting "with other Federal Departments and agencies to supply their goods, services, and construction needs and then subcontract[ing] the actual performance of the work to small business concerns which are owned and controlled by socially or economically disadvantaged persons."*

10. Special help and considerations for minority vendors.

Management assistance: The SBA provides a number of services that are designed to improve the management ability of small business owners:

1. Individual counseling by the SBA's Management Assistance staff.

2. Service Corps of Retired Executives/Active Corps of Executives (SCORE/ACE). Under these programs, volunteer retired executives visit a small firm upon request to study its problems and recommend solutions. The major criticism of the programs is that most volunteers have acquired the major part of their experience in large corporations and are unfamiliar with the unique management re-

---

* Small Business Administration, "SBA: What It Does," publication OPI-6, p. 13.

CAREERS IN GOVERNMENT

quirements of a small business. As we have already learned, the organizational structure of a small business is quite different from that of a large corporation. SCORE/ACE volunteers begin to be successful with firms with sales of $1 million or more; only at this point do small firms begin to need formalized structures.

3. Small Business Institute (SBI). This project represents the combined efforts of the SBA and leading schools of business. On-site management counseling is provided by business students under the direction of a business faculty member. Usually such counseling is restricted to SBA loan recipients and small firms that perform government contracts. It is available to others upon request, however, if the student help is available.

4. Conferences, workshops, clinics, courses, and publications to aid in the general improvement and upgrading of the management expertise of small business owners.

Minority small business: Special help is available to members of socially or economically disadvantaged minority groups who want to own and operate small businesses. This help is extended to women as well as to those groups named earlier. The numerous programs that exist are coordinated by field representatives in the regional offices and in numerous district offices.

OPPORTUNITIES IN GOVERNMENT

Are you a Business student with an interest in government? If so, you may be interested to know that there are a number of business-related opportunities in the civil service, on the Federal, state and local levels.

CAREERS IN THE FEDERAL CIVIL SERVICE

The Federal Civil Service offers diverse career possibilities throughout the United States. There has been a downward trend in Civil Service hiring in the past few years, but there was a projected 23 percent increase in college-level appointments in 1978, and opportunities are particularly good for applicants prepared to be flexible about location and initial hiring grade. The United States Civil Service Commission projected that 15,000 college-level employees would be hired in 1978.

Key areas

Since the range of career possibilities in the Civil Service is so wide, it is not possible to give a complete picture of the jobs open to Business graduates. We can, however, talk about a sample of Business-related Civil Service careers:

■ The Civil Service Commission forecast that 9% of all college-level hires in 1978 would be accountants. The majority of these hires would be employed as accountants or auditors in such agencies as the Internal Revenue Service, the Treasury, the Department of Energy and the Department of Labor.

■ Computer specialists faced limited employment opportunities everywhere in the country except Washington, D.C. The majority of applicants hired would be offered jobs as computer programmers and analysts in the Department of Labor, the Department of Commerce and the General Services Administration.

■ Graduates with a background in Personnel Management in 1978 might have found employment as Equal Employment Opportunity Specialists in the Treasury, Manpower Development Specialists or Labor/Management Relations Compliance Officers in the Department of Labor, or, alternatively, as Manpower Analysts in the Army.

■ Graduates with majors in Marketing might be attracted to work as Supply Management Specialists, while those majoring in Finance could apply for employment as Tax Law Specialists or Financial Institution Examiners.

How do I apply?

It was estimated that approximately 52 percent of the 1978 college-level placements would be nontechnical positions filled through the Professional and Administrative Career Examination (PACE). Some agencies—including the Department of State's Foreign Service, the Central Intelligence Agency, the Federal Bureau of Investigation, the Tennessee Valley Authority and the National Security Agency—require direct applications both for information and placement.

In order to apply for employment in the Civil Service, students should first contact the Federal Job Information Center located in the area in which they want to work. The Center will evaluate their qualifications, give them application forms, and arrange for them to take the Professional and Administrative Career Examination. Applicants are subsequently notified of their scores and of their standing on the Civil Service Commission List. (Generally speaking, only those candidates scoring in the 90s are considered for placement.) Individual agencies fill vacancies by promoting staff, from within their own agency on merit, by hiring qualified candidates who transfer from other agencies, or by requesting names of qualified applicants from the Civil Service Commission List.

What about pay?

Most college-level Civil Service entrants are paid according to the General Schedule (GS) pay system, which ranges from GS-1 to GS-18. College graduates usually enter the pay scale at GS-5 to GS-9, at the first level of that pay grade. GS-5 level pay commences at $9,959, rising to $12,947, and GS-9 commences at $15,090 and rises to $19,617.

Of course, Civil Service employees can also increase their pay through promotion. Whenever possible, agencies fill vacancies by promoting qualified employees, either from within the individual agency or by hiring a Civil Service employee who wishes to transfer from another agency.

CAREERS IN STATE, COUNTY, AND CITY CIVIL SERVICES

Employment opportunities for college graduates are equally varied in these civil services. However, the numbers of job openings and hiring procedures vary according to locality. So, students interested in exploring these career options would be best advised to consult their Placement Office.

APPENDIX

TECHNIQUES FOR ENTERING THE JOB MARKET

THE JOB SEARCH

You've taken your college courses. You know what you're interested in. And now, it's time to begin your job search. This aspect of your career planning is of top importance, and you should think seriously about spending a good deal of time on it. Leading career counselors have observed that the best person doesn't always land the best job, and that only a small portion of the people qualified to fill a job know about it. A person can spend many years getting an education and the proper experience, then not end up with the right job—simply because he or she didn't follow through on a good job search!

There are three fundamental points you should bear in mind as you go about your job search. You are going to have to do the following:

1. Develop a clear understanding of yourself—your aptitudes, abilities, interests, ambitions, resources, and limitations.

2. Learn the key facts about different lines of work. You must know the advantages and disadvantages of each type of work. You must know what kinds of rewards and opportunities each offers. And you must know the requirements for success in these fields.

3. Think about how the above two sets of facts relate to each other. How would each type of work suit *you*? And how well would you do in it? Face these questions honestly.

Likewise, here are some "don'ts."

1. Don't skimp on time—plan to work hard and allocate a considerable amount of time to finding the right job.

2. Don't set unrealistic goals. In some cases, the reason a candidate doesn't get a job is that his or her aptitudes, abilities, education, and experience are not right for the jobs he or she is aiming at.

3. Don't neglect to develop marketable skills in college.

The job search is a challenging process, but it's not impossible. In fact, it can be interesting and even enjoyable. In the pages that follow, we're going to discuss some key points about the job-search procedure. We'll discuss researching the job market, preparing your résumé, using references, filling out applications, going through interviews, and accepting a job offer.

HOW TO RESEARCH THE JOB MARKET

How do you go about researching the job market? Basically, your object is to develop a system for obtaining names of specific employers who might be offering opportunities in the areas you are interested in. The process will require a concerted effort on your part. You'll need to check newspapers, trade journals, and professional publications; make personal contacts; visit the library; talk with placement advisors and professors; make phone calls; and investigate a multitude of other avenues that can lead to job targets. The wise job candidate looks into *all* of these areas in order to find an employer who can meet his needs.

WHERE TO START

The following are some good places to begin your job search.

■ An excellent source for college graduates seeking names and addresses of potential employers in specific fields is the *College Placement Annual*, published by the College Placement Council in Bethlehem, Pennsylvania, and available through most placement offices.

■ Take a look at the job lists posted in your placement office—both the domestic and foreign lists. Most placement offices will have lists of employers, plus job descriptions that give the names of specific people to contact.

■ Other sources include directories such as Moody's; association directories; chambers of commerce; municipal, state, and federal government agencies; and the Yellow Pages. The Yellow Pages are particularly good if you are looking for a job in a specific geographical area. Want ads in selected papers are also a good source of job opportunities, so if you are looking for a job in a specific geographical area, subscribe to a newspaper in that area.

■ Perhaps one of the best—though least frequently used—approaches consists of contacting people in the field and asking them for referrals. Try this—it can open up productive avenues. Trade and professional journals can be very helpful in specific areas. Also, some students find it advisable to attend conventions and meetings of learned societies where they can come in contact with large numbers of employers seeking candidates in their field.

■ Private agencies can very often provide leads, but they are more apt to be helpful to experienced personnel than to fresh college graduates. The United States Employment Service also offers some help to the entry-level graduate, although its emphasis is primarily on hourly rated jobs.

■ Be sure to learn about your placement service's procedures, and take advantage of the aid the staff can offer in planning your job campaign, arranging for interviews, and preparing your résumé and cover letter. Don't forget, the résumé is a very important part of the job campaign; you must take the time to prepare a résumé that will present your qualifications as favorably as possible. (We discuss the résumé below.)

■ Another hint: if you're planning to try the walk-in method, try to make an appointment with the person doing the hiring. If possible, find out all you can about the company's product line, its size, the location of its plants, and the types of jobs available—this will make it easier for you to talk intelligently during the interview. Be sure to bring a résumé with you; it's also a good idea to write a follow-up letter after the interview, indicating your interest in employment with the firm.

YOUR RÉSUMÉ

Your résumé is a personalized summary statement about your background, experience, and ambitions. It should touch on all the things that relate to your qualifications for a particular job or type of employment, e.g. marketing research, teaching French, or rehabilitation counseling.

201 Brayton Road
Fenway, OH 44092

March 10, 1978

Mr. George Duncan
College Relations Manager
Mayfair Industries, Incorporated
74 Shoreline Boulevard
Mentor, OH 44872

Dear Mr. Duncan:

I am interested in pursuing employment possibilities with Mayfair Industries in the Accounting Department. I am an accounting major at Ohio State University, where I will receive my B.A. degree in June of this year. I am particularly interested in cost accounting opportunities, but my accounting background has special strengths in auditing and taxation as well. Summer employment in accounting as well as an internship further heighten my qualifications, which are detailed more extensively in the enclosed résumé.

Does Mayfair Industries have or anticipate openings for a candidate with my qualifications, job interests, and ambition to work? What can you tell me about those positions? Are there job descriptions which you can send? What should I, as an interested applicant, do next? Is there an application form I should complete? May I contact you or one of your staff to arrange a personal interview?

Yours truly,

Nancy A. Hill

NAH
Enclosure

SAMPLE LETTER OF APPLICATION—ACCOUNTING/FINANCE

428 Kinsey Drive
Okemos, MI 48821

March 10, 1978

Mr. Richard Bradley
Director of Marketing
Professional Marketing Services
Detroit, MI 48828

Dear Mr. Bradley:

Dr. William Jones, professor of marketing at Oakland University, recently suggested that I write you concerning the marketing vacancy you have in your organization. He has also described your company to me, and I am very much interested in the position.

During the last two summers, I worked in the Marketing Department of Davis Manufacturing doing market research for a new line of products they hope to merchandise soon. I also had a short stint in their Advertising Department, where I did test marketing in several locations throughout the Midwest.

I have had a long interest in marketing, as demonstrated by the fact that I majored in that subject and had related work experience while attending college. This background, combined with my energies and resourcefulness would, I believe, qualify me for the position you have open. Enclosed is a resume highlighting my background, interests, and abilities.

I would like very much to arrange an interview to talk with you personally about the position you have open. I will call your office next week to make an appointment.

Very truly yours,

Lawrence L. Cooper

llc
Enclosure

SAMPLE LETTER OF APPLICATION—THIRD-PARTY REFERRAL

Essentially, your résumé is your sales message to prospective employers. It should distinguish you from other candidates in the job market and sell the employer on your most desirable qualities. It should be prepared with as much forethought and care as a promotion campaign for a major new product.

WHAT ARE THE PURPOSES OF THE RÉSUMÉ?

The résumé has several purposes. First, it's a self-evaluation tool. Because it requires the individual to list his education and work experience in an objective manner, it helps him identify precisely what he is marketing and think clearly about the demand that may exist for his skills.

Second, it provides information to an employer. It is aimed at encouraging the employer to invite the candidate in for further discussion, and it can provide the employer with information for use during the interview. It also serves as a permanent record for future referrals and consultation.

Third, the résumé can be used to "plant seeds" for future job possibilities. By leaving a résumé with selected people who have contacts in your target field, you may be able to obtain referrals to other sources of job opportunities.

Finally, a résumé should be given to all the individuals you are planning to use as references. If prospective employers contact them, they can use the résumé to answer questions intelligently and accurately.

PLANNING THE RÉSUMÉ: SOME KEY POINTS

The design of the résumé is very important because it projects your personality to the prospective employer. Neatness, color of stationery, layout—all these help convey your image. Equally important is clear organization. The reader should be able to quickly find all the important facts about your employment objective, education, work experience, special interests, and any other information you think is relevant.

Here are some guidelines for preparing your résumé.

ORGANIZATION

Group your information into six or seven categories: (1) PERSONAL DATA, (2) EMPLOYMENT OBJECTIVE, (3) EDUCATION, (4) WORK EXPERIENCE, (5) SPECIAL INTERESTS, SKILLS, AND HONORS, (6) REFERENCES, and (7) MILITARY EXPERIENCE, CERTIFICATES HELD, PUBLICATIONS, or PROFESSIONAL MEMBERSHIPS, where applicable.

SEQUENCE

Beginning with your name, address, and telephone, organize the information in a logical, easy-to-follow sequence. Under education and work experience, list your most recent degree or present job *first.*

LENGTH

Generally speaking, it is best to limit your résumé to one or two pages, unless your employment experience is extensive or unless more detail concerning academic preparation or job responsibilities is required.

EMPLOYMENT OBJECTIVE

State clearly the kind of employment you are seeking. Avoid such generalities as "working with people" and "challenging position in management." (See the sample résumés on pages 536 and 537.)

FORMAT

Readability, eye appeal, and a total positive impression should be your goals. Generous spacing and separation of the components of your résumé will help you achieve this effect. Underline and/or capitalize key headings, job titles, etc.

WRITING STYLE

Choose the style you are most comfortable with (first-person or third-person narrative). Avoid wordiness and excessive detail, especially in job descriptions.

DUPLICATE COPIES

Have your résumé duplicated so that each copy looks as fresh as the original, or type each one individually.

PICTURE

Don't hesitate to use your picture at the top of your résumé near your name. You will find differences of opinion on this; our point of view is that a good picture can make a résumé more interesting. A detachable picture is best; it allows employers who are prohibited by state law to have pictures of candidates in their files to remove the photo easily and still file the résumé.

REFERENCES

The use of references is optional. Today, employers are using them less and less, especially those of the "to whom it may concern" variety. Because of various laws, many professors and employers are reluctant to give negative references, so practically all references are of a positive nature—and many employers recognize this. If they do use references, they frequently telephone, so that they can talk person-to-person about a specific job and how the candidate's qualifications match it.

There's one very useful form of reference, however—your school transcript. You should always have it available to give to employers.

RACHEL L. SUSSMAN

HOME ADDRESS:	294 South Milford Road Traverse City, MI 48042	Phone: 616-685-2064
SCHOOL ADDRESS:	474 South Wonders Hall Michigan State University East Lansing, MI 48824	Phone: 517-357-0142
PERSONAL:	Age: 22 U.S. Citizen	Height: 5'4" Weight: 110

CAREER
OBJECTIVES: Direct sales assignment leading to a position in marketing
development and distribution, marketing research, or other
marketing activities with the opportunity for further specialization in a management field.

EDUCATIONAL
BACKGROUND: BA in Marketing, Michigan State University, June, 1978.
Major GPA 3.85/4.0, overall GPA 3.34/4.0.
Specific areas of study have included consumer behavior, marketing research and forecasting, marketing strategy formulation,
physical distribution management, selling, sales management, and
international marketing. Sales courses introduced conference
leadership roles and conference group selling. Additional
emphasis placed on cost accounting, finance, and data control.

Diploma, Mechanical Engineering and Technical Illustration,
Oakland Vocational Education Center, Oakland, Michigan, 1973-
1974. Overall GPA 3.9/4.0.

EMPLOYMENT
HISTORY: Michigan State University, Departmental Aide, Placement Services;
part-time during school years 1975 through 1978. Duties involved
handling student payroll and assisting with Work-Study Program.

City of Traverse City, Special Program Helper, Traverse City,
Michigan; Summers of 1975 through 1977. Duties included maintenance of specific areas, checking vehicle registration, and
handling admittance fees.

PROFESSIONAL
ASSOCIATIONS: Treasurer, Omicron Chapter, Phi Gamma Nu, Professional Business
Sorority, 1976 through 1978.

Delegate, Phi Gamma Nu National Convention, August, 1976,
Chicago, Illinois.

Member, Undergraduate Student Advisory Council, 1977 through
1978.

Member, Marketing Association, Michigan State University, 1977
through 1978.

REFERENCES: Will be furnished upon request.

SAMPLE RÉSUMÉS: TWO ACCEPTABLE FORMATS

ERIC C. RANDALL

512 Oak Road
East Lansing, MI 48824
517-321-0014

CAREER OBJECTIVE

Capital budgeting and investment analysis or some other area of financial
administration that complements my educational background.

EDUCATIONAL BACKGROUND

September, 1974 - March, 1978: Michigan State University, East Lansing, Michigan
    Major: Financial Administration
    Areas of Study: Finance, Accounting, Management, Marketing
    Date of Graduation: March, 1978
    Degree: M.B.A. in Financial Administration

September, 1969, - June, 1973: Western Michigan University, Kalamazoo, Michigan
    Major: Economics
    Areas of Study: Economics, Statistics, Business Law
    Date of Graduation: June, 1973
    Degree: B.A. in Economics

September, 1967 - June, 1969: Baylor Community College, Lansing, Michigan
    Major: Pre-Engineering
    Areas of Study: Mathematics, English, Chemistry, Social Science, Humanities
    Date of Graduation: June, 1969
    Degree: Associate Degree in Science

EMPLOYMENT HISTORY

September, 1975 - March, 1977: Saginaw Mobil, Lansing, Michigan
    Job Title: Service Station Manager
    Responsible for all phases of operation; purchasing, budgeting, accounting,
    advertising, service, and customer relations.

October, 1969 - June, 1973: Sears, Roebuck and Company, Kalamazoo, Michigan
    Job Title: Automobile Technician
    Became expert in most phases of automobile diagnosis and repair. Often
    assisted in the training of new employees.

Summer, 1967, 1968, 1969: Merrill Construction, Lansing, Michigan
    Job Title: General Laborer
    Worked at various construction sites throughout the state. My work performance
    enabled me to be rehired three straight summers.

REFERENCES

Dr. William Goldman (Professor), Department of Business and Economics, Michigan
State University, 12 Mulder Lane, East Lansing, Michigan 48823.

Mr. Robert B. Lewis, 194 Lakeview, Lansing, Michigan 48842

Mr. Karl Robertson (Vice President), Value Auto Parts, 800 East Dudley, Lansing,
Michigan 48912

A WORD ON FILLING OUT JOB APPLICATIONS

When you get ready to fill out applications, bear in mind the following.

■ If an employer asks you to fill out an application, do not substitute a résumé for application information. The employer usually has a good reason for wanting certain specific types of information included in the application form.

■ If possible, obtain at least two copies of the application form, using one copy for a draft and one copy for final submission to the employer.

■ For the fresh graduate, it's usually a good idea to include information on all jobs—part-time, summer, volunteer, and full-time. Also include co-op programs in which you have participated.

■ Be sure to include a *permanent* address and telephone number on the application. Many graduates lose job opportunities simply because the employer cannot reach them.

■ Before you send in the application, be sure you have answered all the questions, and check the application carefully for misspelled words and improper composition. Above all, make sure that all of your good points are made clear.

THE INTERVIEW

The interview is the most important and decisive stage of the job hunt. Job candidates should make sure they have done all the homework that is necessary to make the interview successful. Even the most impressive credentials cannot overcome a weak and ill-prepared interview performance.

There are many types of interviews. You'll almost undoubtedly go through a preliminary interview, which is simply a quick screening device to determine whether or not the employer is interested in further discussions. Later, you may go through an in-depth interview, which is much more comprehensive and usually takes place in the personnel office or at the site of the job within the organization.

Remember that the interview is a two-way, give-and-take situation; and if you can remember the words

March 14, 1978

Mr. Nathan L. Moore
6243 Endenhall Boulevard
East Lansing, MI 48827

Dear Nathan,

We are very interested in discussing career opportunities with a person having your marketing, leadership, and work background. On Friday, April 14, a team of product management representatives will be on campus interviewing people for product management positions in the Food Service Products Division of Young Industries. If you would be interested in pursuing such an opportunity, please sign up for an interview.

This is the first year that Young will be interviewing and screening candidates for our Food Service Products Division. Therefore, I would like to provide you with an exposure to the fast-growing food service industry that consumes one out of every three dollars spent for food today and is projected to grow to one out of every two dollars by 1985. I think you will find the enclosed *Business Week* article, "America's Eating-Out Splurge," enjoyable reading. With such growth, there are bound to be excellent career opportunities. In addition, our enclosed marketing management brochure should provide interesting reading and provide you with background on our Food Service Management Team.

Our Food Service Products Division sells a line of coffees, desserts, cold beverages, and food products to the "Away From Home" food industry. Our Division has generated the highest percentage profit growth improvement within Young Industries during the past few years. Our sales are projected to grow and to exceed $300 million during the next year. With such growth, we would like to hire several strong MBA graduates to help make this growth happen. We want people who have a high energy level, good interpersonal skills, a good marketing and financial background, and a desire to run a business.

The food service business offers you the opportunity to join a small group in a fast-growing, multi-faceted business environment. We hope you will decide to sign up for an interview when Young Industries is on campus.

Sincerely,

Joseph S. Prior
Product Group Manager

JSP:dgh
Enclosures

SAMPLE PRE-SCREENING LETTER

"Be natural," you will maximize your potential for getting a job. Preparing for the interview requires that you know yourself extremely well. You must know your interests, your likes and dislikes, your geographical preferences, and a multitude of other things.

The second fundamental point to remember is that you must know something about the employer who is doing the interviewing. You will find helpful information in financial statements, brochures, and in talking with employees of the organization. Prior to

PREPARING FOR AN INTERVIEW: HAVE YOU THOUGHT ABOUT THESE QUESTIONS?

QUESTIONS EMPLOYERS OFTEN ASK

1. What was your overall grade-point average all through college?

2. What was your grade-point average in your major field of study?

3. What courses did you enjoy while in college? What courses did you enjoy least?

4. What do you know about our organization?

5. What qualifications do you have that make you feel that you will be successful in your field?

6. How did you happen to apply for this position with our organization?

7. Have you had any part-time or summer employment?

8. What have you learned from some of the jobs you have held?

9. Have you participated in any volunteer or community work?

10. How did previous employers treat you?

11. Do you like routine work?

12. What are your future vocational plans?

13. In what type of position are you most interested?

14. Are you willing to travel?

15. If you could write your ticket, what kind of job would you like to have?

16. What have you done that shows initiative and willingness to work?

17. Tell me about your extracurricular activities.

18. Did you hold any positions of leadership while at school?

19. Do you have any special skills, and where did you acquire them?

20. Have you had any special accomplishments in your lifetime that you would like to speak of?

21. Why did you leave a given job?

22. Do you have any geographical restrictions? (or preferences?)

23. How do you spend your spare time? What are your hobbies?

24. What are your salary requirements?

25. Do you have a girlfriend (or boyfriend)? Is it serious?

26. Why do you think you would like this particular company?

27. Tell me about your home life during the time you were growing up.

28. Have you ever changed your major field of interest while in college? Why?

29. Why did you choose your particular major?

30. What percentage of your college expenses did you earn? How?

31. Do you feel you did the best scholastic work you could?

32. What do you consider your strengths and weaknesses?

33. Is it an effort for you to be tolerant of persons with backgrounds and interests different from your own?

34. What types of people seem to "rub you the wrong way"?

35. Were you in the armed services? If so, what did you do?

36. What have you been doing since your last job (or since you got out of school)?

37. What books have you read recently?

38. If you were fired, what was the reason?

39. If you went to graduate school, what were your purposes and reasons for going?

40. When can you start work?

41. When can you visit our headquarters for further interviews?

QUESTIONS YOU MAY WANT TO ASK THE EMPLOYER

1. Who was the last person on this job and what is he or she doing now?

2. Why was someone not promoted from within the organization to this vacancy?

3. Who will be my immediate supervisor and will I have a chance to speak to that person personally before being hired?

4. What is the growth potential of your organization?

5. What is the organizational pattern, and where do I fit into it?

6. What is the nature of the job?

7. Is there a job description of my job?

8. How long can I expect to be at the location in which I start?

9. Is it anticipated that I will have extended travel?

10. How much time will be spent away from home?

11. What is the normal progression of salary increases? (This should not be an early question.)

12. What are the housing arrangements and conditions in the general area?

Fendler Corporation
1600 Dexter Avenue
Cleveland, OH 44291

March 15, 1978

Mr. Edward McRay
Purdue University
3801 East Newton
Lafayette, IN 46622

Dear Ed,

Mr. T. D. Lewis was pleased with your qualifications and has asked me to extend you an offer of employment as a Marketing Trainee. The starting salary for this position is $1,200.00, plus $29.00, the current cost-of-living allowance, for a total salary of $1,229.00 per month. The COLA increment is figured four times a year, effective on February 1, May 1, August 1, and November 1, and is based on U.S. Government figures.

Our fringe benefits are excellent, including life insurance, hospitalization, surgical, and dental insurance for an employee and his dependents. We are authorized to reimburse you up to $300.00 for moving expenses. A receipted statement from the moving company is required.

Subject to your acceptance, you may start employment whenever convenient. Please inform us by letter of your acceptance and your desired starting date. All offers of employment are contingent upon a physical examination, conducted and then certified as acceptable by our company physician. If you are desirous of taking this examination in advance of obligating yourself for housing, etc., we will be happy to accommodate you.

We are confident that a successful and profitable career awaits you in our marketing organization and we are sincerely hopeful for a favorable reply from you soon.

If you wish to further discuss this offer with me, please do not hesitate to call me collect at (619) 642-1212, ext. 011. If I do not happen to be in, ask for Ms. Gwen Herrygers.

Very truly yours,

Roberta D. Worth
Manager, College Relations

RDW:gh

SAMPLE OFFER LETTER—MARKETING

March 14, 1978

Ms. Joyce Sanford
541 Hedge Avenue
Lansing, MI 49182

Dear Ms. Sanford:

After consideration of your application with members of Lewis Brothers Management, it is our feeling that you will make an outstanding candidate for our Management Training Program.

It is with pleasure that we offer you the opportunity to begin your employment as a management trainee for Lewis Brothers at a salary of $11,000 annually. Your training program will consist of twenty-six (26) weeks of specialized training to insure you a productive avenue of accelerated growth as a manager with our organization. You must, however, understand that you have agreed to relocate to any other Lewis Brothers location within the Midwest region after your training has been completed.

You are to report to Murray Stoneman at our Management Training Facility located at 100 Seaway Park, Creston, New York, on June 12, 1978. He will introduce you to our training manager, his staff, and your fellow trainees.

This offer is contingent upon receipt of your letter of acceptance by May 15, 1978. The offer is also contingent upon the clearance of your school and business references and satisfactory completion of a physical examination. The physical examination will be arranged for you upon your arrival at the training center.

Should you have any questions regarding the availability of housing, or need assistance, please feel free to contact your training coordinator at 408-932-2021.

You have been selected for this outstanding program because Lewis Brothers Management feels that you have a future in management. During this period of training, take advantage of every opportunity to learn; and remember that a great deal of what you learn will be a result of your own initiative.

Congratulations and good luck.

Sincerely,

R. P. Myers
Corporate College Relations

RPM:dgh

SAMPLE OFFER LETTER—MANAGEMENT

---

the interview, arm yourself with as much information about the employer as you can; it can serve you well.

Appearance can be very important in the interview, and all things being equal, employers tend to prefer candidates who dress somewhat conservatively. Recent research on the campus interview has indicated that the first five to ten minutes of the interview is the time when many interviewers decide whether to invite the student in for a plant visit. During this first interval of time, the interviewer is making an initial decision on your appearance, your ability to make eye-to-eye contact, your handshake, and on key application and résumé information such as your grade point average, your degree and your work experience. So make an effort to create a good impression right away.

During the interview, it is important that you emphasize the positive, making sure that you convey all of your good points to the interviewer. Not all interviewers are skilled in finding out what you can contribute to the job, and it is your responsibility to make sure such information is known. Exactly what should you focus on? A recent study investigated this ques-

One more point: it is a good idea to anticipate certain key questions and think out your answers to them. Likewise, there are a number of questions that a candidate might ask an employer to be sure he or she understands the nature of the job and all its implications. For some specifics, see the box on page 539.

ACCEPTING THE JOB OFFER

You got the job! Wonderful! Now, you must formally accept the job offer by writing the employer a letter announcing your decision. It is a good practice to re-state in the letter the conditions of employment as you understand them, including starting salary, reporting location, and other pertinent information. Also, you'll probably want to express your appreciation for the time and consideration given you. This last point can be handled on the telephone or in a personal discussion—but be sure to put it in your letter, too.

Remember that your word, verbal or written, is binding, as is the employer's; and that it is important that both you and the employer understand the conditions of employment. And one last point: you should notify your placement office, and any other agencies that have been involved in your employment campaign, of your decision. They'll need to make changes in their records. Likewise, be sure to notify any friends, past employers, or instructors who have been involved. They'll want to hear the good news.

March 14, 1978

Ms. Susan A. Vincent
941 Drayton, Apartment #3
East Lansing, MI 48825

Dear Ms. Vincent:

Thank you for taking the time to interview with us on February 28, 1978. We enjoyed discussing employment opportunities with you.

Following your interview, we met with our management personnel to see if your experience and educational background matched our position opening. We regret that at this time we cannot utilize your qualifications to our mutual advantage.

In closing, I would like to wish you the best of luck in exploring alternatives to your present situation. I am sure that with your background it is simply a question of time until the right opportunity presents itself.

Your interest in our company is sincerely appreciated.

Sincerely,

Roger Onway
Employment Coordinator

RO:dgh

SAMPLE REJECTION LETTER

---

tion. Employers were asked, "When recruiting fresh college graduates, what are the important factors in your decision to hire a person?" Most important, the study found, were the applicant's knowledge of the business area in question, his or her career or work aspirations, and personality; also very important were previous work-related experience, part-time or summer work, and an ability to think innovatively about the business area.*

* John D. Shingleton and L. Patrick Scheetz, *Recruiting Trends, 1977-1978*, Michigan State University, 1977.

CAREERS: A SELECTED BIBLIOGRAPHY

The following section lists some books that may serve as valuable tools in the pursuit of a satisfying and rewarding career.

- General information books. These books list job titles and descriptions and offer predictions concerning future employment opportunities in business fields.
- "How to" books. These offer bits of practical information, like the best methods of writing a résumé and conducting a job search. This category also lists books that will help you to assess your skills, answering such questions as "Where do I fit in the job market?" "Would a career in accounting be right for me?" "Is my strong point really in personal selling?"
- Books on careers in the Civil Service. These books explore the many employment opportunities in a field that is far more varied than you would think.

Many of these books provide entertaining reading in addition to facts about careers.

GENERAL REFERENCE

U.S. DEPARTMENT OF LABOR. WASHINGTON, D.C.: GOVERNMENT PRINTING OFFICE.

Dictionary of Occupations and Titles, 4th Edition.

Job Guide for Young Workers.

Occupational Outlook Handbook.

Occupational Handbook for Two Years College Graduates, 1977.

Occupational Outlook Handbook for College Graduates.

"HOW TO" BOOKS

BERG, IVAR
Education & Jobs: The Great Training Robbery. Boston: Beacon Press, 1971.

BOLL, C.R.
Executive Jobs Unlimited, New York: Macmillan, 1965.

BOLLES, RICHARD N.
The Quick Job Hunting Map. Berkeley, Calif.: Ten Speed Press, 1976.

BOLLES, RICHARD N.
The Three Boxes of Life and How to Get Out of Them. Berkeley, Calif.: Ten Speed Press, 1977.

BOLLES, RICHARD N.
What Color Is Your Parachute? A Practical Manual for Job-Hunters and Career Changers. Berkeley, Calif.: Ten Speed Press, 1977.

BUSKIRK, RICHARD H.
Your Career: How to Plan It, Manage It, Change It. Boston: Cahners, 1976.

CHAPMAN, ELWOOD N.
Career Search. Palo Alto, Calif.: Science Research Associates, 1976.

CHAPMAN, ELWOOD N.
College Survival: Find Yourself, Find a Career. Palo Alto, Calif.: Science Research Associates, 1974.

CRYSTAL, JOHN C. AND RICHARD BOLLES
Where Do I Go from Here with My Life: A Workbook for Career-Seekers and Career Changers. New York: Seabury Press, 1974.

HOLLAND, JOHN L.
Making Vocational Choices: A Theory of Careers. Englewood Cliffs, N.J.: Prentice-Hall (Counseling and Human Development Service), 1973.

JACKSON, TOM
Twenty-Eight Days to a Better Job. New York: Hawthorn, 1977.

JACKSON, TOM AND DAVIDYNE MAYLEAS
The Hidden Job Market: A System to Beat the System. New York: Quadrangle, 1976.

JOHANSEN, I. NORMAN
Write Your Ticket to Success: A Do-It-Yourself Guide to Effective Résumé Writing & Job-Hunting, 2nd Edition. Annapolis, Md.: Job Hunters Forum, 1976.

JOHANSEN, I. NORMAN
The Best of the Job Hunter's Forum. Annapolis, Md.: Job Hunters Forum, 1977.

LATHROP, ROBERT
Who's Hiring Who. 3rd Edition. Berkeley, Calif.: Ten Speed Press, 1977.

LEMBECK, RUTH
One Thousand One Job Ideas for Today's Woman—A Checklist Guide to the Job Market, New York: Doubleday, 1975.

MARSHALL, AUSTIN
How to Get a Better Job. New York: Hawthorn, 1977.

NOER, DAVID
How to Beat the Employment Game. Radnor, Penn.: Chilton, 1975.

PAYNE, RICHARD A.
How to Get a Better Job Quicker. New York: Taplinger, 1972.

PELL, ARTHUR R.
The College Graduate Guide to Job Finding. New York: Monarch.

CIVIL SERVICE CAREERS

LUKOWSKI, SUSAN AND MARGARET PITON
Strategy and Tactics for Getting a Government Job. Washington, D.C.: Potomac, 1972.

UNITED STATES CIVIL SERVICE COMMISSION. WASHINGTON, D.C.: GOVERNMENT PRINTING OFFICE.

Federal Career Directory: A Guide for College Students.

Federal Job Information Centers Directory.

Federal Jobs Overseas.

Federal Recruiting 1978: Federal Agency College Recruiting Programs.

First See US: Some General Information about Federal Jobs.

The Presidential Management Intern Program.

CHAPTER 1

1. Calvin Coolidge, "Speech to the Society of American Newspaper Editors," January 17, 1925. 2. Rick Lanning, "Tike Miller's Can-Eating 'Goat' Pays for Its Supper and May Gnaw on Litterbugs," *People*, March 13, 1978, p. 52. 3. United States Environmental Protection Agency, "Trends in the Quality of the Nation's Air" (Washington, D.C.: Government Printing Office, March 1977), p. 15. 4. United States Environmental Protection Agency, "Earth Trek . . . Explore Your Environment" (Washington, D.C.: Government Printing Office, October 1977), p. 16. 5. "Landfill Made by Scrubbers," *Business Week*, January 16, 1978, pp. 78B, 78G. 6. Peter Philipps, "Commentary/Environment—Water Pollution: A Case Study in the Art of Compromise," *Business Week*, December 12, 1977, pp. 134, 138. 7. "Taking the Profit out of Pollution," *Business Week*, December 19, 1977, p. 27. 8. Council on Environmental Quality, *Environmental Quality 1977, 8th Annual Report of Council on Environmental Quality* (Washington, D.C.: Government Printing Office, 1977), p. 47. 9. *Environmental Quality 1977*, p. 325. 10. Clare M. Reckert, "Rise Seen in Pollution-Control Cost," *New York Times*, May 15, 1978, pp. D1, D8. 11. Saul Friedman, "Nader Blames Losses on National Anti-Washington Mood," *Dallas Times Herald*, November 27, 1977, Section A. 12. Federal Trade Commission, Debt Collection Practices, "Fair Debt Collection Practices Act" (Washington, D.C.: Government Printing Office, 1978). 13. "Corporate Clout for Consumer," *Business Week*, September 12, 1977, pp. 144, 148 (quote by Stephen E. Upton, vice-president for consumer affairs, Whirlpool Corp. in Benton Harbor, Michigan, appears on p. 144). 14. "Corporate Clout for Consumers" (quote by Joseph B. Danzansky, president of Washington's Giant Food, Inc., appears on p. 144). 15. John Herbers, "Federal Job Program Aids Cities, But Fraud Reports Mar Success," *New York Times*, May 14, 1978, pp. 1, 18. 16. Census Bureau, *Statistical Abstract of the United States 1977* (Washington, D.C.: Government Printing Office, 1977), p. 412. 17. "Furor over Noise Regulations," *Nation's Business*, October 1977, pp. 17-23. 18. "Breaking the Code," *Forbes*, March 6, 1978, p. 50.

CHAPTER 2

1. Marlys Harris, "Do You Have What It Takes?" *Money Magazine*, March 1978, pp. 49-52, 54. 2. Census Bureau, *Statistical Abstract of the United States 1977* (Washington, D.C.: Government Printing Office, 1977), p. 550 (hereafter cited as *Stat. Abstract*). 3. *Stat. Abstract*, p. 551. 4. *Stat. Abstract*, p. 550. 5. Harris, "Do You Have What It Takes?" 6. Harris, "Do You Have What It Takes?" p. 52. 7. *Stat. Abstract*, p. 551. 8. *Webster's New Collegiate Dictionary* (Chicago: Encyclopedia Britannica Education Corp., 1970). 9. *Stat. Abstract*, p. 550. 10. "The Forbes Sales 500," *Forbes*, May 18, 1978, pp. 202-204, 208; and "The Forbes Assets 500, *Forbes*, May 18, 1978, pp. 221, 224, 226, 231. 11. *Information Please Almanac 1978* (New York: Information Please Publishing, 1977), p. 688. 12. *General Motors Annual Report*. 13. *Stat. Abstract*, p. 550; and *The Fortune Directory of the 500 Largest Industrial Corporations*, May 1974, pp. 230-257. 14. "The Great Takeover Binge," *Business Week*, November 14, 1977, pp. 176, 179, 182-184. 15. Census Bureau, " Census of Manufacturers Special Report Series: Concentration Ratios in Manufacturing MC72 (SR-2)" (Washington, D.C.: Government Printing Office, 1975). 16. Miles Howard, " Competing with the Giants," *Dun's Review*, October 1977, pp. 46-52. 17. "The Billion-Dollar Farm Co-ops Nobody Knows," *Business Week*, February 7, 1977, pp. 54-58, 63-64. 18. *Stat. Abstract*, pp. 831, 837. 19. Marlys Harris, "A Freelance Photographer's Comfortably Chancy Life," *Money*, June 1978. 20. Elizabeth Bailey, "Pride Goeth . . . ," *Forbes*, May 1, 1978, pp. 29-30.

CHAPTER IA

1. Bureau of the Census, "Estimates of the Population of the United States, by Age, Sex and Race: 1970-77," *Current Population Reports*, Series P-25, No. 721 (Washington, D.C.: Government Printing Office, 1978). 2. *Information Please Almanac* (New York: Information Please Publishing, Inc., 1977), p. 47. 3. "Hardship in Early Virginia, 1924," *Readings in American History*, ed. Oscar Handlin (New York: Knopf, 1957), p. 31. 4. Census Bureau, *Statistical Abstract of the United States 1977* (Washington, D.C.: Government Printing Office, 1977), p. 136. 5. Census Bureau, *Statistical Abstract*, p. 895. 6. Steve Solomon, "The Great Tuna Story," *Forbes*, May 1, 1978, pp. 96, 100.

PART TWO

1. "With Fashion Coming In, Can Levi Strauss Branch Out?" *Forbes*, August 21, 1978.

CHAPTER 3

1. "Atari's Game Plan to Overwhelm Its Competitors," *Business Week*, May 8, 1978, pp. 50F, 50H, 50L. 2. "Lying High at Delta Air Lines," *Dun's Review*, December 1977, pp. 60-61. 3. "Olin's Shift to Strategy Planning," *Business Week*, March 27, 1978, pp. 102, 104-105. 4. Harold Seneker, "A Day in the Life of Sam Walton," *Forbes*, December 1, 1977, pp. 45-46, 48. 5. Robert Tannenbaum and Warren H. Schmidt, "How to Choose a Leadership Pattern," *Harvard Business Review*, March 1958, pp. 95-101. 6. "How to Choose a Leadership Pattern." 7. "To Be and What to Be—That Is the Question," *Forbes*, May 1, 1978, p. 25.

CHAPTER 4

1. Jim Brokaw, "Dr. Pepper, Sealtest and the Wood Brothers," *Motor Trend*, March 1974, pp. 102-103, 112. 2. "Beatrice Foods Puts It Together," *Dun's Review*, December 1977, pp. 55-57. 3. Charles G. Burke, "How G. M. Turned Itself Around," *Fortune*, January 16, 1978, pp. 87-89, 92, 96, 100. 4. Robert C. Townsend, *Up the Organization* (New York: Knopf, 1970). 5. Karen Elliott House, "Growing Deadwood: At Agriculture Agency, Bureaucracy Is Huge and the Living Is Easy," *The Wall Street Journal*, April 12, 1977, p. 1.

CHAPTER 5

1. "A Manpower Gap at Uranium Mines," *Business Week*, November 7, 1977, p. 32. 2. Fred K. Foulkes, "The Expanding Role of the Personnel Function, *Harvard Business Review*, March-April 1975, pp. 71-84 (quote from p. 71). 3. "How to Forecast Your Manpower Needs," *Nation's Business*, February 1978, pp. 102-107 (quote from p. 103 by Tom Porter of the American Oil Company). 4. "How to Forecast Your Manpower Needs." 5. "The Big Change at EEOC," *Forbes*, February 1978, p. 65. 6. Patrick Oster, "Propose Guidelines on Tests Employers Can Give Workers," *Chicago Sun-Times*, December 23, 1977. 7. "Nucor: One Winner in Troubled Steel," *Business Week*, November 21, 1977.

8. Census Bureau, *Statistical Abstract of the United States 1977* (Washington, D.C.: Government Printing Office, 1977), p. 333. 9. Chamber of Commerce of the United States, "Employee Benefits," 1976, p. 26. 10. Department of Labor, "Bureau of Labor Statistics Reports on Occupational Injuries and Illnesses for 1976," December 1, 1977. 11. Laurence Peter and Raymond Hall, *The Peter Principle* (New York: Bantam, 1970). 12. "How to Earn 'Well Pay'," *Business Week,* June 12, 1978, p. 143. 13. "The Perils in Not Hiring the 'Handicapped'," *Business Week,* March 13, 1978, p. 79.

CHAPTER 6

1. "Litton Hones Its Competitive Edge," *Business Week,* November 7, 1977, p. 36E. 2. Robert L. Simison, "Bold Builder: Mass Output Methods Help Fox & Jacobs Gain Leadership in Housing," *The Wall Street Journal,* March 29, 1978, p. 1.

CHAPTER IIA

1. "Too Many U.S. Workers No Longer Give a Damn," *Newsweek,* April 24, 1972, p. 65. 2. U. S. Department of Health, Education, and Welfare, *Work In America: Report of a Special Task Force to the Secretary of Health, Education, and Welfare* (Cambridge, Mass.: MIT Press, 1973). 3. U. S. Department of Labor, "Current Wage Development," May 1978, p. 28. 4. *Handbook of Labor Statistics* (Washington, D.C.: Government Printing Office, 1977), p. 310. 5. *Handbook of Labor Statistics,* p. 100. 6. Studs Terkel, "A Steelworker Speaks," *Dissent* (Winter 1972). 7. "Selling Soap for Living Happiness?" *Atlanta Journal and Constitution,* December 31, 1976, pp. 16C, 17C. 8. Fritz J. Roethlisberger and William J. Dickson, *Management and the Worker* (Cambridge, Mass.: Harvard University Press, 1939). 9. Abraham H. Maslow, *Motivation and Personality,* 2nd ed. (New York: Harper & Row, 1970). 10. Douglas McGregor, *The Human Side of Enterprise* (New York: McGraw-Hill, 1960). 11. Harry Levinson, "Asinine Attitudes Toward Motivation," *Harvard Business Review,* January 1973, pp. 70-76. 12. "How Successful Managers Manage," *Industry Week,* December 17, 1973, pp. 40-43. 13. "Too Many U. S. Workers No Longer Give a Damn," *Newsweek,* April 24, 1972, p. 65 (quote is by Victoria Bowkers). 14. "Where Skinner's Theories Work," *Business Week,* December 2, 1972, pp. 64-65. 15. Donald N. Scobel, "Doing Away with the Factory Blues," *Harvard Business Review,* November–December 1975, pp. 132-142. 16. "Stonewalling Plant Democracy," *Business Week,* March 28, 1977, p. 88.

CHAPTER IIB

1. "An Airline Rejects Stepped-Up Bargaining," *Business Week,* May 1, 1978, pp. 33-34. 2. "Labor's Big Swing from Surplus to Shortage," *Business Week,* February 20, 1978, pp. 75-77. 3. Matt Witt, "Why Our Labor Laws Don't Work," *MBA,* October 1977, pp. 48, 50, 52, 54. 4. "An Airline Rejects Stepped-Up Bargaining," *Business Week,* May 1, 1978, pp. 33-34. 5. A. H. Raskin, "Today Manny Hanny, Tomorrow the World?" *Forbes,* March 20, 1978, pp. 37-39. 6. Tom Alexander, "How the Tenderfeet Toughened Up U.S. Borax," *Fortune,* December 1974, pp. 159-163, 166. 7. *Handbook of Labor Statistics* (Washington, D.C.: Government Printing Office, 1977), p. 145. 8. *Business Week,* August 19, 1978, p. 88. 9. Barbara Garson, "Luddites in Lordstown," *Harper's Magazine,* June 1972, pp. 68-73.

PART THREE

1. "Betting a Bundle on a New Shampoo," *Business Week,* July 10, 1978, p. 32.

CHAPTER 7

1. Ralph S. Alexander and the Committee on Definitions of the American Marketing Associations, "Marketing Definitions: A Glossary of Marketing Terms" (Chicago: American Marketing Association, 1960), p. 15. 2. "Huffy Puts New Spin in the Bicycle Business, *Business Week,* October 10, 1977, p. 134. 3. "Maryland Cup Sells More Than Just Paper Cups," *Business Week,* May 22, 1978. 4. "Paying $1 Million to Sell a Book," *Business Week,* September 12, 1977, pp. 102, 104.

CHAPTER 8

1. "Tom Swift and His Electric Hamburger Cooker," *Forbes,* October 15, 1977, p. 112. 2. Jean Ross-Skinner, "Ford's Fiesta: $800 Million Bet," *Dun's Review,* August 1977, pp. 62-64. 3. "The Reluctant Invader," *Forbes,* November 1, 1977, pp. 59, 62. 4. *Standard & Poor's Industry Survey,* April 1978, p. C115. 5. "Shasta's Difficult Sales Goal," *Business Week,* December 5, 1977, p. 125. 6. "What You Read Is What You Get," *Sentinel Star,* November 3, 1977, p. 36-E. 7. "Flexible Pricing," *Business Week,* December 12, 1977, pp. 78-81, 84, 88. 8. "Flexible Pricing." 9. "The Idea Marketplace: Give It to R&D!" *Advertising Age,* March 20, 1978. 10. "Gillette Co. Succumbs to Smoke Detector Price Cut," *Advertising Age,* December 19, 1977.

CHAPTER 9

1. M. R. Werner, *Barnum* (New York: Harcourt, Brace & Co., 1923), p. 182. 2. *Advertising Age,* January 23, 1978, p. 14 (hereafter cited as *Ad Age*). 3. *Annual Report of Dr Pepper,* 1977. 4. *Ad Age,* January 9, 1978, p. 1. 5. Joe Cappo, "Lone Entry in Field Wants a Competitor," *Chicago Daily News,* March 23, 1976, p. 36. 6. *Standard Rate and Data Service,* February 27, 1978, p. 475. 7. *Sales and Marketing Management,* February 27, 1978, p. 103. 8. *Ad Age,* December 12, 1977, p. 142. 9. *Ad Age,* December 5, 1977, p. 6. 10. Diane Wagner, "How Beetleboards Put the Bugs into Advertising," *New York Times,* January 8, 1978, p. B3. 11. *Beetleboards, The Extra Mileage Medium* (Los Angeles: Beetleboards of America, Inc.: 1977). 12. Joe Cappo, "He's Aiming for Sound in Middle of the Tunnel," *Chicago Daily News,* May 5, 1976, p. 55. 13. *Ad Age,* May 13, 1978, p. 1. 14. "1976 Survey of Selling Costs," *Sales & Marketing Management,* February 9, 1976. 15. Rena Bartos and Theodore F. Dunn, *Advertising and Consumers* (New York: American Association of Advertising Agencies, 1976). 16. "21st Annual Study—Advertising, Marketing Reports on the 100 Top National Advertisers," *Ad Age,* August 23, 1976, pp. 27-166. 17. "Learning How to Sell Small Cars," *Business Week,* March 27, 1978, pp. 124, 126. 18. "Tonight at the Movies: The Latest National Ads," *Business Week,* October 24, 1977, p. 39.

CHAPTER 10

1. Computer Book Service, Addison, Ill. 2. Census Bureau, *Statistical Abstract of the United States 1977* (Washington, D.C.: Government Printing Office, 1977), p. 829 (hereafter cited as *Stat. Abstract*). 3. *Stat. Abstract,* pp. 429, 831. 4. *Stat. Abstract,* p. 836. 5. *Stat. Abstract,* p. 571. 6. "Nothing Really Changes," *Forbes,* January 23, 1978, p. 68. 7. Glen H. Snyder, "'GM' A Star in New Profit Study," *Progressive Grocer,* January 1978, pp. 62-64, 68. 8. "The Unlimited Limited," *Forbes,* November 15, 1977, pp. 77, 79-80. 9. "Woolworth: The Last Stand of the Variety Store," *Business Week,* January 9, 1978, pp. 84-85. 10. "Cashing In on 'Down East' Simplicity," *Forbes,* January 23, 1978, pp. 61-62. 11. "Theater Owners Work to Ban Blind Bidding," *Business Week,* April 17, 1978, p. 40. 12. "A Hosiery Giant Jumps from L'Eggs to Faces," *Business Week,* August 22, 1977, p. 87; and Julius Duscha, "The Problem of Living Up to L'eggs," *New York Times,* March 5, 1978.

CHAPTER IIIA

1. Census Bureau, *Statistical Abstract of the United States 1977* (Washington, D.C.: Government Printing Office, 1977), p. 5 (hereafter cited as *Stat. Abstract*). 2. *Stat. Abstract*, p. 6. 3. *Stat. Abstract*, p. 81. 4. Robert Reinhold, "Census Data Show Growth Slowing in Part of Sunbelt," *New York Times*, January 26, 1978, pp. A1, A14. 5. "The Most Profitable Magazine in the U.S.," *Forbes*, June 15, 1977, pp. 30-31. 6. June Kronholz, "A Living-Alone Trend Affects Housing, Cars and Other Industries," *The Wall Street Journal*, November 16, 1977, pp. 1, 39. 7. *Stat. Abstract*, p. 6 and "Supplement." 8. *Stat. Abstract*, p. 136. 9. *Stat. Abstract*, p. 452. 10. *Stat. Abstract*, p. 451. 11. *Stat. Abstract*, p. 391. 12. *A Guide to Consumer Markets 1977/1978* (New York: The Conference Board, Inc., 1977), p. 127. 13. *A Guide to Consumer Markets 1977/1978*, p. 143. 14. "The Cable-TV Industry Gets Moving Again," *Business Week*, November 21, 1977, p. 154. 15. Robert Levy, "The Big Buzz in Beepers," *Dun's Review*, November 1977, p. 72.

CHAPTER IIIB

1. "International Financial Statistics," vol. XXXI, no. 10, October 1978, pp. 34-37. 2. "The Reluctant Exporter," *Business Week*, April 10, 1978, pp. 54-57, 60, 65-66. 3. "At War with IBM over Small Computers," *Business Week*, March 21, 1977, p. 43. 4. "Where the Shoe Pinches," *Forbes*, December 15, 1977, pp. 53-54. 5. "Free Trade in Jeopardy," *Time*, October 17, 1977, pp. 48, 53; and "A Push for Protection," *Newsweek*, October 17, 1977, pp. 81, 82, 87. 6. "What Washington May Do for Steel," *Business Week*, October 24, 1977, pp. 35-36; and "Steel Blues," *Newsweek*, October 3, 1977, pp. 80, 83. 7. Census Bureau, *Statistical Abstract of the United States 1977* (Washington, D.C.: Government Printing Office, 1977), p. 5, 889. 8. "A Growing Appetite for U.S. Fast Foods," *Business Week*, April 17, 1978, pp. 52-53. 9. David J. Rachman and Michael H. Mescon, *Business Today*, 1st ed. (New York; Random House, 1976). 10. "Russia Shops for Grain Again,"" *Business Week*, November 21, 1977, pp. 52-53. 11. "Chicago Newsletter," 1978. 12. Rachman and Mescon, *Business Today*, 1st ed. 13. Ibid. 14. "How One US Company Set Up Entry Strategy for Brazilian Joint Venture," *Business Latin America*, August 31, 1977, pp. 274, 276. 15. "Avoiding Faux Pas When Visiting a Foreign Country" (Bradley Hitchings, ed.), *Business Week*, December 12, 1977, pp. 115-116. 16. "The U. S. Trade Gap Will Not Go Away," *Business Week*, January 30, 1978, p. 30. 17. Ibid. 18. GB Bulletin, "Overseas Investment Risks," 1978. 19. Office of Foreign Investigation, "Chilean Politics," 1974. 20. "Pricing Putdown," *Forbes*, February 6, 1978, pp, 51-52. 21. "Pepsi Takes on the Champ," *Business Week*, June 12, 1978, p. 88.

PART FOUR

1. "*Star Wars* Lights Fox's Future," *Business Week*, January 23, 1978, pp. 106, 108.

CHAPTER 11

1. "Downsizing Costlier than Moonshot," *Automotive News*, November 21, 1977, p. 1. 2. Jeremy Main, "A Store or Restaurant of Your Own," *Money*, June 1978, p. 55. 3. Ibid.

CHAPTER 12

1. *Moody's Handbook of Common Stocks*, Spring 1978. 2. *Annual Report*, Sohio, 1977. 3. "Double-Digit Interest Is a Worry Once Again," *Business Week*, February 6, 1978, pp. 40-41. 4. James P. Meagher, "Bond Expertise Commands More Clout Than Ever Before in Market Annals," *Barron's*, October 17, 1977, pp. 7-8, 14. 5. "MAC Set to Sue Moody's in Bid to Regain Investor Faith after Bond Downgrading," *The Wall Street Journal*, June 1, 1976, p. 31. 6. Standard & Poor's, *Standard Corporation Description*, February 1978, pp. 4836-4837. 7. Ben Weberman, "The 8½% Solution," *Forbes*, October 1, 1977, p. 108. 8. Corporate Records, AT&T Treasury Department, 1941-1958. 9. "Municipal Bond Funds," John Nuveen & Co., November 1977, p. 11. 10. Richard R. Leger, "More Companies Sell Tax-Exempt Bonds for Pollution Control, Saving Millions," *The Wall Street Journal*, July 8, 1974, p. 24. 11. *Moody's Industrial Manual 1977*. 12. Wayne Welch, "A Modest Proposal," *Forbes*, November 15, 1977, pp. 37-38. 13. William D. Hartley, "More and More Firms Boost Dividends, Partly Due to Pressure from Stockholders," *The Wall Street Journal*, May 18, 1977, p. 44. 14. Pamela G. Hollie, "More Companies Split Stocks as Alternative to Dividend Increases," *The Wall Street Journal*, January 3, 1972, pp. 1, 12. 15. Robert J. Flaherty, "The Case for Kodak," *Forbes*, December 1, 1977, p. 122. 16. "The Battle of the Lightweights," *Forbes*, May 1, 1978, pp. 23-25. 17. Pamela Archbold, "How to Foil a Raider," *Institutional Investor*, November 1977, pp. 33-34, 180. 18. "How to Survive a Takeover Siege," *Business Week*, July 17, 1978, pp. 75-77.

CHAPTER IVA

1. *Federal Reserve Bulletin*, October 1978, p. A14. 2. Ibid. 3. "A Retreat from the Cashless Society," *Business Week*, April 18, 1977, pp. 80-83, 86-87, 90. 4. "Citibank's New Automated Banking: Are Machines Politer Than People?" *Forbes*, March 6, 1978, pp. 84, 87. 5. "A Retreat from the Cashless Society."

CHAPTER IVB

1. National Association of Securities Dealers Automated Quotations, New York. 2. Census Bureau, *Statistical Abstract of the United States 1977* (Washington, D.C.: Government Printing Office, 1977), p. 540. 3. Jonathan R. Laing, "Computer Formulas Are One Man's Secret to Success," *The Wall Street Journal*, September 23, 1974, pp. 1, 25. 4. "1977 Wiesenberger Investment Companies Services," p. 17. 5. "The Cloudy Skies of Solar Stocks," *Money*, April 1978, p. 77. 6. "The Washington Jet Exchange," *Forbes*, May 1, 1978, p. 78.

CHAPTER IVC

1. "Some Colorado Ski Centers Closing," *Chicago Sun-Times*, February 18, 1977, p. 111. 2. "Insurance Risk Has the Vermont Ski Areas Worried," *Chicago Sun-Times*, November 9, 1977, p. 176. 3. "The Soaring Costs of Workers' Comp," *Business Week*, January 23, 1978, pp. 84B, 84C, 84D, 84I. 4. "The Soaring Costs of Workers' Comp." 5. Ibid. 6. Health Insurance Institute. 7. "New Compresses for Swollen Health Costs," *Money*, January 1978, pp. 71, 73-74. 8. Census Bureau, *Statistical Abstract of the United States 1977* (Washington, D.C.: Government Printing Office, 1977), p. 542. 9. Department of Health, Education, and Welfare, Social Security Administration, Division of Retirees. 10. Health Insurance Institute. 11. A. F. Ehrbar, "Those Pension Plans Are Even Weaker Than You Think," *Fortune*, November 1977, pp. 104-108, 110, 112, 114. 12. "Chicago Newsletter," Chicago, 1978. 13. *Detroit Commodities Data Report*, Detroit, Spring 1978.

PART FIVE

1. Lawrence Minard and Brian McGlynn, "The U.S.' Newest Glamour Job," *Forbes,* September 1, 1977, pp. 32–36.

CHAPTER 13

1. Lawrence Minard and Brian McGlynn, "The U. S.' Newest Glamour Job," *Forbes,* September 1, 1977, pp. 32–36. 2. "The U. S.' Newest Glamour Job," p. 32. 3. "The Controller—Inflation Gives Him More Clout with Management," *Business Week,* August 15, 1977, pp. 84–85, 90. 4. Ralph Blumenthal, "Auditors in Hard Hats: A New Breed," *New York Times,* December 2, 1977, pp. B1, B5. 5. "The U. S.' Newest Glamour Job." 6. "The U. S.' Newest Glamour Job." 7. Susan Lyall, "Corporations Loaded with Cash," *Dun's Review,* January 1978, pp. 54–55 (quote from p. 54). 8. "Steel: Biting the Bullet," *Forbes,* December 1, 1977, pp. 35, 36. 9. " 'Annie's Journey," *Atlanta Journal and Constitution,* May 1, 1977, p. 3-E. 10. "What It Means to Build a Budget from Zero," *Business Week,* April 18, 1977, pp. 160, 162, 164. 11. Stanley Penn, "Securities Analyst Rues Rosy Reports He Wrote for Investors in Mattel Stock," *The Wall Street Journal,* November 5, 1975, p. 42.

CHAPTER VA

1. Thomas O'Toole, "Next: Home Computers," *Chicago Daily News,* February 8, 1978. 2. "General Information Newsletter," New York, 1978. 3. Arnold E. Keller, "Great Expectations," *Infosystems,* January 1978, p. 35. 4. Nancy French, "Dynamic Growth Seen Continuing," *Computerworld,* June 14, 1976, pp. 1–2. 5. "Science: The Numbers Game," *Time,* February 20, 1978, pp. 54–58. 6. "The Smart Machine Revolution," *Business Week,* July 5, 1976, pp. 38–44. 7. Edward F. Pierce, "Best of the Bunch," *Think,* November–December 1977, pp. 27–28, 46. 8. " 'Give Us Your Payrolls, Your Accounts Receivable …' " *Forbes,* January 23, 1978, p. 60. 9. *Electronics,* January 5, 1978, p. 136. 10. *Computer Decisions,* January 1978, p. 48. 11. *Merchandising,* January 1978, p. 56. 12. "The Race for Superiority in Electronic Warfare," *Business Week,* March 20, 1978, p. 45.

CHAPTER VB

1. Yale Hirsch, *Stock Trader's Almanac 1977* (New Rochelle, N.Y.: Arlington House, 1976), p. 125. 2. "Consulting Month-by-Month," *Business Week,* June 12, 1978, pp. 138–140. 3. "Who's Buying Hardlines," *Hardware Age,* September 1977, pp. 61–83. 4. The World Almanac & Book of Facts *1977* (New York: Newspaper Enterprises Association, 1976), p. 419.

PART SIX

1. Richard N. Current, T. Harry Williams, and Frank Freidel, *American History: A Survey* (New York: Alfred A. Knopf, 1979), p. 444. 2. Ibid.

CHAPTER 14

1. A Uranium Pattern Westinghouse Buys," *Business Week,* December 26, 1977, p. 33. 2. "Col. Tom Parker: The Pitchman Who Made Unknown Elvis a King," by Steve Brown," *Chicago Daily News.* 3. Lange v. National Biscuit Co., 211 N. W. 2d 783 (Sup. Ct. Minn. 1973). 4. *Business Week,* June 19, 1978, p. 110. 5. Stanley H. Slom, "Abercrombie's Last Sale Starts Thursday; Firm Isn't Likely to Last Past Christmas," *The Wall Street Journal,* November 15, 1977, p. 10. 6. Steven N. Brenner and Earl A. Molander, "Is the Ethics of Business Changing?" *Harvard Business Review,* January–February 1977, pp. 57–71.

CHAPTER 15

1. Richard Lyons, "Federal Regulation: Is Anybody Happy?" *New York Times,* January 22, 1978, p. E7. 2. "The Regulation Mess," *Newsweek,* June 12, 1978, pp. 86–88. 3. "The Regulation Mess." 4. "The High-Stakes Business of Anti-sub Warfare," *Business Week,* May 8, 1978, pp. 50B, 50C, 50D. 5. R. M. Williams, "Facelift for Detroit," *Saturday Review,* May 14, 1977, pp. 6–8, 10–11. 6. "Cloud over the Superdome," *Forbes,* December 1, 1977, p. 34. 7. "Industry Wins Part of Landsat," *Business Week,* May 8, 1978, pp. 98G, 98H. 8. "The Ski Season is off to a Snowy Start," *Business Week,* December 12, 1977, p. 59. 9. "OPEC's Continuing Impact in Fueling U.S. Inflation," *Business Week,* May 22, 1978, pp. 130–132. 10. "Lykes and LTV Count on an Antitrust Break," *Business Week,* November 21, 1977, p. 64. 11. Russell C. Warren, *Antitrust in Theory & Practice* (Columbus, Ohio: Grid, Inc., 1978), p. 332. 12. "A Test for the Coors Dynasty," *Business Week,* May 8, 1978, pp. 69, 70, 72. 13. *Information Please Almanac 1978* (New York: Information Please Publishing, Inc., 1978), p. 69. 14. Census Bureau, *Statistical Abstract of the United States 1977* (Washington, D.C.: Government Printing Office, 1977), pp. 294, 295 (hereafter cited as *Stat.* Abstract). 15. Richard Phalon, "New Tax Law and Profits," *New York Times,* November 14, 1978, p. D6. 16. *Information Please Almanac,* p. 69. 17. *Information Please Almanac,* p. 693. 18. *Stat. Abstract,* p. 294. 19. *Stat. Abstract,* p. 298. 20. "How Tax Policy Dampens Economic Growth," *Business Week,* April 24, 1978, pp. 61–62. 21. Thomas J. Murray, "The Heyday of Testing Labs," *Dun's Review,* August 1978, pp. 46–48.

CHAPTER VIA

1. Alvin Toffler, *Future Shock* (New York: Random House, 1970). 2. Herman Kahn, The Future of the Corporation (New York: Mason & Lipscomb, 1974), p. 114. 3. Roger Ibbotson and Rex A. Sinqurfield, "Stocks, Bonds, Bills and Inflation: Simulations of the Future, '1976–2000,' " *Journal of Business,* 1976. 4. Michael J. Gaffey, Massachusetts Institute of Technology. 5. "Lighting a Sun on Earth, *Newsweek,* November 21, 1977, p. 132. 6. Barry Commoner, *The Poverty of Power* (New York: Alfred A. Knopf, 1976), p. 114. 7. "The Great American Power Play," advertisement by American Can Company, Greenwich, Connecticut. 8. "Movie Theaters Face Obsolescence by '85, Researcher Asserts," *The Wall Street Journal,* July 18, 1977, p. 6. 9. A. C. Nielsen Company. 10. *Dinner and Diner,* April 30, 1978, p. 23. 11. Alvin Toffler, *Future Shock.* 12. Aric Y. Lewin and J. G. Wiles, "The End of Corporate Enterprise?" *Dun's Review,* October 1977, p. 129. 13. Harlan Cleveland, *The Future Executive, 1972* (New York: Harper & Row, 1972). 14. "Some Potholes on the Road to Metrics," *U.S. News & World Report,* May 29, 1978, p. 49. 15. Mark Gerzon, "Counterculture Capitalists," *New York Times,* June 5, 1977.

CHAPTER 1

Page 22 (f.n. 17): Reprinted by permission from NATION'S BUSINESS, October 1977. Copyright by NATION'S BUSINESS, Chamber of Commerce of the United States. Page 23 (f.n. 18): Based on a FORBES article "Breaking the Code" appearing in the March 6, 1978, issue.

CHAPTER 2

Page 26 (f.n. 1): Adapted from "Do You Have What It Takes?" by Marlys Harris, MONEY Magazine, March 1978, by special permission; © 1978, Time Inc. All rights reserved. Page 28 (box): Adapted from "The 10 Small Businesses Most Likely to Succeed—and to Fail" by Ed Henry, MONEY Magazine, March 1978, by special permission; © 1978, Time Inc. All rights reserved. Page 30 (box): Adapted from "Testing the Entrepreneurial You," MONEY Magazine, March 1978, by special permission; © 1978, Time Inc. All rights reserved. Page 38 (f.n. 14): Adapted from the November 14, 1977, issue of BUSINESS WEEK © 1977 by McGraw-Hill, Inc., 1221 Avenue of the Americas, New York, N.Y. 10020. All rights reserved. Page 39 (f.n. 16): Adapted from the October 1977 DUN'S REVIEW. Reprinted by permission. Page 43 (f.n. 19): Adapted from "A Freelance Photographer's Comfortably Chancy Life" by Marlys Harris, MONEY Magazine, June 1978, by special permission; © 1978, Time Inc. All rights reserved. Page 43 (f.n. 20): Based on a FORBES article "Pride Goeth . . ." appearing in the May 1, 1978, issue.

CHAPTER IA

Page 56 (box): Adapted from a Newsweek article entitled, "In a Pickle Over Soup." Reprinted by permission. Page 59 (f.n. 6): Based on a FORBES article "The Great Tuna Story" appearing in the May 1, 1978, issue.

CHAPTER 3

Page 69 (f.n. 1): Adapted from the May 8, 1978, issue of BUSINESS WEEK © 1978 by McGraw-Hill, Inc., 1221 Avenue of the Americas, New York, N.Y. 10020. All rights reserved. Page 71 (f.n. 3): Adapted from the March 27, 1978, issue of BUSINESS WEEK © 1978 by McGraw-Hill, Inc., 1221 Avenue of the Americas, New York, N.Y. 10020. All rights reserved. Page 74 (f.n. 4): Based on a FORBES article "A Day in the Life of Sam Walton" appearing in the December 1, 1977, issue. Page 74 (f.n. 5): Adapted from Robert Tannenbaum and Warren H. Schmidt, "How to Choose a Leadership Pattern," *Harvard Business Review,* March–April 1958. Copyright © 1958 by the President and Fellows of Harvard College; all rights reserved. Page 76 (box): Adapted from the July 19, 1976, issue of BUSINESS WEEK © 1976 by McGraw-Hill, Inc., 1221 Avenue of the Americas, New York, N.Y. 10020. All rights reserved. Page 80 (box): Based on "Lessons from a Communication Blunder," SUPERVISORY MANAGEMENT, December 1971, pp. 14–17. © 1971 by AMACOM, a division of American Management Associations. All rights reserved. Page 82 (box): Adapted from HOW TO RUN ANY ORGANIZATION by Theodore Caplow. Copyright © 1976 by Theodore Caplow. Reprinted by permission of Holt, Rinehart and Winston and Theodore Caplow. Page 85 (f.n. 7): Based on a FORBES article "To Be and What to Be—That Is the Question" appearing in the May 1, 1978, issue.

CHAPTER 4

Page 88 (f.n. 1): Adapted from an article by Jim Brokaw, entitled "Dr. Pepper, Sealtest and the Wood Brothers, MOTOR TREND, March 1974, p. 102. Reprinted by permission. Page 104 (f.n. 5): Reprinted by permission of THE WALL STREET JOURNAL, © Dow Jones & Company, Inc., 1977.

CHAPTER 5

Page 108 (f.n. 1): Adapted from the November 7, 1977, issue of BUSINESS WEEK © 1977 by McGraw-Hill, Inc., 1221 Avenue of the Americas, New York, N.Y. 10020. All rights reserved. Page 110 (f.n. 3): Reprinted by permission from NATION'S BUSINESS, February 1964; and Donald F. Dvorak. Copyright by NATION'S BUSINESS, Chamber of Commerce of the United States. Page 118 (f.n. 7): Adapted from the November 21, 1977, issue of BUSINESS WEEK © 1977 by McGraw-Hill, Inc., 1221 Avenue of the Americas, New York, N.Y. 10020. All rights reserved. Page 124 (f.n. 12): Adapted from the June 12, 1978, issue of BUSINESS WEEK © 1978 by McGraw-Hill, Inc., 1221 Avenue of the Americas, New York, N.Y. 10020. All rights reserved. Page 125 (f.n. 13): Adapted from the March 13, 1978, issue of BUSINESS WEEK © 1978 by McGraw-Hill, Inc., 1221 Avenue of the Americas, New York, N.Y. 10020. All rights reserved.

CHAPTER 6

Page 131 (f.n. 1): Adapted from the November 7, 1977 issue of BUSINESS WEEK © 1977 by McGraw-Hill, Inc., 1221 Avenue of the Americas, New York, N.Y. 10020. All rights reserved. Page 145 (f.n. 2): Reprinted by permission of THE WALL STREET JOURNAL, © Dow Jones & Company, Inc., 1978.

CHAPTER IIA

Page 154 (f.n. 12): Based on INDUSTRY WEEK, December 17, 1973. Reprinted by permission. Page 154 (box): Based on INDUSTRY WEEK, October 10, 1977. Page 156 (box): Adapted from the May 8, 1978, issue of BUSINESS WEEK © 1978 by McGraw-Hill, Inc., 1221 Avenue of the Americas, New York, N.Y. 10020. All rights reserved. Page 159 (f.n. 15): Adapted from Donald N. Scobel, "Doing Away with Factory Blues," *Harvard Business Review,* November–December 1975. Copyright © 1975 by the President and Fellows of Harvard College; all rights reserved. Page 160 (f.n. 16): Adapted from the March 28, 1977, issue of BUSINESS WEEK © by McGraw-Hill, Inc., 1221 Avenue of the Americas, New York, N.Y. 10020. All rights reserved.

CHAPTER IIB

Page 172 (f.n. 4): Adapted from the May 1, 1978, issue of BUSINESS WEEK © 1978 by McGraw-Hill, Inc., 1221 Avenue of the Americas, New York, N.Y. 10020. All rights reserved.

CHAPTER 7

Page 199 (f.n. 2): Adapted from the October 10, 1977, issue of BUSINESS WEEK © 1977 by McGraw-Hill, Inc., 1221 Avenue of the Americas, New York, N.Y. 10020. All rights reserved. Page 200 (box): Adapted from the October 1977 DUN'S REVIEW. Reprinted by permission. Page 208 (f.n. 3): Adapted from the May 22, 1978, issue of BUSINESS WEEK © 1978 by McGraw-Hill, Inc., 1221 Avenue of the Americas, New York, N.Y. 10020. All rights reserved. Page 209 (f.n. 4): Adapted from the September 12, 1977, issue of BUSINESS WEEK © 1978 by McGraw-Hill, Inc., 1221 Avenue of the Americas, New York, N.Y. 10020. All rights reserved.

CHAPTER 8

Page 214: Adapted from the October 1977 issue of DUN'S REVIEW. Reprinted by permission. Page 216 (f.n. 1): Based on a FORBES article "Tom Swift and His Electric Hamburger Cooker" appearing in the October 15, 1977, issue. Page 217 (f.n. 2): Adapted from the August 1977 DUN'S REVIEW. Reprinted by permission. Page 218 (f.n. 3): Based on a FORBES article "The Reluctant Invader" appearing in the November 1, 1977, issue. Page 224 (f.n. 7): Adapted from the December 12, 1977, issue of BUSINESS WEEK © 1977 by McGraw-Hill, Inc., 1221 Avenue of the Americas, New York, N.Y. 10020. All rights reserved. Page 229 (f.n. 9): Reprinted with permission from the March 20, 1978, issue of ADVERTISING AGE. Copyright March 1978 by Crain Communications, Inc. Page 229 (f.n. 10): Reprinted with permission from the December 19, 1977, issue of ADVERTISING AGE. Copyright December 1977 by Crain Communications, Inc.

CHAPTER 9

Page 232 (f.n. 1): Copyright M. R. Werner. Page 249 (f.n. 17): Adapted from the March 27, 1978, issue of BUSINESS WEEK © 1978 by McGraw-Hill, Inc., 1221 Avenue of the Americas, New York, N.Y. 10020. All rights reserved. Page 249 (f.n. 18): Adapted from the October 24, 1977, issue of BUSINESS WEEK © 1977 by McGraw-Hill, Inc., 1221 Avenue of the Americas, New York, N.Y. 10020. All rights reserved.

CHAPTER 10

Page 257 (box): Based on a FORBES article "Gargling with Peanut Butter" appearing in the October 15, 1977, issue. Page 261 (f.n. 6): Based on a FORBES article "Nothing Really Changes" appearing in the January 23, 1978, issue. Page 263 (f.n. 9): Adapted from the January 9, 1978, issue of BUSINESS WEEK © 1978 by McGraw-Hill, Inc., 1221 Avenue of the Americas, New York, N.Y. 10020. All rights reserved. Page 269 (f.n. 12): Adapted from the August 22, 1977, issue of BUSINESS WEEK © 1977 by McGraw-Hill, Inc., 1221 Avenue of the Americas, New York, N.Y. 10020. All rights reserved; and © 1978 by The New York Times Company. Reprinted by permission.

CHAPTER IIIA

Page 276 (box): Based on BLACK IT'S BEAUTIFUL, *Media Decisions,* April 1977, pp. 73-75. Page 284 (f.n. 14): Adapted from the November 21, 1977, issue of BUSINESS WEEK © 1977 by McGraw-Hill, Inc., 1221 Avenue of the Americas, New York, N.Y. 10020. All rights reserved.

CHAPTER IIIB

Page 291 (box): Based on the UPI article by Gay Pauley entitled "Union Label? It and Clothing Industry Could Be Disappearing." Page 299 (f.n. 20): Based on a FORBES article "Pricing Putdown" appearing in the February 6, 1978, issue. Page 301 (f.n. 21): Adapted from the June 12, 1978, issue of BUSINESS WEEK © 1978 by McGraw-Hill, Inc., 1221 Avenue of the Americas, New York, N.Y. 10020. All rights reserved.

CHAPTER 11

Page 329 (f.n.'s 2, 3): Adapted from "A Store or Restaurant of Your Own" by Jeremy Main from the June 1978 issue of MONEY Magazine by special permission; © 1978, Time Inc. All rights reserved.

CHAPTER 12

Page 344 (box): Chicago Daily News article, May 21, 1974, reprinted with permission. Page 349 (f.n. 18): Adapted from the July 17, 1978, issue of BUSINESS WEEK © by McGraw-Hill, Inc., 1221 Avenue of the Americas, New York, N.Y. 10020. All rights reserved.

CHAPTER IVA

Page 354 (box): © 1977 by The New York Times Company. Reprinted by permission. Page 364 (f.n. 5): Adapted from the April 18, 1977 issue of BUSINESS WEEK © by McGraw-Hill, Inc., 1221 Avenue of the Americas, New York, N.Y. 10020. All rights reserved.

CHAPTER IVB

Page 375 (f.n. 3): Reprinted by permission of THE WALL STREET JOURNAL, © Dow Jones & Company, Inc., 1974. Page 382 (f.n. 5): Adapted from "The Cloudy Skies of Solar Stocks" from the April 1978 issue of MONEY Magazine, by special permission; © 1978, Time Inc. All rights reserved. Page 383 (f.n. 6): Based on a FORBES article "The Washington Jet Exchange" appearing in the May 1, 1978, issue.

CHAPTER 13

Page 414 (f.n. 1), page 415 (f.n. 5), page 416 (f.n. 6): Based on a FORBES article "The U.S.' Newest Glamour Job" appearing in the September 1, 1977, issue.

CHAPTER VA

Page 442 (box): Adapted from "My Pet and I" by Peter Bird Martin, MONEY Magazine, May 1978, by special permission; © 1978, Time Inc. All rights reserved. Page 448 (f.n. 12): Adapted from the March 20, 1978, issue of BUSINESS WEEK © by McGraw-Hill, Inc., 1221 Avenue of the Americas, New York, N.Y. 10020. All rights reserved.

CHAPTER 14

Page 480 (f.n. 1): Adapted from the December 26, 1977, issue of BUSINESS WEEK © by McGraw-Hill, Inc., 1221 Avenue of the Americas, New York, N.Y. 10020. All rights reserved. Page 484 (box): Tony McAdams and Robert C. Miljus, "Growing Criminal Liability of Executives," *Harvard Business Review,* March-April 1977. Copyright © 1977 by the President and Fellows of Harvard College; all rights reserved.

CHAPTER 15

Page 499 (f.n. 4): Adapted from the May 8, 1978, issue of BUSINESS WEEK © by McGraw-Hill, Inc., 1221 Avenue of the Americas, New York, N.Y. 10020. All rights reserved. Page 499 (f.n. 6): Based on a FORBES article "Cloud over the Superdome" appearing in the December 1, 1977, issue. Page 500 (f.n. 7): Adapted from the May 8, 1978, issue of BUSINESS WEEK © by McGraw-Hill, Inc., 1221 Avenue of the Americas, New York, N.Y. 10020. All rights reserved. Page 511 (f.n. 20): Adapted from the April 24, 1978, issue of BUSINESS WEEK © by McGraw-Hill, Inc., 1221 Avenue of the Americas, New York, N.Y. 10020. All rights reserved. Page 511 (f.n. 21): Adapted from the August 1978 DUN'S REVIEW. Reprinted by permission.

CHAPTER VIA

Page 524 (f.n. 14): From a copyrighted article in 'U. S. News & World Report' of May 29, 1978. Page 525 (f.n. 15): © 1977 by The New York Times Company. Reprinted by permission.

Special Acknowledgment

Following are the page numbers and footnote numbers indicating material we have adapted from BUSINESS WEEK © by McGraw-Hill, Inc., 1221 Avenue of the Americas, New York, N.Y. 10020. All rights reserved. The date of issue is included. P. 38 (f.n. 14): Nov. 14, 1977; p. 69 (f.n. 1): May 8, 1978; p. 71 (f.n. 3): Mar. 27, 1978; p. 76 (box): July 19, 1976; p. 108 (f.n. 1): Nov. 7, 1977; p. 118 (f.n. 7): Nov. 21, 1977; p. 124 (f.n. 12): June 12, 1978; p. 125 (f.n. 13): Mar. 13, 1978; p. 131 (f.n. 1): Nov. 7, 1977; p. 156 (box): May 8, 1978; p. 160 (f.n. 16): Mar. 28, 1977; p. 172 (f.n. 4): May 1, 1978; p. 199 (f.n. 2): Oct. 10, 1977; p. 208 (f.n. 3): May 22, 1978; p. 209 (f.n. 4): Sept. 12, 1977; p. 224 (f.n. 7): Dec. 12, 1977; p. 249 (f.n. 17): Mar. 27, 1978; p. 249 (f.n. 18): Oct. 24, 1977; p. 263 (f.n. 9): Jan. 9, 1978; p. 269 (f.n. 12): Aug. 22, 1977; p. 284 (f.n. 14): Nov. 21, 1977; p. 301 (f.n. 21): June 12, 1978; p. 349 (f.n. 18): July 17, 1978; p. 364 (f.n. 5): Apr. 18, 1977; p. 448 (f.n. 12): Mar. 20, 1978; p. 480 (f.n. 1): Dec. 26, 1977; p. 499 (f.n. 4): May 8, 1978; p. 500 (f.n. 7): May 8, 1978; p. 511 (f.n. 20): Apr. 24, 1978.

CHAPTER 1

Page 2: CHARLES COLBY/Photo Researchers, Inc. Page 5: PAUL DEGRUCCIO, PEOPLE WEEKLY ©1978 TIME, Inc. Page 6: LAIMUTE DRUSKIS. Page 8: LAIMUTE DRUSKIS. Page 12: ISADORE SELTZER, based on information in *Environmental Quality 1977, 8th Annual Report of Council on Environmental Quality* (Washington, D.C.: Government Printing Office, 1977), pp. 199, 325, and in United States Environmental Protection Agency, "Trends in the Quality of the Nation's Air" (Washington, D.C.: Government Printing Office, March 1977), p. 15. Page 16: (top): JOEL GORDON; (bottom, left): LAIMUTE DRUSKIS; (bottom, right): LAIMUTE DRUSKIS. Page 20: Vantage Art, based on information from Census Bureau, *Statistical Abstract of the United States 1977* (Washington, D.C.: Government Printing Office, 1977), pp. 136, 389, 451. Page 21: Courtesy, Conoco.

CHAPTER 2

Page 24: MARTIN LUBIN. Page 26: Vantage Art, Inc., and MIKE QUON, based on information from Census Bureau, *Statistical Abstract of the United States 1977* (Washington, D.C.: Government Printing Office, 1977). Page 27: BOB PETERSON. Page 35: MIKE QUON. Page 38: MARTIN LUBIN. Page 39: TOM MCHUGH/Photo Researchers, Inc. Page 40 (top): GEORGE MORAN; (bottom): U.S.D.A. Photograph.

CHAPTER 1A

Page 44: JOEL GORDON. Page 49: Vantage Art, Inc., based on information from Census Bureau, Historical Statistics of the United States, Colonial Times to 1970, Bicentennial Edition, Part 2 (Washington, D.C.: Government Printing Office, 1975), p. 225; Census Bureau, *Current Population Reports*, Series P-25, No. 721, "Estimates of the Population of the United States, by Age, Sex and Race: 1970–1977" (Washington, D.C.: Government Printing Office, 1978); and Census Bureau, *Statistical Abstract of the United States 1977* (Washington, D.C.: Government Printing Office, 1977). Page 50 (top): The Granger Collection; (bottom): N.Y.P.L. Picture Collection. Page 51: The Granger Collection. Page 53 (top): GM Motors, Inc.; (bottom): Fiat Corporation, Inc. Page 55 (both): Culver Pictures, Inc. Page 57: ROY DOTY, Newsweek.

CHAPTER 3

Page 66: DON CARL STEFFEN/Rapho/Photo Researchers, Inc. Page 69: GEORGE HALL/Woodfin Camp & Associates. Page 72: JAMES H. KARALES/Peter Arnold, Inc. Page 77: Vantage Art, Inc. Page 78: Vantage Art, Inc. Page 79: Vantage Art, Inc. Page 80: JOEL GORDON. Page 81: JOEL GORDON.

CHAPTER 4

Page 86: JEFF FOOTT/Bruce Coleman, Inc. Page 89 (left): FRED MAYER/Woodfin Camp & Associates; (right): Vantage Art, Inc. Page 90 (both): Vantage Art, Inc. Page 91: Vantage Art, Inc. Page 92 (right): MIKE QUON. Page 93 (top): Vantage Art, Inc.; (bottom): Betty Binns Graphics and through the courtesy of TIME, Inc. Page 95: MARTIN LUBIN. Page 98: Vantage Art, Inc. Page 99: Vantage Art, Inc. Page 101: Vantage Art, Inc. Page 102: ISADORE SELTZER.

CHAPTER 5

Page 106: DAVID ATTIE. Page 108–109: NASA. Page 112: Vantage Art, Inc., and GEORGE MORAN. Page 118: BETTINA CIRONE/Photo Researchers, Inc. Page 120: Vantage Art, Inc., based on information from U.S. Chamber of Commerce, "Annual Employee Benefits and Earnings per Employee," 1976. Page 122 (top): SYD GREENBERG/Photo Researchers, Inc.; (middle): Newsweek photo by ROBERT R. MCELROY; (bottom): Courtesy, Conoco. Page 123: PETER B. KAPLAN/Photo Researchers, Inc.

CHAPTER 6

Page 126: GUY GILLETTE/Photo Researchers, Inc. Page 128: The Granger Collection. Page 129: L. SIR/Photo Researchers, Inc. Pages 130–131: JOEL GORDON. Page 133: STELLA GOSMAN. Photo 134: MIKE QUON. Page 136: FRANK C. SMITH. Page 140: Vantage Art, Inc., and MARTIN LUBIN. Page 142: Vantage Art, Inc. Page 143: Vantage Art, Inc.

CHAPTER 11A

Page 146: WALLY MCNAMEE/Woodfin Camp & Associates. Page 149: GEORGE MORAN. Page 151: LAIMUTE DRUSKIS. Page 153: GEORGE MORAN. Page 155: The Granger Collection. Page 156: Vantage Art, Inc., and GEORGE MORAN, based on information in MANAGEMENT BY OBJECTIVES by George S. Odiorne, copyright © 1965 by Fearon-Pitman Publishers, Inc., 6 Davis Drive, Belmont, CA 94002. Reprinted by permission. Page 159: MICHIO CHIBOSHI.

CHAPTER 11B

Page 162: JOEL GORDON. Page 164: The Granger Collection. Page 165 (left): Photograph by BYRON. Museum of the City of New York; (right): UPI/JERRY SOLOWAY. Page 170: Reprinted with permission of Macmillan Publishing Co., from *Personnel: Management of People at Work* by Dale S. Beach. Copyright © 1970 by Dale S. Beach. Page 173: ISADORE SELTZER. Page 175: Vantage Art, Inc.

CHAPTER 7

Page 190: DAVID ATTIE. Page 196: JOEL GORDON. Page 197: Vantage Art, Inc. Pages 198–199: N.Y.P.L. Picture Collection. Page 201: GEORGE MORAN. Page 202: MIKE QUON. Page 203: MIKE QUON. Page 205: Vantage Art, Inc. Page 207: MIKE QUON and MARTIN LUBIN, based on information in "Who Gets Your Food Dollar?" American Farm Bureau Federation, August 1977.

CHAPTER 8

Page 210: JOEL GORDON. Page 212: Vantage Art, Inc. Page 213: ISADORE SELTZER. Page 214 (top): Vantage Art, Inc.; (bottom): Vantage Art, Inc., based on information in *1975 Electronic Marketing Data Book*, Electronic Industries Association. Page 220: JOEL GORDON. Page 221: PAOLO KOCH/Photo Researchers, Inc. Page 223: Vantage Art, Inc. Page 225: Vantage Art, Inc.

CHAPTER 9

Page 230: RUSS KINNE/Photo Researchers, Inc. Page 232: Vantage Art, Inc. Page 233: ISADORE SELTZER. Page 235: MIKE QUON, based on information from Census Bureau, *Statistical Abstract of the United States 1977* (Washington, D.C.: Government Printing Office, 1977), p. 845. Page 238: Photo by R. C. ELLINGSEN, courtesy Nielsen, Inc. Page 243: JOEL GORDON.

CHAPTER 10

Page 250: DONALD L. MILLER/Monkmeyer Press Photo Service. Page 252: Vantage Art, Inc. Page 253: JULES BUCHER/Photo Researchers, Inc. Page 254: Vantage Art, Inc. Page 255: Courtesy, Charles Levy Circulating Company. Photo by ARTHUR SEIGEL. Page 258 (top): GEORGE MORAN; (bottom): Vantage Art, Inc., based on information from Census Bureau, *Statistical Abstract of the United States 1977* (Washington, D.C.: Government Printing Office, 1977), p. 831. Page 259: Vantage Art, Inc. Reprinted from STORES magazine. Copyright 1978, National Retail Merchants Association. Page 261: Vantage Art, Inc. Reprinted from STORES magazine. Copyright 1978, National Retail Merchants Association. Page 266: Vantage Art, Inc., reprinted from "Physical Distribution: Key to Improved Volume and Profits," *Journal of Marketing*, 29 January 1965, p. 66, published by the American Marketing Association. Page 267: MIKE QUON, based on information in *Statistical Abstract*.

GLOSSARY/
INDEX

A

Abercrombie & Fitch, 264
 bankruptcy, 488
absenteeism, 148
absorbable risks risks that can be covered by insurance, but for one reason or another they're assumed or absorbed by a business itself. 387–388
access time the amount of time that elapses from the moment the data are asked for until the moment they appear. 440
accountability, and delegation, 95
accountants
 role of, 414–415
 types, 415–416
accounting a system of principles and techniques that permits bookkeepers or computers to record, classify, and accumulate sales, purchases, and other transactions. 414
 key concepts, 416–418
accounting equation assets = liabilities + owners' equity. 416–417
accounting statements records of business operations during a given time period. 414
accounts payable liabilities due in thirty days. 421
accounts receivable the amounts due the business from customers with open-book accounts for items or services the company has sold. 315, 322, 323, 420
accrual basis the method of recording all sales revenues in the year they are made and reporting all expenses in the year in which the associated revenue is reported. 423
accrued expenses expenses incurred for which bills have not yet been received and recorded. 421
acid test ratio (quick ratio) the ratio that shows the ability of a company to meet its short-term debts with its cash, marketable securities, and receivables. 427
Action for Children's Television (ACT), 244
actuary a person employed by an insurance company to compute expected losses and calculate the cost of premiums. 389
advertising any paid form of nonpersonal sales or promotional efforts made on behalf of goods, services, or ideas by an identified sponsor. 232–233
 media, 234–239
 public reaction to, 244–247
 regulation of, 246–247
 superstar endorsements in, 193
 types, 234
advertising agencies the agencies that produce and place nearly all advertising in national magazines and on television networks. 239–241
advisory staff, 99
affirmative action plan a plan for active minority recruitment and training. 113

affirmative action programs programs in which businesses actively recruit members of minority groups and train them specifically for professional-level jobs. 20–21
AFL-CIO the union with which most national unions are affiliated. 173, 176
age, of consumers, 275–277
age discrimination, 115
aged, population growth, 276
agency the legal relationship that exists when one party, known as the principal, authorizes another party, known as the agent, to act in his or her behalf. 484–485
agency shop a working situation that requires non-union workers who benefit from any agreements the union has negotiated to pay dues to that union. 169
agents (or brokers) wholesalers who act as middlemen, but who never actually take title to the products they resell. 253
Agnew, Opus, 88, 89, 90
Agriculture Department, 196
air pollution, 10–12
Alaska Airlines, 177
Alaska pipeline, long-term financing, 332
Alcoa Corp., 50
Amalgamated Clothing Workers Union, 291
American Airlines, computers at, 445
American Association of Advertising Agencies, 492
American Federation of Labor (AFL), 166
American Heart Association, 279
American Management Association, 492
American Marketing Association, 492
American Motors Co., 9, 224
American Stock Exchange, 370
American Telephone & Telegraph Co., 34, 52, 117
 bond interest rates, 336–337
 convertible bonds, 338
American Textile Manufacturers Institute, 291
American Tobacco Trust, 193
American work ethic the belief that work is not only necessary but valuable for its own sake. 4, 149
analytic process breaking down a raw material into one or more different products, which may or may not resemble the original material in form and function. 133–134
Anderson, Robert, 76
Anheuser Busch, 137
Annie, 423
antitrust, current issues, 504–506
Antitrust Improvements Act (1976) the act that required premerger notification for companies, including conglomerates, and also empowered attorneys general at the state level to bring suit on behalf of injured consumers in their state. 504

O